LINCOLN'S UNFINISHED WORK

CONFLICTING WORLDS

New Dimensions of the American Civil War

T. MICHAEL PARRISH, SERIES EDITOR

The New Birth of Freedom
from Generation to Generation

LINCOLN'S UNFINISHED WORK

Edited by
Orville Vernon Burton
and **Peter Eisenstadt**

LOUISIANA STATE UNIVERSITY PRESS
BATON ROUGE

Published with the assistance of the Michael H. and Ayan Rubin Fund

Published by Louisiana State University Press
lsupress.org

Designer: Barbara Neely Bourgoyne
Typeface: Minion Pro
Printer: Sheridan Books

Jacket photograph of the March on Washington is from the Library of Congress,
Prints and Photographs Division.

Cataloging-in-Publication Data are available from the Library of Congress.

ISBN 978-0-8071-7676-4 (cloth: alk. paper) — ISBN 978-0-8071-7815-7 (pdf) —
ISBN 978-0-8071-7814-0 (epub)

Contents

II. The Unfinished Work of Lincoln in American History and the Struggle for Democratic Inclusion

LINCOLN'S UNFINISHED WORK

Introduction

ORVILLE VERNON BURTON and PETER EISENSTADT

During the last years of his presidency, Abraham Lincoln often spoke of the unfinished work ahead. At Gettysburg, Pennsylvania, in November 1863, there to dedicate a cemetery to the Union dead, he told his listeners that the burial ground had already been hallowed by those who had given "the last full measure of devotion" on the battlefield. Their work was finished. But, Lincoln said, it was "for us the living, rather, to be dedicated here to the unfinished work which they who fought here have so nobly advanced." He said much the same thing a year and a half later in the closing words of his second inaugural address: "With malice toward none, with charity for all, with firmness in the right as God gives us to see the right, let us strive on to finish the work we are in."[1]

What was this unfinished work? Was it ever Lincoln's alone? How has it been interpreted and passed down from Lincoln's time to ours? How do we understand and respond to the still-unfinished work of democratic inclusion domestically in the United States and globally in our contemporary world? It was long the ambition of Vernon Burton, author of *The Age of Lincoln,* to assemble a conference of scholars to discuss the sixteenth president's unfinished work in its broadest scope.[2] The conference was held from November 28 to December 1, 2018, on the campus of Clemson University. Peter Eisenstadt assisted him as co-convenor of the conference and as coeditor of the present volume. The question of the unfinished work of democracy is vast. The essays in this book can touch only on some of its aspects. In the conference presentations, Lincoln himself was scrutinized from a number of perspectives. There were talks on his sense of humor, the history of his African American admirers and detractors, the interpretation of his August 1862 letter to Horace Greeley, his Indian policy, and the role of his vision of the American union in the formation of the European Union after World War II. On the Civil War and Reconstruction, there were presentations on the end of the Confederacy understood as a general strike, how Lincoln's Reconstruction might have unfolded, the scope of federal military power during the Reconstruction period, and Reconstruction in the West. There were several papers on Black landownership in the South after 1865: one discussed the famous unfulfilled promise of "forty acres and a mule," another focused on the freedpeople's understanding of the "year of jubilee," and a jointly presented paper explored postbellum African American farm ownership in the South. Papers on Black education stressed the importance of land-grant institutions in the development of historically Black colleges and universities. Other papers explored aspects of women's history, LGBTQ history, the "me-too" movement and the historical profession, and the efforts of the Black Panther Party in the 1960s and 1970s to rethink the unfinished work of American constitutionalism. Pastimes and recreations such as jazz and baseball were viewed from the perspective of the unfinished work of democracy. There was a session on the complex racial history of Clemson University itself, and how, when organized in 1889, the college was largely built on the backs of the unremitting toil and blighted lives of Black convict laborers. One paper discussed Republican attitudes toward Black voting rights in the South in the late nineteenth century. Another examined a very different Republican Party's attitudes toward Black voting rights in the early twentieth-first century. There was an illustrated talk by Cecil Williams, the celebrated African American photographer from South Carolina, who witnessed and documented many of the triumphs and tragedies of the civil rights movement in the state. The conference also included a special program for high school students from underserved communities. They attended sessions of the conference and at one of them presented their thoughts on the importance of history. They interacted with conference speakers, with each student interviewing at least one of the presenters. Burton and the late James W. Loewen, author of the classic *Lies My Teacher Taught Me,* led a workshop for K–12 teachers on how to teach about the history of race relations in public schools.[3] Historian Heather Cox Richardson keynoted the luncheon for the workshop and provided a brief overview for what would become her next book, *How the South Won the Civil War.*[4] The full conference program and the recorded sessions are available for viewing at the conference website.[5]

This volume includes fifteen of the conference papers. These essays use the idea of Lincoln's unfinished work as a jumping-off point. All of them explore aspects of the unfinished work of democracy, particularly the unfinished work of overcoming the legacy of slavery and white supremacy.

The first section, titled "The Unfinished Work of Lincoln in Civil War, Reconstruction, and Post-Reconstruction America," opens with Richard Carwardine's "Humor and Statesmanship: The Instructive Case of Abraham Lincoln." It is the sole essay that is primarily about the president himself. Lincoln, as all of his contemporaries noted, was a funny man, a jokester, a punster, and a great teller of tales. His sharp wit could, depending on the occasion, be dry, broad, ribald, or acerbic. His humor could serve many purposes: self-deprecation, clever defenses of his positions or mocking attacks on those of his opponents without mean-spirited invective, or relating stories that, like those of Aesop, ended with a twist and a sharp moral. For Carwardine, Lincoln's sense of humor formed a part of his "capacity for wise political leadership" and was "an expression of his essential humanity, sense of proportion, and understanding of human foibles." As Carwardine notes, Lincoln's penchant for humor often led critics to accuse him of vulgarity and lapses of taste in his storytelling, but it was for him a way of establishing his enduring political persona as a man of both high seriousness and relatable "commonness." And, perhaps, it was a way to find the human comedy of reconciliation, the overcoming of obstacles, and happy endings amid life's tragedies, with their hard, unappeasable finalities. In wartime America, he knew how to laugh, and he knew how to cry; there have been few politicians as effective as conveying both emotions to their publics.[6]

Eric Foner, in "The Second Founding: How the Civil War and Reconstruction Remade the Constitution," opened the conference with one of the keynotes. In the paper drawn from that address, he argues that "perhaps the most tangible legacies of that era are the Thirteenth, Fourteenth, and Fifteenth Amendments to the US Constitution," the so-called Reconstruction amendments, all adopted between 1865 and 1870. In his opinion, the scope of the amendments constituted a "constitutional revolution" that created "a fundamentally new document." But as Foner notes, quoting US Army officer Thomas Wentworth Higginson, who commanded African American troops, "Revolutions may go backward." Reconstruction was certainly an example of a revolution that reversed direction. The egalitarian potential of the Civil War amendments, both in political practice and by decisions of the US Supreme Court, was whittled away to a shard.

But revolutions can reverse their polarities more than once, and Foner argues "the fact that [Reconstruction] happened at all laid the foundation for another generation a century later to try to bring to fruition the concept of a country that had progressed beyond the tyranny of race." He reminds us that "no historian believes that any important document possesses one single intent or meaning" and that the nature of constitutional interpretation—whatever some legal scholars might say about unambiguous "original" meanings of constitutional texts—is by its very nature unfixed and unfinished. Foner suggests that the full power of the Reconstruction amendments, such as the privileges and immunities clause of the Fourteenth Amendment, has yet to be realized and that, "because the ideals of freedom, equality, and democracy are always contested, our understanding of the Reconstruction amendments will forever be a work in progress."[7]

Lawrence T. McDonnell, in "Lincoln, Du Bois's 'General Strike,' and the Making of the American Working Class," expands on the argument of W. E. B. Du Bois in *Black Reconstruction in America, 1860–1880*, which claims that the final collapse of the Confederacy was in large part a consequence of a general strike by enslaved persons.[8] In his book, Du Bois argues that their refusal to work for their enslavers, either in situ or with their removal of themselves to positions behind US Army lines, undermined the Confederacy.[9] McDonnell argues that this assertion needs to be studied in conjunction with the mass desertion of Confederate soldiers in the final months of the war, that "the role ordinary white Southerners played in wrecking the slaveocracy" shows "the need to study the politics of the battlefield and the home front as an objectively unified revolutionary process," and that this was "the greatest biracial working-class uprising in American history." One reason this has been overlooked, he believes, is that the job of soldiering has often not been viewed as a species of work. In many instances, and certainly in the circumstances of the Civil War, this martial labor took place in a uniquely dangerous, unfree, and unpleasant workplace. Lincoln, at Gettysburg and elsewhere, certainly considered war work as part of the country's unfinished work. Viewed in this way, the Civil War, McDonnell states, becomes part of a longer struggle over the meaning of work in the Reconstruction and post-Reconstruction South and in the Gilded Age labor struggles in the North.

J. William Harris's "Abraham Lincoln's Unfinished Work and the South's Long Self-Reconstruction" argues that most current students of Reconstruction would likely have been disappointed by the president's Reconstruction policies had they been implemented. Lincoln was committed to the "principle of self-reconstruction controlled by southern white unionists," though, as Harris points out, his "confidence that there was a large body of southern men—a real majority—who were still, at heart, devoted to the Union, was, it turned out, quite naive." Lincoln, who never believed that the rebellious Confederate states had actually seceded from the United States, had a fairly robust view of the power of the states, and Harris argues that his strong belief in the importance of property rights makes it unlikely that he would have supported any widespread distribution of farmland to the freedpeople. Harris concludes that Lincoln's idea of his "unfinished work" was the restoration of the Union, not the creation of a truly racially egalitarian society.

Yet nothing on this subject is going to be definitive. As Harris points out, Lincoln was a vastly superior politician compared to the way-over-his-head fumblings of Andrew Johnson. Lincoln would not have alienated the bulk of congressional Republicans, would not have been impeached, and would have undoubtedly responded more forcefully than Johnson to the passage of the Black Codes and the rise of anti-Black violence in the South. Of course, the question of how much he would have changed course after April 1865 in response to events can only be answered with wispy "what-ifs." His famous statement of March 1864—"I claim not to have controlled events, but confess plainly that events have controlled me"—exaggerates his pliability but underlines his pragmatism about the means needed to obtain a predetermined end.[10] How important the maintenance of robust Black voting rights would have been to Lincoln going forward, and how hard would he have been willing to fight to protect them? His Reconstruction would have differed from Johnson's, but Harris suggests it might not have been as different as many Lincoln admirers suspect. We will never know.

The question of Lincoln's Reconstruction raises the broader counterfactual of whether Reconstruction itself was doomed from the outset, even given more optimum circumstances like Lincoln having a full second term. This too is unanswerable; but since it rests less on the unknowable actions of a single individual, it is perhaps a more ponderable matter to consider. Gregory P. Downs, in "The Problem of Enforcement: The Republican Struggle to Protect Voting Rights in Peacetime," does not discuss this directly but argues for the difficulties any Republican administration would have had in the military enforcement of the Civil Rights Act of 1866 and in securing adherence to the several Enforcement Acts in the early 1870s. He argues that the US Army during Reconstruction "launched one of the most spatially ambitious occupations of the mid-nineteenth-century

Atlantic World, creating hundreds of outposts in small crossroads towns and county seats so that they could reach and be reached by freedpeople" to protect Black suffrage. Downs highlights, in this regard, the importance of the use of the commissioner and marshal system, a federal institution often overlooked by historians. But from the outset, the commissioner and marshal system had its own internal weaknesses, along with the political challenge of remaining on a quasi-war footing during "peacetime," all unfolding against the backdrop of the often-violent opposition from white southerners determined to undermine Black voting and civil rights. Downs suggests that, by looking at the challenges of military enforcement, "we may be better prepared to see the postwar Republicans in tragic light, as people who failed but not necessarily for lack of trying," that there were "surprisingly bold nineteenth-century efforts to build governmental structures to protect voting rights," and that Reconstruction was less an "unfinished" than an "overthrown" revolution.

The ultimate problem with Republican efforts to support Black voting rights, Downs suggests, was "the deep, perhaps fundamental, difficulties in sustaining voting rights in a democratic republic where one party is deeply hostile to them." For "if voting rights were not beyond politics but were made the source of political contest, then how could they be protected other than through the one pro-voting party permanently holding power?" Downs notes the parallels between the late nineteenth century and our own era when, "like the zombies so popular in film and television, voting restrictions, once presumed dead, walk again among us." Since Downs presented his paper at the Clemson conference in the winter of 2018, these zombies have only gained in strength, eating away at the heart of our democracy. As we write these words in late 2021, the question of whether a house divided against itself can stand is again the issue of the day.

Another perennial question the destruction of Reconstruction raises is whether comprehensive agrarian reform, through the creation of a relatively economically independent Black yeomanry, would have helped stay the hand of those seeking to return African Americans to economic and political servility. Too many historians, argue Adrienne Petty and Mark Schultz in "Breaking New Ground: African American Landowners and the Pursuit of the 'American Dream,'" have seen the failure of Major General William T. Sherman's Special Order No. 15 ("forty acres and a mule") and similar efforts as the death knell for postbellum Black landownership.[11] But despite the harsh and forbidding realities, "by 1900, a quarter of African American farmers had come to own the land they worked." Black landownership was more pronounced in the Upper South than in the Deep South, but in 1910, there were over 220,000 Black-owned farms on over fifteen million acres, with substantial numbers in every southern state. After 1920, due to the Great Migration and other pressures, African American agricultural landownership began to decline.

Petty and Schultz argue that their story imposes "no clear narrative," calls for "cautious interpretation," and is "neither a celebratory narrative of economic opportunity and political equality nor a dismal and somber tale of chronic impoverishment and civic disengagement." Most of the Black experience in America can be balanced between these two extremes. The advance of African American landownership in the South during the decades that saw the tightening of legal segregation presents something of a paradox. Petty and Schultz argue that African American landownership made a substantial economic, social, civic, and even subtle political difference at a time when alternatives were few: "For freedpeople and their descendants, land represented a decades-long psychic and material refuge from the most vicious attacks and insults of the Jim Crow era. It was a base for developing the social capital of community and community institutions, including decent rural Black schools, as well as an invisible launching pad toward the urban Black middle class. African Americans' sustained quest for land represented an alternative vision of a more equitable, democratic society, even if it was never fully realized"—unfinished work, indeed.

The second half of the book is titled "The Unfinished Work of Lincoln in American History and the Struggle for Democratic Inclusion." Some of these essays directly speak to Lincoln's reputation and reverberations in the twentieth and twenty-first centuries. Others address Lincoln more obliquely. All are concerned with the unfinished work.

In "Our Textbooks and Monuments Have Flattened Lincoln, Just When We Need Him the Most," sociologist James W. Loewen addresses the vagaries of the president's treatment in American history textbooks. His research found that the most oft-quoted text of Lincoln's in recent textbooks is neither the Gettysburg Address nor his second inaugural address—in both of which Lincoln calls us to the "unfinished work"—but his letter to Horace Greeley dated August 22, 1862, especially the following sentence: "If I could save the Union without freeing *any* slave, I would do it; and if I could save it by freeing *all* the slaves, I would do it; and if I could save it by freeing some and leaving others alone, I would also do that."[12] Loewen, as do many recent historians, argues that this is a mis-representation of Lincoln's position. By the time he had written to Greeley, the president had already decided to issue the Emancipation Proclamation. The letter represents special pleading on Lincoln's part to curry favor with the influential editor and "media influencer." Loewen argues that the choice between Lincoln as savior of the Union or Lincoln as Great Emancipator is a false dichotomy, one that flourished starting in the late nineteenth century, when, for most white commentators, the promotion of sectional reunion became a more important political good than the pursuit of racial justice. This was the Lincoln that was celebrated by his memorial on the National Mall. It was also during these decades that the largest wave of monumentalizing Lost Cause statuary was erected. Now that we live in a time when many of these statues are being removed from their pedestals, Loewen argues the time is right for the recovery of a "robust Lincoln, rather than the flattened" portrayals in our textbooks and elsewhere. For Lincoln, while imperfect, was a sincere and dedicated antislavery activist who came to see emancipation and preservation of the Union as a single, indissoluble, cause.

"Looking at Lincoln from the Effigy Mound," by Stephen Kantrowitz, is an extended meditation on another Lincoln monument, depicting the president seated, calm but exuding strength, in a statue that occupies a commanding lo-cation on the University of Wisconsin–Madison campus. The statue has drawn the ire of American Indian activists and members of the Ho-Chunk Nation. The campus was built on their land, and they argue its history shows it was less a land-grant than a "land-grab" university.[13] An Indigenous perspective on Lin-coln, Kantrowitz argues, is necessarily very different from one that views him as a man who spoke of ushering in "a new birth of freedom." Lincoln, like almost all white Americans in the nineteenth century—certainly most of those living in the West—throughout his life and political career maintained an "unambiguous commitment to the American conquest of Indian Country." The ideology of "Free Soil" required land cleared of Native Americans and their claims to sovereignty extinguished. On the question of the expansion of slavery to the territorial United States in the 1850s, if antislavery Republicans such as Lincoln and proslavery Democrats such as Stephen Douglas shared anything in common, it was that any Indian presence on that land was an afterthought and would have to make way as the American republic stretched westward.

In the months he was promulgating the Emancipation Proclamation in late 1862, Lincoln was also involved in the best remembered episode of his presidential Indian policy, the aftermath of the Dakota War. Although he pardoned most of the three hundred members of the Dakota Nation sentenced to hang in Mankato, Minnesota, in December 1862, thirty-eight persons were not pardoned, and their hanging formed the largest mass execution in American history. Kantrowitz argues that in this and other episodes when he might have moderated the worst impulses of white settlers, "Lincoln's conscience is entirely beside the point" because "the entire Republican program was based upon the necessity and the virtue of . . . conquest and settlement." There is no evidence in Lincoln's Indian policy, he argues, of anything besides the standard paternalism and expectation that Native Americans would abandon their land claims and their ways of life to accommodate white settlers. Kantrowitz is agnostic over whether the statue at Madison should be removed, but he argues that a serious reckoning with Lincoln's Indian policy is long overdue. If there is a persistent "what would Lincoln have done if he lived" question for Reconstruction, Kantrowitz believes there is none for his Native American policy. There is no reason to think that the remainder of the 1860s and 1870s would have been any less catastrophic for Native peoples than it actually was.

There is no statue of President Lincoln at Clemson University in South Carolina, but Fort Hill, the plantation estate of US senator, vice president, and secretary of war John C. Calhoun, and his home for many years before his death in 1850, stands in the center of the campus. Calhoun ardently promulgated the proslavery theory in the Senate in 1837, instrumental in changing the idea that slavery was "a necessary evil" to its antebellum elevation as "a positive good." That shift in rhetoric left people in the North like Lincoln no choice but to take a stand on the issue of slavery. With Calhoun's passing and the subsequent death of his daughter, Anna, the estate passed to his Philadelphia-born son-in-law, Thomas Green Clemson, an enslaver who would resign as US superintendent of agriculture in 1861 to follow his adopted state into the Confederacy. After the war, Clemson envisioned creating "a high seminary of Learning" and, upon his death in 1888, bequeathed the 1,100-acre Fort Hill Plantation to the state of South Carolina for that purpose. Governor Benjamin Ryan Tillman, the prototype of the southern racist demagogue, fulfilled his vision for a university and, on the grounds of Fort Hill, made Clemson University a reality. In front of what is still called Tillman Hall, the most iconic building on the campus, stands an impressive statue of Clemson.[14]

Thomas Green Clemson was always opposed to higher education for African Americans. In November 1873, a month after the first Black student was admitted to the College of South Carolina (now the University of South Carolina), he wrote that whites were facing a challenge "from a race entirely distinct from ours . . . [and] not capable of reaching a high degree of civilization," thus white South Carolinians had to "make a stand against the degrading torrent . . . by cultivating to its utmost our superior intellectual facilities."[15] The letter's main point was to argue that, given the Black threat, this was no time to waste money on higher education for white women; only white men should have that privilege. In keeping with his vision of higher education for men only, no women were admitted to Clemson College until 1956. And although some seventy to eighty persons enslaved by Calhoun and Clemson had lived on the site, a number of whom became sharecroppers in the years after 1865, no African American student entered the school until 1963 (and then only after a bitter legal fight on behalf of Harvey Gantt during our Second Reconstruction). On January 19, 1907, the local chapter of the United Daughters of the Confederacy, Rhondda Robinson Thomas writes, "hosted a program in the college chapel to celebrate the centennial birthday of Robert E. Lee," with some fifteen Confederate veterans present. An address was given that day by one of the last surviving signers of South Carolina's ordinance of secession. About a decade later, J. Strom Thurmond attended the college, eventually becoming one of Clemson's most famous graduates and one of South Carolina's most talented and famous politicians. He exemplified constituency service, and after the Voting Rights Act of 1965, this included Black as well as white South Carolinians. Prior to that, he had made a short run for the presidency on the 1948 States' Rights Democratic (Dixiecrat) party platform of segregation and states' rights. He is forever associated with his 1957 filibuster against a civil rights bill.

There could not have been many institutions in the continental United States less interested in or less committed to the realization of Lincoln's unfinished work than Clemson College. On the other hand, Clemson is a land-grant college, one of "democracy's colleges" that Lincoln made possible with the passage of the Morrill Act during the Civil War. Always committed to public education, Lincoln understood the essential role education plays in a democracy.[16] Today, Clemson University has taken hold of that promise of democratic education in the state.

Given this conflicted history, the organizers of this conference were delighted that Thomas was able to present a paper, included here as "The Unfinished Work of Clemson University: Full Recognition for Black Citizens in Its History," part of her ongoing exploration of the forgotten and hidden African American presence at the university. She writes that for most of Clemson University's existence, white males have controlled its history, creating "a narrative of omission regarding the enslavement, oppression, and exploitation of Black laborers on the land and their contributions to the institution's establishment and progress." The college's initial campus was primarily built by African American convict labor, ruthlessly exploited by the convict-lease system. And even as that system lapsed, African Americans "maintained Clemson's infrastructure, labored as field hands, and worked as cooks, janitors, and laundry men and women," forming Clemson's "invisible founders." Professor Thomas has been a leader in the effort to rectify the long history of Black people's invisibility on the campus, to locate unmarked graves on the campus grounds, to recover the names and lives of African Americans who toiled on the college during the Jim Crow era, and to make this a key part of the university's history (and in the process helping make Clemson University a more welcoming and hospitable campus for minority students and faculty). Although there has been some progress in recent years, much remains to be done on campus, and much resistance remains toward realizing what she calls, with justice, Clemson University's "unfinished work."

Among the myriad Lincoln counterfactuals, an easy one to decide is whether, if he were alive today, the "father of the Republican Party" would have anything to do with its contemporary manifestation. The answer, save an ideological about-face while in the realm of the spirits, is clearly a resounding and emphatic No. How the Republican Party devolved from its antislavery past to its neo-Confederate present is a twisted tale. Strom Thurmond is an important part of this story, and so is the marriage between right-wing politics and evangelical Christianity.

Randall J. Stephens, in "Evangelicals, Race, and Reform: From the Age of Lincoln to the Second Reconstruction," takes this story from the antebellum antislavery activism of a prominent evangelical like Charles Grandison Finney to the racial temporizing of a Billy Graham. Along the way he traces the move away from social activism by prominent evangelicals like Dwight Moody, who in the late nineteenth century focused not on social change but on individual salvation. Moody became an epitome of what Stephens calls the "socially disengaged white Protestantism" of postwar evangelicalism. For one of Moody's most noteworthy successors, the flamboyant and energetic Billy Sunday, other than crusading against Demon Rum, the main message was salvation through Jesus Christ and a general racial and social conservatism that made his message attractive to the revitalized Ku Klux Klan. (Sunday and the Klan were mutual admirers.) Stephens observes that, "in broad terms, abolitionism helped create two important later movements: conservative evangelicalism and the liberal to left-leaning Social Gospel movement. These two only began to diverge from each other in the last years of the nineteenth century." There were occasional exceptions to this split, such as the interracial stirrings of the early Pentecostal movement. But by the middle of the twentieth century, evangelicalism was determinedly opposed to both liberal religion and liberal politics. He concludes that, "by the time of the 1950s and 1960s, white evangelicals had long given up on transforming the larger society and fighting societal racism. Leaders and laypeople could do little more than preserve their faith, await the return of Jesus, and rescue lost souls from a fallen world." The next generation of evangelicals, without abandoning their premillennialism, proved to be less otherworldly. In the hands of a Jerry Falwell or a Pat Robertson, the evangelical movement, drawing on white disdain for racial turbulence and Black activism, embraced the worldly snares of politics with the fervor of Christian soldiers at Armageddon, helping create the modern Republican Party.

Jackie Robinson was a Christian activist of a very different sort, and a very different kind of Republican. In his day, he was often compared to Lincoln. "People say Jackie's outspoken, he is. . . . Lincoln spoke up. All great men speak their minds." And for Robinson, Lincoln remained a standard for the measurement of true greatness, as when, in June 1962, he criticized President John F. Kennedy's civil-rights timidity, saying that he might be "a fine man" and "a decent man," but "an Abraham Lincoln—he ain't."[17] Robinson's career, as an ardent Republican who ended up opposing Barry Goldwater in 1964 and Richard Nixon in 1968 and 1972, exemplifies the ways in which the party, with increasing determination, placed itself on the wrong side of the civil rights movement in the 1960s and made the term "Black Republican" a political rarity.

Robinson's stint as a columnist and political commentator was, of course, very much a second career. Peter Eisenstadt, in "Jackie Robinson and the Fight for Effective Black Citizenship; or, How Integration Reached Second Base," looks at Robinson's life as both athlete and activist. When he first played for the Brooklyn Dodgers in 1947, he was hailed (or execrated) for integrating major-league baseball. Eisenstadt argues, however, that most observers understood "integration" narrowly as the breaching of the color line in formerly segregated institutions. Robinson, drawing on a tradition of African American citizenship dating back to the Age of Lincoln and before, saw integration as the full and effective exercise of all of the powers, prerogatives, and responsibilities of citizenship. In his post-baseball career, as he sought to realize this vision, Robinson found himself increasingly at odds with his fellow Republicans, so that, in the last years of his life, he was questioning some of his fundamental assumptions about the possibility of Black citizenship in a racist America.

Jerald Podair, in "Lincoln and the Two Reconstructions: The Unfinished Work of American Equality," also writes about the complex nature of Black citizenship, and makes explicit a theme that underlies a number of the essays in the book: a comparison between the 1860s and 1960s, between Reconstruction (or what is sometimes called the First Reconstruction) and the civil rights movement (or what is sometimes called the Second Reconstruction). He approaches it from a presidential vantage, asking what Andrew Johnson did after 1865 (and what Lincoln might have done) and what Lyndon Johnson did and did not do during his time in office in the 1960s. He argues, like Harris, that Lincoln would probably have been more cautious in Reconstruction than some of his current admirers think—that, in any event, he would not have been able to reverse the growing postbellum conservatism of the Republican Party on economic and social issues, the revived strength of northern Democrats, and the desire of most moderate Republicans to "move on" from the South and its woes. Lyndon Johnson's term in office presents different kinds of counterfactuals—especially imagining his presidency without Vietnam—but raises similar questions. Both reconstructions were disappointing in different ways. Both were committed, in Podair's telling, to expanding economic opportunity rather than directly tackling economic redistribution, each making this concession to political necessity at the expense of needed social transformation. Both reconstructions had similar trajectories. Their initial high expectations were undermined by increasingly equivocal support on the one hand, and, on the other, a determined opposition that steadily gained strength and scope in its efforts to maintain the racial status quo. Podair's sobering look at the two most intense periods of social and presidential action toward making the United States a more racially egalitarian nation raises questions about whether this pattern is doomed to repeat itself or the pattern can be broken.

When, in his December 1862 message to Congress, Lincoln said, "Fellow citizens, we cannot escape history," he was probably arguing that history was not cyclical and that he and his fellow politicians would be judged harshly by posterity if they did not destroy the institution of slavery.[18] However Lincoln understood the meaning of "history," he would have been appalled by History, formerly known as the History Channel. Historian Joshua Casmir Catalano and sociologist Briana L. Pocratsky, in "From Ken Burns's *The Civil War* to History's *Ancient Aliens:* Lincoln's Unfinished Work on Cable Television," urge their fellow citizens to escape History; we hope they do. Far too many Americans, glued to the cable channel's programming, remain in its thrall. In their article, Catalano and Pocratsky trace the descent of history programming on television from Ken Burns's PBS documentary *The Civil War* (1990), which, while stirring, and flawed in some ways, tries to be factual, to the quasi-historical, ahistorical, or simply antihistorical series that have come to dominate the offerings on History. The History Channel started in 1995, with its programming filled with documentaries about US presidents, technology, wars, and weaponry. The target audience was always older white males, and, over time, it started to include more reality programming on "dangerous occupations, survival skills, treasure hunting, and entrepreneurship" that spoke to "the twenty-first century masculinity crisis in the United States and a perceived loss of societal power and privilege among white males," with programs such as *Ice Road Truckers* and *Swamp People.* The channel then left history entirely behind with programs such as *Ancient Aliens,* series on UFOs, and various forms of apocalypse-mongering.

As Catalano and Pocratsky suggest, sober-minded historians ignore such historical swill at their own peril since television, and more recently social media, are the "means by which most people learn about history today." The extent to which History has contributed to the general softening of the American mind is hard to say, but it has certainly played a role. Much of its programming has encouraged conspiratorial rather than critical thinking, to say nothing of reinforcing racial and sexist stereotypes. If too many Americans today follow prating ignoramuses into epistemic black holes, History certainly shares in the blame. The challenge for serious historians is real and urgent. If they do not want to see bad history drive out good history, they must do something about it besides complaining and recognize their responsibility to the general public. To paraphrase Lincoln's most famous apocryphal saying, those who think you can't fool most of the people all of the time never spent an entire month watching the History Channel, as did Catalano and Pocratsky—in doing so, performing a service for the rest of us.

The final essay, "Voting Rights and Economics in the American South" by the economic historian Gavin Wright, examines recent trends in both areas. The essay primarily covers the period from the 1960s through the 2016 election, with a brief coda on the 2020 election. Lincoln is not the only president with a store of un-sourced attributed quotations. Among Lyndon Johnson's most famous statements was a remark, supposedly said after the passage of the Civil Rights Act in 1964, "I think we just handed the South to the Republicans for a long time to come." Wright thinks this is seriously misleading because the Civil Rights Act and the Voting Rights Act (1965) "actually brought to the South more than twenty-five years of vigorous two-party competition." Successful biracial political coalitions in many southern states saw the election of many Democratic governors and legislators, capped by the winning presidential campaigns of two "New South" white Demo-cratic racial moderates, Jimmy Carter in 1976 and Bill Clinton in 1992 and 1996.

By the mid-1990s, however, Johnson's prediction, if that is what it was, was coming true. The South was reemerging as a one-party political region, now dominated by Republicans. The question is why. One of the main interpretations emphasizes the growing racial backlash against African American political and economic success, while another notes the increasing conservative economic climate on such matters as taxes and government spending, and there are varia-tions on these two main positions. Wright offers a third possibility. The opening of the post–Jim Crow South spurred considerable economic development, with growth in the southern states outpacing the rest of the nation from the 1960s to the 1990s. Atlanta and Charlotte blossomed as megacities. But in 1994, Clinton signed and promoted the North American Free Trade Agreement (NAFTA) between the United States, Canada, and Mexico, and in the same year there was the Agreement on Textile and Clothing, negotiated as part of the World Trade Organization's Uruguay Round. Together, they were a one-two punch that devastated the already declining textile industry, and as a result, "the political-economic basis for a biracial coalition was undermined by deindustrialization," along with a decimation of union membership. And once "the structural basis for that [biracial] coalition was removed, it was only to be expected that the attractiveness of alternative appeals was a function of regional culture, including but not exclusively racial attitudes." And in 2016, it was the successful Republican presidential candidate's example (as per George Wallace in 1968) "to take this message national." In doing so, attacks on NAFTA and Chinese imports "were important parts of the package," mixing racial and class resentments. His defeat in 2020 gave hope that perhaps a new coalition, rooted in genuine economic advancement and racial equality, might be emerging. Or perhaps not.

The essays in this book offer pathways to further explorations of the unfinished work of American democracy, but of course no one book, and perhaps no one library of books, will ever be the last word on this inexhaustible subject. In the afterword, the editors offer some thoughts on the nature of Lincoln's unfinished work, how the understanding of it has evolved over the past century and a half, and the image of Lincoln in several recent public controversies, including the 1619 Project and the 1776 Report and suggesting an alternative "1877 Project" for understanding the identity of the United States. They also offer their personal assessments of Lincoln and his unfinished work.

Debates over Abraham Lincoln's legacy have always been too important to be left solely to the historians. The volume closes with a brief, first-person testimonial by an immigrant who was in part lured to America by studying the words and ideas of our sixteenth president. Abraham Lincoln and his unfinished work will continue to inspire, challenge, and perhaps enrage us, continuing to both divide and unite us. To participate in this never-ending conversation is part of our birthright as Americans and, for believers in the possibility of democratic governance everywhere, our unfinished work.

NOTES

1. Abraham Lincoln, *The Essential Lincoln: Speeches and Correspondence,* ed. Orville Vernon Burton (New York: Hill and Wang, 2009), 153–54, 168–70.

2. Orville Vernon Burton, *The Age of Lincoln* (New York: Hill and Wang, 2007).

3. James W. Loewen, *Lies My Teacher Told Me: Everything Your American History Textbook Got Wrong* (New York: Simon and Schuster, 1995).

4. Heather Cox Richardson, *How the South Won the Civil War: Oligarchy, Democracy, and the Continuing Fight for the Soul of America* (New York: Oxford University Press, 2020).

5. "Lincoln's Unfinished Work," Nov. 28–Dec. 1, 2018, Clemson History, College of Architecture, Arts, and Humanities, Clemson University, https://www.clemson.edu/caah/sites/lincoln-conference /index.html.

6. As Carwardine reminds us, though one does not usually think of antislavery and abolitionist writers as having keen senses of humor, there were bitterly comic slavery satirists such as Davis Ross Locke, the antislavery newspaperman who created the ignorant Copperhead character Petroleum Vesuvius Nasby. Carwardine shows that Lincoln was a great fan of Locke and often quoted choice bon mots in meetings. For Lincoln and Shakespearian tragedy, see James Shapiro, *Shakespeare in a Divided America: What His Plays Tell Us about Our Past and Present* (New York: Penguin, 2019), 83–120. We wish there were a way to write about Shakespeare and Lincoln without writing about John Wilkes Booth as well, but alas, it is impossible.

7. This essay draws on material from Eric Foner, *The Second Founding: How the Civil War and Reconstruction Remade the Constitution* (New York: Norton, 2019).

8. W. E. B. Du Bois, *Black Reconstruction in America, 1860–1880* (1935; rept. New York: Atheneum, 1992).

9. The lives of freedpeople in Union refugee camps remains very challenging, as Thavolia Glymph detailed in the paper she delivered at the Clemson University conference in 2018, "Freedom's Price Revisited: Transactional Data and the Business of Making American Freedom," drawn in part from Glymph, *The Women's Fight: The Civil War Battles for Home, Freedom, and Nation* (Chapel Hill: University of North Carolina Press, 2019).

10. Abraham Lincoln to Albert G. Hodges, 4 Apr. 1864, in Abraham Lincoln, *Speeches and Writings: 1859–1865*, ed. Don E. Fehrenbacher (New York: Library of America, 1989), 586.

11. Two other papers at the Clemson conference spoke to the question of Reconstruction land reform: J. Drew Lanham, "Land Legacy and Lost Freedom: What Losing Forty Acres and a Mule Cost a People," and Bennett Parten, "Blow Ye Trumpet Blow: The Idea of Jubilee in Slavery and Freedom." See also J. Drew Lanham, *The Home Place: Memoirs of a Colored Man's Love Affair with Nature* (Minneapolis: Milkweed, 2016). Parten's conference presentation drew on his article of the same title published in *Journal of the Civil War Era* 10, no. 3 (Sept. 2020): 298–318.

12. Lincoln, *Essential Lincoln*, 120–22. For other interpretations of the Greeley letter, see, for instance, David Herbert Donald, *Lincoln* (New York: Touchstone, 1995), 368–69; Eric Foner, *The Fiery Trial: Abraham Lincoln and American Slavery* (New York: Norton, 2010), 228–29; and Burton, *Age of Lincoln*, 162–67.

13. An alternative perspective on land-grant colleges and universities was presented at the 2018 Clemson conference by William Hine, arguing that they were crucial in the development of Black higher education after the Civil War, in "Abraham Lincoln's Great Society and Its Legacy." The paper drew on Hine's full-length study *South Carolina State University: A Black Land-Grant College in Jim Crow America* (Columbia: University of South Carolina Press, 2018).

14. Jerome V. Reel, *The High Seminary: A History of the Clemson Agricultural College of South Carolina* (Clemson, SC: Clemson University Press, 2011).

15. Thomas J. Brown, *Civil War Canon: Sites of Confederate Memory in South Carolina* (Chapel Hill: University of North Carolina Press, 2015), 72. In 1876, when Democrats regained control of the

state legislature, Black students were barred from all the South Carolina colleges and universities; none would be admitted until 1963.

16. Orville Vernon Burton, "Dining with Harvey Gantt: Myth and Realities of 'Integration with Dignity,'" in *Matthew J. Perry: The Man, His Times, and His Legacy,* ed. W. Lewis Burke and Belinda F. Gergel (Columbia: University of South Carolina Press, 2004), 183–220. On Lincoln and education, see "To the People of Sagamo County, March 9, 1832," in Lincoln, *Essential Lincoln,* 3–5. See also "Address to the Wisconsin State Agricultural Society, Sept. 30, 1859," ibid., 65–72.

17. "'Chock Full O' Nuts' Executive Praises Robinson," *Philadelphia Tribune,* May 20, 1960; Jackie Robinson, "Kennedy Not Another Lincoln," *Chicago Defender,* June 9, 1962.

18. "Annual Message to Congress," Dec. 1, 1862, in Lincoln, *Speeches and Writings,* 415.

I

The Unfinished Work of Lincoln in Civil War, Reconstruction, and Post-Reconstruction America

Humor and Statesmanship
The Instructive Case of Abraham Lincoln

RICHARD CARWARDINE

Among the arresting displays at the Chicago Sanitary Fair in 1864 was an exhibit labeled "The Two American Humorists." One of the two busts was that of Dan Rice, a blackface minstrel. The other was of Abraham Lincoln. Few would have quarreled with this description of the president of the United States, for Lincoln was a mold breaker: the first president consistently to make storytelling and laughter tools of the office. His appetite for humor was an essential part of his armory. Few, if any, occupants of the White House have since matched Lincoln's talent. It is no coincidence that the United States' arguably greatest president was also the one who made the most enterprising and best use of a capacious sense of humor.[1]

Lincoln's apparently inexhaustible mental archive of jokes, comic stories, and wit was stocked from his reading, stories he heard from others, and the humorous possibilities of episodes in his own life. Storytelling was a part of everyday conversation in the semifrontier, rural society where Lincoln grew up. Within the family, no storyteller was more accomplished than his father, Thomas, who—according to a relative—"could beat his son telling a story—cracking a joke."[2] Throughout his life, Lincoln's appetite for humor shaped his choice of company. Friends and acquaintances—on the land, in politics, in the courtroom—served as an audience for his storytelling and supplied comic material that he would customize for later use. Riding the judicial circuit and stopping at country taverns, he would sit up all night with "lawyers, jurymen, witnesses and clients" listening to "their life adventures."[3] As president-elect and then in the White House, he enjoyed the convivial and amusing companionship of Ward Hill Lamon. He relished even more the company of John Milton Hay, his young personal secretary; as the historian Michael Burlingame has noted: "Hay's humor, intelligence, love of word play, fondness for literature, and devotion to his boss made him a source of comfort to the beleaguered president in the loneliness of the White House."[4]

Lincoln's reading regularly replenished his reservoir of material. In earlier life he relished the humor of Lord Byron and, above all, Robert Burns, whose poems he committed to memory.[5] Aesop's fables, when embellished and adapted, served as commentaries on people and events.[6] He admired the droll English essayist Sydney Smith. As he traveled the judicial circuit, Lincoln carried with him Joseph Baldwin's satirical sketches of legal life in the southwest of the 1830s and 1840s: the vernacular humor of *Flush Times in Alabama and Mississippi*, with its diet of long-winded comic tales centered on larger-than-life characters, perfectly served his appetite for colorful and inventive narrative. Another of Lincoln's boon companions on the circuit was *Phoenixiana*, a book of Californian drollery, whimsy, and absurdity by "Squibob" (George Horatio Derby).[7]

Other sources of Lincoln's stories included one, possibly two, eighteenth-century English joke books. It is likely that he had sight of *Quin's Jests* since its salacious anecdotes and wordplay are akin to his known tastes.[8] There is no question about his attachment to the stories, quips, and puns in *Joe Miller's Jests.*[9] A judicial colleague concluded that Lincoln had learnt the "entire contents" of *Miller*, having heard him telling the stories around the circuit, "but very much embellished and changed."[10] The Bible and the works of Shakespeare, his two constant literary companions, served him better than any other traditional sources in providing witty analogy and pertinent commentary on events. He illuminated his prose with occasional Shakespearean allusions—sometimes as dry wit, sometimes in broad jest.

During the war years, Lincoln took particular delight in the writings of three young "literary comedians": Charles Farrar Browne, Robert Henry Newell, and especially David Ross Locke. Each was a gifted storyteller whose writings mixed irreverence, absurdity, and degrees of satire. Browne and Locke took on the characters, respectively, of an itinerant showman (Artemus Ward) and an ignorant, proslavery preacher (Petroleum V. Nasby), who spoke idiomatically, wrote phonetically, and provided Lincoln with a low-brow text that, as a gifted performer, he could portray as well as read. Newell's Orpheus C. Kerr character offered a more refined assault on a variety of recognizable American types, including—as his name indicates—the class of political office seekers who also formed a target for the ridicule of Browne and Locke.[11]

There is no evidence that Lincoln kept an extensive paper file of his comic material. Instead, he drew on his extraordinarily retentive memory.[12] Noah Brooks later reflected: "Probably many people who heard him . . . repeat long passages from stories, or comical articles, which he had seen in print, wondered how he ever found time to commit such trifles to memory. The truth was that anything that he heard or read fastened itself into his mind, if it tickled his fancy." When a visitor expressed surprise that he should spend time committing comic writing to memory, the president replied: "Oh, I don't. If I like a thing, it just sticks after one reading or hearing it."[13] Another colleague explained that Lincoln "could recall every incident of his life particularly if any thing amusing was connected with it."[14]

Lincoln's successors in the presidency have generally been cautious in their use of humor for fear of compromising the dignity of the office. John F. Kennedy, for example, although naturally amusing, presented a more serious face in press conferences to avoid appearing unstatesmanlike; Ronald Reagan, probably as good a raconteur as Lincoln, was open to the charge that his jokes were a substitute for thought and—willing to do "anything for a laugh"—risked becoming "a vaudeville routine." Lincoln, however, was hardly circumspect or inhibited: he was happy to be identified as a teller of jokes and comic tales. There was an element of risk in this since many of his stories, as acquaintances politely put it, "would not do exactly for the drawing room." When asked, "why do you not write out your stories & put them in a book," Lincoln reportedly "drew himself up—fixed his face, as if a thousand dead carcusses—and a million of privies were Shooting all their Stench into his nostrils, and Said 'Such a book would Stink like a thousand privies.'" Lincoln's "immodest" stories were more offensive to Victorian sensibilities than to ours.[15]

Even before his election to the presidency, Lincoln's vulgarity was used against him. Democrats berated him for his "smutty jokes" during the senatorial campaign of 1858, and in the presidential canvass of 1860, the opposition press ridiculed a candidate with no qualifications "except that he once drove oxen—went barefooted—split rails—is a passably good lawyer—tells a smutty story in good style—[and] is the ugliest man in the West." As president-elect he was depicted in one cartoon as "Our Presidential Merryman . . . engaged in a lively exchange of wit and humor," drinking with fellow inebriates as a funeral hearse marking the death of the Union passes by.[16]

Throughout the war, critics in both the Union and Confederacy seized on Lincoln's humor as a stick with which to beat him. Their common charge was that the president's appetite for low jokes exposed a disabling lack of gravitas and principle and that he used humor to mask his deficiencies; his jokes measured his cruel disregard for the victims of war. Lincoln the "heartless buffoon" thus became a recurrent theme. In a powerful *Harper's Weekly* cartoon, *Columbia Confronts Her Children,* appearing in the wake of the grievous Union losses at Fredericksburg in December 1862, a female figure with her arm outstretched— Columbia—points at Lincoln and accusingly asks, "Where are my 15,000 sons, murdered at Fredericksburg?" Lincoln's callous answer, "This reminds me of a little joke . . . ," prompts an outraged interruption: "Go tell your joke at Springfield!!" In contrast to Lincoln the incapable buffoon was Lincoln the fanatic, who indulged a love of quixotic humor through savage, unfunny jokes, played by a tyrant laughingly disregarding the Constitution. Emancipation, the suspension of habeas corpus, the draft, armed Black troops, military rule, and a hard war—these were evidence of a warped sense of humor. Disgusted by the president's racial policies, Chauncey Burr told him to "crack your low jokes, Massa Lincoln— / Only white men to ruin are hurled— / So put your foot down, Massa Lincoln, / And trample them out of the world."[17]

The voices of complaint about the national joker in the White House became a vehement chorus of condemnation during the presidential election year of 1864. With the Republican Party in two minds over Lincoln's renomination, James Gordon Bennett, the editor of the *New York Herald,* ran a long article celebrating the claims of Major General John C. Frémont and drumming home one disqualification of the sitting president in particular. Bennett headed his editorial "General Frémont Takes the Presidential Field—Not a Smutty Joker." Listing the general's credentials as a military leader and emancipator, the *Herald* followed each positive recommendation with a stark refrain, repeated thirty times, "Frémont is not a smutty joker." Frémont, or some other new candidate, would "overawe the rebellion and prevent us from having a smutty joker for our next President." The cartoonist Frank Bellew cast Lincoln as the National Joker, a circus jester who was reminded of "a little joke" and "another little story." In one piece he stood grinning under three scenes—the hospital, the battlefield, and Liberty consumed by flames—each emphasizing the grotesque contrast between unpresidential levity and wartime horror.[18]

Democrats insinuated a critique of Lincoln the Joker into each of their key campaigning themes of 1864, especially the charge of shocking levity in the face of numbing military slaughter. Above all, Lincoln faced the bogus accusation that—when visiting the blood-drenched Antietam battlefield in October 1862—he had shattered its sanctity by asking to hear a vulgar comic song as bodies rested "yet warm in their . . . graves." Accompanied by Lamon and Major General George McClellan, Lincoln, "suddenly slapping Marshal Lamon upon the knee, exclaimed: 'Come, Lamon! give us that song about Picayune Butler.' McClellan has never heard it." With a shudder, the general protested: "Not now, if you please Marshal. . . . I would prefer to hear it some other place and time."[19]

This episode offered an ideal target for graphic attack. Especially potent was a cartoon titled *The Commander-in-Chief Conciliates the Soldiers' Vote on the Battlefield.* Lincoln stands at the center, clad in a long cloak and holding a tartan cap—a reminder of "the coward's disguise" he was alleged to have worn when fear of assassination prompted a furtive 1861 journey to Washington as president-elect. Several dead bodies are carried from the field while an officer—evidently McClellan—tends to a wounded soldier. A distraught figure remonstrates as the president demands, "Now, Marshall, sing us 'Picayune Butler,' or something else that's funny."[20]

Lincoln loyalists took alarm at the potential grip of the bogus story on the public imagination. Lamon prepared a reply for the press, but the president considered it too bellicose and fashioned his own rebuttal, to appear over his friend's signature. While traveling on an ambulance from Antietam to Major General Fitz John Porter's corps, Lincoln wrote, "the President asked me to sing [a] little sad song . . . which he had often heard me sing." Then "some one of the party, (I do not think it was the President) asked me to sing something else; and I sang two or three little comic things." But "the place was not on the battle field, the time was sixteen days after the battle, no dead body was seen during the whole time . . . , nor even a grave that had not been rained on since it was made." On reflection, however, Lincoln decided not to release his account, telling Lamon, "You know, Hill, that this is the truth and the whole truth about that affair, but I dislike to appear as an apologist for an act of my own which I know was right."[21]

Given the plentiful evidence of the repugnance prompted by Lincoln's recourse to humor, how is it possible to claim that it served his statesmanship and skill in public affairs? Several lines of argument make the case: first, that Lincoln used anecdotes as a means of political pedagogy and illumination; second, that his jokes, stories, and ready wit helped lubricate his relations with others; third, that Lincoln's appetite for satirical humor, in particular, helped underscore the values that infused his key policies; and fourth, last but by no means least, that Lincoln provides exemplary confirmation of the truth that humor, as a lens on the follies of humankind, may prompt and sustain a more generous, thoughtful, and wise statesmanship.

Lincoln's stories served as a colorful means of political instruction and elucidation. "He seemed never to talk without some definite aim in view," one acquaintance reflected. "The few stories I heard him relate were told in each instance to illustrate some well-defined point." According to Noah Brooks, "His anecdotes were seldom told for the sake of the telling, but because they . . . shed a light on the argument that nothing else could." Lincoln himself told a colleague, "They say I tell a great many stories; I reckon I do, but I have found in the course of a long experience that common people, *common people*, take them as they run, are more easily influenced and informed through the medium of broad illustration than in any other way."[22]

As president, Lincoln was irritated by those who saw him as a simple entertainer. At the Soldiers' Home in June 1863, a group of late-evening visitors found him preparing for bed, his face so lined with anxiety and weariness that one of the callers, Silas W. Burt, felt keenly the presumptuous invasion of his peace. As they were leaving, Burt recalled, a drunken army officer "slapped the President on his knee and said: 'Mr. President, tell us one of your good stories.'" Lincoln "drew himself up, and turning his back as far as possible upon the Major, with great dignity addressed the rest of us, saying: 'I believe I have the popular reputation of being a story-teller, but I do not deserve the name in its general sense; for it is not the story itself, but its purpose or effect, that interests me. I often avoid a long and useless discussion by others or a laborious explanation on my own part by a short story that illustrates my point of view. . . . No, I am not simply a story-teller.'"[23]

Rather, Lincoln used stories as parables to drive home political arguments with engaging economy. When Major General John Pope telegraphed that he had captured 5,000 Confederates, the cabinet asked the president's opinion. "That reminds me," he replied, of an "old woman who was ill." The doctor gave her medicine for her constipation. The next morning he found her "fresh & well getting breakfast." She confirmed that the medicine had worked. "How many movements?" he inquired. "142," she said. "Madame I am serious," the physician replied, "How many?" "142." "Madame, I *must* know," he insisted. "It is necessary I have the exact no. of movements." "I tell you 142," she said, "140 of them *wind*." Lincoln closed the discussion: "I am afraid Pope's captures are 140 of them wind."[24]

Examples of Lincoln's humorous economy in argument are legion. Joseph Gillespie recollected discussing the theory of state sovereignty with the president, who declared that "the advocates of that theory always reminded him of the fellow who contended that the proper place for the big kettle was inside of the little one." Facing objections to the declaration of martial law in Kentucky, since only a few qualified voters had been excluded from the polls there, Lincoln cited the case of Sarah, an unmarried mother, whose plea in extenuation was that "the baby was a little one."[25]

Lincoln recognized that war with foreign powers had to be avoided at all costs—"one war at a time," was his precept. During the *Trent* crisis of late 1861, Orville Browning urged him not to yield to London's demands for the release of the Confederate envoys seized from a British ship: England was bluffing and would not dare fight. Lincoln reminded his friend of a vicious bulldog back in Springfield. Neighbors denied it was dangerous, but he recalled the words of a man who was not so sure: "I know the bulldog will not bite. You know he will not bite, but does the bulldog know he will not bite?" Supported by just one cabinet member during a critical phase of that crisis, the president recalled the drunk who strayed into a church and fell asleep in the front pew. He slumbered on as the revivalist asked, "Who are on the Lord's side?" and the congregation responded by rising en masse. When the preacher then inquired, "Who are on the side of the Devil?" the sleeper stirred and, not fully grasping the inquiry but seeing the minister on his feet, stood up. "I don't exactly understand the question," he said, "but I'll stand by you, parson, to the last. But it seems to me," he added, "that we're in a hopeless minority."[26]

Lincoln's versatility lay not just in finding a story for almost every occasion but also in applying the same tale in different contexts. He several times made use of the story of a barber faced with shaving a lantern-jawed customer with cheeks so hollow that the barber "couldn't get down into the valleys with the razor." Ingeniously, he determined "to stick his finger in the man's mouth and press out the cheeks." But in doing so, "he cut clean through the cheek and into his own finger. He pulled the finger out of the man's mouth and snapped the blood off it and looked at him and said: 'There, you lantern-jawed cus, you've made me cut my finger.'" Horace Porter heard the president tell this to illustrate the dangers England faced in assisting the South: "In the end she will find she has only cut off her own finger."[27] On other occasions, Lincoln used the same anecdote to show that "we've got to be mighty cautious how we manage the negro question."[28]

The story of the Irish teetotaler who wanted whisky added to his glass of lemonade "all unbeknownst to mesilf" offered Lincoln a means of signaling that, given the particular circumstances of the challenge in hand, he was keen to turn a blind eye. So it was with Brigadier General Thomas Ewing's proposal in August 1863 to deport thousands of Missouri civilians from guerrilla-supporting communities and free their enslaved people. When Frank Blair visited Lincoln to seek his views, the president took refuge in the anecdote, leaving his meaning plain. Blair reported later to Major General John Schofield, Union commander in Missouri: "The inference is that old Abe would be glad if you would dispose of the Guerrillas and would not be sorry to see the negroes set free, if it can be done without his being known in the affair as having instigated it. He will be certain to recognize it afterward as a military necessity."[29] With the Confederacy's defeat imminent, Lincoln said he would be saved a deal of bother if his generals allowed Jefferson Davis to escape, "all unbeknownst" to himself.[30]

Other tales that Lincoln often deployed to dodge issues, or to caution against addressing troubles that might never arise, included the farmer who "plowed around" the tree stump that blocked his way. This, Lincoln told Senator James Harlan, was how to handle the "Mormon question." An equally graphic anecdote centered on a group of traveling Methodist ministers who were approaching a river in Illinois that—in Lincoln's words as recalled by George Templeton Strong—was "ugly to cross, ye know, because the waters was up. And they got considerin' and discussin' how they should git across it, and they talked about it for two hours, and one on 'em thought they had ought to cross one way when they got there, and another way, and they got quarrelin' about it, till at last an old brother put in, and he says, says he, 'Brethren, this here talk ain't no use. I never cross a river until I come to it."[31] This, the president explained, was how he handled the pressure to take more radical measures relating to slavery.

The power of Lincoln's humor to enforce his argument was, by one estimate, "irresistible always." It confirmed the president as the representative American. One commentator described his jokes as a "happy device" in prompting public understanding. The women's rights activist and abolitionist Caroline Healey Dall rebuked those "fine ladies" who were repelled by the president's "homely manners" and jokes. "As a nation," she wrote, "we are an intelligent, but not a cultivated people. Mr. Lincoln fairly represents our average attainment, and he has never written a letter that the humble of his constituents cannot understand. . . . Aesop told some stories, and his homely wisdom has kept his name alive. Our Divine Master knew little of classic lore or historic legend," but Jesus did know how to tell a simple, instructive story.[32]

Lincoln's humor gave him a means of turning, deflecting, or smoothing a conversation without giving undue offence. One of his legal associates judged that in the courtroom Lincoln's resort to stories was the sign that he was shoring up a faltering case: he "never indulged in fun when he had a great case—one which he believed was right—then he argued simply but if his case were weak he would tell stories, cover his opponent, the witness etc with ridicule, keep court & jury shrieking with laughter, but when he was *sure,* he was grave."[33] In the political sphere he similarly used anecdotes as a means of deflection. William Cullen Bryant, editor of the *New York Evening Post,* recognized that the president's stories sometimes served to rebuke those who wasted his time with trivialities. Equally, he saw that Lincoln used humor to give himself time when issues could not be hurried; they were not a mark of drift or inaction.[34]

John Hay told how in late 1863 "an infernal nuisance" of a Brooklyn postmaster "fastened himself to the Tycoon . . . and tried to get into conversation about the following year's presidential election": would Lincoln be seeking a second term? The president "quickly put him off with a story of his friend Jesse Dubois," who as state auditor controlled the use of the Illinois State House in Springfield. "An itinerant quack preacher" requested it as the venue for a religious lecture. "'What's it about' said Jesse. 'The Second Coming of Christ' said the parson. 'Nonsense' roared Uncle Jesse, 'if Christ had been to Springfield once, and got away, he'd be damned clear of coming again.'"[35]

One of the president's most stressful tasks upon entering office in 1861 was coping with the surge of applicants for government posts: he was bombarded with far more requests than he had jobs. One day a delegation called to urge the appointment of an acquaintance as commissioner to the Sandwich Islands. They earnestly emphasized not only his fitness for the post but also his poor health, which would benefit from the balmy climate. The president responded with affected regret: "Gentlemen, I am sorry to say that there are eight other applicants for that place, and they are all sicker than your man." To another disappointed office seeker, the president said: "I had in my pig sty a little bit of a pig, that made a terrible commotion—do you know why? Because the old sow had just one more little pig than she had teats, and the little porker that got no teat made a terrible squealing."[36]

Humor also helped deflect protests about conscription. Lincoln supposedly met a deputation from an Illinois village who complained about the draft. As "the Aesop of the new world," he eased their concerns with the story of a "little one-horse village in Maryland, whose quota . . . was one man." The enrolling officer solemnly demanded from the old woman at one of the farmhouses "the name of every male creature" there. She listed them all, including a certain Billy Bray, on whom the lot fell in the draft. When the provost marshal came for his conscript, he discovered that Mr. Bray was the farmer's donkey. "So gentlemen," said Lincoln to his fellow Illinoisans, "you may be the donkey of your town and escape. Therefore don't distress yourselves by meeting trouble half way."[37]

The accusation that Lincoln took pleasure in telling vulgar stories was well founded, but these were just one element in his capacious appetite for humor. At one end of the spectrum, he enjoyed tall tales, absurdity, and larger-than-life characters. At the other, he took cerebral delight in the plasticity, ambiguity, and surprises of language. Between these two poles, Lincoln happily indulged in quick wit, irony, logical fallacy, and satire. His relish for the last of these reveals a key aspect of his wartime statesmanship.

From an early age, Lincoln enjoyed wielding a satirical pen and never lost his admiration for clever writing that exposed hypocrisy, ethical inconsistency, and double-dealing. An ill-judged satirical assault in 1842 on James Shields, the Illinois state auditor, almost resulted in a duel that threatened to ruin Lincoln's reputation, if not cost him his life. From then on, he exercised much more caution. In private, among his lawyer friends, he would occasionally "impale an object disagreeable to him on a sarcastic lance." But his prevailing tone lacked cruelty and malice, and his satirical thrusts were in the main restricted to carefully constructed passages within longer speeches, notably in his contests with his great political rival, Stephen A. Douglas. During the joint debates of 1858, even while "attacking his opponent with keen satire or invective, which, coming from any other speaker, would have sounded bitter and cruel," Carl Schurz reflected, "there was still a certain something in his utterance making his hearers feel that those thrusts came from a reluctant heart, and that he would much rather have treated his foe as a friend."[38]

Several of those sallies related to the Little Giant's appeal to the racial antipathies of white Illinoisans. Faced with the charge that his opposition to slavery meant he was bent upon full equality between the races, Lincoln mocked Douglas for his fallacious logic. At Charleston he declared, to cheers and laughter, "I do not understand that because I do not want a negro woman for a slave I must necessarily want her for a wife. . . . I will also add . . . that I have never had the least apprehension that I or my friends would marry negroes if there was no law to keep them from it."[39] There was also a satirical edge to his reflections on color in a speech at Springfield: "I do not understand the Declaration [of Independence] to mean that all men were created equal in all respects. They are not our equal in color; but I suppose that it does mean to declare that all men are equal in some respects; they are equal in their right to 'life, liberty, and the pursuit of happiness.'"[40]

Lincoln's relish for satire that lampooned the raw race prejudice so rife within the Democratic Party grew keener during the Civil War at the same time that his own views on racial matters became more openly progressive. Above all, he admired the scathing humor of David Ross Locke, a young Ohio newspaperman and merciless satirist of the Peace Democrats, the Copperheads. Locke's comic satire centered on a grotesque creation, the Reverend Petroleum Vesuvius Nasby, a determined enemy of reform, emancipation, and progressive causes. Racist, drunken, greedy, sordid, lying, and bigoted (Locke called him "a nickel-plated son of a bitch"), the fictional Nasby and his illiterate letters to the public first appeared in the columns of Union newspapers in April 1862.[41] His middle name warned readers to prepare for regular, caustic eruptions on pressing wartime issues.

Locke created an imaginative comic narrative for this disciple of the Peace

Democrat Clement Vallandigham. He has Nasby, an inhabitant of a fictional southern Ohio village, taking refuge in Canada to escape the Union draft. Returning home, he is seized and conscripted. He flees to the Confederacy and enlists in an infantry regiment, the Louisiana Pelicans. Disillusioned with the straitened conditions of Confederate service, he again returns home, is arrested for desertion, and imprisoned. Returning to Ohio on his release, Nasby organizes a Democratic church through whose pulpit for the rest of the war he preaches the anti-Black, proslavery peace gospel of "St Valandygum."[42]

By these means, Locke delivered an uncompromising cultural critique. Like all memorable satire, Nasby's letters stake out a conflict between two worldviews, one *explicit* and ridiculed by the resort to absurdity, the other *implicit*. Nasby was the negative photographic print that, when reversed, yielded the positive moral order. Locke himself described his creation as "a convenient vehicle for conveying political truths backwards." The author's implicit voice was that of the New England moralist. Locke was not deeply religious, but the influence of a staunchly antislavery father and an equally devout mother left its mark. He passionately hated slavery and was as close to a racial egalitarian as one could find among white Americans of his time.[43]

Locke's use of the appalling Nasby to ridicule disloyal opponents of the Union administration, and above all their toxic racial views, prompted Lincoln's unrestrained delight. Of the president's satirical sense, Locke declared that it "was at times as blunt as a meat-ax, and at others as keen as a razor"; he located its inspiration in Lincoln's hatred of "horrible injustice. . . . Weakness he was never ferocious with, but intentional wickedness he never spared." Lincoln's friends and acquaintances readily acknowledged this stern trait. According to Leonard Swett: "As he became involved in matters of the gravest importance, full of great responsibility and great doubt, a feeling of religious reverence, and belief in God—his justice and overruling power—increased upon him. . . . He believed in the great laws of truth, the rigid discharge of duty, his accountability to God, the ultimate triumph of right, and the overthrow of wrong."[44]

A sharp sense of the injustice of slavery shaped Lincoln's response to Nasby. So too—albeit with greater complexity—did the injustice of color prejudice. In September 1859 Locke heard Lincoln speak at Columbus, Ohio, and was startled by his defensive and ungenerous statements about race; he thought it "curious" that the speaker denied that he supported Black suffrage and went "out of his way to affirm his support of the law of Illinois forbidding the intermarriage of whites and negroes."[45] Locke could not then know that Lincoln was set on a journey that would see him sign an emancipation edict, press for a constitutional amendment to end slavery, and entertain an embryonic program of Black rights and citizenship. It was a course that gave a keener edge to Lincoln's reading of Nasby and encourages the proposition that in a small way Locke assisted in his radicalization. The president relished no piece more than "On Negro Emigration"—the quintessence of Nasby's ranting on race, which he could quote from memory— and was capable of his own dry humor at the expense of negrophobes.[46] A certain John McMahon of Towanda, Pennsylvania, sent a telegram to the president to educate him in "what is justice & what is truth to all men." Lincoln, he wrote, should respect the proposition: "Equal Rights & Justice to all white men in the United States forever. White men is in class number one & black men is in class number two & must be governed by white men forever." Lincoln drafted a reply purporting to be composed by his secretary; he explained that the president wanted to know "whether you are either a white man or black one, because in either case, you can not be regarded as an entirely impartial judge—It may be that you belong to a third or fourth class of *yellow* or *red* men, in which case the impartiality of your judgment would be more apparant."[47] Lincoln's delight in the egregious Nasby, then, was far more than the relish of a joke—it was the double joy of recognizing a brilliant assault on ugly racial stereotyping, too.

The Nasby Papers was Lincoln's constant companion. He could quote passages from memory. Swett maintained that the president read Nasby "as much as he did the bible."[48] On the final afternoon of his life, Lincoln delayed dinner by reading Nasby aloud to two old Illinois friends. "For the genius to write these things," he declared, "I would gladly give up my office."[49] He admired the great ethical force of Locke's satire, honoring the Union's pursuit of justice. Lincoln's chief pleasure was humor that elicited *righteous* mirth—a *just* laughter occasioned by comic writing that delivered a moral critique.

Lincoln's jesting provides an example of a more universal truth, that humor can yield a perspective on human frailties that enhances the capacity for wise political leadership.[50] Throughout his life, Lincoln used humor to expose the foibles and absurdities of humankind, drawing attention both to his own peculiarities, through self-mockery, and to the shortcomings of others. Possessing a strong sense of self-worth, he happily made a joke at his own expense. Personal characteristics that he might have turned to his credit—such as his abstinence from tobacco and alcohol—he used against himself. He enjoyed recounting his conversational exchange with a Kentuckian who had offered him a plug of tobacco, a cigar, and a glass of brandy. When Lincoln declined, explaining that he did not indulge, the gentleman remarked amiably, "See here, my jolly companion, I have gone through the world a great deal and have had much experience with men and women of all classes, and in all climes, and I have noticed one thing. . . . That those who have no vices have d—d few virtues."[51]

Lincoln made much of his unprepossessing appearance. Conscious of his untypical physical proportions—his height and unusually long limbs—and aware that many considered him an ugly man, he acknowledged that head on. He related a supposed encounter with a stranger in a railroad car, who said, "Excuse me, sir, but I have an article in my possession which belongs to you." Taking a jackknife from his pocket, the man explained: "This . . . was placed in my hands some years ago, with the injunction that I was to keep it until I found a man *uglier* than myself. . . . Allow me *now* to say, sir, that I think *you* are fairly entitled to the property." Lincoln's jesting gave rise to a yarn that, when he was splitting rails while wearing only a shirt and breeches, he found himself looking down the gun barrel of a passerby. "Says Lincoln What do you mean[?]" The man explained "that he had promised to shoot the first man he met who was uglier than himself." Getting a good look at the man's face, Lincoln remarked, while baring his chest, "If I am uglier than you, then blaze away."[52]

This habit of self-deprecation had its uses, notably in enlisting the audience on the side of the underdog, dealing with a dilemma, or taking the sting out of a conversation. When Owen Lovejoy and a western delegation secured Lincoln's agreement to an exchange of soldiers between the eastern and western theaters, the secretary of war flatly refused to implement the scheme, telling Lovejoy that the president was "a damned fool" for ordering it. Bewildered, the Illinois congressman returned to tell this to Lincoln, who paused before saying, "If Stanton said I was a damned fool, then I must be one, for he is nearly always right, and generally says what he means. I will step over and see him."[53]

Lincoln was thus a shining example of one of Reinhold Niebuhr's insights. The theologian found in humor "the capacity of the self to gain a vantage point from which it is able to look at itself." Those with a sense of humor, he noted, "do not take themselves too seriously. They are able to . . . see themselves in perspective, and recognize the ludicrous . . . aspects of their pretensions." By contrast, egotists and narcissists, supposing themselves the planetary center of life, are guilty of absurd pretension—"and its absurdity increases with our lack of awareness of it."[54]

Lincoln appreciated such absurdity in the human condition; it animated the stories he told. Beyond this, his humorous disposition served as a psychological resource on which he could draw to face the world's predicaments and hold them in healthy perspective.

"If it were not for these stories, jokes, jests I should die; they give vent—are the vents—of my moods and gloom," Lincoln confessed to the painter Francis Carpenter. Defending his taste for bawdiness, he explained how "a real smutty story if it has the element of genuine wit in its composition, as most of such stories have, has the same effect on me that I think a good square drink of whisky has to an old toper. It puts new life into me. The fact is, I have always believed that a good laugh was good for both the mental and physical digestion." Jonathan Browning, a gunsmith, told how he and Lincoln swapped yarns when they met as young men. Lincoln chuckled when Browning told him he had got his first Bible by trading a gun for it. Quoting the prophet Isaiah, he quipped that the gunsmith had turned swords into plowshares. Browning, however, confessed that the traded gun had been defective. In mock indignation Lincoln wagged his finger: "You mean that you cheated in a trade for a Bible—a Bible!" "Not exactly," Browning retorted. "When I got to looking through that Bible at home, I found about half the New Testament was missing." The uncontrolled mirth of the two men, in Browning's words, "near to shook the logs" of his cabin.[55] As president, Lincoln rarely knew such unrestrained and untroubled merriment, but he still sought and found peculiar comfort and nourishment from laughing along with those who shared his sense of humor, notably William Seward and John Hay.

In the sphere of politics, Niebuhr considered a sense of humor "indispensable to men of affairs who have the duty of organizing their fellowmen in common endeavors. It reduces the frictions of life and makes the foibles of men tolerable." He did not explicitly cite Lincoln as a model, though he might well have done so, for the Civil War president exemplified the insight that, "in the laughter with which we observe . . . the foibles of others," there is "a nice mixture of mercy and judgment, of censure and forbearance."[56] Humor was an indispensable element in Lincoln's statesmanship.

The political attacks and personal criticism that Lincoln suffered as a self-indulgent humorist are not the whole story. They existed alongside a far more nuanced appreciation of the president's jesting, one encouraged by supporters who seized on his studied use of humor to show how an occupant of the White House could remain a genial man of the people. While the president faced up to the ordeal of wartime office—the setbacks in the field and the high-risk decisions over emancipation, civil liberties, and other divisive policies—his supporters wove his "inveterate habit of telling ludicrous stories to illustrate his opinions" into a larger appreciation of his strength of moral character and determination.[57]

During the course of the war, proadministration newspapers eagerly broadcast "the president's latest story." Hay, Lincoln's private secretary, cultivated a warm relationship with several journalists and saw the benefit of providing examples of the president's wit that passed the test of respectability. Hay's friend Charles Halpine—a War Democrat and writer for the *New York Herald*—mostly served the administration well, particularly following the antidraft riots in New York City in July 1863, when he worked hard to build support for the war among the Irish. To that end, he created an affectionately comic figure, Private Miles O'Reilly, a fervent loyalist whose apparent familiarity with the White House led some readers to mistake fiction for fact. Hay provided his friend with the details that gave spurious authenticity to O'Reilly's meetings with the president and reinforced the image of Lincoln as a man of warmth, humor, and humanity. The defining episode was the president's pardoning of O'Reilly, who languished in prison for writing satirical poems about the Union's military command.[58]

Lincoln's humor allowed the Union presses to characterize the president as the representative American.[59] One commentator described his jokes as a "happy device" in prompting public understanding: "a joke goes for a joke, and not for solemn dogma; an illustration is accepted as such, and not necessarily as a leaf from history which one must swear to." Those distressed by them were "silly people" with "very feeble intellectual digestion." Hearing a presidential story designed to expose the folly of some proposition, "Mr Feeble-mind . . . goes home, consults Plutarch and can't find it there; gets down his Bible, it isn't there; looks in the American Encyclopaedia, it is not there; so he is forced to the conclusion that the President told a wrong story, . . . can not see its truth, and doubts if the war can ever be ended till there is a change of Administrations."⁶⁰ For the New York lawyer T. J. Barnett, this was why "the people can understand him so well, and why the politicians can not comprehend him at all." The people's affectionate regard, he declared, was "absolutely filial" and savored "of the *household*."⁶¹

This benign reading of Lincoln's humor was sufficiently powerful for commercial interests to use it in wartime compilations of jokes and stories, supposedly (but rarely) originating with the president. The publishers of *Old Abe's Joker; or, Wit at the White House* asked, "what could be more natural than to associate with 'quips and cranks and wanton wiles,' the name of one who so greatly enjoys and successfully perpetrates the fine old, full-flavored joke." Graphic advertisements for *Old Abe's Jokes, Fresh from Abraham's Bosom* show the rail-splitter president entertaining a rapt audience of common men wreathed in smiles.

Early in the presidential election year of 1864, Bryant's radical *New York Evening Post* offered a commentary on a wide array of Lincoln's jokes and "little stories," which it characterized as the mark of a purposeful, genial, and wise commander in chief. Bryant's purpose was to show how the tortured mind of a suffering, bone-weary, and patient president found occasional relief "in an appropriate anecdote or well turned jest." His "atrocious" puns brought him innocent delight. He found humor when bedridden with contagious varioloid ("I've got something now that I can give to everybody").⁶²

An understanding of the moral grounding of the president's humor infused mainstream Union opinion. As voters turned out on Election Day, 1864, an infantryman stationed near Nashville distilled in admiring verse the essence of Father Abraham's appeal:

The man who now has nations for beholders,
Who dared to say his Government was made
To lift the weights from off all men's shoulders,
Though for a time its purpose was delayed;
While Treason's banded millions were arrayed,
Displayed the art that made those hosts afraid.

Few would have thought who heard him telling stories,
And jokes that rustic hearers might applaud,
That he would be one of our country's glories,
And live to send those edicts far abroad
That made enslavers tremble and be awed.[63]

As the war drew to an end, Lincoln told a close friend, "die when I may I want it said of me by those who know me best . . . that I always plucked a thistle and planted a flower where I thought a flower would grow."[64] In his strenuous nurturing of the republic, Lincoln the statesman could call on strategic wisdom, clarity of principle, skill in political management and communication, grasp of human psychology, and physical and mental strength. To these ingredients we should add his remarkable and celebrated sense of humor, an expression of his essential humanity, sense of proportion, and understanding of human foibles. Served by an exceptional intellect, flawless memory, quick wit, and mastery of language, Lincoln used his stock of tall tales and jokes to foster friendship, build support, and undermine opponents' arguments, particularly when they reeked of injustice. His example prompts the question: Is wise statesmanship possible without a sense of the ludicrous, of the absurdities and flaws of humankind, oneself included? It is not difficult to identify political leaders who would do well to reflect on this insight: "the less we are able to laugh at ourselves, the more it becomes necessary and inevitable that others laugh at us."[65]

NOTES

1. This essay draws in part on Richard Carwardine, *Lincoln's Sense of Humor* (Carbondale: Southern Illinois University Press, 2017).

2. Douglas L. Wilson and Rodney O. Davis, eds., *Herndon's Informants: Letters Interviews, and Statements about Abraham Lincoln* (Urbana: University of Illinois Press, 1998), 37, 598.

3. Allen Thorndike Rice, ed., *Reminiscences of Abraham Lincoln by Distinguished Men of His Time* (New York: North American, 1886), 428.

4. Michael Burlingame, "Abraham Lincoln: A Life," Lincoln Studies Center, Knox College, chap. 21, p. 2257, https://www.knox.edu/documents/LincolnStudies/BurlingameVol2Chap21.pdf. This is from the complete unedited manuscript of Burlingame's massive biography of Lincoln (published in two volumes in 2008), which is available at https://www.knox.edu/about-knox/lincoln-studies-center/burlingame-abraham-lincoln-a-life.

5. Wilson and Davis, *Herndon's Informants*, 420, 470.

6. Joshua F. Speed, *Reminiscences of Abraham Lincoln and Notes of a Visit to California* (Louisville: J. P. Morton, 1884), 31–32.

7. Ida M. Tarbell, "Humor in the White House," 7–8, Tarbell Collection, Allegheny College; Joseph G. Baldwin, *The Flush Times of Alabama and Mississippi: A Series of Sketches* (New York: D. Appleton, 1854); George H. Derby, *Phoenixiana; or, Sketches and Burlesques* (New York: D. Appleton, 1856).

8. Wayne Lee Garner, "Abraham Lincoln and the Uses of Humor" (PhD diss., State University of Iowa, 1963), 30–34, 57–58.

9. Robert C. Bray, *Reading with Lincoln* (Carbondale: Southern Illinois University Press, 2010), 16–18; Garner, "Lincoln and the Uses of Humor," 74–78.

10. Henry C. Whitney, *Life on the Circuit with Lincoln* (Boston: Estes, 1892), 177.

11. Bray, *Reading with Lincoln*, 200–209.

12. Horace Porter, Speech, Feb. 1889, Scrapbook 15, p. 40, Lincoln Collection, Huntington Library, San Marino, CA.

13. Noah Brooks, "Personal Reminiscences of Lincoln," *Scribner's Monthly* 15, nos. 4–5 (Feb.–Mar. 1878), 563–64.

14. Wilson and Davis, *Herndon's Informants*, 187.

15. Arthur A. Sloane, *Humor in the White House: The Wit of Five American Presidents* (Jefferson, NC: McFarland, 2001), 93–94, 165–68, 183; Wilson and Davis, *Herndon's Informants*, 442.

16. *The Weekly Vincennes (IN) Western Sun*, May 26, 1860; *Harper's Weekly*, Mar. 2, 1861.

17. *Harper's Weekly*, Jan. 3, 1863; *Old Guard* 1 (Oct.–Dec. 1863), 240.

18. *New York Herald*, Jan. 23, Feb. 19, 20, 1864; *Harper's Weekly*, Apr. 2, 1864.

19. *New York World*, Sept. 9, 1864.

20. Unknown artist, *The Commander-in-Chief Conciliates the Soldiers' Votes*, New York, Oct. 1864, Library of Congress.

21. Don E. Fehrenbacher and Virginia Fehrenbacher, eds., *Recollected Words of Abraham Lincoln* (Stanford, CA: Stanford University Press, 1996), 290.

22. Harris, "Recollections of Abraham Lincoln," Scrapbook 45, p. 10, Lincoln Collection, Huntington Library; Rice, *Reminiscences of Abraham Lincoln*, 428.

23. Silas W. Burt, "Lincoln on His Own Story-Telling," *Century Magazine* 73, no. 4 (Feb. 1907): 499–502.

24. As told to Ida M. Tarbell by Albert J. Conant, undated memo, Tarbell Papers. My thanks to Michael Burlingame for this source.

25. Fehrenbacher and Fehrenbacher, *Recollected Words of Abraham Lincoln*, 168.

26. Jay Monaghan, *Diplomat in Carpet Slippers: Abraham Lincoln Deals with Foreign Affairs* (Indianapolis: Bobbs-Merrill, 1945), 187; Alexander K. McClure, *"Abe" Lincoln's Yarns and Stories* (Philadelphia: Elliott, 1901), 442–43.

27. Horace Porter, Speech, Feb. 1889, Scrapbook 15, p. 40, Lincoln Collection, Huntington Library.

28. Burlingame, "Abraham Lincoln: A Life," chap. 27, p. 2931, https://www.knox.edu/documents/LincolnStudies/BurlingameVol2Chap27.pdf.

29. Mark E. Neely, "'Unbeknownst to Lincoln': A Note on Radical Pacification in Missouri during the Civil War," *Civil War History* 44, no. 3 (Sept. 1998): 214.

30. Garner, "Lincoln and the Uses of Humor," 639.

31. Allan Nevins and Milton Halsey Thomas, eds., *Diary of George Templeton Strong*, 4 vols. (New York: Macmillan, 1952), 3:204–5.

32. *San Francisco Daily Evening Bulletin*, Jan. 6, 7, 1864; *Washington Reporter*, Jan. 20, 1864; *The Liberator* (Boston), May 6, 1864.

33. Michael Burlingame, *Abraham Lincoln: A Life*, 2 vols. (Baltimore: Johns Hopkins University Press, 2008), 1:930.

34. *New York Evening Post*, Feb. 17, 1864; *New York Herald*, Feb. 19, 1864.

35. John M. Hay to Miles O'Reilly, Nov. 22, 1863, John M. Hay Papers, Huntington Library.

36. Rice, *Reminiscences of Abraham Lincoln*, 240; Herbert Mitgang, ed., *Abraham Lincoln, a Press Portrait* (Chicago: Quadrangle Books, 1971), 274.

37. Paul M. Zall, ed., *Abe Lincoln's Legacy of Laughter: Humorous Stories by and about Abraham Lincoln* (Knoxville: University of Tennessee Press, 2007), 28.

38. Henry C. Whitney, *Lincoln the Citizen* (New York: Current Literature, 1907), 47; Carl Schurz, *Reminiscences of Carl Schurz*, 3 vols. (New York: McClure, 1907–8), 2:93–94, 96.

39. Lincoln, "Fourth Debate with Stephen A. Douglas at Charleston, Illinois," Sept. 18, 1858, in *The Collected Works of Abraham Lincoln*, ed. Roy P. Basler et al., 9 vols. (New Brunswick, NJ: Rutgers University Press, 1953–55), 3:146.

40. Lincoln, "Speech at Springfield, Illinois," July 17, 1858, ibid., 2:520.

41. John M. Harrison, *The Man Who Made Nasby, David Ross Locke* (Chapel Hill: University of North Carolina Press, 1969), 98.

42. David Ross Locke, *The Nasby Papers: Letters and Sermons containing the Views on the Topics of the Day, of Petroleum V. Nasby, "Paster uv the Church of the Noo Dispensashun"* (Indianapolis: C. O. Perrine, 1864).

43. Harrison, *Man Who Made Nasby*, 14–15, 20, 23–24, 31–32, 85–86, 121; Joseph Jones, "Introduction," *The Struggles of Petroleum V. Nasby by David Ross Locke* (Boston: Beacon, 1963), xi, xviii.

44. Rice, *Reminiscences of Abraham Lincoln*, 442; Wilson and Davis, *Herndon's Informants*, 166, 182–84, 350–51, 507.

45. Rice, *Reminiscences of Abraham Lincoln*, 446–47.

46. Harrison, *Man Who Made Nasby*, 112.

47. John McMahon to Lincoln, Aug. 5, 1864; Lincoln to John McMahon, Aug. 6, 1864; and John G. Nicolay to John McMahon, Aug. 6, 1864, Abraham Lincoln Papers, Library of Congress.

48. Wilson and Davis, *Herndon's Informants*, 167.

49. Archibald Henry Grimké, *Charles Sumner, the Scholar in Politics* (New York: Funk & Wagnalls, 1892), 363.

50. Walter G. Moss, "What Is True Political Wisdom? A Primer for the 2012 Election," History News Network, George Washington University, Mar. 5, 2012, https://historynewsnetwork.org/article /144887 (accessed Jan. 5, 2020).

51. Burlingame, *Abraham Lincoln: A Life*, 1:301; cf. Fehrenbacher and Fehrenbacher, *Recollected Words of Abraham Lincoln*, 139.

52. Francis B. Carpenter, *Six Months at the White House with Abraham Lincoln* (New York: Hurd and Houghton, 1866), 148–49; Fehrenbacher and Fehrenbacher, *Recollected Words of Abraham Lincoln*, 126; Wilson and Davis, *Herndon's Informants*, 85.

53. Benjamin Platt Thomas, "Lincoln's Humor: An Analysis," *Papers of the Abraham Lincoln Association* 3 (1981): 40.

54. Robert McAfee Brown, ed., *The Essential Reinhold Niebuhr: Selected Essays and Addresses* (New Haven, CT: Yale University Press, 1986), 54.

55. Fehrenbacher and Fehrenbacher, *Recollected Words of Abraham Lincoln*, 252, 437–38; Carpenter, *Six Months at the White House with Abraham Lincoln*, 152; Helen Nicolay, *Personal Traits of Abraham Lincoln* (New York: Century, 1912), 16; William H. Herndon and Jesse Weik, *Herndon's Lincoln: William H. Herndon and Jesse W. Weik*, ed. Douglas L. Wilson and Rodney O. Davis (Urbana: University of Illinois Press, 2006), 355n; John Browning and Curt Gentry, *John M. Browning: American Gunmaker* (New York: Doubleday, 1964), 12–13. Cf. Brown, *Essential Reinhold Niebuhr*, 56–57.

56. Brown, *Essential Reinhold Niebuhr*, 51.

57. *Washington Reporter*, June 19, 1862; *San Francisco Evening Bulletin*, Nov. 4, 1862.

58. Charles G. Halpine, *The Life and Adventures, Songs, Services, and Speeches of Private Miles O'Reilly* (New York: Carleton, 1864).

59. *San Francisco Daily Evening Bulletin*, Jan. 6, 1864; *Washington Reporter*, Jan. 20, 1864.

60. *San Francisco Daily Evening Bulletin*, Jan. 7, 1864.

61. T. J. Barnett, *Abraham Lincoln, the Peoples' Candidate. Speech . . . in Richmond, Indiana, October 6, 1864* (N.p.: Union State Central Committee, 1864), 15–16.

62. *New York Evening Post*, Feb. 17, 1864.

63. *The Liberator* (Boston), Dec. 9, 1864.

64. Wilson and Davis, *Herndon's Informants*, 405–6.

65. Brown, *Essential Reinhold Niebuhr*, 54.

The Second Founding

How the Civil War and Reconstruction Remade the Constitution

ERIC FONER

The Civil War and Reconstruction transformed American society in innumerable ways. Many of their effects are still with us today, as are controversies about how these years should be remembered—witness the debates over statues of Confederate leaders. But perhaps the most tangible legacies of that era are the Thirteenth, Fourteenth, and Fifteenth Amendments to the US Constitution. These amendments both reflected and reinforced a new era of individual rights consciousness among Americans of all races and backgrounds. They wrote a new definition of US citizenship and the rights it entails into the Constitution, transforming the relationship between individual Americans and the national state. So profound were these changes that the amendments should be seen not simply as an alteration of an existing structure, but as a "constitutional revolution," in the words of Republican leader Carl Schurz, a second American founding that created a fundamentally new document.[1] But they have not achieved recognition as among the key documents of American history, and their authors—members of Congress such as James Ashley, John A. Bingham, and Henry Wilson—are hardly household names.

Reconstruction was both a time period—the years that followed the Civil War—and a historical process that does not have a clear fixed end—the process by which the United States tried to come to terms with the consequences of the Civil War, the two most important of them the preservation of the nation-state and the destruction of the institution of slavery. One might almost say that we are still trying to work out the consequences of the end of slavery in our country. In that sense, Reconstruction never ended.

I have devoted much of my career to the study of Reconstruction. But I have to acknowledge that most Americans know very little about it. The fact is, however, that Reconstruction remains part of our lives today; or to put it another way, key questions facing American society are in some ways Reconstruction questions. Who is entitled to citizenship? Who should have the right to vote? How should the authorities deal with terrorism—not terrorism from abroad but the home-grown terrorism of the Ku Klux Klan and kindred groups that flourished during Reconstruction? Every session of the Supreme Court adjudicates cases requiring the interpretation of the Fourteenth Amendment. You cannot understand American society today without knowing something about that period a century and a half ago.

Reconstruction is also a prime example of what we sometimes call the politics of history. I am not talking about whether the historian is a Republican or Democrat. I mean the way in which historical interpretation both reflects and helps shape the politics of the time in which the historian is writing. For most of the twentieth century, what we call the Dunning school (after my predecessor at Columbia University, Professor William A. Dunning) shaped historical writing and popular thinking on this period. In that view, Reconstruction was the lowest point in the saga of American democracy, a time of misgovernment and corruption caused by the misguided decision to grant the right to vote to Black men, who, according to these scholars, were innately incapable of participating intelligently in political democracy. In Dunning's view, the Thirteenth Amendment was necessary, the Fourteenth reasonable, but the Fifteenth an unmitigated disaster. This interpretation dominated historical scholarship for over half a century and survives to this day in the popular historical consciousness.[2]

How can we account for the remarkable longevity of that portrait of Reconstruction? The explanation is that it harmonized with the racial system of the United States from 1900 until the civil rights era of the 1960s. The political lessons were clear. First, it was a mistake to give Black people the right to vote; therefore the white South was justified in later taking it away. Second, Reconstruction was imposed by northern outsiders. Perhaps some were motivated by humanitarian concerns, but the result proved that northerners simply do not understand race relations in the South and that the white South should resist outside calls for change in its racial system. As late as 1944, Gunnar Myrdal noted in his influential work *An American Dilemma* that, when pressed about the Black condition,

white southerners "will regularly bring forward the horrors of the Reconstruction governments and of 'black domination.'"[3] The third lesson, which seems
arcane today, was that Reconstruction was created by the Republican Party, and
therefore the white South should remain solidly Democratic. One foundation
of the old Solid South was what we may call, using today's terminology, a fake
history of Reconstruction.

When the civil rights revolution, sometimes called the Second Reconstruction,
took place, the pillars of that old interpretation, especially its overt racism, fell
to the ground, and Reconstruction was completely reinterpreted. Today most
historians see it as a noble if unsuccessful attempt to establish, for the first time
in American history, an interracial democracy, a precursor of the modern civil
rights movement. If Reconstruction was tragic, we now think, it was not because
it was attempted but because it failed and thus left to subsequent generations the
difficult problem of racial justice.

To understand how, despite its immediate failure, Reconstruction reshaped
our history in significant ways, we must remind ourselves of the status of African
Americans when the Civil War broke out. There were about four million slaves
in the United States in 1860. Slavery was powerful, expanding, and economically
thriving. It was not going away—there were more slaves in 1860 in the United
States than at any point in our history. Slavery shaped the definition of American
nationality, giving it a powerful racial dimension. The first Naturalization Act,
approved in 1790, limited the process of becoming a citizen to "white" immigrants. On the eve of the Civil War, no Black person, free or slave, even if born
in the United States, could be a US citizen. Individual states could continue to
recognize African Americans as citizens (as a number of northern ones did),
but neither the federal government nor other states were obliged to recognize
this status. That was what the Supreme Court ruled in 1857 in the infamous Dred
Scott decision. The only people before the Civil War who advocated a nonracial
idea of nationality were abolitionists, Black and white. They not only fought
against slavery but also for equal rights for free Blacks. Black political gatherings
before the Civil War consciously chose to call themselves conventions of "colored
citizens" and put forward a definition of citizenship based on birthright, severed
from the concept of race.[4] That is what came about during Reconstruction.

In discussing the constitutional amendments, let me note that whether courts
should interpret the Constitution in accordance with the authors' original intent

or the original meaning of the language, a doctrine that has become central to conservative jurisprudence, is a political, not a historical question. No historian believes that any important document possesses one single intent or meaning. The Thirteenth, Fourteenth, and Fifteenth Amendments, moreover, were enacted not at one moment but over the course of five years, in response to rapidly evolving political and social imperatives, and in a dynamic situation in which peoples' views underwent rapid change. In the wake of the war and the abolition of slavery, definitions of citizenship and rights were in flux. Opponents of Black suffrage came to support it a few years later. Those who initially rejected federal prohibition of discrimination by private businesses later voted for the Civil Rights Act of 1875, which did precisely that. Freezing understanding of the amendments at the moment of passage or ratification misses this dynamic quality.

It is certainly the job of the historian to try to ascertain what those who framed, voted on, and discussed these amendments hoped to accomplish. But intentions must be examined throughout the society, not simply in congressional debates and court decisions. For example, the Fourteenth Amendment was only ratified by a sufficient number of states because Congress in 1867 mandated the establishment of Black male suffrage throughout the South, resulting in the election of new legislatures, including Black members. Without Black suffrage and Black office holding, no Fourteenth Amendment. Well before the Civil War, Black activists had developed an understanding of the rights of citizenship that encompassed equality before the law, the right to vote, and equal access to public accommodations and transportation. They had also moved beyond the era's meticulously parsed distinctions between natural, political, civil, and social rights toward a more modern definition of equality that encompassed all of these simultaneously. During Reconstruction, constitutional language became far more prominent in Black political discourse. Yet the ways African Americans understood the amendments are almost never considered when their intent or meaning are discussed; in fact, they have been consistently ignored by the Supreme Court when it has interpreted the amendments.

In her memoirs written in the 1890s, Elizabeth Cady Stanton recalled that Reconstruction "involved the reconsideration of the principles of our government and the natural rights of man. The nation's heart was thrilled with prolonged debates in Congress and state legislatures, in the pulpits and public journals, and at every fireside on these vital questions."[5] Those debates are part of the meaning of the Reconstruction amendments. And their meaning changed over time as different Americans sought to make use of the amendments, often in ways not anticipated by those who wrote them. To understand the amendments, we must move beyond the courts and Congress and examine constitutional ideas throughout the society.

The first of the Reconstruction amendments was the Thirteenth, ratified in 1865, which irrevocably abolished slavery throughout the United States (introducing the word "slavery" for the first time into the Constitution—the founders had avoided it, using circumlocutions such as "persons held to labor"). Why was the Thirteenth Amendment necessary anyway? Had the Emancipation Proclamation not freed the slaves? On January 1, 1863, Lincoln declared free over three million slaves, the largest single act of slave emancipation in world history. But his proclamation left in bondage three-quarters of a million persons in the four border slave states that had remained in the Union and in certain portions of the Confederacy. Moreover, while freeing individuals, the proclamation did not abrogate the state laws that had established slavery. Emancipation, in other words, is not quite the same thing as abolition. Slavery is created by state law, and those laws must be repealed, or they must be invalidated by a constitutional amendment, if the institution is to die. Even after issuing the proclamation, Lincoln continued to promote his favored policy of state-by-state abolition. Given the high bar to ratification of an amendment, this route seemed more attainable. Lincoln's Proclamation of Amnesty and Reconstruction of December 1863 required states to abolish slavery as a condition of readmission to the Union.[6]

Contrary to what one might conclude from the 2012 Hollywood movie *Lincoln*, abolitionists, not Lincoln, originated the Thirteenth Amendment. The campaign was coordinated by the Women's Loyal National League, headed by Susan B. Anthony and Elizabeth Cady Stanton. In February 1864, after receiving their massive petitions, the abolitionist senator Charles Sumner proposed an amendment based on France's 1791 Declaration of the Rights of Man and of the Citizen: "All persons are equal before the law, so that no person can hold another as a slave." Jacob Howard of Michigan urged Sumner to "dismiss all reference to French constitutions or French codes, and go back to . . . good old Anglo-Saxon language."[7] And the final language was taken almost word for word from the Northwest Ordinance of 1787, to which it had migrated from Thomas Jefferson's proposed Land Ordinance of 1784, which would have prohibited slavery in all the nation's territories. The amendment states, "Neither slavery nor involuntary servitude, except as a punishment for crime whereof the party shall have been duly convicted, shall exist within the United States, or any place subject to their jurisdiction."

The provision allowing involuntary servitude for those convicted of crime is an excellent illustration of the aphorism that historians write with one eye (at least) fixed on the present. For decades, scholars writing about the Thirteenth Amendment (myself included) paid absolutely no attention to it. But with mass incarceration and the widespread use of prison labor suddenly becoming national issues, it has attracted considerable discussion, including in the 2016 Hollywood documentary *13th,* which draws a straight line from the Thirteenth Amendment to the treatment of prisoners today. Actually, the coupling of a ban on slavery with a criminal exemption long preceded the amendment. Scholars have been unable to explain why Jefferson included it in the Land Ordinance in the first place, except to note that he felt that labor helped build character and would assist in rehabilitating criminals. But this wording was included in most of the constitutions of free states that entered the Union, beginning with Ohio in 1803, and was so familiar by 1865 that almost no one in Congress mentioned it when the amendment was under consideration. It had become what we might call "boilerplate" language. Only Sumner sensed that the exemption might cause problems. He later wrote that he lamented not moving to eliminate that clause but had not done so because his colleagues were impatient and anxious "to get their dinner." "I regret now my forbearance," he added.[8] Inadvertently, the amendment created a loophole that would later allow for the widespread leasing of (mostly Black) convict labor on plantations and in industries in the South and the use of prison labor by businesses down to the present. To this day, courts have ruled that involuntary labor by prisoners does not violate the Thirteenth Amendment. Sometimes, unintended consequences are as important as original intent.

Abolitionists saw the Thirteenth Amendment as the beginning of an even deeper transformation, what today might be called "regime change"—the transformation of a proslavery regime into one committed to the ideal of equality. Most Republicans were not abolitionists, but they agreed on certain principles: slavery had caused the war and the death of three-quarters of a million Americans. It had deprived its victims of the basic rights to which all persons were entitled. It had done more than oppress slaves; it was a cancer that degraded white labor and threatened all Americans' essential liberties, such as freedom of speech and of the press. The amendment intended to change all this and more. Unlike the Emancipation Proclamation, the Thirteenth Amendment applied to the entire country and for the first time made the abolition of slavery an essential part of the nation's legal order. In one respect it was truly revolutionary—it abolished the largest concentration of property in the United States without monetary compensation. This has happened very rarely in history.

"The one question of the age is *settled*," declared one congressman of the Thirteenth Amendment.[9] But if it resolved the fate of slavery, the amendment opened a host of other issues. What, exactly, was being abolished? Property in man? The racial inequality inseparable from slavery? What would be the status of the former slaves and who would determine it? What did it mean to be a free person in postwar America? These were questions on which the politics of Reconstruction persistently turned.

White southerners had their own answers, as became clear when Lincoln was assassinated and Andrew Johnson became president. Once lionized as a heroic defender of the Constitution against the Radical Republicans, Johnson today has a strong claim to being considered the worst president in US history. There are other claimants, but he is certainly a strong contender. Johnson lacked all of Lincoln's qualities of greatness. He was deeply racist, incompetent, had no sense of public opinion, and did not have the ability to work with Congress. In the months after the Civil War ended, Johnson set up new governments in the South controlled entirely by white southerners. These enacted a series of laws called "Black Codes" to define the freedom African Americans now enjoyed. The laws gave Blacks virtually no civil or political rights. They required that all adult Black men at the beginning of each year sign a labor contract to go to work for a white employer or be deemed a vagrant and sold to labor for someone who would pay the fine.

These Black Codes alarmed the Republican Party, which controlled Congress, into thinking that the South was trying to restore slavery in all but name. Most Republicans agreed that the Thirteenth Amendment empowered Congress to ensure, as one senator put it, "that the man made free by the Constitution . . . is a freeman indeed."[10] In 1866, relying on the new amendment, it passed one of the most important laws in American history, the Civil Rights Act of 1866, the first law to declare who is a free citizen of the United States and what rights they are to enjoy.

The Civil Rights Act states that anybody born in the United States—except "Indians not taxed"—is a citizen. Birthright citizenship is a statement that anyone can be a loyal American—race, religion, or national origin do not matter, nor does the legal status of one's parents. It severs citizenship from race, as abolitionists had long demanded. The idea remains controversial. No country in Europe today accords automatic citizenship to everyone born within its borders. President Donald Trump claimed the right to abrogate it in the United States by executive order with regard to American-born children of undocumented immigrants.

The law went on to declare that all citizens must enjoy basic legal equality. States cannot pass one set of laws for Black people—as they had just done—and another set for white people. The Civil Rights Act says nothing about the right to vote—at this point only five northern states with tiny African American populations allowed Black men to vote on the same basis as whites (a sixth, New York, had a prohibitive property qualification for Black, but not white, voters). But it guarantees equality of civil rights, specifically the right to sign contracts, own property, testify in court, and sue and be sued. These are the rights of free labor, necessary to compete in the economic marketplace. No state, or "custom," could deprive any citizen of these basic rights. The language is interesting. All citizens, says the law, must enjoy these rights in the same way as enjoyed by white persons. The concept of "whiteness"—before the war a boundary of exclusion, as in laws stating that only white men could serve in the militia—now became a baseline, a standard for all Americans. The law's intriguing prohibition of customs that deprived citizens of their rights made clear that Congress was acting not only against legal discrimination but also against private behavior, such as efforts of planters to restrict the employment opportunities and other rights of the freedpeople.

Johnson vetoed the Civil Rights Bill, and it became the first important measure in American history to become law over a president's veto. The veto message denounced the bill for what today is called reverse discrimination: "The distinction of race and color is by the bill made to operate in favor of the colored and against the white race."[11] Indeed, in the idea that expanding the rights of nonwhites somehow punishes the white majority, the ghost of Andrew Johnson still haunts our discussions of race.

But, of course, a law can always be repealed, so very soon Congress put these principles into the Fourteenth Amendment, the most important change in our

Constitution since the Bill of Rights. The amendment is long and complicated—the longest amendment to the Constitution. In effect, it constitutionalizes the victorious Republican North's understanding of the consequences of the Civil War. It deals with specific, immediate problems such as the Confederate and Union debts. It contains a convoluted clause depriving states of part of their representation in the House of Representatives if they denied the right to vote to any group of male citizens. This was included because of an ironic consequence of abolition—the end of slavery also ended the three-fifths clause of the Constitution. Now the entire Black population would be counted in apportioning representation in the House of Representatives and Electoral College, so the South would enjoy enhanced political power. This section was a compromise between Republicans who favored Black suffrage and those who feared the idea was too unpopular to win ratification. It raised an outcry among the era's feminist movement because, for the first time, it introduced a gender distinction—the word "male"—into the Constitution. Unlike men, there was no penalty if a state denied women, white or Black, the right to vote, which all of them did.

But the heart of the Fourteenth Amendment is the first section. This constitutionalizes the principle of birthright citizenship and goes on to bar states from abridging the privileges or immunities of citizens, denying to any person (citizen or alien) the equal protection of the law, or depriving them of life, liberty, or property without due process of law. Unlike the Civil Rights Act, the amendment is written in terms of general principles—due process, equal protection—not specific rights. It leaves it to future Congresses and the courts to breathe meaning into these abstract phrases.

Congressman John A. Bingham, with whom most of the wording of Section 1 originated, intentionally couched a radical transformation of the Constitution in familiar terms. "I did imitate the framers," he said; "every word . . . is today in the Constitution of our country."[12] This was not entirely correct. The word "equal" is not in the original Constitution (except with regard to states having equal numbers of senators, and what happens if candidates for president or vice president receive an equal number of electoral votes). The amendment makes the Constitution what it never was, a vehicle through which aggrieved individuals and groups who believe that they are being denied equality can take their claims to federal court. The language is race neutral, which has had enormous consequences in our own time. In recent decades, the courts have used this amendment to expand the legal rights of numerous groups of Americans—lately, gay men and lesbians with regard to the right to marry. Of course, declared Justice Anthony Kennedy's majority opinion, those who wrote the Fourteenth Amendment were not thinking of gay marriage. But our definitions of liberty and equality expand over time, today reaching into the most intimate areas of life—an illustration of the jurisprudence of a "living Constitution," as opposed to original intent or meaning.

Despite controversy over the precise meaning of its language, the first section of the Fourteenth Amendment fundamentally transformed Americans' relationship to their government. It asserted federal authority to create a new, uniform definition of citizenship and announced that being a citizen—or, in some cases simply residing in the country—carried with it rights the states could not abridge. It proclaimed that everyone in the United States was to enjoy a modicum of equality protected by the national government. All in all, to borrow a phrase from the editor George William Curtis, the Fourteenth Amendment changed a Constitution "for white men" into one "for mankind."[13]

The Fourteenth Amendment also marked a significant change in the federal system. It not only put the concept of equal rights into the Constitution but also empowered the federal government to enforce it. The Civil War had crystalized in the minds of northerners the idea of a powerful national state protecting the rights of citizens. You can see the point I am making if you compare the Reconstruction amendments to the Bill of Rights, the first ten amendments, which protect our basic civil liberties—freedom of speech, freedom of the press, separation of church and state, and so on. The Bill of Rights was based on the idea that the main danger to liberty is a too-powerful national state. It begins with the words "Congress shall make no law" and then lists the rights Congress cannot abridge. It does not restrict the state governments. Try to give an abolition speech in South Carolina before the war? State law did not allow it. Did that violate the First Amendment? No, the amendment is about the federal government.

Now look at the final section of each of the three Reconstruction amendments. All end by saying that Congress "shall have the power" to enforce the amendment by appropriate legislation—from "Congress shall make no law" to Congress "shall have the power." Now the federal government is seen as the protector of individual rights and the states as more likely to violate them. This represents a fundamental shift in the federal system. To be sure, the framers of the Reconstruction amendments did not wish to destroy federalism. If the states accorded all citizens equal rights, federal intervention would not be triggered. The national government was ill equipped at this time for continuous intervention in local affairs. But the architects of Reconstruction wanted to bring into being state governments that would make federal intervention unnecessary. The Fourteenth Amendment's third section, barring Confederate leaders from office, was an effort to ensure that such governments would come to power in the South. But if the rights of the former slaves, or other Americans, were flagrantly violated, federal intervention would follow. Overall, the Reconstruction amendments made the federal government, for the first time in our history, in the words of Senator Sumner, "The Custodian of Freedom."[14]

The Fourteenth Amendment said nothing directly about the suffrage, but to guarantee state enforcement of the principle of equal citizenship, Congress in 1867 required that new governments be set up in the South with Black men having the right to vote. And in the Fifteenth Amendment, ratified in 1870, Black male suffrage was extended to the entire nation. The amendment bars states from depriving any citizen of the right to vote because of race. This sounds very sweeping, and in the context of the nineteenth century, when Black voting had been almost unknown, it certainly was. But the amendment outraged the women's rights movement, for it said nothing about discrimination based on sex. Even regarding men, the Radicals preferred a positive statement that all male citizens age twenty-one had the right to vote. What is the difference? The Fifteenth Amendment left open the possibility of other requirements that could deprive Blacks of the right to vote without explicitly mentioning race. Unlike in the debates on the Thirteenth Amendment, Congress was aware of this loophole. Some members warned that states in the future might enact poll taxes, literacy tests, and other ostensibly nonracial requirements that would primarily affect Blacks. But the tradition of state control of voting was deeply rooted, and many northern states did not want to surrender that power. California barred Chinese residents from voting. Rhode Island set different qualifications for immigrants than for native-born citizens. The result was an amendment whose purpose could too easily be circumvented, as indeed continues to happen in the twenty-first century in some states via voter-suppression laws.

The advent of Black male suffrage inaugurated the period we call Radical Reconstruction, when new biracial governments came to power in the South, a massive, unprecedented experiment in interracial democracy. The new governments had many accomplishments. They created the region's first public-education systems. They began the process of rebuilding the southern economy. They tried to protect the rights of Black laborers. Reconstruction created the space in which the Black church emerged as a national institution, the center of African American communities. Families torn apart by slavery were now consolidated. And Black men held office during Reconstruction at every level of government, from the first two Black US senators to members of Congress and state legislatures, down to justices of the peace, sheriffs, and school-board officials. Most power in Reconstruction remained in the hands of white Republicans, but the fact that perhaps two thousand African American men held public office was a revolutionary change in our body politic.

To be sure, the problems of the emancipated slaves were not limited to lacking civil and political rights. Their demands for land redistribution (the famous "forty acres and a mule") remained unmet. One might say that in Reconstruction, the political revolution went forward, but the economic revolution did not. Nevertheless, the political revolution was dramatic enough that it inspired a wave of terrorist violence in the South by the Ku Klux Klan and kindred groups. But hand in hand with that went a retreat on the part of the North from the ideal of equality that had been written into the Constitution. One by one the Reconstruction governments fell by the wayside until, by 1877, the entire South was back under the political control of white-supremacist Democrats, who would dominate the region until the era of the civil rights revolution.

During the next generation, a new racial system was put in place in the South. Its pillars included racial segregation, the disenfranchisement of Black men, a severe cutback in public funding of Black education, a segmented labor market in which most good jobs were reserved for whites, the convict-lease system (alluded to above), and policing the system, lynching, and extralegal mob violence. The alleged misgovernment under Reconstruction became part of the intellectual underpinning of this system, which was invoked as far away as South Africa and Australia to demonstrate the necessity of excluding nonwhite peoples from political rights. This is why W. E. B. Du Bois, in his great 1935 work *Black Reconstruction in America,* saw the end of Reconstruction as a tragedy for democracy not just in the United States, but across the globe.[15]

Did this racial system not violate the Reconstruction amendments? With the conclusion of the second founding came the battle over its meaning. Ultimately, it fell to the Supreme Court to construe the constitutional amendments. And over time, the court played a crucial role in the long retreat from the ideals of Reconstruction. The process was gradual and the outcome never total, with each decision involving its own laws, facts, and legal precedents. Recent scholars have attributed the retreat not simply to judicial racism but also to the persistence of federalism—fear among the justices that too great an expansion of nationally enforceable rights would undermine the legitimate powers of the states. For African Americans, however, the practical consequences were the same. The broad conception of constitutional rights with which they and their allies attempted to imbue the abolition of slavery proved tragically insecure.

A series of interconnected questions cried out for resolution. How substantially had the amendments altered the federal system? Did the Thirteenth Amendment prohibit only chattel bondage or did it extend to the "badges and incidents" of slavery, and what exactly were these? What did key provisions of the Fourteenth Amendment, including the "privileges or immunities" of citizens and the "equal protection of the laws," mean, and did this language apply only to Blacks or to all Americans? Did that amendment protect African Americans against violation of their rights by private individuals and businesses or only by state laws and the actions of public officials—the so-called state-action doctrine? Did it encompass what Blacks called "public rights," such as equal treatment by transportation companies and public accommodations? Did the Fifteenth Amendment's prohibition of disfranchisement "on account of race" prohibit laws, race neutral on their face, clearly intended to limit African Americans' right to vote? On all of these issues, even though alternative understandings were readily available, including among leaders of the Republican Party, the Supreme Court chose to restrict the scope of the second founding. By the early twentieth century, the egalitarian purposes of the Fourteenth and Fifteenth Amendments had been effectively nullified throughout the South. When the court in 1903 threw up its hands and said there was nothing it could do if whites in Alabama chose to disfranchise the state's Black voters, a northern newspaper declared, "We are brought face to face with the consideration that the constitution may be violated with impunity."[16] The result demonstrated a sometimes forgotten point—our Constitution is not self-enforcing.

I do not have space to discuss the individual Supreme Court decisions that eviscerated the second founding. It is worth noting that by the 1890s, the Supreme Court's interpretation of the Reconstruction amendments was powerfully influenced by an emerging national consensus (among whites at any rate) that Reconstruction had been a serious mistake. And well into the twentieth century, Supreme Court decisions reflected this Dunning school outlook. In a dissent in a 1945 case, Justices Owen Roberts, Felix Frankfurter, and Robert H. Jackson wrote that it was "familiar history" that Reconstruction legislation was motivated by a "vengeful spirit" on the part of northerners—so familiar, in fact, that they felt no need to cite any work of historical scholarship to justify their claim.[17]

Because they represented compromises between different factions of the Republican Party, the Reconstruction amendments can legitimately be interpreted in numerous ways. Indeed, the very "indefiniteness of meaning," as George Boutwell, a key member of Congress, put it, was a "charm" to Representative Bingham.[18] Ambiguity creates possibilities. It paves the way for future struggles while giving different groups grounds on which to conduct them. But determining who has the ability to decide which of a range of possible meanings is implemented is very much a matter of political power.

In the late nineteenth century, an alternative, rights-based constitutionalism emerged among Black activists and their allies, one that rejected the key tenets of Supreme Court jurisprudence. In 1889, amid the constitutional retreat, a group of Black lawyers and ministers in Baltimore, calling themselves the Brotherhood of Liberty, published *Justice and Jurisprudence*, the first sustained critique by African Americans of Supreme Court rulings interpreting the Reconstruction amendments. Its anonymous author proposed an alternative reading of the amended Constitution based on a broad conception of federal enforcement power and a rejection of the sharp distinction between civil, political, and social rights that the courts had anxiously adopted. Years earlier, in one of its first decisions interpreting the Fourteenth Amendment, in the *Slaughterhouse Cases*, the Supreme Court had defined the privileges or immunities of citizens so narrowly as to render that clause of the Fourteenth Amendment virtually meaningless. The Brotherhood of Liberty, however, offered a different view of the rights "public and private" that constituted the privileges and immunities of US citizens, which the amendment was meant to protect. These included not only equal treatment in public accommodations, transport, and places of amusement but also the rights of free labor, broadly defined. The book assailed employment discrimination, housing segregation, exclusion of Blacks from labor unions, and lack of access to education, insisting that citizenship carried with it the promise of economic opportunity. "Can a citizen," it asked, "be daily excluded from the paths of industrial progress . . . and yet be a citizen of the United States?" Overall, as one reviewer of *Justice and Jurisprudence* wrote, too many rights had been lost as soon as they reached "that grave of liberty, the Supreme Court of the United States."[19]

Today, the country has gone a long way toward fulfilling the agenda of Reconstruction. The Bill of Rights has been almost entirely "incorporated" so that states must now abide by their guarantees. But this comes via the Fourteenth Amendment's due process clause, not, as Bingham expected, via its guarantee of the privileges or immunities of citizens, which would have been more logical. Yet paradoxically, the recent history of the amendments reveals their ongoing expansion to protect the rights of new groups of Americans alongside their restricted application to questions involving race, for example, affirmative action and limitations on the right to vote. This reflects both current political tendencies and the enduring ramifications of earlier decisions limiting the scope of the second founding. In a legal environment that relies so heavily on precedent, key decisions of the retreat from Reconstruction, with what Justice John Marshall Harlan called the court's "narrow and artificial" understanding of the Thirteenth, Fourteenth, and Fifteenth Amendments, remain undisturbed.[20] With the exception of repudiating *Plessy v. Ferguson,* even the Warren Court did not directly confront the long train of decisions that restricted national power over citizens' basic rights. It could not bring itself to say that, for eighty years or more, the court had been wrong. As a result, the Dunning school view of Reconstruction, long repudiated by historians, remains embedded in our jurisprudence. Moreover, in decisions over the past generation more sympathetic to white plaintiffs complaining of reverse discrimination because of affirmative action than to Blacks seeking assistance in overcoming the legacies of slavery and Jim Crow, we hear again the voice of Andrew Johnson.

But current jurisprudence does not have to be the final word. The counterinterpretation developed in Reconstruction and its aftermath, with its more powerful assertion of the rights enshrined in the Constitution by the second founding and the power of the federal government to enforce them, remains available if the political environment changes. There is no reason why the Fourteenth Amendment's clause related to the privileges or immunities of citizens must remain a dead letter, why it cannot be understood to encompass rights essential to full membership in American society today, such as access to an adequate education or even the "reasonable wages" to which Lincoln said the freed slaves were entitled in the Emancipation Proclamation. There is no reason that "societal discrimination,"[21] cavalierly dismissed by the Supreme Court as a justification for affirmative action and school integration programs, cannot legitimately be taken into account by the courts, or why the state-action doctrine must hamstring federal efforts to protect the rights of all Americans against violation by private parties. The point is not that the counterinterpretation is the one true meaning of the Reconstruction amendments, but that viable alternatives, rooted in the historical record, exist to actual Supreme Court jurisprudence.

We Americans sometimes like to think that our history is a straight line of greater and greater freedom. Actually, as Reconstruction and its aftermath shows, it is a much more complicated story of ups and downs. Rights can be gained, and rights can be taken away, to be fought for another day. As Thomas Wentworth Higginson, who commanded a unit of Black soldiers in the Civil War, wrote when Reconstruction began, "Revolutions may go backward."[22] Reconstruction was a revolution—including a "constitutional revolution"—that went backward, but the fact that it happened at all laid the foundation for another generation a century later to try to bring to fruition the concept of a country that had progressed beyond the tyranny of race.

In his second inaugural address, Abraham Lincoln identified slavery as the fundamental cause of the Civil War and implicitly challenged Americans to think creatively about how to fulfill the aspirations unleashed by its destruction. The three amendments formed part of the nation's response. Because the ideals of freedom, equality, and democracy are always contested, our understanding of the Reconstruction amendments will forever be a work in progress. So long as the legacies of slavery and Jim Crow continue to plague our society, we can expect Americans to return to the second founding and find there new meanings for our fractious and troubled times. And however flawed, the era that followed the Civil War can serve as an inspiration for those striving to achieve a more just society.

NOTES

This essay, the keynote address of the Lincoln's Unfinished Work conference, is based on my book *The Second Founding: How the Civil War and Reconstruction Remade the Constitution* (New York, 2019).

1. *Congressional Globe*, 41st Cong., 2nd sess., 3607.

2. John David Smith, ed., *The Dunning School: Historians, Race, and the Meaning of Reconstruction* (Lexington: University Press of Kentucky, 2013).

3. Gunnar Myrdal, *An American Dilemma: The Negro Problem and Modern Democracy* (New York: Harper and Brothers, 1944), 446.

4. Martha S. Jones, *Birthright Citizens: A History of Race and Rights in Antebellum America* (Cambridge: Cambridge University Press, 2018).

5. Elizabeth Cady Stanton, *Eighty Years and More (1815–1897)* (New York: European Publishing, 1898), 241.

6. Roy P. Basler et al., ed., *The Collected Works of Abraham Lincoln*, 9 vols. (New Brunswick, NJ: Rutgers University Press, 1953–55), 7:36–54.

7. *Congressional Globe*, 38th Cong., 1st sess., 521, 1482.

8. Beverley Wilson Palmer, ed., *The Selected Letters of Charles Sumner*, 2 vols. (Boston: Northeastern University Press, 1990), 2:233.

9. *Memoirs of Cornelius Cole* (New York: McLoughlin, 1908), 220.

10. *Congressional Globe*, 39th Cong., 1st sess., 111.

11. James D. Richardson, ed., *A Compilation of the Messages and Papers of the Presidents 1789–1897*, 10 vols. (Washington: Government Printing Office, 1896–99), 6:399–405.

12. *Congressional Globe*, 42nd Cong., 1st sess., app., 84.

13. Charles Eliot Norton, ed., *Orations and Addresses of George William Curtis*, 3 vols. (New York: Harper and Brothers, 1894), 1:172.

14. Eric Foner, *Reconstruction: America's Unfinished Revolution, 1863–1877* (New York: Harper and Row, 1988), 24.

15. W. E. B. Du Bois, *Black Reconstruction in America, 1860–1880* (New York: Russel and Russel, 1935).

16. *Springfield (MA) Daily Republican*, May 2, 1903.

17. Eric Foner, "The Supreme Court and the History of Reconstruction—and Vice Versa," *Columbia Law Review* 112 (Nov. 2012): 1585–1608.

18. George S. Boutwell, *Reminiscences of Sixty Years in Public Affairs*, 2 vols. (New York: McClure, Phillips, 1902), 2:42.

19. Brotherhood of Liberty, *Justice and Jurisprudence: An Inquiry Concerning the Constitutional Limitations of the Thirteenth, Fourteenth, and Fifteenth Amendments* (Philadelphia: J. B. Lippincott, 1889); *Science: A Weekly Newspaper of All the Arts and Sciences* 15 (Jan. 10, 1890), 26–27.

20. *Civil Rights Cases*, 109 US 3 (1883), 26.

21. *Regents of the University of California v. Bakke*, 238 US 265 (1978), 307.

22. Thomas Wentworth Higginson, *Army Life in a Black Regiment* (Boston: Houghton, Mifflin, 1900), 63–64.

Lincoln, Du Bois's "General Strike," and the Making of the American Working Class

LAWRENCE T. McDONNELL

There is no analysis of war's largest meaning more famous or instructive than the Gettysburg Address. Nor perhaps has any document of such brevity and clarity been so dissected and interpreted by a wider range of scholars.[1] Yet much remains to achieve in coupling the words of that speech precisely to the meaning of the conflict that created it. Reading Abraham Lincoln's words afresh—and taking them seriously—offers a foundation for transforming Civil War studies and rediscovering the origins of an American working class.

In November 1863, the American leader journeyed to the scene of the Great Rebellion's greatest slaughter to dedicate a cemetery to those who fell upon the battlefield.[2] Certainly, Lincoln ranks among the most antiwar presidents the nation has known, and he did not approach his task that day without trepidation. He had seen other cemeteries—too many—and helped dig more than his share of graves. He spoke for less than three minutes.[3]

Lincoln never saw battle firsthand, and in after years he made mock of his short career as a volunteer in the Black Hawk campaign of 1832. By 1860, those who remembered Lincoln's term of service mostly spoke of it as a youthful lark. It was anything but.[4] Chosen by his fellows as company captain, Lincoln at twenty-three showed no knowledge or aptitude for the military demands of his office. He owned no gun, cannot have been much of a shot, and did not know the basic commands of marching and drill. When his men vied with another unit for a campsite, Lincoln was outwrestled for the prize. No wonder they were relegated to bringing up the rear and burying the dead. That must have seemed the nadir of his inglorious soldiering, but there was worse to come. When his company was disbanded mid-campaign, Captain Lincoln reenlisted as Private Lincoln, since he "was out of work . . . and could do nothing better."[5] Soon he was back at the grim war work he knew best, digging a pit at Stillman's Run for the troops slaughtered in that skirmish, carrying their scalped and mutilated bodies one by one to the mass grave, and mounding shovelfuls of earth on top of the corpses. War was dirty, gory, stinking, exhausting work for young Abe Lincoln. And, at the end, on the night before he mustered out in July 1832, someone stole his horse, forcing him to walk all the way back to Peoria, then to canoe it home. Achilles or Alexander, Lincoln was not. Nor did he forget the bloody work of war when he spoke in 1863. It is just that scholars have overlooked Lincoln's central insight on that day in pursuit of more high-flown—and less revolutionary—meanings for his speech.[6]

Lincoln's experience in the Black Hawk War crowned more than fifteen years of trying to survive and escape a life of material privation, unceasing labor, and personal dependence. From the endless toil of his teenage years, much of it under the hypercritical eye of a father he came to detest, Lincoln grew to hate manual work and the abasement that wage labor inevitably entailed.[7] Rail-splitter was no compliment to his mind. He embraced book-learner and, by the time he had advanced to Congress at the hour of the Mexican-American War (1846–48), had seen enough to deplore the job of man-killer. Opposing President James K. Polk's egregious triumph was political suicide, yet he did not flinch. After Lincoln himself was inaugurated president in 1861, we cannot doubt that he drew back initially from smiting southern rebels more strongly at least partly because he had seen the horror and pity of war, knew the awful wreckage, and understood something of the secret character of its pursuit.[8] Sketching the origins of the "mighty scourge of war" he so despised in his second inaugural address, Lincoln could only urge the nation "to finish the work we are in" and move on toward building a lasting peace.[9] Shorn of romanticism, war seen through Abe's eyes was work of the most wretched sort.

Lincoln's description of war as work in March 1865 was no accident of phrasing. He had made the same point in the same terms in that Pennsylvania graveyard in November 1863, drawing on all that he remembered of his own days of youthful soldiering and all that he had experienced of war since the spring of 1861. When he stood up to speak at Gettysburg, looking "a ghastly color," the wonder is that Lincoln rescued meaning from mourning so precisely through political analysis of war's work.[10]

A huge, jostling crowd had gathered for the spectacle, expecting something grand. After military music, a tear-jerking prayer, "Old Hundred" played by the Marine Band, a stony two-hour address delivered by Edward Everett under the cloudless sky of a crisp November afternoon, and yet another hymn, Lincoln's brief words should have been forgettably pro forma.[11] Instead, they were piercing, prophetic, and permanent, summoning hope across continents and generations, promising that humanity's democratic dream might prove other than mortal: *shall not perish.*[12]

In a graveyard? On a battlefield? Admiration of Lincoln's rhetorical achievement has almost entirely shunted aside consideration of the radical political meaning of his words.[13] And so, historians have stared at, quoted to no purpose, and utterly misunderstood this Rosetta Stone of America's sectional conflict for going on eight generations now. What did Lincoln mean at that moment? How does his meaning matter today?

The Gettysburg Address follows a "before-now-but" progression, typical of the jeremiad form, rallying and driving its audience to action. Thrice Lincoln instructs his hearers as to the limits of action, "we can not," culminating in the collision of the centrifugal passive and centripetal active verbs at the heart of his speech. Three statements of common action, "we are engaged," "we are met," "we are come," lead up to the challenge of the moment: "we should do this." Then follow the great "cannots": "dedicate," "consecrate," "hallow." Finally, Lincoln counterposes our inglorious "we say" to the soldiers' everlasting "they did."[14] The link—and the contrast—between military service and civilian life could not be clearer.

It was not just that talk is cheap. The "did" of those dead, Lincoln insists, was the labor of war. By missing that central argument, historians have missed the meaning of the Civil War as contemporaries understood it. Lincoln makes this point explicitly: it is "the unfinished work which they who fought here have so nobly advanced" that focuses his remarks. In contrast to all that Lincoln had experienced of war personally, the horrid work of destruction is ennobled here as a work of construction, though yet incomplete. The "great task" remaining is to give the nation "a new birth of freedom," making imperishable government thrice democratic. As with the Founding Fathers, the work of war in Lincoln's age creates revolutionary freedom.[15]

That the notion of war as work—of military history essentially and everywhere necessarily as a form of labor history—should seem strange or insightful only measures our scholarly shortsightedness.[16] As a rhetorical trope, war described as labor stretches from classical Greece down to the pushbutton conflicts of today.[17] And, to be sure, military historians have labored endlessly to understand how warfare as practiced across time and space, spanning economic, racial, gender, and caste systems, has taken various forms, successful and otherwise. Cynics might wonder whether there is anything at all of significance left to say about warfare's pursuit in human affairs. In recent years, that question has focused the condescension of nonmilitary historians toward the field to great effect.[18] Events, too, have demonstrated the need for a new paradigm. Romantic notions of war as heroic, enlightening, and admirable—so powerfully linked to Western political pursuits from the late eighteenth to the early twentieth centuries—were pulverized by Stalingrad and atomized by Hiroshima, though even Vietnam did not succeed in diminishing Americans' desire to glorify soldiering and war itself. Today, as military historians have shown, that warrior halo is culturally constructed, ethnocentric, and of recent invention.[19] Yet well constructed it is, and well defended.

However much they delight in contending over the details of various conflicts, historians and lay readers unite in a certitude that we know what war means— military veterans more than others, of course. We think we know how it ought to be studied, described, and analyzed. Especially when it comes to the American Civil War, we insist, these men fought for something worthwhile—whether it was for the Union or Dixie, the maintenance of liberty, freedom for the slaves, or the defense of hearth and home. Think of the *Glory* story, of the African American 54th Massachusetts Regiment and their doomed white-savior commander idealized by Hollywood: there cannot be a battle, we know instinctively, without a lesson to learn from it.[20]

Until recently, that lesson was clear: this was an American war and a civil war. Whether wearing the blue or the gray, we imagine, soldiers were brothers in arms.[21] Regardless of the political and social merits of their contending causes, they fought "for cause and comrades," seeking to embody courage, demonstrate manhood, and vivify ideals. Perhaps that was so for some.[22] But motivation is not always the best guide to the meaning of action. Soldiers did tend to grumble when the paymaster was late. In many battles, when push came to shove, not a few came to recognize the better part of valor before it was too late. There were many, too, who served, fought, and died because, like young Abe Lincoln, they could do no better.[23] Before we dive too deep—and too sentimentally—into why men fought, military historians need to understand first what enlistment, service, and combat meant, both objectively and in the eyes of the men who took up the task. The sine qua non across cultures and centuries is simply this: for those who threw a pilum, pulled a trigger, pushed a button, or wrote a code, aiming to make an adversary recoil, rethink, retreat, and perhaps surrender, war at its core has been a labor of killing.[24] Anyone who came to Gettysburg in November 1863 could see that much.

It was the "real earnest work" of war that Private Walter Poor signed up for in the spring of 1861, "hard blows to be given" to the rebels who looked to wreck the republic. Across the next four years, he described that "work, conflict," in murderous detail. "Our work is to slay and not to save," he explained, and though war was "hard work," Poor chafed at hesitation and indirection of all kinds. Despite "work enough" and "blood spilt" in abundance, he seethed at all measures that delayed "the doom of slavery" as "traitorous to the cause of freedom." "When the work is done," he crowed, the rebels would be vanquished and their land "a heap of smouldering ruins." Poor asked only that those incapable or uncommitted to that labor get out of his way—incompetent leaders, listless comrades, even "Granny Lincoln" himself.[25]

Few soldiers match Poor for grim determination, yet thousands echoed his clear-sighted descriptions of war as work. Union and Confederate troops, both high and low, made the same point in letters, diary entries, petitions, and regimental orders that scholars and buffs alike have almost willfully misread, looking out for a different, seemingly better war.[26] Certainly, volunteers early on posed for daguerreotypes with pistols and Bowie knives drawn, trumpeting their bloodlust in letters from the front. What better way to make sweethearts swoon and schoolmates green with envy? But such swagger died away entirely once the shooting started. For most, it did not survive the first days of military training.[27]

War revealed character, men imagined. On the battlefield, a man would have "an opportunity of showing his bravery and patriotism," regardless of previous position. Thousands craved that chance. "Won't it be grand to meet the men from all the States, East and West," thought Robert Gould Shaw, "ready to fight for the country, as the old fellows did in the Revolution?" "When I die I want it to be in the largest battle that was ever fought, since the creation of the world," another Yankee agreed. But such dreams of military service as fraternal celebration and death as glorious sacrifice evaporated as soon as the call to "fall in" came. Then, would-be heroes faced a regime where the individualism and self-direction of civilian life were banished entirely.[28]

Usually within days of enlistment, soldiers' fantasies of heroic fighting and a triumphal return home ran up against a very different reality. Americans had long considered soldiering as one of the lowest forms of wage labor, attracting only unskilled immigrants and the most desperate of native-born whites. "I was never told," one Mexican War veteran complained, "that I would be called on to make roads, build bridges, quarry stone, burn brick and lime, carry the hod, cut wood, hew timber, construct it into rafts and float it to the garrison . . . etc., etc., etc."[29] Such tasks marked soldiers clearly as lumpen proletarians, toiling at the beck and call of a managerial class determined to eradicate independent thought and action.

"[I] belong to the C. S. Army now," one rebel groused, "and do as I am told."[30] Recruits spoke again and again of soldiering as subservience and drudgery, talking not of battle but of their "job," not of killing but of work. Soldiering had nothing of unconstrained manliness about it, recruits discovered quickly. Instead, it was coerced, regimented labor of the lowest sort. Lee's men called Marse Robert "the King of Spades"; Stonewall's footsore troops cursed "Fool Tom Jackson" for overworking his men, on the march and in battle both.[31] The language of labor permeated all aspects of training, camp life, campaigning—even combat. For Thaddeus Capron, victory at Gettysburg meant that the Union armies were "going to work in earnest at last." One hundred twenty casualties at Resaca, Georgia, was reckoned a "small loss for the work that we did." A dead soldier had "done his work," in common parlance, and could now "take his rest."[32] Elisha Hunt Rhodes, one of the central figures of Ken Burns's Civil War documentary, filled his letters home with discussions and descriptions focused on labor, though perhaps these were judged too dull for primetime television. "Great is the shovel and spade," he genuflected. "If I live to get home I shall be fitted for any kind of work, for I have tried most everything since I have been in the army."[33]

The work of war was new for nearly all the 2.75 million Americans who fought in the Civil War, and the gradual process of accommodation to that novel experience bonded men across companies and regiments and between opposing armies. Indeed, for most who volunteered or were drafted, both North and South, Civil War military service marked their first sustained encounter with wage labor under the eyes of a boss. Most found the experience shocking. Soldiers' letters and diaries record their dismay in vivid terms. Common soldiers were "small fry" with "no rights," expecting "nothing but peremptory orders," and "thought no more of . . . than dogs especily privates they are not treated half as well as a negro." "I have been a Government mule for about fifteen months," an Illinois private agreed. "I have been harnessed and driven by all kinds of drivers. I have borne it with all the patience and fortitude at my command. It is no use to kick up, for the harness is strong, and the driver will put on a bigger load and lock the wheel." "If he complains," another added, "he is insulted if not punished. All he dare ask is 'what will you have me to do'? To all this, however, he soon becomes accustomed. . . . [Y]ou would almost think he was a *free man!*" Almost was as far as military discipline would allow. "Most . . . find soldiering very different work from what they expected," Robert Gould Shaw summed up, "but having been sworn in, they seem resigned to the hard work & army rations."[34]

It was not the toil or the food that soldiers complained of. It was the unmanly character of the work they were ordered to perform, degrading in its demands for constant, unthinking obedience. Men on both sides put up with it, mostly, out of political and military necessity, but deep feelings of resentment lingered. The "private soldier is but an automaton," Tennessean Sam Watkins sneered, "a machine that works by the command of a good, bad, or indifferent engineer," with no control over "the shooting and killing, the fortifying and ditching, the sweeping of the streets, the drilling, the standing guard, picket and videt, and [the drawing] of eleven dollars per month and rations."[35] For Watkins, the webfoot was just a waged laborer with a gun. However various his experience—modified by the flag he followed; the function he performed as infantry, cavalry, or artillery; his status as volunteer or conscript; his rank as enlisted man or officer—all was shaped by the labor process itself, what one Indiana volunteer rightly called the "bloody work" that composed Civil War soldiers' service.[36]

For nearly all recruits, the regular pace and tempo of toil, steady oversight by noncommissioned officers, and the inability of men to do as they wished *when* they wished were all profoundly new and degrading aspects of military life. A Georgia private unluckily named Freeman warned his brother against joining up "if you don't want to lose your freedom. . . . for we are nothing better than slaves here." Bound contracts, low pay, hard toil, restricted rights, overbearing bosses, and vicious punishment made the work of common soldiers entirely unlike the labor of freeborn citizens.[37] Military discipline required a species of obedience known only to convicts, apprentices, women, and slaves. And then there was combat, when a man's life might be casually thrown away altogether by the error or incompetence of a superior's order. A soldier's duty was plain, one Confederate explained: "we niggers have to put up with anything that officers choose to do."[38]

But would they? Victory depended on the ability of commanders on each side to enforce obedience and gain the loyalty of the troops they led, willing them to work, kill, and die without dissent. At the heart of the conflict between blue and gray, then, was an all-determining struggle within each army over control of the terms of war's work at the squad, company, and regimental levels. Objectively, this was a struggle over the relations of production between military wageworkers and their bosses, both civil and martial. For those in command, the problem was to establish their ideological construction of the labor process as hegemonic, both imposing new class relations and denying their significance.[39] Objective class ties had to be denied or overridden where competing workers were identified as the "enemy." Conversely, solidarity and submission had to be established between bosses and military laborers even where class divisions were obvious. Military victory was predicated on officers' ability to impose these new relations of production, preventing fraternization with soldiers in the opposing army, mutiny, desertion, and workers' attempts to control the production process. Comprehending the Civil War, its course and outcome, and its place in world history requires us to put this class struggle at the center of the politico-military conflict.[40]

In 1861, Americans both North and South were willing to endure military discipline on a temporary basis as a service to their nation in its hour of crisis. On both sides, soldiers shared a dread of being drawn into the permanent status of a proletarian, a fate that loomed over increasing numbers in the 1850s. A pervasive social and economic system grounded in lifelong toil for wages was "the offspring of the devil," argued Charleston's Frederick Porcher. "It cannot be the will of God that his creatures shall exist in hopeless degradation, toiling harder than slaves, with none of the slaves' security."[41] Whatever their views on chattel slavery, warring Americans agreed that to be condemned to a life of "wage slavery" was antithetical to the ideals of manly competency and self-sufficiency that defined free-labor ideology. Soldiering gave millions of young men their first close look at the fate they feared most.[42]

Common soldiers and their superiors on both sides contested every aspect of military service. Recruits balked especially at the use of time as a tool of labor discipline. "I can't help pitying some of our privates who are nice respectable men," one Yankee officer wrote, "& who have to be treated like the rest." Good or bad, men were "toned down by degrees" and got "into working order" primarily through drill. The accounts of two green soldiers mark the steady imposition of a new class identity. "We drill every morning in companies, and parade every afternoon," Robert Gould Shaw reported. "They keep us trotting pretty steadily."

The Reveille beats at 5 A.M. and at 5 1/2 we march in companies to breakfast, often going double-quick through the town which gives us a good appetite. When we get back Roll is called & at 9 1/2 we have company drill, then nothing to do (unless when on guard duty) until dinnertime, 1 o'cl, & ten of each company can get passes to go out of the grounds. At 3 1/2 or 4 we have a full parade of the whole regt. We march down again to supper at six. Retreat beats at sunset & every one who comes in after that without special permission from the colonel is put in the Guard House. These are the regulations of the U.S. Army. Tattoo sounds at 10 & everyone has to turn in as soon as the Roll is called. The lights are all turned down—the sentinels walk up & down between the rows of sleepers. There is a heavy guard kept up all about the grounds so that not a soul can get in or out without being seen.

"One or two hours" drill was "pretty hard work," he thought, but soon Shaw would be doing double and triple that work on a regular basis. US Army regulations limited a day's work to ten hours in the summer and eight in the winter, but in some regiments troops were routinely drilled six or eight hours daily, apart from their many other duties. "Did nothing but drill," one Iowa boy's diary records laconically. "Did nothing but drill." "Did nothing but drill." "Drilled *ad infinitum*."[43]

The uniformity, routine, and simple boredom of camp life played a powerful role in extinguishing romantic notions of military glory and individual heroism. That men at war had to be fed and clothed, sheltered, moved, penalized, and paid—and that every detail of every aspect of that process had to be recorded in duplicate and triplicate and filed by battalions of clerks—before the labor of killing could even commence came as a stunning—and deflating—revelation. For Thaddeus Capron, quartermaster of the 55th Illinois, it was ink and paper that brought down Vicksburg as surely as shot and shell. "To obtain any one article" to carry out the labor of war, he explained, "we have to make out nine papers, and then have to report it on seven other papers. These are of five different kinds, so you see that there is some writing to be done besides the hard work," by which he meant the labor of killing rebels. By early 1863, the lieutenant looked forward anxiously to the fall of the Confederate citadel on the Mississippi River: so much fighting generated altogether too much writing, and "I am anxious to get my work up to date." Pen pushing was as essential to victory as ramrodding, only a different variety of the same military experience.[44]

In the endless struggle to inculcate discipline, many men came to despise their bosses. Too many could point to a leader "as unfit for his place as the most ignorant private in the ranks." Such men stole and drank, disguised ignorance and blamed virtue, protected their own positions and risked men's lives needlessly—in a word, they "shirked" their duty. "Official incompetence" was everywhere, one Iowa private declared, leaving the men "cold, wet, hungry—foot-sore and worn out added to which the damned lazy, drunken commissarie come from town with nothing to appeas our hunger but a barrel of poisonous whiskey." The upshot was obvious: when cowards, "thieves & blacklegs" were in command, one officer asked, "how can you expect to have good troops?"[45]

As these examples suggest, soldiers were daily confronted by class-based political choices: whether to accept their objectively degraded condition, coupled with the humiliation of personal submission and the possibility of death or dismemberment as a consequence of laboring obediently, or to resist. Many responded as working people have usually responded, denying the possibility of change and resigning themselves to their fate. Men who hoped "to give a good account" of themselves in camp and under fire often simply saw no alternative to gritting their teeth and "going to work." "Such is the lot of a Soldier," one summed up.[46]

In the heat of combat, however, that sort of fatalism might prove entirely too fatal. "It was hard to see our men tumbling over," troops on both sides agreed, especially while toiling as "the subjects of a military despotism" with no "right to think," or "to sigh at the fall of our friends and relatives."[47] Confronted with the chaos of the battlefield and the leadership of commanders they doubted and despised, tens of thousands determined to "stand up to their work" on their own terms. This landscape was, after all, only apparently chaotic. A battlefield was the soldier's workplace, and all that occurred here had been planned, organized, and deliberately produced, like any grand task, by thousands of workers acting in collaborative and oppositional labor. "We know our work well," veterans attested, striving to do the job of fighting and killing according to their own talents and expertise. Again and again, soldiers described combat as "warm work," "murderous work," "hot work," "nasty work," "good work," "bloody work."[48]

Victory or defeat here depended not on some Homeric annihilation of the enemy, but on the collapse of labor discipline. Smoke, noise, fear, and command casualties all undercut labor control, particularly among soldiers on the offensive. Troops were taught to rally on their colors, but those who survived a charge or two soon realized how foolhardy that tactic was. "If [General Ulysses S.] Grant would pull a bag over his eyes, and let the men go forward," declared one Illinois sergeant, "we should succeed." That same logic motivated Bill Fletcher on the second day at Gettysburg. When the dignity of bearing the Stars and Bars was pressed upon him, after five color bearers had been shot down, he gave the banner a kick and a curse and hurried onward. His job, as he figured it, was to kill Yankees, not to provide target practice for the foe. When officers shouted commands and urged troops to close ranks and advance, soldiers submitted— when they could imagine no better course. But after a few good volleys, Hardee's *Tactics* usually went by the board, and men determined to think for themselves. Given the opportunity, they combined self-preservation with the performance of duty in the most careful measure.[49]

Union and Confederate soldiers never simply fought each other. From first enlistment, recruits waged running battles with their superiors over the terms of their service, the measure of independence of action they retained, and the way they conducted themselves in camp and in combat. Mules, slaves, and dogs they might be, but for officers and noncoms North and South, too many soldiers were altogether too recalcitrant to render good service. And once they landed on the firing line, Bill Fletcher argued, "it was nearly impossible . . . to keep a volunteer company under strict discipline." Back in camp, "nearly" became "altogether." This was precisely a struggle over the relations of production between military wage workers and their bosses, both civil and martial. Good leaders both in camp and in battle would guide obedient, well-trained troops in the work of killing against an undisciplined, ill-led foe.[50]

Common soldiers fought this clampdown fiercely. On both sides, recruits resisted and retaliated against stupid or unworthy officers, even shooting down those they could not overmatch by other means. So, too, Federal and Confederate units held informal soldiers' courts sub rosa to try recruits who fled when their comrades stuck.[51] More risky, soldiers refused their labor individually and collectively over a wide range of issues of labor control. Overwork, unequal pay, cowardly and dictatorial officers, suicidal orders, outmoded weapons, degrading assignments, or simple contract disputes all sparked rebellion. If "the perfect military machine" was one where "to hear was to obey" and "the men became the merest puppets," leaders quickly found themselves surrounded by clever Luddites.[52]

Thousands of others on both sides refused to obey commands or perform labor. Some just stacked arms and surrendered when the enemy approached. Indeed, an unsentimental view of the assault on Battery Wagner might conclude that the glory of that day belonged not to the men of the 54th Massachusetts, who proved their manhood by demonstrating their mortality, but rather to the rank and file of the 31st North Carolina, who refused to leave their bombproofs to take part in the battle. What the bosses tarred as mutiny or cowardice we might better recognize as a class-based political choice, a sensible and admirable refusal to perform the work of war.[53]

The most penetrating analysis of that social revolution, W. E. B. Du Bois's 1935 study, *Black Reconstruction in America*, grounds the Union's military victory in class struggle. It was not Gettysburg, Vicksburg, or the fall of Atlanta that doomed the Confederacy, he insists. A "General Strike" decided the war—the deliberate determination of hundreds of thousands of African Americans across the South to withdraw their labor from the Confederate cause and to bestow their strength as workers and soldiers to the cause of freedom, as they understood it.[54]

Du Bois's claim—like Lincoln, insisting that the military conflict was ultimately a labor struggle—has shaped much of the best scholarship of the past half century about the Civil War, from Armstead Robinson's Marxian forays to the rich volumes of the Freedom Project to the gendered analysis of Thavolia Glymph and Stephanie McCurry.[55] But even as these historians have enlarged our understanding of the scope and scale of war, militarizing the labor struggle, the new attention they have drawn to the home front and civil-military relations has come at a cost. As we focus increasingly on how slaves and women "fought" the war, the actions and experiences of millions of men in blue and gray become decentered, displaced, and, inevitably, diminished.[56] What an error of interpretation—and of careful reading.

Strange to say, these scholars have missed clear statements within Du Bois's masterwork that his argument about the "General Strike" was only half fleshed out. "The Southern worker, black *and white,* held the key to the war," he declares, justifying concentration on African Americans because they "held a more strategic place" than white southerners in destroying the Confederacy. Again, he refers to "the general strike of black *and white*" in bringing down the house of bondage.[57] Though Du Bois only briefly sketches the role ordinary white southerners played in wrecking the slaveocracy, he shows the need to study the politics of the battlefield and the home front as an objectively unified revolutionary process.

> This action of the slaves was followed by the disaffection of the poor whites. So long as the planters' war seemed successful, "there was little active opposition by the poorer whites; but the conscription and other burdens to support a slaveowners' war became very severe; the whites not interested in that cause became recalcitrant, some went into active opposition; and at last it was more desertion and disunion than anything else that brought about the final overthrow."

More than unfinished work for Civil War historians, realizing the promise of Du Bois's argument in this passage about the generation of "active opposition" is labor we have hardly begun.[58]

Taking this challenge seriously, weighing its meanings and merits, yields two remarkable conclusions that must reshape our understanding of the American crisis of the mid-nineteenth century. First, if Lincoln and Du Bois are correct in their implications, if not their full argument, historians have utterly missed the greatest biracial working-class uprising in American history. Following from that, it would seem, we have quite mistaken the meaning of the Civil War itself— whether understood as the traditional 1861–65 conflict or the "long Civil War," whose parameters extend beyond those years. If the American crisis was more than a war about Union, even more than a struggle over slavery—if Lincoln was right in calling war work—was the conflict not objectively part of a greater contest over relations of production, stretching from the 1840s down to the late 1870s, in which military conflict itself played a crucial role in the making of an American working class?[59]

If so, we may say, the "new birth of freedom" Lincoln promised at Gettysburg came about precisely because, for some Civil War soldiers, their work remained defiantly unfinished by the time of Lee's surrender. Across 1864 and 1865, tens of thousands of white southerners downed the tools of war and walked away from the Confederate cause. That is how most journeymen and laborers responded when class conflict flared on the shop floor. Contemporaries and historians have often labeled this resistance desertion, a species of soldierly failure. But such men did not just turn tail and run: they made political choices about their refusal to endure a specific set of class relations and acted upon those choices. Du Bois correctly calls the decision of hundreds of thousands of enslaved workers to quit work for enslavers and labor for freedom's cause one of the most notable revolutionary choices of humankind. But whites both North and South participated in their own mass expression of workers' control, which intersected with this uprising and shaped the outcome of the war itself. A Wisconsin boy recalled for his father a chat his unit had with a party of surrendered rebels. "They agreed with us perfectly on one thing, if the settlement of this war was left to the enlisted men of both sides we would soon go home." Come April 1865, former foes "now mingle[d] with each other as if they had always been friends." The labor of killing each other had been a "murderous business," nothing more. Yet their bloody work had laid the foundations of a fraternity of working men that extended far beyond Appomattox.[60]

"We hav done all that we agreed to do," a Yankee private exulted as he mustered out. "Our work is accomplished." "Four years lost and wages cut," a rebel replied. "Then the grave question arises," added a third recruit, "what will a person go to work at?"[61] Indeed. The war had taught powerful lessons of violence and comradeship, agency and submission, capital's power and workers' control. The "General Strike" of whites and Blacks had smashed the regime of chattel slavery for once and all, but the struggle for free labor was still in doubt. Against wage slavery there was unfinished work—which is to say war, more precisely class war—yet to be won.

NOTES

My thanks to Jim Barrett, Vernon Burton, Kathleen Hilliard, John Lynn, Scott Nelson, Bryan Palmer, David Roediger, Craig M. Simpson, and Peter Way for good advice and criticism.

1. See, for example, Garry Wills, *Lincoln at Gettysburg: The Words That Remade America* (New York: Simon and Schuster, 1992); Glen LaFantasie, "Lincoln and the Gettysburg Awakening," *Journal of the Abraham Lincoln Association* 16 (1995): 73–89; Kent Gramm, *November: Lincoln's Elegy at Gettysburg* (Bloomington: Indiana University Press, 2001); James M. McPherson, *Hallowed Ground: A Walk at Gettysburg* (New York: Crown, 2003); Gabor Boritt, *The Gettysburg Gospel: The Lincoln Speech That Nobody Knows* (New York: Simon and Schuster, 2006); Simon Stow, "Pericles at Gettysburg and Ground Zero: Tragedy, Patriotism, and Public Mourning," *American Political Science Review* 101 (2007): 195–208; A. E. Elmore, *Lincoln's Gettysburg Address: Echoes of the Bible and Book of Common Prayer* (Carbondale: Southern Illinois University Press, 2009); James L. Huston, "The Lost Cause of the North: A Reflection on Lincoln's Gettysburg Address and the Second Inaugural," *Journal of the Abraham Lincoln Association* 33 (2012): 14–37; Martin P. Johnson, *Writing the Gettysburg Address* (Lawrence: University Press of Kansas, 2013); Jared Peatman, *The Long Shadow of Lincoln's Gettysburg Address* (Carbondale: Southern Illinois University Press, 2013); Sean Conant, ed., *The Gettysburg Address: Perspectives on Lincoln's Greatest Speech* (New York: Oxford University Press, 2015); and David S. Reynolds, *Abe: Abraham Lincoln in His Times* (New York: Penguin, 2020), 829–52.

2. Wills, *Lincoln at Gettysburg*, 63–89; Boritt, *Gettysburg Gospel*, 40–69.

3. Gabor S. Boritt, "A Question of Political Suicide? Lincoln's Opposition to the Mexican War," *Journal of the Illinois State Historical Society* 67 (1974): 79–100; Amy S. Greenberg, *A Wicked War: Polk, Clay, Lincoln, and the 1846 U.S. Invasion of Mexico* (New York: Vintage, 2013), 251–52; William W. Freehling, *Becoming Lincoln* (Charlottesville: University of Virginia Press, 2018).

4. Douglas L. Wilson and Rodney O. Davis, eds., *Herndon's Informants: Letters, Interviews, and Statements about Abraham Lincoln* (Urbana: University of Illinois Press, 1998), esp. 327–29. The best account of this story is Richard L. Miller, *Lincoln and His World: The Early Years, Birth to Illinois Legislature* (Mechanicsburg, PA: Stackpole Books, 2006), 148–77. See also Freehling, *Becoming Lincoln*, 40–41; and Reynolds, *Abe*, 122–26.

5. Paul M. Angle, ed., *Herndon's Life of Lincoln: The History and Personal Recollections of Abraham Lincoln* (Cleveland: World Publishing, 1942), 82. David H. Donald tells this part of the story, omitting just what Lincoln did during the campaign, along with any ill consequences of his service. See Donald, *Lincoln* (New York: Simon and Schuster, 1995), 44–45.

6. We cannot say how the trauma of war affected Lincoln before 1861. The burden of his wartime presidency, though, was obvious to all, and youthful memories reawakened cannot but have deepened his misery. On this, cf. Jonathan Shay, *Odysseus in America: Combat Trauma and the Trials of Homecoming* (New York: Scribner, 2002).

7. Freehling, *Becoming Lincoln*, 14–18; Gabor S. Boritt, *Lincoln and the Economics of the American Dream* (Urbana: University of Illinois Press, 1994), 80–81; Olivier Fraysée, *Lincoln, Land, and Labor, 1809–60* (Urbana: University of Illinois Press, 1994), esp. 25–39, 50–51, 58–61.

8. On Lincoln's always dark view of war, see Harold Holzer, ed., *Lincoln on War* (Chapel Hill: University of North Carolina Press, 2011), esp. 25, 166, 293.

9. Roy P. Basler et al., eds., *The Collected Works of Abraham Lincoln*, 9 vols. (New Brunswick, NJ: Rutgers University Press, 1953–55), 8:332–33.

10. Armond S. Goldman and Frank C. Schmalsteig Jr., "Abraham Lincoln's Gettysburg Illness," *Journal of Medical Biography* 15 (2007): 104.

11. John G. Nicolay and John Hay, *Abraham Lincoln: A History*, 10 vols. (New York: Century, 1890), 8:189–203; Allan Nevins, *The Ordeal of the Union*, 8 vols. (New York: Charles Scribner's Sons, 1947–71), 7:446–50; Svend Peterson, *The Gettysburg Addresses: The Story of Two Orations* (New York: Frederick Ungar, 1963); Wills, *Lincoln at Gettysburg*, 25–36; Reynolds, *Abe*, 829–41.

12. Cf. Sacvan Bercovitch, *The American Jeremiad* (Madison: University of Wisconsin Press, 1978).

13. See, for example, the lovely but misconceived essays in Allan Nevins, ed., *Lincoln and the Gettysburg Address: Commemorative Papers* (Urbana: University of Illinois Press, 1964). Here, a poet discovers poetry in Lincoln's words, a jurist finds law, a theologian points to religion, and so on.

14. Close analysis of the rhetoric of Lincoln's speech abounds. I learned much from Johnson, *Writing the Gettysburg Address*, esp. 193–96; Freehling, *Becoming Lincoln*, esp. 313; and Craig M. Simpson, "Lincoln and Memory: A New Interpretation of the Gettysburg Address" (unpublished paper, Department of History Seminar Series, Western University, 2019). Missing from these treatments is Lincoln's interpretation of soldierly action as labor.

15. Perceptive on the link between liberty and labor, though this insight deserves elaboration, is William Lee Miller, *President Lincoln: The Duty of a Statesman* (New York: Vintage, 2009), esp. 313.

16. A handful of scholars have developed this argument in recent years. See especially Christian G. Appy, *Working-Class War: American Combat Soldiers and Vietnam* (Chapel Hill: University of North Carolina Press, 1993); Peter J. Way, "Rebellion of the Regulars: Working Soldiers and the Mutiny of 1763–1764," *William and Mary Quarterly* 57 (2000): 761–92; Russell L. Johnson, *Warriors into Workers: The Civil War and the Formation of Urban-Industrial Society in a Northern City* (New York: Fordham University Press, 2003); Lawrence T. McDonnell, "Bloody Work: Toward and Beyond a Labor History of the Civil War" (unpublished paper, British Association for American Studies, 2004); Eric-Jan Zürcher, ed., *Fighting for a Living: A Comparative Study of Military Labour, 1500–2000* (Amsterdam: Amsterdam University Press, 2013); and Mark A. Lause, *Free Labor: The Civil War and the Making of an American Working Class* (Urbana: University of Illinois Press, 2015).

17. See, for example, Xenophon, *The Expedition of Cyrus* (New York: Penguin, 2005), 6–10; Sallust, *The Jurgurthine War / The Conspiracy of Catiline* (New York: Penguin, 1963), 81; Karl F. Friday, *Hired Swords: The Rise of Private Warrior Power in Early Japan* (Stanford, CA: Stanford University Press, 1992); David Parrott, *The Business of War: Military Enterprise and Military Revolution in Early Modern Europe* (New York: Cambridge University Press, 2012); Ernst Junger, *Storm of Steel* (New York: Penguin, 1961), esp. 11, 33, 35, 42, 56–66; Leonard V. Smith, *Between Mutiny and Obedience: The Case of the French Fifth Infantry Division during World War I* (Princeton, NJ: Princeton University Press, 1994); Anthony Swofford, *Jarhead: A Marine's Chronicle of the Gulf War and Other Battles* (New York: Scribner, 2003); Erik Prince, *Civilian Warriors: The Inside Story of Blackwater and the Unsung Heroes of the War on Terror* (New York: Portfolio, 2014); and Shane Harris, *@War: The Rise of the Military-Internet Complex* (New York: Mariner Books, 2014). One recruit tellingly recalled how his staff sergeant chewed him out for "sirring" him like an officer: "I work for a living." Buzz Williams, *Spare Parts: A Marine Reservist's Journey from Campus to Combat in 38 Days* (New York: Gotham Books, 2004), 57.

18. Dennis E. Showalter, "A Modest Plea for Drums and Trumpets," *Military Affairs* 39 (1975): 71–74; Mark Grimsley, "Why Military History Sucked," *WarHistorian.org* (blog), June 2, 2016, http://warhistorian.blogspot.com/2016/06/why-military-history-sucked.html; John A. Lynn, "Rally Once Again: The Embattled Future of Academic Military History," *Journal of Military History* 61 (1997): 777–89; Ronald H. Spector, "Teetering on the Brink of Respectability," *Journal of American History* 93 (2007): 1158–60.

19. Yuval N. Harari, *The Ultimate Experience: Battlefield Revelations and the Making of Modern War Culture, 1450–2000* (New York: Palgrave Macmillan, 2008); John A. Lynn, *Battle: A History of Combat and Culture* (New York: Basic Books, 2004); Brian Sandberg, *Warrior Pursuits: Noble Culture and Civil Conflict in Early Modern France* (Baltimore: Johns Hopkins University Press, 2010); George L. Mosse, *Fallen Soldiers: Reshaping the Memory of the World Wars* (New York: Oxford University Press, 1990); Gregory A. Daddis, *Pulp Vietnam: War and Gender in Cold War Men's Adventure Magazines* (New York: Cambridge University Press, 2020).

20. James M. McPherson, "The '*Glory*' Story: The 54th Massachusetts and the Civil War," *New Republic*, Jan. 8, 1990, 22–27. For current views of the value of and agenda for studying the military history of the Civil War, see the disparate perspectives of Andrew S. Bledsoe and Andrew F. Lang, eds., *Upon the Fields of Battle: Essays on the Military History of America's Civil War* (Baton Rouge: Louisiana State University Press, 2018); and Stephanie McCurry, *Women's War: Fighting and Surviving the American Civil War* (Cambridge, MA: Harvard University Press, 2019).

21. The social construction of that claim is described well in David W. Blight, *Race and Reunion: The Civil War in American Memory* (Cambridge, MA: Belknap Press of Harvard University Press, 2002).

22. On the problem of military motivation in the Civil War, see especially Pete Maslowski, "A Study of Morale in Civil War Soldiers," *Military Affairs* 34 (1970): 122–26; Gerald F. Linderman, *Embattled Courage: The Experience of Combat in the American Civil War* (New York: Free Press, 1987); Larry J. Daniel, *Soldiering in the Army of Tennessee: A Portrait of Life in a Confederate Army* (Chapel Hill: University of North Carolina Press, 1991); James M. McPherson, *What They Fought For, 1861–1865* (Baton Rouge: Louisiana State University Press, 1995); McPherson, *For Cause and Comrades: Why Men Fought in the Civil War* (New York: Oxford University Press, 1997); Earl J. Hess, *The Union Soldier in Battle: Enduring the Ordeal of Combat* (Lawrence: University Press of Kansas, 1997); Joseph A. Frank and George A. Reaves, *"Seeing the Elephant": Raw Recruits at the Battle of Shiloh* (Urbana: University of Illinois Press, 2003); Mark H. Dunkelman, *Brothers One and All: Esprit de Corps in a Civil War Regiment* (Baton Rouge: Louisiana State University Press, 2004); Kenneth W. Noe, *Reluctant Rebels: The Confederates Who Joined the Army after 1861* (Chapel Hill: University of North Carolina Press, 2010); Lesley J. Gordon, *A Broken Regiment: The 16th Connecticut's Civil War* (Baton Rouge: Louisiana State University Press, 2014); and Peter S. Carmichael, *The War for the Common Soldier: How Men Thought, Fought, and Survived in Civil War Armies* (Chapel Hill: University of North Carolina Press, 2018). The need for a more complex analysis has been frequently noted along the lines laid out in John A. Lynn, *The Bayonets of the Republic: Motivation and Tactics in the Army of Revolutionary France, 1791–94* (Urbana: University of Illinois Press, 1984).

23. Fred A. Shannon, "The Mercenary Factor in the Creation of the Union Army," *Mississippi Valley Historical Review* 12 (1926): 523–49; Robert Partin, "The Money Matters of a Confederate

Soldier," *Alabama Historical Quarterly* 25 (1963): 49–69; Eugene C. Murdock, *Patriotism Limited, 1862–1865: The Civil War Draft and the Bounty System* (Kent, OH: Kent State University Press, 1967); Harry N. Scheiber, "The Pay of Confederate Troops and Problems of Demoralization: A Case of Administrative Failure," *Civil War History* 15 (1969): 226–36; James Barnett, "The Bounty Jumpers of Indiana," *Civil War History* 4 (1958): 429–36; William Marvel, *Lincoln's Mercenaries: Economic Motivation among Union Soldiers during the Civil War* (Baton Rouge: Louisiana State University Press, 2018); Brian Luskey, *Men Is Cheap: Exposing the Frauds of Free Labor in Civil War America* (Chapel Hill: University of North Carolina Pres, 2020); Ella Lonn, *Desertion during the Civil War* (1928; rept., Lincoln: University of Nebraska Press, Bison Books, 1998); Richard Bardolph, "Inconstant Rebels: Desertion of North Carolina Troops in the Civil War," *North Carolina Historical Review* 41 (1964): 163–89; Bardolph, "Confederate Dilemma: North Carolina Troops and the Deserter Problem," *North Carolina Historical Review* 66 (1989): 61–86, 179–210; Richard Reid, "A Test Case of the 'Crying Evil': Desertion among North Carolina Troops during the Civil War," *North Carolina Historical Review* 58 (1981): 234–62; Katherine A. Guiffre, "First in Flight: Desertion as Politics in the North Carolina Confederate Army," *Social Science History* 21 (1997): 245–63; Aaron W. Marrs, "Desertion and Loyalty in the South Carolina Infantry, 1861–1865," *Civil War History* 50 (2004): 47–65; Bruce A. Watson, *When Soldiers Quit: Studies in Military Disintegration* (Westport, CT: Praeger, 1997).

24. Drew G. Faust, *This Republic of Suffering: Death and the American Civil War* (New York: Vintage, 2009), 32–60; Joanna Bourke, *An Intimate History of Killing: Face-to-Face Killing in Twentieth-Century Warfare* (New York: Basic Books, 1999).

25. Walter S. Poor to George Fox, Apr. 25, May 15, Oct. 3, 1861, Nov. 28, 1862, Jan. 12, July 16, 1861, Dec. 21, 1863; and Walter S. Poor to Mary Poor Fox, Jan. 14, Oct. 24, 28, 1863, Walter Stone Poor Papers, New-York Historical Society, New York; James J. Heslin, "A Yankee Soldier in a New York Regiment," *New-York Historical Society Quarterly* 50 (1966): 109–49.

26. Phillip S. Paludan, *A People's Contest: The Union and Civil War, 1861–1865* (Lawrence: University Press of Kansas, 1996); Gary W. Gallagher, *The Confederate War* (Cambridge, MA: Harvard University Press, 1999); Gallagher, *The Union War* (Cambridge, MA: Harvard University Press, 2013); Chandra Manning, *What This Cruel War Was Over: Soldiers, Slavery, and the Civil War* (New York: Vintage, 2007); Eric Foner, *The Fiery Trial: Abraham Lincoln and American Slavery* (New York: W. W. Norton, 2011); James Oakes, *Freedom National: The Destruction of Slavery in the United States, 1861–1865* (New York: W. W. Norton, 2012).

27. McPherson, *What They Fought For*, 20–24.

28. Russell Duncan, ed., *Blue-Eyed Child of Fortune: The Civil War Letters of Colonel Robert Gould Shaw* (Athens: University of Georgia Press, 1992), 77, 73; Thomas R. Bright, "Yankees in Arms: The Civil War as a Personal Experience," *Civil War History* 19 (1973): 205.

29. Paul Foos, *A Short, Offhand, Killing Affair: Soldiers and Social Conflict during the Mexican-American War* (Chapel Hill: University of North Carolina Press, 2002), 24; Richard A. Herrera, "Self-Governance and the American Citizen as Soldier, 1776–1861," *Journal of Military History* 65 (2001): 21–52; Marcus Cunliffe, *Soldiers and Civilians: The Martial Spirit in America, 1776–1865* (Boston: Little, Brown, 1968); Edward M. Coffman, *The Old Army: A Portrait of the American Army*

in Peacetime, 1784–1898 (New York: Oxford University Press, 1986); Eugene C. Tidball, "A Subaltern's First Experiences in the Old Army," *Civil War History* 45 (1999): 197–222.

30. Judith Lee Hallock, ed., *The Civil War Letters of Joshua K. Calloway* (Athens: University of Georgia Press, 1997), 46, 35.

31. Douglas S. Freeman, *Robert E. Lee*, 4 vols. (New York: Charles Scribner's Sons, 1934–35), 2:86–101; Sam R. Watkins, *"Co. Aytch": Maury Grays, First Tennessee Regiment; or, A Side Show of the Big Show* (New York: Macmillan, 1962), 32; Harry J. Carman, ed., "The Diary of Amos Glover," *Ohio Archaeological and Historical Quarterly* 44 (1935): 267; Duncan, *Blue-Eyed Child of Fortune*, 194, 196; Albert D. Kirwan, ed., *Johnny Green of the Orphan Brigade: The Journal of a Confederate Soldier* (Lexington: University Press of Kentucky, 1984), 48, 79–80; Ashley Halsey, ed., *A Yankee Private's Civil War* (Chicago: Henry Regnery, 1961), 203; James I. Robertson Jr., ed., "'Such Is War': the Letters of an Orderly in the 7th Iowa Infantry," *Iowa Journal of History,* 58 (1960), 334; Robert S. Dilworth Journal, Apr. 12, 1862, Center for Archival Collections, Jerome Library, Bowling Green State University, Bowling Green, OH (hereafter cited as BGSU); Francis R. Stewart Journal, Aug. 26, 1864, ibid.; John J. Evers to *Perrysburg Journal,* July 4, 1861, John J. Evers Papers, ibid.; T. W. Clements Confederate Journal, [June 18, 1863], Hargrett Library, University of Georgia, Athens (hereafter cited as UGA).

32. "War Diary of Thaddeus H. Capron, 1861–1865," *Journal of the Illinois State Historical Society* 12 (1919): 381, 367, 338; Duncan, *Blue-Eyed Child of Fortune*, 107; W. Nixon to Elijah Whitmore, n.d. [post-Sept. 1863], Elijah Whitmore Papers, BGSU.

33. Robert H. Rhodes, ed., *All for the Union: The Civil War Diary and Letters of Elisha Hunt Rhodes* (New York: Vintage, 1992), 87, 147.

34. "War Diary of Thaddeus H. Capron," 338; Hallock, *Civil War Letters of Joshua K. Calloway,* 46, 35; Halsey, *Yankee Private's Civil War,* 81; Leo M. Kaiser, "Letters from the Front," *Journal of the Illinois State Historical Society* 56 (1963): 153; John K. Mahon, ed., "The Civil War Letters of Samuel Mahon, Seventh Iowa Infantry," *Iowa Journal of History* 51 (1953): 245, 254; Robertson, "'Such Is War,'" 329; John K. Mahon, "Peter Dekle's Letters," *Civil War History* 4 (1958): 14; Francis R. Stewart Journal, Oct. 16, 1864, BGSU; Duncan, *Blue-Eyed Child of Fortune,* 76.

35. Watkins, *"Co. Aytch,"* 19, 22.

36. Lewis B. Jessup, "The 24th Indiana at Shiloh—the Long March to Get into the Battle," *National Tribune Scrap Book: Stories of the Camp, March, Battle, Hospital and Prison Told by Comrades* 3 (1900): 158–59. See also Ida B. Adams, ed., "The Civil War Letters of James Rush Holmes," *Western Pennsylvania Historical Magazine* 44 (1961): 118; Charles W. Turner, ed., *Captain Greenlee Davidson, C.S.A.: Diary and Letters, 1851–1863* (Verona, VA: McClure, 1975), 51.

37. James D. Schmidt, *Free to Work: Labor Law, Emancipation, and Reconstruction, 1815–1880* (Athens: University of Georgia Press, 1998), 7–52; Robert J. Steinfeld, *Coercion, Contract, and Free Labor in the Nineteenth Century* (New York: Cambridge University Press, 2001).

38. H. H. Freeman to family, Oct. 6, 1861, Civil War Correspondence, Ellis Merton Coulter Historical Manuscripts, UGA; J. V. Frederick, ed., "War Diary of W. C. Porter," *Arkansas Historical Quarterly* 11 (1952): 293; Arthur N. Skinner and James L. Skinner, eds., *The Death of a Confederate:*

Selections from the Letters of the Archibald Smith Family of Roswell, Georgia, 1864–1956 (Athens: University of Georgia Press, 1996), 15. The comparison of soldiering to slavery and military labor as work fit for nonwhites only appears everywhere in Anglo-American memoirs of the period 1850–1950. See, for example, Alfred O. Pollard, *Fire-Eater: The Memoirs of a V.C.* (London: Hutchinson, 1932), 31 and passim.

    39. William A. Fletcher, *Rebel Private, Front and Rear: Memoirs of a Confederate Soldier* (New York: Plume, 1997), 31; Halsey, *Yankee Private's Civil War,* 35. On hegemony and class struggle, see especially Eugene D. Genovese, *Roll, Jordan, Roll: The World the Slaves Made* (New York: Vintage, 1974); Genovese, *In Red and Black: Marxian Explorations in Southern and Afro-American History* (New York: Vintage, 1969); Antonio Gramsci, *Selections from the Prison Notebooks* (New York: International, 1971); and Jean-Paul Sartre, *Critique of Dialectical Reason,* vol. 1, *Theory of Practical Ensembles* (London: New Left Books, 1971).

    40. For examples of important labor-history studies that fail to consider the centrality of Civil War military service in the process of working-class formation, see Herbert Gutman, *Work, Culture, and Society in Industrializing America: Essays in American Working-Class and Social History* (New York: Vintage, 1976); David Montgomery, *Beyond Equality: Labor and the Radical Republicans, 1862–1872* (New York: Alfred A. Knopf, 1967); Montgomery, *Workers' Control in America: Studies in the History of Work, Technology, and Labor Struggles* (New York: Cambridge University Press, 1980); Bryan D. Palmer, "Social Formation and Class Formation, 1800–1900," in *Proletarianization and Family History,* ed. David Levine (Orlando, FL: Academic, 1984), 229–309; Amy Bridges, "Becoming American: The Working Classes in the United States before the Civil War," in *Working-Class Formation: Nineteenth-Century Patterns in Western Europe and the United States,* ed. Ira Katznelson and Aristide R. Zolberg (Princeton, NJ: Princeton University Press, 1986), 157–96; David Montgomery, *The Fall of the House of Labor: The Workplace, the State, and American Labor Activism, 1865–1925* (New York: Cambridge University Press, 1989); Sean Wilentz, "The Rise of the American Working Class, 1776–1877," in *Perspectives on American Labor History: The Problem of Synthesis,* ed. J. Carroll Moody and Alice Kessler-Harris (DeKalb: Northern Illinois University Press, 1989), 83–151; Bruce Levine, *The Spirit of 1848: German Immigrants, Labor Conflict, and the Coming of the Civil War* (Urbana: University of Illinois Press, 1992); Iver Bernstein, *The New York City Draft Riots: Their Significance for American Society and Politics in the Age of the Civil War* (New York: Oxford University Press, 1989); David Montgomery, *Citizen Worker: The Experience of Free Workers in the United States and the Free Market during the Nineteenth Century* (New York: Cambridge University Press, 1995); and Bruce Laurie, *Artisans into Workers: Labor in Nineteenth Century America* (Urbana: University of Illinois Press, 1997). More egregious, perhaps, is the face-of-battle treatment soldiers get in otherwise excellent studies, such as Christopher Clark, Nancy A. Hewitt, and Bruce C. Levine, eds., *Who Built America? Working People and the Nation's Economy, Politics, Culture, and Society,* vol. 1, *From Conquest and Colonization to 1877* (New York: Vintage, 2000).

    41. Frederick A. Porcher, "The Conflict of Capital and Labour," *Russell's Magazine* 3 (1858): 289–98; [John Anderson], *Common Sense* (New Orleans: n. p., 1859).

    42. On the fear of "wage slavery," see, for example, *The Liberator* (Boston), Sept. 4, 1846, Apr. 23, 1847; *Anti-Slavery Bugle* (Lisbon, OH), Mar. 26, 1847; *New York Tribune,* June 3, 1850; and *Racine*

(WI) Advocate, Jan. 25, 1860. For a different view, see Eric Foner, *Free Soil, Free Labor, Free Men: The Ideology of the Republican Party before the Civil War* (New York: Oxford University Press, 1970), 23–33.

43. Paddy Griffith, *Battle Tactics of the Civil War* (New Haven, CT: Yale University Press, 2001), 91–98, 105–11; Duncan, *Blue-Eyed Child of Fortune,* 101, 104, 107, 144–45; Halsey, *Rebel Private's Civil War,* 9; US War Department, *Revised United States Army Regulations of 1861* (Washington: Government Printing Office, 1861), 128; Carman, "Diary of Amos Glover," 260, 267; John J. Evers to unknown, May 17, 1861, John J. Evers Papers, BGSU.

44. "War Diary of Thaddeus H. Capron," 362. Cf. Carlton McCarthy, *Detailed Minutiae of Soldier Life in the Army of Northern Virginia, 1861–1865* (Richmond: C. McCarthy, 1882); John D. Billings, *Hardtack and Coffee; or, The Unwritten Story of Army Life. including Chapters on Enlisting, Life in Tents and Log Huts, Jonahs and Beats, Offences and Punishments, Raw Recruits, Foraging, Corps and Corps Badges, the Wagon Trains, the Army Mule, the Engineer Corps, the Signal Corps, Etc.* (Boston: G. M. Smith, 1887); and Bård B. Mæland and Paul O. Brunstad, eds., *Enduring Military Boredom: From 1750 to the Present* (New York: Palgrave Macmillan, 2009).

45. Halsey, *Yankee Private's Civil War,* 17, 86–88; Fletcher, *Rebel Private,* 81; Duncan, *Blue-Eyed Child of Fortune,* 132, 191–92; Carman, "Diary of Amos Glover," 264, 268; Robertson, "'Such Is War,'" 332; Francis R. Stewart Journal, Oct. 9, 1864, BGSU. For a vivid example of the "disgust" Union officers displayed toward their men, see Rev. William L. Lucey, ed., "The Diary of Joseph B. O'Hagan, S.J., Chaplain of the Excelsior Brigade," *Civil War History* 6 (1960): 408–9.

46. Duncan, *Blue-Eyed Child of Fortune,* 137, 186; Fletcher, *Rebel Private,* 65; Robert S. Dilworth Journal, Apr. 12, 1864, BGSU; Francis R. Stewart Journal, Nov. 22, 1864, BGSU; Carman, "Diary of Amos Glover," 261.

47. Carman, "Diary of Amos Glover," 266; Duncan, *Blue-Eyed Child of Fortune,* 188, 205; Watkins, *"Co. Aytch,"* 40, 42; Augustus Bull to "Cousin Roxie," Dec. 23, 1862, Augustus Bull Papers, BGSU.

48. Watkins, *"Co. Aytch,"* 42–44; Francis R. Stewart Journal, Nov. 25, 1864, BGSU; Andrew Altman to John Altman, July 26, 1864, Andrew Altman Papers, ibid.; John Hays Bowen, "An Incident at the Battle of Shiloh," *Tennessee Historical Quarterly* 9 (1925–26): 264; "War Diary of Thaddeus H. Capron," 344, 346, 387–88, 389; Rhodes, *All for the Union,* 64, 73–74, 80, 104, 141, 145, 162, 168, 172, 203; Kirwan, *Johnny Green of the Orphan Brigade,* 25, 27, 54, 99, 137, 151, 155, 180; Duncan, *Blue-Eyed Child of Fortune,* 194; Fletcher, *Rebel Private,* 34, 54, 67; Halsey, *Yankee Private's Civil War,* x, 14, 25, 26, 28, 31, 106, 123, 125, 136–40, 162, 192, 207; Mahon, "Civil War Letters of Samuel Mahon," 245, 247, 248, 266.

49. Watkins, *"Co. Aytch,"* 29–30; Jessup, "24th Indiana at Shiloh," 159; "War Diary of Thaddeus H. Capron," 390; Fletcher, *Rebel Private,* 56–57, 78–79. Notably, prior to the assault on Battery Wagner, the color guard of the 54th Massachusetts attempted to furl its flags because they were drawing so much artillery fire. They were reprimanded, and the attack went forward. Noah A. Trudeau, *Like Men of War: Black Troops in the Civil War, 1862–1865* (Boston: Little, Brown, 1998), 78–80. Excellent on so many points, Griffith, *Battle Tactics of the Civil War,* fails to understand the tactical problem in terms of labor control and discipline, describing it as a "failure of will" (45). This begs the question, whose will? To accomplish what, and why?

50. Fletcher, *Rebel Private,* 14, 31, 36; Kaiser, "Letters from the Front," 155; Mildred Throne, ed., "Letters from Shiloh," *Iowa Journal of History* 3 (1954): 266; Duncan, *Blue-Eyed Child of Fortune,*

185–86; Watt P. Marchman, "The Journal of Sergt. Wm. J. McKell," *Civil War History* 3 (1957): 317–18; Edward G. Longacre, ed., "The Roughest Kind of Campaigning: Letters of Sergeant Edward Wightman, Third New York Volunteers, May–July 1864," *Civil War History* 28 (1982): 338; Halsey, *Yankee Private's Civil War*, 26–27, 35, 173; Bob Crouse to Elijah Whitmore, June 26, 1864; and Warren Whitmore to Elijah Whitmore, June 28, 1864, Elijah Whitmore Papers, BGSU.

51. Kirwan, *Johnny Green of the Orphan Brigade*, 97; Duncan, *Blue-Eyed Child of Fortune*, 185, 189; Watkins, "*Co. Aytch*," 40; Adams, "Civil War Letters of James Rush Holmes," 119; Howard L. Meredith and James L. Nichols, eds., "Letters of a Confederate Soldier: The Andrew J. Fogle Collection," *Library Chronicle of the University of Texas* 8 (1965): 38; Matthew O'Brien, "'The Maddest Folly of the Campaign': A Diarist and a Poet Confront Kennesaw Mountain," *Civil War History* 23 (1977): 243; Rhodes, *All for the Union*, 175; T. Harry Williams, ed., "The Reluctant Warrior: The Diary of N. K. Nichols," *Civil War History* 3 (1957): 17–39; Halsey, *Yankee Private's Civil War*, 17, 39, 189, 203; Fletcher, *Rebel Private*, 87, 90, 109; Francis R. Stewart Journal, Oct. 29, 1864, BGSU; Ira B. Conine to Jennie M. Bysel, Jan. 11, 1863, Ira B. Conine Correspondence, ibid.

52. Halsey, *Yankee Private's Civil War*, 81–92; Billings, *Hardtack and Coffee*, 150–52.

53. Webb Garrison, *Mutiny in the Civil War* (Shippensburg, PA: White Mane, 2001); Francis R. Stewart Journal, Oct. 14, 1864, BGSU; E. Milby Burton, *The Siege of Charleston, 1861–1865* (Columbia: University of South Carolina Press, 1970), 165–66; Mark A. Weitz, "Desertion as Mutiny: Upcountry Georgians in the Army of Tennessee," in *Rebellion, Repression, Reinvention: Mutiny in Comparative Perspective*, ed. Jane Hathaway (Westport, CT: Praeger, 2001), 2–23; Frederick, "War Diary of W. C. Porter," 307; James Barnett, ed., "Some Civil War Letters and Diary of John Lympus Barnett," *Indiana Magazine of History* 37 (1941): 169; "The Diary of Captain Edward Crenshaw of the Confederate States Army," *Alabama Historical Quarterly* 2 (1940): 381–82; Howard C. Westwood, "The Cause and Consequence of a Union Black Soldier's Mutiny and Execution," *Civil War History* 31 (1985): 222–36; B. Kevin Bennett, "The Jacksonville Mutiny," *Civil War History* 38 (1992): 39–49.

54. W. E. B. Du Bois, *Black Reconstruction in America, 1860–1880* (1935; repr., New York: Vintage, 1999), esp. 55–83. Cf. Charles H. Wesley, *The Collapse of the Confederacy* (1937; repr., Columbia: University of South Carolina Press, 2001); and Lause, *Free Labor*, 55–67.

55. Armstead L. Robinson, *Bitter Fruits of Bondage: The Demise of Slavery and the Collapse of the Confederacy, 1861–65* (Charlottesville: University of Virginia Press, 2004); Ira Berlin et al., eds., *Freedom: A Documentary History of Emancipation, 1861–1867*, ser. 1, vols. 1–3 (New York: Cambridge University Press, 1991); Stephanie McCurry, *Confederate Reckoning: Power and Politics in the Civil War South* (Cambridge, MA: Harvard University Press, 2012); Thavolia Glymph, *Out of the House of Bondage: The Transformation of the Plantation Household* (New York: Cambridge University Press, 2008), 97–136; Glymph, *The Women's Fight: The Civil War's Battles for Home, Freedom, and Nation* (Chapel Hill: University of North Carolina Press, 2020).

56. McCurry, *Women's War*, esp. 1–4, 203–12; Brandishing Svetlana Alexievich, *The Unwomanly Face of War: An Oral History of Women in World War II* (New York: Random House, 2018). McCurry chides military historians for ignoring women's experience. But this charge requires her to ignore— for starters—Barton Hacker, "Women and Military Institutions in Early Modern Europe: A Recon-

naissance," *Signs* 6 (1981); 643–71; and the masterful work of John A. Lynn, *Women, Armies, and Warfare in Early Modern Europe* (New York: Cambridge University Press, 2008).

57. Du Bois, *Black Reconstruction in America*, 63, 64 (italics added).

58. Ibid., 80. Du Bois here quotes the British traveler Sir George Campbell, *White and Black: The Outcome of a Visit to the United States* (London: Chatto and Windus, 1879), 165. He mangles the book's title in his citation.

59. This is the subject of my book-in-progress, "Bloody Work: The Civil War and the Making of the American Working Class, 1846–1877."

60. Barnett, "Some Civil War Letters and Diary of John Lympus Barnett," 170; T. W. Clements Confederate Journal, May 3, 1863, UGA.

61. Mahon, "Civil War Letters of Samuel Mahon," 261; Fletcher, *Rebel Private*, 213.

Abraham Lincoln's Unfinished Work and the South's Long Self-Reconstruction

J. WILLIAM HARRIS

The recent historiography of the Reconstruction era has been marked by an expansion of its boundaries, especially geographical boundaries. We now think of a Reconstruction of labor relations in the North, a Reconstruction "west of Appomattox," a Reconstruction in a country without borders, and even a Reconstruction that belongs to a global era of nation-building and war.[1]

In a volume devoted to "Lincoln's Unfinished Work," though, it makes more sense to take what might fairly be called an old-fashioned view of Reconstruction as a time and as a problem. When Abraham Lincoln spoke in the Gettysburg Address of the "unfinished work" and "great task" remaining or urged Americans in his second inaugural "to strive to finish the work we are in," he was not thinking of developments in the West, or northern economic or social issues, or what was happening beyond the borders of the United States. Instead, he was thinking of the need, first, to bring the war to a successful conclusion so that, second, the states of the Confederacy could be restored to "their proper practical relation with the Union" in a way that advanced and protected a "new birth of liberty" in a "government of the people, by the people, for the people."[2]

That was his message throughout the war, even after he issued the Emancipation Proclamation. "I never did as more, nor ever was willing to accept less," he wrote to Major General John A. McClernand in early 1863, "than for all the States, and the people thereof, to take and hold their places, and their rights, in the Union, under the Constitution."[3]

At first, Lincoln argued that, South Carolina excepted, "there is much reason to believe that the Union men are the majority in many, if not in every other one, of the so-called seceded states."[4] Since this majority of whites were Unionists at heart, they could be persuaded to give up secession as soon as the high emotions of the moment subsided. Most importantly, restoration of "proper practical relations" must be the work of loyal southerners themselves; Lincoln "remained committed," in the words of William C. Harris, "to the principle of self-reconstruction controlled by Southern white unionists."[5] In his first inaugural address, he tried to reassure loyal white southerners by quoting his earlier words: "I have no purpose, directly or indirectly, to interfere with the institution of slavery in the States where it exists. I believe I have no lawful right to do so, and I have no inclination to do so."[6] He then endorsed a proposed thirteenth amendment to the Constitution, which had just passed both houses of Congress on the eve of the inauguration with the required two-thirds vote, stating that "no amendment shall be made to the Constitution which will authorize or give to Congress the power to abolish or interfere, within any State, with the domestic institutions thereof, including that of persons held to labor or service by the laws of such state."[7] Four months later, he told Congress that, once the "rebellion" had been suppressed, there would be no change in "the powers, and duties of the Federal government, relatively to the rights of the States, and the people, under the Constitution." In his message to Congress at the end of 1861, he insisted, in an obvious reference to slavery, that the conflict must "not degenerate into a violent and remorseless revolutionary struggle" and that the Union effort must avoid "radical and extreme measures" that would "reach the loyal as well as the disloyal" people of the South.[8]

From the very beginning, then, Lincoln was committed to the idea that reconstruction of the rebellious states should be self-reconstruction led by loyal southerners—although he preferred to speak of restoration rather than "reconstruction (as the phrase goes)."[9] There was a good deal of trial and error in specifics, but the consistent, central idea was that in each state, a core of loyal white Unionists would establish a new government, hold elections, and send representatives and senators to Congress. That core would become the "tangible nucleus," as he wrote to Major General Nathaniel P. Banks in November 1863, that would then attract a growing number of rebels as they grew disenchanted with the Confederacy and their latent loyalty to the Union resurfaced. As early as the spring of 1861, he was seeking to reestablish a loyal government in Virginia. He attempted to do the same, at one time or another, in North Carolina, Tennessee, Arkansas, Florida, Texas, Alabama, and, especially, Louisiana.[10]

In his Proclamation of Amnesty and Reconstruction in December 1863, Lincoln proposed that 10 percent of the 1860 voting population of a state should be sufficient to form this nucleus. To be sure, this 10 percent must be made up of loyal men, "such men only," as he wrote to Governor Andrew Johnson, "as can be trusted for the Union. Exclude all others, and trust that your government [of Tennessee], so organized, will be recognized here, as being the one of republican form, to be guaranteed to the state, and to be protected against invasion and violence."[11] He hoped that Congress would then seat representatives and senators from those states as long as they had been chosen in a reasonable semblance of an election. That, in fact, was the theme of his final speech, delivered three days before his assassination, when he urged Congress to admit to their seats the representatives and senators chosen by Louisiana's new government.[12] Importantly, these loyal men must be genuine (white) southerners. As he wrote to George F. Shepley, military governor of Union-occupied Louisiana, "To send a parcel of Northern men here, as representatives, elected as would be understood, (and perhaps really so,) at the point of the bayonet, would be disgusting and outrageous."[13]

Of course, by mid-1862, Lincoln had become convinced that the Union could not win the war and restore the rebel states to their "proper practical relation" to the Federal government unless he emancipated Confederate slaves. His Proclamation of Amnesty and Reconstruction, issued eleven months after the final Emancipation Proclamation, explicitly excluded slaves from his promise to all rebels, high officers excepted, of a "full pardon . . . with restoration of all rights of property" as long as they took a simple oath to "abide by and faithfully support all acts of Congress passed during the existing rebellion" and "all proclamations of the President . . . having reference to slaves."[14] Still, emancipation was the means, not the end. The very first sentence of his Preliminary Emancipation Proclamation stated, "hereafter, as heretofore, the war will be prossecuted [sic] for the object of practically restoring the constitutional relation between the United States, and each of the states, and the people thereof, in which states that relation is, or may be suspended, or disturbed."[15]

Once issued, the Emancipation Proclamation posed an entirely new question, both for the country and for Lincoln: what would be the status of the formerly enslaved in the restored Union? Lincoln had always believed that slavery must be eventually ended in the United States and that the best solution to the problem of what to do with emancipated slaves was to colonize them outside the country. If he in fact had truly believed that was a practical option, his fitful attempts to promote it during the war showed him otherwise, and after issuing the final Emancipation Proclamation, he never again publicly raised colonization as an option. As he groped his way toward some workable resolution of the practical issues, Lincoln repeatedly emphasized that he preferred some sort of gradual transition to freedom, a transition that should, like other policies, be decided and managed by loyal white southerners, with no fundamental change to the relationship between the states and the national government.[16]

Lincoln stated his preference for such a gradual change on several occasions. In March 1862, when he proposed that Congress provide "pecuniary aid" to any state that chose to "adopt gradual abolishment of slavery," he added, "in my judgement, gradual, and not sudden emancipation, is better for all." In his amnesty proclamation, he said that he would not object to "any provision which may be adopted by such State government in relation to the free people of such State, which shall recognize and declare their permanent freedom, provide for their education, and which may yet be consistent, as a temporary arrangement, for their present condition as a laboring, landless, and homeless class." He had told Congress that if this "vital matter" of managing a transition from slavery to freedom was left to southerners themselves, it might convince the "already deeply afflicted people" of the rebellious states "to give up the cause of their affliction."[17]

In defending his Emancipation Proclamation, Lincoln told McClernand that white southerners could be "nearly as well off" without slavery if they would "adopt systems of apprenticeship for the colored people, conforming substantially to the most approved plans of gradual emancipation." Later that year, as he prodded General Banks to get underway with the creation of a new loyal government in Louisiana, he hoped that such a government would "make a new Constitution recognizing the emancipation proclamation," but that "it would not be objectionable for her to adopt some practical system by which the two races could gradually live themselves out of their old relation to each other, and both come out the better for the new." Several months later, he repeated the point to

Banks: if a new state government in Louisiana "shall think best to adopt a reasonable temporary arrangement, in relation to the landless and homeless freed people, I do not object" as long as "permanent freedom" was assured.[18]

Lincoln never spelled out just what the final status of the formerly enslaved would be once this temporary arrangement ended. His call for the states to provide for education for the freedpeople; his longstanding insistence that the life, liberty, and pursuit of happiness of the Declaration of Independence applied to African Americans; and his championing of "free labor," in which people "of all colors are neither slaves nor masters" and "men with their families—wives, sons, and daughters—work for themselves . . . , taking the whole product to themselves," all strongly suggest that he would have opposed any permanent limitations on the ability of former slaves to work, earn a living, and accumulate property. But this did not necessarily include a wide range of civil rights for African Americans, much less political rights, which had been denied to Blacks even in his own state of Illinois.[19]

Eventually, after meeting with a delegation of free people of color from New Orleans, he urged Michael Hahn, governor of the newly established loyal government in Louisiana, to confer suffrage on "some of the colored people," such as the "very intelligent" and Black soldiers. This was the "only occasion," Eric Foner has noted, "on which Lincoln intervened in a state's Reconstruction process to promote blacks' civil or political rights rather than the abolition of slavery." But the letter stressed that his advice was "for your private consideration" and "only a suggestion, not to the public, but to you alone." In his last speech the president told his audience that he preferred that "the elective franchise" be conferred in Louisiana "on the very intelligent and on those who serve our cause as soldiers"—the first and only time he publicly endorsed Black suffrage. As Don Fehrenbacher writes, Lincoln had a "traditional view of federal relations" and an "orthodox conception of the United States as a relatively decentralized federation in which the state governments played the most active and versatile part." One important part of that conception, as James Oakes argues, was that "it remained an article of faith for Lincoln that political and civil rights were established by the states," not by the federal government.[20]

Central to Lincoln's views of the "unfinished work" was his conviction that the states of the Confederacy had never left the United States and thus retained their essential rights under the Constitution. To him, the very idea of a constitutionally valid secession was a "sophism," the attempt to carry it out was a "farcical pretense," and the very question of whether the "seceded States, so called, are in the Union or out of it" was "a merely pernicious abstraction." Rather, "combinations" of "discontented individuals" had raised an insurrection in some of the states, a rebellion that must be suppressed. He acknowledged that this insurrection had temporarily disrupted the "proper practical relation" between those states and the central government; now, the "sole object of the government, civil and military, in regard to [the Confederate] States is to again get them into that proper practical relation."[21] He never took seriously the arguments of a few Radical Republicans, especially Charles Sumner and Thaddeus Stevens, that the Confederate states had been reduced to the status of territories, either because they had in effect committed constitutional suicide or were now simply "conquered provinces."[22] Thus, whenever he proposed constitutional amendments to bring about the end of slavery, or when he finally gave his full support to the Thirteenth Amendment, which actually abolished slavery, he always assumed that they would have to be ratified, as required in the Constitution, by three-fourths of the states, which would "necessarily include seven of the Slave states."[23]

This view—that the Confederate states were still states under the Constitution, not territories to be governed from Washington—was well within the Republican Party mainstream. Decisions about the franchise had always been made by the states, not the federal government, and many Republicans agreed with Lincoln that any such measure was for the states to decide. The Wade-Davis Bill, the Radical alternative to Lincoln's "10 Percent" plan (and which he pocket-vetoed), included a more stringent eligibility test for voters than the president desired, but it still assumed that fundamental political decisions in the process of Reconstruction would be made by southern voters themselves. Wade-Davis, like Lincoln's plan, claimed justification based on the Constitution's clause that "the United States shall guarantee to every State in this Union a Republican Form of Government." The states, that is, might be part of an insurrection, but they were still states, and as such their governments must be based in some fundamental sense on the votes of their own citizens. Republicans in Congress were also long unwilling to impose Black voting on the rebel states. Most Radicals would have gone further than Lincoln in extending the suffrage to Black men, but the Wade-Davis Bill itself explicitly limited suffrage to adult white men. Representative James Ashley's Reconstruction proposal, debated over the winter of 1864–65, was eventually abandoned in part because there was no congressional majority in favor of Black suffrage in the South. Similarly, in debates on the Thirteenth Amendment, there was no assumption that emancipation would confer the vote on freed slaves. On the contrary, in both congressional debates over passage of the amendment and debates in state legislatures during the ratification process, it was assumed that, while emancipated Blacks would enjoy "natural" rights, they would not automatically receive "political rights," especially the right to vote.[24]

All of this is relevant to a consideration of what Lincoln was thinking of as the "unfinished work." Obviously, the Confederacy had to be utterly defeated militarily, and those states would have to accept emancipation. Beyond that, we are left with "what if" questions—among them, what would Lincoln have either insisted on, or at least encouraged, as part of finishing the "work"? It seems quite likely that he would have continued to think, at least in the first months after the fighting ended, that southerners themselves must reconstruct their states within the Union. According to witnesses from his last cabinet meeting, held on the very day of his assassination, Lincoln had said: "We can't undertake to run State governments in all these Southern States. Their people must do that—though I reckon at first, they may do it badly."[25]

Superficially, at least, Andrew Johnson followed closely Lincoln's official policies in the summer of 1865. Like his predecessor, Johnson assumed that Reconstruction, beyond the basic measures of laying down arms, declaring loyalty, and accepting emancipation, would be self-reconstruction led by white Unionists like himself. He issued a broad amnesty and gave out pardons freely to those initially excluded from it. Even in the case of suffrage, his overt policy was not unlike Lincoln's. In August 1865, he wrote to William Sharkey, provisional governor of Mississippi, that it would be wise to give the vote to "all persons of color" who were literate or who owned real estate worth $250—in broad terms, much like Lincoln's recommendations with respect to Louisiana. Otherwise, though, Johnson left it to the newly reconstituted southern governments to decide on the political status of the formerly enslaved. He offered an adamant defense of this policy in his message to Congress in December 1865, where he denounced the idea that any state could leave the Union of its own volition and insisted that "the perpetuity of the Constitution brings with it the perpetuity of the States." Thus, extended military government was unacceptable, as such a policy implied that the states in rebellion had "ceased to exist." As one step toward restoring the "constitutional relations of the States," Johnson wrote, he had extended "an invitation" to ratify the new Thirteenth Amendment to the Constitution as a kind of "pledge of perpetual loyalty and peace." That done, the states would be ready "to resume their places in the two branches of the National Legislature, and thereby complete the work of restoration." As for the question of suffrage restriction for the formerly enslaved, voting rights had always been left to "each State to decide for itself."[26]

Johnson's views, for the most part, were shared by the great majority of whites in the rebel states, whose outlook was captured well by Edward Pollard, the Richmond editor, in his 1866 book whose title gave the name to the "Lost Cause." Yes, Pollard admitted, the Confederacy was dead. The idea of secession was forever gone: when Lee surrendered, "the public mind of the South was fully represented in that surrender."[27] Slavery, too, was gone for good. But, Pollard goes on to say, the war "did not decide negro equality; it did not decide negro suffrage; it did not decide State Rights." It did not "decide the right of a people to show dignity in misfortune, and to maintain self-respect in the face of adversity. And these things which the war did not decide, the Southern people will still cling to, still claim, and still assert in them their rights and views"; the states' "sons will grow to manhood, and lessons sink deep that are learned from the lips of widowed mothers." The South must not "lose its moral and intellectual distinctiveness as a people" or "superiourity in civilization." This was, of course, an equation of "the South" with the *white* South. And while white southerners after the war were grappling with how to respond to defeat and what might be necessary to change, the overwhelming majority believed that it was they—white southerners—who should "decide" the questions of "negro equality" and the rights of the states to make their own governments.[28]

White southerners proceeded to reconstruct their state governments, with Johnson quickly reversing his denial of amnesty to wealthy or high-ranking ex-Confederates with an indiscriminate use of the pardoning power. There was no serious effort to revive chattel slavery, but there was also no willingness to recognize African Americans as full members of the body politic—even in the limited form that Johnson had suggested to Mississippi. Rather, most southern whites agreed with Edmund Rhett, a member of a commission to revise South Carolina's laws to reflect the reality of emancipation, who believed that whites must keep the former slave "as near to his former condition as Law can keep him, that he should be kept as near to the condition of slavery as possible, and as far from the condition of the white man as is practicable." Especially, he thought, Blacks must be prevented from owning land so that they would "forever labor upon the capital of the white man."[29] Southern whites were afraid of Black violence and determined to make African Americans work, as of old, on the plantations. Aside from the obvious economic imperative, whites found it, in the words of one Mississippi planter, "dreadfully humiliating & disgusting" to negotiate with African Americans, to put up with their "insults" and "impudent demands."[30] Thus the first Black Codes, from Mississippi and South Carolina, singled out "free negroes" for multiple forms of discrimination. In Mississippi, for example, African Americans were forbidden to rent farms and were required to offer proof by mid-January each year of a "lawful home or employment" in the form of either licenses from whites in towns or written contracts approved by planters. Among the many provisions of South Carolina's law regulating "Domestic Relations of Negroes, Pauperism, and Vagrancy" were those regulating relations between "servants" (all "persons of color who may contract for service or labor") and their "masters." "Servants" could be compelled by fines or corporal punishment to return to "masters" should they leave "without sufficient cause." Black shopkeepers and artisans, but not white ones, would have to pay expensive license fees. As Dan Carter has summarized: "White southerners, moderate and radical, unionist and unrepentant rebel, were willing to accept the legal end of slavery, the supremacy of the federal government, and the temporarily diminished political role for the region. But they were unwilling to accept the legal equality of the freedmen or even (as in the case of many of their more cynically astute leaders) to feign such acceptance."[31]

The Republican majority in Congress, of course, rejected Johnson's arguments, refusing to seat the new representatives and senators and establishing the Joint Committee on Reconstruction. Repelled by reports of violence and by the passage of laws in Mississippi and South Carolina that eviscerated the free-labor ideal, they proceeded to enact the Civil Rights Act of 1866, to reauthorize the Freedmen's Bureau and expand its responsibilities, and to pass the Fourteenth Amendment and send it to the states for ratification. Both the bills and the amendment were squarely in the Republican mainstream—the product of moderates, not Radicals.[32] Johnson's political war against the Republicans, and his urging the southern states to reject the Fourteenth Amendment, then pushed the Republicans still further toward a radical form of Reconstruction. Legislation in 1867 imposed military rule on the southern states and gave African American men the right to vote in new elections there; ultimately, Congress approved the Fifteenth Amendment, which straightforwardly outlawed discrimination in voting based on "race, color, or previous condition of servitude."

No one can really know how Lincoln would have reacted to white southerners' actions after the end of the war. His confidence that there was a large body of southern men—a real majority—who were still, at heart, devoted to the Union was, it turned out, quite naive. If he had indeed allowed the southern states to choose new representatives and senators, what would he have done when so many former leaders of the Confederate army and government showed up in December to take seats in Congress? Lincoln had signed into law the first Freedmen's Bureau bill in 1865, and the bureau fit well within his own notion of a period of temporary guardianship, during which former slaves would get access to education and gradually take full responsibility for their own work lives. In his famous prewar debates with Stephen Douglas, he had insisted that "in the right to eat the bread, without leave of anybody else, which his own hand earns," the African American was *my equal and the equal of Judge Douglas, and the equal of every living man.*" So it is hard to imagine that he would have accepted Black Codes like Mississippi's, obstinately vetoed both the Civil Rights Act and the Freedmen's Bureau bill, or campaigned for the southern states to reject the Fourteenth Amendment.[33]

Historians have thus been correct in arguing that Lincoln's views and actions would have been much closer to the those of the Republican majority in Congress than to those of Andrew Johnson. Lincoln, after all, had been a founder of the party, and he was a shrewd politician whose views "occupied the middle ground of Republican opinion," while Johnson was a former Democrat who agreed with Republicans only on crushing the rebellion, not to mention a provincial politician far out of his depth as president. And, of course, they were very different people. When Johnson wrote to Sharkey about suffrage, his argument was that if Mississippi conferred the vote on a small number of African Americans, then "the radicals, who are wild upon negro franchise, will be completely foiled in their attempts to keep the Southern States from renewing their relations to the Union by not accepting their Senators and Representatives."[34] Lincoln had been genuinely moved by the sacrifices of Black soldiers in the war and genuinely impressed by the members of the free Black delegation from New Orleans who had lobbied him. Johnson's motives were cynical and crassly political, in keeping with his temperament and personality. His racism was visceral, while Lincoln's was conventional; as George Fredrickson has put it, Lincoln's "personal" views on race were "much closer to racism as conformity than to racism as pathology."[35]

Perhaps, given his political astuteness, Lincoln might have cajoled both his party and the southern legislatures to come to a compromise similar to the one that white southerners proposed once they realized—too late for them—that northern public opinion was on the side of Congress, not Johnson. A North Carolina version of an alternative Fourteenth Amendment would have left in place most of the wording of the first clause, guaranteeing citizenship, due process, and equal protection of the laws to all persons born in the United States; the fourth clause, guaranteeing the Union's debt and repudiating debt "incurred in aid of insurrection or rebellion"; and a modified version of the second clause, with reduced representation for states that denied the vote "on account of race or color, or previous condition of servitude." The offer to ratify such an amendment came along with a promise to give the vote in North Carolina to every male citizen who could either read and write or who owned property worth at least $250, with a grandfather clause stating that no previous voters would be disfranchised by the new laws. In effect, this language looked forward to the disfranchisement laws passed in the southern states after 1890—offering ostensibly race-neutral language but effectively barring the vast majority of potential Black voters.[36]

In any case, even the radical measures in Congress in 1867–68 were not actually so radical. With few exceptions, the Republicans rejected permanent confiscation and redistribution of land, as this would have violated the constitutional provision that punishment for treason could not "work corruption of the blood, or forfeiture except during the life of the person attainted." As Michael Les Benedict and Herman Belz have both pointed out, most Republican congressmen shared with Lincoln a fundamental conservatism when it came to the basic constitutional relationship of the federal government to the states.[37] They could justify military occupation of the former Confederate states, not on the grounds that they were territories without rights, but rather that they were states temporarily in the "grasp of war." The constitutional guarantee of a "republican" form of government meant that the restored governments would be legitimate only if they "rest[ed] on the authority and voluntary consent of the people of the states" and that "the formation of state governments must be the result of the voluntary action of the people."[38] They could justify the Freedmen's Bureau as a reasonable way to ease the transition from slavery to free labor, but only for a limited period of time; it would not mean any permanent expansion of national power. Similarly, while Republicans were determined to write into law the promise of civil rights for the freedpeople, what Belz calls the "civil rights settlement of 1866" did not call for a "permanent federal presence in the South in order to guarantee blacks' civil rights." He summarizes, "The price of Union continued to be compromise and the essence of the compromise still consisted in the peculiar idea of federalism which regarded states' rights and local self-government as the truest and most effective expression of American nationality."[39] Republicans did not want to rule all the former Confederate states with the bayonet. As U. S. Grant himself later said, the South probably ought to have been placed under military rule for at least ten years, but "the trouble about military rule in the South was that our people did not like it. It was not in accordance with our institutions."[40]

If we return to Lincoln's view that the essence of Reconstruction was to have the rebel states brought back into their "proper practical relation" with the Union, this suggests that Greg Downs was perhaps right to claim that Reconstruction proper ended well before 1877. Southerners held elections, passed constitutions, chose governors and legislators, and sent new representatives and senators to Congress. Those representatives and senators were duly seated, the last ones being from Georgia in 1871—the moment, according to Downs, that civilian rule in the South finally replaced military rule in all states. Or we might place the date somewhat later; in the 1872 elections, the electoral votes from both Louisiana and Arkansas were not counted, and there were some limited military interventions in Louisiana even after that year. But it is quite plausible to see the point at which the southern states were, finally, released from the "grasp of war" as the moment when Lincoln's work, as he conceived it, was finished: when the rebel states had been brought back into their "practical proper relations" with the Union.[41]

At the same time, the idea that the return of the final southern state to civilian rule might represent the completion of the "unfinished work" in Lincoln's eyes is hardly satisfying from a modern point of view. We are concerned above all with the "proper relations" of African Americans in the South—formerly enslaved or not—with the Union. If we take *that* question as the core of the unfinished work of Reconstruction, we have to shift our attention from Lincoln and the national government to the work of southerners themselves after the war because, after a temporary and rapidly diminishing military occupation, the former Confederate states did in fact reconstruct themselves.

Such a policy of self-reconstruction left open a fundamental question and source of conflict: who counted as southerners? Many consistent Unionists, the anti-Confederates among white southerners, would have barred former Confederates from voting and office holding, leaving government in the hands of white men like themselves. But there were too few true Unionists in the region's white population for this to work; the result would hardly have been a "republican form of government." In 1867 Congress decided that African Americans, too, must be full members of the South's body politic.

These Black southerners had their own ideas about the meaning of Reconstruction. They wanted, first, land; they did not get it. President Johnson reversed the tentative efforts of Major General William Tecumseh Sherman to distribute plantation lands to the freedmen along the Atlantic coast. More importantly, northern opinion (Lincoln included) rejected any serious land reform as unwarranted and unconstitutional. If it is easy to imagine Lincoln embracing the civil, and perhaps political, rights of African Americans, there is no hint in the record that he would have pushed for widespread land confiscation and redistribution. On this, as on the central political question of whether the Confederate states were still states under the Constitution and must be treated as such, Lincoln was, as John Rodrigue writes, "a quintessentially centrist, mainstream Republican who adhered to the principle of absolute property rights grounded in a system of law."[42]

African Americans did, though, get a free-labor regime, with a window of protection from the Freedmen's Bureau. That window opened a period—ranging from months to years—of conflict and negotiation between landowners and laborers, ending eventually in the emergence of sharecropping and other forms of tenancy in the cotton South. By the end of the nineteenth century, it also resulted in widespread Black landownership in parts of the South, a result overlooked by many historians.[43]

Beyond land, southern African Americans, even before the war ended, demanded full civil and political equality. In the summer and fall of 1865, from Richmond to Memphis, Blacks demanded the rights to move freely, to choose one's own employment, and to defend Black women and children from harassment by the police.[44] At an Independence Day celebration in Beaufort, North Carolina, one-time fugitive slave Abraham Galloway delivered the keynote address—"a most incendiary harangue," as it was called by a sullen white diarist, James Rumley—demanding Black suffrage.[45] In Nashville that August, the keynote speaker at a freedmen's convention, Union sergeant H. J. Maxwell, insisted on his right to the jury box and the ballot box as fully as he had a right to the cartridge box.[46] At a convention in Raleigh in September, James Hood, a northern-born Black missionary, declared that the time "to give the colored man his rights" was now, including *"the right to testify in courts of justice," "representation in the jury box,"* and *"the right to carry his ballot to the ballot box."*[47]

That same month, Garland White, who had proudly entered Richmond with his Black regiment in April 1865, wrote to the *Christian Recorder* about his alarm at what was happening in the former Confederate states. He demanded that African Americans get the vote so that he and other Black men would "be enabled to protect our families from all the horrors that prey upon a disfranchised people." He urged "both white and colored, who think as we think," to "arouse the mind of the nation to a sense of its duty. . . . until the bonds of ignorance are riven,—till dark oppression is driven from the earth,—till from every land and every sea, one universal, triumphant song is heard, to hail the long-expected jubilee, when every bond is broken, and every slave at liberty." White and his fellow soldiers had left their "wives and little ones to follow the stars and stripes from the Lakes to the Gulf, with a determination never to turn back until it should be proclaimed from Washington that the flag of the Union waved over a nation of freemen. Yes, freemen upon the battle field; freemen in Texas as in Ohio, and freemen at the ballot box, as at the cartridge box."[48]

Southern white intransigence eventually led Republicans to require Black civic equality, and ultimately Black suffrage in the former Confederate states, as a condition of restoring those states to their "proper relation" to the Union. Still, even the constitutional grant of suffrage to African Americans—or, more accurately, the outlawing of discrimination in voting based on race or previous condition of servitude—was designed to keep the policies of the southern states in the hands of southerners. Congressman James A. Garfield, for example, declared that the amendment "confers upon the African race the care of its own destiny. It places their fortunes in their own hands." There would still be self-reconstruction, but now, in theory, the southern loyal Unionists would include Black as well as white men, and the Black voter would, an Illinois paper said, "take his chances in the battle of life."[49]

With occasional limited intervention from the US Army, Black and white southerners proceeded to reconstruct their states. It can be useful to think of the political developments in the next decades in the South in the same way we have come to think of economic developments during the same period: an extended time of conflict, negotiation, and occasional compromise centering on the questions of civil rights, suffrage, and political power. There was no direct challenge by whites to basic civil rights—the right to own property, marry, sue in court, and so forth—although we know that private actors, with little challenge from local or state governments, limited the ability of African Americans to enjoy those rights fully in practice. The Republicans during the Grant administration did pass the Ku Klux Act and other laws designed to protect Blacks from political violence, but actual enforcement over decades proved to be too great a challenge, especially since US courts interpreted the new amendments in extremely narrow ways; regarding the courts, Michael Vorenberg has written, "'equality before the law' did not mean the same thing as equitable justice."[50]

The conflict over Black suffrage was complex and took decades to be resolved. There is no need here to summarize the story; with African Americans outnumbered, outmaneuvered, and outgunned, they could only prevail as long as the national government remained a strong ally. But the contest did not end by any means—the work of white supremacists was not "finished"—with the overthrow of the last state governments controlled by the Republican Party in the South in 1877. Again to refer to Greg Downs, the election of 1876 and withdrawal of federal troops in 1877 was "just one episode in a longer process of peeling back the federal government's authority." A formidable potential for Black political power remained after that point.[51]

Whites used gerrymandering, poll taxes, registration laws, and violence to stifle Black power, but if those measures suppressed African American voting, they did not destroy it, and the question of Black suffrage was contested for another generation. Decades ago, J. Morgan Kousser demonstrated that the Republican Party remained a serious political force in several southern states throughout the 1870s and 1880s.[52] That voting strength translated into Black political power at the state level in many forms. Tennessee, for example, never experienced the full experience of Reconstruction in the form of a return to military rule in 1867, and before 1877, only one African American sat in its legislature. In the 1880s, though, eleven African Americans served there. In Arkansas, eighty-four Black men served in the legislature after the Civil War, and there were still twelve African American legislators as late as 1891. In Florida, Blacks served in the legislature in every session in the 1880s, with a peak of eleven in 1887. In Texas, two dozen African Americans were elected to its legislature after the state was "redeemed." Fewer were elected in the Deep South after 1877, but African Americans continued to serve in the legislatures of South Carolina, Georgia, Alabama, Mississippi, and Louisiana. In North Carolina, more than fifty African Americans served in the legislature after 1877, with fifteen in 1887 alone. Black voters were key allies of the Populist Party in the "Fusion" movement that took power in North Carolina in 1894.[53]

Virginia, like Tennessee, was never governed by an elected Republican government after the war; conservative Democrats maneuvered with a minority of conservative Republicans to shut the Republicans out of power. And yet, from 1869 to 1890, more than ninety Blacks served in Virginia's legislature, and Black voters were part of the Readjuster coalition that won a majority in the legislature in 1879 and again in 1881. Democrats took back power in 1883, but at the end of that decade, there were still five African Americans in the legislature. In 1888, Virginia for the first time elected an African American, John Mercer Langston, to Congress.[54]

It was this continuing contest for political power—the power, to use Edward Pollard's language, to "decide" which southerners would actually count *as* southerners—that so alarmed whites by the late 1880s. In Virginia, the fear of rising Black power led Camm Patteson, a former Confederate officer, member of the Board of Visitors of the University of Virginia, and later a member of the Virginia House of Delegates and Senate, to predict a race war in which the "negroes," their heads filled by enemies of the South with "meanness and impudence," would rise up "with brutal and savage ferocity." The nation's Anglo-Saxons would then have to respond to crush the revolt.[55] Whites there and in the rest of the South did respond, sometimes with violence. Ultimately they created within the southern states a new regime, the one we call Jim Crow. This included segregation law, to stamp people of African descent with a badge of inferiority; disfranchisement, to ensure full white supremacy in politics; and a tolerance, if not encouragement, of widespread violence, to enforce Jim Crow in everyday life. In the 1890s, these new versions of the Black Codes were accepted, and sometimes even endorsed, by all the branches of the federal government.

It was at the end of that decade that the editor of the *Atlantic Monthly* solicited a series of essays on Reconstruction. Woodrow Wilson wrote one; William Dunning of Columbia University wrote another. Dunning concluded that only now—that is, in 1901—was "the undoing of reconstruction . . . nearing completion." The *Atlantic's* editor agreed. "The final stage of the long reconstruction controversy seems to close," he wrote, "singularly enough, in the reversal of the very process which marked its inception. Reconstruction began with enfranchisement; it is ending with disfranchisement."[56]

By the time these articles appeared, Patteson, who in 1890 had written fearfully of a race war to come, was feeling much better. In 1900 he published a volume called *The Young Bachelor,* to which he added, as an appendix, "Essay on the Destiny of the Negro in America." Even though Virginia's disfranchisement law had not yet been passed, he wrote there that "the great battle for supremacy is practically over." In the future, whites could afford to treat "the negro" with "justice and kindness and conciliation"; in turn the Negro "will become more contented when he finds, as he surely will, that he must always occupy a position subordinate to the white race."[57]

Patteson, of course, was mistaken. Black southerners were not content to be permanently subordinate to whites. In January 1901, in the same *Atlantic Monthly* series on Reconstruction, a young Black professor, W. E. B. Du Bois, contributed an essay on "The Freedman's Bureau." Two years later, that essay, little changed, became chapter 2 in *The Souls of Black Folk,* bearing the new title, "Of the Dawn of Freedom." Du Bois opened and then closed that essay with the famous line, "The problem of the twentieth century is the problem of the color line." That "problem" was not what Lincoln conceived as his "unfinished work." In this case, the unfinished work is ours.[58]

NOTES

1. Examples include David Prior, ed., *Reconstruction in a Globalizing World* (New York: Fordham University Press, 2018); Heather Cox Richardson, *The Death of Reconstruction: Race, Labor, and Politics in the Post–Civil War North, 1865–1900* (Cambridge, MA: Harvard University Press, 2001); Richardson, *West from Appomattox: The Reconstruction of America after the Civil War* (New Haven, CT: Yale University Press, 2007); Steven Hahn, *A Nation without Borders: The United States and Its World in an Age of Civil Wars, 1830–1910* (New York: Penguin, 2017).

2. Abraham Lincoln, *Speeches and Writings, 1859–1865: Speeches, Letters, and Miscellaneous Writings: Presidential Messages and Proclamations* (New York: Library of America, 1989), 536 ("unfinished," "task," "new birth"), 687 ("strive"), 699 ("proper").

3. Ibid., 428.

4. Ibid., 258.

5. William C. Harris, *With Charity for All: Lincoln and the Restoration of the Union* (Lexington: University Press of Kentucky, 1997), 10.

6. Lincoln, *Speeches and Writings, 1859–1865*, 215.

7. Daniel W. Crofts, *Lincoln and the Politics of Slavery: The Other Thirteenth Amendment and the Struggle to Save the Union* (Chapel Hill: University of North Carolina Press, 2012).

8. Lincoln, *Speeches and Writings, 1859–1865*, 260, 292, 293.

9. Lincoln, "Speech on Reconstruction," Apr. 11, 1865, ibid., 697.

10. Ibid., 533. Lincoln's efforts in these states are best analyzed in Harris, *With Charity for All.*

11. Lincoln, *Speeches and Writings, 1859–1865*, 504.

12. Ibid., 697–701.

13. Ibid., 384.

14. Ibid., 555, 556.

15. Ibid., 368.

16. Eric Foner, *The Fiery Trial: Abraham Lincoln and American Slavery* (New York: Norton, 2010).

17. Lincoln, *Speeches and Writings, 1859–1865*, 307, 557, 553.

18. Ibid., 428, 486, 534. Similarly, in June 1863, Lincoln wrote to Maj. Gen. John M. Schofield, regarding emancipation in Missouri, that he believed "*gradual* can be made better than *immediate* for both black and white." Ibid., 465.

19. Ibid., 296.

20. Ibid., 579, 699; Foner, *Fiery Trial*, 283; Don E. Fehrenbacher, *Lincoln in Text and Context: Collected Essays*, (Palo Alto, CA: Stanford University Press, 1987), 118; James Oakes, "Natural Rights, Citizenship Rights, States' Rights, and Black Rights: Another Look at Lincoln and Race," in *Our Lincoln: New Perspectives on Lincoln and His World*, ed. Eric Foner (New York: Norton, 2008), 133.

21. Lincoln, *Speeches and Writings, 1859–1865*, 255 ("sophism," "farcical"), 232 ("combinations"), 250 ("discontented"), 699 ("pernicious," "sole object").

22. Examples of "territorialization" arguments are reprinted in Walter L. Fleming, ed., *Documentary History of Reconstruction: Political, Military, Social, Religious, Educational, and Industrial, 1865 to 1906*, vol. 1 (1906; repr., New York: McGraw-Hill, 1966), 144–45 (Sumner), 147–49 (Stevens).

23. Lincoln, *Speeches and Writings, 1859–1865*, 414.

24. Michael Vorenberg, *Final Freedom: The Civil War, the Abolition of Slavery, and the Thirteenth Amendment* (New York: Cambridge University Press, 2001), 64–69, 188–91, 230–33; John C. Rodrigue, *Lincoln and Reconstruction* (Carbondale: Southern Illinois University Press, 2013), 44–74.

25. William C. Harris, *Lincoln's Last Months* (Cambridge, MA: Harvard University Press, 2004), 220–22; David Herbert Donald, *Lincoln* (New York: Simon & Schuster, 1995), 591; Lawanda Cox, *Lincoln and Black Freedom: A Study in Presidential Leadership* (Columbia: University of South Carolina Press, 1981), 142–84; Rodrigue, *Lincoln and Reconstruction*, 143–48; Louis P. Masur, *Lincoln's*

Last Speech: Wartime Reconstruction and the Crisis of Reunion (New York: Oxford University Press, 2015), 175–88.

26. Andrew Johnson, "Message to Congress," Dec. 4, 1865, in *A Just and Lasting Peace: A Documentary History of Reconstruction,* ed. John David Smith (New York: Signet Classics, 2013), 90–106 (quotations, 94, 95, 96, 97, 98).

27. Edward A. Pollard, *The Lost Cause: A New Southern History of the War of the Confederates* (New York: E. B. Treat, 1866), 742.

28. Ibid., 751, 752; Dan T. Carter, *When the War Was Over: The Failure of Self-Reconstruction in the South, 1865–1867* (Baton Rouge: Louisiana State University Press, 1985).

29. John David Smith, *An Old Creed for the New South: Proslavery Ideology and Historiography, 1865–1918* (Westport, CT: Greenwood, 1985), 29; Carter, *When the War Was Over,* 147–75.

30. Carter, *When the War Was Over,* 210.

31. Smith, *Just and Lasting Peace,* 153–57; Fleming, *Documentary History,* 294–310; Carter, *When the War Was Over,* 231.

32. Eric Foner, *Reconstruction: America's Unfinished Revolution, 1863–1877* (New York: Harper & Row, 1988), 239–51.

33. Abraham Lincoln, *Speeches and Writings, 1832–1858: Speeches, Letters, and Miscellaneous Writings: The Lincoln-Douglas Debates* (New York: Library of America, 1989), 512.

34. Foner, *Fiery Trial,* 123; Fleming, *Documentary History,* 177.

35. George M. Fredrickson, *Big Enough to Be Inconsistent: Abraham Lincoln Confronts Slavery and Race* (Cambridge, MA: Harvard University Press, 2008), 84.

36. Fleming, *Documentary History,* 238–40.

37. Michael Les Benedict, "Preserving the Constitution: The Conservative Basis of Radical Reconstruction," *Journal of American History* 61 (June 1974): 65–90; Herman Belz, *Emancipation and Equal Rights: Politics and Constitutionalism in the Civil War Era* (New York: Norton, 1978).

38. Belz, *Emancipation and Equal Rights,* 96, 103. See also Belz, *A New Birth of Freedom: The Republican Party and Freedmen's Rights, 1861–1866* (New York: Fordham University Press, 2000).

39. Belz, *Emancipation and Equal Rights,* 128, 126, 140.

40. Joan Waugh, *U. S. Grant: American Hero, American Myth* (Chapel Hill: University of North Carolina Press, 2009), 151.

41. Gregory P. Downs, *After Appomattox: Military Occupation and the Ends of War* (Cambridge, MA: Harvard University Press, 2015), 211–36.

42. Rodrigue, *Lincoln and Reconstruction,* 5.

43. For an account of the ways in which African Americans in the South did acquire land in the generation after the Civil War, see the essay by Adrienne Petty and Mark Schulz in this volume.

44. Steven Hahn, Steven F. Miller, Susan O'Donovan, John C. Rodrigue, and Leslie C. Rowland, eds., *Freedom: A Documentary History of Emancipation, 1861–1867,* ser. 3, vol. 1, *Land and Labor, 1865* (Chapel Hill: University of North Carolina Press, 2008), 211–12 (Richmond), 275 (Memphis).

45. Judkin Browning, ed., *The Southern Mind under Union Rule: The Diary of James Rumley, Beaufort, North Carolina, 1862–1865* (Gainesville: University Press of Florida, 2009), 181; David S.

Cecelski, *The Fire of Freedom: Abraham Galloway and the Slaves' Civil War* (Chapel Hill: University of North Carolina Press, 2012), 178–80.

46. Philip Foner and George E. Walker, eds., *Proceedings of the Black State Conventions, 1865–1900*, vol. 1 (Philadelphia: Temple University Press, 1979), 112–29.

47. Leon Litwack, *Been in the Storm So Long: The Aftermath of Slavery* (New York: Knopf, 1979), 502–7 (quotation, 505); Cecelski, *Fire of Freedom*, 181–88. For other examples of early claims to political rights, see Joseph P. Reidy, *From Slavery to Agrarian Capitalism in the Cotton Plantation South: Central Georgia, 1800–1880* (Chapel Hill: University of North Carolina Press, 1992), 178–79; Kathleen Clark, *Defining Moments: African American Commemoration and Political Culture in the South, 1863–1913* (Chapel Hill: University of North Carolina Press, 2005), 26–28; Mitchell Snay, *Fenians, Freedmen, and Southern Whites: Race and Nationality in the Era of Reconstruction* (Baton Rouge: Louisiana State University Press, 2011), 111; and Foner, *Reconstruction*, 110–19.

48. *Christian Recorder*, Oct. 21, 1865.

49. Foner, *Reconstruction*, 444–49 (quotations, 449).

50. Michael Vorenberg, "Imagining a Different Reconstruction Constitution," *Civil War History* 51, no. 4 (2005): 416–26 (quotation, 423).

51. Downs, *After Appomattox*, 239.

52. J. Morgan Kousser, *The Shaping of Southern Politics: Suffrage Restriction and the Establishment of the One-Party South* (New Haven, CT: Yale University Press, 1974).

53. These numbers for Black office holders are summarized in Peter Wallenstein, "Race, Representation, and Reconstruction: The Origins and Persistence of Black Electoral Power, 1865–1900," paper in author's possession. On the Fusion movement in North Carolina, see Deborah Beckel, *Radical Reform: Interracial Politics in Post-Emancipation North Carolina* (Charlottesville: University of Virginia Press, 2011), 173–88.

54. Jane Dailey, *Before Jim Crow: The Politics of Race in Postemancipation Virginia* (Chapel Hill: University of North Carolina Press, 2000); Luis-Alejandro Dinnella-Borrego, *The Risen Phoenix: Black Politics in the Post–Civil War South* (Charlottesville: University of Virginia Press, 2016), 164–72.

55. Charles E. Wynes, *Race Relations in Virginia, 1870–1902* (Charlottesville: University Press of Virginia, 1961), 101.

56. William A. Dunning, "The Undoing of Reconstruction," *Atlantic Monthly*, Oct. 1901, 449; "Reconstruction and Disfranchisement," *Atlantic Monthly*, Oct. 1901, 434.

57. Wynes, *Race Relations in Virginia*, 104–5.

58. W. E. B. Du Bois, "The Freedmen's Bureau," *Atlantic Monthly*, Mar. 1901, 354–65; Du Bois, "Of the Dawn of Freedom," in *The Souls of Black Folk*, in W. E. B. Du Bois, *Writings* (New York: Library of America, 1986), 372–91.

The Problem of Enforcement

The Republican Struggle to Protect Voting Rights in Peacetime

GREGORY P. DOWNS

Until the end of the nineteenth century, Republicans struggled not simply to uphold Abraham Lincoln's legacy but also to develop new tools to protect and extend the party's enduring, if sometimes tentative, commitment to freedpeople's rights. Thus, the challenge of the postbellum period was less in sustaining Lincoln's vision than in developing a government capable of delivering upon promises made by the party. Nowhere was this struggle clearer than in the area of voting rights, an issue that has shaped a good deal of Vernon Burton's scholarly and public career. The problem appeared simple but was in fact profound: How could a democracy enforce voting rights for minority groups? Burton's written work on the Civil War era and Reconstruction traced, in part, the way that freedmen and freedwomen demanded the right to vote as a protective measure for the other rights they forced onto the national agenda through military service, political organizing, and activism. Voting was doubly important to many freedpeople, both as a recognition of Black men's standing and as a guard against the retraction of their other rights. There was no clearer way to protect the rights embedded in the Thirteenth and Fourteenth Amendments than to protect the votes of the freedmen who would defend those rights. As Frederick Douglass wrote in the aftermath of the amendments' ratifications: "The revolution wrought in our condition by the Fifteenth Amendment of the Constitution of the United States, is almost startling, even to me. I view it with something like amazement. . . . Henceforth, we live in a new world."[1]

Yet within a decade, Douglass would lament the seeming passing of that "new world." By 1880, he argued: "Our reconstruction measures were radically defective. . . . In the hurry and confusion of the hour, and the eager drive to have the Union restored, there was more care for the sublime superstructure of the republic than for the solid foundation upon which it could alone be upheld." In an even-gloomier reflection in that same speech, Douglass raised the possibility that no structure might have saved freedpeople's rights. "Great and valuable concessions have in different ages been made to the liberties of mankind," he said. "They have, however, come not at the command of reason and persuasion, but by the sharp and terrible edge of the sword."[2]

Douglass in 1870 had good reason for optimism and good reason to hope for change in the superstructure of the republic. After Congress directed the army to oversee the registration of adult Black men in ten ex-Confederate states in 1867, African Americans organized a mass movement to the polls, registering roughly 80 percent of all eligible Black men by the fall of 1867. Between 1868 and 1870, these voters made themselves felt in state constitutional conventions, ratification elections, legislative elections, and congressional races, transforming both the leadership of the South and the laws that shaped education, welfare, tenants' rights, civil rights, divorce, and other fundamental aspects of US life. And that in turn prompted a massive, violent backlash by white southerners desperate to reassert their control of the region's offices and its laws.

Yet by 1880, Douglass had good reason to doubt his optimism and the republic's superstructure and foundations. Over the 1870s he witnessed the start of a process that Vernon Burton has spent much of his public life working to combat: the destruction of voting rights. In that decade, Democrats captured every former Confederate state and went to work preventing Black men from voting by both legal and illegal means, not only relying on fraud and violence but also turning to new forms of suppression by appointing county governments, requiring re-registration, and in other ways stripping from them a right to vote that still seemed to exist on paper. Under these rules, Republican voting in South Carolina fell from 58,071 in 1880 to 13,740 in 1888. In Richmond, Virginia, 2,100 Black men were disfranchised for felony convictions; every ex-Confederate state except Texas passed laws expanding disfranchisement for felons.[3]

Beginning in 1890, ex-Confederate states passed a new wave of state constitutions and constitutional amendments that drove down Black voting through poll taxes, residency requirements, secret-ballot laws, and literacy tests. The consequences of this second wave of disfranchisement are well known. In Mississippi, the standard bearer, African American registration fell from roughly

190,000 to 9,000. In Louisiana, Black registration fell from roughly 130,000 to 1,342. From the beginning, African Americans protested disfranchisement and launched political and legal campaigns to save the vote. After World War II, these started to bear fruit in limited ways in the 1950s and eventually led to 1965's Voting Rights Act (VRA). Burton has devoted a good deal of his talent and energy in his professional life to trying to make the VRA meaningful and turn it against the kinds of voting infringements imposed during the era of Jim Crow segregation. Sadly, however, those fights, once seemed won, returned at ever-increasing pace since 2010. Republicans' decades-long effort to peel back VRA protections was empowered by the 2013 Supreme Court decision in *Shelby County v. Holder*, which ruled Section 4 of the VRA unconstitutional. Since then, at least twenty-five states (some already not covered by the VRA) passed new restrictions on voting rights, including voter-ID laws and limitations on ballot access.[4]

Like the zombies so popular in film and television, voting restrictions, once presumed dead, walk again among us, raising grave moral and political crises and also a new set of scholarly and intellectual questions. While historians have painstakingly captured the push for voting rights and the southern states' efforts at disfranchisement, the question of enforcement—the barrier between federal right and state or local action—has largely stayed in the background. In part, this is due to historians' reluctance to engage with policy or legal histories of bureaucracy. But this scholarly inattention to enforcement also stems from the seeming gap between Reconstruction and the civil rights movement. As the VRA succeeded dramatically in the late 1960s and 1970s, scholars looked to Reconstruction to explore what it lacked—equivalent mechanisms for protecting the vote, especially the expansion of the Department of Justice and the creation of new legal categories that prompted judicial review. Almost ineluctably, these works contrasted a seemingly successful twentieth-century effort to a nineteenth-century failure and diagnosed the problem as a lack of will or lack of foresight. As long as the twentieth-century effort's victories appeared secure, this assumption made sense.[5]

Now, however, in the face of successful attacks on voting rights since the *Shelby County* case, perhaps the time is ripe for a reexamination of the overthrow of voting rights in the nineteenth century, one chastened by our current moment. We are perhaps better placed than we were a decade ago to see how even well-designed and well-intentioned legislation can be made less useful by dogged local disfranchising efforts and courts' determination to look away. Writing now, as voting rights seem imperiled again despite carefully crafted laws and heroic legal and political organizing, we may be better prepared to see the postwar Republicans in tragic light, as people who may have failed, but not for lack of trying. Our own struggles to protect voting rights in the face of determined political opposition may help us ascertain which parts of the earlier failure were attributable to Republicans' limitations, which parts to the triumph of the opposition, and then reassess whether Reconstruction was unfinished or overthrown. This chastened glance may in turn help prompt a reexamination of the surprisingly bold nineteenth-century efforts to build governmental structures to protect voting rights, particularly the tentative moves to fit a government of commissioners and marshals to the project of protecting civil rights.

This essay is by no means an effort to produce a definitive history of Republican enforcement efforts after the Civil War, but instead it seeks to sketch out what such an investigation might look like, what questions it might answer, and why it might be important now, not only to fill out our understanding of the historical past but also, perhaps, to prepare historians to confront the dangerous present. What would it mean to see the commissioner and marshal system as a meaningful effort at state construction; to trace its victories, tentative as they were; to understand the defanging of that system in light of the efforts now to defang the civil rights government constructed in the 1960s and 1970s? We can also reinvigorate the national study of the crucial period between the passage of the Fifteenth Amendment in 1870 and the beginning of the second wave of disfranchisement campaigns in 1890, decades that sit uncomfortably between the gains of early Reconstruction and the overthrow of Reconstruction by Jim Crow but provide what may be a useful—if gloomy—mirror to recognize the dangers of our current moment.

Postbellum Republicans established a commissioner and marshal system, supported by military police, to protect voting rights. It was a system rooted in antebellum slaveowners' efforts to enforce fugitive-slave laws but now went well beyond those powers. It emerged shortly after the Confederate surrenders, even before voting rights, in the Civil Rights Act of 1866. This act protected the rights of citizens to make contracts, testify in court, and enjoy equal treatment under the law. But Republicans well understood that ex-Confederates (and for that matter many white northerners) would not naturally bow to the will of the law. Instead, Republicans made violations of the act a federal misdemeanor and protected freedpeople from oppressive state courts by granting a right to remove cases to presumably more sympathetic federal courts.

To enforce these new civil rights, Republicans expanded the powers of an existing but ill-defined system of commissioners and marshals, attaching those enforcement powers directly to the US military. The act empowered federal commissioners to execute the law with the assistance of federal marshals and deputy marshals and, in the event of resistance, to call out either a posse comitatus or active-duty army and navy personnel. Under the fee system common in federal law at the time, commissioners, marshals, clerks, and their appointed deputies would be paid by the case. Instead of a contemporary bureaucracy with civil-service appointees, the enforcement mechanism depended upon a profit motive. The more cases a commissioner brought, the more money he made. Relying upon fee-based officers was part of the repertoire of nineteenth-century governance, as both Nicholas Parrillo and Richard White have emphasized, that distinguishes it from twentieth-century models. Fearful of a salaried bureaucracy, many nineteenth-century state builders thought that attaching incentives to actions would encourage enforcement of the laws. President Andrew Johnson denounced this use of the fee system in his veto message precisely because it threatened to be too effective. The act created a class of "numerous" commissioners and appointees "whose interest it will be to foment discord between the two races; for as the breach widens, their employment will continue; and when it is closed, their occupation will terminate." Under "the influence of such temptations, bad men might convert any law, however beneficent into an instrument of persecution and fraud."[6]

Even more striking was the Civil Rights Act's explicit reliance upon the military for its enforcement. Section 5 authorized commissioners and their deputies to call upon "such portion of the land or naval forces, or of the militia, as may be necessary" to serve warrants or make arrests. Again, Johnson complained in his veto message that this "extraordinary power" in the hands of unspecified numbers of deputy commissioners "might be made a terrible engine of wrong, oppression, and fraud." And Section 9 vested a surprising and new power in the chief executive's hands. The president could "employ such parts of the land or naval forces of the United States, or of the militia, as shall be necessary to prevent the violation and enforce the due execution of this act." Again, Johnson denounced this creation of a military-enforcement authority "that is to be always at hand, and whose only business is to be the enforcement of this measure over the vast region where it [is] intended to operate."[7]

Where did Republicans find their models for federal law enforcement? They turned to the greatest political power in the antebellum United States: slaveowners. As scholars have frequently acknowledged, the 1866 Civil Rights Act was modeled on the notorious 1850 Fugitive Slave Act. This measure empowered federal commissioners to enforce a national fugitive-slave law for the first time, rewarded them financially for hearing cases through a fee system, commanded "all good citizens" to aid them "in the prompt and efficient execution" of the law, and authorized commissioners to call out bystanders into a posse comitatus for enforcement. Southern slaveowners in 1850 were quite aware of the difficulty of enforcing fugitive-slave laws in the North, as they had contested decades of resistance by northern states and citizens to carrying out the fugitive slave clause of the Constitution and the 1793 Fugitive Slave Act. Thus, southern planters hoped to fashion a stronger national government to enforce unpopular federal laws in localities that resisted them. This is the power that northern Republicans hoped to harness in their 1866 Civil Rights Act and then to extend in their voting rights acts. These commissioners, empowered to protect slavery, were turned in the 1866 Civil Rights Act to the task of tearing down slavery and defending civil rights.[8]

On the use of the military as an enforcement arm, the 1866 Civil Rights Act went further than the Fugitive Slave Act. The latter did not directly authorize the use of the military to execute its provisions, but in 1854 Attorney General Caleb Cushing issued a memorandum arguing that the military constituted part of the available posse comitatus and thus could be called out to support federal commissioners executing the law. These powers were easier to invoke than to use: US officials learned the dangers of utilizing military force in the famed Anthony Burns case, where army troops lined the streets of Boston to return the fugitive Burns to enslavement in Virginia. Northern opinion revolted against this costly and unpopular use of federal force. Still, to some degree, the Fugitive Slave Act and the Cushing memorandum created a new potential for federal enforcement in the states, using the military as not simply a peacekeeping force in emergencies but as an active enforcement arm of the national government. In turn the utilization of the army in Kansas Territory in the late 1850s—while on different legal grounds because of Kansas's territorial status—reinforced the potential of soldiers for federal law enforcement.[9]

The final leg of the commissioner system established in the Civil Rights Act was, as Michael Vorenberg has argued, an entirely new military role in acting preemptively to prevent potential violations. The 1866 law did not only incorporate Cushing's memorandum into the act itself, but Section 9 also granted an entirely new, and in Vorenberg's view revolutionary, power of preemption. The president possessed the authority to deploy the army or navy to "prevent the violation" of the Civil Rights Act. Where, precisely, this power ended was unclear. Until this point, the president's authority to use the army in peacetime was severely limited. The Constitution empowered the chief executive to respond to calls from a state's legislature or governor, if the legislature was out of session, to protect them from "domestic Violence." Early national laws applied this power both to the militia and the newly established US Army, but states had to ask the president for help. The Cushing memo and Civil Rights Act's expansion of this power to request to include federal judges raised the possibility of a president intervening against the will of the state government, as in the Burns case. The Section 9 move to preemption threatened to eliminate the role of the state government in shaping this power entirely.[10]

The Civil Rights Act established the framework for the Republicans' commissioner and marshal system with a military police in reserve, which would be the basis for enforcing voting rights over the rest of the nineteenth century. But to establish those voting rights, Republicans had to reach back one more time to the war powers they had utilized throughout the conflict with the Confederacy. They could rely upon such powers in 1867 because of decisions they had made two years earlier, before African American voting seemed a possible outcome. After the Confederates surrendered in a series of ceremonies from April to June 1865, the United States could have declared the war at an end, as in fact General Robert E. Lee asked of Lieutenant General Ulysses S. Grant at Appomattox. But Grant blithely rejected the request, offering only surrender instead of peace. Thus, he indicated that the war would continue even as Confederates surrendered. In turn President Johnson and the cabinet rejected the idea of peace put forward in the agreement that Major General William T. Sherman offered General Joseph

Johnston near Durham, North Carolina, later in April. Instead, Johnson and the cabinet reaffirmed the endurance of the war even as they accepted the surrender of Confederate armies.[11]

Why did they make such a distinction between war and peace, between a surrender occurring within a war and a peace treaty that ended it? In part this turned on the United States' view that the Confederacy was not a legitimate nation-state and thus could not be the counterparty of a treaty. Soldiers were rebels, Jefferson Davis was a pretend president of a "so-called" country, and the Confederate Congress was a charade. While the United States treated the Confederates at times as belligerents, as for example when exchanging prisoners of war, it repeatedly asserted in international venues that the Confederacy was not actually a country, therefore Great Britain and France should not make treaties or alliances with it, or even recognize its existence. The surrender of rebels thus could not end a war in the way a treaty of peace did. Only the United States could determine when the war against an internal rebellion ended.

That was the rationale, but what was the purpose? Distinguishing between war and peace was no semantic distinction but a crucial way of asserting enduring federal power over states and localities. In peacetime the United States respected, for the most part, the sovereignty of local governments. But neither the Johnson administration nor Congress had any intention of treating any level of the Confederate governments as legitimate. If peacetime prevailed, the United States would have no obvious mechanism to squash ongoing rebellions or to end slavery in restored states, even if federal courts might recognize the freedom of individual people who ran away. To end slavery and to construct even a semblance of civil rights, the United States would need to be able to intervene in states and localities, overriding the governments there. That was only possible in wartime. Additionally, army commanders remained concerned that rebels would rise again and that local courts would imprison US soldiers for carrying out orders to suppress them. The solution to all these problems was to keep the ex-Confederate states in a wartime condition. Everyone from Johnson to Secretary of War Edwin Stanton shared this understanding. Those who dissented, like Major General Sherman, disagreed with the policy precisely because they understood what it entailed.[12]

The extension of wartime made the army the instrument of federal policy in the former Confederate states, often in its own capacity, but at times through its sidecar, the Bureau of Refugees, Freedmen, and Abandoned Lands. Together, army officers and bureau agents did things that would never have been permissible in peacetime: they overrode local laws on Black testimony, slavery, or differential punishment; arrested and deposed judges and sheriffs who refused to recognize the new conditions of things; and pursued and arrested white southerners who attacked freedpeople and white Republicans. The army thus became a police force and, at times, a separate judiciary based upon its war powers. Freedpeople in turn came to the army to press complaints about their treatment. In the process they educated officers—many of whom shared common northern white racial biases—about the actual conditions on the ground and together developed an idea of practical freedom, of what would need to be protected to make freedom meaningful. This would become the basis of the Civil Rights Act of 1866.

In the plantation South, federal enforcement depended upon proximity. An army edict issued from a hundred miles away—or even twenty miles—meant next to nothing, as numerous freedpeople and military officers told congressmen. Since most enslaved people had lived on plantations, authorities had to go toward them. Thus, the army launched one of the most spatially ambitious occupations of the mid-nineteenth-century Atlantic World, creating hundreds of outposts in small crossroads towns and county seats so that they could reach and be reached by freedpeople. Scott Nesbit and I called this proximity the creation of "Zones of Access," where freedpeople could reach the nearest army unit, and "Zones of Occupation," where the army could respond upon hearing about complaints. Military units could move farther and faster because they could more easily call upon horses and railroads for transportation. In general, and with allowances for variation over the vast South, freedpeople in Zones of Access had a chance to counterbalance planter power. Those outside of a Zone of Access but within a Zone of Occupation—people who could not reach the army but lived in an area where the army might reach them—had some chance of help if others could get word. And those beyond the Zone of Occupation were in a region left almost ungoverned, to be contested by the forces of freedpeople and of planters until enough violence erupted to call the attention of the federal government. In some regions, as along the South Carolina and Georgia coasts, freedpeople dominated, but in much of the South, whites' numerical and military strength meant that they ruled these ungoverned zones. What a right meant, therefore, depended upon where one lived. Enforcement thus depended on shrinking those ungoverned zones.[13]

These wartime struggles taught Republicans that enforcement depended upon authority, might, and proximity. Absent those things, they admitted, laws were silent in a place as wild and unruly as the postemancipation South and facing a people as unreconstructed as the planters. Planters' recalcitrance drew upon common agrarian lords' resistance to change, fear of the new labor market, and encouragement from President Johnson, who tried unsuccessfully to return power to white southerners in 1865–66 once the Thirteenth Amendment was ratified. Congressional Republicans, however, denied the legitimacy of the new state governments Johnson tried to create and asserted the continuity of wartime.

Congressional Republicans moved toward the vote as a way to exit wartime. Between 1867 and 1870, through compromise, legislative maneuvering, and chance, congressional Republicans devised a system to transition from wartime to peacetime while sustaining the potential for enforcement. The 1867 Military Reconstruction Acts declared ten of the ex-Confederate states (all but Tennessee) still to be under military rule, dispatched the army to oversee registration, and ordered officers to register all adult-male Black residents regardless of past status. These new voters would elect delegates to state constitutional conventions that would write new state constitutions to be voted on by these reconstructed electorates, then ratify the Fourteenth Amendment. Once done, the newly reconstructed states could apply to Congress for reinstatement. Finally, they would be returned to peace and to whatever balance of powers the new amendments and the Civil Rights Act had created. In the interim, however, the ten ex-rebel states were held under military rule, and the army continued to make arrests, depose local officials, sweep away local laws, and regulate voting in ways unimaginable in the northern or western states. Even as freedpeople registered and voted, enforcement remained under the wartime model, and the army deployed its forces as Election Day neared to keep peace and to protect freedpeople's voting rights. Many states concluded their constitutional process in 1868 and helped ratify the Fourteenth Amendment. Those that did not remained under military rule until 1871 and in turn were required, under military duress, to ratify the Fifteenth Amendment, which made it unconstitutional to deny the right to vote based on race, color, or previous condition of servitude. This was the beginning of federal voting rights.

When Republicans approached voting rights between 1867 and 1870, they possessed antebellum slaveowners' models of governance and their own wartime experimentations to guide them. They also had the chastening experience of fighting ongoing white southern resistance. Thus, even as Republicans passed the Fifteenth Amendment in 1869 and sent it to the states, they expressed grave doubts over the federal government's ability to enforce voting rights by the amendment alone. It would require something more, either the intervention of the military or the creation of a peacetime bureaucracy to support it.

In a series of civil rights acts between 1870 and 1875, Republicans tried to build a system for voting rights upon the mechanisms they had developed for civil rights, which in turn adapted the mechanism used to protect the rights of slaveowners in 1850. The Civil Rights Act of 1870, or the First Enforcement Act, passed in May, addressed a potential gap in the Fifteenth Amendment's language. While the amendment stated that the vote could not be denied upon grounds of race, color, or previous condition of servitude, it did not specifically prevent states from discriminating in voter-registration systems. The First Enforcement Act penalized state and local officials who refused to carry out the Fifteenth Amendment, made it a federal misdemeanor to impose a racial "prerequisite or qualification" to vote, and required judges to count the votes of people who tried to register but were denied by biased clerks or agents.[14]

The act then moved to the always thorny question of intimidation. What constituted access to the vote in the face of public hostility? In nineteenth-century elections, voters often faced menacing crowds, and congressional inquiries into contested elections often stated that men had to show normal physical courage in order to prove that they had tried and been denied the vote. Fear alone could not demonstrate fraud. At the same time, the campaigns of intimidation launched in the South in 1867–68 far surpassed any previous such electoral activity, as the Ku Klux Klan swept through Tennessee, Georgia, and the Carolinas and other vigilante associations claimed power in the Mississippi Valley. Republicans split over the proper response to this violence, and the series of enforcement acts reflects these divisions. The First Enforcement Act made it a misdemeanor to "hinder, delay, prevent, or obstruct" men from registering or voting by "force, bribery, threats, intimidation, or other unlawful means." Such actions could include firing people, taking away their homes, refusing to renew contracts or leases, or threatening violence. The law also made it a felony to conspire together or go in disguise to intimidate voters, a direct shot at the Ku Klux Klan.

The act continued the commissioner and marshal structure for enforcement and increased the number of commissioners "to afford reasonable protection to all persons in their constitutional right to vote without distinction of race, color, or previous condition of servitude." Previously, commissioners or those acting with such authority were appointed by federal judges, but now commissioners could appoint deputies with the same powers to execute the laws and call out "the bystanders or posse comitatus of the proper county, or such portion of the land or naval force of the United States or of the militia, as may be necessary." It also empowered the president to call out the military to enforce the act. To combat fraud (a partisan concern of Republicans in New York, who suspected that Irish immigrants were voting repeatedly and under fake names), the act also made it a crime to cast fraudulent ballots or register falsely or participate in such fraud in a congressional election. Finally, it authorized federal judges to hear cases from losing candidates who claimed their defeat was a product of voter fraud or intimidation.[15] In the Naturalization Act of 1870—best remembered for extending naturalization to Africans and their descendants but not to Asians and other racial groups—Republicans also expanded the electoral system by empowering federal judges to appoint election supervisors and deputy marshals to prevent fraud in large cities.[16]

As the Klan marched through North Carolina in 1870 and claimed control over Georgia, congressional Republicans tried to strengthen the law. As the Senate Select Committee to Investigate the Alleged Outrages in the Southern States heard testimony and received startling War Department reports about the waves of violence in the South, Republicans drafted competing versions of enforcement acts that went beyond the 1870 law. The Second Enforcement Act, passed in February 1871, explicitly expanded the first act's protections for registration for congressional elections (rather than merely the prerequisites of voting) and made it a federal misdemeanor to advise others to violate federal election law. After a great deal of debate about nationalizing voter registration for congressional races, congressional Republicans devised a cynical compromise in which they empowered federal judges to appoint Election Day supervisors in cities of greater than 20,000 residents, a direct challenge to the Democratic dominance in New York City but having little relevance in the South. These supervisors had authority to oversee the vote count, issue their own returns, and appoint special deputy marshals to help protect precincts and arrest violators.[17]

As the Klan violence peaked in the winter of 1870–71, Republicans passed the Third Enforcement Act, which expanded these powers again. This law made it a high crime to conspire to "overthrow, or put down, or to destroy by force the government of the United States"; hinder the execution of federal law; prevent someone from holding office; or go in disguise to intimidate, frighten an officeholder into fleeing, or interfere with voting in a federal election. It also criminalized intimidation and conspiracies to prevent the execution of the law and made it the "duty" of the president to use the land and naval forces to suppress such violence and arrest offenders. If the violence grew so extensive that it thwarted the efforts of federal and state officials, or if local officials worked in complicity with the conspirators, the president was authorized to issue a warning proclamation and then suspend the privilege of the writ of habeas corpus, but it set this power to expire at the end of the next congressional session in hopes of defusing controversy. The act also made it a crime for officials not to intervene to protect rights against conspirators.[18] Finally, in 1872, Republicans tried repeatedly to pass another enforcement act but were blocked by defectors in the House of Representatives. After a great deal of maneuvering, Senate Republicans attached this final enforcement act to the annual appropriations act. They hoped to extend the election-supervisor system over the entire country, but House members blocked this and limited the act in key ways. The final version required a larger number of petitioning citizens before appointing supervisors, then only paid supervisors and empowered them to make arrests in large cities.[19]

The Enforcement Acts provided mechanisms for the United States to respond aggressively to the Ku Klux Klan in South Carolina, initiating hundreds of arrests, suspending habeas corpus in several parishes, and finally breaking up the Klan there while putting the organization on the run elsewhere. But this form of military-style enforcement—almost a continuation of the Civil War, or at least Military Reconstruction methods, in peacetime—was difficult to sustain. Republicans attempted in 1875 to extend the habeas corpus–suspension provisions over a number of states but lost in last-minute parliamentary maneuvering. Democrats in turn used their victories in 1874 and later elections to strip away the army's power to intervene in elections in a series of bitterly contested appropriations and other bills between 1876 and 1880. These fights led to soldiers and officers going without pay for a year, a prolonged government shutdown, and the confusing language of the so-called Posse Comitatus Act of 1878. A rider to that year's army appropriations act, it prohibited the use of troops as a posse comitatus "except in such cases and under such circumstances" as were "expressly authorized by the Constitution or by act of Congress," making any violation a crime.[20] The precise limitations the posse comitatus rider placed on the military were unclear at the time and remain contested today. But Democrats did not see this act as the culmination of their work, only a next step. In 1879 and 1880, in fact, they warred even more brutally with Republicans over their efforts to limit the army.

By the end of the 1870s, the period of direct military policing was over, but the commissioner and marshal system endured, though without the support of military police. By treating this form of governance seriously and tying it to the enduring local power of freedpeople in southern states, we can capture Republicans' enforcement efforts, the nature of late-nineteenth-century federal governance, and the enduring political power of freedpeople. Even as southern Democrats launched a first wave of registration laws and felony disfranchisement acts, African Americans participated politically in every ex-Confederate state, often at reasonably robust levels. At times when white political parties frayed and factionalized, African Americans could continue to wield significant power, as in Readjuster Virginia and, in the 1890s, in Republican-Populist fusions in North Carolina. And in Black-majority districts, African Americans continued to elect Black congressmen and numerous other local officials. In this sense the 1880s represented a continuation of Black political participation and power.[21]

The least-studied aspect of voting rights remains the mechanisms that were in force in the 1880s, ones that helped protect rights in that fragile decade but proved insufficient to the concerted efforts at disfranchisement in the 1890s and early 1900s. This was the commissioner and marshal system. Particularly lost to historians is the role of federal commissioners, the people who often were "an individual's first contact with the administration of federal justice." Their role helps explain the persistence of Reconstruction in the period after the withdrawal of army forces from state legislative halls (though not from the South) in 1877 and after the army's defanging by Democratic legislation in the late 1870s.[22]

Federal commissioners remain relatively mysterious figures even in the burgeoning field of policy history and the history of US state development. This reflects the broader confusion about how to treat fee-based federal officials, in part, and the relative lack of attention to US commissioners' successor title: federal magistrates. Magistrates, created under a 1968 reorganization, became subsidiary judges to serve as special masters. With the increased specialization and legal requirements for magistrates, the work and role of the old commissioners are now scattered among marshals, local FBI agents, magistrates, and other officials. But federal commissioners were present almost from the beginning of the constitutional system. For the first few years after the founding of the federal court system in the Judiciary Act of 1789, federal judges depended upon state officials to handle arrests, bail, and other matters associated with criminal law enforcement. Quickly, the Whiskey Rebellion (1794) and other events exposed the problems with enforcing locally unpopular federal laws through state officials. Federal courts had no recourse if local agents refused to help. And the 1793 Fugitive Slave Law relied upon local magistrates for enforcement because every federal court turned to them. But in 1793 Congress authorized federal circuit courts to appoint commissioners to take bail and affidavits in criminal matters, in 1812 authorized them to collect fees, and then in 1817 allowed them to take depositions in civil cases. Sectional conflicts over slavery increasingly raised doubts about the willingness (or ability) of local officials to carry out federal fugitive-slave laws or enforce federal court orders. At the same time, a general expansion of commissioners' power happened over things like seamen's wages, extradition hearings, enforcement of federal internal-revenue laws, search warrants for certain federal crimes, migratory bird treaties, and federal wildlife and game laws. By 1842, Congress authorized commissioners to issue arrest warrants and to hold people for trial; they had "all the powers that any justice of the peace, or other magistrate, of any of the United States may now exercise" in cases of federal law. They were a kind of national police. When southern congressmen empowered commissioners to enforce the 1850 Fugitive Slave Act, these planter-politicians used a tool that had been sharpened for other purposes.[23] But the great expansions of their power in the postbellum United States were tied to seemingly contradictory practices: civil rights and Chinese exclusion. Along with the special powers granted commissioners under the Civil Rights Act and Enforcement Acts, they now enforced the 1882 Chinese Exclusion Act and sentenced Chinese nationals to deportation. Thus, commissioners expanded into immigration enforcement as a way of overriding recalcitrant state governments and more-lenient state judges.[24]

The number of commissioners expanded dramatically over the nineteenth century, from scattered reports of a handful of officials in circuit courts to roughly two thousand by the late 1870s. As early as 1872, expenses for commissioners approached $100,000 a year, not counting the portions covered under the $2.5 million classified under marshals' expenses as witness fees. As early as 1872, one attorney general argued that the expenses had risen dramatically in part because of the Civil Rights Act and raised questions about both the circuit courts' control of the officers and the fee-based system, which encouraged them to handle more cases so they could collect more money. "These officers are paid by fees, and it is to their interest to have as many examinations and issue as many subpoenas for witnesses as possible, and frequently their warrants are issued on frivolous grounds." Therefore, he requested—but was not granted—power to appoint and relieve commissioners.[25] In 1878 the attorney general complained about the increase in "trivial prosecutions" by the stubbornly large numbers of commissioners.[26] They came under fire for patronage appointments—the son of former president Millard Fillmore notoriously held clerk and commissioner appointments simultaneously—and for their role in enforcing extremely unpopular revenue laws. An 1894 congressional report complained that "some of the commissioners had their professional witnesses whose duty it was to scour out the country for violations of the revenue laws, report, swear out warrants, and attend as a witness in the case, and draw his per diem for attendance and mileage from the place of arresting defendant, irrespective of the place of service of the subpoena." That 1894 report complained that commissioners tried 1,479 cases but had only 616 cases advance, having discharged 462 and the grand jury refusing to indict in 401. In those 401 cases, 1,203 witnesses were resubpoenaed, possibly to increase their fees. Two years later one congressman complained that a commissioner is "Pooh-Bah. He does everything except pay himself."

Flustered, Congress moved to take control over commissioners precisely as political commitment to Black civil rights waned. In 1896 Congress seized power over the office from the federal judiciary, changing its title from "commissioner of the circuit court" to "US commissioner," fixing terms of appointment at four years (instead of indefinite), making each subject to removal by district courts at any time, and prohibiting them from holding other offices. Congress also fixed the fee schedule and did not revise it until 1942. Commissioners, however, still reputedly earned large sums adjudicating prohibition violations and continued to draw higher fees for civil rights and Chinese exclusion cases. In 1946 Congress capped commissioners' total fees, and by 1965, only 613 commissioners remained in the federal court system. Still, in the 1960s a third of commissioners had no legal training. In 1968 Congress overhauled the office in the Federal Magistrate Act, abolishing commissioners and creating US magistrates, with both commissioners' powers and new authority. Since then federal courts have litigated the precise power of magistrate courts, given the constitutional provisions about cases that had to be decided by federal judges with lifetime appointments.[27]

To assess commissioners' effectiveness, we need to examine not just civil rights cases but also antebellum actions to enforce the Fugitive Slave Act. The best guide to this question is R. J. M. Blackett's excellent *The Captive's Quest for Freedom: Fugitive Slaves, the 1850 Fugitive Slave Law, and the Politics of Slavery.* Antislavery northerners denounced the act for its empowerment of commissioners to be police in every northern locality, while some planter-politicians did hope to fashion an extremely robust federal police force. One version of the Fugitive Slave Act of 1850 called for up to three commissioners for every county in the nation. While that provision did not pass, antislavery politicians especially denounced the differential fees—ten dollars for a commissioner who issued a decision in favor of the slaveowner, but only five dollars to a commissioner who did not. Planter-politicians turned to federal commissioners because states had succeeded in blocking their own magistrates from enforcing the 1793 Fugitive Slave Act. Therefore, the 1850 act empowered commissioners to become judges and sometimes enforcement agents. New York abolitionist William Jay denounced this elevation as "among the wonders of the times" as "judges procreate judges for the convenience of slaveholders." When existing commissioners would not enforce the law, judges appointed new commissioners who would. Thus far, this story comports with the idea of an empowered commissioner system enforcing the slaveholders' law.[28]

But Blackett, in fact, shows that the commissioner system was weaker than it might first appear, as federal commissioners were far more vulnerable to local public opinion than post–World War II federal judges. After Harrisburg, Pennsylvania, commissioner Richard McAllister resigned under pressure, he was never replaced, and there appeared to be almost no fugitive-slave enforcement in that city; every local constable who aided McAllister in his renditions was voted out of office in 1853. Other areas had few commissioners and no easy way to fill an unpopular post. By rumor, five Pennsylvania commissioners resigned shortly after the 1850 Fugitive Slave Act passed. Cleveland, Ohio, appears not to have had a commissioner willing to hear cases between 1851 and 1860. When Vincennes, Indiana, commissioner John Moore sent a runaway back south, a grand jury indicted him for kidnapping. Boston commissioner Edward G. Loring lost his job at Harvard Law School for his role in Anthony Burns's rendition and was forced from his commissioner post as well. Additionally, commissioners had a good deal of leeway in interpreting the law. In Chicago, for example, one freed a man because he did not agree with the language used to describe the man's skin color. Blackett credited Philadelphia Black activists with creating public pressure to free Henry Garnett. They and white Quakers packed the hearing room in support of Garnett, then paraded through the streets when the commissioner ruled in their favor. Commissioners in Boston dallied in issuing a warrant for the arrest of William Craft, the marshal doubting he even could arrest Craft in the face of local opposition. At Christiana, Pennsylvania, 150 Black people and a few whites killed a slaveowner who had come to claim his alleged former slaves. When a Syracuse, New York, crowd stormed a hearing with a battering ram and spirited Jerry Henry to Canada, President Fillmore pressed for prosecution, and twenty-four men—twenty of them Black—were charged; the cases collapsed in hung juries and postponements.[29]

The costs of administering a commissioner system to enforce the Fugitive Slave Act were daunting, even to proslavery administrations. When a Harrisburg commissioner billed the government $262.91 for sending a posse to Virginia, the Treasury took months to reimburse him. Commissioners and Treasury auditors frequently squabbled over the proper fees. One federal marshal claimed he was owed $2,000 for advance payments he had to make upon commissioners' claims. When Thomas Sims was arrested in Boston, the military force required to carry him to Savannah, Georgia, as well as the hearing itself, cost between $10,000 and $20,000. Burns's return cost perhaps $40,000, including deployment of 1,500 troops to escort Burns through an angry crowd clamoring to release him. The Christiana trial cost roughly $50,000, as did the trial of the Syracuse men who carried away Henry before he could be captured.[30]

Through painstaking work, Blackett captures "Zones of Enforcement." In some "Zones of Resistance," empowered Black organizations successfully rendered the law mute, particularly around Chicago, Philadelphia, New York City, Syracuse, and Boston at various times. In other regions there were successful Zones of Enforcement where the law was carried out—Cincinnati, Indianapolis, and even Harrisburg for a time. In other areas there were "Zones of Mystery," where it is difficult to discern whether the law was carried out or not. Blackett estimates that of 147 cases heard between September 1850 and April 1851, 105 persons were returned, 16 escaped, 17 were rescued, 7 freed following a hearing, and 2 purchased prior to return. Philadelphia saw 9 cases between October 1850 and October 1851, then just 1 in 1852, 5 in 1853, and 6 between 1854 and 1860, even as numbers of runaways increased. In Albany, New York, many hundreds of runaway slaves passed through (55 aided by the Troy Vigilance Committee alone between September 1856 and September 1857, 287 by Albany steward Stephen Myers, and 187 in 1855 by Jermain Loguen), but only 7 cases were brought before commissioners, ending in one rendition. The vigilance committee that William Still helped organize reported losing only two fugitives in seven years out of perhaps one thousand aided. The Boston Vigilance Committee claimed it aided 163 people in the four years after Burns's rendition. In Syracuse one of Frederick Douglass's correspondents wrote that runaways were "perfectly safe at every point between Buffalo and Albany." "If one measure of the Fugitive Slave Law's effectiveness was the number of slaves retaken and returned as a consequence of hearings before commissioners, then it was woefully ineffective" in northern Illinois, Blackett concludes. "There were less than a handful of hearings during the decade and in only one of these . . . was the suspect returned permanently." He argues, "To function effectively, the Fugitive Slave Law required federal and local authorities to work in tandem: commissioners willing to issue arrest warrants for fugitives beyond their jurisdiction, to arrange expedited hearings, and to employ large police forces." Still, for every person "who was taken and returned, there were countless unnamed slaves who made it to freedom." While Blackett acknowledges the narrow truth of President James Buchanan's claim that in "contested cases" the Fugitive Slave Act worked, he also quotes Buchanan's rueful admission that these only happened at "great loss and inconvenience to the master and with considerable expense to the Government." Blackett concludes, "the law was an inadequate mechanism to address the problem." Vast numbers of enslaved people successfully escaped; while the *New York Times* estimated this rate at 90 percent, Blackett suggests it was much higher still.[31]

In the tumultuous 1850s, the Fugitive Slave Act produced a failed commissioner and marshal system, one that could not make itself felt consistently or thoroughly in the face of intense local opposition. The law itself proved to be slow, cumbersome, and expensive, and people routinely used violence and pressure to resist it. Even when captured, those covered often escaped, with little recourse. The fact that cases prevailed when adjudicated could not obscure the fact that the enforcement was pitifully weak compared to the scope of the problem. Black organizing and white allies had broken the Fugitive Slave Law, in many ways making it a dead letter.

What, then, does this tell us about the mechanism devised to enforce the Civil Rights Acts? If the Fugitive Slave Act could barely be enforced by a vigorously proslavery federal government in the 1850s, what could a civil rights law do with the same structure? Worse, it could never be as strong as the Fugitive Slave Act since offenders were subject to federal court and thus entitled to a due process explicitly denied to enslaved people.

We cannot understand the challenges of enforcing civil and voting rights law if we do not embed them in an analysis of the challenges of enforcing the Fugitive Slave Act. Yet many explanations of the collapse of voting rights turn upon implicit assumptions that enforcement was undermined by particular limitations, whether of racist attitudes, ideological contradictions, or Republican pusillanimity. The juxtaposition of the Civil Rights Acts and the Fugitive Slave Act suggests that those arguments— though plausible—are constructed without regard to the actual nature of the nineteenth-century state, its capacities, and its limitations. The Fugitive Slave Act and the Enforcement Acts arose from precisely opposite racial and ideological views yet shared common limitations, a reminder of the necessity of engaging with state capacity, not merely intention, in explaining the outcomes of federal legislation. From distinct vantage points, the two laws shared the same flaw, one rooted in the challenges of fee-based governance and in the problems of nineteenth-century central governments enforcing their will over democratically and militarily empowered local people, whom central elites could neither easily outvote nor easily outshoot.

Still, explaining whether the commissioner and marshal system actually worked for voting rights enforcement raises questions that have not yet been addressed. There is no equivalent to Blackett's sweeping study of the actual working of commissioners in the face of local opposition. Unsurprisingly, legal historians emphasize court cases, particularly cases around the Ku Klux Klan and the Colfax massacre. But the day-to-day work of federal commissioners remains understudied, as does their basic role and function in this period.

Although the election laws could not duplicate the Fugitive Slave Act's sweeping authority—white southerners remained free citizens—the election laws did expand the federal bureaucracy in new, if temporary, ways. Commissioners themselves became more numerous. Additionally special deputy election officials were appointed by federal marshals at election time—more than 10,000 in New York State in the 1890s. Because they worked to further Republican Party aims and were often Republican leaders, these deputy marshals at once reflected an expansion of the federal state and a continuation of the model of a state of "courts and parties," suggested decades ago by Stephen Skowronek. These election supervisors were selected by federal circuit judges, upon petition from local residents, and had to be appointed from each major political party. But deputy marshals could be appointed by the federal marshal, a political-patronage position. Deputy marshals became, as one scholar has written, "a civilian military, functioning at the command of the party in power in Washington." No wonder, then, that Democrats aimed in 1880 to transfer the appointment of deputy marshals to federal circuit judges as part of their overall effort to empty out federal election law. And no wonder that Republican president Rutherford B. Hayes vetoed the resulting bill. Republicans spent money on deputy marshals in areas where they hoped to regain power, especially in New York City.[32]

But discovering precisely what deputy marshals did in the southern states remains challenging. The best studies focus on special deputies, appointed solely for an election and whose funds could only be spent by law in large cities. But general deputies could and were dispersed in smaller counties, their expenditures hidden in the overall marshals' funds and fees, making them harder to disaggregate. One way to trace their work is through election prosecutions. These had been common in southern states until 1882, then fell in 1884 and throughout President Grover Cleveland's first term. Prosecutions in the South dropped from 367 in 1882 to 19 in 1886. Democrats launched an increased number of prosecutions in 1888, but 91 of the 118 that year were in Tennessee, where the Democratic governor sought help in protecting his seat. Republicans appeared to focus steadily on northern prosecutions to hold their swing states in the 1880s, cases there matching the number of southern prosecutions in 1884, when Republicans lost four northern swing states by less than 1 percent of the vote, then surpassing them from 1888 on. But there remains evidence of ongoing Republican commitment to providing southern states with election supervisors; spending on these officials grew dramatically in the region during the 1880s, reflecting the increased demands from southern Blacks and the circuit judges' attention to local conditions rather than national political trends.[33] Overall, the South received disproportionate attention from federal courts. Between 1871 and 1890, southern states had almost four times the number of criminal cases per capita as northern ones, at 54 cases per 10,000 people compared to 14 per 10,000 respectively. (The West was even higher, at 72 cases per 10,000 residents, in part caused by the number of territorial courts.)[34]

A closer examination of northern Mississippi illuminates one area of heightened enforcement. Along with South Carolina, northern Mississippi was home to a disproportionate number of Enforcement Act cases; 48 percent of all election cases tried in the United States between 1871 and 1884 took place in those two areas, with 1,072 cases in northern Mississippi and 1,504 in South Carolina out of 5,386 nationally. South Carolina famously was the only site of broad habeas corpus suspension against the Klan, with 500 arrests within the first few weeks after the suspension and 1,300 cases by 1873. The South Carolina data also demonstrates the complexity of such prosecutions; there were a total of 168 convictions against 61 acquittals in South Carolina between 1871 and 1884, but 1,275 (or 85 percent) of the cases were nolle prosequi. Election laws nationally had unusually high rates of dropped cases. In South Carolina there was a burst of activity, a bit more than 100 successful convictions, and then a slew of dropped cases and a trickle of new cases (fewer than 200) after 1874. In northern Mississippi, things proceeded quite differently. While only 11 percent of South Carolina cases ended in conviction compared to only 28 percent nationwide, 55 percent of northern Mississippi cases ended with successful prosecutions. The region also stands out for the rural nature of its population; all of the state's major cities were in the Southern District of Mississippi, with the Northern District's offices located in the town of Oxford, population 1,500. The Mississippi cases also point to a transition in civil rights enforcement from reliance on the military as a police force—as in the South Carolina parishes where habeas corpus was suspended and the army directly made arrests—to other forms of enforcement. Through the early 1870s, the US marshal and the US attorney called upon these forces and lobbied Washington to sustain a military presence there. When the army left northern Mississippi in 1877, however, marshals and supervisors had to turn to other enforcement mechanisms. The historian of the Northern District of Mississippi notes that the statutes and convictions do not capture the breadth of the officials' efforts. "One is struck by the fact that US attorneys and marshals did not confine themselves to the formal requirements of their offices. The US attorney did not merely seek indictments and convictions, nor did the marshals confine themselves to serving judicial process and to keeping prisoners." In 1876 the marshal appointed 239 special deputies for the presidential election, though they were overwhelmed by Democratic fraud.[35]

Many of the marshals and attorneys appear stalwart, even heroic, so why did their efforts not succeed? While these officers complained about resources, they blamed broadly held white opposition for suppressing Black voters. "Violators of the law inevitably became heroes," the historian writes. Thus, we face a basic problem not just with the commissioner and marshal system but also with any form of central-state imposition upon the populace: how can a central government force policies upon a deeply recalcitrant local population? This common problem of governance was exacerbated in the nineteenth century by the combination of increased popular demands for central intervention—a product of both politics and technology—and the widespread possession of weapons. When three convicted ballot-box stuffers returned to Clay County, Mississippi, in 1882, a woman wrote a poem in their honor, calling them "our welcome gallant trio, / Clay County's free-born sons! / Convicted of true manhood / Thrice welcomed honored ones." Townspeople raised money to pay the fines assessed on these men. Locals also ran off witnesses, threatened federal agents, poisoned one US attorney, arrested one federal marshal and three deputies on local charges, attacked a marshal in a local courtroom, and ransacked and burglarized their offices. The federal judge tried to sustain the Enforcement Acts by levying light punishments in hopes of convincing local white people that they had latitude to convict in jury trials, but in the process he—perhaps with good intentions—vacated the strict penalties attached to some of the violent crimes. While attorneys general pressed for harsher sentences, they could not control the federal judge, who remained in office until 1892.[36]

Although these laws came under intense federal scrutiny, it is incorrect to say that courts brought them down in the 1880s. Instead, in *ex parte Siebold* (1879) and *ex parte Clarke* (1879), the US Supreme Court refused to grant writs of habeas corpus to local elections officials jailed for violating the Enforcement Acts. In *Siebold* the court explicitly defended the federal government's power to use force to protect voting rights. "The government of the United States may, by means of physical force, exercised through its official agents, execute on every foot of American soil the powers and functions that belong to it," the justices ruled. "Why do we have marshals at all, if they cannot physically lay their hands on persons and things in the performance of their proper duties?" In *ex parte Yarbrough* (1884), the court further denied habeas corpus writs to white men charged with vigilante election violence in Georgia. In a unanimous opinion, the justices asked, "Can it be doubted that Congress can, by law, protect the act of voting, the place where it is done, and the man who votes from personal violence and intimidation and the election itself from corruption or fraud?"[37]

Below the level of court prosecutions lies the still-mysterious figure of commissioners and deputy marshals, who remain hard to pin down in the literature but for a time were widely present. The scale of commissioners is somewhat hard to contemplate. The 1881 federal register of officials lists 1,989 commissioners across the states and territories. The spread of these officials is impressive and raises doubts about my own portrayals of a federal government with no reach. By population, the former Confederate states and slave states had more of them than other states, with 4.2 commissioners per 100,000 people in ex-Confederate states and 4.5 in 1860 slave states compared to 3.8 for all states.[38]

Commissioners were spread across a surprising range of towns, far from the cities containing US district courts. The fifty-eight district courts and marshals in the states were largely centralized (though the Northern District of Mississippi had no large central city). But commissioners were stationed in places like Dardanelle and Eureka Springs, Arkansas; Whitley Court House, Cadiz, and Lebanon, Kentucky; Yanceyville and Mills River, North Carolina; and Wartburg, Ducktown, Milan, and Purdy, Tennessee. Second to post offices, it is likely that these officials represented the second-largest geographical reach of the federal government in the nation's small towns and rural regions.[39] To pick unexceptional federal districts based in Arkansas in 1877, commissioners were reported in Pine

Bluff, Little Rock, Rockport, Saint Charles, Lake Village, Searcy, Magnolia, Des Arc, Jonesboro, Grand Lake, Austin, Dardanelle, Helena, Princeton, Arkansas City, Monticello, Batesville, Desha County, Benton, DeWitt, Ashley County, Lewisville, Hamburg, Prescott, Mount Moriah, Watson, Laconia, Warren, Tulip, Hot Springs, Lonoke, Warren, Washington, Camden, Helena, Fayetteville, Van Buren, Fort Smith, Fort Sill (Indian Territory), and Yellville.[40]

This broad geographical spread raises serious questions about the reach and extent of the federal government in the South, a region that remained deeply rural and where assaults against freedpeople happened frequently far from city centers. Did the commissioners represent an access to government that paralleled, in weaker form, the access provided by the military outposts in 1865–68? Did they create regions of access that in turn opened the possibility, within those regions, of calling upon the federal government through commissioners? It is possible that the presence of commissioners might correlate with responsiveness of other federal officials or even with the outcomes of those responses. It may be possible to map Zones of Access around commissioners' offices that help us denote which freedpeople in the South had access to the federal government and which did not.

It may well be that commissioners did not do much or that the position was simply a title that had lapsed into insignificance. But it is clear that further investigation is warranted into the men who were appointed, the actions they took, the fees they collected, the ways they responded to federal judges, and the variation among regions based on judges' proclivities in appointing these officers. Beyond the understudied role of commissioners, the precise influence of deputy marshals is also hard to pin down.

Republicans and Democrats testified to the potential effectiveness of these officials in their fierce debates over a last round of voting rights laws in the late 1880s and early 1890s. In 1889, when Republicans gained power over the House, Senate, and White House, they launched an ambitious but ultimately unsuccessful effort to expand the power of election supervisors. And in 1893, when Democrats in turn took the House, Senate, and White House in combination for the first time since the 1850s, they launched a successful assault upon a number of election laws. The clearest evidence that these laws mattered lay in the importance both parties granted them.

The proposed elections law of 1890–91, sometimes called the Lodge Force Bill, originated from a Republican realization that no amount of moderation could win over white southern votes and that ongoing fraud and intimidation in the South cost their party perhaps a dozen congressional seats they might otherwise win. A resurgent civil rights wing of the party helped back Benjamin Harrison's nomination, and Massachusetts senator George Hoar lobbied for a broad bill for federal supervision of congressional elections. After Hoar agreed to defer to the House, since the bill would regulate elections to that body, Massachusetts congressman Henry Cabot Lodge became its chief spokesman. The House bill provided for a chief federal elections supervisor for each circuit court and re-quired these officials to cover any city, county, or congressional district where a sufficient number of people petitioned for coverage. The supervisors, backed by special deputy marshals, would observe registration, voting, and tabulation. In covered congressional districts, the circuit court would appoint a federal board of canvassers to report the election returns. If their returns differed from those submitted by state officers, the House should take the returns of the federal agents as prima facie evidence of the proper victor in the race. The bill also defined penalties for people who thwarted the election process or committed fraud. But the bill primarily rested upon presence, not force. "The great safeguard to the public welfare of this country is publicity," Lodge said. "The greatest assurance of honest elections lies in making absolutely public every step and every act by which the Representatives of the people are chosen. . . .The Government which made the black man a citizen of the United States is bound to protect him in his rights as a citizen of the United States, and it is a cowardly Government if it does not do it! . . . If we fail as a people to deal with this question rightly we shall pay for it just as we paid the debt of slavery of which this is a part."[41] The House measure also included a provision for military protection to enforce the laws, but the Senate stripped that in an effort to build support in that chamber.[42]

But the Democrats also saw what was at stake. Mississippi senator James George watched in alarm in 1890 as Republicans pressed this federal elections bill, worried about what was to come. George pressed Mississippi to take the controversial (and deeply contested among whites there) step of calling a state constitutional convention in the summer of 1890 to disfranchise Black people before the federal government could act. The Mississippi disfranchising con-stitution passed in November, quickly and dramatically reducing Black voting from 45-percent turnout of eligible men in the 1880s to roughly 1 percent. After Democrats won control of the House, Senate, and White House in 1892, they repealed parts of the 1870 and 1871 federal elections laws "and all other statutes and parts of statutes relating in any manner to supervisors of election and special deputy marshals" in 1894.[43] Mississippi inspired other southern states to act, particularly after the Supreme Court seemed to open the door to state-level disfranchisement in *Williams v. Mississippi*. Between 1891 and 1908, every other ex-Confederate state reduced Black voting (in Louisiana from 130,000 Black male voters to 5,320 within four years) by a combination of poll taxes, literacy tests, grandfather clauses, and new registration procedures. White southern Democrats hoped to make Black disfranchisement a fait accompli and to convince national Republicans to give up hope of enfranchisement.[44]

Afterward, Senator Hoar, the champion of the elections bill, wrote in despair that "the attempt to secure the rights of the colored people by National legislation would be abandoned until there was a considerable change of opinion in the country, and especially in the South, and until it had ceased to become [a] matter of party strife."[45] His words pose daunting challenges for our interpretations today and for our ability to understand voting rights enforcement. After championing freedpeople's voting rights, Hoar came to believe they depended not on federal legislation, but on public opinion—more dauntingly, on the removal of the issue from partisan politics. Either voting rights had to be secured in a way that elections could not touch or they had to cease to be the source of dispute in electoral contests. Otherwise, Hoar foresaw, parties would run on the promise to undo voting rights, win, and proceed to undo them. Even if the party championing voting rights prevailed, their victories could only be temporary. But he saw no way to move voting rights beyond politics.

From the perspective of the 1970s, it was impossible not to look back with some contempt upon the late-nineteenth-century Republicans who had failed to protect voting rights, to find in Hoar a mealymouthed moderate. In the face of the seemingly massive victories of the Voting Rights Act of 1965 and its subsequent renewals, it was alluring to tell stories of voting as a fundamental American value and of disfranchisement as an exception, one caused by vicious southern Democrats and pusillanimous white northern Republicans. In this telling, enforcement disappeared behind questions of will and intention. But time alters our perspective. From the 2020s, we may well find ourselves dauntingly able to see the challenges that late-nineteenth-century Republicans faced. If great victories, once won, prove impermanent, what then? If voting rights were not beyond politics but were made the source of political contest, then how could they be protected other than through the one provoting party permanently holding power? What mechanisms of governance could plausibly survive partisan defeat and popular apathy?

We may well have opportunity to separate nineteenth-century Republicans' outcomes from their intentions, to see anew the boldness of some of their attempts, and thus to see anew the deep, perhaps fundamental, difficulties in sustaining voting rights in a democratic republic where one party is deeply hostile to them. The barriers that Republicans created were not impregnable, but it may well be that with further study the commissioner and marshal system will look more impressive than it once appeared, its overthrow even more devastating. If our own Justice Department system collapses in the 2020s, we may have a clearer, chastened perspective on the difficulty for even well-designed and executed systems to defend against an empowered and embittered restrictionist party.

But, of course, these reflections should not lead to Hoar's willingness to surrender voting rights. Instead, the proper course may well be to recover the boldness in some of the 1870s–90s Republican dreams: to aim to create positive voting rights, to establish federal regulation of all elections, to lift voting once and for all from the state and local hands that often restrain it, not because voting will be on a certain footing in Washington, DC, but because boldness may represent the only viable path forward once the dreams of an uncontroversial legalism die.

NOTES

1. "Frederick Douglass on the Fifteenth Amendment," *New York Times,* Apr. 11, 1870, 1.

2. Frederick Douglass, *Life and Times of Frederick Douglass, Written by Himself* (Boston: De Wolfe & Fiske, 1892), 604.

3. Pippa Holloway, *Living in Infamy: Felon Disfranchisement and the History of American Citizenship* (New York: Oxford University Press, 2013).

4. Carol Anderson, *One Person, No Vote: How Voter Suppression Is Destroying Our Democracy* (New York: Bloomsburg, 2018); Alexander Keyssar, *The Right to Vote: The Contested History of Democracy in the United States,* rev. ed. (New York: Basic Books, 2009); Allan J. Lichtman, *The Embattled Vote in America: From the Founding to the Present* (Cambridge, MA: Harvard University Press, 2018); "State Voting Laws," Brennan Center for Justice, https://www.brennancenter.org/issues /ensure-every-american-can-vote/voting-reform/state-voting-laws.

5. The greatest works on disfranchisement include J. Morgan Kousser, *The Shaping of Southern Politics: Suffrage Restriction and the Establishment of the One-Party South, 1880–1910* (New Haven,

CT: Yale University Press, 1974); Michael Perman, *Struggle for Mastery: Disfranchisement in the South, 1888–1908* (Chapel Hill: University of North Carolina Press, 2001); Richard M. Vallely, *The Two Reconstructions: The Struggle for Black Enfranchisement* (Chicago: University of Chicago Press, 2004).

6. George A. Rutherglen, *Civil Rights in the Shadow of Slavery: The Constitution, Common Law, and the Civil Rights Act of 1866* (New York: Oxford University Press, 2012); Nicholas R. Parrillo, *Against the Profit Motive: The Salary Revolution in American Government, 1780–1940* (New Haven, CT: Yale University Press, 2013); Richard White, *The Republic for Which It Stands: The United States during Reconstruction and the Gilded Age, 1865–1896* (New York: Oxford University Press, 2017).

7. Michael Vorenberg, "The 1866 Civil Rights Act and the Beginning of Military Reconstruction," in *The Greatest and the Grandest Act: The Civil Rights Act of 1866 from Reconstruction to Today,* ed. Christian G. Samity (Carbondale: Southern Illinois University Press, 2018), 60–88; "Veto of the Civil Rights Bill," Mar. 27, 1866, Teaching American History, https://teachingamericanhistory.org /library/document/veto-of-the-civil-rights-bill/.

8. On Reconstruction generally and on the Republican drive to enshrine new rights for freedpeople, the defining work remains Eric Foner, *Reconstruction: America's Unfinished Revolution, 1863–1877,* updated ed. (New York: Harper Perennial, 2014).

9. See, especially, Gautham Rao, "The Federal 'Posse Comitatus' Doctrine: Slavery, Compulsion, and Statecraft in Mid-Nineteenth Century America," *Law and History Review* 26, no. 1 (Spring 2008): 1–56.

10. Vorenberg, "1866 Civil Rights Act and the Beginning of Military Reconstruction."

11. James E. Sefton, *The United States Army and Reconstruction, 1865–1877* (Baton Rouge: Louisiana State University, 1967); Gregory P. Downs, *After Appomattox: Military Occupation and the Ends of War* (Cambridge, MA: Harvard University Press, 2015).

12. Downs, *After Appomattox.*

13. Gregory P. Downs and Scott Nesbit, *Mapping Occupation: Force, Freedom, and the Army in Reconstruction,* Mar. 2015, http://www.mappingoccupation.org.

14. For the history of Republican efforts in the 1880s and 1890s, see Xi Wang, *The Trial of Democracy: Black Suffrage and Northern Republicans, 1860–1910* (Athens: University of Georgia Press, 1996), 49–133; Charles W. Calhoun, *Conceiving a New Republic: The Republican Party and the Southern Question, 1869–1900* (Lawrence: University Press of Kansas, 2006); Robert Goldman, *A Free Ballot and a Fair Count: The Department of Justice and the Enforcement of Voting Rights in the South, 1877–1893* (New York: Fordham University Press, 2001); William Gillette, *Retreat from Reconstruction, 1869–1879* (Baton Rouge: Louisiana State University Press, 1982); Robert J. Kaczorowski, *The Politics of Judicial Interpretation: The Federal Courts, Department of Justice and Civil Rights, 1866–1876* (Dobbs Ferry, NY: Oceana, 1985).

15. *US Statutes at Large,* 41st Cong., 2nd sess., chap. 114, pp. 140–46.

16. *US Statutes at Large,* 41st Cong., 2nd sess., chap. 254, pp. 254–57; Xi Wang, "The Making of Federal Enforcement Laws, 1870–1872—Freedom: Political," *Chicago-Kent Law Review* 70, no. 3 (1995): 1034–45.

17. *US Statutes at Large,* 41st Cong., 3rd sess., chap. 99, pp. 433–40; Allen W. Trelease, *White Terror: The Ku Klux Klan Conspiracy and Southern Reconstruction* (New York: Harper & Row, 1971); Lou

Falkner Williams, *The Great South Carolina Ku Klux Klan Trials, 1871–1872* (Athens: University of Georgia Press, 2004); Carole Emberton, *Beyond Redemption: Race, Violence, and the American South after the Civil War* (Chicago: University of Chicago Press, 2013); Elaine Frantz Parsons, *Ku-Klux: The Birth of the Klan during Reconstruction* (Chapel Hill: University of North Carolina Pres, 2015).

    18. *US Statutes at Large,* 42nd Cong., 1st sess., chap. 22, pp. 13–15.

    19. Wang, "Making of Federal Enforcement Laws," 1054–56.

    20. *US Statutes at Large,* 45th Cong., 2nd sess., chap. 263, p. 152.

    21. On enduring Black power, see Steven Hahn, *Nation under Our Feet: Black Political Struggles in the Rural South from Slavery to the Great Migration* (Cambridge, MA: Belknap Press of Harvard University Press, 2003); and Justin Behrend, *Reconstructing Democracy: Grassroots Black Politics in the Deep South after the Civil War* (Athens: University of Georgia Press, 2015).

    22. Charles A. Lindquist, "The Origin and Development of the United States Commissioner System," *American Journal of Legal History* 14, no. 1 (Jan. 1970): 1.

    23. Leslie G. Foschio, "A History of the Development of the Office of United States Commissioner and Magistrate Judge System," *Federal Courts Law Review* 4 (1999); Tim A. Baker, "The Expanding Role of Magistrate Judges in the Federal Courts," *Valparaiso University Law Review* 39, no. 3 (2005): 661–92; Lindquist, "Origin and Development of the United States Commissioner System," 3–8.

    24. Foschio, "History of the Development"; Baker, "Expanding Role of Magistrate Judges in the Federal Courts."

    25. *Letter of the Attorney-General, in Compliance with a Senate Resolution of January 20, 1873, Submitting a Statement of Operations for the Department of Justice for the Fiscal Year ending June 30, 1872,* 42nd Cong., 3rd sess. (1873), S. Exec. Doc. 32, 5–7.

    26. *Annual Report of the Attorney-General for the Year 1878* (Washington: Government Printing Office, 1878), 12.

    27. Foschio, "History of the Development," 3–5; Lindquist, "Origins and Development," 8–9.

    28. R. J. M. Blackett, *The Captive's Quest for Freedom: Fugitive Slaves, the 1850 Fugitive Slave Law, and the Politics of Slavery* (New York: Cambridge University Press, 2018), 51–53 (quote, 52). Blackett points to the story of Richard McAllister, commissioner from Harrisburg, Pennsylvania. From one of the last slaveholding families in the state, McAllister returned nine people to the South, ruling in favor of none, and garnering charges of taking bribes. Finally, he resigned and left to lead Kansas territorial actions against John Brown. Blackett's book draws upon prodigious research as well as prior works, including Stanley W. Campbell, *The Slave Catchers: Enforcement of the Fugitive Slave Law, 1850–1860* (Chapel Hill: University of North Carolina, 1968).

    29. Blackett, *Captive's Quest,* 56–59, 62–66, 163, 179, 290, 368, 401.

    30. Ibid., 64, 68–74, 426, 436–38, 458.

    31. Ibid., 179, 268, 337, 355, 360–61, 369, 439, 458–60.

    32. Scott C. James and Brian L. Lawson, "The Political Economy of Voting Rights Enforcement in America's Gilded Age: Electoral College Competition, Partisan Commitment, and the Federal Election Law," *American Political Science Review* 93, no. 1 (Mar. 1999): 115–25; Stephen Skowronek, *Building a New American State: The Expansion of National Administrative Capacities, 1877–1920* (New York: Cambridge University Press, 1982).

33. James and Lawson, "Political Economy of Voting Rights Enforcement."

34. Stephen Creswell, *Mormons and Cowboys, Moonshiners and Klansmen* (Tuscaloosa: University of Alabama Press, 1991), 4.

35. Stephen Creswell, "Enforcing the Enforcement Acts: The Department of Justice in Northern Mississippi, 1870–1890," *Journal of Southern History* 53, no. 3 (Aug. 1987): 421–30 (quote, 428); Everette Swinney, *Suppressing the Ku Klux Klan* (New York: Garand, 1987); Stephen Cresswell, "Resistance and Enforcement: The United States Department of Justice, 1870–1893," in *Mormons and Cowboys;* Robert J. Kaczorowski, *The Politics of Judicial Interpretation: The Federal Courts, Department of Justice, and Civil Rights, 1866–1876* (New York: Fordham University Press, 2005); Robert Michael Goldman, *A Free Ballot and a Fair Count: The Department of Justice and the Enforcement of Voting Rights in the South, 1877–1893* (New York: Fordham University Press, 2001).

36. Creswell, "Enforcing the Enforcement Acts," 431–40 (quote, 432).

37. Richard M. Vallely, "Partisan Entrepreneurship and Policy Windows: George Frisbie Hoar and the 1890 Federal Elections Bill," in *Formative Acts: American Politics in the Making,* ed. Stephen Skowronek and Matthew Glassman (Philadelphia: University of Pennsylvania Press, 2008), 132, 135; Pamela Brandwein, "A Judicial Abandonment of Blacks? Rethinking the 'State Action' Cases of the Waite Court," *Law & Society Review* 41, no. 2 (June 2007): 343–86; Brandwein, *Rethinking the Judicial Settlement of Reconstruction* (New York: Cambridge University Press, 2011). Pamela Brandwein has been particularly clear in assessing the role of federal courts in undoing voting and civil rights.

38. *Official Register of the United States, Containing a List of Officers and Employees in the Civil, Military, and Naval Service on the First of July, 1881; Together with a List of Ships and Vessels Belonging to the United States,* 2 vols. (Washington: Government Printing Office, 1881), 1:695–741; "Table I: Population of the United States, by States and Territories," *Statistics of the Population of the United States at the Tenth Census (June 1, 1880)* (Washington: Government Printing Office, 1883), https://www.census.gov/library/publications/1883/dec/vol-01-population.html. Data was compiled from the *Official Register* and compared to population statistics from the 1880 Census.

39. Examples from *Official Register of the United States,* 695–741.

40. *Official Register of Officers and Agents, Civil, Military, and Naval, in the Service of the United States on the Thirtieth of September, 1877* (Washington: Government Printing Office, 1878), 311–12.

41. *Congressional Record,* June 26, 1890, 51st Cong., 1st sess., 21(7):6538, 6543; Vallely, "Partisan Entrepreneurship," 136–42; Calhoun, *Conceiving a New Republic,* chap. 9; Wang, *Trial of Democracy.*

42. *Congressional Record,* Dec. 2, 1890, 51st Cong., 2nd sess., 22(1):22–26.

43. *US Statutes at Large,* 53rd Cong., 2nd sess., chap. 25, pp. 36–37.

44. David A. Bateman, Ira Katznelson, and John S. Lipinski, *Southern Nation: Congress and White Supremacy after Reconstruction* (Princeton, NJ: Princeton University Press, 2018), 198–211; Kousser, *Shaping Southern Politics;* Perman, *Struggle for Mastery.*

45. George Frisbie Hoar, *Autobiography of Seventy Years,* vol. 2 (New York: Charles Scribner's Sons, 1906), 158.

Breaking New Ground
African American Landowners and the Pursuit of the American Dream

ADRIENNE PETTY and MARK SCHULTZ

Free-soil Republicans like Abraham Lincoln believed that the experiment of American democracy rested upon a foundation of hard-working, independent family farmers standing together in community, casting votes, and making economic choices uncoerced by industrial bosses and slave-owning planters.[1] As the Civil War ended, this Republican vision overlapped with the desperate land hunger of the newly emancipated farmers of the South.[2] To some historical actors of early Reconstruction, the convergence of these forces seemed to have revealed the unfolding of Providence, as victorious Union armies placed the power of confiscation and land reform in Republican hands, and as emancipated women and men insisted that free-soil ideology extend to them.[3] But then the moment passed, and Providence seemed to turn away.[4]

The possibility of Reconstruction land reform has posed an irresistible problem to generations of historians who have debated why it failed and whether widespread landownership would have improved the lives of the freedpeople. Historians have reached greater consensus in assessing Lincoln's role in the process—although as is usual in discussions of Lincoln's vision for the future role of African Americans in the United States, ambiguities remain.

LINCOLN AND LAND FOR ALL
Lincoln took decisive action to strengthen and expand landownership among white citizens and immigrants with the passage of the Homestead Act of 1862 and the creation of land-grant colleges and the US Department of Agriculture (USDA). But when abolitionists and pragmatists in Congress and the US Army

pressed the logic of Republican landownership outward to include African Americans, he restrained and countermanded them. At first he feared alienating the border states, whose support seemed crucial to northern victory and the possibility of emancipation itself. When Republican senator Lyman Trumbull of Illinois proposed the Second Confiscation Act on December 2, 1861, a bill that called for the confiscation of the property of five classes of disloyal citizens, Lincoln objected that it would be found unconstitutional and threatened to veto it. So Congress added an explanatory resolution that limited any confiscation to the lifetime of the guilty party. This action deprived the government of a clear, permanent title to any land it confiscated under this law and undermined later plans to transfer seized land to the freedpeople. Later, at the close of 1863, Lincoln announced his 10-percent plan for reunion with the South. The plan promised pardons "with restoration of all rights of property, except as to slaves," for any former Confederates who would take a simple oath of loyalty. Finally, when Lincoln twice met with members of Confederate delegations, he offered an easy return of confiscated land if the southern states would surrender and accept the Thirteenth Amendment. While the war hung in the balance, Lincoln proved willing to sacrifice any chance for land reform in return for an end to combat and an end to slavery.[5]

At other times, Lincoln seemed more open to freedpeople's vision of landed independence. Because of the intransigence of white southerners, the political assertiveness of the freedpeople, and his relationship with Frederick Douglass, the president changed his position on many issues affecting freedpeople: his constitutional power to free them, their right to remain in the United States, their right to serve in the military, and their right to vote. In 1861, Congress called for a nationwide tax to support the war. But when Union forces captured territory along the Atlantic coast in 1862, Lincoln instructed the tax commissioners in South Carolina to collect unpaid taxes by seizing lands for resale. Among the properties taken, some parcels were to be set aside for "charitable" purposes.[6] Two years later, the government did indeed reserve a small portion of this land (16,000 out of 60,000 acres) for the charitable purpose of redistribution to freedmen in 20-acre lots at the low price of $1.25 per acre.[7] Later, in July 1864, Lincoln told Indiana congressman George Julian that he had come to believe that, as president, he had the authority to confiscate the property of rebels.[8] And, near the end of his life, he approved Major General William T. Sherman's famous Special Field Order

No. 15, which set aside about 400,000 acres of prime farmland for redistribution to the freedpeople in a wide swath along the coasts of South Carolina, Georgia, and Florida.[9] But then he was gone.

Lincoln did not live to see the rise of the Black Codes in the fall of 1865, which reenslaved Black southerners in all but name and forced moderates in Congress to radicalize their approach to Reconstruction. So we do not know if he would have further empowered freedpeople to own their own land.[10] We do know that Lincoln's successor firmly opposed any form of equality for African Americans and boldly acted on his convictions.

Andrew Johnson, who fought a reactionary war with Congress over the course of Reconstruction, used his presidential powers decisively and effectively to block almost all possibility of federal support for the creation of an African American yeomanry. He negated congressional land confiscation by liberally bestowing presidential pardons. He countermanded Sherman's military orders to distribute acreage. He blocked the maneuverings of Freedmen's Bureau officials who offered creative support for freedmen's quest for land. And he finally sidelined the most committed land reformers, men like Brigadier General Rufus Saxton, replacing them with reliable bureaucrats who shared his own intention to alter as little as possible about the southern economic status quo.[11] Johnson changed American history, guaranteeing that emancipation was chained to economic dependency.[12]

Faced by Johnson's determination and their own internal disagreements, the voting majority of Republican congressmen abandoned the idea of meaningful compensation for slavery and of economic independence for the most loyal Unionists in the South. In September 1865, a month after Johnson rescinded Sherman's land grant, Representative Thaddeus Stevens attempted thoroughgoing land reform one last time, proposing to confiscate the land of the wealthiest 10 percent of southern landowners and sell it in forty-acre lots at low prices to freedpeople. Stevens argued that independent Black farm owners would be "the support and guardians of republican liberty." With the land, they could protect themselves from their former masters. But few in Congress supported his plan. The moderates in their ranks ultimately could not bring themselves to undermine property rights, even those of defeated rebels. Instead, they decided that African Americans needed only the vote to protect their own rights and privileges as citizens.[13]

While it is patently obvious that political and economic autonomy intertwine, and each is vulnerable without the other, historical figures felt compelled to choose between them. And so historians have continued the debates of Recon-struction over the decades, with many historians agreeing with this generation's foremost interpreter of Reconstruction, Eric Foner, that Congress had chosen well in prioritizing the ballot over land. According to this reading of events, the Civil War had speeded the process of industrialization and the displacement of small craftsmen and small farmers. The day of Republican free-soil ideology was passing quickly even as congressmen debated whether to apply these values to the freedpeople. According to Foner: "Historical experience and modern scholarship suggest that acquiring small plots of land would hardly, by itself, have solved the economic plight of black families. The fate of the white yeomanry would soon demonstrate the precariousness of small farmers' hold on their land in the postwar South."[14] How, the land-reform critics ask, could we expect former slaves to build a meaningful freedom from small-parcel landownership under such conditions.[15]

But another monumental historian of Reconstruction disagreed. To "have given each one of the million Negro free families a forty-acre freehold," wrote W. E. B. Du Bois, "would have made a basis of real democracy in the United States that might easily have transformed the modern world." And the historian William McFeely believed that if the southern planter class had been forced to pay three hundred years of back wages in the form of land, "perpetual debt" and virtual reenslavement would not have become the central story of postwar Afri-can American history. In the context of contemporary debates over reparations, economist William Darity Jr. has taken the arguments of Du Bois and McFeely one step further: "Had such a racial land reform taken place in the United States during the late 1860s, it is easy to envision that the vast current differences in wealth between blacks and nonblacks would not exist."[16]

To guess what Lincoln might have done, we have to engage in fruitless coun-terfactual speculation. Fortunately, we do not have to do so to learn what land-ownership might have meant to the freedpeople. Their struggle to own land did not end with the betrayal of the federal government or the withdrawal of federal troops. By 1900, a quarter of African American farmers had come to own the land they worked. Even as the number of farm owners began to decline in the 1920s, landownership remained a durable aspiration for many African Amer-icans, as demonstrated by the interviews in the Breaking New Ground collec-tion, the oral-history project we codirect.[17] Yet these surprising facts impose no clear narrative, in part, because the story of African American farm owners is an understudied field with much left to be learned and, in part, because of the ambiguity and variety of their experience. The story of farm ownership among African Americans calls for cautious interpretation. Reflecting the overall story of American farm owners during these years, it is neither a celebratory narrative of economic opportunity and political equality nor a dismal and somber tale of chronic impoverishment and civic disengagement. The costs and benefits varied from state to state and from family to family, depending on the broad historical context and the narrow family and community circumstances that shaped their tenure. For many, owning land gave them power to make meaningful choices: to plant food crops instead of staple crops, or to send their children to school or withdraw them as labor. Many farm owners and their descendants have testified that this widened degree of choice improved the quality of their lives on the farm under the Jim Crow regime and launched their descendants toward more desirable professional and business careers in towns and cities. African American landowners, then, stood as a rebuke to Jim Crow and a reminder of what emancipation could and should have achieved for American society.

So we have at least a partial answer to the question, what if African Americans had begun freedom with the economic resources to build their rural American dream? What if Lincoln had been able to include Black people in his Republican vision of a virtuous, democratic society springing up from the soil of small family farms?

CLOSED DOORS

For the first two generations of freedom, landownership seems to have been the widest economic path forward for the largest number of people, but only because all other paths were even more blocked. Even as the freedpeople petitioned Reconstruction officials for land, their former owners began to devise methods to deny it to them. By the fall of 1865, planters in Mississippi and South Carolina had devised the blunt instrument of the Black Codes to maintain African Americans as a dependent and dependable work force for staple-crop production. Edmund Rhett, a South Carolina planter who helped draft his state's codes, wrote a friend that the former slave "should be kept as near to his former condition as Law can keep him." Accordingly, his first proposed law would prohibit "all Freedmen . . . from ever holding or owning real Estate in South Carolina, or their posterity after them." Rhett wrote that this act was "essential in order to uproot the idea which has now run the negroes crazy all over this state—namely that they are all to have forty acres of their own." If that idea took root, he continued, "they will never work for the white man, or upon any land but their own." Therefore, the white elite's monopoly on land was "the most vital Law that can be made for our future prospering."[18] Not trusting in the efficacy of law, white vigilantes across the South began carrying out violent campaigns against both African Americans who bought land and the white people who sold it to them.[19]

In the decades following Reconstruction's disappointments, Black farmers who aspired to improve their circumstances faced not only their region's poverty but also disfranchisement, lynching, limited education, and the endless ways that landlords could rob them of their share of the crop. Most freedpeople found themselves transformed into wage laborers or sharecroppers, with white landlords dictating what they could plant, controlling their access to credit, keeping the books, and enjoying legal rights to the crop their tenants produced.[20]

While sharecropping became ever more entrenched as an institution ensnaring landless southerners regardless of color, small farm owners in the South and the Great Plains faced new difficulties in holding on to their land. From the late 1870s through the 1890s, falling farm prices sank them deeper into debt. Federal policies added to their troubles, as high tariffs protected manufacturers but forced farmers to pay more for factory-produced goods. Federal hard-money policies made currency scarce, forcing farmers to pay off their heavy debts with a deflated money supply. To make matters worse, Redemption-era state legislatures gradually repealed safeguards that had traditionally protected yeoman farmers. These included the homestead exemption, which protected farmers from losing their homes because of debt, and the open range, which made it harder for small farmers to remain self-sufficient.[21]

As thousands lost their land, farmers embraced the old agrarian ideas of economic and political cooperation with a new desperation. Beginning in the mid-1870s, they formed a multitude of state-level organizations, which coalesced into the national Farmers' Alliance, the white-only Southern Farmers' Alliance, and the Colored Farmers' National Alliance and Co-Operative Union, founded in Houston County, Texas, in 1886. At the height of its six-year history, the Colored Alliance counted perhaps one million members.[22]

Most of the leaders of the Colored Alliance were farm owners like Isaiah Williams, a graduate of Hampton Institute who owned 160 acres in South Carolina. "My aim is farming and merchandise," he reported in a publication about Hampton alumni.[23] Men like Williams needed the leverage of a mass movement, so they invited propertyless farmers to join.[24] Across the South, local chapters of the Colored Alliance promoted self-help, improved farming methods, and mutual aid, much as the other branches of the movement did. They encouraged farmers to avoid liquor and debt and to raise their own food. They organized teaching demonstrations, and established alternate institutions for buying supplies, marketing their crops, and making a living. The chapters set up farming exchanges and cooperatives, such as the three hundred members of an alliance in Eatonton, Georgia, who worked to open a general merchandise store.[25] With ten thousand members, the Colored Farmers' Alliance of Richmond, Burke and Columbia Counties in Georgia raised $100,000, most likely through dues and donations, to open an alliance store in Augusta.[26] Another group in Wateree, South Carolina, established a molasses mill.[27] Some chapters also established financial institutions, including one in Charleston that worked to establish a bank with $100,000 of starting capital.[28]

When they emphasized self-help activities, the Colored Alliance reflected the programs of the white alliances, but unlike them, their economic critique included a consciousness of racism. As one Colored Alliance leader declared: "We perform the greater part of the manual labor of the South, and we see the fruits thereof, but very seldom enjoy them as we should. We see the white man growing fat by our toil." Drawing upon a masculine ideal, he continued: "Certainly we are responsible for walking in the dust, with our wives and children following us, while we are making our way wearily to church after a hard week's work. Meanwhile, our merchant and master carries his family in a fine vehicle, drawn by fast stock."[29] Accordingly, the alliance engaged in political agitation to protest injustices that disproportionately targeted Black people, including the convict-lease system, segregated facilities, lynching, the poll tax, the exclusion of Black jurors from cases involving Black defendants, and the corrupt election process that held sway in many of their communities.[30] Because they represented such a challenge to the status quo, the Colored Alliance conducted some of its work in secret through a network of African American churches and other institutions.[31]

In addition to its critique of racism, the Colored Alliance far more forcefully defended the interests of landless farmers than did the white alliances. They promoted landownership and homeownership for tenants to "prevent their being at the mercy of the landlords by placing them in homes of their own."[32] The boldest action of the Colored Farmers' Alliance was the cotton-picking strike that they called for September 12, 1891, "as the day upon which all our people shall cease from and absolutely stop picking cotton, except their own, and shall pick no more before about November 1, unless their just demands for wages shall be sooner acceded to by planters and others interested."[33] This extraordinary move was only sporadically implemented, but it led to severe repression by the planters and the dissolution of the Colored Alliance in 1892.[34]

Before that happened, however, all the strands of the Farmers' Alliance movement united to form the national People's, or Populist, Party during an 1890 meeting in Ocala, Florida. The creation of the Populist Party had special significance for the members of the Colored Farmers' Alliance because, as a convention in Richmond, Virginia, put it, the Alliance resolved that "the salvation of the colored man rests not in either of the old political parties, and that he is no longer a slave to them. . . . We are uniting to protect ourselves and wives and children, and to build up enterprises among ourselves, and thus free the toiling masses of our race from the deadly fangs of . . . liens, rings, and trust companies."[35]

Yet the Populists' interracial coalition was pulled apart by racism and the divergence of interests between landlords and tenants. For instance, Georgia's white Populists, who were mainly yeoman farmers and small planters, supported the poll tax and the crop-lien system that hurt so many sharecroppers and tenant farmers.[36] Regardless of these differences, the cross-racial unity achieved by voters so threatened the southern merchant class that they defeated them with violence and widespread voter fraud, then divided them with a white supremacist call for full Jim Crow segregation and disfranchisement.[37] The destruction of Populism must have left many African Americans agreeing with an Alabamian quoted by Booker T. Washington in 1900: "I ain't got but six feet of land, and I is got to die to git dat."[38] At the same time, the Colored Alliance and the Populist movement had a tremendous influence on African Americans' economic strategies, political connections, and the cooperative spirit that sustained them in their quest for land during the first two decades of the twentieth century.[39]

Landed independence remained an aspiration for Black southerners, even after the economic volatility and political defeats of the late nineteenth century, in part because opportunities outside of agriculture were even more limited. Most nonagricultural jobs for African American men lay in menial labor, earning the lowest wages and with little chance of upward mobility. Meanwhile, Black women found work off the farm as domestic workers and laundresses. In the late nineteenth century, they made up nine-tenths of domestic servants in southern cities. Washerwomen in Atlanta struck for higher wages in 1881, gaining important concessions from their employers. Yet as the historian Jacqueline Jones argues, they still made "the meagerest wages" because "they had virtually no other employment opportunities."[40] A family could patch together a livelihood when both parents and the older children sought out this kind of work, but it did not afford much for savings, much less economic independence.

There were other, better-paying jobs to be sure. An estimated 80 percent of all southern artisans in 1865 were African American. But at the turn of the twentieth century, Du Bois launched a series of sociological conferences at Atlanta University and determined that competition from white artisans and the prejudice of white employers had driven most African American workmen from the high-skilled positions or had forced them to work for half the wages that similarly skilled white workers were paid.[41] Some jobs truly could support a family in modest comfort. But there were too few openings in the ranks of ironworkers, coalminers, Pullman porters, and skilled seamstresses to offer a path forward for the masses. A tiny business and professional class continued to grow from its origins in the antebellum period, but an overabundance of systemic racism and a paucity of paying customers meant that this could not be the way out for many. Meanwhile, in the North, racist labor unions blocked Black migrants from access to the new industrial jobs that were providing some economic opportunity for European immigrants. As an African American newspaper in Kansas put it in 1899, "They hang the Negro in the South, but they aren't so bad in the North; they just simply starve him to death by labor unions."[42]

NONGOVERNMENT PATHWAYS TO LAND

So, although the road to landownership was hard, for two generations after emancipation, it was the most important single pathway toward economic security for the majority of African Americans. Sometimes alone, and sometimes combined with urban trades and professions, or even with part-time domestic work or agricultural wage labor, farm ownership was the livelihood in which the largest number of African Americans were not entirely dependent on white employers. As Loren Schweninger's pathbreaking study has demonstrated, African American farm ownership began in the colonial period, grew very slowly through the antebellum period and the immediate aftermath of slavery, and then surged from the 1880s until about 1920, decades in which white yeomen were losing their own grip on the land.[43] In 1870, only 5 percent of African American farmers owned their farms, and a disproportionate number of these had previously been free people of color, with educations and kinship ties to white patrons.[44] But by 1900, 24 percent had become landowners, the great majority of whom were former slaves.[45] By 1910, over 200,000 Black families had risen to landowner status, owning more than fifteen million acres, almost equal in size to the state of West Virginia (see fig. 6.1). How did these new arrivals navigate their way to landownership against the opposing currents of poverty, inadequate schooling, and violence?[46]

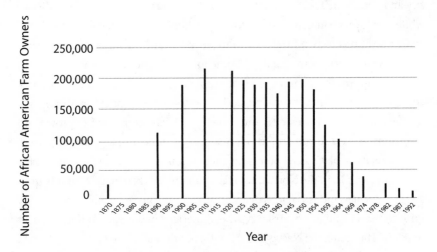

Figure 6.1. African American Farmers and Landownership, 1870–1992
Sources: For 1870, 1890, and 1900 data: Schweninger, *Black Property Owners,* 174; for data after 1900, *Agricultural Census.*

In the first generation of freedom, many people worked cooperatively with others in their community to obtain land because planters preferred to sell their land as a block instead of as smaller, more affordable plots. Sometimes, African American churches organized communities to pool their resources and purchase entire plantations before subdividing them in proportion to the amount of money each family put up. For example, in 1866, the freedpeople of Hampton, Virginia, founded the Lincoln's Land Association. Under the leadership of Reverend William Thornton, the association bought several hundred acres locally.[47] Later, in the 1870s and 1880s, some ministers led their congregations into wilderness areas of Texas, where they squatted on unclaimed land.[48] Pastors from Tennessee and elsewhere helped organize the Exoduster movement to claim homesteads in Kansas, Oklahoma, and Colorado beginning in 1879.[49] Black veterans of the Union army likewise purchased land cooperatively by bundling their bounties, back pay, and savings as squads, companies, and regiments. The men of twenty Black regiments pooled their money to buy land in different parts of Louisiana, including one regiment that raised $50,000 to buy four or five plantations along the banks of the Mississippi.[50] Across the South, freedmen also formed independent land associations, bought blocks of land, and then subdivided it. In the fall of 1865, African Americans in northeastern Georgia pooled their resources to buy property locally. An officer of the Freedmen's Bureau advised them to purchase land in southwestern Georgia instead, which had better soil and was more sparsely settled, so the group sent two of their leaders to scout for land there. With the assistance of another Freedmen's Bureau official, they contracted to buy a 2,200-acre plantation. A few months later, 150 pioneers made the two-hundred-mile trek to southwestern Georgia, began to farm, and set aside money to care for the elderly and build a school. Another nine hundred people followed them. Their community was highly active politically, sending uncompromising representatives to the state legislature and even organizing a militia to defend themselves. Yet this ambitious community does not seem to have survived Reconstruction.[51]

Lumber and railroad companies provided yet another means for the formation of all-Black farm-owning communities. In Arkansas, from the 1880s through the 1920s, lumber companies pursued a policy of "cut out and get out," completing these projects with unwanted land on their hands.[52] In some places, they offered their lumber workers land in lieu of wages. As sawmill crews were segregated, this policy also fostered segregated settlements.[53]

However African American farmers acquired land, they developed their own approach to land use. Rarely did they fully rationalize their property toward production for the market, as increasing numbers of white farmers did. Rather, according to the criticisms of Freedmen's Bureau officers during Reconstruction and the praise of rural sociologists and agricultural-extension agents in the twentieth century, they dedicated a higher proportion of their acreage to subsistence crops than did white farmers.[54] Yet with few exceptions, the evidence suggests that African Americans sought both subsistence and marketable crops and that, when they purchased it together, they almost always divided the property among themselves to farm separately. Traditions of neighborly cooperation and kinship often bound these communities together, but the land was operated at the unit of the family, not by the entire community.[55] Frequently, Black land associations drew up carefully worded contracts that distributed varying amounts of acreage on the basis of the investment of members.[56] Sometimes, wealthier Black individuals bought land, either singly or in concert with others, and resold it in parcels at a profit to poorer farmers in their community.[57] Later in the nineteenth century, communal purchasing became rarer. Instead, nuclear or extended families worked together to buy land. Sometimes grown brothers bought land together, worked it together until they paid it off, and then subdivided it between them.[58]

While not communal anticapitalists, African American farm owners represent something equally interesting: a core of Black separatism in rural America. When General Sherman met with representatives of freedpeople in Savannah in 1864 to ask what their people wanted, these men told him that they wanted land of their own, preferably separate from white people.[59] In the decades that followed, organizers of all-Black towns in the West, as well as newspaper editors and the influential Tuskegee leadership, invited aspiring landowners to take part in the building of vibrant, free communities rising from the soil.[60]

After Reconstruction, much variation appeared in the strategies African Americans used to gain land. They were deeply opportunistic, adopting any form of agriculture that would pay, taking any pathway, and making any sacrifice. When separatism afforded opportunity, they formed cooperatives to buy a space of their own. When white patrons opened a door to ownership, they seized on these means as well, cultivating relationships with these landowners to buy a corner of their estate—sometimes after working it as tenants for decades.

Much variation appears between states. In central Florida, African Americans found early success with citrus crops. Later, with some guidance from county extension agents, they raised produce to ship cooperatively to northern cities. In time, half of all Black Florida farmers worked their own land.[61] West Virginia coalmines drew Black farmers from surrounding states who hoped to raise money to buy land back home. But with encouragement from the state government, they began to invest instead in small plots of land in West Virginia. Although fewer than 1,000 Black farmers lived in the state, and their holdings remained small, nearly 80 percent of them became owners, a higher percentage than in any other state.[62] In late-nineteenth-century North Carolina, African American farmers were able to purchase land from turpentine producers that had tapped out the trees and were eager to sell it and move on to fresh pine forests in Georgia, Alabama, and Florida.[63] In Arkansas, African American farmers seemed to find their path to land without much personal aid from white planters, while in plantation-belt Georgia, paternalistic assistance seemed necessary to break down local hostility to the economic independence of Black farm owners.[64] And, beyond the South, Black farm-owning communities were sprinkled across the Midwest.[65]

There were some region-wide themes of land acquisition. After emancipation, some former masters gave portions of their estates to a few favored slaves or, on truly rare occasions, to all of their former slaves.[66] The sociologist Gerald Jaynes argues that "the practice" of giving land to freedpeople "was widespread, if not deep." A Missouri freedman, interviewed by the Works Progress Administration in the 1930s, agreed: "I do know some of dem old slave owners to be nice enough to start der slaves off in freedom wid somethin' to live on . . . but dey wasn't in droves, I tell you."[67]

Some white southerners found it expedient to sell small portions of their land to freedpeople to keep them close as a pool of seasonal labor. An Edisto Island planter, in an address to the Agricultural Society of South Carolina, called for a Black "laboring class to be settled with their little farms around our broad acres; with their little comforts, their cow, pig and poultry," satisfied with their station in life and "always at hand to hire you their services in cultivating your fields and attend you to the ballot-box in support of intelligence and honesty."[68] An attitude of self-interest among Sea Island planters made African American landownership—albeit in very small plots—more widespread in this area than in any other part of the Deep South.[69]

Particularly in the long-settled eastern portions of the South, some tenants also relied on kinship ties and close connections with well-heeled white landowners who advanced funds or ran interference for them when they were bidding on land. In central Georgia and elsewhere, some white fathers successfully willed land to their interracial children. When state laws forbade bequeathing property to children born out of wedlock, white fathers sometimes sold their estates for a dollar or two to a friend, who would be trusted to later resell the estate to the original owner's children of color. White extended-family members in some cases provided other aid across racial lines, such as a bale of cotton, livestock, the free use of a plot of land, or crucial loans to help their Black kin begin the climb to landownership. Sometimes they simply acted as financial intermediaries, buying land to resell to their Black family members. Aid flowing through interracial kinship accounted disproportionately for the rise of the highest strata of the rural Black elite. For example, in 1910 the five wealthiest African Americans in Hancock County, Georgia, had received significant aid from white kin.[70] But obviously, having wealthy ancestors was not an advancement strategy that could be widely recommended for the masses.

In the absence of recognized ties to white kin or more effective and transformative state and federal support, the majority of freedpeople took matters into their own hands. As the second generation of freedom came of age, African Americans increasingly sought land as nuclear or sometimes extended families, combining the earning powers of all the relatives. As Sharon Ann Holt's study of Granville County, North Carolina, suggests, most freedpeople acquired land after slow but steady capital accumulation. Working together, sharecropping families made money little by little by marketing eggs, garden vegetables, butter, cream, and homebrewed wines and liquors. The widely acknowledged withdrawal of women's labor from the fields was a strategy freedpeople enacted so that women could concentrate their efforts on this household economy. Children also contributed to this capital accumulation by working in the fields and gardens and by gathering berries, grapes, pecans, and other edibles. Supplying their own household goods by "living out of the garden" served both short- and long-term goals. It improved their day-to-day living by supplementing the meager and seasonal pay of sharecropping, freed them from the trap of debt, and helped them accumulate capital to invest in land. In addition to using cash on hand, freedpeople leveraged merchants' new instruments of credit to their own advantage when they could, using chattel mortgages to fund land acquisition.[71] As they assembled the down payment, families usually timed their attempted leap to farm ownership for when they could employ the labor of both parents as well as a number of children old enough to plow. Individuals did not rise to landowner status, families did.

Some farms maintained a clear sexual division of labor, with men plowing and planting, women weeding and hoeing, both harvesting, and all the children leveling up from about the age of five into increasingly responsible labor. On tobacco farms, the youngest children were initiated into the family vocation with the most unpleasant task: crushing tobacco hornworms by hand before they could devour the valuable leaves. Ruth Royster, who was raised on a farm in North Carolina, allowed that all of her chores were demanding, "but chopping the tobacco and pulling the suckers," she explained, "that was the worst."[72] On cotton farms, everyone—woman, man, girl, and boy—worked the harvest. "I loved to pick cotton," declared Naomi James, who grew up on a Louisiana farm during the 1940s and 1950s. Her grandparents paid her $2.50 for every 100 pounds she picked, and she averaged 150 to 200 pounds a day. James also made money for school clothes or to help her family with expenses by harvesting corn and cotton "for white folks in the community."[73]

Families also strategically accumulated cash for a down payment through seasonal paid farm work, construction work, or occasional labor on the railroads. The family history of Carl Hodges illustrates this point. His grandfather, Samuel Hodges, took advantage of some northern businessmen's need for labor during the early years of Reconstruction in order to gain two hundred acres of land. These businessmen built a cotton mill in North Carolina and bought woodland to fuel their operation. "My grandfather was working for them, driving the wagon and horses and what have you," Carl Hodges explained. "They asked him to find somebody that . . . would cut the wood and haul it to the mill. Grandpa made a deal with them. If they give him the land, he would cut the wood. So he took my father and his youngest brother, Andrew, and cut the wood at night and hauled it to the mill and that's how he got the land to start with." Carl's grandfather told him that he had worked a double shift, cutting wood at night and hauling it to the mill, where he continued working a day shift. His focus and sacrifice was representative of that of many first-generation Black land owners.[74]

African Americans who lived near towns or cities had additional means of earning money to buy or maintain a farm: public work in town or truck farming. In 1898, Du Bois studied Black landowners on small five- to thirty-five-acre farms in one Virginia village. He learned that they supported themselves in part by working in a nearby town. Women along the Georgia coast bought their own farms with money they made by carrying shellfish, fish, fruit, handwoven mats and brooms, and garden produce for sale in nearby towns.[75] Generally, the more urban a state was, the higher a percentage of its Black farmers achieved landownership.

Women were central to African American land acquisition. Their household production and sale of surplus farm products saved money and provided capital for down payments. During the Jim Crow era, boys were generally pulled out of school early to plow, so women developed greater literacy, which enabled them to read contracts and deeds for family members who could not read. Members of Black farm-owning families generally described their parents as a collaborative team, with joint decisions being represented publicly as those of the husband, whose masculine identity gave him greater public power.[76]

Nate Shaw, in his famous oral history, repeatedly affirmed the key role his wife, Hannah, played as they climbed from sharecropping to landownership together as a young couple in Alabama during the first decades of the twentieth century. Whereas Nate was illiterate, he recognized that Hannah had "a pretty good education," so "she transacted my business after me and her married." As an old man looking back, he recalled: "Sometimes she'd say, 'Darlin, you know what's best to do. But you can't decide *what* to do until you knows every side of the proposition. And bein that you can't read and write, it's profitable for us all for you to make me your partner.'" Shaw recognized that Hannah "was valuable" to him. "I told her, one day and many a time, 'I'm married to you. And I think my best business should be in your hands. If anybody knows the ins and outs of it, you the one to know.' She was in a way of speakin, the *eyes,* and I was the mouthpiece."[77] Shaw's observation holds generally for African American farm-owning families. The Breaking New Ground project also recast some women as family leaders, not just partners. Interviewees reported their grandmothers and mothers running the farm with their children while the men in their lives held jobs on other farms, in construction, or on the railroad. Rachel Petty, who grew up in Richland County, South Carolina, said that her grandmother found, negotiated, and purchased her family's farm, running it with the help of her children and workers hired during the harvest season while Petty's grandfather traveled around the South as a brick mason. Her work as a farmer was not a directive from her husband but a life that she initiated herself.[78]

Another strategy that mixed a variety of income streams and contributions from all household members was dual tenure, the practice of holding more than one form of land tenure that African American farmers first embraced during Reconstruction. On their own farms, families engaged in the practice of maintaining gardens for their own subsistence in ways reminiscent of how their ancestors had survived during slavery. At the same time, they raised cash crops on other people's land under sharecropping or tenant-farming arrangements. For example, in Brookhaven, Mississippi, Robert Robinson's father, N. Z., bought forty acres of land during the 1940s. "All this was wooded," he recalled. "We had to clear it. Until we got this place cleared enough, he rented land." Harold Carter, who was born in 1948 and grew up in the Shiloh community of Gaston County, Florida, marveled at how his father juggled two farms. In addition to running his own operation, Fred Carter managed a one-hundred-acre farm for a white landowner who had three hundred head of cattle. "It was amazing how . . . he worked there in the daytime on them and then he come back home in the afternoon and he ran his farm."[79] Because these farmers tended to have their own tools and work stock, dual tenure enabled them to enter into more favorable rental arrangements with landowners than could those who were strictly sharecroppers. It also allowed Black farm owners to fly under the radar of racists bent on intimidating or meting out violence on those who dared to own land. By continuing to work as tenant farmers or sharecroppers, they were able to mitigate some of the dangers of appearing too successful or "uppity" to their white neighbors.[80]

African American families who sought land generally had to accept what white society was willing to begrudge them. So like Robinson's father, they had to make do with land that had not yet been cleared of trees, was deemed too rocky or sandy, or was considered too poor for use by white farmers. Others had to take the risk of farming in bottomland, where the rich, alluvial soil promised flourishing harvests, but the proximity to waterways promised floods every few years that would wash away their crops. They also frequently had to work farms that lay deep in the woods, were isolated from the main roads and out of sight from white society, or were inaccessible in rainy seasons.[81]

THE STATISTICAL ACHIEVEMENTS OF BLACK FARM OWNERS

Most Black farm-owning families also emphasized the role of hard work as a key to their success. But table 6.1 below, showing the great variation in the percentage of landed Black families in each state, demonstrates that, although it was no doubt important, hard work could not have been the critical factor. In Virginia, 67 percent of Black farmers had come to own land by 1910. Meanwhile, in Georgia, only 12.8 percent did. Clearly, Black farmers in Virginia did not work five times harder than those in Georgia.[82]

Table 6.1. Black-Owned Farms in 1910

State	Black Farm Owners as % of All Black Farmers	State	Total Black-Owned Acres	State	Number of Black Farm Owners
West Virginia	78.8	Mississippi	2,227,314	Virginia	32,228
Maryland	74.1	Texas	1,866,293	Mississippi	25,026
Virginia	67.0	Oklahoma	1,600,025	North Carolina	21,443
Missouri	57.5	Alabama	1,467,344	Texas	21,232
Oklahoma	53.9	Virginia	1,382,581	South Carolina	20,372
Kentucky	50.5	Georgia	1,350,028	Alabama	17,082
Florida	49.6	Arkansas	1,203,750	Georgia	15,698
North Carolina	32.7	North Carolina	1,196,519	Arkansas	14,662
Texas	30.4	South Carolina	1,098,051	Oklahoma	11,150
Tennessee	27.9	Louisiana	834,405	Louisiana	10,725
Arkansas	23.1	Tennessee	590,640	Tennessee	10,700
South Carolina	21.0	Florida	458,314	Florida	7,298
Louisiana	19.5	Kentucky	255,540	Kentucky	5,929
Alabama	15.5	Maryland	142,109	Maryland	4,599
Mississippi	15.2	Missouri	131,602	Missouri	2,109
Georgia	12.8	West Virginia	25,947	West Virginia	558
Regional Average	**24.7**	**Total**	**15,259,420**	**Total**	**220,811**

Source: US Bureau of the Census, *Thirteenth Census of the United States, 1910,* vols. 6 and 7, *Agriculture, 1909 and 1910* (Washington, DC: US Census Office, 1913). "Farm owners" included part owners who farmed their own land and rented additional land to farm. For more information on definitions in the census, see note 45.

Overall, the Upper South had more widespread Black ownership of property, at 44 percent, but a smaller average farm size, at fifty acres in comparison to the Deep South's 19 percent and eighty acres. The plantation belt, with its large African American population, held the majority of Black farm owners and Black-owned acreage. Five states (Virginia, Mississippi, North Carolina, Texas, and South Carolina) contained 120,301 Black farm owners, more than the rest of the country combined. And four states (Mississippi, Texas, and Oklahoma, and Alabama) held nearly half of the nation's total of Black-owned land.[83]

Why did African Americans fare so much better in their quest for land in some states than in others? In large part, the answer lies in the overall opportunity structure of a state. In general, those with low percentages of white farm ownership had even lower levels of Black ownership.[84] And poor Black and white farmers struggled to get land wherever cotton dominated.[85] Cotton required larger plots for competitive farming, making it more difficult for landless farmers to purchase land in cotton-dominant states. White cotton planters also tended to hold on to their land longer than tobacco or rice growers did, making less land available for sale.

THE CHANGING PUBLIC PERCEPTION OF BLACK FARM OWNERS

In the late nineteenth century, African American scholars and activists regularly cited the rise of farm ownership and literacy as the clinching evidence of Black people's ability to thrive in freedom.[86] Of course, Booker T. Washington championed the ongoing expansion of rural Black economic independence through his writings and speeches as well as through the Tuskegee Institute's farmers' conferences and its newspaper, *The Negro Farmer*. Each edition of *The Negro Farmer* celebrated accounts of Black men and women across the South who had used their resourcefulness and self-discipline to gain economic independence on their own land and, with it, opportunity for their children and the respect of their community. In 1913, at the fiftieth anniversary of the Emancipation Proclamation, African American farm ownership took pride of place in civic celebrations and publications nationwide. Monroe Work, the sociologist who headed Tuskegee's Department of Records and Research, produced a widely consulted publication, *Fifty Years of Negro Progress*. This book pointed out that Black-owned property at emancipation had been worth $20 million nationwide. But fifty years later it was worth $700 million. Of that total, the value of Black-owned farms and farm buildings in 1913 stood at $273 million. When $36 million in farm machinery was added to it—largely owned by Black farm owners—the total surpassed 40 percent of all Black-owned property. If livestock is added to the total—and again, farm owners disproportionately owned this—the total could rise above half of all Black wealth in America.[87] And in 1913, the trajectory pointed toward more of the same. After all, the value of Black-owned land had increased almost 177 percent between 1900 and 1910.

Some white observers celebrated the rise of Black agricultural independence at venues like the first Mohonk Conference on the Negro Question in 1890.[88]

But fear-mongering white observers argued that the rapid expansion of African American farm ownership would quickly dispossess small white farmers across the South. In 1913, Clarence Poe, editor of *The Progressive Farmer,* launched a region-wide campaign to impose rural segregation explicitly to prevent such an outcome.[89] But Poe's fear was Kelly Miller's hope. Miller, a Howard University sociologist, wrote in 1904 that Black residents were already replacing white farmers in the Deep South. He welcomed "separateness rather than separation" and imagined a prosperous Black farm-owning civilization rising up from the soil that white planters and poor whites were abandoning.[90] Miller's rural Black-separatist vision dovetailed with the economically independent Black civilization that Washington was boostering and that was taking shape in all-Black towns scattered across the South but heavily concentrated in Texas, Oklahoma, Kansas, and Nebraska.[91]

Then the story of African American progress took an unexpected turn. Just as World War I witnessed the peaking of African American farm ownership, the war also opened new opportunities, and the Great Migration shifted popular and scholarly attention from the fields to the cities. While the Harlem Renaissance bloomed and African Americans went to work for Henry Ford, Black farm owners stumbled through decades of a deepening economic quagmire: eternally falling cotton prices, increasing competition globally and from domestic agribusiness, the mounting hostility of the USDA, and apparently even the wrath of God, made manifest in weevils, floods, and droughts. Astute observers took note. Although he had begun the study of African American farm ownership in the nineteenth century, after the Great Migration, Du Bois stopped paying them attention. At about the same time, Marcus Garvey came to the United States. He had been planning to meet with Washington in preparation for launching a Tuskegee-inspired agricultural program in Jamaica. But when he arrived in 1916, Washington was dead, and the Great Migration was exploding, so he instead focused his attention on opportunities in New York City, although ironically, as Mary Rolinson discovered, he drew the majority of his funding from the membership dues of rural Black southerners—including farm owners.[92]

OWNERS REMAINED DESPITE DECLINE

When the attention of the publishing world turned elsewhere, African American farm owners did not disappear, but they did decline in number—a bit faster than the decline in farmers overall—and the rising generation, marked by hopefully striving ex-slaves, transitioned in many families to generations of dutiful children and grandchildren doggedly clinging to the land and to their ancestors' dreams. The federal government never compensated for its original betrayal of the promise of forty acres of independence. But beginning in the late nineteenth century, it did provide limited support for those who continued to pursue lives on their own farms. Because African Americans were excluded from the original Morrill Act land-grant colleges in the South, in 1890, the USDA cooperated with existing agricultural-extension programs at Tuskegee and Prairie View A&M in Texas to fund additional agriculture departments and extension programs at selected Black colleges and universities. Passage of the Smith-Lever Act in 1914 expanded this extension work among African American farmers. These programs advised landless farmers in seeking land and tried to help landowners keep their holdings. Fanning out across rural space, home-demonstration agents and agricultural-extension agents helped communities maintain their hybrid strategies through programs that included marketing their produce cooperatively and sharing time at community canning centers.[93]

The New Deal, like Reconstruction, raised hopes that the federal government would enact land reform but quickly proved disappointing. Although a limited number of Black families obtained land through the Farm Security Administration, the more far-reaching consequence of the New Deal was to hasten the consolidation of agribusiness by giving America's largest farmers capital to invest in machinery. African Americans, overwhelmingly the smallest farm owners, faced stiffening competition from better-financed large farm owners.[94]

WHAT DIFFERENCE DID LAND MAKE?

So for fifty years after emancipation, farm ownership remained the primary hope of economic advancement for most African Americans. Working singly or cooperatively, they found ways to overcome the barriers of illiteracy, poverty, and white supremacy until they held approximately half of the wealth of Black America. In West Virginia, Maryland, and Virginia, almost 70 percent of African American farmers owned their own land, while in Missouri, Oklahoma, Kentucky, and Florida, over 50 percent did. Their accomplishments received pride of place in the defenses of Black potential mounted by African American intellectuals and spokespersons. But how significant were Black farm owners,

given that they declined both in numbers and in prestige in the decades following
World War I. What difference did landownership make in the lives of the men
and women who sought this rural version of the American dream? And did it
leave a lasting impression in the story of American equality?

Owning land did not exempt Black farmers from the humiliations and social
costs of Jim Crow. Like other African Americans, they were denied the protection of the law and were subject to racist violence. Black farm owners were
barred from libraries, parks, and other all-white spaces and were segregated
on trains, buses, and in movie theaters. Their schools were underfunded, with
graduates having difficulty finding remunerative work. Away from their farms,
Black landowners faced the casual humiliations of the southern caste system.
Indeed, they may have had to demonstrate their acceptance of the etiquette of
white supremacy in word and gesture more assiduously than did others, to signal
that their personal privilege of property did not pose a direct threat to white
supremacy generally. They were generally disfranchised, although in some areas
they continued to exercise their right to vote throughout the Jim Crow period.
Black farm owners faced economic hurdles, being charged more for loans, lev-
ied higher taxes, and sometimes paid less for their agricultural products. These
hurdles often made it less feasible and desirable for them to hold on to their
land. With these liabilities, many Black farm owners struggled to save money or
to rise in material comfort. Truly, theirs was an ambiguous privilege, hemmed
in by the restrictions of racism and inequality. The racist limitations placed on
African American farm owners had consequences that extended beyond themselves. Although they shared class interests with similarly situated white farm
owners, the twisted ideology of Jim Crow prevented the two groups from finding
common cause in pushing for their economic, social, and political well-being.

QUALITY OF LIFE AND INDEPENDENCE

In many parts of the rural South, particularly on the richest parts of the plantation
belt, landlords insisted their tenants plant cotton right up to their porches and
buy all of their food at commissaries. So, many tenants and rural wage-laboring
families worked long hours, fed only with cornmeal, lard, and a bit of molasses.
High rates of pellagra and short lifespans resulted. In contrast, African American
farm owners always planted big gardens and frequently cultivated fruit orchards
and a variety of crops for their own tables. Willie Essick of southwest Georgia

expressed a refrain common among narrators in the Breaking New Ground collection: "Yes, we always had a garden. We always had cattle. We always had hogs. We always had stock. And let me explain to you. Back at that time, that's the way people lived." So farm owners suffered less hunger and fewer diseases from nutritional deficiencies than landless farmers did. Emmie Mae Harper, a rural schoolteacher, grew up on the 107 acres of sandy soil that her father had cleared to farm in the early twentieth century. She remembered him saying that their land provided "all they needed and some of what they wanted." And it did. According to Harper, "we didn't know nothing in the world about the grocery store."[95] John Fluker, a retired federal judge in Little Rock, was born into a self-sufficient family in 1936. They raised their own food, and his grandmother made family clothes by hand from cotton. "I have good memories of my childhood," he said. "We didn't have to go hungry even though it was the Depression. We never knew hard times. And folks who had property didn't."[96]

Yet the privilege of Black landowners was only relative. A North Carolina study found that white farm owners had more abundant and varied gardens than their African American counterparts, who nevertheless had more varied gardens than sharecroppers of any race. One Georgia study found that, among African American farmers in the piedmont, sharecroppers grew only half as much food as landowners did over the course of a year and ate only one-third the meat.[97] The quality of gardens and, of course, the overall quality of life varied from place to place depending on the time, size of the farming operation, quality of the terrain, and numerous other factors. Not all African American farm owners shared in the type of bounty Fluker's family enjoyed. Roy Anderson of Mississippi had trouble understanding how some made ends meet. "When I was a kid . . . there were some elderly neighbors had five acres, and that's all they farmed," he recalled. "Of course, we couldn't understand because my daddy had eighty acres here and forty acres here, but he had nine children. They were old men that had no one but themselves, but they had to farm to survive. They had five acres and they would plant corn and cotton on those five acres and that was their way of surviving. Now I don't know how much money that they was getting to plant that, but that was their only source of income."[98]

Having a stable home was another benefit of landownership—and another feature of life in a civil society that should have been a given. The stability, dignity, and permanence of homeownership meant a great deal to African American farm owners and their descendants. Lillian Glass Hunter embraced the advice her great-grandmother passed to her through her oldest uncle. The older woman had been an eight-year-old Tennessee slave at emancipation. If you own your own land, Hunter learned from her, "nobody can ask you to move."[99] Samuel Lee spoke of the value of having "a piece of land that you can call your own and nobody can put you off it. You don't have to worry about a man being able to tell you, 'I don't need you anymore.'"[100] A stable sense of home persisted in many families even long after they ceased farming. In recent decades, Black-owned farmland has become a magnet for far-flung members of extended families, as whoever has title has welcomed home kin as they retire from the North and offered lots on which to build homes.[101]

Black farm owners in the twentieth and twenty-first centuries resonated with the powerful sense of connection to place that had motivated so many newly emancipated slaves to demand a piece of the land that held their sweat and their ancestors' bones. Many of them cherished a sense of connection to their local communities. They took pride that their grandparents or great-grandparents had donated the land to build the local schools as well as the churches that continue to hold these rural communities together. They frequently held positions of honor and responsibility in their community, serving disproportionately as deacons or mothers of the church as their ancestors had a century ago.[102] Some spoke of their love of nature or connection to departed family members as they walked across fields or along streams that their forebears had known. Others prized their relationships with farm animals or took pride in watching the seeds they planted spring up out of the soil.

In the hundreds of interviews Breaking New Ground has conducted, African American farm owners and their descendants frequently expressed the meaning of land in terms of values that their family developed and passed on. They spoke of a fierce independence that landowners learned but that many tenants were denied. Roy Carter, who was raised on a family farm in Mississippi, put it this way: "The boss man say 'I'll take care of you,' and he would, but he wouldn't pay you nothing either." In contrast, his landowning grandfather "cherished the idea of being his own boss." According to Travis Benford of Texas, "Owning the land meant that nobody would ever tell me to quit doing what I'm doing that's important to me and my family to go do something that's important to him."[103] This independence had practical implications. Farm owners could gin their own cotton and market it without having to trust a landlord to report these transactions fairly. They could shop where they wanted and could keep their own books. Ownership gave them meaningful choices that helped them stay out of debt and maintain their independence. Personally meaningful choices like these were the bone and sinew of freedom.

VIOLENCE AND SELF-DEFENSE

Yet Black farm owners could be lynched. Sometimes jealous white neighbors targeted them specifically because of their material success. It is likely that the highest rates of violence against Black farm owners took place in the turbulent and poorly recorded decade following emancipation. And many more fell victim to white murderers and lynch mobs during the high tide of recorded white violence, the period from 1880 to 1920.[104] Yet in the lists of lynch victims compiled after 1882 by the *Chicago Tribune,* Tuskegee, and the National Association for the Advancement of Colored People (NAACP), the names of African American farm owners appear far less frequently than their proportion of the overall population.

This longstanding interpretive contradiction seems to have been finally resolved by a recent statistical study by the sociologists Amy Bailey and Stewart Tolnay. Their book *Lynched* has demonstrated that, of all African Americans in the South, farm owners were the safest from lynching, though only if they lived in areas where African American landownership was common. In contrast, of all African Americans in the South, they were the most in danger of being lynched when they lived in areas where whites saw them as an aberration. In addition to individually targeted lynchings, Black farm owners were also targeted by jealous poor whites in the whitecapping movement of the late nineteenth and early twentieth centuries. Finally, some were also swept up in the mass anti-Black pogroms that sometimes swept through a community, as happened in Wilmington, North Carolina; Rosewood and Oconee, Florida; Slocum, Texas; and Elaine, Arkansas.

Yet despite the danger they passed through, the great majority of African American farm owners interviewed for Breaking New Ground described having been unafraid of white people. Even people born in the early twentieth century claimed to have felt secure on their own land. About a dozen interviewees volunteered that they had heard their parents or grandparents talking about Black farm owners being lynched in their own time. Yet narrator after narrator shared that they thought of land as a sanctuary from the violence of the Jim Crow era.

Andre Vann reminisced that his family had "our own little kingdom" in Vance County, North Carolina. The county was about 80 percent African American, and Vann's entire community was owned by family or friends. "It was pretty safe," he remembered. "I always felt safe because I knew wherever I moved around in my neighborhood or outside the neighborhood, somebody always knew who I was." In the locally intimate setting of his rural community, "I've never had problems because they knew my family. They knew they didn't play." His family's reputation gave him a sense of protection. "I'll be honest," he said, "I never feared nobody where I went."[105]

EDUCATION

Black farm owners' greater autonomy also laid bare the educational inequalities of the Jim Crow era that have had far-reaching consequences. In the late nineteenth and early twentieth centuries, the education of African American children largely depended on the tuition and book expenses paid by parents. Black farm owners were better able to bear these costs as well as the cost of forgoing their children's labor while they attended school. Also, being freer from the coercive demands of white planters, they could choose whether or not to send their children to school at all. Most of them chose to educate their children longer than their landless neighbors did. Many even sent some of their children to board in town so that they could attend high school. As one learns by attending the family reunions and church anniversaries of Black farm owners, they also sent their grandchildren to college. The descendants of African American farm owners appear regularly in business, professional, and academic settings. Breaking New Ground even found landowning families from Georgia, Arkansas, and Florida in which members worked for NASA as mathematicians or engineers. Gary Grant of Tillery, North Carolina, grew up with "two distinct communities," the children of landowners and the children of sharecroppers. He estimated that 80 percent of the landowners' kids finished high school and 50–60 percent finished college. In contrast, the first descendant of Tillery's African American sharecroppers to attend college did so in 2003.[106] So the urban descendants of landowners actually carried with them heritages from the land—even from families who lost their property. They described their success as growing from their education as well as from a sense of confidence that they could find a way to achievement or make one.[107]

Because African American farm owners were permanent members of their community with the resources to build local institutions, their presence in rural spaces also aided non–farm owners. They established the country stores where neighbors could gather around wood-burning stoves and swap stories. They frequently donated pieces of land to build churches, lodges, and schools. In particular, landowners contributed heavily to the building of excellent Rosenwald high schools, when that building fund kicked off in 1917. Rosenwald administrators tended to place their schools in areas where there were a number of Black farm owners, apparently believing that these communities could most successfully follow through on the building campaigns and the maintenance of the facilities. In testimony from landowners and tenants alike, we also learned that some landowners provided aid during hard times to landless neighbors: a basket of produce for a widow, books or shoes for impoverished schoolchildren, or, on their farms or at the cotton gins, stores, and other rural businesses they founded, the opportunity to work for someone who was not white. By helping raise these institutions, farm owners lifted all those who shared the community with them.[108]

Much later, during the civil rights movement, they also continued to serve the common good by taking leading roles in rural spaces. Charles Payne, in his landmark study of the movement in Mississippi, found that African American landowners and their descendants were twice as likely as tenants to attend civil rights rallies early in the movement and four times more likely to register to vote. They also housed voter registrants in rural areas, where their farms stood like citadels during the struggle for fuller freedom against the shotgun culture of the planters and their allies. According to Diane Nash, who helped direct the Student Nonviolent Coordinating Committee as it organized in rural Mississippi, African American farm owners "were strong and bad, meaning they didn't back down."[109]

Their political activism did not emerge out of thin air in the 1960s. Certainly, Black farm owners were often disfranchised along with dependent farmers, as Du Bois found in Lowndes County, Alabama, in 1906. There, he learned that fifty "thrifty, striving men" who had bought land together had nonetheless been denied the vote.[110] But in other communities, African American landowners continued to vote throughout the Jim Crow era. Unlike sharecroppers, they often had the resources to pay the poll tax, the educational background to pass the literacy test (if honestly administered), and the patronage ties with white leaders. Where allowed to vote, their numbers at the polls were always small. But by continuing to vote for decades after disfranchisement, Black farm owners formed a living bridge between Reconstruction and the civil rights movement.[111]

LAND LOSS

Today, relatively few African Americans are involved in farming, and fewer than 49,000 farm their own land. Many overlapping reasons lowered their numbers even more precipitously than that of farmers generally. Some chose to leave agriculture. After World War I, rural young people of all races drained from the farms as new economic and social opportunities beckoned in the cities. Many young African Americans in particular said that farming—even if done independently— carried too much of the flavor of slavery and rural Jim Crow repression.

Others were forced off the land. The boll weevil, droughts, floods, a tightening global market for agricultural commodities, and the ongoing march of mechanized agribusiness led to farm bankruptcies, abandonments, and consolidations suffered by Black and white farmers alike. A disproportionate number of African American farmers avoided drafting formal wills. Their land was then shared equally among descendants, which contributed to dispossession through the forced partition of heirs' property.[112]

But African American farm owners also suffered from many racially targeted mechanisms for dispossession. Their inability to seek protection through the courts or local sheriff subjected them to livestock poisoning, violence, threats of violence, and records manipulation at the courthouse.[113] According to the historian Andrew Kahrl, during the Jim Crow era, county tax assessors overvalued property owned by African Americans, leading to tax delinquency for many Black landowners and cheap acquisitions for white speculators and developers.[114] The historian Justin Randolph uncovered a particularly egregious example of this in which a local sheriff and landowner in Mississippi falsely alleged that an African American landowner was behind in his taxes in order to buy the land and reap the benefits of the matured pines growing there.[115] Paradoxically, these practices only intensified during the 1960s, when the freedom struggle was at its height. Simultaneously, from the 1960s through the 1980s, local USDA administrators increasingly sabotaged African American farmers' hold on their land by denying or delaying their springtime planting loans.[116]

When, in 1999, North Carolina farmer Timothy Pigford led a class-action lawsuit against the USDA in *Pigford v. Glickman,* a federal district court ruled that the department had discriminated against Black farmers and called for damages to be paid amounting to nearly one billion dollars, the largest civil rights settlement in history.[117] To continue making reparations for generations of official discrimination, President Joe Biden's administration proposed to set aside four billion dollars in 2021 to help nonwhite farmers pay off their farm debts.[118]

CONCLUSION

Despite more than a century of contestation over land, the freedpeople and their descendants never experienced widespread landed independence. President Andrew Johnson's disastrous, history-altering reversals of Sherman's and Congress's land-reform measures represented the first of many betrayals that short-circuited democracy and denied African Americans any measure of restitution for centuries of slavery. Yet even if the federal government had supported widespread land reform, would that have "transformed the modern world" as Du Bois believed? The evidence provided by the lived experience of African American farm owners suggests a reading that falls between the optimism of Du Bois and the pessimism of Foner.

The emergence of industrial-capitalist agriculture after the Civil War unleashed a period of enclosure, dispossession, and consolidation, as wealthy farmers and industrialists expropriated land for large-scale agriculture and timber production, which only expanded over the course of the twentieth century. Even the strongest Black farm-owning communities, struggling with fewer resources, burdened by systematic racism, and stripped of the ultimate prerogative of citizenship—the right to defend their interests through the democratic process—fared worse than did white yeomen in resisting this tidal wave.

Yet for freedpeople and their descendants, land represented a decades-long psychic and material refuge from the most vicious attacks and insults of the Jim Crow era. It was a base for developing the social capital of community and institutions, including decent rural schools, as well as an invisible launching pad toward the urban middle class. African Americans' sustained quest for land represented an alternative vision of a more equitable, democratic society, even if it was never fully realized.

NOTES

1. Eric Foner, *Free Soil, Free Labor, Free Men: The Ideology of the Republican Party before the Civil War* (New York: Oxford University Press, 1970); Heather Cox Richardson, *To Make Men Free: A History of the Republican Party* (New York: Basic Books, 2014), 1–54.

2. Edward Magdol, *A Right to the Land: Essays on the Freedmen's Community* (Westport, CT: Greenwood, 1977).

3. For testimony of the freedpeople's land hunger, see Steven Hahn et al., *Freedom: A Documentary History of Emancipation, 1861–1867,* ser. 3, vol. 1, *Land and Labor, 1865* (Chapel Hill: University of North Carolina Press, 2007).

4. Our thanks to Bill Harris, Michael Fitzgerald, and Sydney Nathans for critiquing earlier drafts of this essay. We also thank Drea George for creating figure 6.1.

5. Daniel W. Hamilton, *The Limits of Sovereignty: Property Confiscation in the Union and Confederacy during the Civil War* (Chicago: University of Chicago Press, 2007); David Herbert Donald, *Lincoln* (London: Jonathan Cape, 1995), 364–65, 560, 578; John C. Rodrigue, *Lincoln and Reconstruction* (Carbondale: Southern Illinois University Press, 2013), 146–47.

6. Abraham Lincoln to David Hunter et al., Feb. 10, 1863, in *Collected Works of Abraham Lincoln,* vol. 6, *1809–1865,* https://quod.lib.umich.edu/cgi/t/text/text-idx?c=lincoln;rgn=div1;view=text;idno=lincoln6;node=lincoln6:196 (accessed Jan. 10, 2020).

7. Willie Lee Rose, *Rehearsal for Reconstruction: The Port Royal Experiment* (London: Oxford University Press, 1964), 212, 272.

8. James M. McPherson, "The Ballot and Land for the Freedmen, 1861–1865," in *Reconstruction: An Anthology of Revisionist Writings,* ed. Kenneth M. Stampp and Leon F. Litwack (Baton Rouge: Louisiana State University Press, 1969), 151.

9. Orville Vernon Burton, *The Age of Lincoln* (New York: Hill and Wang, 2007), 259.

10. Those with the best authority to speculate, Lincoln's biographers, concur that the president would not have supported land reform had he not been assassinated. After detailing the many ways that Lincoln had changed his mind to extend more civil rights to African Americans, David Donald concludes, "Unlike the Radicals, he gave no thought to dividing up the estates of the defeated Southern planters and giving each black family forty acres and a mule." Donald, *Lincoln,* 583. See also Rodrigue, *Lincoln and Reconstruction;* Louis P. Masur, *Lincoln's Last Speech: Wartime Reconstruction and the Crisis of Reunion* (New York: Oxford University Press, 2017).

11. William S. McFeely, *Yankee Stepfather: General O. O. Howard and the Freedmen* (New York: Norton, 1968); Claude F. Oubre, *Forty Acres and a Mule* (Baton Rouge: Louisiana State University Press, 1978); David Warren Bowen, *Andrew Johnson and the Negro* (Knoxville: University of Tennessee Press, 1989).

12. In 1866, Congress passed the Southern Homestead Act, which offered to sell unclaimed public lands in five states to ex-slaves for one year. But few African Americans were able to take advantage of the opportunity for the very good reason that these public lands had frequently been unclaimed because they were nonarable. Additionally, the land offices were hard to access and required prohibitive processing fees. It was very difficult for African Americans to travel to obtain title to land because of the key role of "regional knowledge, kinship networks and white resistance to non-local

African Americans." Quoted in Neil Canaday, Charles Reback, and Kristin Stowe, "Race and Local Knowledge: New Evidence from the Southern Homestead Act," *Review of Black Political Economy* 42, no. 4 (Dec. 2015): 399. After January 1876, Congress allowed speculators to bid on this public land, and they snapped up most of it for logging and speculation. See Michael Lanza, *Agrarianism and Reconstruction: The Southern Homestead Act* (Baton Rouge: Louisiana University Press, 1990). In the end, only about 5,000 of 28,000 settlers on public lands were African American. Keri Leigh Merritt, "Land and the Roots of African American Poverty," *Aeon*, Mar. 11, 2016, https://aeon.co /ideas/land-and-the-roots-of-african-american-poverty (accessed Mar. 25, 2018).

13. Burton, *Age of Lincoln*, 260; David Montgomery, *Beyond Equality: Labor and the Radical Republicans, 1862–1872* (Champaign: University of Illinois Press, 1981). Some limited, state-sponsored programs benefited freedpeople seeking land. Once the Reconstruction Act of 1867 passed, Black South Carolinians began to use their votes to promote meaningful compensation to freedpeople. The state legislature established the South Carolina Land Commission to purchase plantations worth a total of $700,000 to subdivide into plots, ranging from 25–100 acres each, and then to distribute them to both African American and white applicants. When conservatives regained control of the state government, they tightened requirements for gaining title to land and eventually abolished the Land Commission. But before they did so, between 1870 and the 1890s, close to 1,000 African Americans received title to more than 44,500 acres of land in South Carolina. The program had the potential to have a larger impact. About 14,000 Black families took occupancy on Land Commission lands but never owned the property outright. See Carol K. Rothrock Bleser, *The Promised Land: The History of the South Carolina Land Commission, 1869–1902* (Columbia: University of South Carolina Press, 1969), xi–xii; Elizabeth Rauh Bethel, *Promiseland: A Century of Life in a Negro Community* (Philadelphia: Temple University Press, 1981); Elizabeth Almlie et al., "Prized Pieces of Land: The Impact of Reconstruction on African-American Land Ownership in Lower Richland County, South Carolina" (2009), Books and Manuscripts 3, https://scholarcommons.sc.edu/pubhist_books/3 (accessed June 28, 2019).

Texas also experimented with a state land commission. And the federal government forced Oklahoma Native Americans not only to free their slaves but also to provide them with land. Apparently taking land from whites to give to poor Blacks set a dangerous constitutional precedent. But taking it from Indians was a well-established American tradition. See George H. Moneyhon, "George T. Ruby and the Politics of Expediency in Texas," in *Southern Black Leaders of the Reconstruction Era*, ed. Howard N. Rabinowitz (Urbana: University of Illinois Press, 1982), 370; David A. Chang, *The Color of the Land: Race, Nation, and the Politics of Landownership in Oklahoma, 1832–1929* (Chapel Hill: University of North Carolina Press, 1910), 39–40; M. Thomas Bailey, *Reconstruction in Indian Territory: A Story of Avarice, Discrimination, and Opportunism* (Port Washington, NY: Kennikat, 1972), 60–72.

14. Eric Foner, *Reconstruction: America's Unfinished Revolution, 1863–1877* (New York: Harper and Row, 1988), 109.

15. The historian John B. Boles agreed with Foner, writing that the "wrenching economic conditions" of the 1860s and 1870s "were so severe that land ownership would probably not have made a substantial difference in the long run unless blacks had opted for a peasantlike existence outside

the market-crop market." Boles, *Black Southerners, 1619–1869* (Lexington: University Press of Kentucky, 1983), 202. The economist Jay R. Mandle agreed, drawing on W. E. B. Du Bois's arguments against Washington that property could not be defended without equal legal and political rights. See Mandle, *The Roots of Black Poverty: The Southern Plantation Economy after the Civil War* (Durham, NC: Duke University Press, 1978), 106–10.

16. W. E. B. Du Bois, *Black Reconstruction in America, 1860–1880* (New York: Harcourt, Brace, 1935), 602; William S. McFeely, "Unfinished Business: The Freedmen's Bureau and Federal Action in Race Relations," in *Key Issues in the Afro-American Experience,* ed. Nathan I. Huggins et al., 2 vols. (New York: Harcourt Brace Jovanovich, 1971), 2:15, 22, 23; William Darity Jr., "Forty Acres and a Mule in the 21st Century," *Social Science Quarterly* 89, no. 3 (Sept. 2008): 661. Yet another historian, Keri Leigh Merritt, shows that white southerners, along with other white Americans, benefited from the Homestead Act of 1862. See Merritt, *Masterless Men: Poor Whites and Slavery in the Antebellum South* (Cambridge: Cambridge University Press, 2017), 327. See also Katherine Franke, *Repair: Redeeming the Promise of Abolition* (Chicago: Haymarket Books, 2019). By drawing on international evidence from a wide range of disciplines, Peter Coclanis builds a concise argument for the value of small landholding in improving an owner's health and economic wellbeing in "What Made Booker Wash(ington) the Wizard of Tuskegee in Economic Context," in *Booker T. Washington and Black Progress: "Up from Slavery" 100 Years Later,* ed. W. Fitzhugh Brundage (Gainesville: University Press of Florida, 2003), 90–95.

17. The Breaking New Ground oral-history collection is available through the Southern Oral History Program Interview Database, University of North Carolina at Chapel Hill, https://dc.lib.unc .edu/cdm/landingpage/collection/sohp. For the interviews in the project, see U. 19. Long Civil Rights Movement: Breaking New Ground Project, https://dc.lib.unc.edu/cdm/search/collection/sohp /searchterm/U.19.%20Long%20Civil%20Rights%20Movement:%20Breaking%20New%20Ground /mode/exact.

18. Stephen Budiansky, *The Bloody Shirt: Terror after Appomattox* (New York: Viking, 2008), 23–24.

19. Michael W. Fitzgerald, *The Union League Movement in the Deep South: Politics and Agricultural Change during Reconstruction* (Baton Rouge: Louisiana State University Press, 1989), 139–40.

20. Gavin Wright, *Old South, New South: Revolutions in the Southern Economy since the Civil War* (Baton Rouge: Louisiana State University Press, 1997); Leon F. Litwack, *Trouble in Mind: Black Southerners in the Age of Jim Crow* (New York: Knopf, 1989); Neil R. McMillen, *Dark Journey: Black Mississippians in the Age of Jim Crow* (Urbana: University of Illinois Press, 1989).

21. Harold D. Woodman, "Post–Civil War Southern Agriculture and the Law," *Agricultural History* 53, no. 1 (Jan. 1979): 333.

22. *Freeman,* Sept. 6, 1890, 6; Omar H. Ali, *In the Lion's Mouth: Black Populism in the New South, 1886–1900* (Oxford: University Press of Mississippi, 2010), 53; Patrick J. Dickson, "Out of the Lion's Mouth: The Colored Farmers' Alliance in the New South, 1886–1892" (master's thesis, Cornell University, 2000), 91; Charles Postel, *The Populist Vision* (New York: Oxford University Press, 2007), 42. See also Robert C. McMath Jr., *Populist Vanguard: A History of the Southern Farmers' Alliance*

(Chapel Hill: University of North Carolina Press, 1975), 45; Gerald H. Gaither, *Blacks and the Populist Revolt: Ballots and Bigotry in the "New South"* (University: University of Alabama Press, 1977), 4.

23. *Twenty-Two Years' Work of the Hampton Normal and Agricultural Institute at Hampton, Virginia* (Hampton, VA: Normal School Press, 1891), 236.

24. Ali, *In the Lion's Mouth*, 75.

25. *Savannah Tribune*, Sept. 7, 1889, 2.

26. "Race Gleanings," *Freeman*, Aug. 30, 1890, 2.

27. *Cleveland Gazette*, Oct. 25, 1890, 1.

28. *Cleveland Gazette*, July 18, 1891, 1.

29. "Colored Farmers' Alliance: A Co-operative Movement in Texas," *New York Age*, Dec. 22, 1888.

30. Ali, *In the Lion's Mouth*, 80.

31. Postel, *Populist Vision*, 41.

32. "Colored Farmers' Alliance," *New York Age*, Dec. 1, 1888; Ali, *In the Lion's Mouth*, 55.

33. *Raleigh (NC) News and Observer*, Sept. 16, 1891.

34. Gaither, *Blacks and the Populist Revolt*, 14–16.

35. "Colored Farmers' Alliance," *Huntsville (AL) Gazette*, Aug. 15, 1891, 3.

36. *Meriden (KS) Advocate*, Aug. 26, 1891, 8.

37. Ali, *In the Lion's Mouth*, 139.

38. Booker T. Washington, "Signs of Progress among the Negroes," *Century* 59 (Jan. 1900) in *The Black Man and the American Dream: Negro Aspirations in America, 1900–1930*, ed. June Sochen (Chicago: Quadrangle Books, 1971), 159.

39. Ali, *In the Lion's Mouth*, 149–50.

40. Tera Hunter, *To 'Joy My Freedom: Southern Black Women's Lives and Labors after the Civil War* (Cambridge, MA: Harvard University Press, 1997), 88–97; Jacqueline Jones, *Labor of Love, Labor of Sorrow: Black Women, Work, and the Family from Slavery to the Present* (New York: Basic Books, 1985), 128.

41. C. Vann Woodward, *Origins of the New South, 1877–1913* (Baton Rouge: Louisiana State University Press, 1951), 360. W. E. B. Du Bois dedicated two Atlanta University conferences, both called The Negro Artisan, in 1902 and 1912 to the status of Black artisans, and found the situation bleak.

42. Philip S. Foner, *Organized Labor and the Black Worker, 1619–1973* (New York: International Publishers, 1974), 79. For excellent overviews of the barriers that African Americans faced in finding decent work after the Civil War, see the early chapters of Steven A. Reich, *A Working People: A History of African American Workers since Emancipation* (New York: Rowman and Littlefield, 2013); Robert H. Zieger, *For Jobs and Freedom: Race and Labor in America since 1865* (Lexington: University Press of Kentucky, 2007); Jones, *Labor of Love*; and Jones, *American Work: Four Centuries of Black and White Labor* (New York: W. W. Norton, 1998).

43. Loren Schweninger, *Black Property Owners in the South, 1790–1915* (Urbana: University of Illinois Press, 1990). For a study of mulatto planters in antebellum Louisiana, see Gary B. Mills, *The Forgotten People: Cane River's Creoles of Color* (Baton Rouge: Louisiana State University Press, 1977). For a study of a Black farm-owning community in antebellum Virginia, see Melvin Patrick

Ely, *Israel on the Appomattox: A Southern Experiment in Black Freedom from the 1790s through the Civil War* (New York: Vintage Books, 2005).

44. Robert Tracy McKenzie, *One South or Many? Plantation Belt and Upcountry in Civil War–Era Tennessee* (Cambridge: Cambridge University Press, 1994), 143.

45. Schweninger, *Black Property Owners,* 160, 183. These figures are drawn from the Agricultural Census, which underreports farm ownership by listing only individuals with at least three acres of farmland or plots of less than three acres that required the continuous labor of at least one person or produced and sold agricultural products of a prescribed minimum value in the previous year. In 1850, that figure was set at $100; in 1870, 1880, and 1890, $500; and in 1910, $250. These were obviously arbitrary lines, drawn to separate "farmers" from "gardeners," a necessary distinction for statisticians charged with constructing a coherent view of the national economy. But the line raises questions for historians interested in the lived meaning of "farm" and "farmer." The Department of Agriculture was far more concerned with tracing changes in the national market economy than in understanding the flexible family strategies of poor southerners who farmed small plots to raise a variety of food for their own tables and to earn a bit of money for taxes and new shoes and clothing for the upcoming school year. Additionally, the Agricultural Census did not count as "farmland" any acreage dedicated to raising feed for one's own livestock or woodland for hunting, fishing, foraging, and firewood collection, all crucial sources of support for smallholders. These definitions would have eliminated many of the actual farming families whose small plots gave them a permanent presence in their communities, sustenance, and a base from which family members could go out and engage as paid labor on nearby farms, domestic servants, or as skilled or unskilled workers in towns. Such families were scattered across the South, and some areas like the Atlantic coast and the Sea Islands were filled with them. J. William Harris, *Deep Souths: Delta, Piedmont, and Sea Island Society in the Age of Segregation* (Baltimore: Johns Hopkins University Press, 2001), 15–26.

The 1910 Agricultural Census included an intriguing discussion of the evolving official "definition of a farm" from 1850 to 1910 and admitted that tens of thousands more people viewed themselves as "farmers" in the General Census than were officially designated as such in the Agricultural Census. US Bureau of the Census, *Thirteenth Census of the United States, 1910,* vols. 6–7, *Agriculture, 1909 and 1910* (Washington: US Census Office, 1913), 22–24 (hereafter cited as *Agricultural Census*). Loren Schweninger came at this problem from another direction. Based on comparisons of the tax digest and Agricultural Census figures in selected counties of Maryland and South Carolina, he has estimated that in the 1860s, approximately 10 percent of African American property owners were not included in the census. Schweninger, *Black Property Owners in the South,* 376.

46. Robert Kenzer, *Enterprising Southerners: Black Economic Success in North Carolina, 1865–1915* (Charlottesville: University Press of Virginia, 1989); Schweninger, *Black Property Owners,* 57, 149.

47. Robert Francis Engs, *Freedom's First Generation: Black Hampton, Virginia, 1861–1890* (Philadelphia: University of Pennsylvania Press, 1979), 91.

48. Thad Sitton and James H. Conrad, *Freedom Colonies: Independent Black Texans in the Time of Jim Crow* (Austin: University of Texas Press, 205), 18.

49. Nell Irvin Painter, *Exodusters: Black Migration to Kansas after Reconstruction* (New York: Knopf, 1976).

50. Wilbert Jenkins, *Climbing Up to Glory: A Short History of African Americans during the Civil War and Reconstruction* (Wilmington, DE: Scholarly Resources, 2002), 117; Oubre, *Forty Acres*, 28–29.

51. Paul A. Cimbala, "A Black Colony in Dougherty County: The Freedmen's Bureau and the Failure of Reconstruction in Southwest Georgia," in *African American Life in the Post-Emancipation South*, ed. Donald G. Nieman, vol. 2, *The Freedmen's Bureau and Black Freedom* (Hamden, CT: Garland, 1994); Hahn et al., *Freedom: A Documentary History of Emancipation*, ser. 3, vol. 1, *Land and Labor, 1865*, 688, 690, 721–22, 731–35; Susan Eva O'Donovan, *Becoming Free in the Cotton South* (Cambridge, MA: Harvard University Press, 2007), 147–48, 226–27, 244–45. Communal purchasing continued into the 1920s in many places, organized by pastors, teachers, or college graduates. Steven Hahn, *A Nation under Our Feet: Black Political Struggles in the Rural South from Slavery to the Great Migration* (Cambridge, MA: Harvard University Press, 2004), 63, 79, 81, 142, 167.

52. George W. Balogh, *Entrepreneurs in the Lumber Industry: Arkansas, 1881–1963* (New York: Garland, 1995); Kenneth L. Smith, *Sawmill: The Story of Cutting the Last Great Virgin Forest East of the Rockies* (Fayetteville: University of Arkansas Press, 1986); Jami Marie Forrester, "From Swamp Forest to Cotton: Three States Lumber Company and the Development of Burdette, Arkansas, in the Early Twentieth Century" (PhD diss., University of Arkansas, 2011).

53. Robert Johnson, interviewed by Mark Schultz, Birdsong, AR, Aug. 18, 2012, recording in author's possession. Johnson moved to Birdsong, in northeastern Arkansas, in the 1940s and came to know some of the first settlers of the community. They told him the town had been established as a final payment made to an all-Black lumber camp in 1901. William P. Jones has found that seasonal lumbering work supported African American farm-owning communities, particularly in the late nineteenth and early twentieth centuries. Jones, *The Tribe of the Black Ulysses: African American Lumber Workers in the Jim Crow South* (Urbana: University of Illinois Press, 2005), 15, 19, 32.

54. John Eaton, general superintendent of freedmen in Mississippi, reported that freedpeople in Natchez "seem determined to do what they can to thwart the project of raising cotton." Rev. Joseph Warren, ed., *Extracts from Reports of Superintendents of Freedmen: Records in the Office of Col. John Eaton Jr., General Superintendent of Freedmen, Department of the Tennessee and State of Arkansas* (Vicksburg, MS: Freedmen's, 1864), 30. In his classic 1936 study of two Georgia counties, Arthur F. Raper remarks, "The Negro owner is as near a live-at-home farmer as one finds in the Black Belt: he has hogs, cows, chickens, and a permanent garden." Raper, *Preface to Peasantry: A Tale of Two Black Belt Counties* (New York: Atheneum, 1974), 140.

55. For a recently published example, see Zora Neale Hurston, *Barracoon: The Story of the Last "Black Cargo"* (New York: HarperCollins, 2018), 66–68.

56. Jaynes, *Branches without Roots: Genesis of the Black Working Class in the American South, 1862–1882* (New York: Oxford University Press, 1986), 292–93.

57. Ibid., 296.

58. Mark Schultz, *The Rural Face of White Supremacy: Beyond Jim Crow* (Urbana: University of Illinois Press, 2005), 49–50; Sydney Nathans, *A Mind to Stay: White Plantation, Black Homeland* (Cambridge, MA: Harvard University Press, 2017), 142.

59. *New York Tribune*, Feb. 13, 1865.

60. Hahn, *Nation under Our Feet*; frequent articles and advertisements, *The Negro Farmer*, 1914–15.

61. Canter Brown Jr., *In the Midst of All That Makes Life Worth Living* (Tallahassee: Sentry, 2001), 116.

62. Annual Reports of the Bureau of Negro Welfare and Statistics of the State of West Virginia (Charleston: [State Press of West Virginia], 1921–52), Drain-Jordan Library, West Virginia State University, Institute.

63. Adrienne Monteith Petty, *Standing Their Ground: Small Farmers in North Carolina since the Civil War* (New York: Oxford University Press, 2013), 39–40.

64. At this point, it is not possible to properly compare patterns among the states, as there is currently only one thorough state account of Black farm ownership. See Sitton and Conrad, *Freedom Colonies.* May this excellent study serve as a model for future work.

65. Stephen A. Vincent, *Southern Seed, Northern Soil: African American Farm Communities in the Midwest, 1765–1900* (Bloomington: Indiana University Press, 1999).

66. Sitton and Conrad, *Freedom Colonies,* 19–20; James J. Harrison Jr., interviewed by Mark Schultz, rural Stephens County, GA, July 22, 2005; Carolyn Jarrett Crawford, interviewed by Mark Schultz, Stephens County, GA, July 2005.

67. Jaynes, *Branches without Roots,* 104; Foner, *Reconstruction,* 131.

68. Jaynes, *Branches without Roots,* 105.

69. Harris, *Deep Souths,* 15–26.

70. Mark Schultz, "Interracial Kinship Ties and the Emergence of a Rural Middle Class," *Georgia in Black and White,* ed. John Inscoe (Athens: University of Georgia Press, 1994), 141–72; Adele Logan Alexander, *Ambiguous Lives: Free Women of Color in Rural Georgia, 1789–1879* (Fayetteville: University of Arkansas Press, 1991); Kent Anderson Leslie, *Woman of Color, Daughter of Privilege: Amanda America Dickson, 1849–1893* (Athens: University of Georgia Press, 1995); Katie Hunt and Mae Warren, interviewed by Mark Schultz, Hancock County, GA, Sept. 1994.

71. Sharon Ann Holt, *Making Freedom Pay: North Carolina Freedpeople Working for Themselves, 1865–1900* (Athens: University of Georgia Press, 2000), 10–15, 51.

72. Ruth Royster, interviewed by Michael Verville, Roxboro, NC, Aug. 16, 2011, U-0784, Southern Oral History Program, Collection 4007, Southern Historical Collection, Wilson Library, University of North Carolina at Chapel Hill (hereafter SOHP).

73. Naomi James, interviewed by Veronica Dominach, Mount Hermon, LA, June 18, 2012, U-0864, ibid.

74. Carl Hodges, interviewed by Michael Verville, Durham, NC, June 6, 2011, U-0776, ibid.

75. W. E. B. Du Bois, "The Negroes of Farmville, Virginia: A Social Study," in *Contributions by W. E. B. DuBois in Government Publications and Proceedings,* comp. and ed. Herbert Aptheker (New York: Kreus-Thompson Organization Limited, 1980); Karen Cook Bell, *Claiming Freedom: Race, Kinship, and Land in Nineteenth-Century Georgia* (Columbia: University of South Carolina Press, 2018), 63–64.

76. Holt, *Making Freedom Pay,* 10–19. The majority of Breaking New Ground interviewees, both male and female, who were asked to discuss the topic testified that husbands consulted their wives in family financial strategies. See, for example, Gary Grant, interviewed by Michael Verville, Tillery, NC, Aug. 17, 2011, U-0773, SOHP.

77. Theodore Rosengarten, *All God's Dangers: The Life of Nate Shaw* (New York: Knopf, 1974), 91, 107, 266, 267. Usually, the Shaws' partnership was hidden at home. Once, Hannah accompanied Nate to the bank when he was planning to take out a loan and buy a plot of land so that she could read the agreement that was given to him to sign. She warned him that the note used all of his property as collateral against the loan, not just the land he was planning to buy, so he refused to sign until the terms were changed.

78. Rachel Petty, interviewed by Ayana Flewellen, Washington, DC, June 18, 2012, U-0883, SOHP.

79. Rob Robinson, interviewed by Kelly Davila, Brookhaven, MS, June 1, 2012, U-0835, SOHP; Harry K. Holt, interviewed by Allen Copeland, Quincy, FL, June 10, 2012, U-0813, ibid.

80. Holt, *Making Freedom Pay*, 93.

81. Mark R. Schultz, "The Dream Realized: African American Landownership in Central Georgia Between Reconstruction and World War II," *Agricultural History* 72, no. 2 (Spring 1998): 298–312.

82. Statistics are from the *Agricultural Census, 1910.*

83. Black Oklahoma farmers averaged holdings of 144 acres per farm in 1910, much larger than Black-owned farms in Mississippi, which were the second largest on average at 89 acres per farm. The average size of Black-owned farms across the South was 69 acres.

84. A powerful positive statistical correlation (Pearson .691) describes the percentage of Black farm owners in 1920 relative to the percentage of white farm owners across the southern states. Inexplicably, the correlation in 1910 is relatively weak, at Pearson .380. But the correlation strengthens in the following years (.759 for 1925; .887 for 1930; and .733 for 1940). *Agricultural Census*, 1910, 1920, 1925, 1930, 1940. Our thanks to Rick Kloser for helping us run these correlations.

85. We correlated the percent of Black farm owners relative to cotton acreages in each state, divided by the number of improved acres per state. The Pearson correlation linking cotton with Black farm ownership in 1920 was -.815. In 1925, it was -.776; in 1930, -.900; and in 1940, -.825. (Pearson correlation figures for white farmers hovered just below those of African American farmers, at -.796, -.681, -.885, and -.780, respectively. What stunted opportunity for white farmers did so to an even greater extent with Black farmers.) When we ran multiple-regression analysis on our data, both backward-elimination regression and stepwise regression for these years, the percent of acres dedicated to cotton was the only factor that emerged as a significant predictor of the percent of Black farm ownership in all years and for both types of regression. Of course, correlation is not causation, so these factors may both be affected by a third, possibly cultural, influence.

86. For example, in 1882, the leading Black Episcopalian bishop and intellectual Alexander Crummell rebutted a white Episcopalian bishop's claims that African Americans had deteriorated morally and materially since slavery by emphasizing the "wide domain of land" that they had accumulated, "equal in extent to the size of the STATE OF CONNECTICUT." See "A Defense of the Negro Race in America from the Assaults and Charges of Rev. J. L. Tucker, D.D. of Jackson, Mississippi," *Civilization and Black Progress: Selected Writings of Alexander Crummell on the South*, ed. J. R. Oldfield (Charlottesville: University Press of Virginia, 1995), 72. W. E. B. Du Bois is largely associated with urban professionalism, but his early studies for the US Census Bureau, from 1898 to 1906, celebrated Black farm ownership, and before World War I, he regularly defended African American thrift and work ethic by praising the "simply astounding" advancement of African American farm owners

since slavery. Du Bois, "Violations of Property Rights," in *Writings by W. E. B. DuBois in Periodicals Edited by Others*, comp. and ed. Herbert Aptheker, vol. 2, *1910–1934* (New York: Kreus-Thompson Organization Limited, 1982), 61–64. According to Aptheker, this paper was given at a conference on behalf of the NAACP in 1911 or 1912.

87. Robert J. Norrell, *Up from History: The Life of Booker T. Washington* (Cambridge, MA: Harvard University Press, 2009); Monroe Work, *Fifty Years of Negro Progress* (Hampton, VA: Press of the Hampton Normal and Agricultural Institute, 1913), 10–11. Work notes that the twenty million acres that African Americans owned was equal to the combined size of Vermont, New Hampshire, Massachusetts, and Rhode Island.

88. *First Mohonk Conference on the Negro Question, Held at Lake Mohonk, Ulster County New York, June 4, 5, 6, 1890*, ed. Isabel C. Barrows (Boston: George H. Ellis, Printer, 1890), 18. The conference brought together white scholars, editors, businessmen, and politicians.

89. Elizabeth A. Herbin-Triant, *Threatening Property: Race, Class, and Campaigns to Legislate Jim Crow Neighborhoods* (New York: Columbia University Press, 2019).

90. Kelly Miller, "Darkest America," *New England Magazine*, Mar. 1904, 14–21.

91. Painter, *Exodusters;* Norman L. Crockett, *The Black Towns* (Lawrence: Regents Press of Kansas, 1979); Kenneth Marvin Hamilton, *Black Towns and Profit: Promotion and Development in the Trans-Appalachian West, 1877–1915* (Urbana: University of Illinois Press, 1991); Quintard Taylor, *In Search of the Racial Frontier* (New York: W. W. Norton, 1998); Selena Ronshaye Sanderfer, "For Land and Liberty: Black Territorial Separatism in the South, 1776–1904" (PhD diss. Vanderbilt University, 2010).

92. Mary Rolinson, *Grassroots Garveyism: The Universal Negro Improvement Association in the Rural South, 1920–1927* (Chapel Hill: University of North Carolina Press, 2007).

93. Debra A. Reid, *Reaping a Greater Harvest: African Americans, the Extension Service, and Rural Reform in Jim Crow Texas* (College Station: Texas A&M University Press, 2007); Allen W. Jones, "The South's First Black Farm Agents," *Agricultural History* 50 (Oct. 1976): 636–44; Carmen V. Harris, "'A Ray of Hope for Liberation': Blacks in the South Carolina Extension Service, 1915–1970" (PhD diss., Michigan State University, 2002).

94. Robert Hunt Ferguson, *Remaking the Rural South: Interracialism, Christian Socialism, and Cooperative Farming in Jim Crow Mississippi* (Athens: University of Georgia Press, 2018).

95. Essie Mae Harper, interviewed by Mark Schultz, Hancock County, GA, Sept. 23, 1991.

96. John Fluker, interviewed by Mark Schultz, Little Rock, AR, June 9, 2012.

97. Willie Essick, interviewed by Brittney Owens, Albany, GA, July 19, 2011, U-0665, SOHP; Schultz, *Rural Face of White Supremacy*, 29; Harris, *Deep Souths*, 257–60.

98. Roy Anderson, interviewed by Robert Hunt Ferguson, Lexington, MS, June 27, 2011, U-0657, SOHP.

99. Lillian Glass Hunter, interviewed by Heidi Dodson, New Madrid, MO, July 6, 2012, U-0848, ibid.

100. Samuel Lee, interviewed by Hudson Vaughan, Ripley, TN, May 31, 2012, U-0986, ibid.

101. Carol B. Stack, *All Our Kin: Strategies for Survival in a Black Community* (New York: Harper & Row, 1975).

102. Raper, *Preface to Peasantry,* 128, 383; Thomas Jackson Woofter Jr., "Negro Migration: Changes in Rural Organization and Population of the Cotton Belt" (PhD diss., Columbia University, 1920), 90.

103. Travis Benford, interviewed by Priscilla Martinez, San Antonio, TX, June 19, 2011, transcript in authors' possession; Nathans, *A Mind to Stay,* 186–87, 206.

104. William Lynwood Montell, *The Saga of Coe Ridge* (Knoxville: University of Tennessee Press, 1970); Horace Mann Bond and Julia W. Bond, *The Star Creek Papers,* ed. Adam Fairclough (Athens: University of Georgia Press, 1997); Elizabeth Robeson, "An 'Ominous Defiance': The Lowman Lynchings of 1926," in *Toward a Meeting of the Waters: Currents in the Civil Rights Movement of South Carolina during the Twentieth Century,* ed. Winifred B. Moore Jr. and Orville Vernon Burton (Columbia: University of South Carolina Press, 2008), 65–92.

105. Andre Vann, interviewed by Michael Verville, Durham, NC, May 20, 2011, U-0787, SOHP.

106. Gary Grant, interviewed by Michael Verville, Tillery, NC, Aug. 17, 2011, U-0466, ibid.

107. Zora Neale Hurston came from the Black town of Eatonton, Florida, which stood on the shoulders of its farmers. She stated that her own sense of confidence grew from the independent spirit of that community. Valerie Boyd, *Wrapped in Rainbows: The Life of Zora Neale Hurston* (New York: Scribner, 2004). Lynette Parker recently researched participants in Kenneth and Mamie Clark's doll studies from the 1940s to learn more about the girls who had chosen the Black doll. Celestine Parson Lloyd told her that her sense of independence and self-confidence originated in two generations of farm ownership. Parker, "Brown and Board & Reparations: What We Can Learn from Children Who Chose the Black Doll" (paper presented at the American Educational Research Association, San Francisco, 2020). This is also a central theme of Natalie Baszile, *We Are Each Other's Harvest: Celebrating African American Farmers, Land, and Legacy* (New York: Amistad, 2021).

108. Julius Rosenwald Foundation papers in the Alabama Department of Archives and History, the Georgia Archives, the Louisiana State Archives Research Library, and the State Archives of North Carolina; Clemmie Whatley, interviewed by Mark Schultz, Chubbtown, GA, July 8, 2018.

109. Charles Payne, *I've Got the Light of Freedom: The Organizing Tradition and the Mississippi Freedom Struggle* (Berkeley: University of California Press, 1996), 141, 281–83; Diane Nash, personal communication with Mark Schultz, spring 2012.

110. W. E. B. Du Bois, "The Rural South," *Quarterly Publications of the American Statistical Association* 13, no. 97 (1912): 84.

111. Schultz, *Rural Face of White Supremacy,* 188–200. In Louisiana, African American farm owners and businessmen served as political leaders during the Jim Crow period and into the early years of the civil rights struggle. Greta de Jong, *A Different Day: African American Struggles for Justice in Rural Louisiana, 1900–1970* (Chapel Hill: University of North Carolina Press, 2002), 48–49, 170, 179; Jarod Roll, "'The Lazarus of American Farmers': The Politics of Black Agrarianism in the Jim Crow South, 1921–1938," in *Beyond Forty Acres and a Mule: African American Landowning Families since Reconstruction,* ed. Debra A. Reid and Evan P. Bennett (Gainesville: University Press of Florida, 2012), 132–52. In Hancock County, Georgia, the tax digest reveals that farm owners made up 10 percent of all African Americans paying the poll tax in 1900 at the onset of systematic disfranchisement but composed nearly 70 percent by the demise of the poll tax in 1945. Dozens of

interviews with Black farm owners and white politicians in Hancock confirmed the persistence of voting by independent Black farmers.

112. Thomas W. Mitchell, "From Reconstruction to Deconstruction: Undermining Black Land-ownership, Political Independence, and Community through Partition Sales of Tenancies in Common," *Northwestern University Law Review* 95, no. 2 (2001): 505–80.

113. Vann R. Newkirk II, "The Great Land Robbery," *Atlantic Monthly* 324, no. 3 (Sept. 2019): 74–85. In 2001 Associated Press reporters Todd Lewan and Dolores Barclay published a three-part series on African American land loss. The series was the culmination of an eighteen-month in-vestigation, more than a thousand interviews, and a deep dive into archival records at the county, state, and federal level. It found that courthouse corruption, planter deception, and simple violence had stripped African Americans of farmland across the South. Lewan and Barclay, "Torn from the Land: Black Americans' Farmland Taken through Cheating, Intimidation, Even Murder," *Seattle Times*, Dec. 2, 2001; Barclay, Lewan, and Allen G. Breed, "Lynched for Their Land: Violence Used to Separate Blacks from Their Acreage," *Seattle Times*, Dec. 3, 2001.

114. Andrew Kahrl, *The Land Was Ours: How Black Beaches Became White Wealth in the Coastal South* (Chapel Hill: University of North Carolina Press, 2012), 94–104.

115. Justin Randolph, "Civil Rights Arrested: The Black Freedom Movement and Mass Incarcer-ation in Rural Mississippi, 1938 to 1980" (PhD diss., Yale University, 2019).

116. Pete Daniel, *Dispossession: Discrimination against African American Farmers in the Age of Civil Rights* (Chapel Hill: University of North Carolina Press, 2013).

117. Valerie Grim, "Between Forty Acres and a Class Action Suit: Black Farmers, Civil Rights, and Protest against the US Department of Agriculture, 1997–2010," in Reid and Bennett, *Beyond Forty Acres and a Mule*, 271–96.

118. Jack Healy, "Windfall for Black Farmers Roils Rural America," *New York Times*, May 23, 2021.

II

The Unfinished Work of Lincoln in American History and the Struggle for Democratic Inclusion

Our Textbooks and Monuments Have Flattened Lincoln, Just When We Need Him the Most

JAMES W. LOEWEN

Since the first publication of *Lies My Teacher Told Me* in 1995, I have spoken to more than five hundred audiences about how high school textbooks mistreat American history.[1] About Abraham Lincoln, I often ask, "What speech, address, letter, etc., by Lincoln do you think textbooks would be sure to include?"

Invariably, audiences chorus back to me, "The Gettysburg Address."

Of course, this might be because it is the *only* title of a talk by Lincoln that they remember! But no, I suggest it is an intelligent choice, partly because it is so short. It can fit on a quarter of a textbook page; and indeed, six of the eighteen textbooks I studied for the 2018 edition of *Lies* do exactly that—stick it in a corner of a page in a box.[2] I suspect publishers put it there so that, when a school district official or adoption panel asks, "Does your textbook have any primary sources?" they can reply, "Yes! Look on page 464—the whole of Lincoln's Gettysburg Address." A couple of other textbooks quote only a single phrase, "that government of the people, by the people, for the people, shall not perish from the earth."

But it is not the right answer.

By far their favorite statement of Lincoln's, quoted or paraphrased by fifteen of the eighteen textbooks I studied, is *not* the Gettysburg Address, nor perhaps an even more useful choice, his second inaugural address, but a letter he wrote on August 22, 1862, to the *New York Tribune,* Horace Greeley's antislavery Republican newspaper. And they all excerpt the same passage:

I would save the Union. . . . If I could save the Union without freeing *any* slave, I would do it; and if I could save it by freeing *all* the slaves, I would do it; and if I could save it by freeing some and leaving others alone, I would also do that. What I do about slavery and the colored race I do because I believe it helps to save this Union; and what I forbear, I forbear because I do not believe it would help to save the Union.[3]

Moreover, they present these words to convey to students Lincoln's motivation in pursuing the Civil War "in his own words."

With this quote and their discussion of it, our textbook authors teach students to venerate Abraham Lincoln because "he saved the Union." Period. They specifically deny that Lincoln sought to end slavery. The two sides in the Civil War thus can both claim moral equivalence.

This is bad history. To make this claim, textbooks first leave out the political context. Lincoln wrote to seek support for the war from Northern defenders of slavery. Excepting Greeley, New York City, then and now, was one of the most Democratic jurisdictions in the nation. Democrats then were openly white supremacists—they called themselves "the white man's party" into the 1920s. Lincoln could *never* appeal to downstate New Yorkers generally to support the Civil War on the basis that it would help end slavery. Such an argument would only intensify their opposition to the war effort. So he made the only appeal he could that would find favor with them: support the Civil War to hold the nation together. Frederick Douglass would have made the same appeal had he been president and seeking support from New York City.

To get their false point about Lincoln across, most textbooks even edit this letter to omit his next and final point: "I have here stated my purpose according to my view of *official* duty, and I intend no modification of my oft-expressed *personal* wish that all men, everywhere could be free [Lincoln's emphasis]." That says something very different about slavery and about Lincoln. So textbooks leave it out.

Saving the Union had *never* been Lincoln's sole concern. In 1835, at the onset of his political career, he was one of just five members of the Illinois House of Representatives to vote against an anti-abolitionist resolution.[4] In 1860 he rejected the eleventh-hour Crittenden Compromise, a proposed constitutional amendment seeking to ward off secession by preserving slavery forever and by extending the Missouri Compromise line for its expansion westward. Lincoln specifically used these words: "On the territorial question, I am inflexible. . . .

You think slavery is right and ought to be extended; we think it is wrong and ought to be restricted."[5]

Moreover, a month before he wrote the *Tribune,* Lincoln had already presented the Emancipation Proclamation to his cabinet as an irreversible decision, but no textbook notes this when claiming that the Greeley letter is the guide to the president's war aims. Nor does a single textbook tell of Lincoln's encouragement that same summer to a group of abolitionist ministers to "go home and try to bring the people to your views" because "we shall need all the anti-slavery feeling in the country, and more." If textbooks did, students might grasp how Lincoln, like every political leader, modified his words depending upon his audience.[6] Here he was cultivating antiracist opposition on his "left" so he could use it to counter Democratic white supremacists on his "right."[7] Surely students would see that indifference was not Lincoln's only response to the issue of slavery in America.

Why might the authors of history textbooks omit such facts?

Because after 1890, the Confederates—or, more accurately, since it was a new generation, neo-Confederates—won the Civil War. Of course, the war ended in 1865. But they won it, or won what it was about, in 1890 and the years that followed, setting in motion the nadir of race relations—that terrible era between 1890 and 1940 when racism grew ever stronger, North and South.

Their victory came in several forms. Late in 1890, white supremacist Democrats in the Senate defeated the Federal Elections Bill, more or less by a single vote. Republicans had put it through the House, and President Benjamin Harrison would have signed it into law happily. After the bill's defeat, Democrats responded as they usually did: tarring Republicans as "nigger-lovers," often using that precise term. In the past Republicans had replied to this, yes, it is an outrage how you Democrats use violence and fraud in every election against Black voters; but in 1891 Republicans gave a new response: no we are not. So it transpired that during the 1890s, African Americans increasingly found themselves without political allies, hence powerless.[8]

Also in 1890, the US Army committed the Massacre at Wounded Knee (in South Dakota). Rationalizing this act raised racism still higher toward Native Americans. Worst of all from the standpoint of Black civil rights, Mississippi passed its new state constitution, openly barring African Americans from voting, holding office—indeed, from citizenship. Although it flagrantly violated the Fourteenth and Fifteenth Amendments, the federal government did nothing, thus indirectly encouraging every other southern state and even the Oklahoma Territory to follow suit by 1907.

Neo-Confederates also won the war on the ground, with Confederate monuments. Most people put up monuments after they win, and neo-Confederates were no exception. For the most part, these monuments went up during and after the destruction of Reconstruction. At first, most of the statuary honored Confederate veterans collectively, valiant but war weary, often with the names of local dead soldiers on the pedestals. After 1890, when Jim Crow began to tighten its vise on the South, the monuments became larger and more heroic, such as the equestrian statue of Robert E. Lee erected in Richmond in 1890, sitting on a horse with bulging muscles, its hooves forty feet in the air, devoid of commentary save the three letters "L-e-e." Later nadir monuments often wield triumphant words as well as images, claiming Confederates seceded for "states' rights" rather than slavery and implying—"Deo Vindice"—that their cause had god on its side. These triumphant monuments not only went up across the old Confederacy but also came to dominate Maryland, Kentucky, and Missouri. They even appeared in places far distant from the South, such as California, Washington State, Montana, and even Wisconsin!

Neo-Confederates even challenged the name of the war, and during the nadir—and occasionally even today—it became known as "The War between the States." This is anachronistic; during the war itself, it was called—duh!—the Civil War. I examined the six largest South Carolina newspapers for the period 1860–65 and found not one use of "War between the States."

Meanwhile, across the North as well as the South, whites increasingly limited the social and legal rights of African Americans. Schools such as Harvard University and the University of Minnesota still let Black students attend class but now shut them out of dormitories. Town after town across the West and North went "sundown," driving out their Black populations, sometimes violently, or taking steps to ensure that none ever moved in. Chinese Americans, Jews, Natives, and Mexican Americans were often likewise targeted. Organizations like the Union League Clubs, founded by Jews as well as Christians, now went anti-Semitic. Eugenics became popular and "scientific."

In this cultural climate, Abraham Lincoln's very real, though inconsistent, antislavery and antiracist thinking had become an embarrassment. So, it had to go. It became unseemly to remember Lincoln for anything *other* than saving the

Union.[9] Thus, in 1922 the Lincoln Memorial was dedicated in Washington, DC, with the inscription, "In this temple, as in the hearts of the people for whom he saved the Union, the memory of Abraham Lincoln is enshrined forever." Art critic Royal Cortissoz, who wrote it, deliberately omitted slavery: "By saying nothing about slavery," he noted, "you avoid the rubbing of old sores."[10] At the memorial's dedication, African Americans were segregated into a distant part of the audience, prompting nineteen to walk out in protest.[11]

Ironically, this "Lincoln" who did not care about slavery or have much regard for African Americans is also the man whom Black nationalists present to African Americans to persuade them to stop thinking well of him. He was merely *Forced into Glory,*" as the title of Lerone Bennett's book proclaims.[12] Neo-Confederates like James Ronald Kennedy and Walter Donald Kennedy in *The South Was Right!* present the same Lincoln as part of their false argument that secession and the Civil War had little to do with slavery or white supremacy.[13] No wonder that Abraham Lincoln remains little used as an antecedent by today's young people.

Regrettably, if students do not learn about Lincoln in high school, they will hardly do so afterward, for most Americans, even if they go to college, never take a course in US history. Meanwhile, we conflated his and George Washington's birthdays into a single holiday, gradually coming to be called "Presidents' Day," whose main function now seems to be to spur retail sales, not to ponder the moral or intellectual legacy of either man. For that matter, Presidents' Day is supposed to honor *all* of our presidents! Buying something on sale might be a rational response to a call to honor the moral and intellectual legacy of, say, James Buchanan or Andrew Johnson.

Thus, it can come as no surprise that when I ask college students who their heroes are in American history, only one or two in a hundred pick Lincoln. Even those who do choose him know only that he was "really great"—they do not know why. Their ignorance makes sense—after all, textbooks present him almost devoid of content.

Sadly, it is not just Lincoln that our textbooks and public history misrepresent. Other antiracist idealists get the same treatment. Almost none gets any attention except John Brown, and during the nadir, textbook authors eliminated him as a serious moral or political ancestor by focusing on whether or not he was mentally ill, an emphasis that persists in today's textbooks. As a result, white students who would be antiracist have to reinvent the genre from scratch.

Conversely, just as textbook authors suggested mental illness so students did not have to take Brown seriously, they did the same thing so students did not have to take John Wilkes Booth seriously. "A half-crazed, fanatically pro-Southern actor, John Wilkes Booth, slipped behind Lincoln as he sat in his box and shot him in the head," according to the authors of *The American Pageant*, still available in its seventeenth edition (list price $159.95) as of 2019. This description of Booth dates to the original 1956 edition by Thomas Bailey.[14] The other five recent textbooks I sampled for the current edition of *Lies My Teacher Told Me* do not question Booth's sanity but also never mention white supremacy. Each merely uses the phrase "Southern sympathizer."

In fact, the incident that pushed Booth over the edge was a speech Lincoln gave from the White House balcony on April 11, 1865. There, he repeated what he had said to a Black crowd in Richmond a week earlier, when he walked to the "Confederate White House" the day after the United States liberated the Virginia city. As well as I can tell, in Richmond Lincoln said, "As long as I live *no* one shall put a shackle on your limbs, and you shall have *all* the rights which God has given to every other free citizen of this Republic." From the White House, he proposed specifically that at least some African Americans, North and South, should have the right to vote. Booth was in the crowd that night and said to two companions: "That means nigger citizenship. That is the last speech he will ever make. . . . By God, I'll put him through."[15] So Abraham Lincoln was murdered in the cause of white supremacy—just like Medgar Evers, Viola Liuzzo, Martin Luther King, and so many others, including the nine parishioners in Charleston, South Carolina, in 2015, and Heather Heyer in Charlottesville, Virginia, two years later.

Imagine the effect on a young Black student of realizing that a white supremacist killed Lincoln! Imagine the effect on a young white student! Yet not one textbook mentions white supremacy or racism as Booth's motivation.

Indeed, authors rarely use either term at all. Why not? Because both remain controversial. Is Donald Trump racist? Did the Confederacy embody white supremacy? Questions like these might pitch some parents against others in a high school PTA meeting. We cannot have that! "When you're publishing a book," as a Holt, Rinehart, and Winston representative once said to me, "if there's something that is controversial, it's better to take it out."

Unfortunately, by suppressing the racism in our past, history textbooks make it hard for students to understand racism in our present society. And by suppressing the antiracist idealism of Abraham Lincoln, textbooks withhold from students a role model who might inspire them to deal with that racism. And for what? Surely American civilization will endure if textbooks no longer "protect us" from Lincoln's ideas, or even—shudder—his words.

Ironically, then, the first task facing those of us—academics and not—who want to carry forward Lincoln's unfinished work is to rehabilitate Abraham Lincoln himself, so he can be our ally. That rehabilitation must not be based on one-sided scholarship. Part of his meaning includes a full consideration of his flaws, especially in the area of race. If Lerone Bennett ignores, minimizes, or explains away most of Lincoln's positive acts and utterances in the area of race, which he does, he has also performed a service by reminding us of occasions when Lincoln was clearly guilty of remarkably racist deeds and statements.

We must admit that on occasion Lincoln was a racist, but we must also point out that he was an *anti*racist. We need not cherry-pick his speeches and writings to present his most uplifting and equalitarian phrases out of context. Rather, we can point to the arc of Lincoln's career, the ideological and cultural context of his speeches and writings, and the fact that his actions throughout his presidency always proved barely doable politically. Then we can justly extract the meaning of his life for our time.

Abraham Lincoln believed in America because he believed its basic dynamic ultimately stood for true equality of opportunity for all. As he wrote to Congress on the Fourth of July, 1861, the "leading object" of government is "to lift artificial weights from all shoulders—to clear the paths of laudable pursuit for all—to afford all, an unfettered start, and a fair chance, in the race of life."

True equality of opportunity underlies the Morrill Act of 1862, which set up public universities in every state, most having no or low tuition. Surely we can extrapolate to conclude that Lincoln would favor making college affordable for all.[16] When Republicans next compiled a party platform after his assassination, it included "liberal and just" immigration policies, advocated "removal of the disqualifications and restrictions imposed upon the late rebels" if they accepted "impartial justice and equal rights," and even declared "sympathy with all the oppressed people which are struggling for their rights." These ideas clearly accord with Lincoln's thinking. They help explain why, around the world, people still cherish his memory.

Today's new outcries against Confederate monuments provide a welcoming milieu for recovering a robust Lincoln, rather than the flattened Lincoln now provided by our textbooks and monuments. Let us make use of this opportunity. "It is for us, the living," quoting the president at Gettysburg, to dedicate ourselves first to putting back into our culture a true image of Lincoln's idealism, and then to use it to carry on the unfinished work which he so nobly advanced.

NOTES

1. James W. Loewen, *Lies My Teacher Told Me* (1995; repr., New York: New Press, 2018).

2. Actually one textbook, from the long-ago "inquiry text" movement around 1980, actually asks students questions about the speech, thus bringing it into the main narrative. The other seven just leave it in the corner.

3. Burton, *The Essential Lincoln,* 120–22. Eight of the eighteen textbooks I studied for *Lies My Teacher Told Me* do include the second inaugural, but seven only quote the "safe" final paragraph, "With malice toward none. . . ." Only one includes anything about slavery.

4. He also favored women's suffrage in that early year. See Burton, *The Age of Lincoln,* 111.

5. Lincoln to John A. Gilmer, Springfield, IL, Dec. 15, 1860, in *Abraham Lincoln: Speeches and Writings, 1859–1865,* ed. Don. E. Fehrenbacher (New York: Library of America, 1989), 190–92.

6. See Moncure D. Conway, *Autobiography: Memories and Experiences* (London: Cassel and Co., 1903), 307. Conway (1832–1904) was a prominent American abolitionist.

7. Presciently, he also said to them, "When the hour comes for dealing with slavery, I trust I will be willing to do my duty though it cost my life." Ibid. And, of course, it did.

8. Of course, this term rarely saw print. Even in the Lincoln-Douglas debates, attended by stenographers, "nigger" routinely got changed to "negro." Harold Holzer, interviewed by Brian Lamb, Booknotes: *The Lincoln-Douglas Debates,* C-Span, July 21, 1993, c-span.org/video/?49145-1 /the-lincoln-douglas-debates. Nevertheless, some contemporaneous newspapers do make the point verbatim, including *Martinsburg (TN) Herald,* quoted by *Shepherdstown (WV) Register,* Oct. 21, 1892; J. F. Stone, "Roast for Republicans," *St. Paul Daily Globe,* May 2, 1894; and "Opening their Eyes," *St. Landry Clarion* (Opelousas, LA), Jan. 2, 1897. (The *Clarion* mischaracterized the *New York Herald* but makes the point nonetheless.) Cf. Joe B. Wilkins, "The Participation of the Richmond Negro in Politics, 1890–1900" (master's thesis, University of Richmond, 1972); and Donna A. Barnes, *The Louisiana Populist Movement* (Baton Rouge: Louisiana State University Press, 2011), 203–4.

9. See Barry Schwartz, *Abraham Lincoln and the Forge of National Memory* (Chicago: University of Chicago Press, 2000).

10. Scott Sandage, "A Marble House Divided," in *Race and the Production of Modern American Nationalism,* ed. R. J. Scott-Childress (Abingdon-on-Thames: Routledge, 2014), 277–78.

11. Decades earlier, Lincoln had specifically invited African Americans to social and business occasions at the White House.

12. Lerone Bennett Jr., *Forced into Glory: Abraham Lincoln's White Dream* (Chicago: Johnson, 2000).

13. James Ronald Kennedy and Walter Donald Kennedy, *The South Was Right!* (1991; repr., Gretna, LA: Pelican, 1994), 26–32. Thomas J. DiLorenzo makes a similar false claim in *The Real Lincoln* (New York: Three Rivers, 2003).

14. Bailey, who actually wrote the first edition of this textbook, much of which is still his prose, is now not even listed as an author of it. This puts the listed authors, David M. Kennedy and Lizabeth Cohen, into the position of plagiarism. This is ironic, for as I showed in *Lies My Teacher Told Me* (315–21) and brought to public awareness in the *New York Times* (Diana Jean Schemo, "Schoolbooks Are Given F's in Originality," July 13, 2006, nytimes.com/2006/07/13/books/13textbook .html [subscription]), today's listed authors are the ones who never wrote "their" textbooks, and my conversations with Kennedy convinced me he never wrote this one. See also Ray Raphael, "Thomas A. Bailey: Dead and Forgotten by His Publisher?," History News Network, Apr. 26, 2015, historynewsnetwork.org/article/159214.

15. David D. Porter, *Incidents and Anecdotes of the Civil War* (New York: Appleton, 1886), 295. On Booth, see, for example, William Hanchett, *The Lincoln Murder Conspiracies* (Urbana: University of Illinois Press, 1983), chap. 2, n.9.

16. Amy Sherman, "Was College Once Free in [the] United States, as Bernie Sanders Says?" Politifact Florida, Feb. 9, 2016, politifact.com/florida/statements/2016/feb/09/bernie-s/was-college -once-free-united-states-and-it-oversea/.

Looking at Lincoln from the Effigy Mound

STEPHEN KANTROWITZ

As activists turned critical eyes on the American commemorative landscape in 2020, Abraham Lincoln did not escape. Protestors toppled one of his statues in Portland, Oregon, and officials dismantled another in Boston; it is not clear how much longer he will stand in Lincoln Park in Washington, DC.[1] The Lincoln question remained a minor part of the year's upheaval, but it reverberated loudly at the University of Wisconsin–Madison, where a larger-than-life statue of the sixteenth president occupies Bascom Hill, one of the most prominent sites on campus. After years of simmering challenges, a coalition of students called on the chancellor to remove the Lincoln statue, in part for reasons that Civil War scholars and teachers will find familiar.[2] Their bullet-point broadside against the statue began with two ways that the memorial reflects the history of anti-Black racism. First, they quoted Lincoln's infamous line from the 1858 Charleston, Illinois, debate with Stephen Douglass—"I am not, nor ever have been, in favor of bringing about in any way the social and political equality of the white and black races."[3] Second, they argued that Madison's Lincoln sprang from an ugly seed: it was the brainchild of the virulently racist newspaper editor Richard Lloyd Jones, whose *Tulsa Tribune* is often charged with having provoked the Tulsa Massacre of 1921.[4]

After twenty-five years of teaching Civil War–era history at the University of Wisconsin–Madison, I feel reasonably well prepared for a debate about Lincoln in relation to the freedom and standing of African Americans. It stands beyond dispute that for most of his life Lincoln imagined and sought to build a free, white republic. In 1858, he did not believe white Americans would accept African Americans as equals and knew that to insist that they should would be the end of his political career, which was dedicated not to abolition or equality but to preventing the further expansion of slavery. I also think that our assessment of Lincoln's life and legacy must move beyond 1858 to take account of the remarkable transformation of his last years. During the Civil War, Lincoln learned to heed the voices and examples of African American activists and freedom seekers. As those lessons came home, he began to speak and make policy as though African Americans belonged to what he called the "family of freedom," entitled to equal standing and even equal suffrage.[5] This ability to evolve in response to radical demands for equality makes Lincoln special, perhaps unique, among US presidents. But one can believe this and at the same time believe, as his admirer Frederick Douglass did, that while white people were the "children of Abraham Lincoln," African Americans were "only his step-children, children by adoption, children by force of circumstances and necessity." Without the opening the Civil War created for African Americans to make themselves essential to the Union cause, Lincoln's awakening would not have occurred.[6] On the students' second point, while there's no evidence that Jones's racism figured directly in his affection for the sixteenth president, there's also no whitewashing the statue's origin story.

But the 2020 challenge to Lincoln featured an element that many observers found new and disquieting: Lincoln's unambiguous commitment to the American conquest of Indian Country. The second half of the students' broadside against the statue focused on the Homestead Act and the Pacific Railway Act, 1862 laws for which Lincoln and the wartime Republican Party have generally been celebrated, not criticized. These laws, they noted, promoted the conquest of Native homelands. Native resistance to invasion brought the US military to the plains, where it waged the bloody and calamitous Indian Wars of the late nineteenth century. These ended with Native nations stripped of most of their land and autonomy.

What happens when Lincoln's career is told not as a story of antislavery commitment and egalitarian awakening, but as a strikingly if not uniquely bloody chapter in the history of conquest and colonialism? What if conquest is, with rare exceptions, the story of the American presidency as seen from Indian Country? The conversation about Lincoln opened by Native American history is complex and multilayered, but it cannot be told as a story of growth, and it may not provide us with a Lincoln for our time—at any rate, not one deserving honor or emulation. Indeed, it opens the door to questions about American history that strike at the core of national narratives of progress, inclusion, and equality. To those for whom the national history is an essential resource for contemporary civic life, the implications are troubling. Under such circumstances, historians, myself included, are wont to fall back on words such as "balance" and "complexity." "History is complex and nuanced and a lot of the figures we revere, like [George] Washington or Lincoln, are not perfect in all things," one historian who opposed removing the statue told the UW–Madison student newspaper. "We should be able to tell that complex story instead of saying, 'This guy was all bad and we should get rid of him.'" For this scholar, toppling Lincoln on the basis of his Indian policy alone was a bridge too far. It was an existential challenge to the national story. "You could destroy our entire history because it's based entirely on dispossession of Native Americans," she worried.[7]

Such hyperbolic concerns reflect the profound discomfort that can accompany what ought to be an uncontroversial statement: like every other president of his era, Lincoln was unwavering in his commitment to the conquest of Indian Country. If that language sounds harsh, it is only because we are more accustomed to acknowledging its truth via euphemistic slogans that come from the Civil War era itself: "Manifest Destiny" and "Free Soil." It may be easy to see the first slogan as raw propaganda, but the second is more seductive. Many of us who teach the Civil War era consciously or unconsciously align ourselves with the forces of antislavery and emancipation rather than with its foes. Even though we understand that opposition to the extension of slavery was a far cry from egalitarian abolitionism, we also know that the antiextensionist program signified by "Free Soil" played a crucial role in building an antislavery coalition. Lincoln embodies this history. Although he found slavery morally repugnant—"If slavery is not wrong, nothing is wrong," he concluded in 1864—for most of his career, Lincoln did not call for its abolition; instead, his strategic goal was to prevent it from spreading beyond its current borders so that a white society based on free labor, not a slaveholding society, could populate the West.[8] "Free Soil," despite the racism of many of its proponents, represents part of the broad antislavery coalition that brought the Republican Party to power, supported the war against the Confederacy, helped transform that fight into a war against slavery, and took enormous if insufficient steps toward creating a more just and equal nation. But when we use "Free Soil" in this way, we obscure the violence kenneled in its terms, an assumption that was fundamental to Lincoln's career and the nation's expansion: that western soil was "free" for the taking.

At universities such as Wisconsin's flagship, this assumption is literally foundational. The Madison students pointed to the Homestead Act and Pacific Railway Act, but they could easily have focused on the third 1862 law that realized the Republican program, the Morrill Land Grant College Act. This law granted states 30,000 acres of the public domain for each of their congressional seats; the proceeds from the sale of these lands were used to found new agricultural and mechanical colleges or support existing ones, such as the University of Wisconsin. The "public domain," of course, was land extracted from Native nations by war, coercive diplomacy, or the desperation born of previous acts of conquest. But this is not how conventional narratives of American history describe land-grant universities, homesteading settlers, railroad workers, or the triumph of the "golden spike" that completed the Pacific railroad. The university's official position is that the Morrill Act earned Lincoln a place of honor at the state's land-grant university. "Abe is actually here because he was the person who really created public universities in the states throughout this country in a very real way," the chancellor told the student newspaper.[9]

Land-grant universities are the pride and economic engines of many states, including Wisconsin, so it is disquieting to be reminded of their dual character as optimistic promoters of the common good and engines of Native dispossession. In the 2020 Land Grab Universities project, scholars and journalists at *High Country News* documented the enormous benefits that accrued to American universities through the Morrill Act—the value of nearly eleven million acres of what had been Indigenous land, which has now grown into about a half-billion dollars in endowment wealth that supports institutions that overwhelmingly serve non-Native students. UW–Madison reaped modest benefits from the Morrill Act, but that law was only one of the many state and federal land seizures and land grants through which public higher education in Wisconsin profited from the dispossession of Native people. It is not what the chancellor had in mind, but UW–Madison's Lincoln statue is as good a place as any to begin thinking about this tradition of land taking and the way universities have profited from and celebrated it.[10]

The disquieting dual character of land-grant universities is in fact common to American institutions and American places. In her history of the early Wisconsin Territory, aptly titled *The Settler's Empire*, historian Bethel Saler asks us to consider antebellum America as "both a postcolonial republic and a contiguous domestic empire."[11] The development of republican institutions coexisted, and not just incidentally, with the forcible transformation of Indian homelands into American farms, fields, and towns. These interwoven projects of building a state and seizing a territory created what we call "the American West," and they reached new heights with the wartime enactments of the Lincoln administration. Scholars frequently describe this process as "settler-colonialism," a project of conquest and replacement that entailed the dispossession or destruction of Native nations.[12] Like it or not, the duality of conquest and creation was fundamental to the nineteenth-century United States.

The figure of Lincoln atop one of the university's highest hills actually makes that duality concrete. In order to explain how, we must move beyond abstractions such as "conquest" and "Indians" to acknowledge that the university was built on land seized from the Ho-Chunk people. Madison, Wisconsin, has been a dot on the Jeffersonian grid of township and range for less than two centuries. But it has been a Native homeland for at least 12,000 years, known for much of that time by another name, Teejop, which means "Four Lakes" in the language of the Ho-Chunk. Their fields, villages, and hunting grounds long girdled the region's shores and riverbanks, and they have never stopped considering this place part of their homeland. They live here today. Ho-Chunk people hold sacred the region's abundant water, plant, and animal life, not to mention its many burial mounds. Before the US conquest, the region contained a thousand or so of these mounds, ranging from dozens to hundreds of feet in length. Many of them are effigies, representing bears, geese, water spirits, or other figures that are elements of the Ho-Chunk clan system. Settlers destroyed 90 percent of the mounds during the first century after the US invasion of Teejop, including dozens that once stood on the current university's grounds.[13]

Teejop was a small part of the much larger territory claimed by the Ho-Chunk, which embraced a large proportion of what is today southern Wisconsin and northwestern Illinois. Across this domain, Ho-Chunk families lived in semi-autonomous bands. They did not share one perspective as to how to respond to the growing pressure on Indian Country from the United States. Many traveled east to take up arms with Tecumseh's confederation in the second decade of the nineteenth century, but others did not. As Americans began to invade their territory in the 1820s, the Ho-Chunks strove to avoid direct confrontation. But they could not ignore the squatters who took possession of their lead diggings, and some retaliated proportionally for acts of violence. These small-scale conflicts brought a massive response from the US military, which ended in 1829 when the United States forced the Ho-Chunk nation to cede the southern third of its territory. This traumatic rupture was only the beginning of broader conflict and land loss. When the Sauk leader Black Hawk defied a treaty and brought his followers back across the Mississippi River in 1832, some Ho-Chunk bands sided with him, others strove to remain neutral, and some sought to improve their bargaining position by offering their services to the Americans. This was the conflict we know as the Black Hawk War.[14]

Those who are familiar with Lincoln's early life can now see where this is heading. In the early summer of 1832, when the Illinois militia traveled to the outskirts of Teejop, young Captain Abraham Lincoln was among them. Although these troops were led by American officers, they were guided through the territory by locals—that is, by Ho-Chunk and other Native people who had (or at least claimed to have) cast their lot with the United States. Among the two hundred or so Ho-Chunk, Menominee, and Potawatomi fighters who accompanied the American forces under Generals Dodge and Atkinson, Lincoln might well have noticed Ho-Chunk leaders such as White Crow and Spotted Arm, whose villages lay on Teejop's lakeshores.[15]

While some Ho-Chunks served alongside the US troops in this campaign, it seems pretty clear that many, if not most, sought only to defuse the conflict and move both Black Hawk's band and the Americans out of their territory as quickly as possible. They hoped that by doing so they could prevent a wider war that they feared would result in another calamitous treaty of cession.[16] These efforts failed. Soldiers massacred Black Hawk's band a month later as they tried to escape across the Mississippi, after which the US government followed its traditional pattern. It assigned collective guilt and forced all the Ho-Chunks—including those allied with the United States—to cede another vast portion of their territory in the Treaty of 1832, which the American negotiators unapologetically described as taking place "on the blended grounds of conquest & contract."[17] This cession included Teejop, where White Crow's village stood. Just five years later, in 1837, US officials coerced and cheated Ho-Chunk negotiators into another treaty, which stripped them of the rest of their Wisconsin homelands and assigned them to territory across the Mississippi. The Ho-Chunks never accepted the validity of this treaty, and over the next fifty years, large numbers of them persistently returned to Teejop and other parts of Wisconsin. By the 1870s, their determination and their canny navigation of evolving US policies finally gained them the right to remain in Wisconsin, where they today comprise the federally recognized Ho-Chunk Nation.[18]

The Black Hawk War plays an inconsequential part in most accounts of Lincoln's life, in part because Lincoln diminished his own role in it. "I had a good many bloody struggles with the mosquitoes," he joked in Congress.[19] But, in fact, Lincoln was right up against the edge of this conflict. His unit once arrived just after the ambush and massacre of a militia company. Just days before mustering out, he and his men unwittingly camped less than a day's march from the swamps where Ho-Chunk villagers sheltered and fed Black Hawk's band. Much more importantly, Lincoln's dismissal of his role misleads us in a fundamental way about the significance of his service. Militia volunteers on the frontier—the kind of service Lincoln experienced—were an essential component of the nineteenth-century conquest of the West. They were the white men through whom the American state asserted its authority to demand that Indians trade their land for an uncertain peace—the shock troops of this phase of "Manifest Destiny."

This is not how we have learned to think about Lincoln the soldier. Consider the only well-known story—perhaps a fable—of Lincoln and Indians drawn from the Black Hawk War, one of the reminiscences solicited by William Herndon following the president's assassination. During the war, the story went, an old Potawatomi man entered the Illinois militiamen's camp. Some assumed he was a spy and reached for their weapons to kill him. Lincoln courageously interposed himself between the soldiers and the Native man.[20] The story's factual basis is unclear, but its moral was plain: Lincoln was no Indian hater but a fearless defender of the downtrodden.

But there is a better-known and less-reassuring story about Lincoln and the violence of frontier conflict: his role in the execution of the Dakota 38. This event is well known to many people in the upper Midwest and across Indian Country, but its outlines bear repeating. In brief, the US conquest and settlement of the Minnesota Territory during the 1850s forced several bands of Dakotas (known to Americans as "Sioux") onto small territories in exchange for annual payments guaranteed by treaty. In 1862 the government failed to make these payments on time, causing serious hunger as well as conflict between Dakotas and American traders unwilling to extend them credit. In August, the Dakotas responded by going to war against the US invasion and occupation of their homeland, killing many settlers over a number of weeks and inducing many more to flee the region. The United States retaliated with overwhelming force. By the end of September, its soldiers had defeated, put to flight, or captured many Dakota combatants and noncombatants. Military officials subjected nearly five hundred Dakota men to hasty and irregular military tribunals. They sentenced more than three hundred of them to death, frequently on the basis of hearsay.[21] Lincoln reviewed the cases and commuted a large majority of the sentences, but he also let more than three dozen stand. On the day after Christmas, 1862, US officials hanged thirty-eight Dakota men from a giant gallows in the center of Mankato, Minnesota. It remains the largest mass execution in US history.[22]

Although this history was not central to the 2020 Lincoln controversy in Madison, the execution of the Dakota 38 had driven a wave of protests against the statue only three years earlier. In 2017, UW–Madison's American Indian student organization called for an interpretive plaque on the statue to acknowledge Lincoln's role in the 1862 executions. The university's student government endorsed this demand; its chair described the mass execution as a "massacre" for which the president bore responsibility.[23] The university chancellor rejected their demands. The student newspaper quoted her as saying that Lincoln played a "restraining role," insisting on "personally weeding through all of this, and he ends up saying 'I'm only going to take the sentences of those who we have evidence, witness evidence, that they were involved in either killing or raping, and everyone else we are going to dismiss charges on.'" The moral was that Lincoln was striving to do right in circumstances not of his choosing.

If the chancellor's version of the story sounds familiar, it is because so many historians have written it this way. The common account places Lincoln's actions in the context of the aftermath of the US–Dakota War, when vengeful settlers threatened to massacre the prisoners and rebel against the Republican Party politically unless the executions went forward. If one accepts these premises as facts beyond Lincoln's control, his commutation of the great majority of the death sentences becomes an example of his pragmatic but humane response to moral and political crisis. Another leader might have allowed all three hundred executions to go forward, but this one did not. Lincoln himself framed his decision in moral terms—"I could not afford to hang men for votes"—and many historians have followed suit.[24] So it is not surprising that, when preparing her response to the students' demands, the chancellor's conclusion closely matched the historians' consensus: Lincoln, facing a tragic choice, moderated the white frontier's worst impulses.[25]

The story of Lincoln, the commutations, and the executions, like the oft-told story of Lincoln, emancipation, and equality, focuses our attention on the dance of morality and pragmatism in his mind and heart. But what if this is an insufficient frame through which to view the mass execution in Mankato? What if we turn our attention away from Lincoln's heart and consider instead that the policies he championed throughout his life were guaranteed to produce conflicts such as the US–Dakota War and outcomes such as the tribunals and sentences of death? Certainly from a Dakota perspective, this is true. But why only from a Dakota perspective? Nothing prevents the non-Dakota, non-Native majority from contemplating Lincoln's decisions—who should live or die—as just one moment in a centuries-long history of colonial decision making. Viewed in this way, his commutations form a minor note in a broader story of the rise and triumph of "Free Soil" settler-colonialism.

Take the Kansas-Nebraska Act of 1854, which Lincoln said brought him back into political life. At the moment the Kansas Territory was "opened" to settlement, it was literally Indian Territory—land promised in perpetuity to tribes removed from the East. When the act passed in May 1854, not one acre had been treated for or purchased from its Indian inhabitants. Jayhawkers and border ruffians murdered one another over the fate of slavery in that territory. But on a more fundamental question, they agreed with one another—and with speculators, railroad companies, and US officers: all that Indian land was going to waste. By the end of the 1860s, virtually all of eastern Kansas was in non-Indian hands.[26] Here as elsewhere, the most persistent violators of treaties—squatters—generally got what they wanted. Once these white settlers established themselves within Indian country, the US government sooner or later arrived to demand new treaties and removals. Congress passed preemption laws that allowed squatters to recoup their illegal investments and be made whole as legitimate American settlers. But Lincoln only publicly condemned "squatting" when it seemed to be part of proslavery men's designs on territory that in his view ought to be designated "Free Soil."[27]

Or consider President Lincoln's response to the representatives of Southern Plains tribes who visited the White House in March 1863.[28] Prior to the war, the

United States had entered into treaties with the Apaches, Arapahos, Caddos, Cheyennes, Comanches, and Kiowas, but, as settlers and soldiers moved west, the government prevented or punished settler encroachments on those nations' territories only occasionally. During the Civil War, it did not even do that, and plains peoples at the edge of US settlement had good reason to fear the land-hungry and gold-seeking people now breaching their borders. In the 1863 meeting, Cheyenne chiefs Lean Bear and Spotted Wolf "pledged their tribal friendship but expressed dire concern about the encroachment of white settlers on their land." Lincoln promised to do his best to see the treaties were enforced—"we make treaties with you, and will try to observe them." But he had a few other things to say.

Through interpreters, Lincoln presented the delegates with a bleak choice of futures. They could adopt the habits and customs of American life and become numerous and prosperous like the Americans, or they could maintain their current way of life and risk annihilation. He set forth the age-old dichotomy between savagery and civilization in terms both self-serving and absurd. His own "palefaced people" were numerous and prosperous for two reasons, he explained. First, he said, Americans farmed rather than hunted. This was a red herring, of course: many Native peoples farmed, the Ho-Chunks among them, and not even the adoption of American-style farming and other elements of US "civilization" had protected Native nations from being forced from their homelands. This had been the fate of Cherokees, Choctaws, Creeks, Chickasaws, Potawatomis, and many more. The United States did not dispossess Indians because they did not farm but because white settlers wanted their land. Lincoln's second argument was even worse. Unlike Native Americans, he told the delegation, whites were "not, as a race, so much disposed to fight and kill one another as our red brethren." Lincoln made this claim, one assumes with a straight face, midway between the Battles of Stones River and Chancellorsville, which together left nearly 50,000 men killed, wounded, or missing in action. Yet as empirically indefensible as these arguments were, they were essential to the project of the settlement of the American West by free white people. And this was the project Lincoln spent his career pursuing.

The president spoke to a particular group of delegates, but he was not talking about particular Native people or peoples, their ways of life, or their histories. He instead articulated a monolithic idea of "Indianness" as a savage and static prehistory that must, sooner or later, give way to a progressive civilization—to Lincoln's idealized free-labor civilization.[29] Indians could only escape that prehistory if they abandoned being Indian—not just in adopting particular American habits and customs, but in literally surrendering their ways of talking, thinking, and being. This assumption was baked into Lincoln's view of American expansion, as it was for countless other Americans. A few viewed the consequences for Native people with more concern than Lincoln did, but many with much less. Only a handful of US citizens thought that Native sovereignty should stand in the way of American expansion to any significant degree.[30] Lincoln was not among them.

Perhaps this explains his cautious phrasing to the Southern Plains delegation: "we make treaties with you, and will *try* to observe them; and if our children should sometimes behave badly, and violate those treaties, it is against our wish."[31] Lincoln's qualification told the tale. A thoughtful man with a deep knowledge of his country's history, he knew that treaties with Indians were made to be broken. No one looking even briefly at the relations between the United States and the Indian nations in 1863 could argue otherwise. Even as the president and the delegates spoke, white soldiers and settlers prepared to strip the Ho-Chunks of their Minnesota treaty lands, though they had played no significant role in the US–Dakota War. Americans would deport the Ho-Chunks to a barren reservation in the West simply because angry settlers demanded their land.[32]

Lincoln could not make good on even his slenderest promises to the 1863 delegation. One of its members, Lean Bear, left Washington with a peace medal and a letter in Lincoln's hand declaring him a friend. In May 1864 US troops mistook Lean Bear for a hostile and shot him to pieces, the medal still around his neck and the letter still in his pocket. Six months later, on November 29, Colorado volunteers under Colonel John Chivington massacred and mutilated more than a hundred peaceful Cheyenne and Arapaho people in Black Kettle's village. Two more members of the delegation to the White House, War Bonnet and Standing in the Water, were among the dead.[33] But even the special horror of the Sand Creek Massacre is not the point.[34] Even if Lincoln could somehow have prevented these particular atrocities, he could not under any circumstances have stopped the flood of the US free-labor settlement of the West, nor did he wish to. The entire Republican program was based upon the necessity and the virtue of that conquest and settlement.[35] Lincoln's conscience is entirely beside the point.

*   *   *

In June 2019, after several years of negotiation and the labor of Ho-Chunk community members from Teejop to the tribal headquarters in Black River Falls, UW–Madison's chancellor and the president of Ho-Chunk Nation took part in a ceremony to install a plaque on Bascom Hill just a hundred feet from where the Lincoln statue sits. Its brief text acknowledges that the university sits on ancestral Ho-Chunk land, that the United States engaged in a half century of ethnic cleansing to dispossess them, and that despite this, Ho-Chunk people remain here. It invokes the vision of a "shared future" between the university and the state's twelve Native nations. At the ceremony, Ho-Chunk Nation president Wilfrid Cleveland offered his hope for the university community "that this plaque will cause them to dig a little deeper, that it will be a spark for them to learn about the Ho-Chunk people and the sacredness we hold for this land." In response, the chancellor committed the university to beginning a conversation "that moves us from ignorance to awareness."[36] In the two years since, Our Shared Future has become a campus-wide project of education and events, including an observance recognizing the anniversary of the 1832 treaty that gives the non-Ho-Chunk people the right to be in Teejop.[37] But to make this work meaningful requires more than intentions and attention; it requires resources.

To think seriously about a shared future, we must confront our shared past. In one sense, a reckoning with Lincoln can only scratch the surface of this history. But at the same time, the veneration of Lincoln is so deeply woven into the US national story that to explore him from this angle can be unsettling. Ho-Chunk people know this history, and they know that most non-Native people do not. As Ho-Chunk tribal member and UW–Madison graduate student Kendra Greendeer writes, the Lincoln statue is a reminder "that this institution was not built with the intention of including me." And Ho-Chunk people know that even when they protest the statue, the university resists their demands.[38]

Over the past two years, as I have tried to tell these stories with various audiences in mind, I have resisted announcing a verdict of my own on "the Lincoln question." Indeed, I have resisted reaching one. This has at least two roots. Part of it stems from my skepticism about the value of many fights over symbols. I am aware of the deep investment that many past and present members of the university community feel in the statue. They touch Lincoln's foot for good luck; they climb into his lap for graduation photos.[39] I worry that simply removing the statue will produce great ill will without producing either greater understanding or a campus that is a better home for its Native students and other students of color. I fear being drawn into a fight that may generate more heat than light.

Another part of my resistance is rooted in a hope: if any institution in our society can take the time to listen, learn, deliberate, and decide, it should be a university. I understand the long tradition of students making demands on the officials who command institutional power and resources. I am mindful of the equally long tradition of university administrations waiting out student protestors, knowing that sooner or later they will graduate. But if we take the challenge posed by Our Shared Future seriously, neither a demand nor a capitulation is sufficient. Not all conflicts can be talked away, but the students, staff, faculty, and alumni of the university have a responsibility to respond, thoughtfully and deliberately, to the actual question before us. From my point of view, that question is not about whether Lincoln was a sinner (who isn't?) or a saint (who is?) or about "balance." It is not really about Lincoln at all, but about the university—how it came to be, what it has been, what it is, and what we hope it can become. In that conversation, the campus's Native past and present must play the central role.

That conversation must be followed by a thoughtful reallocation of resources that reshapes the relationship between the university, Native people, and Native nations. In the past two years, the university for the first time has established a full-time director of tribal relations and a half-time Indigenous education coordinator. This is a start. What comes next is not for me alone to say, but some obvious possibilities include extending these staffing commitments and—in recognition of the people on whose land the university sits, and the land sold for its benefit—providing free tuition to the members of the state's twelve Native nations. And surely there are ways to better support Native students once they arrive on campus, heeding Greendeer's reminder that the institution—like nearly all American colleges and universities—was not created to include them. Such questions and conversations about resources are under way on a growing number of campuses, from Cornell to the University of California.[40]

Whatever happens, we are unlikely to be finished with Lincoln any time soon. I know I will not be. I will probably always teach the speech by Frederick Douglass that names him both as "near and dear to our hearts" and as "pre-eminently the white man's president." I still find his journey out of anti-Blackness moving and instructive. But now, as I walk up the hill from my office toward the statue, that twentieth-century rendering of a nineteenth-century politician no longer seems so permanent and immovable, not in comparison to the 12,000-year history of Native life in Teejop. The people who made that history are still here, not relics of the past, but a people, a culture, and a nation. I consider what this landscape looks like to them—how the veneer of Madison presses down upon Teejop, and how Teejop remains. The signs of it are everywhere, now that I know to look.

You can look, too. Stop near the top of the hill, just west of the campus's oldest building. Here, a stone's throw from the statue, burial mounds stood for a thousand years until they were flattened during construction in 1851.[41] Stand where they used to be, where the remains of Ho-Chunk ancestors still lie, somewhere down below. Stand there, and look at Lincoln as if from Indian Country.

NOTES

1. John Hart, "UW–Madison Students Call for Removal of Abraham Lincoln Statue on Bascom Hill," *Wisconsin State Journal* (Madison), June 27, 2020, https://madison.com/wsj/news/local/education /university/uw-madison-students-call-for-removal-of-abraham-lincoln-statue-on-bascom-hil /article_b12c83c9-38a1-5e68-9964-beabe4046d02.html (accessed Apr. 19, 2021); Sergio Olmos, Ryan Haas, and Rebecca Ellis, "Portland Protesters Tear down Roosevelt, Lincoln Statues during 'Day of Rage,'" *OPB*, Oct. 12, 2020, https://www.opb.org/article/2020/10/12/portland-protesters-tear-down-roosevelt-lincoln-statues-during-day-of-rage/ (accessed Apr. 23, 2021); William J. Kole, "Statue of Slave Kneeling before Lincoln Is Removed in Boston," Associated Press, Dec. 29, 2020, https:// apnews.com/article/marty-walsh-us-news-1bbe10800ca102f9af56a6a04615adb5 (accessed Apr. 21, 2021); Aishvarya Kavi, "Activists Push for Removal of Statue of Freed Slave Kneeling before Lincoln," *New York Times*, June 27, 2020, updated Dec. 29, 2020, https://www.nytimes.com/2020/06/27/us /politics/lincoln-slave-statue-emancipation.html (accessed Apr. 21, 2021).

2. "UW–Madison Students Call for Removal"; Student Inclusion Coalition of UW-Madison (@ SICofUW), "Reasons to Remove Abe: A History of Racism and Violence," Twitter, June 13, 2020, 11:44 a.m., https://twitter.com/SICofUW/status/1271845999569440768/photo/1 (accessed Apr. 19, 2021).

3. National Park Service, "Fourth Debate: Charleston, Illinois," Lincoln Home National Historic Site, updated Apr. 10, 2015, https://www.nps.gov/liho/learn/historyculture/debate4.htm (accessed Apr. 19, 2021).

4. University of Wisconsin–Madison Archives (uwmadarchives), "How Abe Came to Be on Bascom Hill," Tumblr, https://uwmadarchives.tumblr.com/post/162629610036/how-abe-came-to-be-on-bascom/embed (accessed Jan. 1, 2020); "Tulsa Race Riot: A Report by the Oklahoma Commission to Study the Tulsa Race Riot of 1921," Feb. 28, 2001, https://www.okhistory.org/research /forms/freport.pdf (accessed Jan. 1, 2020), esp. 54–60; Scott Ellsworth, *Death in a Promised Land: The Tulsa Race Riot of 1921* (Baton Rouge: Louisiana State University Press, 1982); Alfred L. Brophy, *Reconstructing the Dreamland: The Tulsa Race Riot of 1921—Race, Reparations, and Reconciliation* (New York: Oxford University Press, 2002); Tim Madigan, *The Burning: Massacre, Destruction, and the Tulsa Race Riot of 1921* (New York: Macmillan, 2001).

5. Lincoln to Gov. Michael Hahn, Mar. 13, 1864, Documents, Teaching American History, https://teachingamericanhistory.org/library/document/letter-to-governor-michael-hahn/ (accessed Apr. 23, 2021).

6. "Douglass on Lincoln," *New York Times,* Apr. 22, 1876.

7. "UW—Madison Students Call for Removal"; Jenny Whiddent, "In Land of Lincoln, What's Wrong with Statues of Honest Abe?," *Chicago Tribune,* Mar. 5, 2021, https://www.chicagotribune.com/politics/ct-chicago-monuments-controversy-lincoln-20210305-gkqw3jupzrdy5aa2gedts43kpi-htmlstory.html (accessed Apr. 21, 2021).

8. Lincoln to Albert G. Hodges, Apr. 4, 1864, in *Collected Works of Abraham Lincoln,* ed. Roy P. Basler et al., 9 vols. (New Brunswick, NJ: Rutgers University Press, 1953–55), 7:281.

9. Lawrence Andrea, "Blank Says There Will Not Be a Plaque Honoring Natives on Lincoln Statue," *Daily Cardinal,* Oct. 9, 2017, https://www.dailycardinal.com/article/2017/10/blank-says-there-will-not-be-a-plaque-honoring-natives-on-lincoln-statue (accessed Dec. 31, 2019).

10. For an introduction to the project, see Robert Lee and Tristan Ahtone, "Land-Grab Universities," *High Country News* 52 (Apr. 2020): 32–45. The searchable database and reporting can be found at https://www.landgrabu.org/universities/ (accessed Apr. 19, 2021). On the array of other legislation that turned Native land to universities' benefit, see, for example, Alyssa Mt. Pleasant and Stephen Kantrowitz, "Campuses, Colonialism, and Land Grabs before Morrill," *NAIS: Journal of the Native American and Indigenous Studies Association* 8 (Spring 2021): 151–56.

11. Bethel Saler, *The Settlers' Empire: Colonialism and State Formation in America's Old Northwest* (Philadelphia: University of Pennsylvania Press, 2015), 1.

12. For an introduction to this mode of analysis, see Patrick Wolfe, "Land, Labor, and Difference: Elementary Structures of Race," *American Historical Review* 106 (June 2001): 866–905; and Wolfe, "Settler Colonialism and the Elimination of the Native," *Journal of Genocide Research* 8 (Dec. 2006): 387–409.

13. My description of preconquest Teejop draws on research conducted by members of the Teejop Community History Project, including Omar Poler, Tara Tindall, Janice Rice, Kyla Beard, Kendra Greendeer, Chloris Lowe, and Missy Tracy. I am grateful to them for inviting me to participate in this work. It also draws on research conducted by UW–Madison graduate student Molli Pauliot and by Aaron Bird Bear, UW–Madison director of tribal relations. On the effigy mounds, see Robert A. Birmingham, *Spirits of Earth: The Effigy Mound Landscape of Madison and the Four Lakes* (Madison: University of Wisconsin Press, 2010); George Christiansen III, "Archaeological Investigations: University of Wisconsin–Madison Campus," Great Lakes Archaeological Research Center Project 04.005, June 2005, https://lakeshorepreserve.wisc.edu/wp-content/uploads/sites/27/2017/01/2005_Christiansen_UW_campuswide.pdf (accessed Jan. 1, 2020); and Kendra Greendeer, "The Land Remembers Native Histories," *Edge Effects,* Nov. 21, 2019, https://edgeeffects.net/native-histories/ (accessed Apr. 24, 2021).

14. This simplified account of Ho-Chunk history draws on the following: Nancy O. Lurie, "Winnebago," in *Handbook of North American Indians,* ed. William C. Sturtevant, vol. 15, *Northeast,* ed. Bruce G. Trigger (Washington: Smithsonian Institution, 1978), 690–707; Lucy Eldersveld Murphy, *A Gathering of Rivers: Indians, Métis, and Mining in the Western Great Lakes, 1737–1832* (Lincoln:

University of Nebraska Press, 2000); Kathleen Neils Conzen, "The Winnebago Urban System: Indian Policy and Townsite Promotion on the Upper Mississippi," in *Cities and Markets: Studies in the Organization of Human Space,* ed. Rondo Cameron and Leo F. Schnore (Lanham, MD: University Press of America, 1997), 269–310; Lawrence W. Onsager, "The Removal of the Winnebago Indians from Wisconsin in 1873–1874" (master's thesis, Loma Linda University, 1985); and Tom Jones, Michael Schmudlach, Matthew Daniel Mason, Amy Lonetree, and George Greendeer, *People of the Big Voice: Photographs of Ho-Chunk Families by Charles Van Schaick, 1879–1942* (Madison: Wisconsin Historical Society Press, 2011). On the Black Hawk War, see Libby Rose Tronnes, "Corn Moon Migrations: Ho-Chunk Belonging, Removal, and Return in the Early Nineteenth-Century Western Great Lakes" (PhD diss., UW–Madison, 2017); John Hall, *Uncommon Defense: Indian Allies in the Black Hawk War* (Cambridge, MA: Harvard University Press, 2009); and Patrick J. Jung, *The Black Hawk War of 1832* (Norman: University of Oklahoma Press, 2007).

15. On the movement of armies and Native allies, see Hall, *Uncommon Defense;* Jung, *Black Hawk War;* Alfred Augustus Jackson, "Abraham Lincoln in the Black Hawk War," in *Wisconsin Historical Collections 14* (Madison: State Historical Society of Wisconsin, 1898), 118–36; and *The Lincoln Log: A Daily Chronology of the Life of Abraham Lincoln,* http://www.thelincolnlog.org/Home.aspx (accessed Jan. 1, 2020). The locations of Ho-Chunk villages in the early 1830s, as noted by agent John Kinzie, are reproduced in Norton William Jipson, "History of the Winnebago Indians," unpublished ms., Chicago Historical Society.

16. This point is made persuasively in Tronnes, "Corn Moon Migrations."

17. "Ratified Treaty No. 169: Documents Relating to the Negotiation of the Treaty of September 15, 1832, with the Winnebago Indians," Indigenous Peoples of North America, Gale Primary Sources (from National Archives), http://tinyurl.galegroup.com/tinyurl/8qVeY6 (accessed Jan. 21, 2019), 9.

18. See Onsager, "Removal of the Winnebago Indians," and Stephen Kantrowitz, "'Not Quite Constitutionalized': The Meanings of 'Civilization' and the Limits of Native American Citizenship," in *The World the Civil War Made,* ed. Gregory P. Downs and Kate Masur (Chapel Hill: University of North Carolina Press, 2015), 75–105.

19. Don E. Fehrenbacher, ed., *Abraham Lincoln, Speeches and Writings,* vol. 1, *1832–1858* (New York: Library of America, 1989), 214. Even the one book explicitly about Lincoln in relation to Native Americans mentions his war service only in passing. See David Nichols, *Lincoln and the Indians: Civil War Policy and Politics* (1978; repr., St. Paul: Minnesota Historical Society Press, 2012).

20. Douglas L. Wilson and Rodney O. Davis, eds., *Herndon's Informants: Letters, Interviews, and Statements about Abraham Lincoln* (Urbana: University of Illinois Press, 1998), 18–19.

21. Carol Chomsky, "The United States–Dakota War Trials: A Study in Military Injustice," *Stanford Law Review* 43 (Nov. 1990): 13–98.

22. Scott W. Berg, *38 Nooses: Lincoln, Little Crow, and the Beginning of the Frontier's End* (New York: Vintage, 2012).

23. Andrea, "Blank Says There Will Not Be a Plaque."

24. Quoted in David Herbert Donald, *Lincoln* (New York: Simon & Schuster, 1995), 395.

25. Until recently, this subject has been so peripheral to mainstream analyses of Lincoln that some works passed over it entirely. See, for example, Richard J. Carwardine, *Lincoln* (London:

Pearson, 2003). The exculpatory tradition includes Donald, *Lincoln;* Stephen B. Oates, *With Malice toward None: A Life of Abraham Lincoln* (1977; repr., New York: Harper & Row, 1994), 368 ("Lincoln himself had intervened in the Minnesota Indian war of 1862 and prevented vengeful whites from executing a number of innocent Sioux"); and various opinion pieces, including David Von Drehle, "Abraham Lincoln Didn't Deserve Portland's Wrath," *Washington Post,* Oct. 13, 2020 ("265 lives were saved solely by the conscience of one man"); and Ron Soodalter, "Lincoln and the Sioux," *New York Times,* Aug. 20, 2012 ("the president oversaw the suppression of a violent American Indian uprising—and dealt with it with surprising clemency"). Eric Foner's brief analysis acknowledges Lincoln's commitment to dispossessing Indians of their land and the "free rein" he gave to western military commanders who went on to massacre Native people at Sand Creek and elsewhere. It nonetheless juxtaposes his commutations to the exterminationism of "Indian haters." Foner, *The Fiery Trial: Abraham Lincoln and American Slavery* (New York: Norton, 2010), 261. A handful of Lincoln-centered works focus squarely on his part in the conquest of Indian Country, notably Nichols, *Lincoln and the Indians,* and Berg, *38 Nooses.* A developing historiography seeks to reframe how we think about the relationship between the Civil War and Native American history. See, for example, Boyd Cothran and Ari Kelman, "How the Civil War Became the Indian Wars," *New York Times,* May 25, 2015; Megan Kate Nelson, *The Three-Cornered War: The Union, the Confederacy, and Native Peoples in the Fight for the West* (New York: Scribner, 2020).

26. Craig Miner and William E. Unrau, *The End of Indian Kansas: A Study of Cultural Revolution, 1854–1871* (1978; repr., Lawrence: University Press of Kansas, 1990).

27. See, for example, Lincoln's speech in the debate with Stephen Douglas at Quincy, Oct. 13, 1858, in Basler, *Collected Works of Abraham Lincoln,* 3:279. On squatters in antebellum political life and culture, see John Suval, "Dangerous Ground: Squatters, Statesmen, and the Rupture of American Democracy, 1830–1860" (PhD diss., University of Wisconsin–Madison, 2018).

28. My account of this meeting follows Clifford Krainik and Michele Krainik, "Photographs of Indian Delegates in the President's 'Summer House,'" White House Historical Association, https://www.whitehousehistory.org/photographs-of-indian-delegates-in-the-presidents-summer-house (accessed Jan. 1, 2020). Quotations from Lincoln in this and the next paragraph are from Basler, *Collected Works of Abraham Lincoln,* 6:151–52.

29. Robert F. Berkhofer Jr., *The White Man's Indian: Images of the American Indian from Columbus to the Present* (1978; repr., New York: Vintage, 1979); Steven Conn, *History's Shadow: Native Americans and Historical Consciousness in the Nineteenth Century* (Chicago: University of Chicago Press, 2004).

30. Natalie Joy, "The Indian's Cause: Abolitionists and Native American Rights," *Journal of the Civil War Era* 8, no. 2 (June 2018): 215–42. On the self-styled "benevolence" of plans to dispossess Native people of their homelands, see Nicholas Guyatt, *Bind Us Apart: How Enlightened Americans Invented Racial Segregation* (New York: Basic Books, 2016).

31. Italics mine.

32. "An Act for the Removal of the Winnebago Indians, and for the Sale of their Reservation in Minnesota for their Benefit," 12 *Stat.* 53, pp. 658–60 (Feb. 21, 1863).

33. Krainick and Krainick, "Photographs of Indian Delegates."

34. But see Ari Kelman, *A Misplaced Massacre: Struggling over the Memory of Sand Creek* (Cambridge, MA: Harvard University Press, 2013).

35. For an effective summary, see Megan Kate Nelson, "Today's Republicans Are like Lincoln in Only One Way," *New York Times,* Feb. 13, 2020.

36. Doug Erickson, "UW–Madison Heritage Marker Honors Ho-Chunk, Recognizes Land as Ancestral Home," June 24, 2019, https://news.wisc.edu/uw-madison-heritage-marker-honors-ho-chunk-recognizes-land-as-ancestral-home/ (accessed Apr. 19, 2021).

37. See Our Shared Future, https://oursharedfuture.wisc.edu/ (accessed Jan. 1, 2020).

38. Greendeer, "Land Remembers Native Histories."

39. Jenny Price, "Abraham Lincoln Statue," Tradition, *On Wisconsin,* Spring 2010, https://onwisconsin.uwalumni.com/traditions/abraham-lincoln-statue/ (accessed Apr. 23, 2021).

40. Jessica Douglas, "Cornell University Addresses Stolen Indigenous Land in New Project," *High Country News,* Oct. 23, 2020, https://www.hcn.org/issues/52.11/latest-cornell-university-addresses-stolen-indigenous-land-in-new-project (accessed May 6, 2021); Centers for Educational Justice and Community Engagement, "The University of California Land Grab," https://cejce.berkeley.edu/uc-land-grab (accessed May 6, 2021).

41. I thank UW–Madison Historic and Cultural Resources Manager Daniel Einstein for his "Summary of References to Burials within UW–Madison's ASI DA 573 on Bascom Hill, March 14, 2019," in author's possession.

The Unfinished Work of Clemson University

Full Recognition for Black Citizens in Its History

RHONDDA ROBINSON THOMAS

As late as 1945, the imprint of John C. and Floride Calhoun's Fort Hill Plantation was still visible on the Clemson Agricultural College of South Carolina's campus.[1] The Calhouns' home sat prominently at the top of a hill near the cadets' barracks and main classroom building, preserved "for the inspection of visitors" by a stipulation in their son-in-law Thomas Green Clemson's will that offered the property to the state for the establishment of the higher-education institution. Several plantation outbuildings and pieces of equipment also remained.[2] Thomas Clemson had not provided instructions for their use, however.

Instead of demolishing these elements of Fort Hill's built environment, Rudolph E. Lee, the first director of the college's architecture program, devised "Suggestions for the Restoration of Colonial Farm Life at Clemson College" to preserve them. At that time, several other plantation houses were located on the college's land, including Woodburn and Altamont,[3] along with log cabins more than a century old, the foundation stones for Fort Hill's quarters for enslaved field hands, an overseer's kitchen, a gristmill building, and antebellum farm machinery and tools. Lee conceptualized an attraction that "would be landscaped, using shrubbery and trees of colonial days, the streets lighted by the old type of oil lamps on posts (electrified); the streets topsoiled (oiled) and a post and rail fence built along each side of the property."[4] To cover the cost of establishing the farm, he proposed that rental apartments be developed in the Woodburn Plantation house before then transforming the home into a "magnificent Club House," a rental facility for groups to host receptions, meetings, luncheons, or games. Additionally, he suggested that the college could rent some of the cabins to older students, unmarried faculty, or veterans to generate revenue. Architecture students would be required to "study the design, plan and details of the buildings, a very important part of their training," Lee further recommended. "Properly landscaped this Restoration will be as attractive as a 'Little Williamsburg' and in connection with the John C. Calhoun mansion will be a show place, drawing many tourists to the Campus."[5]

Between Lee's introduction of a plan for a "Little Williamsburg" for Clemson and his retirement a few years later, the college's Buildings and Grounds Committee made several recommendations for memorialization on the campus. On May 16, 1945, committee members began by identifying nine buildings that could be named for "prominent men who had been connected with Clemson College in various capacities."[6] Clemson president Robert F. Poole may have been involved in this process, for a letter that committee chair David Watson wrote to him prior to the meeting indicates that the list of proposed names were "in line with your suggestions of several days ago."[7] Clemson trustees approved three of the committee's recommendations: The Administration Building, the most iconic structure on campus, was named for Benjamin R. Tillman, self-avowed white supremacist, influential South Carolina politician, and original Clemson successor trustee; two of the cadets' residential halls, Barracks No. 1 and Barracks No. 2, were named for Richard W. Simpson and Alan Johnstone, respectively.[8] Simpson signed South Carolina's Articles of Secession and served as a Confederate officer, as Thomas Clemson's lawyer, and as one of the college's first successor trustees. Johnstone, who had been elected as a state representative and senator and appointed as legislative and then a successor Clemson trustee, had hoped to serve in the Confederate army at age sixteen, but the Civil War ended before he could enlist. Clemson trustees eventually approved recommendations for renaming seven additional buildings in honor of influential white male trustees and past Clemson professors who were also Confederate veterans.[9]

Around this time, the Buildings and Grounds Committee also endorsed at least three memorial projects for Black people in Clemson history. They proposed the naming of a street for Sawney Sr., John C. Calhoun's "favorite" enslaved person; the installation of signage for the enslaved- and convicted-laborer burial ground located adjacent to the Calhoun family plot in Woodland Cemetery; and the naming of the new camellia test garden and a street for a longtime Black employee, Judge Crawford.[10] Clemson trustees approved only one of these recommendations, creating and naming Sawney Street.

For most of the university's existence, white males have controlled its history, creating a narrative of omission regarding the enslavement, oppression, and exploitation of Black laborers on the land and their contributions to the institution's establishment and development. Lee's well-intentioned efforts to create a "Little Williamsburg" focused on nostalgic, romanticized views of the Old South devoid of any references to the enslaved Black people owned by the Calhouns and Clemsons who had labored on the land. White renters could live in a beautifully restored plantation home filled with antiques and artwork. White visitors could socialize in a "magnificent" big house as if they were cast in scenes from *Gone with the Wind*. White Clemson cadets could lease rustic log cabins and attend classes in buildings built by mostly Black convicted laborers, unnamed and unhonored. Salamishah Tillet states: "The impact of such purged histories has been the denial of one of the constitutive markers of American citizenship, the right to recognition. . . . Americans can begin the process of racial healing and reconciliation only by remembering our murky history."[11]

Slavery and its legacies create the murkiness of Clemson University history, which itself is a microcosm of American history. Before a predominately Black convicted-laborer workforce built this university named for honorable diplomat, former enslaver, Confederate veteran, agricultural scientist, and Calhoun son-in-law Thomas Clemson, enslaved Black people, sharecroppers (freedmen and freedwomen), tenant farmers, and wage workers lived and labored on the Fort Hill Plantation. After the land-grant higher-education institution opened for white male cadets in 1893, Black wage workers maintained Clemson's infrastructure, labored as field hands, and were employed as cooks, janitors, launderers, and cooperative-extension agents. Archeologist and anthropologist Lynn Rainville characterizes such Black laborers as "invisible founders."[12] Their only visible memorials at Clemson are historical markers and banners that briefly note the history or contributions of mostly nameless enslaved persons, sharecroppers, and convicted laborers. In the Gettysburg Address, Abraham Lincoln spoke of the need for Americans to complete "the unfinished work which they who fought here so nobly advanced," the work of social and political reconstruction in a fractured nation.[13] Public commemoration of the lives and contributions of Black laborers is Clemson University's unfinished work, for it acknowledges their "right to recognition" as the foundation of the institution's existence, development, and success and encourages an honest reckoning with the institution's complete and complex history.

THE LABOR OF ENSLAVED PERSONS ON CLEMSON LAND

When John C. Calhoun's widow, Floride, and their daughter Cornelia sold the 1,102-acre Fort Hill Plantation to Andrew Pickens "A. P." Calhoun, the Calhouns' oldest son, in 1854, the deed included the names of fifty enslaved Black people. They ranged in age from Caty, "zero year old," to Phoebe, "one-hundred years old." Most were women and children. The names of the enslaved first appear in a paragraph on the second page of the deed, which describes the property. Following their names, the deed stipulates that the sale also includes "plantation tools and implements, Stock of Horses & Mules & Cattle, C[?] provisions & provender, Household & Kitchen furniture, being the entire property of every description connected with or belonging to the Fort Hill premises."[14] The Calhouns were members of a plantocracy that could not imagine a society in which they did not force enslaved persons to provide the free labor they deemed essential for operating plantations like Fort Hill and undergirding the nation's economy. On Fort Hill, enslaved laborers worked as domestics, field hands, gatekeepers, weavers, horse groomers, gardeners, carpenters, and blacksmiths. At least one, Susan Calhoun, was given as a wedding present by her owners to their daughter Anna Maria when she married Thomas Green Clemson in 1838.

Some of the enslaved persons listed on the 1854 deed may have been moved to Fort Hill in 1826 after John C. Calhoun relocated his family from the expansive Dumbarton Oaks mansion in Georgetown in the District of Columbia to a four-room manse for the Old Stone Church known as Clergy Hall in upcountry South Carolina. By this time, Calhoun had completed his studies at Yale University and at Judge Tapping Revere's School of Law in Connecticut; married Floride Colhoun, his first cousin once removed, with whom he had five children; opened a law office in Abbeville, South Carolina; and been elected to Congress and appointed secretary of war. Enslaved carpenters slowly enlarged the four-room home he had rented from his mother-in-law, Floride Bonneau Colhoun, into a fourteen-room, white-pillared, green-shuttered plantation house situated on land that he eventually christened Fort Hill. In 1836, Calhoun gained ownership of the property after his wife relinquished her dower rights to the land she had inherited when her mother died. Thomas Clemson helped manage Fort Hill after his marriage but also purchased forty-five enslaved persons and his own 1,000-acre plantation, Cane Break, in Saluda, South Carolina, in 1843. A decade later, he sold that plantation for $38,000 ($1,265,296 in 2020 currency, adjusted for inflation) after his appointment as US diplomat to Belgium ended.[15]

Enslaved persons worked on Fort Hill until the end of the Civil War. The April 26, 1865, appraisal of A. P. Calhoun's Fort Hill estate includes 122 field hands, seven domestics, and five skilled craftsmen (gardener, coachman, blacksmith, miller, and carpenter) listed among the property.[16] A. P. Calhoun had died about a month earlier, leaving his estate on the brink of foreclosure due to his failure to keep the mortgage payments current. His mother eventually regained ownership of Fort Hill and willed most of it to Anna, who resided there with her husband until their deaths in 1875 and 1888, respectively.

Until 2014, enslaved persons were still identified as "servants" in tours of the Fort Hill Plantation historic house when A. D. Carson published "See The Stripes." Carson's spoken-word poem drew attention to the deliberate omission of information about enslavement or enslaved persons in these tours.[17] Although the labor of enslaved persons had sustained the plantation for nearly forty years, helping prepare the way for the eventual founding of a college on the property, recognition of their lives and labors on Clemson University's built landscape is still limited to a few banners hung near and a few newly installed interpretative panels inside the Fort Hill Plantation house in the center of campus.

THE LABOR OF SHARECROPPERS ON CLEMSON LAND

After the Civil War ended, recently emancipated Black Americans on the Fort Hill Plantation pursued a variety of means to experience freedom as citizens during Reconstruction. Some relocated to nearby communities. Others moved to towns situated miles away from the plantation and adopted new last names, such as Sharper, Caroline, and their children Matilda and Solomon who took the surname Brown and settled in Calhoun Falls, South Carolina. Still others who remained at or moved to Fort Hill were hired by Thomas Clemson as servants, including Thomas and Franny Fruster, or as sharecroppers and tenant farmers.

Between 1865 and 1877, at least forty-four freedmen and freedwomen signed four annual agreements to work for Thomas Clemson as sharecroppers under

a system similar to enslavement. Sixteen children were also included in the signature area of the contracts as "boys" or "half-hands." These contracts reflected
the complexities of the paradigm shift from master-slave to employer-employee
within the southern plantation system. On the first day of the year, each man
or woman affixed his or her signature as an X mark to work for Clemson, reflecting their inability to sign their actual names likely due to illiteracy. Sharecroppers agreed to complete tasks that enslaved persons had previously done on
the plantation, including being called to and dismissed from work at the sound
of a horn and laboring from dawn to dusk. They could not leave the property
during workhours or sell any produce without Clemson's permission. But missed
days of work now meant a fine or firing; injured animals or broken tools meant
paying for either's repair or restoration. Their homes were liable to inspection
by Clemson or his agent at any time. They were assumed guilty and immediately
dismissed if stolen property was found in their residence. Their employer was
duty bound to treat them with "justice & kindness," provide housing and feed for
their animals, and allow them to gather firewood on the property, but the only
evidence permissible in court in the event of a dispute was the agent's logbook.[18]

Not only were their living conditions restrictive, but their wages fluctuated.
In 1868, they were required to purchase their bread rations using their pay, and
Clemson reserved the right to refuse to give them five bushels of every one
hundred or the equivalent wages after they had harvested the crop planted the
previous fall.[19] During the 1874 season, sharecroppers were promised "one third
of the fodder, shucks, cotton, potatoes, and one half the peas, and forty bushels
of corn out of every hundred made. Of oats or other small grain one third of
the grain."[20] Yet they could not claim any part of the grain crops harvested each
fall and were required to reimburse Clemson for the cost of seed or its market
value out of their wages. They were forbidden from cultivating and selling a
profitable cotton crop. Like the enslaved persons who worked on the Fort Hill
Plantation before them, sharecroppers ensured that the land on which Clemson
University would be built remained viable and valuable. Although the names
of many of these Black American citizens who labored there are included on
the contracts and the rolls of local churches and in US Census records, there is
no public recognition of any identifiable sharecropper or tenant farmer on the
university's built landscape.

THE FOUNDING OF CLEMSON UNIVERSITY ON RACIST IDEOLOGIES

While Thomas Clemson benefited from the labor of recently freed American citizens during Reconstruction, he solidified his plans for a new agricultural college for white males and widely shared his racist views about Black people. On November 23, 1873, he wrote a letter to Mary Amarinthia Snowden, who had formed the Ladies' Calhoun Monument Association in 1854, to convince her to redirect the monies she had raised to commission and install a monument for John C. Calhoun in Charleston, South Carolina, to the fund he had established for the development of a college on Calhoun's former upcountry plantation. Snowden, who had enjoyed a close friendship with Calhoun, had also established the Soldiers' Relief Association in 1861 to support the Confederate army. Her husband, William Snowden, had died while serving as a physician for the Confederacy. After the war ended, she founded the Ladies' Memorial Association in 1866 to install monuments that commemorated Confederate soldiers who were killed in the Civil War and to educate children about what became known as the "Lost Cause."[21]

Thomas Clemson resorted to racist fear tactics to convince Snowden to support his efforts to build a college on the site of Calhoun's plantation that would both honor the American stateman and ensure his legacy while also preserving and protecting white people through the education of their bright young males. He began his letter with an expression of concern that white southerners would be "entirely overwhelmed by the foreign race, which now governs us." At the time, Black Republicans and their allies controlled the South Carolina General Assembly. He further asserted, "the Negro is not 'a black white man,' but a race entirely distinct from ours, in all physical and mental attributes—in my opinion not capable of reaching a high degree of civilization, and certainly never the same as that of the white man."[22] Clemson assured Snowden that white people could solidify their supremacy by "cultivating to its utmost our superior intellectual faculties." He admitted that he had "thought, spoken, and written *constantly* on this subject [emphasis mine]." Additionally, he held up the "great and good man" John C. Calhoun, who had been revered as one of the "founding fathers" of the Confederacy, as the model for young white men and expressed his desire to connect Calhoun's name with their "regeneration" or "resurrection" and Black American citizens' disempowerment.[23] Clemson believed that he and Snowden could convince distinguished white men in southern and northern states who revered Calhoun to join South Carolinians in raising money for a segregated college for "their own Sons." He argued that the new school should be located on Fort Hill, the southern statesman's "favorite spot," where trains would connect the institution eastward to low-country South Carolina and to the North and South through railroad lines to New York and New Orleans, respectively. This location would make the school attractive for America's white sons from the East Coast through the Mississippi Delta. Clemson also assured Snowden that he supported the education and advancement of white women and the eventual creation of a "female branch" for the college.[24]

Snowden declined the invitation to collaborate and remained focused on achieving her objective of honoring Calhoun. Her fundraising led to the installation of a one-hundred-foot Calhoun monument in Marion Square in Charleston in 1887 that overlooked The Citadel, which had been built to provide military resources to better control enslaved persons in Charleston after Denmark Vesey's failed insurrection in 1822. In his reflections on the significance and purpose of the Calhoun monument, William Zachariah Leitner, Confederate veteran and South Carolina secretary of state, expressed his hoped that it would "stimulate the boys and young men of South Carolina to emulate the virtues of the great statesman."[25] South Carolina's sons would literally look skyward to see the image of Calhoun, the influential leader who had declared slavery to be a positive good and crafted a nullification doctrine regarding states' rights that had helped lead to the Civil War.

Undeterred by his failure to convince Snowden to support his efforts, Clemson wrote William W. Corcoran, his investment banker and one of the "distinguished men" he referenced to Snowden, about five years later on October 29, 1878, requesting financial support for his college project, which he asserted would ensure the "prosperity of the state."[26] He also conveyed his concerns about the potential influence of an interracial state legislature on the institution, writing, "The project for this time would be untrammeled as a private enterprise, whereas the contrary might occur in the hands of the Legislature representing two different races."[27] Clemson worried that, despite the white conservative Democratic takeover of the General Assembly in 1877, a time might come in the future when Black Republicans would again win the majority in the statehouse and could integrate or otherwise alter his institution as they had the South Carolina College (later the University of South Carolina) immediately after the Civil War ended. If his college was established as a state school, he would need to devise a means for it to remain "untrammeled" by a mixed-race, majority-Black General Assembly. Corcoran later replied that he was unable to contribute due to other pressing financial obligations.[28]

Nevertheless, Clemson moved forward with his plans to establish an agricultural college on Fort Hill Plantation. In an early draft of his will, he conveyed a desire for the college to be named "the Calhoun-Clemson Scientific Institute of the South."[29] As he further developed his plans, he devised a unique configuration for governance that included seven successor trustees, with lifetime terms, and six others appointed by the state, who would serve six-year renewable terms, to protect his college from state interference. In his will, Clemson stipulated, "The seven trustees appointed by me shall always have the right, and the power is hereby given them and their successors, *which right the legislature shall never take away or abridge,* to fill all vacancies which may occur in their number by death, resignation, refusal to act, or otherwise [emphasis mine]."[30] In "The Origin of Clemson College," Tillman later affirmed Clemson's fears, asserting, "Having in view the possible danger of the Negroes, who are so largely in the majority in our state, at some time getting control of the State Government, we suggested the scheme of seven trustees who would be self-perpetuating, and thus make it impossible for an adverse Legislature to shipwreck the college or make it a school to which negroes would be admitted."[31] But Richard Simpson, Clemson's lawyer, provided a different explanation for the configuration of the trustees. He suggested that the successor trustees on the board were selected to protect Thomas Clemson's property if the state rejected the terms of the will.[32] But the effect of Tillman's and Simpson's explanations is the same: both would lead to successor trustees maintaining control of the college.[33]

All of the initial successor trustees that Clemson empowered to direct the development of his "high seminary" had direct ties to the system of slavery and its legacies. Tillman and John Edward Wannamaker had grown up in South Carolina families of enslavers. Tillman's parents, Sophia and Benjamin Ryan Tillman, were enslavers; Wannamaker's father, enslaver John Jacob Wannamaker, signed South Carolina's Articles of Secession. Robert Esli Bowen, John E. Bradley, Milton L. Donaldson, Daniel K. Norris, and Simpson were Confederate veterans. Additionally, four were politicians: State Representative Bradley, State Senator Donaldson, Governor-elect Tillman, and Simpson, who during his time a state representative from 1874 to 1881 asserted that his goal was to establish an agricultural college in the "upper part of the state amidst the *white* counties [emphasis mine]."[34] Of the six trustees appointed by the state legislature, five—James L. Orr, Berryman W. Edwards, Jesse H. Hardin, Eli T. Stackhouse, and James E. Tindal—had served in the Confederate army; the sixth, Johnstone, as previously stated, had desired to serve but was ineligible before the war ended.[35] Both Clemson and the General Assembly chose trustees who had been devoted to the practice and the preservation of the enslavement of Black people for a college that was established for the "regeneration" and "resurrection" of white American men. Two trustees, Tindal and Johnstone, however, supported segregated education for Black youth.[36] None advocated for the integration of Clemson College. Additionally, Tillman had publicly identified the two goals of the Farmers' Association to which he belonged: to support the development of the college through the bequest of Fort Hill in Clemson's will as stated and to "safeguard white supremacy."[37]

Yet former Clemson University historian Jerome Reel notes: "Even more extraordinary was what [Clemson's] will did not say. It did not limit admissions by state (South Carolina), by gender (male), or by race (white). This was most unusual given the era and climate in which the will was drafted, and it was unusual given the sentiments, at least, of Tillman."[38] Reel's analysis of Clemson's will contradicts successor trustee Tillman's assertion, "We were anxious to keep down negro domination of the school and at the same time to prevent the prostitution of the institution to ends not intended by its founder."[39] I suggest that Thomas Clemson omitted references to state, gender, and race from his will because there was no compelling reason for him to include such stipulations. Indeed, few if any Confederate veterans and sons of enslavers were interested in developing interracial, coeducational higher-education institutions during the post–Civil War era. None challenged Tillman's successful efforts to legalize the disenfranchisement and disempowerment of Black South Carolinians. Furthermore, Clemson College became coeducational in 1955 due to a dramatic drop in white-male student enrollment after World War II, but the institution did not desegregate until 1963—when legally forced to do so after administrators lost an appeal to the US Supreme Court to overturn the positive ruling in Harvey Gantt's class-action lawsuit to gain admission as the first Black student.

This history of Clemson's founding trustees' ties to enslavement and its legacies is missing from the university's public history on the built landscape. Although new historical markers were installed on campus in 2018 as part of the

Trustees' Task Force on the History of Clemson in which they vowed to share the university's "complete history," none include details about earlier trustees' ties to slavery or to the Confederacy. Older signage inside buildings named for trustees, faculty, or administrators who were Confederate veterans also omits such connections. One must read Reel's "High Seminary," conduct research in Clemson University Libraries' Special Collections and Archives, or search for obscure online resources to locate this information.

THE WORK OF STATE CONVICTED LABORERS ON CLEMSON LAND

Tillman and Simpson's political connections helped ensure that the white, Democratic-controlled state legislature eventually accepted Thomas Clemson's bequest of Fort Hill for a new higher-education institution in the South Carolina upstate region. Although Clemson provided land and some funds and the state and federal governments provided additional funding, the trustees needed a cheap labor source for the establishment of the school.

Clemson trustees' decision to lease incarcerated persons to build the college further solidified the institution's ties to the legacy of enslavement. Historian Douglas A. Blackmon has asserted, "The South's highly evolved system and customs of leasing slaves from one farm or factory to the next, bartering for the cost of slaves, and wholesaling and retailing of slaves regenerated itself around convict leasing in the 1870s and 1880s."[40] When members of the General Assembly enacted the legislation that created Clemson College, they authorized the state penitentiary to lease up to fifty "able-bodied convicts" to the school's trustees to prepare the grounds, create materials, and erect the buildings. The trustees would be responsible for the convicted laborers' transportation, medical fees, food, and lodging.[41] In their first annual report, the trustees noted that the fifty convicted laborers supplied by the state had "saved to the Board the expenditure of a large amount of money, but they are not sufficient to do all the work required, without the hire of much additional labor."[42] They requested that the legislature authorize one hundred additional "able-bodied" convicted laborers who were "skilled, or have some skill, as carpenters, brickmasons and blacksmiths." The board reported spending $736.42 for convicted-laborer expenses, $187.12 to build a stockade, and $4.20 to transport convicted laborers.[43]

Between 1890 and 1915, the state penitentiary assigned nearly seven hundred convicted men and boys to work at Clemson College. They ranged in age from twelve to sixty-seven when they were processed into the penitentiary. They were sent to work at the school in groups of twenty-five, fifty, or one hundred. Most were Black American citizens, convicted of some form of felonious larceny, such as stealing a piece of jewelry or boy's clothing and a toy drum. By the time the college opened in 1894, Clemson trustees stated:

> We are pleased to be able to report that the small force of three or four carpenters and the convicts have during the year accomplished very satisfactory results. They have completed the kitchen, room for the boilers, placed the boilers, built smoke-stack and baking department, and the kitchen is now ready for use. They have completed the inside work of the Dormitory, except painting, and it is now ready to be occupied, and is capable of accommodating six hundred students, being perhaps the largest house in the State. They have completed the dining room, finished building the walls of the Chapel, put on the roof, put in the windows and floored it. They have completed the walls of the President's house and put the roof thereon. They have nearly completed the Infirmary and have built a brick house for Laundry, 40 by 50 feet. They have built another brick Professor's house and covered it in. They have built the tower to [the] main building above the roof, and would have completed it but for want of necessary material we were not able to purchase, and are now flooring, ceiling and plastering the Main College Building, which work we hope to finish in about a month from this date unless the material therefor be exhausted. They have also made 900,000 bricks, sufficient probably to complete the buildings as planned by the Board.[44]

Clemson trustees requested additional convicted laborers to work on remote farmland, improve creek and river bottoms, and transform steep land into pastures.[45]

By 1900, the US Census noted that twenty-five convicted laborers were working and living on campus. Twenty-three were Black; three were white. They ranged in age from eighteen to fifty-three years old.[46] That year, Clemson trustees reported $1,519.03 for expenses related to the convicted laborers. Reviewing developments for the college in their annual report, the trusted noted: "We visited the farm and found it in a state of excellent cultivation. In this connection, and in view of much necessary work about to be undertaken, it would be a matter of much saving if the full quota of convicts that has been allotted here was furnished without delay."[47] After convicted laborers completed building construction, they enhanced the campus infrastructure and developed satellite sites. According to the board minutes of July 9, 1907, the convicted laborers were employed in "improving the roads, walks, and campus" and working on the development of the Coast Experiment Station in Summerville, South Carolina.[48]

By 1909, however, Clemson trustees would report that expenditures for convicted laborers working on the college farm were "exceedingly costly," characterizing the $4,100 they were paying to lease convicted laborers as "wastefully expended." They sought to restrict these workers to "improving the farm, cultivating crops, clearing land, ditching, etc."[49] Within five years, the president reported to the board that no "convict gang" was working for the college, and the school could no longer afford to pay $100 per month for the supervision of such a workforce.[50]

While convicted laborers completed most of the initial construction projects, Clemson College began hiring hundreds of Black wage workers during the Jim Crow era for domestic and manual-labor jobs. Black Americans were employed in the dining hall, laundry, greenhouse, farm, dairy, transportation, and grounds departments. Several professors and administrators hired Black Americans as live-in servants to care for their families, often as nurses for children. Most of Clemson's Black employees were literate, though few had completed any formal education.[51] During the late nineteenth and early to middle twentieth centuries at the college, Black American citizens were either forced to work as convicted laborers or hired as low-paid wage workers or cooperative-extension agents. In the twenty-first century, no public recognition of the university's past and present indebtedness to wage workers exists on campus, though recently installed historical markers note the labor of the nameless "predominately African American state convict crew" who built the school's oldest buildings.

THE RIGHT TO RECOGNITION FOR BLACK LABORERS IN CLEMSON HISTORY

In *The Souls of Black Folk*, W. E. B. Du Bois asserts that "the problem of the twentieth century is the problem of the color-line,—the relation of the darker to the lighter races of men in Asia and Africa, in America and the islands of the sea."[52] When afforded the opportunity during Reconstruction, Black American citizens throughout the South demonstrated their desire to establish an equitable, inclusive, and integrated society. They reunited with family members, obtained literacy, purchased land, founded churches, established businesses, sought employment, and participated in elections, Yet in his letter to Snowden, Thomas Clemson characterized these signs of Black progress as a hinderance to white achievement, asserting, "Our only hope to make a stand against the degrading torrent, that is fast overwhelming us, is by cultivating to its utmost our superior intellectual faculties."[53] Thus, he exacerbated the "problem of the color line" in South Carolina by establishing a college where young white men could learn how to preserve and enact white supremacy by following in the footsteps of John C. Calhoun. Clemson continued, "yet at this very moment, we are, and have been neglecting the ordinary culture of civilized nations, and unless we act speedily, the men of the rising generation, will come on the stage even less armed than ourselves to compete in the deadly struggle before them."[54] For him, the struggle for supremacy was a matter of life and death, the survival and success of white people.

The establishment of land-grant higher-education institutions like Clemson College not only served as incubators for white supremacy but also marked a shift in how many white Americans perceived agriculture. Clemson, Thomas Jefferson, George Washington, and other well-educated planters had experimented with raising various plants in their gardens while enslaved persons were forced to cultivate and harvest cash crops like rice, cotton, and indigo in their vast fields. After slavery was outlawed, young white men began to pursue farming as a respectable profession by earning a degree in agricultural science. According to its 1893 catalog, Clemson College was founded "to give practical instruction in agriculture and in the mechanical arts" along with courses in English, economics, and history to provide a "rounded education."[55] Furthermore, "It is considered of supreme importance that students should be taught, not only theoretic methods, but practical work in these methods. Young men need to learn to work. With this end in view, a certain amount of manual labor is required of all students."[56] Although Clemson was established during a period of intense industrialization in America, the "value and virtue of physical dexterity and diligence" was still emphasized at land-grant institutions.[57] Heretofore, enslaved people had been forced to do most of the manual labor, including on the Fort Hill Plantation, where sharecroppers also tilled the land during Reconstruction, after which a predominately Black American workforce of convicted laborers helped build Clemson College in the late nineteenth and early twentieth centuries. That work was now characterized as an "experiment" for white male students at land-grant institutions throughout the South. For Black Americans associated with Clemson history, however, manual labor was the enactment of slavery and its legacies on the land where the higher-education institution was established.

As the cadets earned degrees, including compulsory manual labor, they also cultivated an admiration of and appreciate for the Lost Cause through programming sponsored by the Calhoun Chapter of the United Daughters of the Confederacy, a group with close ties to the Ladies' Calhoun Monument Association. On January 19, 1907, the Calhoun Chapter hosted a program in the college chapel to celebrate the centennial birthday of Robert E. Lee, "our hero," as characterized by a staff writer of the *Tiger*, Clemson's student newspaper: "Some fifteen of the old veterans were present. At the close of the exercises crosses of honor were presented to all who had not previously received them. The address of the occasion was prepared by Col. [Robert Anderson] Thompson, one of the three survivors of the signors of the ordinance of secession. At the close of the exercises the veterans marched to the President's mansion, where the ladies had prepared a sumptuous dinner."[58] At this time, Clemson's president was Patrick Henry Mell. His father was proslavery minister Patrick Hues Mell, who eventually served as the chancellor of the University of Georgia. In effect, by commemorating secession, venerating the Confederacy, and memorializing its veterans, the Calhoun Chapter was finishing and expanding the work of the Ladies' Calhoun Memorial Association and other organizations established to create "a positive memory of the Confederacy. . . . This nostalgia for the past accompanied a collective forgetting of slavery, while defining Reconstruction as a period of 'Yankee aggression' and black 'betrayal.'"[59]

Despite the school's connections to the Confederacy, the Lost Cause, and white supremacy, some Clemson faculty and administrators have continued to argue that the higher-education institution has offered varied means to educate all South Carolinians, even during the Jim Crow era. The "History" section of the current Clemson Board of Trustees' Manual, for example, asserts that "the college was an early leader in the movement to provide education to all citizens through extension. The 'Clemson Model' of extension linked directly to the land grant college became the basis for the Smith-Lever Act of 1914 (Extension), which extended that model to all part of the United States."[60] Representative A. Frank Lever, cosponsor of the Smith-Lever Act, was serving as a successor trustee when the law was enacted, creating an extension program at Clemson College that was racially separate and unequal. Extension programs for white South Carolinians were based at Clemson, while those for Black South Carolinians operated out of the Colored Normal Industrial Agricultural and Mechanical College of South Carolina (renamed South Carolina State University in 1954) in Orangeburg. White extension employees far outnumbered their Black counterparts and received better pay and more resources. In 1921, for example, when the state population was 51.4 percent white and 48.6 percent Black, there were thirty-five white extension agents but only seven Black agents. That year, white agents provided 827 corn demonstrations, while Black agents conducted 51. White agents assisted with the construction of 244 new farm buildings, while Black agents helped with the erection of 69.[61] Furthermore, the first Black county extension agent, Ellis D. Dean, was not appointed until 1970, nearly a decade after desegregation in 1963. Dean had worked for Clemson's Extension Service for twenty-six years before his promotion.[62] Although several theses, dissertations, journal articles, and books have been written about the school's Black extension workers, there is no public recognition of their contributions to the development of Black communities throughout South Carolina during the Jim Crow era on either the main campus or in extension offices throughout the state.

Two years before Clemson hired Dean to work for the extension service in 1944, the Buildings and Grounds Committee made several recommendations to commemorate Black laborers on campus. At the March 11, 1946, meeting when they proposed that buildings be named for prominent white men in Clemson history, committee member Charles Carter Newman, professor of horticulture and Clemson's first student to earn a degree, "stated that it was his understanding that on Cemetery Hill are buried some 200 to 250 slaves and convicts. After some discussion . . . the Committee unanimously voted to recommend that some type of marker be established on Cemetery Hill to indicate this colored graveyard."[63] This burial ground likely originated in the early 1800s after the enslaved African Americans began living, laboring, and dying on the land. The first group of enslaved persons were owned by Reverend James McElhenny, pastor of the Old Stone Presbyterian Church in nearby Pendleton, who established a parsonage known as Clergy Hall on the site. Additionally, enslaved persons owned by the Calhouns and Clemsons and who labored on the Fort Hill Plantation from about 1826 to the end of the Civil War and sharecroppers who worked there during Reconstruction may also be buried there. Historical records suggest that convicted laborers who died while helping build the college are also interred in this cemetery. Wage workers who lived on campus during the Jim Crow era are believed to have buried their loved ones on the site as well. The committee's recommendation for a marker for the burial ground was not enacted in 1946. In 1960, Clemson administrators sought and received permission from the Oconee County Court to disinter the graves of Black Americans from the west side of the cemetery and reinter them on the south side of the cemetery to facilitate campus development.[64] Eventually, the university hung a sign on the black chain-link fence around the newly designated burial ground that reads, "Unknown Burials, ca. 1865," though the burials were known to likely date back into the antebellum period.

Seventy years after the original recommendation for a marker, Clemson trustees approved another request, initiated by a faculty member, for the installation of a double-sided South Carolina historical marker at the entrance of Woodland Cemetery that would include a brief description of the "Fort Hill Slave and Convict Cemetery." In the summer of 2020, temporary signs for the African American burial ground were added throughout the cemetery after 667 unmarked graves, believed to be those of African Americans, were identified using ground-penetrating radar. Clemson trustees have committed to developing a preservation plan and memorial for the site as well as providing more resources for local African American communities.[65]

During the mid-twentieth century, the Buildings and Grounds Committee was also interested in including the history of Black Americans in the campus streetscape. Nearly six months after they discussed a sign for the "colored graveyard" in 1946, committee members recommended naming several streets on campus for Black laborers. One of these would honor an enslaved man who worked on the Fort Hill Plantation: "Sawney Street is a street in the process of being developed and was named for one of John C. Calhoun's favorite slaves who lived down on the branch in this area."[66] Here, the committee was still playing favorites with Clemson's Black history, choosing to honor an enslaved man whom Calhoun favored but whose children had rebelled against enslavement by setting fire to an overseer's tent and attempting to burn down the plantation house.[67] A street named for Sawney was added to the campus in the late 1940s but later removed during campus expansion. In 2016, one side of another double-sided state historical marker, authorized by the trustees, notes the previous naming of the branch of a creek in his honor.[68]

Despite little success in marking Clemson's landscape with the history of African Americans, the Buildings and Grounds Committee continued its efforts to commemorate Black laborers at Clemson eight years later. In October 1952, committee members returned their attention to Lee's plans for "a colonial restoration consisting of several antebellum homes and a re-production of John C. Calhoun's farm-hand quarters and other small log buildings, such as a weave shed, corn crib, and grist mill."[69] They recommended that the "Restoration of Colonial Farm Life" plans Lee had prepared in 1945 be submitted to Perry, Shaw, & Hepburn, Kehoe & Dean, an architectural firm that had developed a renovation plan for Colonial Williamsburg, for review and approval.[70] Lee's plans—including a reproduction of the quarters for Fort Hill's enslaved field hands—were not fully implemented, though Clemson maintains several historic properties on campus, including the Fort Hill Plantation house, Hanover House, and the Hopewell Plantation house, and has recently begun to more fully incorporate the stories of enslaved persons into tours of Fort Hill.

Six months after resurrecting Lee's initiative, the committee "recommended . . . that the test garden located southeast of the cemetery be named 'Judge Crawford' Camellia Garden. This is in honor of the old colored gardener who worked for Clemson College for approximately 50 years."[71] Crawford had arrived there in 1890 at the age of sixteen just after the South Carolina General Assembly gave the trustees permission to begin building the college. During his employment at Clemson, he supervised leased convicted laborers who helped build the school and cadets who completed compulsory farm work, maintained farm equipment and tools, worked in the greenhouse, and landscaped the campus. Crawford retired in 1947 after working for Clemson for fifty-seven years.[72] His widow also requested that a street on campus be named in his honor. There is no record of trustees discussing or approving either recommendation. The camellia test garden, operated by the South Carolina Camellia Society and the American Camellia Society, was not named in honor of Judge Crawford either.[73] It was eventually incorporated into the South Carolina Botanical Garden (SCBG), which includes a camellia demonstration garden.[74] The SCBG acknowledges its "humble beginning as a camellia collection" on its website but does not mention Crawford.[75]

Indeed, no building, street, monument, or memorial on the Clemson University campus currently bears the name of a Black laborer who helped build the institution. Instead, trustees have continued the practice of naming spaces for prominent white men who contributed to Clemson's development or wealthy white families who have purchased naming rights to spaces or structures.

In 2015, however, the trustees signaled a willingness to document and share the university's complete and complex history. After a white supremacist murdered nine parishioners at the Mother Emanuel African Methodist Episcopal Church in Charleston, they issued a statement repudiating the gunman's white supremacist ideologies, supported the removal of the Confederate flag from the South Carolina statehouse grounds, and authorized the appointment of the Trustee Task Force on the History of Clemson.[76] After interviewing stakeholders and collecting ideas through a website, the trustees recommended a series of initiatives, including installing the aforementioned historical markers on campus. On these new markers, Clemson's Black laborers remain mostly nameless and are instead identified as slaves, sharecroppers, domestic workers, and a predominately African American state convict crew. The final report of the Clemson History Task Force Implementation Team, a group of staff and faculty that university president Jim Clements appointed to enact the trustee task force's recommendations, includes instructions to "enhance the existing recognition of the slave quarters and burial sites, [and] include names if we have them"; to "develop a way to recognize the [convicted laborers] who constructed the first buildings on campus"; and to "develop a tribute to the early wage earners and staff who helped build the campus and shape the early student experience."[77]

Five years later, after initiating their history project, Clemson's trustees addressed a different aspect of the university's history: requests for the removal of the names of white supremacists and enslavers from buildings and programs. For many years, they had refused to publicly respond to the demands of students and their allies to rename Tillman Hall and the Calhoun Honors College. Students and their allies now intensified their efforts to bring about these changes through their "Reclaim Old Main" and "Reclaim&Rename" campaigns.[78] About a month after the murder of George Floyd on May 25, 2020, however, trustees approved a request to change the name of the honor's program to the Clemson University Honors College. They announced their decision the Friday before Clemson football players held their peaceful protest in support of the Black Lives Matter movement. The trustees also requested a one-time exemption from the South Carolina Heritage Act to revert the name of Tillman Hall to Old Main.[79] Nearly a year after this second recommendation, the General Assembly still has not formally responded to the request. The Heritage Act, compromise legislation enacted in 2000 when the General Assembly agreed to remove the Confederate battle flag from the statehouse dome and reinstall it and place an African American monument on the statehouse grounds, requires a two-thirds vote in both the house and senate for approval of any change to a monument or memorial on state property that is associated with specific cultural and war history. In May 2021, the South Carolina Supreme Court heard arguments regarding the constitutionality of the "two-thirds" requirement, which opponents to the law view as an insurmountable "supermajority."[80] Six months later, the court upheld the law but struck down its supermajority requirement.[81]

Thomas Clemson and the trustees that he and the General Assembly appointed achieved their goal of establishing a "high seminary of learning" in upcountry South Carolina to shape young white men in the mold of John C. Calhoun. Snowden and the Ladies' Calhoun Monument Association achieved their goal of building a memorial that commemorated Calhoun's contributions to the development of a distinct southern identity of white supremacy and states' rights. (The City of Charleston recently removed the statue of Calhoun from Marion Square, circumventing the restrictions of the Heritage Act because the memorial was on private property.)[82] Clemson trustees achieved their goal of providing recognition to white male founders—American citizens who were mostly enslavers, Confederate veterans, white supremacists, and segregationists—who helped establish the higher-education institution by naming buildings and streets in their honor.

Without the commemoration of Black laborers and Black people to whom it is indebted for its establishment and success in its public history, however, Clemson University's work of documenting and sharing its history is incomplete. Although Harvey Gantt desegregated the school in 1963, the school did not commemorate this historic event on its landscape until forty years later. The South Carolina historical marker installed in 2003 reduced Gantt's two-year quest to gain admission, culminating in a class-action lawsuit, to "Integration with Dignity."[83] Yet through his enrollment in Clemson, Gantt ensured that Thomas Clemson's vision for a college where young white men learned to emulate Calhoun and a nation in which Black people were viewed as "a race entirely distinct from [white people], in all physical and mental attributes" rather than as American citizens, was not fulfilled. Yet in the Gantt historical marker, the university places the most emphasis on then president Robert C. Edwards's efforts to ensure that Gantt's enrollment was peaceful, thus protecting the college's reputation and drawing attention away from the fact that South Carolina was the last state to integrate its public schools.

More often than not, Clemson University's current efforts to commemorate its history have positioned Black Americans in classifications—enslaved, sharecropper, convict, wage worker—diminishing their humanity and minimizing their struggle for recognition as citizens in post–Civil War America. On most recently installed historical markers, for example, the description of the mostly Black men and boys who built Clemson as a "state convict crew" leads many to believe they were hardened criminals, not Black American citizens struggling for recognition in South Carolina where white supremacist, powerful politician, and Clemson trustee Benjamin Tillman unduly influenced and controlled politics and policies designed to suppress or expel them. Yet from the antebellum period though the Jim Crow era, unheralded Black people—both those denied citizenship and those who never fully experienced the rights and privileges of citizenship— helped build and sustain the Fort Hill Plantation and the college later built on its grounds. Commemorating their lives and contributions and affirming their "right to recognition" as US citizens by inscribing their names on buildings, streets, memorials, and monuments; incorporating their stories fully into the institution's public history; including their history in numerous educational opportunities, ranging from courses to tours; and providing scholarships to their descendants is Clemson University's unfinished work. Doing this work will help the higher-education institution fulfill its mission to generate, preserve, communicate, and apply knowledge both locally and globally.

NOTES

1. The Eastern Band of the Cherokees lived in the town of Esseneca (Isinugu or Seneca), which the colonists burned down during the American Revolution, killing most of the inhabitants. In 2016, a South Carolina historical marker was installed near the site of the town on the campus of Clemson University to acknowledge this history. The Hopewell Plantation house, where representatives of the Cherokee, Choctaw, and Chickasaw Nations signed treaties in 1785 and 1786 ceding most of their land to the US government in exchange for hunting grounds, trading rights, and federal protection, is also located on the campus.

2. "The Will of Thomas Green Clemson," Clemson University, https://www.clemson.edu/about /history/tgc-will.html (accessed May 28, 2020).

3. In 1808, Col. Thomas Pinckney Jr. built the Altamont house on property he had purchased from Joseph Whitner Sr. In 1832, South Carolina lieutenant governor and low-country planter Charles

Cotesworth Pinckney built the four-story, wood-and-clapboard Woodburn Plantation house as a summer home.

4. Rudolph Lee, "Suggestions for the Restoration of Colonial Farm Life at Clemson College," Rudolph Lee Papers, Mss 002, Box 2, Special Collections and Archives, Clemson University Libraries, Clemson, SC, 1.

5. Ibid., 2.

6. "Report of the Buildings and Grounds Committee for the Fiscal Year 1945–46," in Clemson University, "Faculty Senate Minutes, 1946 Meetings" (1946), Faculty Senate Minutes 11, https://tigerprints.clemson.edu/faculty_senate/11.

7. "Minutes of the Buildings and Grounds Committee, March 11, 1946," Folder 6, Pres. Robert F. Poole Committee Files, ser. 7, Special Collections and Archives, Clemson University Libraries.

8. Board of Trustees, Clemson University, "Clemson Trustees Minutes, 1946 June 28" (1946), *Minutes,* 427:600–601, https://tigerprints.clemson.edu/trustees_minutes/427.

9. Clemson trustees renamed the following buildings: the Chemistry Laboratory became Hardin Hall in 1954, honoring Confederate army officer and Clemson's first chemistry professor, Mark Hardin; the Food Industries Building became Newman Hall in 1966, named for Confederate army veteran and Clemson's first agricultural professor, James S. Newman, and his son, Charles C. Newman; Barracks No. 4 was renamed Donaldson Hall in 1966 for Confederate army veteran, state legislator, and Clemson successor trustee Milton LaFayette Donaldson; Barracks No. 5 became Bowen Hall in 1966 to honor Confederate army officer and state legislator Robert Esli Bowen; Barracks No. 7 was renamed Bradley Hall in 1966 for Confederate army veteran, amateur soils engineer, and Clemson trustee John E. Bradley; Barracks No. 8 became Norris Hall in 1966, named for original cotton planter, Confederate army officer, and successor trustee Daniel Keating Norris; and Strode Tower in 1969 was named for Confederate army veteran and Clemson's first president Henry Aubrey Strode. For more information, see "Building Legacies: Clemson Campus Namesakes," Clemson University Libraries, https://www.arcgis.com/apps/MapJournal/index.html?appid=7a4b63694a374180a86faf6d2a3aac65 (accessed June 1, 2020); Clemson Board of Trustee Minutes, TigerPrints, https://tigerprints.clemson.edu/trustees_minutes/; and Clemson University Board of Trustees Records, 1881–1991, ser. 30, Special Collections and Archives, Clemson University Libraries, http://media.clemson.edu/library/special_collections/findingaids/archives/Administrative/Series30BoardofTrustees.pdf (accessed June 2, 2021).

10. Clemson College president Walter Riggs conceived of the idea for Woodland Cemetery as a place where white employees who had served at least three years could be buried. The cemetery opened in the summer of 1924 a few months after Riggs died; Anna P. Schwarz Sterns was the first person interred there in 1927.

11. Salamishah Tillet, *Sites of Slavery: Citizenship and Racial Democracy in the Post-Civil Rights Imagination* (Durham, NC: Duke University Press, 2012), 38, 45.

12. Lynn Rainville, *Invisible Founders: How Two Centuries of African American Families Transformed a Plantation into a College* (New York: Berghahn Books, 2019).

13. Abraham Lincoln, "Gettysburg Address," Cornell University Library, https://rmc.library.cornell.edu/gettysburg/good_cause/transcript.htm (accessed May 26, 2020).

14. Deed to Real and Personal Estate, Thomas Green Clemson Papers, Box 1, Folder 25, Special Collections and Archives, Clemson University Libraries.

15. "Thomas Green Clemson," The Clemson Story—History, Clemson University, https://www.clemson.edu/about/history/bios/thomas-g-clemson.html (accessed May 28, 2020).

16. Inventory and Valuation of the Estate of Colonel A. P. Calhoun, Clemson Papers, Box 5, Folder 2.

17. A. D. Carson, "See The Stripes [Clemson]," 2014, AyDeeTheGreat.com, https://aydeethegreat.com/see-the-stripes/ (accessed June 8, 2021).

18. "Articles of Agreement between Thos. G. Clemson Trustee on the one part, and the under-signed freedmen, and women on the other part," Jan. 1, 1874, Clemson Papers, Box 5, Folder 10.

19. "Articles of Agreement between Thos. G. Clemson of the one part, and the undersigned freedmen & women on the other part," Jan. 1, 1868, Clemson Papers, Box 5, Folder 5.

20. Ibid.

21. John W. Dubose, "Beloved Daughter of South Carolina," *Confederate Veteran* 26, no. 1 (Jan. 1918): 9–11; Bruce E. Baker, "Snowden, Mary Amarinthia," *South Carolina Encyclopedia,* Aug. 1, 2016, http://www.scencyclopedia.org/sce/entries/snowden-mary-amarinthia/ (accessed May 29, 2020); Thomas Green Clemson to Mary Amarinthia Snowden, Nov. 23, 1873, Mary Amarinthia Snowden Papers, 1846–1958, South Caroliniana Library, University of South Carolina, Columbia.

22. Clemson to Snowden, Nov. 23, 1873.

23. Ibid.; Robert Elder, *Calhoun: American Heretic* (New York: Basic Books, 2021), 528.

24. Clemson to Snowden, Nov. 23, 1873.

25. Ladies' Calhoun Monument Association, *A History of the Calhoun Monument at Charleston, S.C.* (Charleston, SC: Lucas, Richardson, 1888), 131.

26. Thomas Green Clemson to William Wilson (W. W.) Corcoran, Oct. 29, 1878, Clemson Papers, Box 5, Folder 14.

27. Ibid.

28. W. W. Corcoran to Thomas Green Clemson, Nov. 1, 1878, Clemson, Thomas Green—1807–1888—Correspondence, W. W. Corcoran Papers, Library of Congress, Washington, DC.

29. Thomas Green Clemson, Draft of Will, 1880, Clemson Papers, Box 5, Folder 16.

30. "Will of Thomas Green Clemson," https://www.clemson.edu/about/history/tgc-will.html.

31. Benjamin Ryan Tillman, "The Origin of Clemson College," n.d., Benjamin Ryan Tillman Papers, Mss. 0080, Box 70, Folder 1064, Special Collections and Archives, Clemson University Libraries, 5.

32. Richard Simpson, Letter to the Editor of *The State,* 1909, Richard W. Simpson Papers, Mss. 96, Box 1, ibid.

33. By 1910, however, a vote of nine trustees was required to change the "rules, orders, regulations, resolutions, and by-laws" that govern the board's operations. See Board of Trustees, "Board of Trustees Manual, Chapter V—Organization and Operating Rules," Clemson University, https://www.clemson.edu/administration/bot/manual/chapter5.html (accessed May 30, 2020); Walter Merritt Riggs, "Clemson Catechism," nos. 12–15, ClemsonWiki, https://clemsonwiki.com/wiki/Clemson_Catechism (accessed May 22, 2020).

34. Jerome V. Reel, *The High Seminary: The History of the Clemson Agricultural College of South Carolina,1889–1946*, vol. 1 (Clemson, SC: Clemson University Press, 2011), 45.

35. Ibid., 69–71.

36. Ibid., 71.

37. Ibid., 57; *Pickens (SC) Sentinel,* May 3, 1888.

38. Reel, *High Seminary,* 47.

39. Tillman, "Origin of Clemson College," 5.

40. Douglas A. Blackmon, *Slavery by Another Name: The Re-enslavement of Black Americans from the Civil War to World War II* (New York: Vintage Books, 2008), 6.

41. "An Act to Provide for the Building and Maintenance of Clemson Agricultural College, No. 188," sec. 5, Dec. 23, 1889, *Acts and Joint Resolutions of the General Assembly of the State of South Carolina Passed at the Regular Session of 1889* (Columbia: James H. Woodrow, 1890), 302, https://babel .hathitrust.org/cgi/pt?id=nyp.33433007186814&view=1up&seq=64.

42. Board of Trustees, Clemson University, "Annual Report of the Clemson Board of Trustees, 1890" (1890), *Annual Reports,* 7:642, https://tigerprints.clemson.edu/trustees_reports/7.

43. Ibid., 642, 645.

44. Board of Trustees, Clemson University, "Annual Report of the Clemson Board of Trustees, 1892" (1892), *Annual Reports,* 9:6, https://tigerprints.clemson.edu/trustees_reports/9.

45. Ibid., 18.

46. Twelfth Census of the United States, Population Schedule, Oconee County, SC, Clemson Agricultural College, Seneca Township, June 6, 1900, Sheet 8, Ancestry.com.

47. Board of Trustees, Clemson University, "Annual Report of the Clemson Board of Trustees, 1900" (1900), *Annual Reports,* 17:9, 31, https://tigerprints.clemson.edu/trustees_reports/17.

48. Board of Trustees, Clemson University, "Clemson Trustees Minutes, 1907 July 9" (1907), *Minutes,* 497:480, https://tigerprints.clemson.edu/trustees_minutes/497; Board of Trustees, Clemson University, "Clemson Trustees Minutes, 1908 July 14-16" (1908), *Minutes,* 357:511, 520, https:// tigerprints.clemson.edu/trustees_minutes/357.

49. Board of Trustees, Clemson University, "Clemson Trustees Minutes, 1909 September 15" (1909), *Minutes,* 338:610, https://tigerprints.clemson.edu/trustees_minutes/338.

50. Board of Trustees, Clemson University, "Clemson Trustees Minutes, 1914 November 18–19" (1914), *Minutes,* 346:951, https://tigerprints.clemson.edu/trustees_minutes/346.

51. US Census Bureau, 1900, 1920, 1930, and 1940, Population Schedules, Oconee County, SC, Clemson Agricultural College, Seneca Township, Ancestry.com.

52. W. E. B. Du Bois, *The Souls of Black Folk: Essays and Sketches,* 7th ed. (Chicago: A. C. Mc-Clurg, 1907), 13.

53. Clemson to Snowden, Nov. 23, 1873.

54. Ibid.

55. Clemson University, "Clemson Catalog, 1894, No. 2" (1894), *Clemson Catalog (undergraduate announcements),* 162:8, https://tigerprints.clemson.edu/clemson_catalog/162.

56. Ibid.

57. Earle D. Ross, "The Manual Labor Experiment in the Land Grant College," *Mississippi Valley Historical Review* 21, no. 4 (Mar. 1935): 513.

58. "Local News," *Tiger* (Clemson College), Jan. 28, 1907, 3, TigerPrints, https://tigerprints.clemson .edu/tiger_newspaper/2.

59. Caroline E. Janney, *Burying the Dead but Not the Past: Ladies' Memorial Associations and the Lost Cause* (Chapel Hill: University of North Carolina Press, 2012), 2, 3.

60. Board of Trustees, "Board of Trustees Manual, Chapter II—History," Clemson University, https://www.clemson.edu/administration/bot/manual/chapter2.html.

61. W. W. Long, Cooperative Extension Service, Clemson University, "Extension Service Annual Report, 1921" (1921), *Cooperative Annual Reports,* 1:17–28, https://tigerprints.clemson.edu/coop _reports/1.

62. "Dean Becomes 1st Negro County Agent in South Carolina," *Greenville (SC) News,* Sept. 16, 1970.

63. "Minutes of the Buildings and Grounds Committee, March 11, 1946."

64. State of South Carolina, County of Oconee, Court of Common Pleas, Ex parte: The Clemson Agricultural College of South Carolina, In Re: The Purported Cemetery of Unknown Deceased Persons, Petition, Aug. 22, 1960, and Order, Sept. 3, 1960, Box 2, Folder 17, Carrel Cowan-Ricks Papers, Clemson University Libraries' Special Collections and Archives.

65. "History of the African American Burial Ground," Woodland Cemetery Historic Preservation, www.clemson.edu/cemetery (accessed June 8, 2021).

66. "Report of the Buildings and Grounds Committee for the Fiscal Year 1946–47," in Clemson University, "Faculty Senate Minutes, 1947 Meetings" (1947), *Faculty Senate Minutes,* 10, https:// tigerprints.clemson.edu/faculty_senate/10.

67. In the spring of 1842, Sawney Jr. set fire to the overseer's tent. About year later, his sister Issey attempted to set Fort Hill on fire by dropping hot coals on a feather pillow in an upstairs bedroom. Both could have been hanged, the punishment for arson. Instead, they were sent to Andrew P. Calhoun's plantation in Alabama. Their whereabouts thereafter are unknown. "The African American Experience at Fort Hill," Department of Historic Properties, Clemson University, https:// www.clemson.edu/about/history/properties/documents/AfricanAmericansatFH.pdf and "Floride [Colhoun] Calhoun to Lt. Patrick Calhoun, 'Fort Towson, Choctaw Nation, Arkansaw,'" Apr. 3, 1843, in *The Papers of John C. Calhoun,* ed. Clyde Norman Wilson, vol. 17 (Columbia: University of South Carolina Press, 1959), 136.

68. A branch is a very small stream of water, usually six inches wide or less, that feeds off of a larger stream or creek but is located further inland.

69. "Minutes of the General Faculty of Clemson Agricultural College, January 3, 1945–September 24, 1945," in Clemson University, "Faculty Senate Minutes, 1945 Meetings" (1945), *Faculty Senate Minutes,* 12, https://tigerprints.clemson.edu/faculty_senate/12.

70. "Minutes of the General Faculty of Clemson Agricultural College, January 30, 1953–September 6, 1954," in Clemson University, "Faculty Senate Minutes, 1953 Meetings" (1953), *Faculty Senate Minutes,* 4:2, https://tigerprints.clemson.edu/faculty_senate/4.

71. Ibid., 2–3.

72. "Aged Negro Helped Build College: Judge Crawford Still Serves the Institution He Helped Build," *Tiger* (Clemson College), Apr. 23, 1930, 5, TigerPrints, https://tigerprints.clemson.edu /tiger_newspaper/949/; Clemson University, "President's Report to Board of Trustees, 1947" (1947), *President's Reports to the Board of Trustees*, 50:31, https://tigerprints.clemson.edu/pres_reports/50.

73. "Camilla Test Garden Open," *Greenville (SC) News*, Feb. 27, 1954, 11.

74. Mary Taylor Hague, "South Carolina Botanical Garden," *South Carolina Encyclopedia*, Aug. 1, 2016, https://www.scencyclopedia.org/sce/entries/south-carolina-botanical-garden/ (accessed May 27, 2021).

75. "South Carolina Botanical Garden," Clemson University, https://www.clemson.edu/public /scbg/ (accessed May 29, 2020).

76. "Sense of the Board Regarding Accurately Portraying Clemson University's History," July 17, 2015, Clemson University, http://media.clemson.edu/bot/documents/resolution-clemson-history -16Q1.pdf (accessed May 31, 2020).

77. "History Task Force Implementation Team Final Report," Oct. 2019, Clemson University, 9–10, https://www.clemson.edu/about/history/taskforce/documents/HistoryProjectFinalReport.pdf.

78. See Reclaim&Rename, https://www.reclaimandrename.com (accessed June 8, 2021); and Nathaniel Cary, "'Reclaim Old Main' Group Chants in Clemson March on Tillman Hall," *State* (Columbia, SC), Sept. 16, 2015, https://www.thestate.com/news/state/south-carolina/article35510736.html.

79. "Protection of Certain Monuments and Memorials," Public Buildings and Property, Code, S.C. Code Ann. Sec. 10-1-165, South Carolina Legislature, https://www.scstatehouse.gov/code/t10c001. php (accessed June 8, 2021).

80. Zoe Nicholson, "SC Supreme Court Hears Arguments on Heritage Act, Constitutionality of 'Two-Thirds' Vote," *Greenville (SC) News*, May 25, 2021, https://www.greenvilleonline.com/story/ news/2021/05/25/sc-heritage-act-south-carolina-supreme-court-is-it-legal/7427842002/.

81. Seanna Adcox, "SC Supreme Court Keeps Part of Heritage Act Intact, Strikes Supermajority Vote Approval," *Charleston (SC) Post and Courier*, Sept. 22, 2021, https://www.postandcourier.com /politics/sc-supreme-court-keeps-part-of-heritage-act-intact-strikes-supermajority-vote-approval /article_ecocfoba-162a-11ec-aeff-6f6399a9b169.html (accessed Sept. 27, 2021).

82. Meg Kinnard, "Slavery Advocate's Statue Removed in South Carolina," Associated Press, June 24, 2020, https://apnews.com/article/us-news-ap-top-news-sc-state-wire-slavery-south -carolina-a88ad98372bbb810d1261d61acb5350f.

83. Brian Scott, "Integration with Dignity, 1963," Historical Marker Database, July 25, 2008, updated Sept. 17, 2020, https://www.hmdb.org/m.asp?m=9530 (accessed June 8, 2021).

Evangelicals, Race, and Reform

From the Age of Lincoln to the Second Reconstruction

RANDALL J. STEPHENS

In the same year that Abraham Lincoln formed a new law partnership and served out his fourth term in the Illinois state legislature, a radical abolitionist church took root among Yankees in the Northeast and West. The Wesleyan Methodist Connection, established in Utica, New York, in 1843, splintered off from the Methodists. Its members would help lead a new kind of politically and socially engaged evangelicalism. The Wesleyans combined theological perfectionism with a vibrant egalitarianism. Perfectionists called for total abstinence from sin on the individual level and the societal level. The doctrine found some of its strongest supporters in the Wesleyan tradition and some of its fiercest opponents among Calvinists. Still, it had a wide influence among evangelical and nonevangelical Christian reformers. For the schismatic Wesleyans, the Methodist Church was hopelessly weak and impure on the issue of slavery; or worse, it was a church that actively supported "man stealing."

Fittingly, leading voices within the antislavery movement championed the Wesleyans and their cause. In Rochester, New York, Frederick Douglass had close contact with its members. He spoke in one of their congregations, and in 1848 he noted that there were numerous "pro-slavery congregations of this city." Yet the Wesleyans had distinguished themselves as "a small band of men and women [who] meet to hear the Gospel of Freedom and Love for all."[1] They also received high praise from the suffragist, abolitionist, and controversial editor William Lloyd Garrison. The students and instructors at Oberlin College in Ohio clearly saw the Wesleyans as close allies.[2] Like other perfectionist saints, the Wesleyans eagerly took part in spiriting the enslaved out of the South through the underground railroad.[3]

While the Wesleyans may have stood out for their brazenness, there were many others in the evangelical fold who took up the cause of abolitionism or championed any number of other antebellum reforms. These included the Free Methodists, United Brethren, Congregationalists, United Presbyterians, Free Church Presbyterians, Reformed Presbyterians, and Quakers.[4] They established missions, international-aid societies, and educational institutions. In some instances, evangelicals promoted a democratized form of religion.

Just how to define evangelicalism has become a matter of contention among scholars. Some give greater weight to theology, while others stress a variety of cultural and social factors. Surely, a universal definition of evangelicalism across space and time is impossible.[5] Daniel Walker Howe suggests, "Most antebellum American religion was, in one way or another, evangelical." Yet he points out that the defining features of the movement included an "insistence upon a new birth, that is a conscious commitment to Christ, undertaken voluntarily at an identifiable moment and generally conceived (depending on the theology of the particular evangelical group) as a response to divine grace." In the North, evangelicalism was defined by its revivalist impulse, the rage to reform society and the individual, an emphasis on discipleship and church discipline, an idealization of the Christian home, a pronounced biblicism, anti-Catholicism, and, as Howe puts it, "the longing for a personal relationship with Christ."[6] Definitions of the movement that privilege theology tend to minimize the importance of class, race, and ethnicity; gender; manners; regionalism; or activism. Of course, those should rank as critical factors as well. By the early twentieth century, American Protestantism would be fractured, and evangelicalism would lose some of the status, position in society, and coherence it once had.

In the antebellum years, perfectionist evangelicalism had revolutionary implications. In 1835, Oberlin College admitted African Americans into its programs. With Presbyterian minister and leading voice of the Second Great Awakening Charles G. Finney as its new president, it was the first college in the nation to do so. This was at a time when the state of Ohio was still debating whether or not Black and white children could attend school together. It was also a period in which, following Nat Turner's slave rebellion in 1831, southern states had made it a crime to teach Blacks to read and write.[7]

Other leading evangelicals—including Theodore Weld, Jonathan Blanchard, Arthur and Lewis Tappan, and Angelina and Sarah Grimké—attracted national and international attention to the cause. As Carol Berkin puts it, for those like "Angelina Grimké, the message of this 'second great awakening' was a mixture of hope and urgency, the belief that America must purify itself in preparation for the impending judgment day."[8] A kind of pragmatic Arminianism inspired many. Evangelical abolitionist and educator Beriah Green believed that the Bible clearly taught that "professed piety towards God is . . . base and spurious on the ground that it is not united with benevolence for men."[9] The Wesleyans agreed. The Western Anti-Slavery Society took note of the new denomination's hard-line stance and activism. "Of the religious sects in Ohio," observed the group's Executive Committee, "no one has furnished so many members in proportion to their number, that are ready to embrace ultra Abolitionism, as the Wesleyan Methodists." The church's members included "true hearts—many noble spirits, who were delirious to learn and willing to embrace the truth."[10]

Of course, as Charles Irons and Donald Mathews remind us, evangelicals in the South also promoted a new Bible-based proslavery Christianity. Indeed, abolitionist evangelicals were certainly in the Protestant minority. As Richard Carwardine observes of the 1840s, "even within the free states most evangelicals held abolitionism and its political expression at arm's length, regarding it at best with distaste and more commonly with horror."[11] Still, a minority of radical evangelical reformers took part in the antislavery cause, the early women's rights movement, prison reform, peace campaigns, and other related work.

Some of the reforms that stalwarts supported would adjust with the times. With the start of the Civil War, the Wesleyans altered their stance on pacifism and joined in the Union effort with full force. Leaders in the denomination took part with others in the northern states, serving as soldiers or chaplains or supporting the war effort from the home front.[12] In their zeal, many within the church pushed for an even stronger response. They were not entirely satisfied, for instance, with what seemed like President Lincoln's half measures. Church officials sent a letter to the president after Lincoln signed the Emancipation Proclamation in 1863. The Wesleyans at Adrian College in Michigan wrote a letter of support and encouragement to "His Excellency." They introduced themselves to the president and wrote of their founding. They were firm believers who only seceded from the Methodist Church "on account of her then notoriously pro-slavery principles and practices." Wesleyans would not "fellowship with the slaveholder, his aider, or apologist." They praised Lincoln for issuing the proclamation: "We thank you in the name of that God who has revealed himself as the friend, and protector, and avenger of the poor and needy. We thank you in the name of the millions of the oppressed of our land. We thank you in the name of universal humanity." Still, the writers regretted that the Emancipation Proclamation, "noble as it is, is too partial and discriminating in favor of those States, and parts of States not in open rebellion, but whose treason against God's moral government only the more clearly shows that their treasonable proclivities are but scarcely concealed; and their protestations of loyalty are but for the basest and most selfish purposes." The Michigan petitioners went on to further criticize the president, telling him that they "often felt grieved and disappointed at the apparent reluctance exhibited in adopting such measures as would ere now have struck a fatal blow to the very heart of rebellion."[13]

Others were even more critical of Lincoln. Charles Finney, the country's foremost evangelical minister, had written and spoken out against his 1860 and 1864 presidential candidacies. He thought that Lincoln was far too slow to act, or worse, compromised on emancipation.[14] Shortly after Lincoln's nomination at the Republican Convention in Chicago on May 18, 1860, Finney reported on him in the *Oberlin Evangelist*. He admitted that the Illinois lawyer had won "laurels on the score of his intellectual ability and forensic powers" in his 1858 Senate race against Stephen A. Douglas. Yet "his ground on the score of humanity towards the oppressed race was too low. It did him no honor."[15]

For Finney and others like him, proslavery and irreligion were closely linked. Though revivalism and evangelicalism influenced white southerners in profound ways, one of those being missions and outreach to the enslaved, he would not have recognized that fact. In part that is why Finney was so unwavering about what he saw as a kind of false religion that took hold in the slave South. It seemed that the revival of the so-called Second Great Awakening, which swept through the North, could not take hold south of Mason-Dixon Line. "Slavery seemed to shut it out from the South," Finney lamented in his memoir. "The people there were in such a state of irritation, of vexation, and of committal to their peculiar institution . . . that the Spirit of God seemed to be grieved away from them."[16]

All of this flurry of evangelical reform, social perfectionism, and political engagement had its limits. "Although few evangelicals could have suspected it at the time," notes Randall Balmer, "the evangelical benevolent empire had reached its apotheosis by 1860. With the Civil War, the shining aspirations of evangelical social amelioration began to dim for several decades as Americans coped with the devastation of the war and addressed the delicate task of mending the torn fabric of the republic."[17] Certainly, northern Methodists, Baptists, Congregationalists, Presbyterians, and others worked with the Freedmen's Bureau, supported Reconstruction, and turned to urban reform. But much of the initial energy was dissipating.

Already in the decade after the Civil War, some influential evangelicals began to question the emphasis on Christian activism and the commitment to the uplift of former slaves. New initiatives like the decidedly middle-class and social-striving Chautauqua movement picked up where more aggressive social reform left off. Some postwar evangelicals wondered if fellow believers had spent too little time cultivating personal piety. Baltimore minister Richard Fuller made these concerns central to his 1873 address to the Evangelical Alliance in New York City. Fuller observed that he lived in an age of activist energies and social-reform societies. But the danger of the era was in "mistaking what we do for what we are, and consequently the neglect of our own spiritual health and prosperity, while we engage in the diversified systems of concerted movements which incessantly claim our attention."[18] In the coming decades, the logic shifted so that to be overly engaged in social reform, from a white-evangelical point of view, meant that one had jettisoned theological orthodoxy and abandoned a commitment to personal piety.

By the early decades of the twentieth century, evangelicals, and those who would later be called fundamentalists, downplayed social reform and had turned away from the radical causes of their progenitors.[19] The early years of the century marked a period when more liberal Protestants, inspired by the ideals of the Social Gospel and political progressivism, now appeared quite unlike their conservative brethren. There were some within the Social Gospel camp, like midwestern Congregational minister Harlan Paul Douglass, who actively opposed the racism and discrimination that dominated early twentieth-century America.[20]

In this process of transformation, conservative and liberal Protestants came to define themselves against one another. By then, the political radicalism and social innovations of the early Wesleyans had become an embarrassment to fundamentalists. From the fundamentalist vantage of the first decades of the twentieth century, the steadfast abolitionists, women's rights activists, and pacifists of the antebellum era seemed misguided. Later ministers in the movement sanitized the writings of Charles Finney, scrubbing them of their social activism and reformist ideals to better suit the needs of twentieth-century conservatives.[21]

The change in the basic evangelical outlook on society and reform was enormous. One hundred years after their founding, the Wesleyan Methodists, like most other white evangelicals, had become conservatives, battling liberal Protestantism and defending their faith against theological modernism. Aligned with what became known as fundamentalism, such Protestants hoped to preserve the fundamentals of the faith against the acids of modernism.

From his pulpit at First Presbyterian Church in Manhattan, the influential liberal Protestant minister Harry Emerson Fosdick retaliated. Fundamentalists were threatening to "divide the American Churches," he intoned. "Their apparent intention," Fosdick warned in May 1922, "is to drive out of the evangelical churches men and women of liberal opinions." He proclaimed that "the Fundamentalist program is essentially illiberal and intolerant." Fosdick lamented how closed off his conservative foes had become to the larger world. "They have even endeavored to put on the statute books of a whole state binding laws against teaching modern biology," he recounted, in reference to a growing antievolution movement, which culminated in the 1925 Scopes Trial. Kentucky's antievolution bill was only defeated by the narrowest of margins in March 1922. Indeed, during the 1920s, there were at least twenty-seven antievolution bills, resolutions, and riders introduced at the state level across the country. Fittingly, Fosdick pleaded for "the cause of magnanimity and liberality and tolerance of spirit."[22] Yet his appeal typically only drew the ire of fundamentalists. In their estimation, Fosdick was a heretic, plain and simple. James M. Gray, president of Moody Bible Institute, shot back at Fosdick and his question, "Shall the fundamentalists win?" "Win what?" snapped Gray. The true Christian, in his estimation, would know that the very things Fosdick assailed were fundamental principles of scripture. Liberalism, said Gray, rejected "the Saviour."[23]

While Quakers and Congregationalists, and later members of the Lutheran Church in America, would go on to support civil rights, ecology, and other matters of social justice, most evangelicals like Gray turned sharply from such public crusades.[24] Such developments are particularly interesting, in part, because historians like Balmer, Donald Dayton, and Nancy Hardesty have described a sharp break in the tradition. In such a view, modern twentieth-century fundamentalism and conservative evangelicalism bear little resemblance to what came before.

James Brewer Stewart, a historian of nineteenth-century antislavery and reform movements, observes: "Contemporary fundamentalists ought to think again, hard, before claiming the abolitionists as their historical ancestors. Standards of historical accuracy confirm such claims as specious. Second, today's religious right finds political agency a straightforward exercise. For abolitionists it was not. Obedient to established authority, fundamentalist activists today embrace prevailing governance in order to conform it to God's will by mobilizing voters, winning elections, discouraging dissent, and passing laws."[25] Those evangelicals who were abolitionists had strong ideas about the greater good and the role that faith could play in changing the social order and redeeming society. Their efforts would bring about the kingdom of God on earth, they thought.

Modern, conservative, and politicized fundamentalists and evangelicals, in Stewart's view, have tended to be far more pessimistic about human agency. In the 1970s, as evangelicals embraced conservative politics in new ways, there was a minority of left and liberal evangelicals who tried to chart a different path. Many of these turned to their own history for guidance. One was University of Chicago–trained historian Donald Dayton. In 1976, the year that born-again Christian Jimmy Carter won the presidency, Dayton looked back at the history of his own denomination, Wesleyan Methodism. To his surprise, he discovered that the abolitionist church was a forerunner to the modern civil rights movement. He observed that twentieth-century fundamentalism and evangelicalism "in many ways stood for the opposite of what an earlier generation of Evangelicals had affirmed. . . . Revivalist currents that had once been bent to the liberation of the slave now allied themselves with wealth and power against the civil rights movement."[26] The historian Steven Miller has described this rediscovery and reorientation. Younger adherents were asking themselves, "What had happened to the abolitionist legacy of Charles Finney, the Tappan brothers, and the early administrators of Oberlin and Wheaton Colleges?"[27]

If Dayton was right, why did these changes happen when and where they did? There were a number of variables. Some were theological; others were so-cial, cultural, and ethnographic. The regional center of the movement, too, had changed with the shifting of the population westward in the late nineteenth and early twentieth centuries. In addition, the conservative South would become one of the most vital centers of evangelicalism, fundamentalism, and Pentecostal-ism in the new century.[28] Like the larger political establishment in the twenty years after Lincoln's death, white evangelicals slowly turned away from African American relief work and from the causes of the freedmen. By the end of the century, a growing number of believers had become convinced that society could not be improved or redeemed in ways that their predecessors had thought. This shift, observes Martin Marty, changed the relationship of believers to the world around them. Marty writes that such stalwarts were now asking themselves, "Why devote energies to making peace between nations, management and labor, men and women, or religious groups . . . if to do so distracted from the first work of Christians, the task of rescuing people from the world?"[29] This transformation to an inward-looking, pessimistic detachment took place between roughly 1900 and 1930, though it was well underway in the last decades of the nineteenth century. Believers became more reactionary, lashing out at anarchists, new immigrants, Roman Catholics, evolutionary scientists, liberal theologians, and social reformers. Prohibition was one of the last great causes that a large group of Protestants could unite behind. For the most part, however, progressive social concern, especially as it was linked to more liberal Protestants who espoused the Social Gospel, came under much suspicion.[30]

One might ask, however, if it is even possible to talk about the trajectory of a religious tradition from the Age of Lincoln to the Roaring Twenties. Certainly there are risks to charting the changes of a movement over a decade, much less fifty years. Can the social and cultural identity of a group in one era be compared to that in a much different era? These were the kinds of questions that C. Vann Woodward explored in 1962 in his correspondence with Richard Hofstadter. Woodward, who could be quite tone deaf when it came to religious topics, challenged Hofstadter's use of the term "fundamentalist" to describe certain Christians in the nineteenth century. That term was only in general usage in the 1920s, though it is applicable to the early twentieth century. Woodward wrote to Hofstadter: "if you mean by fundamentalists those addicted to 'literal scanning of Scripture' you take in a hell of the proportion of the population from the seventeenth down through the nineteenth centuries—including a hell of a lot of intellectuals, even some leading ones way down into the nineteenth century." One of the main dangers, as he saw it, was "anachronism, for a lot of people would be accused of opposing things that did not really exist in their time."[31] It can be difficult to compare one era to another, and such efforts always risk such anachronism. But the trajectory of white evangelicalism tells us much about how conservative stalwarts walled themselves off in the early twentieth century, defined themselves against their liberal brethren, and broke from an earlier tradition. Some of these basic transformations are apparent in the lives of the movement's most high-profile and influential preachers.

The most famous evangelist in the post–Civil War era set the tone for much of white conservative Protestantism for decades to come. "Brother [Dwight] Moody's success has been well nigh phenomenal," rhapsodized a reporter in 1899 in the *Chicago Tribune.* "There have been many evangelists in his time, but not one of them has so closely commended himself to the people or reaped such great results from his labor." In the writer's estimation, "no man is better known. Certainly no man is more highly esteemed."[32]

Moody, who reporters dubbed "God's Man for the Gilded Age," had started his professional career humbly enough as a Chicago shoe salesman before launching a ministerial career in that city. Scoffers called him "Crazy Moody" because of his religious zeal. He established a Sunday school in Chicago's slums before serving as an evangelist and relief worker for the Union war effort. When President-elect Lincoln visited Moody's popular Chicago Sunday school in 1860, it leant the young minister a great deal of clout. But it was Moody's postwar career as an urban evangelist that brought him transatlantic fame and widespread influence. Massive revivals in the large cities of Great Britain and in Boston, Chicago, Brooklyn, and Philadelphia made him and his music minister partner, Ira Sankey, household names.

Moody's social outlook in this era became increasingly individualistic. He also aligned with wealthy industrialists as he accepted the logic of segregation. Moody seems to have reacted against the radical evangelicals of the antebellum years. In the process, he turned his attention to the inner spiritual lives of the devout. The Chicago evangelist, reflecting the new values of the movement, focused a great deal on the sins of the flesh, but sins of social oppression, race prejudice, or greed he largely ignored.[33]

Moody may have believed, at least privately, that racial justice and the plight of African Americans in the Jim Crow era were worth greater attention. As a young man living in Boston in the 1850s, the abolitionist cause appealed to him. He attended antislavery meetings in Faneuil Hall and even took part in the raid on the old courthouse to free the runaway slave Anthony Burns.[34] But in his work as a professional evangelist, Moody was willing to make compromises. At a spring 1876 revival in Augusta, Georgia, he had at first wanted to hold integrated services but quickly caved to pressures from local whites. Ongoing worries about how any such signals would be read by his white audience remained foremost for the famous minister. As one historian put it years ago, "he could not risk the unpopularity of such a stand in public."[35] Moody conformed to prevailing conservative southern white opinion. But that did not go unchallenged. When he held segregated meetings in Louisville, Kentucky, in 1888, African American ministers in town chastised him. One proclaimed, "I recognize no color line in the church of God."[36] The African American journalist and antilynching activist Ida B. Wells criticized both Moody and temperance crusader and suffragist Francis Willard. Neither, said Wells, was willing to take a stand against segregation in the Jim Crow South.[37]

But there was something more at work in the case of Moody. For conservative evangelicals like him, the reform campaigns of the antebellum and Civil War eras seemed out of date or just plain wrong. Moody liked to speak about a change he underwent on how he thought of reform in general. "I used to make a mistake on that point," he lamented.

> When I was at work in the City Relief Society, before the [Great Chicago Fire of 1871], I used to go to a poor sinner with the Bible in one hand and a loaf of bread in the other. . . . My idea was that I could open a poor man's heart by giving him a load of wood or a ton of coal when the winter was coming on, but I soon found out that he wasn't any more interested in the Gospel on that account. Instead of thinking how he could come to Christ, he was thinking how long it would be before he got another load of wood. If I had the Bible in one hand and a loaf in the other the people always looked first at the loaf; and that was just contrary to the order laid down in the Gospel.[38]

Accordingly, Moody adopted the perspective that social injustices were a kind of natural, brutal reality. Changing someone's station in life would bring them no closer to God. Though Moody died in 1899, his ideas about relief work and reform would live on in the movement.

It is not entirely surprising that the church Moody had founded in Chicago bowed to the dictates of Jim Crow. In 1915, the *Crisis* reported that Paul Rader, the pastor at that time, "objects to colored people in his church."[39] The Moody Bible

Institute did nothing to challenge Jim Crow justice. As Timothy Gloege notes, it also "considered the benefits of the Ku Klux Klan to be an open question in the early 1920s."[40] Indeed, a pastor from western New York wrote to the *Moody Monthly* in late 1923 with the matter of the resurrected KKK on his mind. Why had not the magazine taken a definitive position on the Klan, he wondered. He had noticed many ministers who were leaving their pulpits to lend their support to this organization. "If the thing is right and necessary, why not help to give it momentum," he advised, "if wrong, sound the alarm, or at least give a warning before it is too late."[41]

Like Moody and the institutions he founded, the Wesleyans slowly turned away from an array of causes. A committed Christian, in the outlook of many of them, could do little more than save souls and prepare for the second coming of Jesus. The Wesleyans never officially adopted the end-times theology of premillennialism. Still, numerous individuals in the denomination became staunch premillennialists.[42] These and other proto-fundamentalists from the 1890s to about 1920 read and sat at the feet of American and British divines who preached about the urgency of the last days at prophecy conferences, in church halls, and in mass revivals. The simple message was that mankind was fallen and hopeless. Only Christ could rescue the saints from a broken and evil world. Before Christ returned in judgment, a select few saints would be raptured into heaven, sparing them the suffering and tribulation that awaited the unrepentant.[43] In the middle of the nineteenth century, premillennialism had been a rather marginal theology. Its adherents, like the Millerites and the Seventh-day Adventist in the United States or the Plymouth Brethren in England, lacked the social capital and influence of Methodists, Baptists, and Presbyterians. Yet, by the last part of the century, this apocalyptic theology had gained a growing following.

A typical adopter of the new theology was B. F. Haynes, a southern Methodist minister who would eventually join the holiness Church of the Nazarene. Haynes looked back on the misguidedness of his earlier views. He had been taught that the "Church was gradually to overspread the earth with salvation until all mankind were saved, and that then the millennium would come." By the end of the nineteenth century, he "plainly saw that such was not being done."[44] A whole array of white evangelicals in this era embraced premillennialism, which well fit their growing pessimism about society, politics, and race relations.[45] In the words of one historian, for those who adopted it, "only the supernatural return of Christ on the clouds of glory would arrest the growing corruption of human history, hold its downward spiral, and inaugurate the kingdom of God on earth."[46]

Premillennialism, a theology of the past and of the future, shaped some of the basic ways Wesleyans and other evangelicals thought about reform and imagined their place in the world. It is not surprising that they made new compromises with Jim Crow in the same period that this outlook began to dominate. The Wesleyans, for instance, established a separate African American conference in southern Ohio and in Alabama in 1891.[47]

When it came to race and segregation, there were some exceptions to the rule. A minority that fit broadly in the evangelical or fundamentalist camp maintained interracial churches, promoted integration, and featured Black leaders. The Azusa Street Revival in Los Angeles in April 1906, one starting point of Pentecostalism, was led by the southern African American preacher William J. Seymour. Whites and Blacks who attended some of these early, rowdy meetings thought that the interracial element was a sure sign of divine approval and of Holy Ghost power; what else could explain something so odd, they wondered. A. A. Boddy was a white Englishman from the shipbuilding and coalmining center of Sunderland who had made his way to the Azusa Street Mission. Writing in his Pentecostal newspaper *Confidence*, Boddy rhapsodically recalled the stunning sight of Blacks and whites worshiping and praying together.

> One of the remarkable things [at Azusa] was that preachers of the Southern States were willing and eager to go over to those negro people at Los Angeles and have fellowship with them, and through their prayers receive the same blessing. The most wonderful thing was that, when those white preachers came back to the Southern States, they were not ashamed to say before their own congregations that they had been worshiping with negroes, and had received some of the same wonderful blessings that had been poured out on them.[48]

Much of this faded by midcentury. But there were some so-called oneness (non-trinitarian) Pentecostals who maintained a commitment to integration. Even a temporary or liminal interracial aspect in the Jim Crow South was quite extraordinary. Some groups, like the relatively small Church of God of Prophecy, were quite bold in their pronouncements. A 1965 piece in the church's bulletin in Cleveland, Tennessee, warned: "To have racial distinction would be against the will of God or the purpose of the Church. . . . The speckled bird has many different colored feathers, and so is [sic] the Church of the last days."[49]

Other Christian organizations, like the Salvation Army, remained firmly committed to poor relief and urban slum work. Its dedicated members devoted a great deal of time and energy working with and for the white and Black underclass.[50] There were other rare experiments in social justice, like the racially integrated evangelical community of Koinonia Farm. Clarence Jordan and Martin England founded the four-hundred-acre experiment near Americus, Georgia, in 1942. The group dedicated itself to pacifism, agricultural education, racial justice, and economic equality. As Koinonia Farm challenged the southern status quo, it was met with fierce opposition. Locals accused the residents of having communist sympathies. Rehoboth Baptist Church expelled Jordan and his followers in 1950. They also faced economic boycotts as well as violent attacks from the local Klan. Yet they remained, even in the face of bombings, shootings, and other acts of terrorism.[51]

Regardless, the vast majority of white evangelicals shunned social innovations like racial integration, pacifism, and other kinds of progressive reform. By the 1920s and 1930s, new leaders of the fold represented a much more strident and reactionary brand of white conservatism. Well-known ministers acted like righteous warriors, battling against Roman Catholics, racial integrationists, bootleggers, immigrants, liberal theologians, Bolsheviks, and a range of other "enemies" of the faith.

In the 1920s, the famous fundamentalist crusader Billy Sunday inspired evangelicals with a homespun gospel and a lively stage routine. Like his predecessor Moody, Sunday focused his attention on sinners in need of salvation and disparaged most reform work.[52] He conducted integrated revivals in the North. But when traveling in the South, he had no trouble holding separate meetings for Blacks and whites. The African American newspaper New York Age pointed out the popular revivalist's blind spot on race. It ran a short paragraph in the spring of 1915 noting, "Billy Sunday speaks out emphatically, acrobatically and ungrammatically against almost every wrong in the country—except race prejudice." Then it challenged his manliness, stating, "If he wants to show that he is a real brave man, not afraid to tackle anything, and do some good where it is most needed, let him speak out against race prejudice."[53]

But for Sunday, race was never at the root of the nation's trouble. An ardent prohibitionist, he believed that alcohol was responsible for the gravest social problems of the day. The former professional baseball player did not traffic in the kind of anti-Semitism and anti-Catholicism so common in his era. Nonetheless, his moral authoritarianism and nationalism, as well as his use of racial epithets and violent rhetoric from the pulpit, drew the support of the relaunched Ku Klux Klan. Sunday made some efforts to keep his distance from the KKK, which by the mid-1920s may have numbered as many as 5 million members. But Klansmen nonetheless tended to see the revivalist as a kindred spirit. Without cozying up too much to the organization, Sunday found ways to praise the robed terrorists.

Other traveling preachers like Bob Jones, Alma White, B. B. Crimm, J. Frank Norris, Charlie Taylor, and Raymond T. Richey heaped praise on white suprem-acists in their sermons or openly and enthusiastically supported the Klan.[54] At the same time, numerous liberal white and African American Protestants casti-gated Klansmen and their violent organization.[55] The *Christian Century* warned its readers of the pernicious influence of the KKK. One writer cautioned, "if it succeeds, Christianity fails, no matter what other gains may be thought won."[56] Editors and writers were well aware that hooded visitors were making large donations at churches across the United States on Sunday mornings. But, such critics declared, ministers who accepted these gifts did great harm to the church.

Stories of the Klan's association with white Protestant laypeople and ministers were common enough that novelist Sinclair Lewis took note. In *Elmer Gantry* (1927), a parody of a morally compromised preacher, Lewis paints a picture of the connections. "Many of the most worthy Methodist and Baptist clergymen supported it and were supported by it," he narrates. Gantry "admired its prin-ciple—to keep all foreigners, Jews, Catholics, and Negroes in their place, which was no place at all, and let the country be led by native Protestants, like Elmer Gantry."[57] Lewis modeled another character in the book, the faith-healing re-vivalist Sister Sharon Falconer, on Pentecostal celebrity minister Aimee Semple McPherson. McPherson praised the work of the Klan as a force for righteousness and old-fashioned values. Other Pentecostals took a stand against it because it was a secret society, not because of its ethnic bigotry and promotion of violence. Some within the movement also saw the anti-Catholicism of the KKK as a sign of the end of the world.[58]

Other high-profile ministers were strong proponents of the Klan's ideals and actions. The influential fundamentalist "Fighting Bob" Shuler, a southern Methodist who pastored Trinity Methodist Church in Los Angeles, claimed to have conducted a twelve-month study of the KKK in order to find out about its "ideals, principles, teachings and activities." He reported his finding in the *Moody Monthly*. "First, the Klan is the positive and active friend of Protestant Christianity," he claimed.

> Second, the Klan is undoubtedly the strong defender of our public schools and stands unhesitatingly for the return of the Word of God to that institution. . . . Third, the Klan stands all over the nation as an active defender of virtue in American womanhood. . . . Fourth, the Klan, whatever may be the claim of her foes, is today an active and powerful factor in behalf of law enforcement. . . . Fifth, the Klan opposed stubbornly the driving back of American idealism by the combination of foreign ideals that have today massed for the destruction of American ideals and standards of living.[59]

Shuler came away from his study "thoroughly convinced" by the good of the secret society. *Moody Monthly* and other fundamentalist publications found it difficult to take a strong, official position for or against the Klan. Yet Shuler urged his brethren to find out about the society for themselves.[60]

Billy Sunday was never so forthcoming. But there are numerous hints about what he thought of the Klan and its crusading white supremacists. More importantly, the KKK roundly supported him. Sunday's biblical literalism and nativism won effusive praise from Klan members. In 1922, a South Bend, Indiana, newspaper even joked about their mutual affection. "Down in West Virginia the other day," wrote an editor, the Klan "slipped Billy Sunday the sum of $200. With Sunday's O.K., that ought to put the K.K.K. in good standing with old St. Peter."[61]

Sunday returned the favor with positive pronouncements about Klansmen who valiantly aided police in vice raids. The Jackson, Mississippi, Klan No. 22 gave the revivalist a donation of $195 on January 29, 1925, for Sunday's "incomparable, militant, Christian work." His reply appeared in the *Winona Times* of Mississippi a week later. "Some folks think the Ku Klux are trying to overthrow the government," he began. "Forget it, they are trying to keep others from doing this very thing, and if the government ever wants an organization 100 percent American, they will find it in this crowd."[62] After receiving a KKK donation of $650 in Spartanburg, South Carolina, Sunday assured the congregation, "if you are on the right side the Ku Klux won't get you anyway."[63] One of his mass meetings, which drew 15,000 to the Memphis City Auditorium, was dubbed "Klan night."[64]

The revivalist accepted other larger-than-average gifts from the Klan at revivals in Indiana, Tennessee, South Carolina, West Virginia, and Louisiana between 1922 and 1925. In 1922, his secretary claimed that the Klan had made donations in every city the revivalist had visited that year.[65] Klansmen in Richmond, Indiana, attended a revival wearing their full regalia to publicly offer Sunday their gift. Not surprisingly, in 1923 a Klan-supporting Texas editor proclaimed: "I find the preachers of the Protestant faith almost solid for the Klan and its ideals, with here and there an isolated minister . . . who will line up with the Catholics in their fight on Protestantism, but that kind of preacher is persona non grata in most every congregation in Texas."[66]

Members of the Klan were fluent in the sentimental language of evangelicalism and fundamentalism, drawing on imagery and themes that believers would have found deeply familiar.[67] For instance, the popular song "The Old Rugged Cross" appeared in a Klan hymnal with new lyrics and a new title. The altered anthem was copyrighted by George Bennard and Homer A. Rodeheaver. The latter was Sunday's music evangelist and ministerial partner. Rodeheaver likely received royalties from the revised version. "The Bright Fiery Cross" drew on standard sentimental themes in order to win allegiance to the cause:

To the Bright Fi-ery Cross, I will ev-er be true;
All blame and reproach gla-dly bear,
And friend-ship will show, to each Klans-man I know;
It's glo-ry for ev-er we'll share
So I'll cherish the Bright Fiery Cross
Till from duties at last I lay down;
Then burn o'er me a Bright Fiery Cross,
The day I am laid in the ground.[68]

At roughly the same time that Sunday had become the most popular preacher in the United States, other Protestants charted a different path. The Quaker American Friends Service Committee, a humanitarian group founded in 1917, campaigned against racism and the mistreatment of prisoners and coordinated relief efforts for refugees. The international organization received the 1947 Nobel

Peace Prize for its work during World War II. The Congregationalists' Council for Social Action, founded in 1934, also took a strong stand on racial equality. Other church and parachurch groups inspired by figures who promoted the Social Gospel—Washington Gladden, Walter Rauschenbusch, Jane Addams, and Lyman Abbott, among others—were similarly motivated.[69]

In the middle of the twentieth century, Billy Graham was the obvious successor of Billy Sunday. Yet Graham would shed the vaudevillian vulgarities of his predecessor just as he rejected explicit bigotry and racism. He opened up his tents and crusade auditoriums to Blacks and whites in the Jim Crow South. The color line was at odds with Christianity, he came to insist. *Ebony* magazine's September 1957 issue included his essay "No Color Line in Heaven." The Billy Graham Association widely advertised that piece in newspapers around the country. On tours in Asia and Africa, he said much the same. During his crusade at Madison Square Garden in New York City, Graham shared the platform with Martin Luther King Jr. Graham told the multitudes that King had started a "great social revolution" in the United States. Yet the two would chart radically different paths when it came to social action and relating faith to politics.[70]

Graham skillfully skirted the issue but occasionally spoke more directly about race and segregation. He addressed 17,000 who gathered at the May 1964 Southern Baptist Convention in New Jersey. There, he called for a moral and spiritual revival, hitting on a common theme. "I've never understood how, in the church, you can say 'this church is for one race only,'" Graham said to the crowd. Yet the denomination put forth only vague statements on the matter.[71] Graham himself remained suspicious about the power of government at the national, state, or even local level, believing real change would not come as a result of Supreme Court decisions or acts of Congress. He tended to spiritualize the issue, claiming that it was most important for people to repent. Men and women first had to give their lives to Jesus, then right thinking and action would follow.

Certainly, there were some who pegged Graham as a white nationalist. With rhetorical flair, Malcolm X used the famous minister as a key example in his "The Ballot or the Bullet" speech of April 3, 1964. "I have watched how Billy Graham comes into a city, spreading what he calls the gospel of Christ, which is only white nationalism," he told his audience at Cory Methodist Church in Cleveland, Ohio. "Billy Graham is a white nationalist; I'm a black nationalist," he said bluntly. So, he concluded, "we're going to take a page from his book."[72]

Graham would have classed himself a moderate who only acted on firm biblical principles and certainly would have winced at Malcolm X's characterization.
Most importantly, Graham, like millions of other white evangelicals in the 1950s
and 1960s, considered the sin of racism to be a private, personal matter that had
little or nothing to do with institutions or social structures. This line of reasoning
was on display when he addressed those gathered for a prayer breakfast in April
1964. The Southern Baptist evangelist spoke of the pressing problems of the era:
the threats of communism, the arms race, and racial tensions. Racism was sin-
ful. People should not be treated unequally, he declared. Yet neither civil rights
marches nor legislation could really address the problem. "It has to come from
the hearts of the people," he preached. "That's the answer to the race problem."[73]

Over a decade before, the president of Youth for Christ responded to charges
of racism with similar language. Bob Cook, who had worked closely with Graham, told a reporter, "We find there is no race relations problem when people
have God in their hearts."[74] White evangelicals' focus on personal conversion,
their commitment to free market ideals, and their resistance to federal government power influenced such views on race.[75]

Why had this outlook come to predominate, though? Baptist minister and
University of North Carolina religious studies professor Samuel Hill Jr. had spent
a great deal of time studying that question before addressing it directly in his 1966
book, *Southern Churches in Crisis.* And though he focused on one region, his
argument applied to the wider Christian movement as well. White evangelicals
were indifferent to issues of racial justice, he observed, because of a "general
Evangelical stance, which simply does not view responsibility toward God or
man in the light of a social ethic." White believers felt called by God to convert,
not to meddle with social arrangements.[76]

The historian George Marsden sheds light on this brand of disengaged white
conservative Protestantism with reference to the Social Gospel. "To understand
the fundamentalists' strong reaction against anything that even looked like the
Social Gospel, it is necessary to distinguish the liberal Social Gospel from . . .
evangelical social concern," he writes. Conservative evangelicals demanded that
"public or private social programs be understood as complementary outgrowths
of the regenerating work of Christ which saved souls for all eternity."[77] In broad
terms, abolitionism helped create two important later movements: conservative
evangelicalism and the liberal to left-leaning Social Gospel movement.[78] These

two only began to diverge from each other in the last years of the nineteenth century.

The Wesleyan historian Lee M. Haines has described how the first generation of his church thought of themselves and their work. In his estimation, they "prided themselves in being radical, liberal, the vanguard of the righteous host which would soon bring in the millennial reign of Christ on earth."[79] One hundred years later, the church's leading lights had a rather different vision. One of those reflected on the changes his denomination had undergone over the century. Writing in 1942, the minister cautioned fellow Wesleyans to "observe the peculiar danger of the reformer." Previous generations had spent too much time and energy on social reform and had obscured "the whole field of religious and spiritual truth."[80] This was largely true of British evangelicals as well. By the 1920s, even those who tended to be more liberal were now withdrawing from the reform work that inspired a previous generation. In both the United States and the United Kingdom, the Salvation Army remained one of the few evangelical denominations that maintained active social work.[81] By the time of the 1950s and 1960s, white evangelicals had long given up on transforming the larger society and fighting societal racism. Leaders and laypeople could do little more than preserve their faith, await the return of Jesus, and rescue lost souls from a fallen world.

NOTES

1. Douglass called their congregation "an oasis in a desert." "The Meeting on Main Street," *North Star* (Rochester, NY), Jan. 14, 1848, 2. See also Milton C. Sernett, *North Star Country: Upstate New York and the Crusade for African American Freedom* (Syracuse, NY: Syracuse University Press, 2002), 83–85, 115.

2. "The True Wesleyan," *Oberlin Evangelist*, Jan. 17, 1844, 15. See also "The True Wesleyan," *Voice of Freedom* (Brandon, VT), Jan. 11, 1844, 114; and L.B. Gallien, "The 'Double-Conscious' Nature of American Evangelicalism's Struggle over Civil Rights during the Progressive Era," in *The Wiley-Blackwell Companion to Religion and Social Justice,* ed. Michael D. Palmer and Stanley M. Burgess (Malden, MA: Blackwell, 2012), 522–25. The Wesleyan Church in North America had an average weekly attendance in 2016–17 of 240,000. Ron McClung, "North American Worship Attendance at All-Time High," Wesleyan Church, www.wesleyan.org/north-american-worship-attendance-time -high (accessed May 15, 2019).

3. "Sound Conference Testimonies," *The Liberator* (Boston), Mar. 30, 1849, 1. Wilbur H. Siebert, *The Underground Railroad: From Slavery to Freedom* (New York: Macmillan, 1898), 32, 50, 95, 235. Douglas Strong, *Perfectionist Politics: Abolitionism and the Religious Tensions of American Democracy* (Syracuse, NY: Syracuse University Press, 1999), 129. This research first began as a more detailed

exploration of the Wesleyan Methodists and their social, political, and religious evolution: Randall J. Stephens, "From Abolitionists to Fundamentalists: The Transformation of the Wesleyan Methodists in the 19th and 20th Centuries," *American Nineteenth Century History* (May 2015): 159–91.

4. Richard S. Taylor, "Beyond Immediate Emancipation: Jonathan Blanchard, Abolitionism, and the Emergence of American Fundamentalism," *Civil War History* 27, no. 3 (Sept. 1981): 273.

5. For a sampling of attempts to define the movement at various places and times, see Marguerite Van Die, "The Rise of the Domestic Ideal in the United States and Canada," in *Turning Points in the History of American Evangelicalism,* ed. Heath W. Carter and Laura Porter (Grand Rapids, MI: Wm. B. Eerdmans, 2017), 103–6; Mark A. Noll, *America's God: From Jonathan Edwards to Abraham Lincoln* (New York: Oxford University Press, 2002), 5–7; Frances FitzGerald, *The Evangelicals: The Struggle to Shape America* (New York: Simon & Schuster, 2017), 164; Linford Fisher, "Evangelicals and Unevangelicals: The Contested History of a Word, 1500–1950," *Religion and American Culture* 26, no. 2 (Summer 2016): 184–226; and Thomas S. Kidd, *Who Is an Evangelical? The History of a Movement in Crisis* (New Haven, CT: Yale University Press, 2019).

6. Daniel Walker Howe, *Making the American Self: Jonathan Edwards to Abraham Lincoln* (New York: Oxford University Press, 2009), 114, 117.

7. Pam Hollister, "Oberlin College," in *International Dictionary of University Histories,* ed. Mary Elizabeth Devine and Carol Summerfield (Chicago: Fitzroy Dearborn, 1998), 315.

8. Carol Berkin, "Angelina Grimké's Evangelical Passion to End Slavery," *Huffington Post,* Jan. 9, 2013, updated Dec. 6, 2017, www.huffingtonpost.com/carol-berkin/angelina-grimke-evangelical -passion-to-end-slavery_b_2435248.html (accessed Nov. 26, 2018).

9. Beriah Green, *Four Sermons Preached in the Chapel of the Western Reserve College* (Cleveland: Office of the Herald, 1833), 11.

10. "Fifth Annual Report of the Executive Committee of the Western Anti-Slavery Society," *Anti-Slavery Bugle* (Lisbon, OH), Sept. 3, 1847, 1.

11. Richard J. Carwardine, *Evangelicals and Politics in Antebellum America* (New Haven, CT: Yale University Press, 1993), 139. On the broad regional outlines of evangelicalism at the start of the Civil War, see ibid., xix, 382. By 1850, roughly 70 percent of America's protestants were members of the two main evangelical groups: Methodists and Baptists. Most other evangelicals were members of the Disciples of Christ, Presbyterian, and Congregational churches. Jon Butler, Grant Wacker, and Randall Balmer, *Religion in American Life: A Short History* (New York: Oxford University Press, 2011), 182–83.

12. "Section XXI: On Peace," *Discipline of the Wesleyan Methodist Connection of America* (Syracuse, NY: A. Crooks for the Wesleyan Methodist Connection, 1867), 124; Lee M. Haines, "Radical Reform and Living Piety," in *Reformers and Revivalists: The History of the Wesleyan Church,* ed. Wayne E. Caldwell (Indianapolis: Wesley, 1992), 55.

13. Luther Lee and John McEldowney, "To His Excellency Abraham Lincoln, President of the United States," June 6, 1864, Adrian College, Adrian, MI, in *Of the United States of America, during the Great Rebellion,* ed. Edward McPherson (Washington, DC: Philp and Solomons, 1864), 546, 547.

14. Charles E. Hambrick-Stowe, *Charles G. Finney and the Spirit of American Evangelicalism* (Grand Rapids, MI: William B. Eerdmans, 1996), 288.

15. "The Republican Convention at Chicago," *Oberlin (OH) Evangelist,* May 23, 1860, 83.

16. Charles G. Finney, *Memoirs of Rev. Charles G. Finney Written by Himself* (New York: A. S. Barnes, 1876), 444. James David Essig writes that "the progress of revivals and abolition," for Finney, "formed a part of a single process by which men hastened the onset of the millennium." Essig, "The Lord's Free Man: Charles G. Finney and His Abolitionism," in *Abolitionism and American Religion*, ed. John R. McKivigan (New York: Garland, 1999), 319.

17. Randall Balmer, "'An End to Unjust Inequality in the World': The Radical Tradition of Progressive Evangelicalism," *Church History and Religious Culture* 94, no. 4 (2014): 525; Mark A. Noll, *The Civil War as a Theological Crisis* (Chapel Hill: University of North Carolina Press, 2006), 53.

18. Richard Fuller, "Personal Religion, Its Aids and Hindrances," in *History, Essays, Orations, and Other Documents of the Sixth General Conference of the Evangelical Alliance, Held in New York, October 2–12, 1873*, ed. Philip Schaff and S. Irenæus Prime (New York: Harper and Brothers, 1874), 335; Melvin E. Dieter, *The Holiness Revival of the Nineteenth Century* (Lanham, MD: Scarecrow, 1996), 101–3; Brian Steensland and Philip Goff, eds., *The New Evangelical Social Engagement* (New York: Oxford University Press, 2014), 21; Timothy W. Gloege, "A Gilded Age Modernist: Reuben A. Torrey and the Roots of Conservative Activism," in *American Evangelicalism: George Marsden and the State of American Religious History*, ed. Darren Dochuk, Thomas S. Kidd, and Kurt W. Peterson (South Bend, IN: University of Notre Dame Press, 2014), 199–229.

19. Even Oberlin College, once a center of abolitionism and interracial cooperation, made considerable adjustments in the Jim Crow era. In 1903, the school's debate and literary societies started to exclude Blacks. By 1909, the college had established segregated dorms. Ten years later, Black women were barred from admittance. J. Brent Morris, *Oberlin, Hotbed of Abolitionism: College, Community, and the Fight for Freedom and Equality in Antebellum America* (Chapel Hill: University of North Carolina Press, 2014), 244.

20. Mark Noll, *God and Race in American Politics: A Short History* (Princeton, NJ: Princeton University Press, 2009), 81.

21. Gary J. Dorrien, *The Remaking of Evangelical Theology* (Louisville, KY: Westminster John Knox, 1998), 155; Balmer, "'End to Unjust Inequality in the World,'" 505–30.

22. Harry Emerson Fosdick, "Shall the Fundamentalists Win?," in *Contemporary Forum: American Speeches on Twentieth-Century Issues*, ed. Ernest J. Wrage and Barnet Baskerville (New York: Harper & Brothers, 1962), 98, 100; R. Halliburton Jr., "Kentucky's Anti-Evolution Controversy," *Register of the Kentucky Historical Society* 66, no. 2 (Apr. 1968): 97; "Pros and Cons in Anti-Darwin Bill Controversy," *Louisville Courier Journal*, Feb. 18, 1922, 4.

23. James M. Gray, "The Deadline of Doctrine around the Church," *Moody Monthly* 23, no. 3 (Nov. 1922): 105.

24. On the Wesleyan's growing fundamentalism, see Ira Ford McLeister and Roy Stephen Nicholson, *History of the Wesleyan Methodist Church of America* (Marion, IN: Wesley, 1959), 372, 476–78.

25. James Brewer Stewart, "Reconsidering the Abolitionists in an Age of Fundamentalist Politics," *Journal of the Early Republic* 26, no. 1 (2006): 7.

26. Donald W. Dayton, *Discovering an Evangelical Heritage* (New York: Harper & Row, 1976), 4, 134 (quote).

27. Steven P. Miller, *The Age of Evangelicalism: America's Born-Again Years* (New York: Oxford University Press, 2014), 36; Molly Worthen, *Apostles of Reason: The Crisis of Authority in American Evangelicalism* (New York: Oxford University Press, 2014), 178–79. For contemporary accounts of this evangelical reevaluation of the faith during the Nixon years, see Claire Cox, "Christian Debate Ending?," *Daily Capital News* (Jefferson City, MO), Apr. 14, 1973, 6; and David Anderson, "Evangelicals Reconsider Social Role," *Boston Globe,* June 17, 1973, 33.

28. On the regional dimensions, see Randall J. Stephens, *The Fire Spreads: Holiness and Pentecostalism in the American South* (Cambridge, MA: Harvard University Press, 2008); Samuel S. Hill Jr., *Southern Churches in Crisis Revisited* (1966; repr., Tuscaloosa: University of Alabama Press, 1999); and Darren Dochuk, *From Bible Belt to Sunbelt: Plain-Folk Religion, Grassroots Politics, and the Rise of Evangelical Conservatism* (New York: W. W. Norton, 2010).

29. Martin E. Marty, *Modern American Religion: The Noise of Conflict, 1919–1941,* vol. 2 (Chicago: University of Chicago Press, 1997), 174.

30. George M. Marsden, *Fundamentalism and American Culture: The Shaping of Twentieth Century Evangelicalism, 1870–1925* (New York: Oxford University Press, 1980), 86.

31. C. Vann Woodward to Richard Hofstadter, May 11, 1962, in *The Letters of C. Vann Woodward,* ed. Michael O'Brien (New Haven, CT: Yale University Press, 2013), 227.

32. "Prostration of Brother Moody," *Chicago Tribune,* Nov. 19, 1899, 36.

33. Other prominent figures—including the minister Henry Ward Beecher, novelist Harriet Beecher Stowe, and temperance crusader Francis Willard—turned away from the cause of recently freed slaves. Mark Noll, *God and Race in American Politics: A Short History* (Princeton, NJ: Princeton University Press, 2009), 79–80.

34. Paul Dwight Moody and Arthur Percy Fitt, *The Shorter Life of D. L. Moody,* vol. 1, *His Life* (Chicago: Bible Institute Colportage Association, 1900), 19.

35. James F. Findlay, *Dwight L. Moody: American Evangelist, 1837–1899* (Chicago, University of Chicago Press, 1969), 279, 281. On Moody's preaching to segregated troops in the late nineteenth century, see Edward J. Blum, *Reforging the White Republic: Race, Religion, and American Nationalism, 1865–1898* (Baton Rouge: Louisiana State University Press, 2005), 242.

36. Louisville minister quoted in Findlay, *Dwight L. Moody,* 280.

37. Glenda Elizabeth Gilmore, *Gender and Jim Crow: Women and the Politics of White Supremacy in North Carolina, 1896–1920* (Chapel Hill: University of North Carolina Press, 1996), 56.

38. Edward Leigh Pell, ed., *Dwight L. Moody: His Life, His Work, His Words* (Richmond, VA: B. F. Johnson, 1900), 472–73.

39. "The Ghetto," *Crisis* 10, no. 3 (July 1915): 117.

40. Timothy Gloege, *Guaranteed Pure: The Moody Bible Institute, Business, and the Making of Modern Evangelicalism* (Chapel Hill: University of North Carolina Press, 2015), 218.

41. H. F. Dudley, "South Lima Baptist Church," *Moody Monthly* (Dec. 1923): 163.

42. "He Will Come," *Wesleyan Methodist,* Jan. 25, 1893. See the 1908 resolution in Michigan Conference of the Wesleyan Methodists, *Minutes of the Sixty-Sixth Annual Session of the Michigan Conference of the Wesleyan Methodist Connection, or Church, of America, Held at Hastings, Mich-*

igan, Aug. 12–15, 1908 (Syracuse, NY: Wesleyan Methodist Publishing, 1908), 25. The Michigan representatives likely meant this as a response to denominations that had embraced the decidedly postmillennial Social Gospel. L. L. Pickett, "A Question," *Wesleyan Methodist*, Jan. 21, 1903, 9. See also the premillennial material in the ministerial "Course of Study," *Discipline of the Wesleyan Methodist Connection (or Church) of America* (Syracuse, NY: Wesleyan Methodist Publishing, 1939), 188.

43. Paul Boyer, *When Time Shall Be No More: Prophecy Belief in Modern American Culture* (Cambridge, MA: Harvard University Press, 1992), 86–90; Timothy P. Weber, "Premillennialism and the Branches of Evangelicalism," in *The Variety of American Evangelicalism*, ed. Donald W. Dayton and Robert K. Johnston (Downer's Grove, IL: InterVarsity, 1991), 6.

44. B. F. Haynes, *Tempest Tossed on Methodist Seas; Or, A Sketch of My Life* (Louisville: Pentecostal Publishing, 1921), 73.

45. William Kostlevy, *Holy Jumpers: Evangelicals and Radicals in Progressive Era America* (New York: Oxford University Press, 2010), 25–26, 30, 71; J. Lawrence Brasher, *The Sanctified South: John Lakin Brasher and the Holiness Movement* (Urbana: University of Illinois Press, 1994), 62–63; Briane Turley, *A Wheel within a Wheel: Southern Methodism and the Georgia Holiness Association* (Macon, GA: Mercer University Press, 1999), 196–98, 365–79.

46. James Moorhead, "The Quest for Holiness in American Protestantism," *Interpretation: A Journal of Bible and Theology* 53, no. 4 (1999): 372.

47. Ira Ford McLeister, *History of the Wesleyan Methodist Church of America* (Syracuse, NY: Wesleyan Methodist Publishing, 1934), 281 (quote). See also ibid., 283. On similar church segregation in Alabama in 1891, see ibid., 326. On Wesleyan fundamentalism, see ibid., 331. See other examples of holiness groups becoming fundamentalist in Timothy L. Smith, *Called unto Holiness: The Story of the Nazarenes, the Formative Years* (Kansas City, MO: Nazarene Publishing, 1962), 315–21; and Paul M. Bassett, "The Fundamentalist Leavening of the Holiness Movement: 1914–1940," *Wesleyan Theological Journal* 13 (Spring 1978): 65–91.

48. A. A. Boddy, "The Southern States," *Confidence*, Sept. 1912, 209, quoted in *Bridegroom's Messenger* (Atlanta), Sept. 1, 1912, 1. See also reports from the Azusa Street newspaper, *The Apostolic Faith*, Feb.–Mar. 1907.

49. Quoted in David Edwin Harrell Jr., *White Sects and Black Men in the Recent South* (Nashville: Vanderbilt University Press, 1971), 95–96; Harold D. Hunter, "A Journey toward Racial Reconciliation: Race Mixing in the CGP" (paper delivered at the Annual Meeting of the Society for Pentecostal Studies, Marquette University, Milwaukee, WI, Mar. 2004), 8–9.

50. Norris Magnusson, *Salvation in the Slums: Evangelical Social Work, 1865–1920* (Eugene, OR: Wipf & Stock, 2004), 118–26; Lillian Taiz, *Hallelujah Lads & Lasses: Remaking the Salvation Army in America, 1880–1930* (Chapel Hill: University of North Carolina Press, 2001), 15–16, 22, 53.

51. Andrew S. Chancey, "'A Demonstration Plot for the Kingdom of God': The Establishment and Early Years of Koinonia Farm," *Georgia Historical Quarterly* 75, no. 2 (Summer 1991): 321–53; Tracy Elaine K'Meyer, *Interracialism and Christian Community in the Postwar South: The Story of Koinonia Farm* (Charlottesville: University Press of Virginia, 1997); "Integrated Georgia Farm to Continue Operation," *Alabama Journal* (Montgomery), Mar. 2, 1957, 11; Ed Creagh, "Koinonia

Leader to Brave Foes," *Daily Press* (Newport News, VA), Apr. 6, 1957, 2; Juanita Nelson, "Koinonia Farm, 'Where the Saints Go Marching On!'" *Pittsburgh Courier,* July 20, 1957. On the founding of interracial churches in the post–World War II period, see Quinton H. Dixie and Peter R. Eisenstadt, *Visions of a Better World: Howard Thurman's Pilgrimage to India and the Origins of African American Nonviolence* (Boston: Beacon, 2011), 177–79.

52. "Rev. Sunday Calls Modernists Liars: Famous Evangelist Attacks Methodists Who 'Claim They Are Progressive,'" *Asbury Park (NJ) Press,* Aug. 27, 1929, 3; "Fine Tribute Paid Klan by Billy Sunday," *Missouri Valley Independent* (St. Joseph), Mar. 12, 1925, 6; "Jackson Klan Number 7 to the Reverend Billy Sunday," *Jackson (MS) Clarion-Ledger,* Feb. 3, 1925, 5.

53. *New York Age,* May 6, 1915, 4. See the same in the African American newspaper *Saint Paul (MN) Appeal,* Mar. 18, 1916, 2. See also the letter of the African American clergyman Francis J. Grimke to Billy Sunday in "Segregation," *Crisis* 9, no. 6 (Apr. 1915): 282. On Billy Sunday and race, see Josh McMullen, *Under the Big Top: Big Tent Revivalism and American Culture, 1885–1925* (New York: Oxford University Press, 2015), 79–80.

54. Arnold S. Rice, *The Ku Klux Klan in American Politics* (Washington, DC: Public Affairs, 1962), 24–25, 33, 88; Charles C. Alexander, *The Ku Klux Klan in the Southwest* (Lexington: University of Kentucky Press, 1965), 87–90; Linda Gordon, *The Second Coming of the KKK: The Ku Klux Klan of the 1920s and the American Political Tradition* (New York: Liveright, 2017), 14–15, 118–21; Adam Laats, *Fundamentalism and Education in the Scopes Era: God, Darwin, and the Roots of America's Culture Wars* (New York: Palgrave Macmillan, 2010), 164; Kenneth T. Jackson, *The Ku Klux Klan in the City, 1915–1930* (Chicago: Ivan R. Dee, 1992), 84, 98, 150, 176, 209. On the Wesleyans' ambiguous stance on the Klan, see Robert E. Black, "Becoming a Church: Wesleyan Methodism, 1899–1935," in Caldwell, *Reformers and Revivalists,* 207–8.

55. See, for instance, reports in the African American *New York Age,* "Activities of the Invisible Empire Are on the Increase," June 24, 1922, 1, 5; and "Mayor Hylan Takes Issue with Ku Klux," Dec. 2, 1922, 1. See also "Notes of the Friends of Negro Freedom," *Messenger* (New York) (Mar. 1922): 379.

56. *Christian Century* quote and other material on Protestant reactions against the Klan in Robert Moats Miller, "A Note on the Relationship between the Protestant Churches and the Revived Ku Klux Klan," *Journal of Southern History* 22, no. 3 (Aug. 1956): 357. See also "The Protestant Ku Klux," *Christian Century* (Chicago), Mar. 9, 1922, 293; Alva W. Taylor, "The Ku Klux Klan," ibid., July 6, 1922, 850–51; "Anti-Ku Klux," *Congregationalist* (Boston), Nov. 23, 1922, 655; and Frank L. Moore, "What of the Ku Klux Klan? Methods and Results of the Movement," ibid., Apr. 5, 1923, 428–29. In 1923, the attendees of the Wisconsin Congregational Conference officially denounced the KKK. "Ku Klux Klan Repudiated at the Congregational Meeting," *Wisconsin Rapids Daily Tribune,* Oct. 4, 1923, 1.

57. Sinclair Lewis, *Elmer Gantry* (New York: Dell, 1954), 378–79.

58. Matthew Avery Sutton, *Aimee Semple McPherson and the Resurrection of Christian America* (Cambridge, MA: Harvard University Press, 2007), 33–34, 115–16, 146–47. On holiness and Pentecostal attitudes, see Smith, *Called unto Holiness,* 318; Frank Boyd, "Romanism: What Is Its Place in the Last Days," *Pentecostal Evangel* (Springfield, MO), Aug. 16, 1924, 8; and "Question Box: Is It Right for Our Preachers to Endorse the Ku Klux Klan?," *Pentecostal Holiness Advocate,* Nov. 8, 1923, 9. Thanks to Jesse Curtis for pointing me to the "Question Box" source.

RANDALL J. STEPHENS

59. Bob Shuler, "Investigate the Ku Klux Klan," *Moody Monthly* (Dec. 1923): 182.

60. "Joining the Ku Klux Klan," *Moody Monthly* (Oct. 1923): 70; Matthew Avery Sutton, *American Apocalypse: A History of Modern Evangelicalism* (Cambridge, MA: Belknap Press of Harvard University Press, 2014), 128; Kelly J. Baker, *Gospel According to the Klan: The KKK's Appeal to Protestant America, 1915–1930* (Lawrence: University Press of Kansas, 2011).

61. Lyle W. Dorsett, *Billy Sunday and the Redemption of Urban America* (Grand Rapids, MI: William B. Eerdmans, 1991), 149; Rory McVeigh, *The Rise of the Ku Klux Klan: Right-Wing Movements and National Politics* (Minneapolis: University of Minnesota Press, 2009), 148; Michael Newton, *White Robes and Burning Crosses: A History of the Ku Klux Klan from 1866* (Jefferson, NC: McFarland, 2014), 55–57; Bill Armstrong, "The Tower of Babel," *South Bend (IN) News-Times,* Apr. 20, 1922, 6; "Ku Klux Pastor Speaks Tonight: Dr. C. A. Ridley of Atlanta, Will Deliver Address in Local School Auditorium," *High Point (NC) Enterprise,* Jan. 25, 1922, 1. For other links between the Klan and fundamentalists, see Stewart Grant Cole, *The History of Fundamentalism* (New York: Richard R. Smith, 1931), 25, 209, 275–78; and "Ku Klux Klan Will Take up Fundamentalist Fight," *Marysville (OH) Journal-Tribune,* Aug. 21, 1925, 1.

62. "Ku Klux Klan Pays Tribute to Evangelist," *Winona (MS) Times,* Feb. 6, 1925, 6.

63. "Ku Klux Present: White Hooded Knight Presents Billy Sunday with $650," *Yorkville (SC) Enquirer,* Feb. 21, 1922, 1. Sunday made similar remarks in the early 1920s. "The Klan is like the Sherriff," one newspaper reported him as saying, "it will not molest you as long as you obey the laws of the U.S.A." He continued: "The Klu [*sic*] Klux Klan believes in being 100 per cent American, obeying the laws and the supremacy of the white race." "Fiery Cross Leaves Trail of K.K.K in Many Eastern Towns," *American Falls (ID) Press,* June 29, 1922, 4. Similarly, after the secret terrorist organization made a public donation in Richmond, Indiana, in May 1922, Sunday was reported as commenting, "I guess if you behave yourself they won't bother you." "Ku Klux Klan in Robes at Tabernacle: Twelve Members of Mysterious Order March to Front and Hand Evangelist Letter Containing $50," *Richmond (IN) Palladium and Sun-Telegram,* May 15, 1922, 1, 2 (quote).

64. "Fine Tribute Paid Klan by Billy Sunday," *Missouri Valley Independent* (St. Joseph), Mar. 12, 1925, 6.

65. "Ku Klux Klan in Robes at Tabernacle," 14.

66. "On the Side Lines of the Billy Sunday Evangelistic Campaign," *Charleston (WV) Daily Mail,* Mar. 13, 1922, 6; "They Were at Charleston Too," *Richmond (IN) Item,* May 18, 1922, 7; *Colonel Mayfield's Weekly,* Dec. 8, 1923, quoted in Alexander, *Ku Klux Klan in the Southwest,* 90.

67. See Leonard J. Moore, *Citizen Klansmen: The Ku Klux Klan in Indiana, 1921–1928* (Chapel Hill: University of North Carolina Press, 1991), 41; and George Marsden, *Understanding Fundamentalism and Evangelicalism* (Grand Rapids, MI: William B. Eerdmans, 1991), 54–55.

68. Alvia O. DeRee, "The Bright Fiery Cross: Our Song" (Indianapolis: George Bennard and Homer A. Rodeheaver, 1923). Thanks to Paul Matzko for pointing me to the hymn. See also Danny O. Crew, *Ku Klux Klan Sheet Music: An Illustrated Catalogue of Published Music, 1867–2002* (Jefferson, NC: McFarland, 2003), 36.

69. Smith, *Called unto Holiness,* 200.

70. Billy Graham, "No Color Line in Heaven," *Ebony* (Sept. 1957): 102; John Pollock, "Evangelist Became an Early Supporter of Integration," *Morning Call* (Allentown, PA), Sept. 24, 1966, 3; "Reach Decision Today," Paterson (NJ) *News,* July 19, 1957, 12 (Graham quote about King). See also "Has Religion Changed Segregationist Karam?," *Ebony* (Nov. 1962): 30; and Billy Graham, "'Jim Crow Must Go': Billy Graham Speaks out on Segregation Question," *Tampa Bay Times,* Apr. 16, 1960, 36. For advertisements of the color-line article, see *Pittsburgh Courier,* Aug. 17, 1957, 5; *New York Age,* Aug. 17, 1967, 5; *Atlanta Constitution,* Aug. 13, 1957, 6; and *Baltimore Evening Sun,* Aug. 13, 1957, 17.

71. Billy Graham quoted in "Billy Graham Denounces Segregation," *Franklin (IN) Daily Journal,* May 25, 1964, 11.

72. Malcolm X, "The Ballot or the Bullet," in *The Will of a People: A Critical Anthology of Great African American Speeches,* ed. Richard W. Leeman and Bernard K. Duffy (Carbondale: Southern Illinois University Press, 2012), 291.

73. Graham quoted in "Graham Speaks at N.Y. Meeting," *Charleston (SC) News and Courier,* Apr. 7, 1964, 9-A. For one of the most insightful treatments of Graham and race, see Steven P. Miller, *Billy Graham and the Rise of the Republican South* (Philadelphia: University of Pennsylvania Press, 2009).

74. Cook quoted in Jay Edgerton, "A New 'Billy' Spurs Religious Revivalism Boom," *Des Moines Register,* Apr. 23, 1950, 12.

75. Miles S. Mullin, "Neoevangelicalism and the Problem of Race in Postwar America," in *Christians and the Color Line: Race and Religion after Divided by Faith,* ed. J. Russell Hawkins and Philip Luke Sinitiere (New York: Oxford University Press, 2013), 15. See also Carl F. H. Henry, *The Uneasy Conscience of Modern Fundamentalism* (1947; repr., Grand Rapids, MI: Eerdmans, 2003), 3–4, 22. For a moderate take on civil disobedience, see "Editorials: The Bible and Civil Disobedience," *Eternity* (Oct. 1966): 6. For San Diego pastor Tim LaHaye asking the NAE for "the scriptural position" on the "racial situation," see Tim LaHaye, San Diego, CA, to the National Association of Evangelicals, Whittier, CA, Mar.16, 1964, ser. 5, executive director files, subseries 2, Clyde W. Taylor, box 52, folder 11, Civil Rights, 1964–65, National Association of Evangelicals Records, Wheaton College, Wheaton, IL. See also Adam Laats, *Fundamentalist U: Keeping the Faith in American Higher Education* (New York: Oxford University Press, 2018), 229–37.

76. "Dr. Sam Hill to Write Book on Protestantism in South," *Daily Tar Heel* (Chapel Hill, NC), Oc. 17, 1962, 1; Hill, *Southern Churches in Crisis Revisited,* lxvi (quote), 106–7, 114–15; Charles Marsh, *God's Long Summer: Stories of Faith and Civil Rights* (Princeton, NJ: Princeton University Press, 1997), 113; Carolyn Renée Dupont, *Mississippi Praying: Southern White Evangelicals and the Civil Rights Movement, 1945–1975* (New York: New York University Press, 2013), 35–36.

77. Marsden, *Fundamentalism and American Culture,* 91. See also Matthew Bowman, *The Urban Pulpit: New York City and the Fate of Liberal Evangelicalism* (New York: Oxford University Press, 2014), 16–17; and George M. Marsden, *The Soul of the American University: From Protestant Establishment to Established Nonbelief* (New York: Oxford University Press, 1994), 17–20.

78. Strong, *Perfectionist Politics,* 166.

79. Lee M. Haines, "The Grander Nobler Work: Wesleyan Methodism's Transition, 1867–1901," in Caldwell, *Reformers and Revivalists,* 118.

80. Rev. Leslie D. Wilcox, "The Origin and History of Wesleyan Methodism," *Wesleyan Methodist*, May 20, 1942, 4.

81. D. W. Bebbington, *Evangelicalism in Modern Britain: A History from the 1730s to the 1980s* (London: Unwin Hyman, 1989), 213–17.

Jackie Robinson and the Fight for Effective Black Citizenship; or, How Integration Reached Second Base

PETER EISENSTADT

As early as 1940, there was speculation that Jackie Robinson, UCLA's "baseball wizard," would "turn his attention to the professional diamond" once his college days were over.[1] This, of course, meant the Negro Leagues, but he was also mentioned, as in a 1942 article, in reference to the growing determination of the "Negro baseball integration fight."[2] In December 1944, the *Pittsburgh Courier* interviewed the venerable Connie Mack, who had managed the Philadelphia Athletics since 1900, on the question of the "integration of Negroes into the ranks of organized baseball." Mack acknowledged that the ongoing war was "fast changing the complexities of the world" and that "vast progress was being made in the field of inter-race relationships." He was sure that Blacks would play in the Major and Minor Leagues, but only when "everything is satisfactory to everybody." He was specifically asked about the case of "Example A," Lt. Jackie Robinson, the "shortstop deluxe" recently discharged from the service and seeking a big league tryout. Mack said he had heard of Robinson, that he was a fine athlete, but questioned whether Black ballplayers actually wanted to play in the Major Leagues since, according to what he had read, "integration in the sport was not the race's aim."[3]

Mack was not entirely mistaken. A careful reader of the Black press during the war years could find a number of articles by and about ballplayers and Negro League owners that questioned whether the integration of white professional baseball was wise or prudent. But there were many more articles that held the opposite view, that integration was an absolute necessity. That was certainly Robinson's view. After he was signed by Branch Rickey for the Brooklyn Dodgers organization in October 1945, articles about Robinson and integration went from a trickle to a deluge. More than anyone else, he became integration's living embodiment, its synonym, its "Jackie Robinson." Some have argued that Robinson's joining the Brooklyn Dodgers was the "most fruitful step taken by Negroes since the Civil War towards social integration" or that he "changed the pattern for the black man . . . sports, and baseball, did more for integration than anything did."[4] These claims are pardonable exaggerations, but what is important is that many people, both then and now, have believed this to be so. There seems little reason to challenge Jules Tygiel's assertion that "in the years before Martin Luther King Jr. Robinson, more than any individual, personified the era's liberal optimism and reaffirmed the possibility of racial integration."[5] In what follows, I am presuming a basic familiarity with the story of Jackie Robinson, especially his signing by Rickey and his years with the Brooklyn Dodgers.

Most people think that Robinson integrated baseball when he became the first acknowledged person of African descent in the twentieth century to play in what the white baseball establishment called "Organized Baseball."[6] On one level, this is of course true. But the mere puncturing of the color line is not what Robinson, millions of other African Americans, and many of their allies understood by integration in the 1940s. Integration was not defined by race mixing, that is, inclusion in previously all-white organizations and institutions. It was the quest for effective Black citizenship, with all of the privileges and responsibilities this entailed. Citizenship had to be full and effective, not nominal. It had to be Black. Citizenship did not have to be earned; African Americans were—and were ready to be—full citizens now, without having in any way to uplift, transform, or assimilate themselves. Of course, forced segregation was inimical to citizenship and had to end—in all of its forms. But at its core, segregation was not about Black separation from whites, but Black separation and exclusion from the powers, privileges, and responsibilities of citizenship.

Racial integration is a complex and often badly misunderstood idea, and like all "keywords"—terms on the political barricades—it is blessed or cursed with a multiplicity of meanings.[7] This essay will concentrate on two understandings of integration: integration as effective Black citizenship, and integration as the inclusion in previously segregated institutions. There is some overlap between them, but they are distinct. For a number of reasons, over time, by the 1950s and 1960s, the main sense of integration had become seen as the entrance into white institutions. But this was to define it down and make "race mixing" the goal of integration, rather than a byproduct. Integration's fate in America's culture and politics traced a parabola; a rapid ascent, a brief apogee, and a sudden fall to earth. Jackie Robinson's life and career rode its curve.

Integration is both a word and an idea, and if it is easier to trace the uses of a word, it is more important to find the history of the idea behind it. As for the word, the emergence of "integration" into the racial vocabulary can be marked with a fair degree of precision. In early 1934, W. E. B. Du Bois, editor of the NAACP's journal, *The Crisis,* created a furor by writing a series of editorials that defended segregation. By "segregation," Du Bois meant voluntary Black separation from white institutions and not compelled Black exclusion from them by whites. Although he was widely misunderstood on this point, he did not defend white supremacy. Rather, Du Bois argued that African Americans should develop their own internal economy, utilizing Black-owned cooperatives, and should limit contact with white America as much as possible. He urged that "the thinking colored people of the United States must stop being stampeded by the word segregation," that it would "be idiotic simply to sit on the sidelines and yell: 'No Segregation' in an increasingly segregated world."[8]

Although some supported Du Bois's newfound enthusiasm for segregation, most of the comments in the Black press were lacerating in their hostility. There were many who thought the sixty-six-year-old was suffering from "mental sterilization" or that he had become a "quitter," a "coward," or even a "race traitor." Some offered eulogies: "My Du Bois is dead."[9] Walter White, the executive secretary of the NAACP, in his response to Du Bois—the two men detested one another— argued that Du Bois was correct that the fight against segregation had been a wearying struggle of attrition, with many defeats and only the occasional victory. Nonetheless, "the mere difficulty of the road should not and will not serve as a deterrent" to persisting. White insisted that voluntary segregation by "submerged, exploited and marginal groups" means "a distinctly inferior position in national and communal life" and would only lead to "spiritual atrophy." Acknowledging its challenges, he claimed that "the Negro must, without yielding, continue the grim struggle for integration, and against segregation, for their bodies and their souls, and the spiritual well-being of America, and of the world."[10]

From White and others, "integration" emerged in the Black press as the opposite and alternative to "segregation" and Du Bois's notion of voluntary self-separation. Although there were a few earlier uses of "integration" in a racial context, it was only after the Du Bois controversy that the term became popular in the Black press, with 1934 as the breakthrough year.[11] (The term as applied to African Americans remained uncommon in the mainstream white press for the better part of a decade.)

The most significant and searching response to the Du Bois segregation controversy was by James Weldon Johnson, the former executive secretary of the NAACP (Walter White's predecessor), Du Bois's friend, and the only other possible claimant to the title of grand old man of African American letters. In the opening pages of his book-length response, *Negro Americans, What Now?*, appearing in late 1934, Johnson considers several political alternatives for Black Americans, rejecting a return to Africa and Marxist-inspired revolution as unfeasible and unlikely to change white prejudice. This left only two real options, "isolation or integration." This, he argues, had been the basic tension in Black political and intellectual opinion from the outset, the choice between fighting for "the common rights and privileges, as well as duties, of citizenship" versus acknowledging "our isolation and the determination to accept and make the best of it." It was not an easy decision. There were times, writes Johnson, "when the most persistent integrationist becomes an isolationist, when he curses the White world and consigns it to hell." There are times when fighting for equal citizenship seems futile, an exercise in wishful thinking, "shooting at the stars with a pop-gun." But to point out the reality of prejudice was to make the isolationists "apostles of the obvious." Calling on Blacks to "realize that prejudice is an actuality" was to place an "emphasis on what has never been questioned." Black Americans' problem, Johnson concludes, was not a failure to acknowledge "that we are segregated, but in acknowledging it too fully." Of course, he adds, Blacks needed to make their separate institutions—their schools, their business enterprises, their newspapers, and so on—as strong as possible. But Johnson urges African Americans to consider them "as a means, not an end." The strength gained from them "should be applied to the objective of entering into, not *staying out of* the body politic." Integration did not mean "suddenly doing away with voluntary groupings in religious or secular organizations or of abolishing group enterprises." But it did mean following the stony path that "leads to equal rights."[12]

If integration was a new word in this context, the idea of effective Black citizenship was not. This dates back at least to incendiary tracts such as David Walker's

Appeal to the Colored Citizens of the World (1829). Writing of the campaign for effective citizenship among Black abolitionists, Stephen Kantrowitz has noted that they sought "to create a world in which 'colored citizen' was not a contradiction." They wanted an "entire enfranchisement" that "would mean being able to move through the world without being constantly reminded that they belonged to a suspect class, sharing the experiences of daily life without wondering when they would next be rebuked, mocked, excluded, or set upon; joining the rituals and customs of public life without apology and apprehension."[13] When the Colored People's Convention, which met in Charleston, South Carolina, in November 1865, stated that they were "Americans by birth" and "Americans by feeling," they were saying much the same thing.[14] But after the destruction of Reconstruction, there was a desperate fight to maintain the merest traces of Black citizenship. Comprehensive or effective Black citizenship would have to wait.

For Du Bois, in 1934, segregation was "more insistent, more prevalent, and more unassailable by appeal or argument" than ever.[15] For others, the ongoing Depression was both a catastrophe and an opportunity in a country whose basic institutions now seemed newly malleable. Black New Dealers often spoke of integration, including Mary McLeod Bethune, who after a 1937 meeting with President Franklin Roosevelt reported that he was "deeply interested in the forward steps that Negroes are taking toward a more definite integration into the American program."[16] Some thought that the economy so toxic that US workers just might place their common economic interests ahead of their racial biases. Guy Johnson, also writing in 1937, suggested that, while heretofore there had two "significant Negro philosophies"—that of Booker T. Washington, who "preached patience and good will," and that of the NAACP, which used "the idea of militant legal tactics to enforce the recognition of the rights of Negroes"—now "the stage is now set for a third great movement, based upon the united efforts of black and white workers to change the economic order."[17] Perhaps for the first time since Reconstruction, it was not outlandish to think of the possibility of effective Black citizenship. These hopes were the impetus for the new calls for integration.

Within a few years, the idea of racial integration had been widely disseminated in places far from the centers of Black intellectual opinion (and places where crossing the color line was politically impossible). After years of brutal racial attacks, the African American citizens of Cheraw, South Carolina, established a local chapter of the NAACP in 1938. Their founding manifesto read in part:

To be set aside as a subject group by social prejudice and government sanction, subject to the domination of all and any who many assume authority to command, is to be robbed of the same native rights which others demand and for which they barter their lives. . . . What the Negro needs is integration, instead of segregation. These conditions are exact opposites. They are to each other as plus is to minus. The one affirms, the other denies. All the blessings of life, liberty, and happiness are possible in integration, while in segregation lurk all the forces destructive of their values.[18]

In Cheraw, segregation was death, integration was life. Integration still had its skeptics and caustic critics, but they were underrepresented in the major Black newspapers. Still, in the *Chicago Defender* in 1940, Violet Moten Foster made an impassioned "Plea for More Segregation," calling on Blacks to reject the "pseudo-freedom that insidiously weakens our common resolve" and recognize that "in segregation lies the only hope of economic freedom and, in rapid sequence—social, political, and intellectual equality." If Foster echoed Du Bois's call for segregation, unlike him, she evidently was a baseball fan. When "the light of reason breaks through the red haze of emotionalism," Blacks should "give up such childish projects as trying to get one or two Negro ballplayers in the 'big leagues.'" Instead, she and other Blacks should "voluntarily segregate ourselves into our own ball parks where Negro teams are playing against each other and [playing] against the mighty drawbacks of lack of proper training facilities, lack of regulated diets, and (worst of all) lack of support from members of their own race."[19]

But the more prevalent view was expressed the following year, also in the *Chicago Defender,* by Rebecca Stiles Taylor in "Integration Versus Disintegration Is Question of Hour." In it, she observes that "the word *integration* has become so popular today it has almost become a byword." Its popularity, she notes, had been heightened by the fight against a Jim Crow military. "If for Shakespeare," writes Taylor, "'to be or not to be' was the question," the new version for Black Americans was "to integrate or to disintegrate: that is the question." Integration, far from lessening a sense of racial cohesion, required it and would only strengthen it. It was the opposite of assimilation or amalgamation. There was no time to waste. "The time is *now* for Negroes to pool their strength and everything that is theirs for the proper recognition of their citizenship rights."[20]

*   *   *

This is the world into which Jackie Robinson came of age. Jack Roosevelt Robinson was born on January 31, 1919, in Cairo, Georgia, about three months after the end of World War I and about three weeks after the death of Theodore Roosevelt, the source of his seldom-used middle name.[21] Nonetheless, one way to think of Robinson is as a belated, Black Teddy Roosevelt progressive. Both men were outspoken in their patriotism, Republicans who so despised the conservative wing of their party that they left it altogether. They were both muscular Christians of the body and spirit who pushed themselves relentlessly and impatiently. Both died young and left behind a complex legacy.

Jackie's mother, Mallie McGriff Robinson, was an incredibly resourceful woman. She left Georgia permanently with her son and his four older siblings when Jackie was less than two years old, moving to Pasadena, California, where her step-brother had relocated. (Robinson's father, Jerry Robinson, was never a part of his life.) If young Jackie had no direct memories of life in Georgia, his maternal grandmother, Edna Simms McGriff, born into slavery in the late 1850s and who came to live with her relatives in Pasadena when he was a young boy, told him stories of her childhood, once declaring that "when the slaves were freed they wanted no part of freedom. They were afraid of it." Jackie was disbelieving. "Can you imagine anyone born in the United States being afraid of freedom?" It is no longer fashionable to think of a "slave mentality" or of enslaved people being predisposed to docility. But the idea of integration thrived on sharp contrasts between Black people's attitudes to white authority then and now and the conviction that, indeed, Black people had been cowed and intimidated into meekness, thus a break with the past was urgent. Robinson sometimes described himself as a "'refugee' from Georgia." For him, Georgia represented not only a place but also a way of life from which he spent his life trying to escape.[22]

Pasadena was described in the 1939 WPA *Guide for California* as being "something of a paradox."[23] The paradoxes of Robinson's Pasadena were not the same as those of the guide's authors, but they abounded. The *Guide* claimed it was "the richest city, per capita, in America," but Robinson and his family knew poverty, precarity, and food insecurity. Pasadena had been officially segregated until 1917, with specific zones set aside for the residences of racial minorities, until the US Supreme Court, in *Buchanan v. Warley*, outlawed the practice. But as in many cities, this was replaced by restrictive covenants in the city, culminating in the founding of the Pasadena Improvement Association in 1939. Its mission was to limit property sales to only members of the "white or Caucasian race." This organization was needed, according to one of its representatives, because there were "too many nigger lovers in the city." Regardless, by 1941, 7,500 lots in the city, or 60 percent of all residential properties, had legally enforceable restrictive covenants, while a study released that year reported that a whopping 89 percent of whites surveyed were in favor "of a regulation requiring Negroes to live in a section of the city by themselves." A majority were opposed to any Black children in their local schools, a sentiment shared by almost half of the city's teachers—all of whom, of course, were white. There were a series of formal and informal but equally onerous restrictions on where Black people could live, where and how they could work, and where they could play.[24] The author of the 1941 survey concluded that most whites continually fretted about what to do about the "Negro Problem," while "the constant and all-powerful impact of white dominance is probably the strongest influence on [Black] lives."[25]

Unlike in Georgia, African Americans were a relatively small minority in Pasadena, rising from about 2 percent to 5 percent of the population during the interwar years. (The Great Migration came to California during World War II, not World War I.) In 1922, Mallie, on a maid's salary, managed to buy a house for her brood on Pepper Street. They were not welcomed by their neighbors.[26] Robinson remembered that "Pasadena regarded us as intruders" and that "in certain respects Pasadenans were less understanding than Southerners and even more openly hostile."[27] His sister, Willa Mae Robinson Walker, remembered a cross burning on their front lawn.[28] A Black newspaper in Southern California wrote in 1924 that the racial situation in Pasadena was "nothing less than nauseating."[29]

Unlike in Georgia, African Americans were not the only nonwhite ethnicity treated with disdain by the white majority. There were substantial numbers of Mexicans, Japanese, and Chinese residents, and if there were occasional tensions among them, they knew that most whites simply lumped them together as non-Caucasian outsiders. The adolescent Robinson became the ringleader of a group of Blacks, Mexicans, and Japanese boys who called themselves the Pepper Street Gang. Their mischievousness consisted of throwing clods of dirt at passing cars, robbing fruit from grocers, and stealing golf balls from the rough of a local course only to sell them back to their owners. The gang members had a "growing resentment at being deprived of some of the advantages the white kids had."[30] There were run-ins, almost weekly, with local police, some of them involving arrests.[31] Robinson later wrote that, if he continued on this path, "I suppose I might have become a full-fledged juvenile delinquent."[32]

At the same time, Pasadena certainly gave Robinson and his siblings opportunities that would have been unavailable in Georgia. The city's public schools were not segregated and undoubtedly better than the south Georgia alternatives. Robinson and his siblings provided differing accounts of how they were treated in school. Some teachers befriended the children and made sure that they did not go hungry.[33] Others in the higher grades were less welcoming. As one Japanese classmate of Robinson remembered: "Discrimination against the blacks and Japanese was obvious, though it was a subtle statement. And there was nothing you could do about it. You felt it from the teachers."[34] Still, there was at least a chance in Pasadena that one's talent and achievements would be fairly evaluated.

And as Robinson the budding athlete, coming of age in sports-mad Pasadena, discovered when he was about eight, there was "one sector of life in southern California I was free to compete with whites on equal terms—in sports."[35] Or in his case, it was on superior terms. Robinson was always eager to demonstrate his prowess to Blacks and whites alike. His fourth-grade soccer team beat the sixth graders. In the cruel childhood sport known as dodgeball, Robinson was always the last person left standing. (He was, from his earliest years, a great dodger.)[36] From elementary school to the "jockocracy" of the playground to more organized athletic competition, Robinson excelled in "any kind of game with a ball," to say nothing of his prowess as a swimmer and in track and field, where he set national collegiate records in the long jump.[37]

Robinson evidently was not alone among the city's young Black men in seeing victory on the playing fields of Pasadena as a battle in a wider war.[38] The local YMCA had no Black members, but it did sponsor boys' clubs in local churches or organizations, most of which were segregated, though they occasionally came together for city-wide athletic tournaments. The tournaments' director told a researcher in 1941: "One problem which attends this program is the fact that Negro teams [representing less than a fifth of the participants] consistently win the greater portion of the athletic contests. This is true to such an extent that white boys sometimes become discouraged. The director of the club activities explained this Negro supremacy due to two factors. The first of these is natural ability, and the second, compensation for a lack of a real chance to compete with whites in other lines."[39] If the comment about "natural ability" was a damnable stereotype, a way of reducing Black athletes to mere brawn, on an individual basis, we are not created athletically equal, and Jackie Robinson was one of the most extraordinarily gifted and versatile athletes of his generation. Above all, he excelled in the triumvirate of team sports that, then and now, stand at America's athletic apex—baseball, football, and basketball.

Sports needs and creates heroes. That is certainly one reason for their enduring popularity. Young men and women, by dint of their athletic prowess, have greatness thrust upon them. As Gerald Early has written, "high-performance athletics is perhaps the most theatrical and emotional form of ritualized honor we have left in the world."[40] Other than boxing, the only major mainstream American sport at the time that permitted Black athletes to compete on its highest levels as equals with whites was big-time college athletics. (Albeit, this was far from universal in the country, only outside of the South, and even then with informal quotas and restrictions.) From the time he entered Pasadena Junior College in the fall of 1937 until he left UCLA in 1941, Robinson was a star, attracting national attention in the Black press. The *Pittsburgh Courier,* employing the adjective-clotted sportswriter-ese characteristic of the era, described him during his Pasadena Junior College days as a "cyclone-gaited hellion" who had performed his "razzle-dazzle hocus-pocus" before appreciative crowds of 30,000–60,000 fans, now "riding prophetic winds across gridiron domains."[41] He performed before even bigger crowds at UCLA, which played its home games in the Los Angeles Coliseum, which had been the main stadium for the 1932 Olympics. The 1939 UCLA Bruins team had, remarkably, three African Americans in their starting backfield, and Robinson, a "climax runner, needle-threading passer, coffin-corner punter, and vicious tackler and blocker on the football field," was one of the "sepia horsemen."[42] Indeed, in 1939, there were, according to the *Atlanta Daily World,* "twelve million Negroes hoping UCLA will receive Rose Bowl bid"; but alas, a tied game against crosstown rival USC ended that dream.[43] His basketball coach thought Robinson had a chance to become one of the all-time greats.[44] As early as 1940, there was speculation about UCLA's "baseball wizard" having a possible professional career.[45] (Indeed, had he been white, it is entirely possible that Robinson, perhaps signed directly out of high school, could have made his Major League debut by 1940. These were, as Arnold Rampersad has suggested, the years of his "lost baseball youth, never to be recovered.")[46]

By the end of his second year at UCLA, and the end of his college eligibility, Robinson's encomia inflation continued. He was now being hailed as one of the greatest African American athletes "in all history."[47] But Robinson was a distinctive type of Black sports hero, a new variety, the Black sports hero as interracial trailblazer. With the exception of his few months with the Kansas City Monarchs, in all of his major athletic endeavors, Robinson played for white coaches, with mostly white teammates, and before mostly white crowds. The interracial trailblazer had to win the approval of white America while retaining the respect of Black America, neither falsely humble nor vainglorious, with enough self-confidence not to be rattled by the myriad minor encounters with incidents of racial hostility and enough pride and confidence to address major racial episodes directly and forthrightly. Robinson took his Black heroism seriously and early on felt he was carrying the burden of expectations of "the race" on his broad shoulders. Even his Black teammates noticed his standoffishness. He was sober, abstemious, and monogamous; did not hang around with white women; exhibited God-fearing behavior and was well-spoken; and was determined not to embarrass himself on or off the field.[48] Throughout his career, Robinson was accused, especially by unsympathetic white sportswriters, of being an "angry" athlete, a hair-trigger taker of umbrage. This is to profoundly misunderstand him. The anger and rage was, to be sure, present, but it was latent, not kinetic, and carefully hoarded, a way of warding off confrontations rather than seeking them out. It was the ethic of integration.

Robinson's embrace of integration as a combination lifestyle and ideology was to a certain extent instinctive; it was also, by the late 1930s and early 1940s, in the air, spreading among young African Americans as if by osmosis. It could also be taught. For Robinson, integration's main teacher was Karl E. Downs, the pastor of Pasadena's Scott Methodist Church. Robinson credited Downs with keeping him, as a teenager, on the straight and narrow, turning him away from his Pepper Street Gang years of adolescent petty-criminality.[49] Downs was a living embodiment of integration. Only six years older than Robinson, he came to Pasadena in 1938 after his undergraduate days at Samuel Huston College in Austin and graduate studies at Gammon Seminary in Atlanta and the Boston University School of Theology.[50] In Pasadena, the charismatic Downs had a ministry that reached out to young people. At Mallie's request, he soon snared the teenage Robinson, who became a devotee, often rousing himself to teach Sunday school after a Saturday's gridiron pounding. If, as was likely, Jackie was in attendance for the annual Lincoln Day service in 1941, he heard the great Duke Ellington preach a patriotic sermon on how "this kicking, yelling, touchy, sensitive, scrupulously-demanding minority" had "recreated in America the desire for true democracy."[51] He probably was in attendance as well that fall when Ellington, with his orchestra at their early 1940s peak, returned to Pasadena for a full-length concert in Downs's Starlight Fiesta of Negro Music, including selections from their anti–Jim Crow musical, *Jump for Joy*.[52]

Downs helped start a regular, monthly interracial church service at alternating Black and white area churches.[53] He had definite ideas about how Blacks needed to conduct themselves in such settings. A 1936 article by Downs in *The Crisis*, "Timid Negro Students," praised interracial efforts but, as its title indicates, condemned those who were overly deferential to their white counterparts. Although "racial adjustment must be made through fearless, rational comprehensive and cooperative ventures of both races," all too often, Blacks became "overly enthusiastic and overly cautious." Some suffered from "figments of self-glorification" and placed themselves above the masses of African Americans; others sacrificed "racial pride" for the often gossamer thinness of "racial goodwill."[54]

Downs was a fighter for effective Black citizenship. In Atlanta, he had been active in campaigning for voting rights for Black Georgians. He is credited with coining the enduring catchphrase "A voteless people is a hopeless people."[55] As a Methodist, he fought against the creation of a separate, segregated "Central Jurisdiction" of African American Methodists within the new Methodist Church. (This was a demand of southern Methodists that was agreed to by their northern counterparts for ending the antebellum North/South split within the denomination. The Central Jurisdiction existed from 1939 to 1968.) Downs was one of the leaders of an interracial youth Methodist league that condemned the jurisdiction's creation as "anti-social, anti-ethical. and anti-Christian."[56] He attended the annual General Council of the Methodist Episcopal Church in Chicago in 1938 to deliver an address on a largely nonpolitical topic, "What we expect of our church."[57] His expectations were not met.

When Downs arrived in Chicago, he discovered that he and the other three hundred African American delegates—four thousand total delegates attended the conference—would not be accommodated at the hotel hosting the convention despite a previous church ruling that no meeting would be held in a segregated setting. When he protested, Methodist officials told Downs that he was out of line. This angered him more than the initial refusal by the hotel, as he was "bowed with disgust and shame and seething with the human accompaniment of mental anguish," fighting back "the deep passion of hatred and despair which involuntarily boiled within me." What to do? He thought of leaving the conference but decided against it. He could "blast the thing wide open" in his speech, but that was not what he intended to speak about, and it would just reinforce the perception among whites that "every speaker of a minority group is expected to 'harp' upon injustice." (Many Blacks speaking before white audiences in these years faced this catch-22: to limit themselves to speaking about white racism would be to give the impression that Blacks could speak of nothing else; to not speak about it would seemingly be an act of appeasement.) So Downs gave his speech as planned, then wrote a blistering article about his experiences in a prominent Methodist journal, quoting the final defiant words of Johnson's *Negro Americans, What Now?* which had become a sort of credo for integration: "I would not allow one prejudiced person or one million or one hundred million to blight my life. I would not allow prejudice or any of its attendant humiliations [to] bear me down to spiritual defeat."[58] In the article, he attacked "the timidity of namby-pamby leaders" who accommodated themselves to segregation, as a result of which, "we Negroes have been forsaken."[59] When Downs returned to Pasadena, he no doubt told his congregation all about his Chicago experience and how he felt he had to control the passionate emotions that "boiled within" him in order to combat white prejudice in the most effective manner. It was a lesson that Branch Rickey—who, fervent Methodist that he was, was another featured speaker at the convention—did not have to teach Robinson.[60]

In 1943, Downs published his only book, *Meet the Negro,* a short collection of sixty profiles of accomplishments of prominent Blacks in a variety of fields.[61] (Downs, no mean accomplisher himself, that fall became president of his alma mater, Samuel Huston College, at age twenty-nine, supposedly the youngest college president in the country.) *Meet the Negro* opens with the statement, "America is deeply concerned about the 'Negro Problem,' and it is pitifully blind to the 'Negro possibility.'" Downs rejects the "shibboleth of a 'Lily White God'" and states that "fourteen million Black Americans stand before the judgment seat of American democracy, pleading for cooperation and understanding, not pity and sympathy."[62] The message of *Meet the Negro* to whites is clear: help Black Americans take what is rightfully ours or stand aside. An irony of the book is that Robinson was not profiled, though given his remarkable collegiate athletic achievements, he already more than qualified. Nonetheless, he likely read the book and certainly knew its sentiments. He and Downs remained in close contact. When Robinson ran into legal trouble in the army, Downs was one of the first persons he contacted. The minister returned to Pasadena in February 1946 to officiate at Robinson's marriage to Rachel Isum, just before the start of his first spring training with the Dodgers.[63]

Probably the main reason Downs is not better remembered is that he died, suddenly and tragically, in 1948 in an Austin, Texas, hospital at age thirty-five. Robinson believed that he died "a victim of racism" because, after an operation, "he was wheeled to the Negro ward of a hospital," where he was left, largely unsupervised, as complications set in rather than "being rushed to the emergency room in the white wing."[64] Robinson thought that, "in ability and dedication," Downs ranked with "Roy Wilkins, Whitney Young, and Dr. Martin Luther King, Jr.," and that had he lived, he could well have had a similar career.[65] This seems entirely possible. One eulogy of Downs stated that he "thrilled at the game of life and accepted its challenges. He played it hard, he played it clean, and he played it fair."[66] As Robinson later wrote of his own life, "I played hard, and always to win."[67] That was the way to play the game of integration.

As Robinson approached graduation in 1941, however, his big-time sports days seemed largely over. All the major professional team-sports leagues were segregated. He dropped out of UCLA in the spring of 1941 when his athletic eligibility expired, in part because he "was convinced that no amount of education would help a black man get a job"; that he was "living in an academic and athletic dream world"; that his brothers had studied hard and ended up as porters, elevator operators, taxi drivers, and bellhops; and that "long hours over books were a waste of time."[68] That September he played on the College All-Stars team in an exhibition game against the Chicago Bears before almost 100,000 people at Soldier Field in Chicago. The mighty Bears had routed the Washington Redskins in a legendary 73–0 drubbing in the NFL title game the previous December, but the College All-Stars were not shut out, with halfback Robinson shining and scoring a touchdown. But if the main purpose of the game for the college players was to exhibit their wares before pro scouts, Robinson was taboo—"exhibit A," wrote the *Pittsburgh Courier*, of the "inviolate proscriptions practiced against us sons of Ham in professional football."[69] A few months later, after he and another Black athlete had a fruitless spring-training tryout with the Chicago White Sox, they complained that they had to "fight to defend this country where [we] can't play." Both men were resigned to join what the *Pittsburgh Courier* called, with some irony, the "fight for democracy."[70]

Robinson had no particular interest in joining the military and tried to get a hardship deferment, but he was drafted in April 1942.[71] With him and hundreds of thousands other African Americans in the military, the force of integration met an adamant opposition determined to maintain Jim Crow even in the ranks. This was because, in large part, the military leadership agreed with Secretary of War Henry Stimson that Blacks were the intellectual, emotional, and martial inferiors of their white counterparts. Therefore, as General George Marshall stated on December 8, 1941, a war was no time to undertake a "sociological experiment."[72]

But the war was a sociological experiment on the grandest possible scale. Despite the best efforts of the brass, the fight against segregation continued and had some success in nibbling away at its corners. This was why, in November 1942, Robinson, then stationed at Fort Riley, Kansas, was a member of the first integrated class of the Officer Candidate School (OCS) in the history of the US Army. The following January he was commissioned a second lieutenant and assigned as morale officer to his Black company at Fort Riley, dealing with, among other matters, the myriad injustices of Jim Crow on the base. Rachel Robinson later speculated that he was made morale officer because otherwise he would have been a troublemaker.[73] Things got worse when, in April 1944, Robinson was transferred, along with a dozen other Black officers, to Camp Hood in Texas. (It had opened in 1942 and was named after the Confederate general John Bell Hood in what must be the uniquely American custom of naming military installations after traitors who took up arms against their own country.) It was Robinson's first extended stay in the South since his infancy. He did not like it. On July 6, he refused to sit in the back of a bus on the base, knowing that a month previously, in response to numerous incidents, the army had prohibited segregation on its installations, though it seems that many officers responsible for enforcing this standard had yet to read the memorandum. His action sparked an incident, and tempers escalated. The commander of Camp Hood's military police ordered Robinson arrested; he was handcuffed and placed in leg irons.

Charges were subsequently pressed for exhibiting disrespect and disobedience to superior officers.[74]

The Black press took some note. The *Chicago Defender* wrote, "Lt. Jack Robinson, Camp Hood—You're learning what some of us know, a colored man can't win in the South, truth, honor, or anything else notwithstanding."[75] The court-martial took only four hours—Robinson was acquitted of all charges. The case against him was weak, and a conviction would have angered Black public opinion. By the summer of 1944, the army was probably happy to bury the incident quickly. Robinson knew he had been lucky, luckier than he at first realized. Without an acquittal and without an honorable discharge, surely his subsequent career in the Major Leagues would been unlikely. At the same time, if he had not been brought up on charges, he likely would have gone overseas with his battalion, would not have spent the spring and summer of 1945 playing baseball, and would not have been in a position to become Rickey's first candidate to break Major League Baseball's color barrier. But a quick acquittal on ridiculous charges that should never have brought in the first place offered a very mixed message about the American system of justice.

Robinson's court-martial and acquittal was ignored in the white press, and received some, but not all that much, attention in the Black press.[76] It later became a nonevent in the Black press after his signing by the Dodgers in October 1945. For nearly four years afterward, despite thousands of articles on Robinson, his court-martial received nary a mention in the major papers of the Black or mainstream press.[77] (In Robinson's first autobiography, *Jackie Robinson: My Own Story,* ghost-written by a *Pittsburgh Courier* sportswriter in 1948, his entire military career is dispatched in all of two anodyne sentences.)[78] Black and white journalists had their reasons for not wanting Robinson's court-martial to receive much attention.

After his acquittal and "pretty much fed up with the service," Robinson wanted out of the army.[79] He would always be a patriot, but one who always knew that he came close to having his life chances destroyed by a few racists in Texas. Patriotism is a key to understanding the life and thought of Jackie Robinson, and it is a key to understanding the history of integration. Believers tried to summon into existence an America capacious enough to transcend its racial contradictions. As Langston Hughes famously wrote in the late 1930s: "America was never America to me / And yet I swear this oath— / America will be!"[80] World War II only made this more immediate and urgent.

Wartime integrationist patriotism was the theme of the popular 1944 book by the Black journalist Roi Ottley, *New World a-Comin'*, about Black America and its aspirations for the future.[81] Its thesis is contained in the title. It was time for Americans to turn the page. The tragedies, the setbacks, the unfulfilled promises should not be forgotten, but they were in the past. Ottley wrote in an article about his book in the *Amsterdam News,* "Negroes may quarrel among themselves about minor issues, but on the question of their rights—which mean to them the right to integration in American life, they form a solid bloc, each member of it being fiercely group conscious."[82]

Coming out of the war, the cause of integration was as militant as it ever would be. In 1945, Adam Clayton Powell Jr., just elected to Congress as the first African American member from New York State, published *Marching Blacks.* Powell was, as he proudly proclaims in his book, a radical: "I was born to be a radical—it is in the blood of all my people—it's in the blood of every American. This country has gone forward only as the ferment of radicalism produced men and women of daring." (The book has very flattering things to say about the Communist Party, to which Powell had close ties to since the late 1930s.) He states that the war had unleashed a clash between the "irresistible force" of "the awakened and united new Negro" and their white allies and the "immovable object" of "intolerant, anti-democratic, fascist prejudice concentrated in the South but spreading rapidly, especially during the war period, into every section of America." And what did politically active Blacks want? "Today there is not a handful of Negroes in America who believe in any other way to solve the problem than by way of integration." For Powell, integration had nothing to do with assimilation, vague promises, or favored nostrums of the "case-study crack pots," the "social-work mercenaries," or the "swivel-chair liberals."[83] It had nothing to do with liking or trusting white people. As he had once written, he wanted "Negroes to be Americans by becoming so integrated in American life that the white race couldn't hurt a Negro without hurting the white race."[84] Keep your friends close and your enemies closer—this was effective Black citizenship. Robinson, the Black Republican, would have some fierce conflicts with the Harlem Democrat over the course of Powell's somewhat wayward career. But if the athlete probably would have expressed himself somewhat differently, he no doubt would have agreed with the congressman's sentiments. Robinson had left the army but was still a soldier in what Powell called Civil War II. And like Powell, he helped push the question of the status and rights of African Americans into the center of American awareness and politics for the first time since Reconstruction—a place it has yet to relinquish.

Out of the army, Robinson needed a job. His first position, in the winter of 1944–45, was at Samuel Huston College, where Downs hired him as athletic director and basketball coach. But Downs could not pay him much of a salary, so Robinson, seeking to capitalize on his remarkable talents, turned to what seemed to be the most lucrative alternative: Negro League baseball. He contacted the Kansas City Monarchs to see if they would be interested in his services. They were, and he played shortstop for the team in 1945, batting .387 and attracting plaudits for his fielding, base running, and general hustle.[85] When Robinson played his only season in the Negro Leagues, African Americans had been playing professional baseball, organized by themselves, since the nineteenth century. As the color line tightened in baseball and in American society overall after Reconstruction, the Major and Minor Leagues rooted out its few Black anomalies. "In no other profession," Black baseball's first historian, Sol White, wrote in 1907, "has the color line been drawn more rigidly than in base ball."[86] In response, African Americans organized their own teams and leagues. The term "Negro Leagues" covers a wide spectrum of professional and semiprofessional baseball teams of varying degrees of ability and stability. African American baseball, after some rough years early in the Depression, was on the upswing in the late 1930s. The war years, extending to 1946, were the best years for the Negro Leagues.[87]

As a business, Black baseball suffered from problems endemic to all Black businesses, starting with the hard fact that 90 percent of the American market was not very interested in what they had to sell, and the 10 percent who were tended not to have a lot of money. Without much in the way of white capital (although there were some white owners) or customers, Black baseball always had a weak and semi-improvisational structure. Leagues came and went, teams appeared and disappeared; players, often lacking contracts, jumped from team to team, with no reserve clause to restrain them; home teams often provided their own umpires; the difference between "official" games and "exhibitions" was often not clear; and statistical records were maintained haphazardly. Negro Leaguers toiled to the near complete indifference of white America. The attention given to Negro League Baseball in recent decades has distorted this reality. Few whites knew, and fewer cared, about Black baseball at the time. Through the end of 1945, Babe Ruth had been mentioned in the *New York Times* 6,103 times. By comparison, to pick of a few of the most prominent Negro League players, the *Times* had mentioned Satchel Paige 46 times, Josh Gibson 12 times, Oscar Charleston once, and James "Cool Papa" Bell not at all. An important aspect of integration was simply being acknowledged and recognized in the national and white-controlled media for one's achievements. "Many a time I said it didn't matter," said Negro Leagues and later New York Giants star Monte Irvin, "but it really did. You wanted to be known for what you did best."[88]

This lack of interest in the Negro Leagues sometimes extended to Black fans as well. An April 1939 editorial in the *New York Amsterdam News* decrying "Naziism [*sic*] in Baseball" lamented the fact that "thousands of Negroes will be in the stands on opening day in every ball park in the country" for Black-less Major League franchises and encouraged them to see baseball "where they won't be insulted."[89] Even for these baseball fans, the main source of information would have been the weeklies of the Black press rather than the daily sports sections of white papers. If avid Black fans of all-white segregated baseball teams might seem strange in retrospect, it is perhaps no odder than African Americans going to movies with all-white casts, reading newspapers with all-white staffs, or, when allowed to vote, having to choose between only white candidates.

Jules Tygiel has argued that the Negro Leagues, unlike the Black church, Black musical or theatrical performances, or historically Black colleges and universities, "lacked any legitimacy outside of a segregationist context."[90] This seems unduly harsh. Sol White may have been a bit biased when, in 1930, he called Negro League Baseball "one of the great institutions of the race," but he was not alone in these sentiments.[91] The idea of integration cannot be separated from the evolving complex of emotions that African Americans had for their institutions, which combined great pride at what had been accomplished under incredibly difficult circumstances, with a resentment at the limitations imposed on their institutional life by white racism. In the 1930s and 1940s, there was a growing sentiment, led by African American intellectuals such as Ralph Bunche and E. Franklin Frazier, that whatever was wrong with Black institutions, there would no remedy without an end to segregation.[92] Perhaps the central dilemma of integration for most African Americans was the future status of their institutions in an integrated world. As much as Sol White prized Black baseball, he did not want Black players excluded from the Major Leagues. For the most part, through the 1930s, their exclusion was, if not accepted, not foremost in the minds of Black ballplayers and fans. Black sportswriters spent relatively little time focused on the exclusion of African Americans from white baseball, instead writing about the splendors and miseries of the Negro Leagues.[93] This began to change in the 1930s, and toward the end of that decade, as Brian Carrol has argued, the cause of Blacks in the Major Leagues was moving "from the sports pages to the front pages" of the Black press.[94] By 1942, the clamor had become sufficiently vociferous to lead Baseball Commissioner Kenesaw Mountain Landis, who for two decades had stood athwart any effort to change the color line, to declare in July 1942, "there is no rule, formal or informal, or any understanding—unwritten, subterranean, or sub-anything—against the hiring of Negro players by the teams of Organized Baseball."[95] The leagues are not blocking Blacks from playing, said Landis, they just are not hiring them.

One reason why Landis could get away with such a bald-faced evasion was that the pressure to change was fairly minimal, save for some ire from sportswriters. The Major and Minor Leagues' exclusion of Blacks broke no law since they and their teams were private businesses. The onus was on Black ballplayers to demonstrate that they belonged, not on the teams to justify their absence. There was a widely shared conventional wisdom, an example of what Gunnar Myrdal called the "convenience of ignorance," that Black ballplayers, a few exceptionally talented persons perhaps excepted, were not of Major League caliber.[96] (Branch Rickey was by no means free of this bias, telling the *New York Times* shortly after signing Robinson, "my scouts inform me that there is not a single Negro player ready for the big leagues," modifying this only slightly in July 1947 to the extent that he "did not think too many colored players could make the grade in the big leagues.")[97] In many ways, a color line that excluded Blacks because of their supposed inferiority was just as rigid, less honest, and straightforward than legal discrimination.

World War II raised the stakes. The question of whether to break the color line seemed even more arbitrary as major-league teams attempted to fill their war-depleted ranks with castoffs and oddities (like one-armed outfielders) rather than available African American ballplayers. And the ambiguities of fighting a war for democracy with a Jim Crow army could not be separated from playing the national pastime with the conspicuous exclusion of a large percentage of the nation. Then, just about the same time Robinson received his honorable discharge,

Landis died. With his removal from the scene, it became far easier for someone like Rickey to take the late commissioner at his word that there were no formal or informal bars against Blacks in mainstream baseball. And so, the famous secret meetings that culminated, on October 23, 1945, with Rickey's announcement that the Brooklyn Dodgers had signed Robinson to a minor-league contract for the following season. Reactions in the mainstream press and white baseball ranged from the approving, with varying degrees of enthusiasm, to curt no-comments, to the splenetic, with the head of Minor League Baseball calling Rickey a selfish "carpetbagger."[98] The chief sportswriter of the *New York Times* thought the move showed "moral courage" but lacked "hard-headed practicality," reminding Rickey that he had somehow overlooked "the cold fact that race prejudice exists in some parts of the United States." He concluded that "there may be some who are wondering if Rickey is rushing things too rapidly."[99]

In the Black press, there was unanimous praise for Rickey's move—"Democracy has finally invaded baseball, our great national pastime"—and no concerns whether the signing of Robinson was somehow too precipitous.[100] But sportswriters were very concerned about the consequences of his signing on the Negro Leagues, especially because Rickey refused to compensate the Monarchs for Robinson's move.[101] Many writers held an animosity toward Negro League owners. When the owners of the Kansas City Monarchs avowed that they "would not do anything to impede the advancement of any Negro ball player . . . [or] do anything to keep any Negro ball player out of the white major leagues," many sportswriters did not believe them.[102] This had been a longstanding complaint. In 1943, Lem Graves Jr., a sportswriter for the *Norfolk Journal and Guide,* had observed that the "principal enthusiasm" for breaking the color line in baseball was the preserve of "Negro sportswriters and a few white sportswriters," while the "the issues of democracy, justice, job opportunities, fair play seldom occur to Negro ball players [or] Negro club owners." A Black club owner posed Graves a question: Would the owner of his newspaper sell its best talent to the *Norfolk Virginian-Pilot* "simply for the novel experience of seeing a Negro" on the staff of a white newspaper? Graves admitted it was a tough question. His answer was that, once integrated, baseball would provide new entrepreneurial opportunities for Negro League owners; they were properly skeptical.[103]

Many Black ballplayers were skeptical as well. Sportswriter Sam Lacy reported in 1939 that Negro Leaguers were "indifferent about entering [the] major leagues," worrying that those teams would hire the Negro Leagues' most talented one-tenth, leaving the rest without a job, and that most were "none too anxious to face the miserable inconveniences of traveling with white teams and meeting discrimination on a daily basis."[104] This was the view of Satchell Paige, the best-known Black ballplayer, who in 1942 stated: "You might as well be honest about it. There would be plenty of problems, not only in the South, where the colored boys wouldn't be able to stay or travel with the teams. . . . All the nice statements in the world from both sides aren't going to knock out Jim Crow."[105]

Most Black sportswriters told Paige to stick to pitching.[106] Nonetheless, his comments spoke to a real ambivalence. Most supporters of the integration of baseball wanted both the Negro Leagues and having Black players in Major and Minor League Baseball. Many thought that the resulting competition would strengthen the Negro Leagues and force them to finally get their house in order.[107] Some owners thought the Major Leagues could incorporate the Negro Leagues as part of the Minor Leagues, a farm system of the Majors.[108] Paige himself thought the solution might be an all-Black Major League team.[109] A writer in the *Norfolk Journal and Guide* suggested in late 1945 that if Robinson could play in the Major Leagues, then whites could play in the Negro Leagues.[110] But integration has never worked both ways, in part because whites have never had to join Black organizations to exercise their citizenship rights.

One of those who tried to have it both ways, preserving the Negro Leagues while entering the Majors, was Robinson himself. He felt little loyalty to the Negro Leagues and had not particularly liked his time there. For one accustomed to intercollegiate sports on the highest level and the roar from the stands after scoring touchdowns before crowds of 90,000 fans, he found the Negro Leagues to be disconcertingly slipshod and haphazard, poorly organized, and poorly supported by fans, along with having low salaries, difficult traveling logistics, excessive postgame carousing, and often execrable accommodations. Robinson offered this critique in a 1948 article in *Ebony*, "What's Wrong with the Negro Leagues," while also calling out the "low class . . . character and morals" of some his former teammates. He recognized that some of the problems with the Negro Leagues were the problems of being Black in America, marginalized in almost every possible way. Still, he asserted that he left the Negro Leagues to improve them. "When I first joined the Montreal team [in 1946], I was convinced that my leaving Negro baseball would stimulate interest in the colored leagues." And

Robinson hoped that this new attention would be a catalyst of reform and "improve the status of all Negro ballplayers and place Negro baseball on a par with the rest of organized baseball."[111]

Some astute observers of the fight to integrate baseball have called these sorts of arguments, the belief that the entrance of Blacks into Major League baseball helped or might help the Negro Leagues, "paradoxical."[112] And in hindsight, these arguments, if not paradoxical, were just wrong. Sometimes your adversaries can see your situation more clearly than can you or your friends. *The Sporting News,* that self-proclaimed "Bible of Baseball" and longtime opponent of Major League integration, was notably clear eyed, if more than a little hypocritical, when it editorialized in 1942: "The country has a great Negro major league, which draws heavy support from the colored folk. If its ranks were raided by the American and National Leagues, with their tremendous resources, it would have fewer stars and the caliber of ball which has made it an attraction would be so lowered that the Negro loop, of necessity, would sink to the status of an inferior minor circuit, with subsequent decline in enthusiasm by fans and prestige of performers."[113] But Black supporters of integration never believed that the price of entering white institutions would—or should—be the involuntary destruction of Black ones.

This is, of course, what happened. Black sportswriters who had spent years haranguing the Negro Leagues for their limitations and selfishness in their hostility to integration, by 1948, became the leagues' biggest boosters, urging, with increasing desperation, that "Negro League Baseball Must Survive."[114] But the Black press itself was focusing more and more of its attention on the handful of African American ballplayers in the Major Leagues rather than the many more in the Negro Leagues.[115] Although the speed of the demise of the Negro Leagues surprised most observers, it was by then a lost cause. After 1950, they were no longer playing on a major-league level. A few years thereafter, the Negro Leagues were no more. Of the five hundred or so players in the Negro Leagues in 1947, only about fifty played in the Major Leagues.[116] The Negro Leagues employed not only Black ballplayers but also Black coaches, managers, publicists, and front-office personnel, all the while supporting (mostly) Black club owners. They all, too, needed new jobs. It would not be until 1962 that a Major League team hired a Black coach, not until 1966 that the Major Leagues had their first Black umpire, not until 1975 their first Black manager, and not until 2010, their first Black owner.

The Negro Leagues became the first, though certainly not the last, Black institution to be extinguished by integration. The Negro Leagues soon became more honored in death than in life. The organization is now universally considered to have been, at its peak, a legitimate major league, equal in talent to white baseball. This was certainly not the view of Branch Rickey, other club owners, and perhaps not even Jackie Robinson. It has become common to argue that the Negro Leagues played a different brand of baseball, one based more on guile and speed than the home-run-happy power game of the Major Leagues.[117] But at the time, few Black sportswriters praised the Negro Leagues for any such distinctive style. They wanted to demonstrate the equal capacity of Black ballplayers to their white peers, and the only place to do this was in the Major Leagues. As Jules Tygiel has written, "few in the 1940s posited it [sustaining the Negro Leagues] as a preferable alternative to major league integration."[118] But sometimes institutions, like people, need to die to become revered. Should Robinson be held responsible for the death of the Negro Leagues? This was the verdict of Amiri Baraka, who grew up as a fan of the Negro League Newark Eagles and later wrote that Robinson was a "synthetic colored guy" who was fashioned "out of the California laboratories of USC [sic]" and proceeded to "rip off" what Blacks had in the Negro Leagues "in the name of what you ain't never gonna get," forcing Black fans who wanted to go to a baseball game to "sit next to drunken racists . . . and watch our heroes put down by slimy cocksuckers."[119] Many others, less immoderately, have expressed similar sentiments.[120] Defenders of integration would have responded, with the African American religious thinker Howard Thurman, that without the freedom to have choices and alternatives, even the most beloved of Black institutions risks becoming a prison.[121]

But if Robinson and most Black commentators saw integration as a step toward effective Black citizenship, Rickey saw the inclusion of African Americans in white institutions as integration itself. He did not care about the viability of Black institutions. He hated the Negro Leagues. Shortly after signing Robinson, Rickey stated: "There is no Negro League as far as I am concerned. Negro baseball is in the zone of a racket and there is not a circuit that could be admitted to organized baseball."[122] In addition, his politics were complicated. Rickey was a conservative Republican Christian who was an avid reader of the latest social science on African Americans and convinced that segregation was an evil, one that that required immediate remedying.[123] Robinson's career with the Dodgers was a watershed in the understanding of integration. Afterward, more and more observers, Blacks as well as whites, interpreted integration as Rickey did, simply the inclusion of minorities in previously all-white institutions, disconnecting it from the broader African American political campaign for effective citizenship. (If anything about Rickey that follows sounds harsh, it is offered in full admiration for his courage, skill, and fortitude in hiring and playing Robinson.)

It was by no means foreordained that the first major postwar venue for a challenge to segregation would be professional baseball. The 1944 Myrdal Report, of which Rickey was an admirer, gave baseball a single passing mention among its 1,483 pages.[124] For advocates of Black civil rights, there were many more pressing issues than sports and baseball—the Jim Crow military, discrimination by defense contractors, all-white primaries and voting rights, segregated housing and schooling, police brutality, mob violence, and so on. African Americans and their allies protested many things during the 1930s and the war years, but the first demonstration against segregation in organized baseball, with a not very impressive turnout of some twenty picketers, evidently took place on opening day in 1945 at Yankee Stadium.[125] Other than sportswriters, with their professional obligation to write about sports, segregation in baseball was usually not a first-tier issue. Rickey's hiring of Robinson stood outside the general trajectory of postwar civil rights activism. It did not involve the courts, such as Thurgood Marshall and the NAACP's careful fight against legal segregation. It did not set any sort of binding precedent other sports teams were obliged to follow. If hiring Robinson was in some ways a labor question, it had nothing to do with unionization efforts, like the CIO's Operation Dixie. It obviously did not in any way address the situation of Black women. It was not even, once Rickey hired Robinson, really a battle between outsiders and an entrenched power elite determined to keep them at bay. Major and Minor League Baseball had no greater insider than Branch Rickey.

At the same time, this made it relatively easy for Rickey to breach the color line. He did not have to negotiate or engage in a long campaign to hire Robinson. He had no constituency to report to, no real boss. He was almost entirely in control. He rejected the idea that Black political pressure in any way entered into his decision. If Robinson told the Black press after his hiring that he knew that his "position was obtained only through the constant pressure of my people and their press," Rickey had a very different view.[126] "I have not been pushed into this. I signed Robinson in spite of the pressure groups who are only exploiting the Negroes instead of advancing their cause."[127]

One of the central paradoxes of the idea of integration was that, while it was a Black movement for Black citizenship, its success, unavoidably, depended on its acceptance by whites, who almost always were the persons with the economic and political power to determine its fate. Robinson joined the Dodgers on Rickey's terms. Rickey's understanding of integration was top-down and voluntary. It is true that he applauded the Ives-Quinn Act, passed in early 1945, that banned discrimination in employment and education in New York—the first state to pass such a law—making, he thought, his plans to hire a Black ballplayer legally and politically unassailable; Rickey told his wife, "they can't stop me now."[128] But this was an exception to his general view of civil rights legislation, especially its application to discriminatory practices by private companies, such as the Brooklyn Dodgers. As late as 1950, Rickey could state that "legislative force can delay rather than accelerate the problem" of racial progress.[129] (He subsequently changed his mind about civil rights legislation.)

Rickey's vision of integration was frictionless. It was something he would arrange and manage. Black agitation for integration or for Robinson, or even Black admiration too vocally expressed, was something to be avoided. He told a middle-class African American audience in Atlanta in 1956 that he was worried that Robinson's Black fans would have expressed themselves through "over-adulation, mass attendance, dinners, of one kind or another of such a public nature that it would have a tendency to create a solidification of the antagonisms and misunderstandings—over-doing it. . . . The greatest danger, the greatest hazard, I felt, was the Negro race itself. . . . Not people of this crowd. . . . Those of less understanding, those of a lower grade of education, frankly."[130] He was always afraid that too much identification with Black political aspirations would damage Robinson's chances of success.

Rickey's view of integration was incremental, seeding an all-white institution with a few test cases, extraordinarily well-qualified minority candidates, waiting for change to percolate, trying to convince skeptical/racist whites to recant. This put extraordinary pressure on the individuals challenging the standing racial order, much less so on its upholders. Robinson said in late 1945, "I feel that if I flop, or conduct myself badly—on or off the field—then I'll set this advancement back a hundred years."[131] But the emphasis on the success or failure of a single exemplar unavoidably distracted attention from the reality that segregation in baseball was structural, not personal, and had little to do with the achievements or failures of a single individual. Nonetheless, integration often became identified with its courageous pioneers—the Little Rock Nine, Rosa Parks, James Meredith, Jackie Robinson.

While it may have been prudent advice, Rickey's famous injunction to Robinson to have the courage not to fight back against the racist taunts he would face ensured that the emotional and at times physical brunt of breaking the color line would be borne by the man challenging it. It placed little pressure on other clubs. No other team was obliged to follow Rickey's initiative, and few did. By the end of 1947, only four other African Americans played in the Major Leagues. Every team that broke the color line, including the Dodgers, soon established an informal quota system for Blacks in Major League clubs with relegation to the Minor Leagues for others; this led to steady Major League employment for the Willie Mayses of the world, but less so for more ordinary Black ballplayers.[132] Despite the excellence of Robinson and his African American peers, there was no stampede to hire Blacks. By the opening of the 1953 season, there were only twenty Black players in the Major Leagues, and these on the rosters of only six of the sixteen teams. The Boston Red Sox, notoriously, did not field its first hire of its first African American player until 1959.

Were there other ways to proceed? Could there have been some way, as Negro League owners suggested, to preserve some institutional viability for Black baseball by incorporating the Negro Leagues into lower levels of the existing structures of white baseball? What if, say, in July 1948, when President Harry Truman issued Executive Order 9981 mandating an end to segregation in the military, Baseball Commissioner Happy Chandler had followed suit with a similar order for the Major Leagues? To be sure, for the armed forces, the end of segregation took several years to achieve, was met with recalcitrance by some authorities, and certainly did not end all racial tension in the ranks. Still, by 1954, all segregated units had been eliminated in an organization vastly larger (and vastly more important) than Major League Baseball—long before the first African American played for the Red Sox.[133] Whether or not such changes were practical or possible is a question for further discussion. But the broader point is that there were alternatives to Rickey's view of integration, ones that, perhaps, could have preserved Negro League baseball in some fashion or that would not have relied so heavily on individual standouts. And for the most part, in the 1950s and 1960s, it was baseball's approach to integration, not the military's, that became the favored model in society, an always cautious and delicate toe gingerly testing the waters.

Jackie Robinson retired after the 1956 season. He had been an exemplary ball-player and citizen. Despite his great baseball acumen and his universally acknowl-edged competitiveness, he was never offered a position in baseball management, which, if it now valued Black baseball talent, was still indifferent to Black baseball expertise. Whether Robinson wanted such a position or would have accepted one if it had been offered soon became moot with his rather bitter divorce from the sport that had made him a household name. "Baseball was good to me, but I don't owe it anything," he said in 1967. "Fun to play, but now that I am out of it, I'm just not interested." He continued: "Jackie Robinson would have made more if he were white. Or if he was meek and mild. But that's not me, that's not my way."[134]

But finding his way in a world in which he was neither white nor meek and mild would not prove an easy task. Robinson would try his hand at several businesses, with some success and some failure. His first position after leaving baseball was as a vice president in a midsized, white-owned company, Chock Full o' Nuts, a chain of New York City coffee shops with a largely African American workforce. The company was an example of "welfare capitalism." The employees were treated generously, but this was intended as an alternative to unionization. As William Black, the company president, stated, "I hired Jackie because a major-ity of the people who work for me are colored—and I figured they would worship him."[135] Robinson liked the job but left after 1964, when he felt he was becoming a figurehead. He then tried his hand at several Black-owned companies, notably Freedom National Bank in Harlem, which suffered, like many such businesses, from undercapitalization and would have a troubled history until its eventual failure in 1990. If Black-owned businesses were, as Robinson said in 1967, "the kind of Black Power that I advocate, the wise use of our dollar, the wise use of our political sense," he experienced in his working life one of the quandaries often posed by integration: the choice between relative tokenism in white-owned companies, on the one hand, and the inherent limitations of capital-poor Black-owned businesses, on the other.[136]

But, arguably, the main interest of Robinson after leaving the Dodgers was lending his extraordinary fame to the cause of integration and effective citizen-ship for Black Americans. In 1956, as he prepared to retire, he was awarded the prestigious Spingarn Medal by the NAACP, the first athlete to win the honor, and in 1957 served as the chairman of the organization's Fight for Freedom campaign. Again and again in the late 1950s and early 1960s, he lent his time and name to a long parade of demonstrations, protests, and assorted civil rights causes.[137] Robinson also would disseminate his views as a columnist both in the mainstream and Black press.[138]

By 1956, integration had entered the political mainstream. But as it widened for many, it also seemed to slow, like a great river. In its first article about Martin Luther King Jr., in March 1956, the *New York Times* quoted him as standing "for immediate integration. Segregation is evil and as a minister I cannot condone evil."[139] The key word here is "immediate." When integration arose as a demand, it was often viewed as something that could be implemented in the near future, only requiring the requisite political will. Typical was Earl Conrad, a white journalist for Black newspapers, who wrote in 1947 that, "in so very many areas of American society, since the beginning of WWII, there has occurred so much integration" that it "has even penetrated the hidebound South so that it can no longer be said to be a Solid South."[140] But as integration advanced, its realization also became seen as something less proximate, an ideal with a distant goal to be aimed for without perhaps being realized. A new intermediate vocabulary then developed. For this, a new word emerged in the early 1950s, as defined in 1952: "*Desegregation*—i.e., the mere admission of Negro students to existing institutions for white people—does not constitute *integration*." The term "de facto segregation," referring to informal segregation patterns, especially in housing and education, and promoted by the NAACP in northern civil rights struggles, first appeared in the *New York Times* in 1956.[141]

Also in the early 1950s, integration was increasingly "defined down" to mean only race mixing. Sometimes this was done by diehard segregationists with one-track minds. Strom Thurmond, running for president as candidate of the segregationist States' Right Party in 1948, proclaimed: "We believe in racial integrity. We are opposed to racial 'integration.'"[142] But just as often, integration was viewed as simply the breaching of the color line, counting and amassing small victories in hopes they presaged a better future. But integration as effective Black citizenship could not easily be reduced to a number, to something easily measurable.[143]

For many, touting the positive measures of integration, often consisting largely of stories of middle-class "first Negro" trailblazers or tentative breaches of the color line, rang increasingly hollow. In 1955, Langston Hughes declared, "We are being rapidly integrated into every phase of American life, from the army to the navy to schools to industry, advancing, advancing," only to have Simple, his Harlem everyman, respond: "I have not advanced one step. Still the same old job, same old salary, same old kitchenette, same old Harlem, and the same old color."[144]

Hughes's article appeared in the Black press the same week the US Supreme Court handed down its decision in *Brown II*, the decree that permitted school desegregation to advance "with all deliberate speed." As for Robinson, he did not expect overnight transformation, but his idea of integration was much speedier than the Court contemplated. He told the *Los Angeles Times* in 1954 that "anything done overnight is dangerous, but if you do it slowly, seeing all along what is happening, that that is the type of foundation that lasts." While he said that "integration in schools in the south must be taken a step at a time," there "should be a goal which makes 1956 better than 1954 and 1958 better than 1956. Then, maybe in 1960 the schools would be fully integrated."[145] This would have to be fought for. Robinson did not expect it to be granted. He wanted to do, he said in 1957, "everything short of violence to achieve our rights."[146]

This would be within the context of the United States realizing its implicit promise of equal citizenship to all Americans, and it would demonstrate the superiority of American democracy over its alternatives worldwide. Robinson's conception of integration as effective Black citizenship could not be separated from liberal Cold War goals. In 1950s America, the two issues were often juxtaposed. (The *Brown* decision, handed down on May 17, 1954, temporarily took the nation's attention away from its primary political preoccupation that spring, the ongoing Army-McCarthy hearings in the Senate.) Robinson believed that the Ku Klux Klan and the White Citizens' Council violence and intransigence just "feed the anti-American propaganda mills of the Communist powers."[147] In 1949, in perhaps the most controversial episode of his career, he criticized the singer, actor, and leftist activist Paul Robeson before the assorted racists and segregationists comprising the House Committee on Un-American Activities (HUAC). He had been asked to speak on Robeson's comments about the readiness and willingness of African Americans to take up arms against the Soviet Union; Rickey urged him to do so.[148] Whatever one makes of the episode—Robinson was at once defiant and ambivalent in his later accounts, saying he had "never regretted" his appearance but implying that he could have handled it differently—he was not alone among Black civil rights activists in thinking the cause was not being aided by a too-close identification with the Communist Party.[149] But if Robinson was the epitome of an African American Cold War civil rights liberal, it would be a great mistake to think that he was in any way less ardent in his civil rights commitments than his brothers and sisters to his left.[150] He told the committee that "white people must realize that the more a Negro hates Communism because it opposes democracy, the more he is going to hate the other influences that kill off democracy in this country—and that goes for racial discrimination in the Army, segregation on trains and buses, and job discrimination."[151] He also insisted that condemning Communism did not mean he was also condemning Communists' legitimate agitation for African American civil rights, telling the congressmen that if a Communist "denounces injustice in the courts, police brutality, and lynching," it is no less true because a Communist says it.[152] In 1960, at a time when the American Communist Party was a spent political force, former president Truman claimed that Communists were behind the recent sit-in demonstrations; Robinson called him senile.[153]

Robinson's natural political home was in the Republican Party, but he had the misfortune to be a prominent Black Republican during the decades when the label "liberal Republican" was beginning its slow, painful transition from an ideology to an oxymoron.[154] He did not trust the Democrats because of their continuing ties to southern segregationists, but he supported civil rights activists whatever their political affiliation. He supported Richard Nixon in the 1960 presidential race, but not before campaigning for Hubert Humphrey in the Democratic primaries. (He came to bitterly regret his decision to back Nixon, claiming in the 1968 campaign that the "Nixon candidacy imperils America.")[155] If Robinson had a political idol, it was that epitome of liberal Republicanism, Nelson Rockefeller, the longtime governor of New York and frequent presidential aspirant. For Robinson, he was "the one man in public life in whom I had complete faith and confidence."[156] He campaigned for Rockefeller in 1964 and urgently wanted him to run again in 1968. From 1966 to 1968, Robinson was on Rockefeller's gubernatorial staff as a special assistant.

Increasingly, however, Robinson was without a real political home. In 1964, furious at Barry Goldwater, George Wallace, and what he called "bleeding heart" northern liberals more concerned with racial abuses in Alabama than in their own neighborhoods, he warned that "the counterrevolution of white people in America against the aims and aspirations of Negro people in America is ugly."[157] In 1966, he castigated the GOP as increasingly a haven for "far out, right-wing kooks, goons, and bigots."[158] In the summer of 1968, he wrote that "the Republican Party has told the Black man to go to hell. I offer them a similar invitation."[159] Robinson voted for the Democratic candidate for president in 1964 and 1968; had he lived, he probably would done so again in 1972, albeit reluctantly, much more out of a detestation of Nixon than an admiration for George McGovern.

Integration was increasingly defined as inclusion or race mixing and thus viewed as a failure. If defenders of the older definition, such as Kenneth Clark and Charles Silberman, insisted that "integration should not be confused with the mere mixing of Negroes and whites in the same classroom, or in the same school, or in the same neighborhood," it was a message that integration's growing ranks of opponents, Black and white, did not want to hear.[160] Malcolm X skyrocketed to fame in large part due to his coruscating attacks on integration. "We don't want to be wiped out with the white man, we don't want to integrate with him, we want to separate from him," he said in 1962.[161] White liberals, sharing little with Malcolm X except a definition of integration as race mixing, were similarly disparaging. The same year, when the sociologist Nathan Glazer used a title to ask "Is 'Integration' possible in New York Schools?" he answered his rhetorical question with a negative: "Much of the professional integrationist 'reasoning' is based on the fallacious assumption that learning aptitude is somehow improved by race mixing per se."[162]

By the late 1960s, integration had been turned on its head; rather than a synonym for race pride, it became equivalent to race extinction. Prominent advocates of Black power decried integration as "unrealistic," "despicable," "cultural genocide," or a "government plot to enslave Blacks," or argued that the first integrationist was the slave-owning "rapist racist."[163] Martin Luther King Jr. in his final book, *Where Do We Go from Here?*, quoted the prominent African American novelist John O. Killens: "Integration has never been the main slogan of the revolution. The oppressed fights to free himself from his oppressor, not to integrate with him." King responded that what he wanted for Black people was to be "integrated, with power, into every level of American life," that "liberation cannot come without integration and integration cannot come without liberation."[164] But on this issue, it was King's opponents who would carry the day.

It is not easy to summarize Robinson's politics in his later years. As some observers of his career have noted, he often exhibited a testy outspokenness. If he was perhaps the most admired African American of his generation, he was destined to be a relative loner in his racial politics, often finding mainstream Black leaders too complacent and Black radicals too incendiary. As Patrick Henry observed, "each of his actions seemed to alienate someone."[165]

In the early 1960s, Robinson tangled repeatedly with Malcolm X, who accused him of "shifty base running," "still trying to win 'the big game' for your white boss," and by doing the white man's bidding, of having "never shown appreciation for the support given you by the Negro masses."[166] For his part, Robinson called Malcolm X a "racist" peddling his "vicious theories" while exhibiting "sick leadership," making his accusations against civil rights leaders from relative safety while badmouthing activists risking their lives in Alabama and Mississippi.[167] In 1964, Robinson stated, "the masses of the Negro people, in cities all over the country, are demonstrating, some at the risk of their lives, to give witness that they want integration—the exact opposite of segregation," and wish "to be integrated into the mainstream of American life, not invited to live in some small cubicle of this land in splendid isolation."[168] At the same time, as much as he disliked the ideology of Malcolm X, he disliked some of his white critics even more. In 1962, when HUAC was considering investigating the Nation of Islam, Robinson wrote, "In spite of my differences with the Black Muslims, they have as much right to hate the white man—if it is true that they do—as any white man has the right, legally, to hate the Black man."[169]

Robinson never gave up faith in the mainstream civil rights movement. In 1969, he wondered why "shouldn't Whitney Young be the hero of the Black community rather than Eldridge Cleaver?"[170] But he also wanted to listen to what the Cleavers had to say. Robinson met with the Black Panthers and, if not supporting their positions, defended their right to hold them without persecution from the police.[171] When armed Black radicals staged an attention-attracting takeover of the student union at Cornell University in April 1969, Robinson contacted its leaders in order to better understand them.[172] In time, he even mellowed on Malcolm X, seeing him less as a contradiction than as a possible complement to his integrationist views—an alternative path to Black equality. Writing in late 1967 on the subject of the proposed boycott of the 1968 Olympics by Black athletes, Robinson admitted to mixed emotions but declared: "Maybe we as Negro athletes have 'been around' too long, accepting inequities and indignities and accepting worn-out promises about how things are going to get better. If this is the way youngsters feel, believe me, I can sympathize with their point of view. Malcolm X, the late and brilliant leader, once pointed out to me in the course of a debate that: 'Jackie, in days to come, your son and my son will not be willing to settle for things we are willing to settle for.'"[173]

For a long time, Robinson was a stubborn supporter of the war in Vietnam. In 1965, when his son, Jackie Robinson Jr., was serving in the military, he wrote an article that argued "Foes of Vietnam Policy Should Pause to Fight Dixie Murderers."[174] He insisted as late as the fall of 1967 that Americans had "a moral commitment we have to live up to" in Vietnam, urging President Lyndon Johnson to stay the course and to continue the bombing of North Vietnam.[175] Robinson's deepest belief at the time was that the United States "must defeat Communism in Vietnam. And fascistic bigotry at home." There is little doubt that he really believed that the two causes could not be sundered.[176]

Of course, many did not agree. He was very disappointed when, in April 1967, King announced his opposition to the war, and Robinson told him so, both in person and in print. But always he added that he completely respected King's right to his opinion and did not want "bigots and those who secretly hate Dr. King to find comfort in me disagreeing with him."[177] He said much the same about Stokely Carmichael, defending his right to outspokenness and rejecting the often-heard argument in 1968 that Black radicalism gave white America an opportunity to fold their tents on civil rights.[178] By August of that year, after the Tet offensive and with King lying in a freshly dug grave, Robinson began sounding more like Carmichael than the erstwhile cold warrior of the past. "Black people are not afraid to die and there are hundreds of thousands of young Black people who would rather make a last-ditch stand for freedom in the ghettoes of their cities than in the jungles of Vietnam."[179]

That fall, Robinson asserted that he was "Black first, American second," and "if that is racism so be it."[180] Given these sentiments, it is perhaps understandable (but still rather surprising) that in the fall of 1968, in the fierce parting of the ways between white liberals and Black nationalism that was the New York City teacher's strike, Robinson, the lifelong supporter of integration, took the side of the Black nationalist–inspired school decentralization experiment in Ocean Hill–Brownsville. He thought the strike had been "directed against the good and welfare of the Black community."[181] In that turbulent fall, one did not have to be a radical or a nationalist to feel, like Robinson, that local community control of education was not to be anti-white but simply pro-Black.[182] In a lambasting of Bayard Rustin, one of the most prominent Black supporters of the strike, one observer noted that Robinson, in effect, called him an Uncle Tom, saying he was not really a Black leader at all but really just wanted to "curry favor with white folks."[183] (This was an accusation, as noted above from Malcolm X, that had often been leveled at himself.)

In his last years, at times Robinson sounded as if he had lost his faith in America. Symbols he once embraced as bringing Americans together he now rejected as divisive and implicitly anti-Black. He told the *New York Times* on the Fourth of July 1971 that he "wouldn't fly the flag on the Fourth of July or any other day. When I see a car with a flag pasted on it, I figure the guy behind the wheel isn't my friend."[184] In the last months of his life, Robinson even turned his back on Rockefeller, his greatest political idol, in the wake of Attica, writing the governor that he had lost the "sensitivity and understanding" he once had, sacrificing "doing what is right" for political expediency.[185] Rockefeller responded that "liberalism ceases to work if it is not controlled by realism."[186] But for Robinson, Rockefeller's realism was the realism of fools, one that had become the coin of wisdom in large stretches of white America (and, usually for very different reasons, in Black America as well): that serious efforts to achieve integration had been made, they had been found wanting, and now it was time to move on.

In his final years, Robinson, says biographer Arnold Rampersad, moved beyond the "misty dream of true racial integration in America in the 1930s."[187] Robinson had certainly moved beyond "misty dreams," but integration had never been just that for him or for many Black Americans. The belief in integration was the practical product of an intense, concentrated, and burning anger at the way white America treated its Black citizens. It had never been premised on illusions about the benevolence of white people. And for him, its realization was perhaps more distant in the fall of 1972, when the rulers of Major League Baseball were shamed into acknowledging the dying Robinson at the World Series, than it had been a quarter century before, when he first walked onto the infield at Ebbets Field. Robinson called his autobiography, published earlier that year, *I Never Had It Made* because, in part, "I cannot say that I have it made while our country drives full speed ahead to deeper rifts between men and women of varying color, speeds along a course toward more and more racism."[188] He went on to say, "There was a time I deeply believed in America. I have become bitterly disillusioned."[189] Still, he hoped that "some day the pendulum will swing back to the time when America seemed ready to make an effort to be a united state."[190] He had not given up his belief in integration as effective Black citizenship. But he had come to the conclusion that its realization would take something more than another Jackie Robinson.

NOTES

1. "Jackie Robinson of UCLA," *Atlanta Daily World*, Mar. 8, 1940.

2. Lucius "Melancholy" Jones, "Satchel Paige (West), Josh Gibson (East) in Dream Game Today," *Atlanta Daily World*, Aug. 16, 1942.

3. "Connie Mack Vague on When Negroes Will Crash Majors," *Pittsburgh Courier*, Dec. 12, 1944.

4. Ted Page, "A Day with Jackie Robinson," *New Pittsburgh Courier*, July 15, 1972; John "Buck" O'Neil quoted in John B. Holway, *Black Diamonds: Life in the Negro Leagues from the Men Who Lived It* (Westport, CT: Meckler Books, 1989), 103.

5. Jules Tygiel, *Extra Bases: Reflections on Jackie Robinson, Race, and Baseball History* (Lincoln, University of Nebraska Press, 2002), 36.

6. "Organized Baseball" was the common term for the Major Leagues and their farm systems. By using the term, I am not implying that baseball elsewhere was not "organized."

7. Raymond Williams, *Keywords: A Vocabulary of Culture and Society* (New York: Oxford University Press, 1985).

8. W. E. B. Du Bois, "Segregation," *The Crisis* 41, no. 1 (Jan. 1934): 20; "The N.A.A.C.P. and Race Segregation," *The Crisis* 41, no. 2 (Feb. 1934): 52–53.

9. Charles F. Lane, "Is Dr. DuBois Growing Weary? Has He Quit?," *Chicago Defender*, Mar. 24, 1934; Rev. A. Wayman Ward, "He Fought in Vain," ibid.; Dewey R. Jones, "Why Fight Segregation—Dr. DuBois: Distinguished Race Leader Sees Nothing to Be Gained by Opposing Jim Crow System in the United States, Tells Chicago Audience We Should Make of Situation, No Relief in Sight, Is He a Quitter?," ibid.; "Calls Du Bois a Traitor to His Race," Ibid., Apr. 14, 1934; Samuel Williams, "An Elegy to Dr. Du Bois," *Pittsburgh Courier*, Apr. 14, 1934.

10. Walter White, "Segregation—A Symposium," *The Crisis* 41, no. 3 (Mar. 1934): 80–81.

11. In four widely circulated Black newspapers—*Pittsburgh Courier, Chicago Defender, New York Amsterdam News*, and *Baltimore Afro-American*—the word "integration" appeared a total of 13 times before 1930, 14 times from 1930 to 1933, 34 times in 1934, and 48 times in 1935–36 before achieving ubiquity, being used 261 times in 1937–40 and 1,227 times from 1941 to 1945. By contrast, in the *New York Times* there were forty-two articles that included "Negro" and "integration" through 1940, ninety-eight during the war years, and its regular use in a racial context really took off after the war.

12. James Weldon Johnson, *Negro Americans, What Now?* (New York: Viking, 1934) 12–18.

13. Stephen Kantrowitz, *More than Freedom: Fighting for Black Citizenship in a White Republic, 1828–1889* (New York: Penguin, 2012), 32–33.

14. "Address of the Colored State Convention to the People of South Carolina, November 24, 1865," in *Reconstruction: Voices from America's First Great Struggle for Racial Equality*, ed. Brooks D. Simson (New York: Library of America, 2018), 129–33.

15. W. E. B. Du Bois, "Segregation in the North," *The Crisis* 41, no. 4 (Apr. 1934): 115–16.

16. Mary McLeod Bethune, "My Conference with the President," *Atlanta Daily World*, Feb. 9, 1937.

17. Guy B. Johnson, "Negro Racial Movements and Leadership in the United States," *American Journal of Sociology* 43, no. 1 (July 1937): 57.

18. Edwin D. Hoffman, "The Genesis of the Modern Movement for Equal Rights in South Carolina, 1900–1939," *Journal of Negro History* 44, no. 4 (Oct. 1959): 346–69. See also Peter F. Lau, "Mr. NAACP: Levi G. Bird and the Remaking of the NAACP in State and Nation," in *Toward a Meeting of the Waters: Currents in the Civil Rights Movement of South Carolina during the Twentieth Century*, ed. Winnifred B. Moore Jr. and Orville Vernon Burton (Columbia: University of South Carolina Press, 2008), 146–55.

19. Violet Moten Foster, "Plea for More Segregation," *Chicago Defender*, July 6, 1940.

20. Rebecca Stiles Taylor, "Integration Versus Disintegration Is the Question of the Hour," *Chicago Defender*, Sept. 13, 1941.

21. The literature on Robinson is mountainous. See, for example, Arnold Rampersad, *Jackie Robinson: A Biography* (New York: Ballantine, 1997); Jackie Robinson, *I Never Had It Made*, with Alfred Duckett (New York: G. P. Putnam's Sons, 1972); and Jules Tygiel, *Baseball's Great Experiment: Jackie Robinson and His Legacy* (New York: Oxford University Press, 2008).

22. Carl T. Rowan, *Wait Till Next Year: The Life Story of Jackie Robinson* (New York: Random House, 1960), 203.

23. *California: A Guide to the Golden State*, American Guide Series (New York: Hastings House, 1939), 245–49.

24. Rampersad, *Jackie Robinson*, 21; Andrew Wiese, *Places of Their Own: African American Suburbanization in the Twentieth Century* (Chicago: University of Chicago Press, 2004), 35.

25. James E. Crimi, "The Social Status of the Negro in Pasadena, California" (master's thesis, University of Southern California, 1941), 72–75, 59–60, 48.

26. Rampersad, *Jackie Robinson*, 19.

27. Jackie Robinson, *Baseball Has Done It* (Philadelphia: Lippincott, 1964), 29.

28. Maury Allen, *Jackie Robinson: A Life Remembered* (New York: Franklin Watts, 1987), 25–26.

29. Rampersad, *Jackie Robinson*, 22.

30. Robinson, *I Never Had It Made*, 18.

31. Ibid. This included an adolescent arrest at gunpoint for swimming in the city reservoir, which he felt justified in doing because of the ban on Blacks swimming in the municipal pool other than Tuesdays, and an arrest as a teenager after an altercation with a police officer. Ibid., 34, 51–52.

32. Ibid., 18–19.

33. Rampersad, *Jackie Robinson*, 26; Robinson, *Baseball Has Done It*, 30.

34. Peter Golenbock, *Bums: An Oral History of the Brooklyn Dodgers* (New York: Putnam, 1984), 117–18. Although he was still living in Pasadena in early 1942 as the Japanese internment began, Robinson nowhere comments on this.

35. Rampersad, *Jackie Robinson*, 27.

36. Ibid.; Robinson, *Baseball Has Done It,* 30–31.

37. Robinson, *Baseball Has Done It,* 31.

38. Robinson's older brother, Mack, was an example of the precariousness of Black athletic victory in Pasadena. A silver medalist at 200 meters in the 1936 Olympics, second only to Jesse Owens, Mack returned home to be largely snubbed and ignored by Pasadena's city fathers, which hurt him deeply. Rampersad, *Jackie Robinson*, 31, 41.

39. Crimi, "Social Status of the Negro," 82–83.

40. Gerald L. Early, *A Level Playing Field: African American Athletes and the Republic of Sports* (Cambridge, MA: Harvard University Press, 2011), 5.

41. Randy Dixon, "Riding Prophetic Winds across Gridiron Domains," *Pittsburgh Courier,* Sept. 9, 1939.

42. Lucius "Melancholy" Jones, "Slants on Sports," *Atlanta Daily World,* Aug. 3, 1940.

43. Lucius "Melancholy" Jones, "Twelve Million Negroes Hoping UCLA Will Receive Rose Bowl Bid," *Atlanta Daily World,* Nov. 12, 1939.

44. Randy Dixon, "The Sports Bugle," *Los Angeles Sentinel,* July 13, 1939.

45. "Jackie Robinson of UCLA," *Atlanta Daily World,* Mar. 8, 1940.

46. Rampersad, *Jackie Robinson,* 55.

47. "Famous Jackie Robinson to Play Here," *Chicago Defender,* Dec. 7, 1940.

48. Rampersad, *Jackie Robinson,* 71. While in the army, Robinson was treated for a case of gonorrhea. Ibid., 99.

49. Robinson, *I Never Had It Made,* 18–19.

50. The Austin college was named for Samuel Huston, an Iowa Methodist, not to be confused with the antebellum Texas politician and enslaver Samuel Houston. For Downs, see Ada Anderson, "Downs, Karl Everette (1912–1914)," *Handbook of Texas,* Dec. 1, 1994, https://www.tshaonline.org/handbook/entries/downs-karl-everette (accessed June 16, 2019). See also Michael G. Long and Chris Lamb, *Jackie Robinson, a Spiritual Biography: The Faith of a Boundary-Breaking Hero* (Louisville, KY: Westminster John Knox Press, 2017), 28–35.

51. "We, Too, Sing America," in *The Duke Ellington Reader,* ed. Marc Tucker (New York: Oxford University Press, 1993), 146–47; Alemena Davis, "Duke's 'Symphonic' Classical Jazz," *Pittsburgh Courier,* Sept. 6, 1941.

52. Davis, "Duke's 'Symphonic' Classical Jazz."

53. For the Fellowship Church (Interracial) in Pasadena, see E. Stanley Jones, *The Christ of the American Road* (New York: Abingdon, 1944), 97; and "Here's Today's Events in Mission's Program," *Los Angeles Times,* Mar. 18, 1941.

54. Karl E. Downs, "Timid Negro Students," *Atlanta Daily World,* Apr. 6, 1936, reprinted in *The Crisis* 43, no. 6 (June 1936).

55. "To Stress the Value of the Ballot," *Atlanta Daily World,* May 5, 1935; "Dr. Logan Optimistic over Franchise Gains," *Baltimore Afro-American,* June 8, 1946. Downs was also credited as author of another, less enduring slogan on the same theme, "the man without a vote is the public's goat." Ibid.

56. "Methodist Youth Oppose Plan of Church," *Pittsburgh Courier,* Sept. 19, 1936. For the central jurisdiction, see Peter C. Murray, *Methodists and the Crucible of Race, 1930–1975* (Columbia: University of Missouri Press, 2004).

57. Karl E. Downs, "Did My Church Forsake Me? A Negro Methodist Asks a Question," *Zion's Herald,* Mar. 9, 1938.

58. Johnson, *Negro Americans, What Now?,* 103.

59. Downs, "Did My Church Forsake Me?"

60. Lee Lowenfish, *Branch Rickey: Baseball's Ferocious Gentleman* (Lincoln: University of Nebraska Press, 2007), 289–90.

61. Karl E. Downs, *Meet the Negro* (Los Angeles: Methodist Youth Fellowship Southern California–Arizona Annual Conference, 1943), 21, 24.

62. Ibid., 21, 24, 27.

63. Rampersad, *Jackie Robinson,* 113–14.

64. Robinson, *Baseball Has Done It,* 30.

65. Robinson, *I Never Had It Made,* 82–83.

66. R. E. Dixon, "Skipper's Southwest Sports-o-Graph," *Atlanta Daily World,* Mar. 3, 1948.

67. Robinson, *Baseball Has Done It,* 31.

68. Robinson, *I Never Had It Made,* 23; Robinson, *Baseball Has Done It,* 32.

69. Randy Dixon, "Exhibit A in a So-Called Democracy: The Case of Jackie Robinson," *Pittsburgh Courier,* Sept. 6, 1941.

70. Herman Hill, "Chi White Sox Reject Race Players," *Pittsburgh Courier,* Mar. 21, 1942.

71. Rampersad, *Jackie Robinson,* 89–91.

72. Philip McGuire, *He, Too, Spoke for Democracy: Judge Hastie, World War II, and the Black Soldier* (New York: Greenwood, 1988), 9, 29.

73. Golenbeck, *Bums,* 132.

74. Rampersad, *Jackie Robinson,* 97–109.

75. Charlie Cherokee, "National Grapevine," *Chicago Defender,* Aug. 12, 1944.

76. The only notice in the major Black newspapers was "Jackie Robinson Freed at Army Court-Martial," *Pittsburgh Courier,* Sept. 9, 1944.

77. The earliest account I could find was an autobiographical account: Jackie Robinson, "Cleared on Charges in the Army," *Washington Post,* Aug. 27, 1949.

78. Jackie Robinson, *My Own Story,* as told to Wendell Smith (New York: Greenberg, 1949), 19.

79. Robinson, *I Never Had It Made,* 34.

80. "Let America Be America Again," in *The Collected Poems of Langston Hughes,* ed. Arnold Rampersad (New York: Vintage Books, 1994), 189–91.

81. Roi Ottley, *"New World a-Coming": Inside Black America* (Cleveland: World Publishing, 1943).

82. Roi Ottley, "New World A-Comin," *New York Amsterdam News,* Apr. 1, 1944.

83. Adam Clayton Powell Jr., *Marching Blacks: An Interpretive History of the Rise of the Common Black Man* (New York: Dial, 1945), 3, 204.

84. Gamewell Valentine, "Theme and Variations," *Atlanta Daily World,* Feb. 16, 1940.

85. Rampersad, *Jackie Robinson*, 113–34.

86. Sol White, *Sol White's History of Colored Base Ball, with Other Documents on the Early Black Game, 1886–1936*, ed. Jerry Malloy (1907; repr., Lincoln: University of Nebraska Press, 1995), 74.

87. The literature on African American baseball is voluminous. See, for example, Neil Lanctot, *Negro League Baseball: The Rise and Fall of a Black Institution* (Philadelphia: University of Pennsylvania Press, 2004).

88. Donn Rogosin, *Invisible Men: Life in Baseball's Negro Leagues* (1983; repr. Lincoln: University of Nebraska Press, 2007), 219.

89. "Naziism in Baseball," *New York Amsterdam News*, Apr. 15, 1939. See also Lucius Harper, "Dustin' off the News," *Chicago Defender*, May 21, 1938. If Major League teams barred Black players, they generally welcomed Black fans. Sportsmen's Park in St. Louis, home of the Cardinals and the Browns, was the last stadium to officially end segregated seating in 1944, though informal restrictions evidently remained; Brian Carroll, *When to Stop the Cheering? The Black Press, the Black Community, and the Integration of Professional Baseball* (New York: Routledge, 2007), 132; George Vecsey, "A Journal from Ebbets Field to the Steps of the Capitol," *New York Times*, Jan. 17, 2009.

90. Tygiel, *Baseball's Great Experiment*, 348.

91. Sol White, "The Grand Old Game," *New York Amsterdam News*, Dec. 18, 1929, reprinted in White, *Sol White's History of Colored Base Ball*, 153.

92. Jonathan Scott Holloway, *Confronting the Veil: Abram Harris, Jr., E. Franklin Frazier, and Ralph Bunche, 1919–1941* (Chapel Hill: University of North Carolina Press, 2002).

93. Carroll, *When to Stop the Cheering?*, 65.

94. Ibid., 86–87.

95. *The Sporting News*, July 23, 1942, cited in Rick Swaine, *The Integration of Major League Baseball: A Team by Team History* (Jefferson, NC: McFarland, 2009), 22.

96. Gunnar Myrdal, *An American Dilemma: The Negro Problem and American Democracy* (New York: Harper and Brothers, 1944), 40–42.

97. "Rickey Takes Slap at Negro Leagues," *New York Times*, Oct. 25, 1945; "Rickey Predicts Complete Integration by Big Leagues," *Cleveland Call and Post*, July 5, 1947.

98. Fay Young, "End of Baseball's Jim Crow Seen with the Signing of Robinson," *Chicago Defender*, Nov. 3, 1945; "Rickey Cites Wire to Refute Critics," *New York Times*, Oct. 26, 1945.

99. Arthur Daley, "Short Shots in Sundry Directions," *New York Times*, Oct. 25, 1945. A few months later, Daley thought a skit in which a reporter in blackface said, "Massa Rickey done bote me from da Kansas City Monarchs," was the height of hilarity. Daley, "At the Baseball Writer's Show," ibid., Feb. 4, 1946.

100. Young, "End of Baseball's Jim Crow Seen with the Signing of Robinson."

101. Later signings of Negro League players by Major League teams usually included some compensation to the parent clubs.

102. "Will Appeal to Chandler," *New York Times*, Oct. 24, 1945; "Rickey Takes Slap at Negro Leagues."

103. Young, "End of Baseball's Jim Crow Seen with the Signing of Robinson."

104. Sam Lacy, "Players Indifferent about Entering Major Leagues," *Baltimore Afro-American*, Aug. 12, 1939.

105. Dan Burley, "Purely Baseball and Satchell Paige," *New York Amsterdam News*, Aug. 15, 1942.

106. Ibid.; Lucius Jones, "Satchell Paige Admits He Wouldn't Risk Present Fame for Big Leagues," *Atlanta Daily World*, Aug. 8, 1942.

107. Jones, "Satchel Paige (West), Josh Gibson (East) in Dream Game Today."

108. "Branch Rickey and the Future," *New York Amsterdam News*, Aug. 14, 1948.

109. Burley, "Purely Baseball and Satchell Paige."

110. "Why Not White Players on Negro Teams?," *New Journal and Guide*, Dec. 29, 1945.

111. Jackie Robinson, "What's Wrong with Negro Baseball," *Ebony* (June 1948): 16–18.

112. Carroll, *When to Stop the Cheering?*, 93.

113. Quoted in Dan Burley, "Confidentially Yours," *New York Amsterdam News*, Aug. 15, 1942.

114. Alvin Moss, "Negro League Baseball Must Survive," *Atlanta Daily World*, Feb. 5, 1948.

115. Carroll, *When to Stop the Cheering?*, 167.

116. Ibid., 149.

117. See, for example, Rogosin, *Invisible Men*, 79–82. There were some differences between Major League and Negro League baseball, in part because the Black teams had only fourteen to sixteen men on their rosters. For an argument that the dissimilarities between the way Negro League and Major League baseball was played have been exaggerated, see Bill James, *The New Bill James Historical Baseball Abstract* (New York: Free Press, 2001), 320–22.

118. Tygiel, *Baseball's Great Experiment*, 348.

119. Amiri Baraka, *The Autobiography of Leroi Jones* (Chicago: Lawrence Hill Books, 1997), 51.

120. For a discussion, see Tygiel, *Baseball's Great Experiment*, 347–49.

121. See Peter Eisenstadt, *Against the Hounds of Hell: A Life of Howard Thurman* (Charlottesville: University of Virginia Press, 2021), 375.

122. "Rickey Takes Slap at Negro Leagues."

123. For Rickey's enthusiasm for the Myrdal report, see Lowenfish, *Branch Rickey*, 351. See ibid., 415–16, for his interest in Frank Tannenbaum's *Slave and Citizen* (New York: Vintage Books, 1946).

124. Myrdal, *American Dilemma*, 989n2.

125. Henry D. Fetter, "The Party Line and the Color Line: The American Communist Party, the Daily Worker, and Jackie Robinson," *Journal of Sports History* 28, no. 3 (Fall 2001): 375–402 (quote, 382).

126. "Jackie Tells Afro He 'Won't Let 'Em Down,'" *Baltimore Afro-American*, Nov. 3, 1945.

127. "Rickey Takes Slap at Negro Leagues."

128. Lowenfish, *Branch Rickey*, 358–59.

129. Tygiel, *Extra Bases*, 37.

130. Branch Rickey, "One Hundred Percent Wrong Club" Speech, Atlanta, GA, Jan. 20, 1956, By Popular Demand: Jackie Robinson and Other Baseball Highlights, 1860s–1960s, Library of Congress, https://www.loc.gov/collections/jackie-robinson-baseball/articles-and-essays/baseball-the-color -line-and-jackie-robinson/one-hundred-percent-wrong-club-speech/ (accessed May 27, 2019).

131. Michael Carte, "It's a Press Victory, Says Jackie Robinson," *Baltimore Afro-American*, Nov. 3, 1946.

132. Tygiel, *Baseball's Great Experiment*, 246–64, 306–8.

133. Kimberley L. Phillips, *War! What Is It Good For? Black Freedom Struggles and the Military from World War II to Iraq* (Chapel Hill: University of North Carolina Press, 2012); Charles C. Moskos and John Sibley Butler, *Black Leadership and Racial Integration the Army Way* (New York: Basic Books, 1996).

134. "Major Leagues Ignore Colored Stars," *Norfolk (VA) Journal and Guide*, May 27, 1967.

135. For Robinson at Chock Full o' Nuts, see Rampersad, *Jackie Robinson*, 303–4, 320–23 (quote, 322).

136. "Negro Businesses in Harlem Rising," *New York Times*, Aug. 28, 1967.

137. See, for example, "Robinson Heads March at City Housing Bill," *New York Amsterdam News*, Oct. 26, 1957; "3,000 to March on DC: Jackie Robinson Will Lead Way," ibid., Oct. 25, 1958; "Jackie Urges Students to Continue Picketing," *Baltimore Afro-American*, Mar. 19, 1960.

138. Robinson was a columnist for the *New York Post* from April 1959 to November 1960—he was let go for his support of Nixon in the 1960 election—and at the *New York Amsterdam News* from 1962 through 1968. In these endeavors, he used his friend Al Duckett Jr. as a ghostwriter, who also collaborated with Robinson on his autobiography.

139. "Battle against Tradition: Martin Luther King Jr.," *New York Times*, Mar. 21, 1956.

140. Earl Conrad, *Jim Crow America* (New York: Duell, Sloan, and Pearce, 1947), 167.

141. Martin D. Jenkins, "Problems Incident to Racial Integration and Some Suggested Approaches to these Problems," *Journal of Negro Education* 21, no. 3 (Summer 1952): 411–21. Leonard Buder, "City Schools Open a Major Campaign to Spur Integration," *New York Times*, July 24, 1956. The article explained the concept of "de facto segregation" to its readers.

142. "Thurmond Expects 100 Elector Votes," *New York Times*, Oct. 1, 1948.

143. A good example of the mid-1950s quantitative overoptimism about integration is David Loth and Harold Fleming, *Integration North and South* (New York: Fund for the Republic, 1956).

144. Langston Hughes, "No Civil War without an Atomic Bomb, Says Simple," *Chicago Defender*, May 28, 1955.

145. "Jackie Robinson Urges Race Integration Case," *Los Angeles Times*, Feb. 16, 1954.

146. "Jackie Robinson Urges Negroes to Uphold Rights," *Washington Post*, Sept. 18, 1957.

147. "Jackie Robinson Says NAACP Shuns Force," *Washington Post*, Apr. 1, 1957.

148. For Robinson's HUAC appearance, see Rampersad, *Jackie Robinson*, 211–16.

149. Robinson, *I Never Had It Made*, 94–98.

150. For a spirited defense of the NAACP during the 1940s and early 1950s as a progressive civil rights organization domestically and internationally, see Carol Anderson, *Bourgeois Radicals: The NAACP and the Struggle for Colonial Liberation, 1940–1960* (Cambridge: Cambridge University Press, 2015).

151. "Text of Jackie Robinson's Statement to House Unit," *New York Times*, July 19, 1949.

152. Ibid.

153. *New York Post*, Mar. 25, 1960, cited in *Beyond Home Plate: Jackie Robinson on Life after Baseball*, ed. Michael G. Long (Syracuse, NY: Syracuse University Press, 2013), 69; Jackie Robinson, "HST—Man from Nowhere Going Home," *New York Amsterdam News*, June 10, 1961.

154. See Joshua D. Farrington, *Black Republicans and the Transformation of the GOP* (Philadelphia: University of Pennsylvania Press, 2016).

155. Jackie Robinson, "Nixon Candidacy Imperils America," *New York Amsterdam News*, Aug. 17, 1968.

156. Michael G. Long, *First Class Citizenship: The Civil Rights Letters of Jackie Robinson* (New York: Times Books, 2007), 314–15.

157. Jackie Robinson, "Serious Trouble," *New York Amsterdam News*, Apr. 25, 1964.

158. Jackie Robinson, "New Challenges," *New York Amsterdam News*, Feb. 26, 1966.

159. Jackie Robinson, "Note to GOP: Go to Hell," *New York Amsterdam News*, Aug. 17, 1968.

160. Charles Silberman, *Crisis in Black and White* (New York: Random House, 1964), 304; Peter Eisenstadt, *Rochdale Village: Robert Moses, 6,000 Families, and New York City's Great Experiment in Integrated Housing* (Ithaca, NY: Cornell University Press, 2010), 159–60.

161. "Malcolm X and James Farmer: Separation or Integration: A Debate" (1962), in *Black Protest Thought in the Twentieth Century*, ed. August Meier et al., 2nd ed. (Indianapolis, Bobbs-Merrill, 1971), 395–96.

162. Nathan Glazer, "Is 'Integration' Possible in New York Schools?," in *American Race Relations Today*, ed. Earl Raab (Garden City, NY: Doubleday, 1962), 135–63 (quote, 148).

163. Stokely Carmichael and Charles V. Hamilton, *Black Power: The Politics of Liberation in America* (New York: Vintage Books, 1967), 54; Robert S. Browne and Bayard Rustin, *Separatism or Integration: Which Way America?* (New York: A. Philip Randolph Educational Fund, 1969), 10; Ivan Brandon, "SCLC Head Urges Pan Africanism: Integration Called Conspiracy," *Washington Post*, Sept. 7, 1970.

164. Martin Luther King Jr., *Where Do We Go from Here: Chaos or Community?* (Boston: Beacon, 1967), 62.

165. Patrick Henry, "Kareem's Omission? Jackie Robinson, Black Profile in Courage," in *Jackie Robinson: Race, Sports, and the American Dream*, ed. Joseph Dorinson and Joram Warmund (Armonk, NY: M. E. Sharpe, 1998), 209.

166. Malcolm X, "Malcolm X's Letter" *New York Amsterdam News*, Nov. 30, 1963.

167. Jackie Robinson, "Jackie Robinson again Writes to Malcolm X," *New York Amsterdam News*, Dec. 4, 1963.

168. Jackie Robinson, "Cassius Did More Than Just Win," *New York Amsterdam News*, Mar. 14, 1964.

169. Jackie Robinson, "The Right to Hate," *New York Amsterdam News*, Aug. 25, 1962.

170. "Toward a Black Middle Class: Sea Host, Inc. [interview with Jackie Robinson]," *Fast Food: The Magazine of the Restaurant Business* (Nov. 1969), in Long, *Beyond Home Plate*, 63–64.

171. Jackie Robinson, "The Police and the Black Panthers," *New York Amsterdam News*, Apr. 12, 1968; Robinson, "West Coast Action! Reaction in New York?," *New York Amsterdam News*, Sept. 21, 1968; Robinson, *I Never Had It Made*, 280–81.

172. Robinson, *I Never Had It Made*, 281–82.

173. Jackie Robinson, "Mixed Emotions over Boycott of Olympics," *New York Amsterdam News*, Dec. 16, 1967.

174. Jackie Robinson, "Foes of Vietnam Policy Should Pause to Fight Dixie Murderers," *Philadelphia Tribune*, Dec. 28, 1965.

175. Jackie Robinson, "LBJ Deserves Support in Vietnam," *New York Amsterdam News*, Oct. 21, 1967.

176. Jackie Robinson, "Don't Forget the Home-Style Enemy," *New York Amsterdam News*, June 3, 1967.

177. Jackie Robinson, "What I Think of Dr. Martin King," *New York Amsterdam News*, July 1, 1967.

178. Jackie Robinson, "Mr. Cellar Sounds off Again," *New York Amsterdam News*, May 6, 1967; Clayton Willis, "Draft Arrests Aimed at Stokely: Jackie Robinson Says They Are," ibid., Jan. 13, 1967.

179. Robinson, "Nixon Candidacy Imperils America."

180. Jackie Robinson, "A Reply to Bill Buckley," *New York Amsterdam News*, Sept. 7, 1968.

181. Alfred Duckett, "Jackie in Hot Answer to Rustin," *New York Amsterdam News*, May 10, 1969.

182. For the strike, see Eisenstadt, *Rochdale Village*, 191–214.

183. Duckett, "Jackie in Hot Answer to Rustin."

184. Jon Nordheimer, "Flag on July 4th: Thrill to Some, Threat to Others," *New York Times*, July 4, 1971.

185. Jackie Robinson to Nelson Rockefeller, May 2, 1972, in Long, *First Class Citizenship*, 314–15.

186. Nelson Rockefeller to Jackie Robinson, May 8, 1972, ibid., 315–16.

187. Rampersad, *Jackie Robinson*, 313.

188. Robinson, *I Never Had It Made*, 277.

189. Ibid., 203.

190. Ibid., 251.

Lincoln and the Two Reconstructions
The Unfinished Work of American Equality

JERALD PODAIR

On the evening of April 11, 1865, Abraham Lincoln stood at a White House window before a joyous crowd gathered on the lawn to celebrate the surrender of Robert E. Lee's Army of Northern Virginia at Appomattox two days earlier. It had to be a moment of deep gratification for this much-maligned man, who had suffered so deeply over the past four years. But now the people of Washington had come to cheer and honor him. The expectant crowd was somewhat taken aback by the tenor of Lincoln's brief speech. Eschewing triumphalism, as he had in his second inaugural address a month earlier, the president spoke generally about Reconstruction, promising a more detailed set of plans in the future and gingerly suggesting that certain categories of African Americans be given the right to vote. It was clear, however, that victory was at hand.

But who had won? And what had won? That was much less clear as Lincoln spoke. The Union had won, of course. Grant had won. Lincoln had won. One could also say that emancipation and a northern culture of free labor, enterprise, and growth had won. Almost four million freedpeople, participants in and beneficiaries of history's single greatest act of human liberation, had certainly won because slavery was doomed. Beyond these, the future was as misty as that April evening.

Both the political and economic ramifications of slavery's demise would need to be sorted out under singularly unpropitious circumstances. The northern white population was deeply divided over the question of what rights the freedpeople were entitled to, with a substantial number questioning the very nature of their humanity. The Democratic Party in the North, tarnished as it was by its association with opposition to what was now a popular war, still possessed the power to mobilize a potent constituency. The white South lay in ruins, yet remained unrepentant and unreconstructed. The victorious Republican Party itself was divided. A left flank called for a root-and-branch transformation in political and economic conditions in the South, the logical climax of a war viewed in revolutionary terms. A more numerous and cautious group of moderates, with less-well-defined views of the direction of the postwar South, understood the "rights" to be enumerated, legislated, and enforced there more in terms of the legal and procedural than in the material and substantive.

Then, of course, there was Lincoln himself. It is impossible to divine the inner thoughts of this complex and elusive man. But as he looked to the futures of those he had helped free and pondered a South without slavery, Lincoln was impelled by a series of principles, beliefs, and impulses that he projected on the conditions that lay before him, all filtered through the prism of his own experiences. As is also so often the case, the implications of those principles, beliefs, and impulses clashed, competed, and contradicted.

Lincoln believed deeply in human equality, which he defined not as an inherent equality of ability or an expectation of equality of life outcomes but as the equality conferred by the doctrine of free labor, under which every individual, including African Americans, enjoyed the right to keep the fruits of what they had worked for and earned. Lincoln held to this understanding of economic equality even before he began to come around to broader understandings of political equality—that is, even before he advocated voting and other civil rights for African Americans—because of his commitment to free labor. It was one of his lodestars, and he articulated it many times, notably during his 1858 debates with Stephen Douglas, when he averred that he had "no purpose to introduce political and social equality between the white and black races" and agreed with Douglas that the Black man "is not my equal in many respects," nevertheless, "in the right to eat the bread, without the leave of anybody else, which his own hand earns, he is my equal and the equal of Judge Douglas, and the equal of every living man."[1]

Free labor and its corresponding "right to rise" defined Lincoln's life. He wanted his story to be every American's story, North and South. Lincoln was intensely proud of his personal narrative of success, as embodied by his status as an attorney. The home he cherished the most was not the White House or even the Kentucky cabin in which he was born, but his two-story home on Eighth and Jackson Streets in Springfield, Illinois, because it symbolized his free-labor ascension to a respectable professional position. That house meant that he had worked, acquired property, and left his humble origins far behind. It meant America had worked. "I want every man," Lincoln said in 1860, "to have the chance—and I believe a black man is entitled to it—in which he can better his condition—when he may look forward and hope to be a hired laborer this year and the next, work for himself afterward, and finally to hire men to work for him! That is the true system."[2] It was Lincoln's hope, and that of his fellow Republicans, that this would be the trajectory of freedpeople in the emancipated South.

We know, unfortunately, what happened next. A tragic assassination, only three days after Lincoln's April 11 speech; a new president, whose devotion to free-labor principles, to the extent that they existed, extended only to white men; a defiant white South determined to preserve its social, political, and racial cultures and prerogatives as much as possible; institutions such as the Freedmen's Bureau that did not realize their full transformational potential; laws and constitutional amendments aimed at conferring legal and political rights, effective for a brief window of time, then eviscerated by redeemed southern governments, a hostile judiciary, and white terror; and, finally, the collective failure of will of most in the North to continue the struggle for change in the South in the face of financial crisis, labor unrest, and a growing, gnawing sense that the South would not and could not change—at least not then.

Neither did there develop a systematic and effective program of land redistribution to the freedpeople: Not from the Freedmen's Bureau, which did not transfer lands that had been confiscated from rebels. Not from President Johnson, whose generous pardons ensured that most white former Confederates would keep their lands. Not from Congress, which rejected appeals by Congressman Thaddeus Stevens to make land available to the freedpeople. And not even from Major General William T. Sherman's famous January 1865 Special Field Order No. 15, setting aside lands along the South Carolina and Georgia coasts for Black settlement and cultivation, most of which eventually wound up back in white hands.

Land, of course, was no cure for all ills. The freedpeople would have also required access to credit, viable markets, and the legal rights and political power with which to protect their interests. As Adrienne Petty and Mark Schultz have shown elsewhere in this volume, the process of land acquisition by African American farmers was much more advanced than scholars have assumed, with some 25 percent of southern Black farmers owning land by 1900.[3] That this positive development was nonetheless accompanied by Jim Crow and disenfranchisement in the late nineteenth and early twentieth centuries challenges the idea that landownership was the precondition to African American independence and empowerment. Perhaps this rate of acquisition was simply not enough to exert any substantial force on the southern edifice of white supremacy. But land, and as much of it as possible, would have at least partially fulfilled Lincoln's free-labor aspirations for African Americans, launching them on a journey that bore at least some resemblance to his own—not from rags to riches, but from rags to a reasonably secure and independent respectability.

This, of course, makes Lincoln's death all the more devastating. We may console ourselves with the idea that events would have taken a different turn had he lived, that Lincoln would have achieved the metamorphosis in postwar southern life that we today desire to see. But perhaps we ask too much of Lincoln. Perhaps we invest him too thoroughly with our own desires, aspirations, and hopes. Lincoln was the product of many contravening forces, and they did not lead him in a single, unwavering direction. His devotion to free labor and its implications, in fact, may well have constrained his responses to the land question in the postbellum South and the larger question of American equality with which it was intertwined.

For Lincoln, the right to rise was predicated on the dignity of work and the sanctity of its proprietary rewards. Lincoln the constitutionalist had trod very carefully on property rights before and during the war. He was, after all, willing to guarantee the continuance of southern property rights in human beings in a desperate attempt to avert secession, and his articulation of the Emancipation Proclamation as an exercise of presidential war power subject to constitutional legitimization is also well known. Lincoln approved Sherman's Special Field Order No. 15, but this too was a product of war and subject to ratification and modification.

The pre-emancipation Lincoln was willing to protect ill-gotten human property in the rebellious states, albeit reluctantly and unhappily. It required extraordinary circumstances—a state of national emergency constituting a mortal threat to the continued existence of the United States—to force the president to elide his instinctive reverence for property rights in issuing the Emancipation Proclamation as an executive order.

But with the war concluded and the emergency at an end, would Lincoln have been willing to extend the idea of "ill-gotten" gains to real property, even that held by rebels, in the face of his constitutionalism and respect for the prerogatives of individual gain? The process of land acquisition in the South was deeply implicated in the system of human bondage, and Lincoln knew this. He also held the egalitarian principles of the Declaration of Independence in high regard. Lincoln had built his political philosophy, public persona, and war leadership around them. The land-for-freedpeople issue forced Americans, North and South, to define equality with uncomfortable precision. It has been observed that Americans integrate by class almost as reluctantly as they do by race, and the word "redistribution," especially when applied to economic resources, has not been a popular one in most eras of American history. Nor was it favored by Lincoln, who prized the right of Americans to retain the product of their labors.

Accordingly, in the remainder of his second term as president and in the years after 1869 as the elder statesman of the Republican Party and the nation, there is a question as to whether Lincoln would have been willing to do the things he would have had to do to ensure that the freedpeople received what was essential to any real condition of equality in a reconstructed America, what he himself had famously articulated as a national goal at the beginning of the Civil War: "to lift artificial weights from all shoulders—to clear the paths of laudable pursuit for all—to afford all, an unfettered start, and a fair chance, in the race of life."[4] A "fair chance in the race of life" for all was very close to Lincoln's heart, but would he have been willing to risk a second Civil War—and we know what transpired in the South after 1865 in the face of politically egalitarian measures, to say nothing of economic ones—in order to achieve it? Lincoln desired economic justice for the freedpeople, but as a fervent American nationalist, he also wanted a reunified nation. It may not have been so much a question of what he wanted, but what he wanted more.

By the mid-1870s, then, Lincoln may very well have been where so many of his fellow Republicans were, whipsawed between a series of competing impulses: A desire not only for some form of economic equity in the South but also for a stable, reintegrating southern economy that was safe for northern investment;

not only a lingering sense of anger at white southern recalcitrance, at political fraud, and at acts of domestic terrorism but also a sense of exhaustion at the high cost of effecting change in the South, of the amount of blood and treasure already expended, and how much more would have to be expended to protect that change; not only a belief in the promise of free labor, even in the face of the rising force of postwar industrial capitalism and finance that threatened to make a mockery of it, but also a deference to property rights and constitutionalism; a longing not only for a new nation but also for a reconciled nation, even with many of its promises to African Americans left unfulfilled; and not only an understanding of the importance of land to the African American vision of equality and freedom but also a fear of the implications of property redistribution in the South for a North in economic turmoil and rent by class and labor strife.

Republicans, torn as they were between these competing impulses, followed those that best served their own interests. Lincoln would have as well. He would doubtlessly have worked assiduously to build up the Republican Party in the South after the war, creating a constituency of poor and working-class whites, northern transplants, and newly enfranchised African Americans. But it is possible that his inherent sense of caution would have run up against the limits of his commitment to social, political, and economic change in the South.

Speculations as to how Lincoln would have approached the issues of economic and political equality in the years following the Civil War are inherently unprovable. There is value in the attempt, however, because of the contingencies inherent in what was done and left undone by the historical actors who made the decisions that Lincoln would have faced had he lived. We do not and cannot know what he would have done, but we do know what Ulysses S. Grant did when confronted with the issues of equality, freedom, and citizenship that Lincoln would have confronted later in his second term as president and as the titular leader of the Republican Party afterward. We know that Grant, after a vigorous effort to advance the rights of African Americans in the postwar South, had concluded by the mid-1870s that the price of Reconstruction—in social turmoil, diverted resources, and damage to the Republicans nationally—could no longer be borne. We also know what a later president, Lyndon Johnson, did during another civil rights era that bore more than a passing historical resemblance to the years of Reconstruction.

*   *   *

Abraham Lincoln and Lyndon Johnson inhabited eras with different political cultures, social arrangements, economic systems, stages of technological and scientific advancement, and levels of American global hegemony. But there was still much they had in common: southern roots, humble beginnings, a talent for self-promotion, the qualities of the self-made man, ambitions that knew no rest, and, most significantly, commitments to equal opportunity and the right to rise for every American. Both knew all too well "the short and simple annals of the poor," as Lincoln described his childhood, as well as the sting and shame of failure.[5] Both were master politicians with an instinct for recognizing what was possible and what was beyond reach, which they leavened with an idealized view of America as, in Lincoln's immortal phrase, "the last best hope of earth."[6]

But for all their romanticized notions of America as a land of unbridled promise, neither man was comfortable with the idea of redistribution of economic resources, preferring policies that would offer opportunity and training in an open, growth-oriented society rather than a guaranteed outcome in the American race of life. This was the foundation on which Johnson based his War on Poverty. Even as he assembled the legislative edifice of what would be aptly characterized as a "Second Reconstruction," Johnson was much more willing to redistribute political power, in the form of voting rights and access to public accommodations, than to transfer economic resources from one group of Americans to another. It is thus possible that an examination of the path of Lyndon Johnson's Reconstruction, and its ultimate fate, could shed light on what Lincoln's may have resembled.

Lyndon Johnson saw in his unexpected presidency an opportunity to reunite his native South with the rest of the United States. For the better part of a century, it had been a region apart, with its own set of economic relations, social structures, historical traditions, and, of course, racial systems. But Johnson viewed civil rights legislation, as well as his planned War on Poverty, as mediums through which the South could be reconstructed and brought back into the mainstream of American life. The civil rights bill that John F. Kennedy had hoped to pass, and which the new president was determined to enact, along with the voting rights legislation that Johnson also planned, would secure African Americans the legal and political equality they had been denied in the South since the failure of the first Reconstruction. The programs of the War on Poverty, which Kennedy had envisioned and Johnson also intended to realize, would offer a measure of economic support to disadvantaged Americans, including African Americans, whose median family income in 1965 was approximately 55 percent that of whites.[7]

Johnson viewed the re-enfranchisement of southern African Americans and the institution of antipoverty programs both as matters of simple justice and means to strengthen the Democratic Party, with the combination of high-minded idealism and ruthless opportunism that was the sum of his career in American politics. "I think we just gave the South to the Republicans," Johnson mused after he signed the Civil Rights Act on July 2, 1964, although he still held out hope that an influx of Black voters, combined with a segment of racially moderate whites, could preserve some degree of Democratic electoral power in the region.[8]

But as much as Johnson desired to make the South and America as a whole more just and equitable, and as much as he wished to offer African Americans full political citizenship, there were still places he would not go as well as places that whites, both South and North, would not let him go. An illustration came at the Democratic National Convention in August 1964, when Johnson moved to squelch a challenge to the seating of the all-white "Regular" Mississippi state delegation, an action brought by the integrated Mississippi Freedom Democratic Party (MFDP) and the voter-activist Student Nonviolent Coordinating Committee (SNCC).

Johnson had planned the convention as a triumphant coronation, which a racially charged battle over delegate credentials would disrupt, and he went so far as to hold an impromptu press conference on a pretext in order to preempt testimony by voting rights crusader Fannie Lou Hamer detailing the brutalities she had suffered at the hands of Mississippi authorities. Still hoping to somehow appease the white South, the president insisted on the seating of the Regular Mississippi delegation, with two "at-large" votes promised to the MFDP as a consolation offering. That, along with Johnson's promise that future Democratic national convention delegates would be selected on a nondiscriminatory basis, was viewed by MFDP and SNCC leaders as merely a continuation of racial politics as usual and a signal that the president wanted to have it both ways, courting the Black South while pandering to the white South. They rejected the compromise and walked out of the convention.

The MFDP controversy showed that, even as he pursued long-delayed racial justice, Johnson would have to navigate a narrow path between African American aspirations and southern white fears. He would also need to reckon with the fears of the essential element of the Democratic Party's base in the North: urban white and ethnic voters. These men and women had been the beneficiaries of New Deal policies that had propelled them from poverty to middle-class, or at the least stable working-class, status. The New Deal had taken them out of the slums and in the direction of the expanding suburbs, increasing their spatial and social distance from the nonwhites who were left behind. If these northern whites wished to be as far away from nonwhites, and especially African Americans, as possible, and Johnson pressed ahead with civil rights legislation that would effectively shrink that distance, how would they respond?

By 1964, these heretofore loyal Democrats had alternatives. Accepting the Republican presidential nomination in July of that year, and speaking as a serious racial disturbance was beginning in New York City's Harlem neighborhood, Senator Barry Goldwater, a states' rights Arizona conservative, pointedly used the words "freedom" or "free" more than thirty times in his acceptance speech, only mentioning "equality" twice, as he railed against "those who seek to live your lives for you" and "the growing menace in our country tonight, to personal safety, to life, to limb and property."[9] Goldwater's rhetoric was calibrated to resonate among whites concerned about crime rates, civil disorders, school integration, and "neighborhood change" in the North and the imminent demise of Jim Crow in the South.[10] Although Johnson won an overwhelming victory in November's presidential election, the warning signs for him and his party were clear. Segregationist Alabama governor George Wallace, running in the Wisconsin and Maryland Democratic presidential primaries that year, had polled at 34 and 43 percent, respectively, receiving a majority of ballots cast by whites in the latter state.[11] In California, a proposed fair-housing act had been overwhelmingly rejected by referendum, and Republican George Murphy, an opponent of the act and self-avowed spokesman for white middle-class homeowners, was elected to the US Senate.

These results gave Johnson pause, and his fears of losing his party's electoral backbone played a major role in his planning for the War on Poverty. The president believed in opportunity, not largesse. Growing up in poverty in rural Texas, he had been repelled by the humiliations of charity, and these instincts led him to foreshorten the scope of his antipoverty visions. His War on Poverty was as significant for what it did not do as for what it did. Even while it was in its initial stages during the Kennedy administration, its progenitors were told not to employ the terms "redistribution of income or wealth" and "inequality" for fear they would be interpreted as proposals to transfer resources from the middle to the lower classes.[12] In one of his last conversations on antipoverty initiatives, Kennedy emphasized that it was "also . . . important to make clear that we're doing something for the middle-income man in the suburbs."[13]

Johnson was cautious as well. The War on Poverty, he insisted, could and should be funded from the wealth and output of a growing US economy, one that had been expanding consistently since the end of World War II, without the necessity of major tax increases, significant deficit spending, or confiscatory class legislation. The president rejected the idea of a guaranteed national income as part of the program, viewing it as demeaning and initiative stifling, not to mention prohibitively expensive. Similarly, a federal employment program, in Johnson's view, was a potential budget breaker as well as a threat to the health and viability of the private-sector economy.[14] The president had seen how nationally administered jobs programs worked during the New Deal; indeed, he had helped run one of them, the National Youth Administration. He had also been in Congress in the 1940s during the fight to pass a full-employment bill that was criticized as socialistic and ultimately failed.[15] Now, as president, he resolved to build his War on Poverty around education and training, not redistribution, offering the opportunity to rise in an expanding economy without requiring white middle- and working-class Americans to make substantial sacrifices on behalf of the marginalized.

Johnson did speak of making social and economic conditions for African Americans more equitable, as when, during his 1965 Howard University commencement speech, he averred, "you do not take a person who, for years, has been hobbled by chains and liberate him, bring him up to the starting line of a race and then say 'you are free to compete with all the others,' and still justly believe that you have been completely fair."[16] There were also elements of the War on Poverty, including Medicaid, an expanded Social Security program, and Head Start, that involved direct grants of services and resources. But Johnson's intentions were not redistributionist in nature, and his understanding of "opportunity" included a respect for property rights, both inherited and earned. If the impoverished were to be lifted up to economic security, it would not be at the expense of those who were already there.

But even this was too much for millions of white Democrats, North and South, who responded to civil and voting rights legislation and the War on Poverty, as well as civil disorders and upsurges in crime rates, with a pronounced rightward shift that came to be known as "white backlash." The 1966 congressional elections produced Republican gains of three Senate and forty-seven House seats, including twenty-three in the South, creating the largest GOP constituency there since the first Reconstruction era.[17] The party also added some seven hundred seats in state legislatures around the country and won eight governorships, notably in California, where Ronald Reagan channeled anger at campus unrest, open housing, high taxes, and urban violence to defeat liberal Democratic incumbent Edmund Brown by almost one million votes.[18] Four years earlier, Governor Brown had won a resounding reelection victory over Richard Nixon, presumably ending the latter's political career. But now, resurrected as a spokesman for white voters who would soon be known as the "Silent Majority," Nixon became a viable candidate for the Republican presidential nomination in 1968.

The GOP gains of 1966, coupled with the stresses of the escalating war in Vietnam, which robbed domestic initiatives of funds, ticked inflation upward, and diminished his party support, dampened Johnson's remaining enthusiasm for transformational social and economic policy through the mechanism of the War on Poverty. Its programs, especially in the controversial area of community action, where local groups, often based in minority neighborhoods, challenged white-dominated urban political machines for federal funds, began to lapse into stasis. Johnson ignored the 1966 proposal of his political ally, civil rights leader Bayard Rustin, for a "Freedom Budget" that proposed to spend $185 billion over ten years on national jobs and incomes programs that aimed to eradicate poverty in the United States, and he barely acknowledged Dr. Martin Luther King Jr.'s Poor People's Campaign, which had similar goals, even after King's martyrdom in 1968. In November of that year, white-backlash presidential candidates Nixon and Wallace together won 57 percent of the popular vote in a stunning repudiation of the results of four years earlier.

Johnson and the Democrats lost more than the South. Northern white Democratic voters who had likely never pulled a lever for a Republican candidate in their lives had done the unthinkable. While class and cultural resentments played significant roles in this shift away from the Democratic Party, race was the essential wedge, and even Johnson, that legendarily skilled political operative, could do little to stem the tide. Nixon, a redeemer for the twentieth century, would bring the War on Poverty to a close. He would defend inherited property rights, reject the idea of redistributive justice, and embrace a modern version of the free-labor creed of equal opportunity, self-invention, and upward mobility that would not have been out of place in the America of a hundred years earlier. Johnson, whatever his dreams may have been for a truly equitable Great Society, was overcome by forces and impulses among white Americans that he could not control. As well, his own free-labor ethos of work, merit, and individual responsibility, as well as his hard-headed political calculations, limited the directions he would and could go.

In the arc of Johnson's trajectory, we can see the rough outlines of Lincoln's, had he survived to put his own stamp on the years of Reconstruction as president and party elder. Would Lincoln have been willing to support ex-Confederate land confiscation and redistribution on the order of Radical Republican Stevens's 1865 proposal?[19] Would he have been willing to expand the 1866 Southern Homestead Act's land-sale program, which as it stood offered freedpeople access to a limited amount of substandard property with no buyer-financing provisions and a short purchasing window, into a program that provided more-generous opportunities for land acquisition?[20] Would he have been willing to order the Freedmen's Bureau to distribute abandoned and confiscated rebel lands to the freedpeople? Would he have issued pardons to large numbers of high-ranking Confederate political and military officials, restoring their property in the interest of sectional healing and national reconciliation?

After leaving office in 1869 and assuming the role of eminence grise in both party and nation, would Lincoln have endorsed the arguments of the Liberal Republicans—many of whom, including David Davis, Orville Browning, and Lyman Trumbull, were old friends and political allies—that continued federal intervention in southern affairs was counterproductive and futile and instead proposed an alliance of the respectable and responsible "men of property and enterprise" in both regions to thwart rising labor and social unrest?[21] Would he have modified his free-labor principles to support government protection of a restive and rising organized-labor movement?[22] Would he have been willing to endorse the stationing of federal troops in the South indefinitely, sometimes on the floors of state legislatures themselves, or would he have agreed with Grant, the man with whom Lincoln had worked with most closely to save the Union, that the cost of quelling the "annual autumnal outbreaks" of southern violence was by the mid-1870s too high, especially in terms of diminishing northern white support for the Republican Party?[23] Would Lincoln have seconded President Grant's calculation that attempting to save Mississippi for the Republicans in 1875 would lose Ohio, and would he have supported Grant's stand down in the former to make possible the election of future president Rutherford B. Hayes in the latter's governor's race?[24]

Finally, would a now elderly but still influential Lincoln even have been willing to support the Compromise of 1877, which brought the first Reconstruction to an end in the hopes of finally calming the waters of sectional discord and allowing the South to redeem itself through what Hayes overoptimistically termed "honest and capable local self-government," with the added incentive of retaining Republican control of the White House?[25]

When during the Civil War Lincoln claimed famously "not to have controlled events, but confess plainly that events have controlled me," he was not, as some believe, being disingenuous.[26] It is possible that he, like Lyndon Johnson a century later, would have been drawn along by both the momentum of events and by the implications of his own belief systems to promises only partially fulfilled for African Americans. Indeed, he may well have ended his journey through the years of the first Reconstruction essentially where Grant did in 1877. This is less a commentary on Lincoln than on the American people—in Lincoln's time, in Johnson's, and in ours—who, despite their professions to egalitarian ideals, do not truly wish to be equal and cannot even reach a consensus on what the term means.

It is also a commentary on the enduring power of American racism, in all three eras, to attenuate even the nation's most vigorous egalitarian impulses. Where the American impetus toward material success and unequal economic life outcomes ends and racism's sway begins will determine whether the project of completing Lincoln's unfinished work is worth undertaking. Lincoln did not approach the idea of American equality as a literalist, conceding that individual ability was a variable that could not be controlled. But he insisted that every American had an equal right to rise, and he made that principle, expressed in the language of the Declaration of Independence, the motivating force of his public life. Today, many argue that the systemic nature of American racism makes Lincoln's goal of true equality of opportunity impossible to attain. There is much in US history to support this view. But giving up on Lincoln's unfinished work, as enticing as it may appear to those who either have lost their illusions or never had them in the first place, is not a viable option. It would eventually substitute the diktat of the tyrant for the democratic will, however imperfect that will might be. It would thus negate the idea of America itself. Lincoln understood this, even if his contemporaries, North and South, did not. It was why he was willing to fight and to shed lives so that an imperfect Union could go on. It is also why, in an imperfect twenty-first-century Union, Lincoln's unfinished work must go on as well.

NOTES

1. Lincoln-Douglas Debate, Ottawa, IL, Aug. 21, 1858, Lincoln Home National Historic Site, updated Apr. 10, 2015, https://www.nps.gov/liho/learn/historyculture/debate1.htm (accessed Feb. 10, 2020).

2. Abraham Lincoln, Speech at New Haven, CT, Mar. 6, 1860, *Abraham Lincoln: Speeches and Writings, 1859–1865*, ed. Don E. Fehrenbacher (New York: Library of America, 1989), 144.

3. See Adrienne Petty and Mark Schultz's essay in this volume, "Breaking New Ground: African American Landowners and the Pursuit of the American Dream."

4. Abraham Lincoln, Message to Congress in Special Session, July 4, 1861, *Abraham Lincoln: Speeches and Writings*, 259.

5. See Stephen B. Oates, *With Malice toward None: A Life of Abraham Lincoln* (New York: HarperCollins, 1994), 4.

6. Abraham Lincoln, *Great Speeches* (New York: Dover, 1991), 97.

7. US Bureau of the Census, Current Population Reports, ser. P-60, no. 51, "Income in 1965 of Families and Persons in the U.S.," US Government Printing Office, Washington, DC, 1967, https://www2.census.gov/prod2/popscan/p60-051.pdf (accessed Sept. 25, 2021).

8. Quoted in Nicholas Lemann, *The Promised Land: The Great Black Migration and How It Changed America* (New York: Alfred A. Knopf, 1991), 183.

9. "Goldwater's 1964 Acceptance Speech," *Washington Post*, www.washingtonpost.com/wp-srv/politics/daily/may98/goldwaterspeech.htm (accessed Sept. 18, 2018).

10. See Charles J. Holden, Zach Messitte, and Jerald Podair, *Republican Populist: Spiro Agnew and the Origins of Donald Trump's America* (Charlottesville: University of Virginia Press, 2019), 66–69.

11. Ibid., 69; "Wallace for President," *American Experience*, PBS.org, https://www.pbs.org/wgbh/americanexperience/features/wallace-president/ (accessed Sept. 25, 2021); Patrick J. Buchanan, *The Greatest Comeback: How Richard Nixon Rose from Defeat to Create the New Majority* (New York: Crown Forum, 2014), 290.

12. Lemann, *Promised Land*, 131.

13. Ibid., 134.

14. Ibid., 131–32, 154, 170.

15. See Alan Brinkley, *The End of Reform: New Deal Liberalism in Recession and War* (New York: Alfred A. Knopf, 1995), 227–71.

16. Lyndon B. Johnson, "To Fulfill These Rights," June 4, 1965, American Presidency Project, https://www.presidency.ucsb.edu/documents/commencement-address-howard-university-fulfill -these-rights (accessed May 22, 2021).

17. Holden, Messitte, and Podair, *Republican Populist*, 69, 72.

18. Ibid., 71–72.

19. See Orville Vernon Burton, *The Age of Lincoln* (New York: Hill and Wang, 2007), 260.

20. Ibid.

21. Eric Foner, *Reconstruction: America's Unfinished Revolution, 1863–1877* (New York: Harper & Row, 1988), 500, 501.

22. See Burton, *Age of Lincoln*, 313.

23. Ibid., 306.

24. Ibid.

25. Foner, *Reconstruction*, 567.

26. Abraham Lincoln to Albert G. Hodges, Apr. 4, 1864, *Abraham Lincoln: Speeches and Writings*, 585–86.

From Ken Burns's *The Civil War* to History's *Ancient Aliens*

Lincoln's Unfinished Work on Cable Television

JOSHUA CASMIR CATALANO and BRIANA L. POCRATSKY

In the fall of 1990, PBS aired an eleven-hour documentary series on the Civil War that captured the imagination of millions of viewers. Like Abraham Lincoln over a century before him, producer Ken Burns hoped that the "mystic chords of memory" could elicit personal introspection and in the process help heal the nation's wounds. The commercial success of the documentary caught the eyes of historians and media executives alike, as an estimated 13.9 million Americans watched the first episode and nearly 40 million tuned in to at least one broadcast.[1] As of 2020, it is estimated that 80 million Americans have seen the documentary.[2] As historian Robert Toplin commented, the documentary's "extraordinary reception demonstrated that a single television series could stimulate millions of people in the United States and the world to think seriously about the experiences of the past."[3]

The film received nearly universal acclaim for its ability to turn static black-and-white photographs into emotionally moving narratives. But it was not without its critics. Many white southerners accused the film of northern bias and were upset with its "emphasis on slavery as the principle cause of the fighting and racial justice as a centrally important issue in the war."[4] At the same time, many historians wished there would have been a stronger focus on race and were bothered by the inclusion and subsequent celebrity of Confederate apologist Shelby Foote. In the words of Leon Litwack, "Foote is an engaging battlefield guide, a master of the anecdote, and a gifted and charming storyteller, but he is not a good historian."[5] Military historians also found it lacking, as it left viewers with "a skewed sense of the war's military dimension."[6] Historians of gender criticized the production for its inadequate portrayal of women. As Catherine Clinton asserted, "Burns has demonstrated that when it comes to women, he not only doesn't get it, he doesn't seem to care."[7]

Historians also critiqued the documentary for its treatment of race and the legacy of the war. Eric Foner found the film to contain "disturbing echoes" of older romantic and reconciliationist interpretations of the war as it "recapitulate[d] the very historical understanding of the war 'invented' in the 1890s as part of the glorification of the national state and nationwide triumph of white supremacy."[8] Gary Edgerton argued that the film "reaffirmed for the members of its principal audience (which skewed white, male, 35 to 49, and upscale in the ratings) the relevance of their past in an era of unprecedented multicultural redefinition."[9] These concerns, evident to historians in the 1990s, have led to the recent call for a new documentary on the Civil War. As historian Keri Leigh Merritt has argued, "the documentary had an outsized effect on how many Americans think about the war, but it's one that unfortunately led to a fundamental misunderstanding about slavery and its legacies—a failing that both undergirds and fuels the flames of racism today."[10]

In spite of, or perhaps because of, its flaws, Burns created a widely popular documentary that was substantive enough to elicit scholarly debate and critique in the first place. As Toplin concluded, the "debates about *The Civil War* became intense, because the documentary represented perhaps the best modern American example of film's potential to teach history on a mass scale."[11] As Clinton herself acknowledged, this "documentary *Wunderkind* has rejuvenated serious interest in history—from networks, corporations, and perhaps, even the viewing public."[12]

The success of *The Civil War* led to an explosion of history-related programming, including the creation of The History Channel. These developments allowed Edgerton to conclude in 2000 that *"television is the principal means by which most people learn about history today."*[13] Despite the continued popularity of museums and online resources, this assertion remains largely true. Yet the historical programming now presented on television is no longer dominated by the "biographies and quasi-biographical documentaries" of decades past.[14] While PBS and a few other outlets continue to produce educational programming that presents historical content rooted in archival research and scholarly expertise, such as *Reconstruction: America after the Civil War* (2019), other networks such as History (formerly The History Channel) have shifted to more financially profitable programming that is only loosely based on historical content and gives little regard to topical representativeness and nuanced interpretation.[15] As Edgerton noted in 2020, historical programming is now an "entirely new and different kind of programming altogether" that comprises a spectrum of quality, from "comprehensive, complex, and penetrating to trash TV."[16] Ann Gray and Erin Bell have argued that these changes are the result of larger industry forces, such as the intensification of competition, the fragmentation of the audience, branding, and celebrity culture, that are driving content creation. Accordingly, the "search for 'niche' audiences has shaped the requirements of history programmes in relation to choice of periods and topics considered to be attractive to these target audiences."[17] Many of these pressures, in addition to a host of new factors, also apply to the creation of content for streaming services.[18] In the United States, reality television has profoundly reshaped historical programming within a changing political, economic, and social landscape.[19]

The content and quality of this programming deserves sustained and focused academic scrutiny and financial and intellectual resources. Scholars have argued that film and television, and by extension History and its programming, play an important role in historical knowledge production and the present shaping of collective memory, especially in relationship to how audiences engage with historical content in everyday life.[20] As Maurice Halbwachs has explained, our collective memory is sustained by social frameworks, which can include "borrowed memory" from newspapers, books, and family. This allows individuals and societies to acquire memories of events that they did not live through.[21]

One of today's most influential social frameworks is television. If History is in fact transgressing the boundary of infotainment and is directly influencing our social frameworks, what kind of discourses are circulating on the channel? How do those discourses shape the historical understanding of the audiences who are consuming content from sources that are framed as authoritative? As Litwack reminds us, "over the past century, the power of historians and filmmakers to influence the public, to reflect and shape attitudes and popular prejudices, has been amply demonstrated, often with tragic consequences."[22] Burns himself has warned that "television is rapidly eroding the strength of our republic from within (just as Lincoln predicted)," for it has "equipped us as citizens to live only in an all-consuming, and thereby forgettable and disposable, present, blissfully unaware of the historical tides and movements that speak not only to this moment, but to our vast future as well. This environment ensures that we have no *history.* And by so doing, [it] ensures that we have no *future.*"[23]

This essay highlights some of Lincoln's unfinished work by exploring the discursive means by which History assigns value to and legitimizes certain methodologies, ideas, and identities. Using distant reading and close textual analysis of thirty consecutive days of History's programming, it is clear that the majority of the network's aired programming is reality television in the guise of historical content. By filming the day-to-day operations of small businesses or micro-industries, such as alligator hunting, the network is able to capture the drama and interpersonal conflict that fuels the interests of television audiences. This "raw" footage is then edited together with short historical-trivia asides that create a veneer of educational merit. This programming reproduces a narrow conception of masculinity that emphasizes whiteness, manual labor, patriotism, and the mythic frontier situated within a capitalist framework. By entangling this construction of masculinity with a nostalgic, decontextualized, and meritocratic understanding of the American Dream, History caters to an older, predominantly white male demographic and offers programming that aligns with and legitimizes their worldview. Finally, History supplements its reality-television shows with conspiratorial programming that promotes racist ideologies and profits off of a problematic orientation to the factual and evidence-based framework that humanistic and scientific inquiry is built upon. When it comes to historical television programming, Lincoln's work remains unfinished.

THE HISTORY OF HISTORY

Following the success of *The Civil War* in 1990, cable companies looked to tap into a new market for entertaining and informative programming. In 1995, A&E Networks launched The History Channel, and it soon became a standard part of cable packages.[24] Since its launch, what is now known as History has grown to become one of the most popular networks on television, consistently receiving high ratings among older men. As Brian Taves explains, "The History Channel's bedrock support is considered to be men, middle-aged and older; hence the emphasis on programming dealing with war, weapons, and technology, especially during its weekend lineup, as a counteroffering to sports broadcasting."[25]

With successful and informative shows and miniseries such as *Modern Marvels, The Presidents, The American Revolution, Civil War Journal,* and a variety of other documentary-style programming, The History Channel as a brand name developed an authoritative credibility among audiences despite criticisms regarding its US/Eurocentric bias and proclivity for World War II programming and Great (White) Man history.[26] While History now moves further and further away from scholarly content, it continues to enjoy a scholarly authority regarding the past. Its authoritative presence has been reinforced through educational partnerships such as "History in the Classroom" and its collaboration with and/or financial support of museums and historical associations, including the National Park Service; the Smithsonian Institution; the Library of Congress; Mount Vernon; the Ellis Island National Museum of Immigration; the Intrepid Sea, Air, and Space Museum; the National Council for Public History; the American Historical Association; and the Organization of American Historians.[27] These associations legitimize the brand name as a trustworthy and respected source of historical information. While History continues to enjoy a significant amount of intellectual credibility among audiences, the quality and content of its programming has changed significantly.

In 2004, The History Channel was pulling beyond its traditional audience as ratings among men aged 18–34 and 18–49 increased.[28] With the success of shows such as *History's Mysteries, UFO Files, Conspiracy?, Wild West Tech,* and *Mail Call,* the network found an audience for both conspiratorial and nontraditional historical programming. Other programs, such as *Extreme History with Roger Daltrey,* began incorporating elements of reality television and drawing upon a fascination with survivalism and rugged individualism.[29] Under the leadership of Nancy Dubuc, the network revamped its programming. Building off of its growing audience and catering to changing tastes, Dubuc convinced the network to expand an episode of *Modern Marvels* into a full series modeled off of Discovery's *Deadliest Catch.* In 2007, The History Channel fully entered the reality-television market with *Ice Road Truckers,* a series about truck drivers who navigate dangerous driving conditions.[30] Its success resulted in The History Channel moving further into entertainment programming, specifically reality-television shows that featured "gritty jobs," "dangerous conditions," and "the wilds of nature."[31] This programming regularly focuses on white men engaged in blue-collar occupations and is sometimes referred to as the "real-men-in-danger" or "testosterone reality" subgenre, which is popular among young male viewers.[32]

Soon after the premiere of *Ice Road Truckers,* The History Channel rebranded itself as History in 2008. Dubuc hoped to make history more fun, explaining that the word "history" carried the "baggage" of having an "academic connotation." In her view, "we needed to evolve the definition of history."[33] More reality-television programming, centering on what can be categorized as blue-collar work, followed with *Ax Men* (2008–16), *Swamp People* (2010–), *American Restoration* (2010–16), *American Pickers* (2010–), *Only in America with Larry the Cable Guy* (2011–13), *Mountain Men* (2012–), and *Appalachian Outlaws* (2014–15). The shift in programming included new promotions. History's slogan changed from "Where the Past Comes Alive" to "History, Made Every Day." Describing the success of this new genre of programming, Bill Koenigsberg, CEO of Horizon Media, stated, "take a look at the Duck Dynasty guys" and "take a look at the guys from Pawn Stars. Middle America can relate to these people."[34] What he did not explicitly state was that by "middle America," he meant white, middle-aged men holding conservative views and a nostalgic understanding of the American past.

Some media scholars attribute the rise in popularity of programming featuring dangerous occupations, survival skills, treasure hunting, and entrepreneurship to the twenty-first-century masculinity crisis in the United States and a perceived loss of societal power and privilege among white men who adhere to a construction of masculinity rooted in labor.[35] Blue-collar occupational reality-television programming centers on a narrow understanding of masculinity that legitimizes whiteness, maleness, and rurality situated within an industrial economy. These shows construct authentic masculinity as involving physical force and control, occupational achievement, familial patriarchy, frontiersmanship, and heterosexuality.[36] As media scholar Gareth Palmer explains, these series "remind us that some men are still engaged in primitive struggles to sustain both the economy and the definition of heroic hegemonic masculinity."[37]

Reality-television programming that emphasizes frontiersmanship in particular, whether it is logging, mining, hunting, or survival, are escapist in the sense that they, according to William Trapani and Laura Winn, "eliminate the presence of others from its imagery," offering a "perfectly sanitized space free from political strife."[38] The main goal of this type of programming is a "disconnection and mastery over social space" in which "men are once again in charge even if it is because all others have been evacuated from the scene."[39]

History also expanded its reach among evangelicals with its miniseries *The Bible* (2013). Created by Roma Downey and reality-television producer Mark Burnett, the opening episode attracted 13.1 million viewers, rivaling the debut of Burns's *The Civil War.*[40] Downey and Burnett boosted their viewership numbers by giving previews to "influential Christian pastors at megachurches around the country."[41] The show elicited a fair amount of controversy, as the actor playing Satan had a resemblance to President Barack Obama.[42] This casting decision was all the more important considering that the few programs on History that have focused on people of color, such as *Gangland* (2007–10), have portrayed racial and ethnic minorities as drug dealers and murderers.

The new formula has worked. In 2011, ratings showed that History "attracted more middle-aged men than any other cable channel except ESPN." The network was fifth among primetime cable viewership, trailing only USA, the Disney Channel, TNT, and ESPN.[43] In May 2018 (the period of data collection for this study), it was rated ninth among cable networks.[44] As of 2020, History reaches 380 million homes worldwide, and much of its content is now accessible via Hulu, Netflix, YouTube, and its own streaming service, History Vault.[45]

These programming changes have not come without criticism from scholars and media critics who have called out History's production of inaccurate, fabricated, and purposefully ambiguous content that continues to move further away from historical scholarship and closer to conspiracy narratives and reality television. The title of one critique questioned, "Where's the History on History?"[46] Another asked, "Is The History Channel Making Us Stupid?"[47] While History is not the only scholastic television network to move away from research-based educational programming (see Discovery Channel, formerly The Discovery Channel, and TLC, formerly The Learning Channel), its authoritative presence makes this shift deeply concerning and worthy of further analysis. As Dubuc herself has stated: "At the end of the day we're [History] not an education resource. We're an entertainment brand."[48]

METHODS

In order to demonstrate the extent to which History has shifted away from evidenced-based historical programming, we employed a mixed-methods and interdisciplinary approach to analyze thirty consecutive days of 2018 programming aired on History in the United States. To critically understand the themes and messages of the channel's programming both in aggregate and as individual shows, we supplemented close reading with topic models generated from the episode titles and descriptions.

Topic modeling is a method of computational analysis, often referred to as distant reading, that uses word co-occurrences to analyze the themes or topics of a text corpus.[49] To create the corpus, we collected episode titles and descriptions from History's website for all of the programs aired from May 15 through June 13, 2018. This encompassed 905 total programs with 510 unique episodes. From the corpus, the model generates a specified number of topics based on word co-occurrences and provides a breakdown of what percentage of each topic is contained within a particular text, or in this case, episode title and description. In this way, the themes of History's programming across shows can be seen in aggregate. To improve the output, we removed duplicated episodes and pruned the vocabulary, omitting proper names and other words unique to the corpus that skewed the model. After creating several topic models, we concluded that twelve topics was the optimal number for the corpus.[50]

In addition to topic modeling, we performed a close textual analysis of History's four most frequently aired shows and their most frequently aired episode in the sample. Close textual analysis allows for a detailed and contextualized reading of content present in History programming that works in conjunction with topic modeling, providing a richer analysis of discourse production on the network.

RESULTS AND ANALYSIS

The results of the topic model showed a general lack of historic themes. The model contains twelve topics and displays the top-twenty most significant words associated with each one (figures can be accessed at www.joshuacatalano.org /lincoln). We assigned labels to each topic based on the content or words in each:

1. Apocalyptic/Prophecy
2. Treasure Hunting
3. Bladesmithing
4. Collecting/Cars
5. Space and Technology

6. Competition/Killing

7. Collecting/Antiques

8. American Military

9. Mixed

10. Aliens

11. Classic Cars

12. Capitalism

As this topic model shows, the themes of History's programming have very little to do with history as it is traditionally understood.

To gain an understanding of the overall prevalence or frequency of these topics on History, not just their mere existence or inclusion in the topic model, we counted the number of times a particular word appeared in an episode title or description. The most frequently used were "ancient," "old," "world," "rare," "collection," "final," "car," "war," "fire," "history," "take," "offer," and "gets."

Many of these words are more associated with specific topics. For example, the word "ancient" appears in the description of nearly every episode of *Ancient Aliens* as do the words "fire" and "final" in the show *Forged in Fire* (the names of the shows were not included in the model). Other words related to the themes of Capitalism and Collecting/Antiques, such as "buy," "take," "offer," "car," "war," and "get," are present in the descriptions of several shows, including *Pawn Stars, American Pickers,* and *Counting Cars.*

After examining the models, we performed a close textual analysis of several episodes of the most frequently aired programs. The most frequently aired shows were *Pawn Stars, American Pickers, Forged in Fire, Ancient Aliens, SIX,* and *Counting Cars.* A close reading of these shows revealed not only the themes of capitalism and conspiracy but also an underlying thread of masculinity.

MELDING MASCULINITY, CAPITALISM, AND AMERICANA

Capitalism tied to a narrow conception of masculinity that emphasizes whiteness, manual labor, patriotism, and the mythic frontier was the most prominent theme in the sample and wove many of the topics together. Since its debut, History has emphasized capitalism as a content focus, with programming such as the failed launch of *The Spirit of Enterprise.*[51] The network has continued in this area, creating the miniseries docudrama *The Men Who Built America* (2012), which focuses on titans of industry such as Vanderbilt, Rockefeller, Carnegie, and Ford. Recently, History has also ventured into programming that celebrates and documents capitalism in action. The two most aired shows during the thirty-day sample period, *Pawn Stars,* which aired 153 times, and *American Pickers* and *American Pickers: Bonus Buys,* which aired a combined 141 times, fall into this category.

Pawn Stars, a hit show on History since 2009, is a reality-television program that features the Gold & Silver Pawn Shop in Las Vegas and follows "three generations of the Harrison family" as they "jointly run the family business."[52] These men are depicted as no-nonsense, well-networked business experts who are concerned with making a profit. In the opening to each episode of *Pawn Stars,* Rick Harrison states, "at my shop, family comes first and money comes second . . . depending on who you ask." A typical scene consists of someone entering the shop with an item, the Harrisons or family friend Chumlee verifying its authenticity (often with an outside appraiser's help), a price negotiation, and finally a sale of the item.

Harrison goes beyond the confines of his History timeslots to celebrate capitalism. In an interview on Fox News's *Life, Liberty & Levin,* Harrison stated that capitalism is the "survival of the fittest" and that "in the end, everyone has a better life because of it," relying on an example of the watchmaking business in the 1850s to support his claim.[53] He used the interview as an opportunity to promote libertarianism, his support of Donald Trump, and his personal success story in relation to the American Dream. Harrison noted his lower-middle-class background, his self-education, and his father's strong work ethic, meanwhile condemning government regulation and socialism. His appearance on Fox News and the blending of his on- and off-screen personalities promoted a meritocratic understanding of success and connected the ideological messages of both networks. This is not the only example of the History–Fox News relationship, as *Ancient Aliens* framed an entire episode around Fox News host Tucker Carlson in 2019.[54]

The existence and popularity of *Pawn Stars* is due in part to capitalism itself. Reality television appeals to producers not only because it is popular programming but also because it is cheap. Sending a film crew to a pawn shop to film "regular" people was a low-risk and cost-effective way to produce content.[55] Ironically, the show's popularity came about at the exact historic moment that capitalism seemed to be failing. As one of the show's stars, Corey Harrison, has explained:

The show definitely hit at the right time. It couldn't have been a better time for it to hit. . . . Going back to the recession when the show popped off, people were broke. People were looking for what they could sell and make money on. And I think that's one of the reasons it became such a big hit and why people started watching it, because everybody kind of had that thing in their attic or their garage that might be worth some money and they didn't know. And in those times, I think people were really interested in finding out what stuff was worth.[56]

With over 570 episodes, *Pawn Stars* is now reaching audiences in 150 countries and in thirty-eight different languages.[57]

Pawn Stars was not the only show that rode economic anxiety to large profits and high ratings. Cable networks released a slew of shows, including *Storage Wars* (A&E), *Barter Kings* (A&E), *Shipping Wars* (A&E), *Hardcore Pawn* (USA), *Pawn Queens* (TLC), *Flea Market Flip* (HGTV), *Garage Gold* (DIY), and others that captivated audiences with the idea that financial security was only one family heirloom away. *Pawn Stars* was also not the only one on History to do this. Network executives spun off two shows with appraisers who appeared on *Pawn Stars*, blending Americana with capitalism. Both *Counting Cars* and *American Restoration* proved to be hits.

The biggest success growing out of this formula, and the second most aired show, *American Pickers,* also highlights History's construction of masculinity and strongly ties to the topics of "collecting," "treasure hunting," and, to a lesser extent, "capitalism." Premiering in 2010, it is a reality-television show that features two midwesterners, Mike Wolfe and Frank Fritz, as they travel the rural United States in search of Americana to restore and resell at their antique shops. *American Pickers* repackages the antiquing genre, as featured in programs such as PBS's *Antiques Roadshow,* into a manly quest for rusty gold or "mantiques." As Madeleine Shufeldt Esch explains, "where *Antiques Roadshow* focuses on traditional appraisal techniques, provenance and conservative valuations from licensed experts, the new appraisal TV formats defy images of stuffy antique shops or high-end auction houses." In this way, the show "emphasizes the rugged physicality of picking and the macho business tactics of brokering deals while narratively excluding traditionally feminine aspects of collecting and the feminized sphere of antiques retail."[58]

Mike and Frank present themselves as intelligent but approachable guys' guys who wear basic t-shirts and worn-in blue jeans and appear to embrace the hunt for "mantiques" and what they signify, no matter how dirty or sweaty the hunt may be. History's description of the show begins with "[t]his isn't your grandmother's antiquing" and states that Mike and Frank are "on a mission to recycle America, even if it means diving into countless piles of grimy junk or getting chased off a gun-wielding homeowner's land."[59]

On the show, Mike and Frank are usually in search of vintage cars, bicycles, and motorcycles, in addition to oilcans, signage, and memorabilia tied to US patriotism and industrial labor. Episodes often feature sellers who are older white men in rural America. For example, in the most aired *American Pickers* episode in the sample, "Space Ranger," Mike and Frank visit a father and son in rural Minnesota. The father owned and operated a children's carnival for over thirty years, building rides by hand. While on site, Mike moves dusty, rusty, and heavy objects with excitement and vigor in order to clear a path and hunt for picks to take back to his antique shops. During the segment with the seller, there are regular cuts to grainy photographs and video footage. One video features people waving small US flags on the Fourth of July. Other videos and photos depict the rides operating in their full capacity. These images construct a childlike nostalgia for "simpler times" or "the good old days" when the rides were not covered in rust.

The overall framing of the show and of the sellers reinforces Mike and Frank's "everyday, hardworking guys" and "expert buyers" personas. In the same segment, Mike and the seller are discussing a price for parts of a carnival ride, and the seller offers a price that is low. Mike, having a better understanding of the market, insists that he pay the man more in order for the transaction to be a fair deal. The show constructs the pickers as "good guys" trying to make fair deals with sellers and who respect the value the owners assign to items and the stories and memories associated with the objects.[60] In the same episode at a different seller's house, Mike and Frank visit a divorced man and pick through his house filled with 1940s and 1950s memorabilia. The seller laments, "it's hard to find a woman that likes this stuff." At the end of the episode, Frank, a bachelor who collects vintage toys, tells the seller to "keep on buyin'."

Mike and Frank are able to momentarily keep industrial white nostalgia alive for themselves, sellers, and audiences as they rummage through remnants of an ephemeral time and place amid a changing US economy. But unlike many sellers and audiences, the pickers profit off of both the industrial and postindustrial economy. Despite their efforts to appear as average Joes who are just like the sellers, the act of "picking" itself, and the framing of Mike and Frank as "experts" who understand the market better than the sellers, creates a power dynamic where they have the choice to buy. While sellers may exhibit agency through refusing to sell or by haggling, the pickers' mobility and flexibility as businesspeople who get to leave and travel to another location and participate in a changing economy act as a contrast to the sellers, who are often rooted in time and place.[61] Both *Pawn Stars* and *American Pickers* are part of what media scholar June Deery calls hyperconsumption as spectacle. Collecting is portrayed as an acceptable way to spend beyond one's means because it is framed as educational or as an exercise in skill.[62] In addition to *American Pickers,* several other shows in the sample focus on collecting and automobiles, including *Counting Cars* (36 episodes), *Top Gear* (6 episodes), and *Truck Night in America* (2 episodes).[63] Even History's more traditional documentary-style programming has emphasized nostalgic automobiles with the release of *The Cars That Made America* (2017).

Coming in a distant third for most aired programming on History was the reality television competition *Forged in Fire* (50 episodes) and its related series *Forged in Fire: Cutting Deeper* (19 episodes) and *Forged in Fire: Knife or Death* (11 episodes). *Forged in Fire* contributes to the construction of masculinity on History and includes topics such as competition/killing, capitalism, and blade-smithing. In the show, bladesmiths forge iconic weapons from metal. The show repackages the popular television format of cooking and singing competitions in a way that emphasizes violence and rewards lethality. Their weapons are judged by a panel of experts who determine the winner of a $10,000 prize.[64] History describes *Forged in Fire* in the following way:

> *Forged in Fire* is an original competition series hosted by weapons expert and US Army and Air Force veteran Wil Willis featuring world-class bladesmiths competing to create history's most iconic edged weapons. In each episode, four of the nation's finest bladesmiths come together to put their skill and reputations on the line, trying to avoid elimination and win the $10,000 prize. They use sweat, fire, force of will, and a well-equipped forge to turn raw material into authentic, fully functional implements of war.

The forge itself evokes imagery of gritty, sweaty, and tiresome work in the US popular imagination. Contestants on the show, often men, are featured frantically heating, hammering, pressing, and grinding steel as sweat drips off of their faces in front of a glowing fire.[65] Judges test the strength, durability, and sharpness of the weapons produced in addition to a final "kill test" involving animal carcasses and ballistic dummies. Brandon Weigel explains that the show is a "callback to our country's height as an industrial powerhouse, when red-blooded American men could make a good living using their hands, and so much of what we bought proudly said 'Made in the U.S.A.'"[66] For example, in the most played episode in the sample, "The Two-Handed Sword," a contestant says in reference to blade-smithing and his family's occupations and hobbies, "we always have taken a lot of pride in doing stuff with our hands and being creative."

In this episode, the four contestants are tasked with fashioning blades by harvesting steel parts from a motorcycle. For the third round, the final two contestants must create an Indian two-handed sword. In this segment of the show, History sprinkles in some historical content. In order to decide who wins the $10,000, the sword must pass "the kill test" (later changed to the "KEAL" test, which stands for "Keep Everyone Alive").[67] A boar carcass is used to determine if the weapon "will kill." In addition to the kill test, the judges perform a "bone chop" with the blades and a sharpness test in which a judge uses the contestants' swords to cut pumpkins in half and ultimately select the champion for the episode.

While *Forged in Fire* is a competition show, the contestants are framed in a way that perpetuates the "hardworking, good guy" narrative present on *American Pickers.* Sabotage and unsportsmanlike conduct are not featured on the show, which has a strong emphasis on honest competition. Contestants are often supportive of one another, giving each other a pat on the back when their blade does well in one of the rounds or complimenting one another's bladesmithing. When a contestant is eliminated, it is often depicted as personal failure as opposed to a wrongful decision by the judges.

SURVIVING AND SCRIPTING HISTORY

History also has had a successful run of programs that mix elements of survival, occupational hazards, and capitalism. *Swamp People* (36 episodes) and *Swamp People: Blood and Guts* (8 episodes) were the most played occupational programming during the sample period. *Swamp People* is an occupational reality-television series that follows hunters, primarily in Louisiana, on their quest find, kill, and sell alligators. While *Swamp People* dominated the number of episodes aired during the sample, it has previously shared this occupational programming genre with *Appalachian Outlaws, Ax Men, Ice Road Truckers,* and *Mountain Men.* The success of these shows also led History to refocus its non-reality programming. The release of *The Men Who Built America: Frontiersmen* in 2018 is an example of this influence. These shows meld together the themes of masculinity and capitalism and are situated within a larger media landscape that reinforces specific articulations of masculinity and gendered expectations. As Deery has noted, shows that depict women engaged in "extreme spending" and men engaged in "extreme earning" serve as "another affirmation perhaps of the old trope of woman as consumer and man as provider."[68]

History's recent production of scripted dramas also appeared in the sample. Cancelled after two seasons, *SIX* (2017–18) was the most-aired scripted drama in the sample. The show depicts the lives of Navy SEAL Team Six members both at home and abroad. The second season "follows Navy SEAL Team Six in a mission to destroy the terrorist network responsible for the shooting of their former team leader."[69] Many of the plotlines focus on the rescue or saving of some individual. *SIX* was part of History's growing lineup of scripted dramas that include the successful historical-fiction show *Vikings* (2013–20), the more recently debuted *Knightfall* (2017–19), and the series *Blue Book* (2019–20). These scripted historical dramas are becoming a more important part of the channel's business model. As Executive Vice President of Programming for History Eli Lehrer states, "whether it's the legendary Knights Templar, the extraordinary tale of medieval Norsemen, or the story of a formerly classified United States Air Force program investigating UFOs during the Cold War, these series reflect our commitment to bringing the defining, big canvas stories of history to life."[70]

ANCIENT ALIENS AND RACIST CONSPIRACY THEORIES

Another prominent topic in the model consisted of aliens, prophecies, and speculative content that frequently contained racist themes. *Ancient Aliens* (49 episodes) was the most frequently aired and emblematic program of this topic in the sample.[71] History describes the show in the following way:

[*Ancient Aliens*] explores the controversial theory that extraterrestrials have visited Earth for millions of years. From the age of the dinosaurs to ancient Egypt, from early cave drawings to continued mass sightings in the US, each episode in this hit HISTORY series gives historic depth to the questions, speculations, provocative controversies, first-hand accounts and grounded theories surrounding this age old debate. Did intelligent beings from outer space visit Earth thousands of years ago?[72]

The premise of *Ancient Aliens* is anything but novel, rather it is part of the long tradition of alternative archaeology or pseudoarchaeology. The fascination with the possibility of extraterrestrial ancestors can be traced back to the Victorian era and the early twentieth century works of H. P. Lovecraft.[73] By the 1920s, many of the topics and theories of modern alternative archaeology or pseudoarchaeology were already present, including "giants; ancient space travelers; magic as occult science and wisdom; druids; megaliths; poor 'sounds alike, is alike' linguistics; secret texts in unknown languages; a particular interest in the Aryan race; lost continents; 'looks alike, is alike' comparisons between places like Egypt, the Maya homeland, Peru, and Easter Island; myth as history; and a high handed disdain for foolish, materialist scientists and benighted religious leaders."[74] These same themes can be seen in the questions posed by *Ancient Aliens:*

Could giant ancient drawings found etched into the desert floor be part of an ancient alien code? Could black holes exist not just in outer space, but here on Earth? And if so, could Earth's Black Holes [*sic*] have caused strange disappearances and other inexplicable phenomena for centuries? What is the meaning behind secret messages found throughout Washington, D.C.? Did America's Founding Fathers know something about ancient aliens that the general public did not? And if so, could this knowledge have been incorporated into the symbols, architecture, and even the founding documents of the United States of America? If ancient aliens visited Earth, were they responsible for catastrophes, wars and other deadly disasters to control the fate of the human race? The story of the Great Flood sent by deities to destroy civilizations exists in many prehistoric cultures. There are ancient descriptions of extraterrestrial battles that caused wide-scale destruction, and even reports of UFOs lurking in the shadows of recent natural disasters. The Book of Revelations [*sic*] and the Dead Sea Scrolls describe a future apocalyptic battle between good and evil that will destroy our world. Are these ancient texts proof that aliens are hostile and planning a violent return? Or might they be our saviors, ensuring our survival as a species during times of devastation?[75]

Episodes of *Ancient Aliens* consist of a carefully selected group of what are called "ancient astronaut theorists" who attempt to explain historical and archaeological questions about ancient civilizations through the past visitation of extraterrestrial beings. The lack of credentialed and respected archaeologists on this show is a hallmark of pseudoarchaeology. As Jeb Card explains, "anyone willing to wear the old symbols of preprofessional archaeology can claim the archaeological legacy and its mythic social currency even if their ideas or methods have no significant tie to archaeological practices past or present."[76]

Through the examination of archaeological sites and artifacts, these ancient astronaut theorists attempt to bring credibility to their often unsupported, fantastical, and extraterrestrial explanations.[77] By continuously posing often unanswerable questions without any conclusive answers and cherry-picking evidence, the show erodes the basis for proof and understanding that science and humanistic inquiry are founded upon, thus promoting the acceptance of highly unlikely and unsupported theories as legitimate possibilities. The testimony of ancient astronaut theorists and their ideas is constructed as just as legitimate as that of professional archaeologists and their peer-reviewed research.[78] In some respects, they are portrayed as more legitimate because of their lack of an academic training that would have prevented them from seeing the bigger picture. As Card has pointed out, the one unifying theme of alternative archaeology is its "opposition to professional mainstream archaeology and, more broadly, science."[79]

By providing adherents to alternative archaeology or pseudoarchaeology with a platform to promote their ideas, History legitimizes their perspectives and threatens to undermine or delegitimize the research methods and conclusions of professional archaeologists. As Evan Parker argues: "The proliferation of these [infotainment] programs becomes problematic when we consider that they are purported to be educational and lay claim to authenticity and scientific truth.... Even if audiences grasp the inauthenticity of such programs, it does not diminish many of the negative externalities generated by the scientific claims made by hosts."[80] The Smithsonian has taken notice. In a review of *Ancient Aliens,* Riley Black opines: "What results is a slimy and incomprehensible mixture of idle speculation and outright fabrications which pit the enthusiastic 'ancient alien theorists,' as the narrator generously calls them, against 'mainstream science.' I would say 'You can't make this stuff up,' but I have a feeling that that is exactly what most of the show's personalities were doing."[81]

Alternative archaeology has already contributed to the proliferation of conspiracy narratives and the undermining of scientific truth. Conspiracy theorists such as Alex Jones and Jim Marrs cite Lovecraft's "Call of Cthulhu" as inspiration for their work.[82] As Donald Holly Jr. has noted, many archaeologists and historians have laughed at the memes of Giorgio Tsoukalos and the absurdity of many of the show's claims, but he has started to wonder if "we are the only ones laughing. A lot more people seem to be listening, and even nodding in agreement."[83] Demonstrating the extent and dangers of conspiratorial groups, Jason Colavito has bluntly warned, "It's easy to dismiss UFOs as a fantasy or a fad, but the money, the connections, and the power wielded by a group of UFO believers—embedded in the defense industry and bent on supplanting material science with a pseudoscientific mysticism straight from the History Channel's *Ancient Aliens*—poses a danger to America more real than a flying saucer."[84]

History and its shows such as *Ancient Aliens* are also responsible for platforming racist ideologies and pseudoscience. As Card cautions, "Alternative archaeology can be a major vector for spreading old racist ideologies into the present."[85] Sarah Bond has similarly argued that *Ancient Aliens* and pseudoarchaeology has a racial dimension whereby practitioners deny the agency of non-Western peoples and diminish their accomplishments.[86] A common theme among this conspiratorial programming is a belief in an ancient white civilization existing in the Americas. As Colavito has shown, the fantasy of a "lost white race" has been embraced by white supremacists from the nineteenth century through the present.[87] *Ancient Aliens* also features episodes focused on eugenics and the search for a "leadership gene."[88]

The questioning of professional research is not limited to the discipline of archaeology. As Card has argued, "the explosion of cable television and Internet media, the declining government funding of educational media, and the resulting privatization and outsourcing of documentary production [has] replaced academic and specialist media figures with telegenic presenters of mysterious themes."[89] Within this changing economic environment, History found the construction of ambiguous, unresolved narratives to be a profitable endeavor with shows such as *Ancient Aliens, America Unearthed, Search for the Lost Giants, The Secret of Skinwalker Ranch, Haunted History, History's Mysteries, UFO Files, The UnXplained, Conspiracy?, MonsterQuest, Nostradamus Effect,* and *Decoding the Past,* among others.

The prevalence of pseudoarchaeology and the growing public interest in it have led to a call for archaeologists to more carefully consider how to reach different publics and address misconceptions in introductory courses.[90] As part of this effort, the entire review section of an issue of *American Antiquity* was devoted to works of pseudoarchaeology.[91] It is time for historians to push back against pseudoarchaeology and pseudohistory and demand responsibility from companies and organizations that continue to platform and legitimize this dangerous rhetoric.

CONCLUSION

The themes that weave History's programming together in the sample are capitalism, masculinity, and conspiracies. These topics are overrepresented on History. Largely absent from the network are discussions of race (except for ancient aliens or "lost white races"), ethnicity, class, gender, (neo)colonialism, slavery, politics, LGBTQ+ history, and nearly all other topical foci of the modern history discipline. Only military history remains as a prominent theme on the television network, and even it occupies only a small percentage of aired programming in the sample. While History moves further and further away from scholarly content, it continues to enjoy a scholarly authority regarding the past. Its partnerships with prominent historical organizations and museums legitimizes the brand name as a trustworthy and respected source of historical information. This adds a dangerous degree of legitimacy to its conspiratorial programming.

Given History's popularity, it is important for scholars of all disciplines to critically examine what messages are being sent and received through the seemingly authoritative medium of History and other cable-television networks. There is an urgent need for scholars to pay close attention to the kind of programming on network television and streaming services in this increasingly diverse media environment. While streaming services such as Netflix have consciously attempted to respond to the changing economic, social, and political landscape in the United States and the demand for better representation by offering a variety of programming with more inclusive narratives, television networks often have to adapt to older and less diverse cable/satellite audiences to remain profitable. Taves explains that, "as a commercial channel, The History Channel lacks the possibility of the uninterrupted attention of a PBS audience, so much of The History Channel's original programming is created in recognition of the fact that it must appeal to the fragmented attention of the channel surfer."[92] Couched in a historical period of divisive politics and the "alternative facts" of the Trump administration, discourse production concerning conspiracy theories and white masculinity on History is of pressing importance.

In regard to cable television, Lincoln's unfinished work seems to be an increasingly daunting task, but as Burns reminds us, "we mustn't throw the medium out, turn away, or surrender its great power to those disingenuous people for whom it is merely the tool of some temporal or financial end."[93] This is why Merritt's call for a new documentary is essential. It would serve as an important educational tool in homes and classrooms across the world. Perhaps a new generation of historical documentarians will help us find the better angels of our nature. As Barbara Fields reminds us, the Civil War "is still to be fought, and regrettably, it can still be lost."[94]

NOTES

Portions of this essay were first published in *Current Research in Digital History.* We would like to thank our fellow panelists and the audiences at the American Sociological Association and Lincoln's Unfinished Work conferences for their comments and suggestions. We would especially like to thank the members of the Clemson University Humanities Hub who provided feedback on the essay.

1. Robert Brent Toplin, ed., *Ken Burns's "The Civil War": Historians Respond* (New York: Oxford University Press, 1996), xv.

2. Gary R. Edgerton, "The Past Is Now Present Onscreen: Television, History, and Collective Memory," in *A Companion to Television,* ed. Janet Wasko and Eileen R. Meehan, 2nd ed. (John Wiley & Sons, 2020), 82.

3. Toplin, *Ken Burns's "The Civil War,"* xxvi.

4. Robert Brent Toplin, "Ken Burns's *The Civil War* as an Interpretation of History," in *Ken Burns's* The Civil War, 32.

5. Leon F. Litwack, "Telling the Story: The Historian, the Filmmaker, and the Civil War," in Toplin, *Ken Burns's "The Civil War,"* 137.

6. Gary W. Gallagher, "How Familiarity Bred Success: Military Campaigns and Leaders in Ken Burns's *The Civil War,*" in Toplin, *Ken Burns's "The Civil War,"* 43.

7. Catherine Clinton, "'Nobel Women as Well,'" in Toplin, *Ken Burns's "The Civil War,"* 66–67.

8. Eric Foner, "Ken Burns and the Romance of Reunion," in Toplin, *Ken Burns's "The Civil War,"* 116, 117–18.

9. Gary R. Edgerton, *Ken Burns's America* (New York: Palgrave, 2001), 20.

10. Keri Leigh Merritt, "Why We Need a New Civil War Documentary," Smithsonian Magazine, Apr. 23, 2019, https://www.smithsonianmag.com/history/why-we-need-new-civil-war-documentary-180971996/.

11. Toplin, *Ken Burns's "The Civil War,"* xxvi.

12. Clinton, "'Nobel Women as Well,'" 66.

13. Gary Edgerton, "Television as Historian: An Introduction," *Film & History* 30, no. 1 (2000): 7 (italics in original).

14. Ibid., 7.

15. Smithsonian, HBO, Netflix, and even ESPN have started producing engaging and insightful documentaries and historical dramas. History has recently made an attempt to include more substantive programs such as *Washington* (2020) and *Grant* (2020).

16. Edgerton, "Past Is Now Present Onscreen," 82–83.

17. Ann Gray and Erin Bell, *History on Television* (London: Routledge, 2013), 10.

18. Sylvia Harvey, "Broadcasting in the Age of Netflix: When the Market Is Master," in Wasko and Meehan, *Companion to Television*, 105–28; Antonio Gomez-Aguilar, "Content Bubbles: How Platforms Filter What We See," in *Handbook of Research on Transmedia Storytelling, Audience Engagement, and Business Strategies*, ed. Victor Hernandez-Santaolalla and Monica Barrientos-Bueno (Hershey, PA: IGI Global, 2020), 238–350.

19. Eli Lehrer, executive vice president and head of programming at History, recently discussed the challenge faced by the network to balance its scripted programming with "big premium event docs." The network's leadership is hoping that its two recent series *Washington* (2020) and *Grant* (2020) will help achieve a happy medium. Christie Brendan, "History in the Making: Inside the First 25 Years of One of Cable's Top Brands," *Realscreen* (blog), Jan. 22, 2020, https://realscreen.com/2020/01/22/history-in-the-making-inside-the-first-25-years-of-one-of-cables-top-brands/.

20. Gary R. Edgerton and Peter C. Rollins, eds., *Television Histories: Shaping Collective Memory in the Media Age* (Lexington: University Press of Kentucky, 2001); Alison Landsberg, *Prosthetic Memory: The Transformation of American Remembrance in the Age of Mass Culture* (New York: Columbia University Press, 2004); George Lipsitz, *Time Passages: Collective Memory and American Popular Culture* (1990; repr., Minneapolis: University of Minnesota Press, 2001); Paul Grainge, ed., *Memory and Popular Film* (Manchester, UK: Manchester University Press, 2003).

21. Maurice Halbwachs, *On Collective Memory*, ed. Lewis A. Coser (Chicago: University of Chicago Press, 1992).

22. Litwack, "Telling the Story," 122.

23. Ken Burns, "Four O'Clock in the Morning Courage," in Toplin, *Ken Burns's "The Civil War,"* 175–76.

24. Brian Taves, "The History Channel and the Challenge of Historical Programming," in Edgerton and Rollins, *Television Histories*, 261.

25. Ibid., 276.

26. Andrew J. Bacevich, "History That Makes Us Stupid," *Chronicle of Higher Education*, Nov. 1, 2015, http://www.chronicle.com/article/History-That-Makes-Us-Stupid/233971; Alex Knapp, "An

Archaeologist Watches the History Channel and Questions the Part about the Aliens," Forbes, Sept. 19, 2011, https://www.forbes.com/sites/alexknapp/2011/09/19/an-archaeologist-watches-the -history-channel-and-questions-the-part-about-the-aliens/#2ee1787f3e65; Stanley I. Kutler, "Why the History Channel Had to Apologize for the Documentary That Blamed LBJ for JFK's Murder," History News Network, Apr. 7, 2004, https://historynewsnetwork.org/article/4504; Mark Schone, "Media Circus: All Hitler All the Time," Salon, May 8, 1997, https://www.salon.com/1997/05/08/media_90/; Riley Black, "The Idiocy, Fabrications, and Lies of Ancient Aliens," Smithsonian Magazine, May 11, 2012, https://www.smithsonianmag.com/science-nature/the-idiocy-fabrications-and-lies-of-ancient -aliens-86294030/; Zach West, "The History Channel? Historical Content by Show," Cracked.com, June 30, 2010, http://www.cracked.com/funny-5720-the-history-channel/ (page removed); Taves, "History Channel and the Challenge of Historical Programming."

27. "National Museum of American History's New Exhibition Examines 250 Years of American Military Conflicts," National Museum of American History, Oct. 20, 2004, https://americanhistory. si.edu/press/releases/national-museum-american-history%E2%80%99s-new-exhibition-examines- 250-years-american; "Smithsonian National Museum of Natural History—Washington D.C.," *McCann Systems* (blog), June 28, 2010, https://www.mccannsystems.com/audio-visual-projects /smithsonian-natural-museum-of-history/; "Discovering George Washington," George Washington's Mount Vernon, http://www.mountvernon.org/the-estate-gardens/museum/education-center- galleries/ (accessed Mar. 16, 2020); ESI Design, "ESI Design Brings Sweeping New Dynamic and Interactive Exhibits to Ellis Island's New National Immigration Museum," press release, May 12, 2015, https://esidesign.com/esi-design-brings-sweeping-new-dynamic-and-interactive-exhibits- to-ellis-islands-new-national-immigration-museum/; Lonnie G. Bunch III, "How Lonnie Bunch Built a Museum Dream Team," book excerpt, Smithsonian Magazine, Sept. 19, 2019, https://www .smithsonianmag.com/smithsonian-institution/how-lonnie-bunch-built-museum-dream-team -1-180973132/ (accessed Mar. 16, 2020); Anne Becker, "The History Channel Teams Up with the Library of Congress," Broadcasting & Cable, Apr. 12, 2008, https://www.broadcastingcable.com /news/history-channel-teams-library-congress-32110; "The History Channel Partners with Intrepid Museum," *Chief Marketer* (blog), July 7, 2004, https://www.chiefmarketer.com/the-history-channel -partners-with-intrepid-museum/; Libby Haight O'Connell, "The History Channel and History Education," *Perspectives on History* 33, no. 7 (Oct. 1, 1995), https://www.historians.org/publications -and-directories/perspectives-on-history/october-1995/the-history-channel-and-history-education.

28. Allison Romano, "On a Roll: History Channel Touts Younger Appeal and Clever Marketing," *Broadcasting & Cable* 134, no. 28 (2004): 18.

29. Gary R. Edgerton, "'Where the Past Comes Alive': Television, History, and Collective Memory," in *A Companion to Television,* ed. Janet Wasko (Malden, MA: John Wiley & Sons, Ltd, 2005), 366.

30. Felix Gillette, "A+E Networks CEO Nancy Dubuc, the Duck Whisperer," *Bloomberg.Com,* June 20, 2013, https://www.bloomberg.com/news/articles/2013-06-20/a-plus-e-networks-ceo-nancy- dubuc-the-duck-whisperer.

31. Brian Stelter, "Channel's Swift Rise Attracts Ads and Envy," Media, *New York Times,* Dec. 18, 2011, https://www.nytimes.com/2011/12/19/business/media/now-in-top-tier-history-channel -struggles-to-stay-there.html.

32. Amy Chozick, "What Real Men Watch: Cable TV Finds Elusive Upscale Audience for 'Swamp Loggers,' 'Pawn Stars,'" *Wall Street Journal*, Nov. 18, 2010, https://www.wsj.com/articles/SB1000142 405274870464860457562054068459912.

33. Gillette, "A+E Networks CEO Nancy Dubuc."

34. Ibid.

35. Burton P. Buchanan, "Portrayals of Masculinity in the Discovery Channel's Deadliest Catch," in *Reality Television: Oddities of Culture*, ed. Alison F. Slade, Amber J. Narro, and Burton P. Buchanan (Lanham, MD: Lexington Books, 2014); William C. Trapani and Laura L. Winn, "Manifest Masculinity: Frontier, Fraternity, and Family in Discovery Channel's Gold Rush," ibid., 183–201.

36. Buchanan, "Portrayals of Masculinity in The Discovery Channel's Deadliest Catch."

37. Gareth Palmer, "The Wild Bunch: Men, Labor, and Reality Television," in *A Companion to Reality Television: Theory and Evidence*, ed. Laurie Ouellette (Malden, MA: John Wiley & Sons, 2014), 255.

38. Trapani and Winn, "Manifest Masculinity," 184–85.

39. Ibid., 185.

40. Gillette, "A+E Networks CEO Nancy Dubuc, the Duck Whisperer."

41. Ibid.

42. Lily Rothman, "After Obama Uproar, Satan Removed from 'Bible' Movie," *Time*, Feb. 18, 2014, https://time.com/8290/bible-without-obama-satan/ (accessed Apr. 25, 2020).

43. Stelter, "Channel's Swift Rise Attracts Ads and Envy."

44. A. J. Katz, "Here Are the Top Cable Networks for May 2018," TVNewser, June 1, 2018, https://adweek.it/2H9JWW1.

45. Brendan, "History in the Making."

46. Brad Lockwood, "High Ratings Aside, Where's the History on History?," *Forbes*, Oct. 17, 2011, https://www.forbes.com/sites/bradlockwood/2011/10/17/high-ratings-aside-wheres-the-history-on -history/#317474e6ffod.

47. Marvin DeBose, "Is The History Channel Making Us Stupid?," *Mind of Marvin* (blog), Mar. 19, 2013, https://themindofmarvin.wordpress.com/2013/03/19/is-the-history-channel-making-us-stupid/.

48. Gillette, "A+E Networks CEO Nancy Dubuc, the Duck Whisperer."

49. For topic modeling, see David M. Blei, Andrew Y. Ng, and Michael I. Jordon, "Latent Dirichlet Allocation," *Journal of Machine Learning Research* 3 (2003): 993–1022; Matthew L. Jockers, *Macroanalysis: Digital Methods and Literary History* (Urbana: University of Illinois Press, 2013); and *Journal of Digital Humanities* 2, no. 1 (Winter 2012), http://journalofdigitalhumanities.org/2-1/.

50. The code and data used for this project is available at https://github.com/jccatalano/CRDH _history_channel.

51. Taves, "History Channel and the Challenge of Historical Programming"; Robert Wright, "The Way We Were? History as 'Infotainment' in the Age of History Television," in *The River of History: Trans-National and Trans-Disciplinary Perspectives on the Immanence of the Past*, ed. Peter Farrugia (Calgary, AB: University of Calgary Press, 2005), 35–57.

52. "Pawn Stars: About," History, 2018, https://www.history.com/shows/pawn-stars/about.

53. "Rick Harrison Opens up about His Journey to 'Pawn Stars,'" Fox News, Aug. 5, 2018, https://www.foxnews.com/transcript/rick-harrison-opens-up-about-his-journey-to-pawn-stars; "Rick Harrison on 'Life, Liberty & Levin': Capitalism Is 'Survival of the Fittest,'" Fox News, Aug. 5, 2018, http://insider.foxnews.com/2018/08/05/rick-harrison-life-liberty-levin-capitalism-survival-fittest.

54. *Ancient Aliens,* season 14, episode 21, "Countdown to Disclosure," aired Nov. 22, 2019, on History. For more on the relationship between conservative media and History, see Jason Colavito, "How Washington Got Hooked on Flying Saucers," *New Republic,* May 21, 2021, https://newrepublic.com/article/162457/government-embrace-ufos-bad-science.

55. June Deery, "Mapping Commercialization in Reality Television," in Ouellette, *Companion to Reality Television,* 11–28.

56. Christopher Lawrence, "'Pawn Stars' Cast Reflects on Road to Monday's 500th Episode," *Las Vegas Review-Journal* (blog), Jan. 20, 2018, https://www.reviewjournal.com/entertainment/entertainment-columns/christopher-lawrence/pawn-stars-cast-reflects-on-road-to-mondays-500th-episode/.

57. Ibid.

58. Madeleine Shufeldt Esch, "Picking through History: 'Mantiques' and Masculinity in Artifactual Entertainment," *European Journal of Cultural Studies* 20, no. 5 (Oct. 1, 2017): 510.

59. "American Pickers: About," History, 2018, https://www.history.com/shows/american-pickers/about.

60. Esch, "Picking through History."

61. Ibid.

62. Deery, "Mapping Commercialization in Reality Television," 24.

63. *Counting Cars* (2012–), a spin-off of *Pawn Stars,* is a reality television series that follows Danny "The Count" Koker, who "walks, talks and breathes classic American muscle cars," and his crew as they restore and customize classic cars and motorcycles at Count's Kustoms. *Truck Night in America* (2018–) is a reality competition show that features trucks and jeeps, focusing on the customization, performance, and limits of various vehicles. "Counting Cars: About," History, 2018, https://www.history.com/shows/counting-cars.

64. "Forged in Fire: About," History, 2018, https://www.history.com/shows/forged-in-fire/about.

65. Brandon Weigel, "This Will Kill: History Channel's 'Forged in Fire' and American Economic Anxiety," *City Paper,* July 5, 2017, https://www.baltimoresun.com/citypaper/bcp-070517-screens-forged-in-fire-20170705-story.html.

66. Ibid.

67. In a YouTube video, Doug Marcaida, one of the judges on *Forged in Fire,* explains that the popular saying from the show "it will kill" has changed to "It will KEAL" (Keep Everyone Alive) to ensure that the show stays family friendly and is in line with the meaning of martial arts, which, according to Marcaida, is about protection, not destruction. Doug Marcaida, "The Meaning behind 'It Will Kill,'" Morning Coffee with Marcaida, Dec. 12, 2017, 8:04, https://www.youtube.com/watch?v=loNG-HFEHzQ&t=55s.

68. Deery, "Mapping Commercialization in Reality Television," 25.

69. "Six: About," History, 2018, https://www.history.com/shows/six/about.

70. Joe Otterson, "'Knightfall' Renewed at History, Mark Hamill Joins Cast," *Variety*, Aug. 13, 2018, https://variety.com/2018/tv/news/knightfall-renewed-season-2-history-mark-hamill-1202903138/.

71. Programming focusing on prophecies and the paranormal also had a strong presence with five airings of the *Nostradamus Effect* and four airings of *Haunted History*.

72. "Ancient Aliens: About," History, 2018, https://www.history.com/shows/ancient-aliens/about.

73. Jason Colavito, *The Cult of Alien Gods: H. P. Lovecraft and Extraterrestrial Pop Culture* (Amhers, NY: Prometheus Books, 2005); Jeb J. Card, *Spooky Archaeology: Myth and the Science of the Past* (Albuquerque: University of New Mexico Press, 2018).

74. Card, *Spooky Archaeology*, 15.

75. Selection of questions and statements posed by the *Ancient Aliens* series from the episode descriptions.

76. Card, *Spooky Archaeology*, 11.

77. For an episode-by-episode debunking of *Ancient Aliens*, see Jason Colavito, *A Critical Companion to* Ancient Aliens *Seasons 3 and 4: Unauthorized* (Albany, NY: Jason Colavito, 2012).

78. Richard K. Popp, "History in Discursive Limbo: Ritual and Conspiracy Narratives on the History Channel," *Popular Communication* 4, no. 4 (2006): 253–72.

79. Card, *Spooky Archaeology*, 259–60.

80. Evan A. Parker, "The Proliferation of Pseudoarchaeology through 'Reality' Television Programming," in *Lost City, Found Pyramid: Understanding Alternative Archaeologies and Pseudoscientific Practices*, ed. Jeb J. Card and David S. Anderson (Tuscaloosa: University Alabama Press, 2016), 150, 155.

81. Black, "Idiocy, Fabrications, and Lies of Ancient Aliens."

82. Card, *Spooky Archaeology*, 251.

83. Donald H. Holly, "Talking to the Guy on the Airplane," *American Antiquity* 80, no. 3 (2015): 615.

84. Colavito, "How Washington Got Hooked on Flying Saucers."

85. Card, *Spooky Archaeology*, 267.

86. Sarah E. Bond, "Pseudoarchaeology and the Racism behind Ancient Aliens," Hyperallergic, Nov. 13, 2018, https://hyperallergic.com/470795/pseudoarchaeology-and-the-racism-behind-ancient-aliens/.

87. Jason Colavito, *The Mound Builder Myth: Fake History and the Hunt for a "Lost White Race"* (Norman: University of Oklahoma Press, 2020).

88. *Ancient Aliens*, season 6, episode 7, "Emperors, Kings, and Pharaohs," aired Nov. 8, 2013, on History.

89. Card, *Spooky Archaeology*, 263.

90. David S. Anderson, Jeb J. Card, and Keneth L. Feder, "Speaking Up and Speaking Out: Collective Efforts in the Fight to Reclaim the Public Perception of Archaeology," *SAA Archaeological Record* 13, no. 2 (2013): 24–28; Cerisa R. Reynolds, "Fighting Ancient Aliens in the Classroom: Restoring Credit to Peoples of the Past in Introduction to Archeology Courses," *Teaching Anthropology* 21, no. 1 (2015): 1–8.

91. See *American Antiquity* 80, no. 3 (2015).

92. Taves, "History Channel and the Challenge of Historical Programming," 272.

93. Burns, "Four O'Clock in the Morning Courage," 177.

94. Commentary of Barbara Fields in Ken Burns, *The Civil War,* DVD (PBS Home Video, 2004).

Voting Rights and Economics in the American South

GAVIN WRIGHT

Voting rights for African Americans are undeniably part of Abraham Lincoln's unfinished legacy. Lincoln himself, in his confidential 1864 letter to Louisiana governor Michael Hahn, expressed only cautious support for extending the franchise "to some of the colored people . . . as, for instance, the very intelligent, and especially those who have fought gallantly in our ranks." But when he expressed these sentiments in a public address on April 11, 1865, the prospect of Black voting infuriated audience member John Wilkes Booth and cost Lincoln his life. We will never know with confidence how his views and policies would have evolved had he lived, but Black enfranchisement soon became a priority for congressional Republicans, embodied in the Military Reconstruction Acts of 1867 and the Fifteenth Amendment to the Constitution, ratified on February 3, 1870.[1]

The keyword here is "unfinished." We now know that Black southerners responded to enfranchisement quickly and in large numbers, electing Black political officials in every state of the former Confederacy. Voting and office holding were purposeful, reflected in efforts to raise taxes, support public schools, and expand access to landownership.[2] But we also know that these efforts were crushed by southern white opposition, beginning with violent intimidation in the 1870s and culminating in legal disfranchisement between 1890 and 1910. Although Black registration and voting gradually increased over the next fifty years, the political effect in the South was slight until the landmark Voting Rights Act of 1965 (VRA).

The VRA revolutionized Black political participation in the South. Black voter registration rates jumped almost overnight in targeted areas and then rose steadily, though voting differences in turnout between the North and the South in federal elections only first closed up completely in 2014.[3] The increase in Black elected officials was longer and slower, requiring extensive litigation to overcome "vote dilution" tactics on the part of white politicians. Subsequently, the number of Black elected officials in the South continued to rise throughout the 1980s and 1990s, nearly doubling the non-South numbers by the end of the century. Small wonder that the VRA has been hailed as the most successful civil rights law in history.[4]

In *Sharing the Prize*, I show that enhanced political participation was not just of moral and symbolic value but also contributed positively to the economic well-being of Black southerners and the South as a whole. The most immediate gains were in municipalities and counties, where post-VRA surveys found more paved roads and streetlights in Black residential areas, better access to city and county services, and increased Black hires into public-sector jobs, including policemen and firemen. Advances were also observable at the state level, though Blacks were not close to a voting majority in any southern state. Economists Elizabeth Cascio and Ebonya Washington show that the VRA's elimination of literacy tests was systematically associated with greater increases in state transfers to counties with higher Black population shares. These shifts occurred well before any major Black representation in state government.[5]

The economic gains from broadening the franchise were not limited to African Americans. Contrary to Lyndon Johnson's oft-quoted remark that the Civil Rights Act had "handed the South to the Republicans for a generation," what the VRA actually brought to the South was more than twenty-five years of vigorous two-party competition. Aided by new Black voters, moderate Democrats like John West of South Carolina, Reubin Askew of Florida, and Jimmy Carter of Georgia defeated segregationist opponents in 1970, changing the political landscape for most of the region. Knowing the divisiveness of the race issue, these new-breed governors stressed economic development and education as unifying themes. For a somewhat later period, political scientist Kerry Haynie reports that greater Black representation in state legislatures tended to raise spending on health, education, and social welfare, benefiting southerners of all races.[6] Energized or at least not deterred by these policies, growth in the southern states outpaced the rest of the nation from the 1960s to the 1990s.

This essay extends the account to address the question: if the reconfigured political economy of the post–civil rights South was so beneficial for almost all concerned, why was it largely abandoned with the consolidation of conservative majorities beginning in the 1990s? One perspective views this outcome as the culmination of a long-term realignment between the ideologies of white southerners and their partisan identities, a process that took time because state party organizations and officeholders were historically Democratic.[7] Another school of thought stresses the creation of majority-minority districts in response to vote-dilution litigation, reducing incentives toward coalition building and moderation.[8] However this may be, state boundaries were not redistricted, yet southern white voting in statewide elections clearly shifted to the right from the 1990s onward. The power of reformulated ideological appeals can hardly be denied, but another important contributor was the end of rapid regional growth, specifically the massive loss of manufacturing jobs after 1994. This development undermined an important structural basis for biracial political cooperation.

THE HISTORICAL PATH OF THE SOUTHERN BLACK VOTE

The Fifteenth Amendment to the US Constitution provided that the right to vote could not be denied on the basis of "race, color, or previous condition of servitude," and African Americans participated actively in southern state and local politics for the next two decades, electing more than six hundred Black state legislators overall.[9] With the withdrawal of federal troops in 1876, however, white southerners intensified efforts to repress Black voting. After 1890, disfranchisement became formalized in legislation and, in many cases, in new state constitutions. By 1910, southern Black disfranchisement was virtually complete.[10]

It is worth noting that although the racial motivations of southern legislators were blatant and unconcealed, the laws themselves were ostensibly race-neutral in ironic deference to the Fifteenth Amendment, among the most effective instruments being literacy tests and poll taxes (that typically cumulated each year if unpaid). The most direct economic consequences were racial in character, primarily the sharp decline in both absolute and relative spending on Black schools.[11] But whether by intention or inadvertence, voting by lower-income white southerners was also substantially curtailed by the disfranchisement package, and this group, too, suffered economic consequences. Statistical studies show a strong three-way association among disfranchisement, plantation tenancy, and educational inequality for both Blacks and whites.[12] The dual-inequality pattern extended even to North Carolina, exemplifying what J. Morgan Kousser calls "progressivism for middle-class whites only."[13] Such scenarios gave rise to V. O. Key's classic formulation: fixation on race stifled both political competition and progressive economic policies in the South, to the ultimate detriment of low-income members of both races.[14]

Black political leaders never accepted disfranchisement as settled, waging a legal struggle for the vote for more than half a century and achieving periodic breakthroughs. As early as 1915, the NAACP persuaded the US Supreme Court to invalidate Oklahoma's grandfather clause exempting whites from literacy tests if a linear ancestor had been entitled to vote on January 1, 1866. With the court's overthrow of the Texas white primary in 1944 (after three decades of litigation), southern Black voter registration began a slow climb, from an estimated 3 percent of the voting-age population in 1940 to 12 percent in 1947 and 20 percent in 1952.[15] Black voters in this era were mainly in cities and could sometimes exercise political influence in competitive elections. But progress during the 1950s was painfully slow, and this stasis was hardly changed by the Civil Rights Acts of 1957 and 1960. Between 1960 and 1962, the estimated southern Black registration rate barely budged, from 29.1 to 29.4 percent.[16]

The historic break came in 1962 with the launch of the Voter Education Project, a mass-registration effort sponsored by five civil rights organizations and encouraged by the Kennedy administration. The campaign registered approximately 700,000 voters in two and a half years. But it also provoked considerable resistance and retaliation, and some states (notably Alabama, Louisiana, and Mississippi) saw minimal gains at best. Thus, the Johnson administration was preparing more aggressive federal legislation even before the dramatic showdown at Selma on March 7, 1965.[17]

The Voting Rights Act of 1965 rewrote the rules of southern politics almost overnight. Sections 2 and 3 restated the principles of the Fifteenth Amendment nationally. Section 4 defined a "coverage formula" for federal action: jurisdictions that imposed a literacy test or similar device *and* where voter turnout was less than 50 percent in the 1964 presidential election. These criteria covered six southern states fully (Alabama, Georgia, Louisiana, Mississippi, South Carolina, and Virginia) and about forty counties in North Carolina. Literacy tests were banned entirely in covered areas, and the attorney general was authorized to assign federal examiners to enroll qualified voters in these areas. Within the first three months of enactment, Attorney General Nicholas Katzenbach sent examiners to thirty-two counties in four states. By the end of 1967, examiners had registered more than 150,000 Black southerners in fifty-eight counties. More than twice this number were registered by local voting registrars elsewhere under the threat of federal intervention, if prior practices did not change.[18]

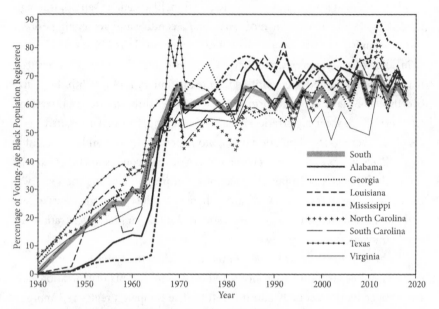

Figure 14.1. Southern Black Voter Registration Rate, 1940–2018

Sources: (1940–1971) Voter Education Project, *Protest at Selma,* comp. David J. Garrow (New Haven, CT: Yale University Press, 1978), 7, 11, 19, 189, 200; (1976–1980) Voter Education Project, *Voter Mobilization and the Politics of Race,* comp. Harold W. Stanley (New York: Praeger, 1987), 97; (1980–2018) US Census Bureau, Current Population Survey, Reported Voting and Registration by Sex, Race, and Hispanic Origin, for States.

Figure 14.1 shows the sharp jump in Black voter registration between 1965 and 1970 in the seven original VRA states and in the South as a whole. The increase was substantial even in states where growth was fairly steady from 1940 onward, but the discontinuity was particularly marked in Alabama, Mississippi, and South Carolina. The figure also shows that these higher registration levels were largely maintained in subsequent decades, albeit with fluctuations. By the 1980s, southern Black registration rates were typically higher than those of Blacks in other regions, at times exceeding white registration rates in the same state and year.

The VRA was an emergency measure set to expire in five years. President Richard Nixon came into office intending to get the voting rights "monkey . . . off the backs of the South" by extending coverage nationwide and eliminating Section 5, which required "preclearance" of any change in election procedures in covered areas. In the end, however, the VRA was renewed in 1970 for another five years little changed, though the ban on literacy tests did indeed become national at that time. The 1975 renewal was for seven years and extended coverage to language minorities, a provision championed by Barbara Jordan of Texas, the first Black woman ever elected to Congress from the South. By that time, the VRA had acquired significant support from within the South: in the House, fifty-two of seventy-eight southern Democrats voted in favor, and ten of twenty-seven southern Republicans; in the Senate, a regional majority of eleven Democrats and two Republicans from the South voted for renewal. Some of the change may have been merely a matter of acquiescence to what had become a national consensus. But it also reflected the observation that experience under the VRA had by no means been as calamitous as white southerners anticipated. As Louisiana Democratic senator J. Bennett Johnston put it: "We found that the sky did not fall under the 1965 Voting Rights Act, that things worked pretty well in the South, the deep South of the old Confederacy, which readjusted their patterns of voting, readjusted their attitudes towards all people. It worked." As if in confirmation of the emerging consensus within the region, every southern governor joined in designating July 1976 "Voter Registration Month," urging all unregistered persons to register and vote in the bicentennial year.[19]

The VRA survived even the Reagan revolution of the 1980s, which curtailed or reversed many other aspects of civil rights policy. Encouraged by Senator Strom Thurmond of South Carolina, President Ronald Reagan initially favored extending Section 5 to all of the states, a transparent means of diluting enforcement in the South. Despite vigorous efforts by Reagan's team, strong congressional majorities voted not only for a twenty-five-year renewal in 1982 but also to reverse the Supreme Court's 1980 ruling that vote dilution was actionable only if discriminatory intent could be established. This time the final votes in both houses were nearly unanimous, with only four of twenty-two southern senators in opposition. Thurmond himself, not wanting to antagonize South Carolina's Black voters, supported renewal for the first time. It would hardly seem possible that the VRA consensus could grow any stronger, but in fact the 2006 renewal vote continued the trend. Majorities for another twenty-five-year renewal then were even more overwhelming in both the Senate (98–0) and the House (390–33).[20]

BLACK ELECTED OFFICIALS

The surge in Black voters was accompanied by an upward jump in Black candidates for office. There were several striking early successes in Black-majority areas. Newly enfranchised voters in Macon County, Alabama, elected a Black sheriff for the first time in 1966. The Freedom Democratic Party of Mississippi successfully backed Robert Clark of Holmes County in his election to the state house of representatives in 1967. By 1974, in the states covered by the VRA, nearly a thousand Black officials were serving, compared to just seventy-two in 1965. Nonetheless, a report by the US Commission on Civil Rights on the tenth anniversary of the VRA found that Black representation was still far below its demographic potential so that "minorities have not yet gained a foothold on positions of real influence."[21]

A central reason for the lag in Black representation was the adoption of an array of measures by southern jurisdictions to weaken the effectiveness of Black voting, a practice known as "vote dilution." The Civil Rights Commission devoted more than half of its 1968 report to documenting these practices, which included changing from district to county-wide elections, consolidating adjoining counties to increase the share of white voters, abolishing elective offices contested by Black candidates, imposing additional filing fees and requirements for elective office, withholding essential information for contesting a public office, and many others.[22]

Particularly egregious actions by the state of Mississippi led to the decision in *Allen v. State Board of Education* (1969) in which the Supreme Court declared that *all* changes in electoral procedures in covered areas must be submitted to the attorney general for preclearance, giving an expansive reading to the VRA's language authorizing "all actions necessary to make voting effective." The court's pendulum later swung the other way in *Mobile v. Bolden* (1980), which held that vote dilution was only actionable if discriminatory intent could be established. This restriction was promptly reversed by Congress in the 1982 renewal of the VRA, illustrating the strength of the national consensus in support of meaningful

Black political participation. The new language provided that voting violations need only have a "discriminatory effect," not necessarily a "discriminatory purpose," to be proscribed. The Supreme Court revisited the issue in *Thornburg v. Gingles* (1986), a case emerging from a North Carolina redistricting plan that spread Black voters across seven new congressional districts in such a way that no Black candidate was likely to be elected. This time the court ruled that six of the new districts violated the VRA, endorsing criteria based on the "totality of circumstances" in the area, including the size and cohesiveness of racial voting blocs and the history of racially polarized voting. The outcome of this historical process was in essence a conclusion that the VRA required the creation of Black-majority legislative districts in the South.[23]

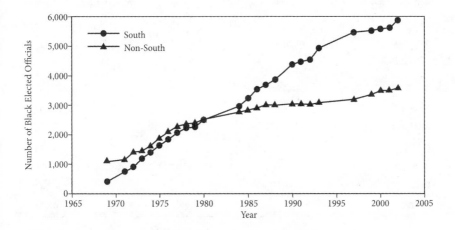

Figure 14.2. Black Elected Officials, South and Non-South, 1969–2002
Source: Joint Center for Political and Economic Studies, *Black Elected Officials,* various issues.

Figure 14.2 illustrates the results for Black elected officials, comparing the eleven-state South to the rest of the nation (see also table 14.1). The litigation-driven accelerations of the 1980s and 1990s are evident. It is notable that by 1984, the number of Black elected officials in the South surpassed that of the non-South, where progress on this front stagnated. A statistical analysis published in 1994 concluded that the transition was largely driven by Black-majority districts compelled by enforcement of the VRA.[24]

Table 14.1. Share of Black Elected Officials Relative to Share of Voting-Age Population, 2001

	State Senate	State House	County Commission	Mayor	City Council	School Board	All Elected Offices
Alabama	0.927	1.04	0.979	0.427	0.979	0.427	0.717
Arkansas	0.562	0.85	0.0	0.434	0.0	0.434	0.432
Florida	1.316	1.068	0.503	0.269	0.503	0.269	0.339
Georgia	0.713	0.789	0.512	0.196	0.512	0.196	0.350
Louisiana	0.762	0.723	0.661	0.362	0.661	0.362	0.468
Mississippi	0.62	0.863	0.749	0.539	0.749	0.539	0.565
North Carolina	0.673	0.76	0.913	0.288	0.913	0.288	0.42
South Carolina	0.621	0.721	0.836	0.377	0.836	0.377	0.496
Tennessee	0.607	1.013	0.155	0.06	0.155	0.06	0.176
Texas	0.546	0.782	0.112	0.248	0.112	0.248	0.155
Virginia	0.672	0.591	0.505	0.117	0.505	0.117	0.429
SOUTH							0.375
NON-SOUTH							0.095
Illinois							0.098
Michigan							0.150
New Jersey							0.213
New York							0.079
Ohio							0.143
Pennsylvania							0.071

Sources: Charles S. Bullock III and Ronald Keith Gaddie, *The Triumph of Voting Rights in the South* (Norman: University of Oklahoma Press, 2009), table 12.4; Joint Center for Political and Economic Studies, *Black Elected Officials: A Statistical Summary* (Washington, DC: Joint Center for Political and Economic Studies, 2001), table 3.

Intentional creation of majority-minority districts was controversial at the time and continues to be so. On the one hand, grouping voters by race may reduce incentives for interracial cooperation and coalition building. Against this, there is much evidence that a visible Black presence in elected leadership positions makes a difference, both subjectively and objectively. A Black political organizer in Mississippi remarked, "The number of victories isn't as important as the fact that they symbolize a bit of black authority, a gradual return to respect for those accustomed to having their lives manipulated by white hands."[25] Tom McCain, the first Black candidate for office in Edgefield County, South Carolina, since Reconstruction argued: "There's an inherent value in office-holding that goes far beyond picking up the garbage. A race of people who are excluded from office will always be second class."[26] Beyond mere perceptions are the many services that Black representatives provide for their constituents. Studies of Congress show that, although the racial composition of delegations has little effect on roll-call votes, Black representatives make a decisive difference for constituency services, hiring Black staff members, locating district offices, and establishing a sense of trust with Black voters.[27] A Black official in Panola County, Mississippi, noted, "Blacks feel they can come to me and get answers to problems; they have a connection with the system."[28]

Because federal and state legislative districts have been subject to change through judicial and political processes, this essay concentrates on statewide elections, where no redistricting has occurred. Indeed, one of the clearest indications that race remains politically salient in the South is that elections of Black candidates to statewide offices there has been and continues to be extremely rare. In modern times, no Black candidate has been elected to a state constitutional office in Alabama, Arkansas, Louisiana, Mississippi, Tennessee, or Texas. The two most conspicuous counterexamples—Douglas Wilder of Virginia and Tim Scott of South Carolina—are both exceptions that prove the general rule. Wilder was first elected as lieutenant governor in 1985, then governor in 1989; both elections were extremely close, and the bulk of Wilder's white votes came from northern counties and Hampton Roads, fast-growing areas with large nonnative populations.[29] Tim Scott is a conservative Republican who was appointed to a vacant US Senate seat by Governor Nikki Haley in 2013 and then elected for the remainder of the term in 2014. Although Scott's election confirms that southern white attitudes toward race have changed since civil rights days, his political isolation also underscores the extent to which race and partisan polarization have become closely intertwined in the contemporary South.

ECONOMIC GAINS FROM VOTING RIGHTS

A large question looming over this discussion is whether the advent of voting rights actually enhanced the wellbeing of African Americans in the South. One direct effect was to reduce and then virtually eliminate the extreme racial rhetoric that had long characterized southern campaigns. Knowledgeable observers of South Carolina politics reported, "The increase in African-American voter registration and turnout almost immediately ended the white supremacist rhetoric that had been a hallmark of the state's political leaders."[30] In the 1967 Mississippi gubernatorial election, "neither of the two major candidates dared praise segregation as overtly as had the candidates four and eight years earlier."[31] True, a diehard segregationist candidate like Lester Maddox could make a political splash, becoming governor of Georgia in 1967. But even Maddox in office moderated his racial rhetoric, and he was succeeded in 1971 by Jimmy Carter, an outspoken racial progressive. The year 1970 marked something of a turning point in which traditional racial rhetoric proved politically unsuccessful throughout the South. In that year, former Dixiecrat Thurmond backed a segregationist gubernatorial candidate who lost to moderate Democrat John West. Having gotten the message, Thurmond became the first southern senator to appoint a Black staff aide and the first to sponsor an African American for a federal judgeship. For the rest of his career, Thurmond actively sought Black votes, achieving moderate success.[32] Five years after passage of the VRA, Black voting seemed clearly to be a force for political moderation.[33]

Moderation in local politics also generated improved access to city and county services, such as police and fire protection, paved roads and street lights, recreational facilities, and appointments to boards, commissions, and civil service jobs.[34] Systematic evidence compiled by political scientist James Button for six Florida counties shows that the percentage of streets paved in Black neighborhoods was far below the white norm in 1960 but rose rapidly in that decade, eventually becoming at or near parity with white areas by the 1980s. As the white mayor of Titusville explained: "Through the early 1960s the city council was composed of an old-line group of people—rural, southern, been here all their lives, and some of whom still carried Civil War memories. Blacks did not receive their fair share of services because they were considered second-, or even third-class citizens."[35]

Black voting and representation produced tangible economic benefits by changing the racial composition of public-sector employment.[36] The biggest increases were realized in large cities with Black city councils and mayors. When Atlanta first elected a Black mayor in 1973, Black employment rose from 38.1 to 55.6 percent of the total; Black administrators jumped from 7.1 to 32.6 percent, and professionals from 15.2 to 42.2 percent.[37] In Richmond, Virginia, Black city employment was restricted to service and maintenance jobs until 1963. African Americans attained a majority on the city council in 1977 after redistricting in response to a Supreme Court ruling rejecting a proposed annexation. As a direct result, the parity score for minority employment increased from 0.756 to 1.10. As in Atlanta, employment shares rose most rapidly in administrative and professional categories.[38] Some of these gains may have happened even without local political voice because the 1972 amendments to the Civil Rights Act extended Title VII coverage to the public sector. But Black political representation also clearly made a difference. Using a national panel of cities and metropolitan areas for 1971–2004, economists John V. C. Nye, Ilia Ranier, and Thomas Stratmann find that election of a Black mayor in a city with a large Black population had a large positive impact on Black employment in both public and private sectors, labor-force participation, and income.[39]

Similar effects are found in studies of VRA impacts at the county level. Comparing covered and noncovered North Carolina counties in the mid-1980s, political scientist Joel Thompson reported that the VRA counties had not only greater increases in Black voter registration and elected officials but also more rapid growth in Black incomes and occupational status, and they attracted more revenue from both county and outside governmental sources. A later study by Abhay P. Aneja and Carlos F. Avenancio-Leon compares covered and noncovered counties throughout the South between 1950 and 1980, showing that coverage reduced Black-white wage gaps by expanding public-sector employment opportunities for Black workers and by support for antidiscrimination policies. Economists Andrea Bernini, Giovanni Facchini, and Cecelia Testa find that southern counties more strongly affected by the VRA—those compelled by litigation to switch to single-member districts—elected more Black officials, gained more revenue from state and federal transfers, and provided more public goods and services, primarily education. Giovanni Facchini, Brian G. Knight, and Cecelia Testa report that in counties covered by the VRA with large numbers of new Black voters, Black arrest rates fell.[40]

Most of the foregoing examples are from jurisdictions in which Black voters constituted a majority or near majority of the electorate. There is evidence, however, that economic gains were also realized through the policies of states, none of which had Black majorities even after the registration surge impelled by the VRA. The most thoroughly documented study is by Elizabeth Cascio and Ebonya Washington, who track the share of state transfers (chiefly for education) to counties with higher Black population shares, comparing states with literacy tests (and therefore covered by the VRA) and those without. The authors estimate that the mean county in a literacy-test state saw an increase of 16.4 percent in per-capita transfers over the period. Citing contemporary testimony, Cascio and Washington interpret the result as an indication that Blacks were part of new statewide coalitions. The shift in state resource allocation was strongly associated with increased turnout in presidential elections but occurred well before any major Black representation in state government.[41]

The case for positive economic benefits for African Americans from voting seems strong. A further question raised in *Sharing the Prize* is whether these advances came at the expense of white southerners or instead were part of a broader restructuring by which most white southerners also gained. If we define progress in terms of shares—of fund transfers, public services, or employment—then the game is zero-sum by definition. But if Black political participation facilitated biracial cooperation toward mutually beneficial goals, then both races may have been net winners. Many local studies describe precisely this outcome. Returning to Panola County, Mississippi, after a twenty-year absence, Frederick Wirt found: "Among white leaders of Panola County there was a general sense that voting changes had benefited not merely blacks but whites as well. . . . Whites reported that black empowerment had helped them overturn the old power holders and the planters who had blocked racial and economic change."[42] Cooperation to attract community health centers into underserved areas is a good illustration of the potential return to interracial coalitions. Healthcare historian Bonnie Lefkowitz writes, "In South Carolina, Mississippi, and Texas, the centers not only drew strength from the civil rights movement, they irrevocably altered the white power structure that controlled the economic and environmental determinants of disease."[43]

Major southern cities also developed biracial coalitions in the wake of Black political empowerment. In Birmingham, Alabama, a city beleaguered by racial conflict and industrial decline, new Black voters supported long-stymied city-government reform and bond issues to improve municipal services. The twenty-year administration of the first Black mayor, Richard Arrington, was marked by collaboration with the largely white business community and a development program centered on the University of Alabama–Birmingham and its medical complex.[44] Another successful biracial coalition was in Charlotte, North Carolina, which struggled to an uneasy compromise on school integration and busing in the 1970s. A move to district representatives in 1977 increased Black participation and contributed to passage of an airport bond issue in 1978, reversing an earlier defeat. The election of civil rights hero Harvey Gantt as mayor in 1981 seemed to symbolize the post–civil rights consensus around economic growth, helping Charlotte become the third-largest banking center in the nation.[45] Perhaps the most famous example of biracial growth is Atlanta, which emerged from 1960s turmoil to the status of world-class city—fourth-largest concentration of Fortune 500 companies, world's busiest airport, home of prominent universities and high-tech industries—with Black political leadership since 1974. Atlanta's progress has been sufficient to attract an influx of young, educated, predominantly white people since 1990.[46]

THE VOTING RIGHTS ACT AND THE TWO-PARTY SOUTH

The most stringent test for the proposition that Black voting rights were broadly beneficial is the effect on the political climate in statewide elections. Among the best-known quotations from the civil rights era is Lyndon Johnson's reported remark to Bill Moyers after signing the historic 1964 bill, "I think we just handed the South to the Republicans for a generation." The statement is repeated because it seems prophetic: the twenty-first-century South is solidly Republican, and the region has been voting that way in presidential elections since the 1970s. But as commonly used, the quote is deeply misleading. Johnson knew that the Civil Rights Act had damaged him with the white South, but he also believed that the VRA would repair much of this loss by making moderate southern Democrats competitive. In a memo entitled "Negro Vote in the South," presidential aide Lawrence O'Brien pointed out that Black voters had provided Johnson's margin of victory in four southern states.[47] Martin Luther King Jr. expanded on this argument in a January 1965 phone conversation with Johnson: "It's very interesting, Mr. President, to note that the only states you didn't carry in the South . . . have less than forty percent of the Negroes registered to vote. . . . It's so important to get Negroes registered in large numbers in the South. It would be this coalition of the Negro vote and the moderate white vote that will really make the new South."[48]

King's vision of a successful biracial coalition was largely borne out in state-wide elections over the next twenty-five to thirty years. Figure 14.3 shows the distribution of US senators and governors by party in the South from 1960 to 2019. Republican strength rose from nearly zero between 1965 and 1970, but Democrats continued to be competitive through the 1990s. Southern Democratic governors outnumbered Republicans as late as 2002.

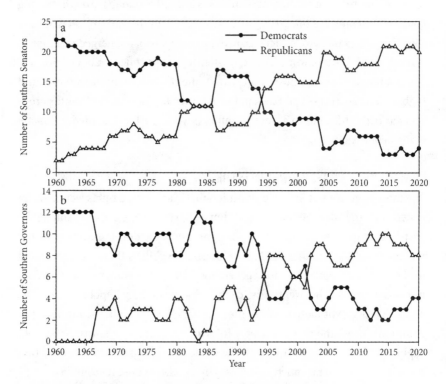

Figure 14.3. Southern Senators and Southern Governors by Party, 1960-1921
Source: Proquest Statistical Abstract of the United States, various years.

A count of officeholders is not necessarily a good measure of interparty competition because it does not tell us what was happening within the states. A tool commonly used by political scientists is the Ranney Index, which aggregates each party's proportion of success (percentage of votes for governor, percentage of legislative seats), duration of success (length of time under party control), and frequency of divided government. As adapted to federal elections by J. David

Woodard, the picture is much the same as in figures 14.3a and 14.3b. For 1956–62, all the southern states were classified as One-Party Democrat. Between 1964 and 1978, five states became Two-Party Competitive (Florida, South Carolina, Tennessee, Texas, and Virginia). Between 1980 and 1994, nine of the eleven states were Two-Party Competitive. Illustrating that these categorizations are far from permanent, two states (North Carolina and Virginia) actually reverted from One-Party Republican to Two-Party Competitive between periods. True, a strong rightward shift after 1994 is clearly visible. The point is that the move into One-Party Republican rule is historically very recent in most southern states.[49]

Such indices do not necessarily capture the changes in voting behavior we are after because differences between presidential and state voting can persist for long periods and congressional elections (both state and federal) are subject to influence by redistricting. Figure 14.4 (top) displays the Democratic share of the vote in all southern statewide elections from 1960 to 2016. The trend from 1970 to 1992 is barely perceptible, the average falling by less than 2 percentage points. The trend is slightly faster when only Senate votes are included (figure 14.4 bottom), but here, too, the decisive shift came in 1994.[50]

Because 1994 was the year in which the Republicans gained control of the House of Representatives (for the first time since the 1950s), the relatively sudden shift in partisan balance is often attributed to the redistricting decisions of the early 1990s. But Ebonya Washington compares congressional political outcomes (party and ideology) in redistricted states' litigation with those in southern states not covered by the VRA, finding no significant difference between the two. Political scientists John R. Petrocik and Scott W. Desposato show that the direct effect of reshuffling Black and white voters had no more than a minor influence on short-term partisan results. The critical factor, in their view, was a "pro-GOP surge, independent of redistricting . . . [and] an impossible-to-anticipate, large, anti-Democratic tide."[51] In any case, the shares in figures 14.4a and 14.4b are for states, whose boundaries did not change. In 1994, Republicans won five of six southern senate races and four of seven governorships. It appears that the trend as well as the level shifted, a genuine regime change in regional politics.

Looking back from the twenty-first century, many writers are inclined to see the transition to a Republican South as inevitable, a "process [that] took decades to completely sort itself out" but was nonetheless bound to happen. On this view, realignment was constrained only by the need to build an infrastructure of Re-

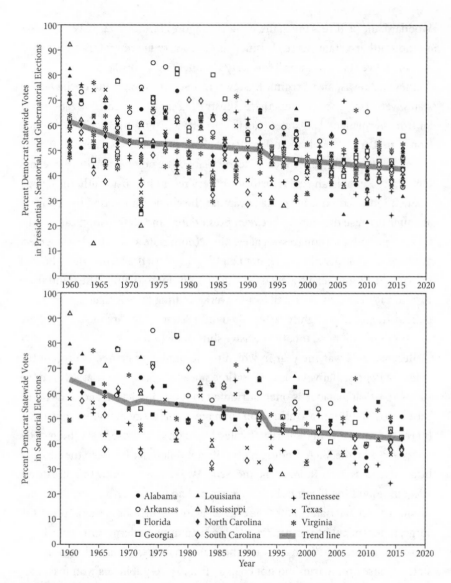

Figures 14.4. Democratic Shares of Statewide Votes in the South, 1960-2016

Source: America Votes: A Handbook of Contemporary American Election Statistics (Government Affairs Institute), various years. Odd-year elections have been assigned to the following calendar year.

publican support networks and "viable Republican candidates who campaigned on a message that was in step with the views of white southerners." The premise of this interpretation is that the white South "has never changed fundamentally, in a political sense or even a cultural one." As one recent observer puts it: "Why did Democrats lose the white South? . . . Because the party became too liberal on civil rights and racist white Southerners didn't like it."[52]

Such interpretations are unhistorical. Knowledgeable observers of southern politics during the 1970s and 1980s did not portray a shaky temporary waystation on the road to conservative restoration. They thought they were seeing the wave of the future, a region that at long last had shaken off the race issue, freeing its politics for realignment along economic lines. Surveying the scene in 1976, Jack Bass and Walter DeVries write: "The political liberation of southern blacks, important as it is, may be of less significance than the liberation of southern whites. . . . The South retains some distinctive regional qualities, but it has joined the nation's political mainstream."[53] Alexander Lamis published the first edition of *The Two-Party South* in 1984, opening with the observation: "By the early 1970s . . . one could discern a distinct lessening of racial tension in the region. . . . [T]he altered racial environment contributed to the development of two-party politics." He concludes, "Party competition has now firmly settled into the region."[54] These statements were not revised in the edition of 1988, which noted that "the most striking feature of the recent period is continuity with the patterns described in the original edition."[55] Writing in 1990, political scientist Laurence W. Moreland held, "there is no evidence to suggest that a new one-party Republican South looms in the future."[56] Even in the decade following the transformative election of 1994, the eminent scholars Earl Black and Merle Black wrote: "If the old solid Democratic South has vanished, a comparably solid Republican South has not yet developed. Nor is one likely to emerge."[57]

An analysis of patterns of party identification among native white southerners in the early 1990s confirmed the emergence of a class-based partisanship that had been missing in earlier decades: higher-status individuals favored Republican identification, while those whites who remained Democrats had "tendencies similar to whites in the rest of the nation: older, Catholic, union members, blue-collar, working-class, less educated, and less affluent."[58] An update ten years later confirmed the shift toward "normal," class-based polarization among white southerners and the "movement away from race as the sole issue of importance

to Southern voters."[59] In their 2006 reassessment of postwar southern political history, political scientists Byron Shafer and Richard Johnston found that
southern-white party identification was tightly linked to social class, refuting the
notion that the politics of race provided a "reliable and consistent contribution"
to Republican ascendancy.[60]

To be sure, from the information in figures 14.4a and 14.4b alone, one could
not distinguish an old-line segregationist Democrat from a new-breed progressive. In fact, the 1970s South saw a wave of "New South" Democratic governors,
including such prominent and successful figures as Reubin Askew of Florida,
Dale Bumpers and David Pryor of Arkansas, Jimmy Carter and George Busbee
of Georgia, Edwin Edwards of Louisiana, and John West of South Carolina. All
were moderates by national standards, and all had similar programs to replace
the divisive race issue with unifying support for economic development through
education and other infrastructure investments. Nor was this a one-generation
affair. The first wave of the 1970s was succeeded by a second wave in the 1980s,
featuring names such as Bob Graham of Florida, Dave Treen of Louisiana, William Winter of Mississippi, Richard Riley and Carroll Campbell of South Carolina, Chuck Robb of Virginia, and Bill Clinton of Arkansas. Historian Gordon
Harvey writes that since 1970, every southern state except Alabama has elected
at least one New South governor.[61]

The picture was much the same for southern Democrats in the US Senate.
Not only did their numbers remain high through the 1980s, but their average
ADA liberalism ratings continued to rise during this period. Well-known names
include former governors Hollings, Bumpers, and Pryor plus Ralph Yarborough
of Texas and Albert Gore Sr. of Tennessee. Yarborough and Gore were defeated
for reelection in 1971 largely over the Vietnam War rather than race or economics. But only Gore lost to a Republican, and in that case the seat was retaken six
years later by progressive Democrat Jim Sasser, who served until 1995. Clearly,
these experienced politicians did not believe they were out of step with their
constituencies.[62]

RACE, ECONOMY, AND REALIGNMENT IN THE SOUTH

If this characterization of the two-party South is accurate, the obvious question
is, why did the region's voters move so decisively to the right from the mid-
1990s onward? Broadly speaking, historians and social scientists have offered

two main interpretations of realignment: the first emphasizes race and racial backlash, featuring the emergence of a new "coded" language reframing issues in ostensibly race-neutral terms; the second argues that the main driving force has been economic development, including the shift of population into suburbs, attracted by conservative positions on economic issues such as taxes and government spending. Other accounts feature innovations in political rhetoric and outreach, such as the mobilization of evangelical Christians on issues such as abortion and homosexuality; but the question of racialized appeals versus economic interests persists even in this broader frame.[63]

A reasonable person can believe that there is truth in both interpretations. The superficial race-neutrality of modern southern political discourse cannot be taken at face value. Ilyana Kuziemko and Ebonya Washington find that holding racially conservative views is the single strongest predictor of the shift in southern-white party identification between 1958 and 1980, a period when regional survey responses on race questions were moving toward national norms.[64] Although the openly racist rhetoric of earlier times was no longer acceptable, unobtrusive measures of racial attitudes—designed to remove the effects of social desirability—pointed to distinctly higher levels of racial prejudice in the South than in the non-South even in the 1990s.[65] Political scientists Nicholas Valentino and David Sears find a strong association between southern ideological conservatism and "modern" or "symbolic" racial attitudes, reflected in beliefs that Black disadvantages are caused by poor work ethic or that Blacks make excessive demands and get too many concessions from government.[66] At times, the racial appeals were not even disguised, as in the blatant images deployed by Jesse Helms during his North Carolina senatorial campaigns against Harvey Gantt in 1990 and 1996.

The pervasiveness of southern race consciousness, however, does not imply that economic considerations did not matter. V. O. Key famously writes, "Whatever phase of the southern political process one seeks to understand, sooner or later the trail of inquiry leads to the Negro." But his very next sentence reads: "Yet it is far from the truth to paint a picture of southern politics as being chiefly concerned with the maintenance of the supremacy of white over black."[67] That disclaimer is as apt for later decades as it was in the Jim Crow era. Whatever their racial attitudes, the median southern white voter cast a ballot for a moderate-to-liberal Democrat until 1994. Veteran observers of southern politics saw this break as a discontinuity that could not have been foreseen even a few years before.

Alexander Lamis, for example, in a sequel to his earlier books on the two-party South, stressed that the trends down to 1990 did not foretell the Republican surge.[68] Writing two decades later, Charles Bullock III remarked: "After seven elections in which between 45 percent and 55 percent of whites voted Democratic, support fell [in 1994] to barely a third and has yet to rise."[69]

There are no official records of voter choices by race, and the archival inventory of exit polls for nonpresidential elections is not complete. But the basic mathematics of southern electoral demography confirms the truth of Bullock's statement in light of the facts that the Black share of state electorates was essentially stable from 1980 to 2014 (ranging between 15 and 30 percent in most states), and Black voters remained solidly Democratic, playing no part in the realignment process. Throughout the period, the share of Hispanic voters was too small to have political significance outside of Texas and Florida. The implication is that figures 14.4a and 14.4b understate the discontinuity of the 1990s, which was entirely a white-voter phenomenon. Available exit polls confirm this general picture. For senatorial elections in the 1980s, for example, Democratic incumbents were comfortably returned to office with biracial majorities, while open-seat competition for white votes was essentially even.[70]

What happened between 1990 and 1994 to precipitate such a drastic political response? Ronald Gaddie and Donna Hoffman observe that unlike previous "critical realignment" elections, the 1994 voter revolt defies easy categorization in terms of issues or events, even in the South: "The potential culprits in this mystery, in short, are numerous. . . . [T]he elections of the 1990s might be characterized as realignment by a hundred cuts."[71] Many observers point to the congressional-redistricting measures of the early 1990s, which created Black-majority districts and allegedly drove the parties to extremes. But statewide elections displayed the same trend shift at the same time. Political scientists Adam Bonica and Gary Cox argue that the prospect of Republican control of the House (for the first time since the 1950s) focused the attention of activists, donors, and party leaders on the battle for majority status, a process that may have had spillover effects on statewide elections.[72] But if so, what was the substantive content of this intensified mobilization? Lamis and others emphasize the personal unpopularity of President Clinton in 1994, reflecting an apparently successful Republican effort to "nationalize" House elections in that year. According to Gary Jacobsen, "fully 44 percent of [sampled] white southern males said that their House vote was a vote against Clinton."[73] But Clinton and his vice president, Al Gore, were both southerners and ran about even in the South against George H. W. Bush and Dan Quayle in 1992. What could have changed so dramatically in just two years?

It seems to have escaped attention in this literature that much of the South experienced wrenching economic dislocation at precisely this time, as the manufacturing industries that had formed the core of the regional economy began their historic descent in response to import competition. Figure 14.5 conveys some sense of the magnitude of employment losses. North Carolina lost the most jobs, mainly because it was the largest manufacturing state. But in proportionate terms, the patterns were similar and the falloffs nearly as great in all the southern states. Research by David Autor, David Dorn, and Gordon Hanson documents the geographic concentration of trade-exposed local labor markets in these states.[74]

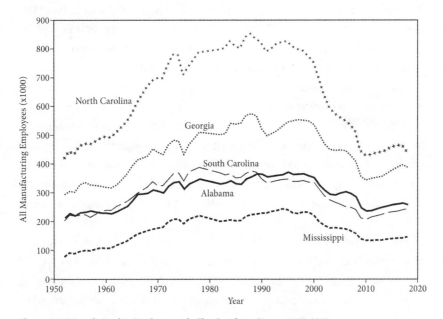

Figure 14.5. Manufacturing Employment in Five Southern States, 1952–2018
Source: Bureau of Labor Statistics. Figures for 2018 are from Proquest Statistical Abstract of the United States, 2021, table 1041.

Could this global economic restructuring have affected regional partisan voting? Indeed, it was front and center. One highly visible object was the North American Free Trade Agreement (NAFTA), enacted in November 1993, with vigorous backing from President Clinton, and implemented January 1, 1994. Although supported by some parts of the industry, NAFTA was strongly opposed by workers and unions in textile areas (as well as the industrial Midwest). The origins of the pact were bipartisan, but most of the blame focused on Clinton, and Democrats voting in favor of the agreement suffered badly at the polls in 1994. The most famous example was Tom Foley of Washington, the first House speaker to lose his seat since the Civil War. But southern Democrats supporting NAFTA were also hard hit. Those who lost seats included six-term incumbent Buddy Darden of Georgia and David Price of North Carolina. Rising star Clete Johnson of Georgia lost his reelection bid by 31 percentage points, the largest margin of the year. A handful of other incumbents barely survived.[75]

Of more direct relevance for the textiles and apparel industry was the 1994 Agreement on Textile and Clothing, negotiated as part of the World Trade Organization's Uruguay Round. The agreement phased out the import quotas of the Multi-Fibre Arrangement (MFA) over the ten-year period 1994–2004. The two issues interacted when Clinton sent letters to textile-and-apparel-state representatives shortly before the vote on NAFTA, promising that an extended phaseout of fifteen years would be secured. Instead, a month after the NAFTA vote, US negotiators accepted the ten-year plan. Figure 14.6 shows that employment in these sectors, which had been drifting downward through the 1980s, began a precipitous decline in 1994 in every southern textile state. Although textiles and apparel composed less than 10 percent of US manufacturing employment in 1990, they accounted for nearly one-third of the employment contraction between 1990 and 2003.[76]

Business leaders, workers, and their unions clearly understood the importance of import quotas to the industry's survival. Maintaining them was the object of lobbying and grassroots mobilization for decades. A landmark of sorts was the Textile and Apparel Enforcement Act of 1985, passed by both houses but vetoed by President Reagan. As the vote to override the veto neared, thousands of workers bombarded their representatives with pleas for support. Many writers bolstered their case by pointing out that in the wake of the civil rights movement, textiles and apparel now provided employment for women and minorities in large num-

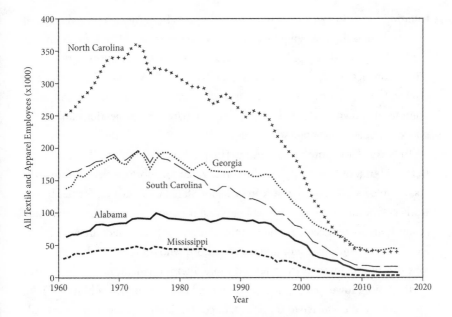

Figure 14.6. Textiles and Apparel Employment in Five Southern States, 1961–2016
Source: Annual Survey of Manufactures, Geographic Area Series.

bers. Within five days of the override vote, Reagan announced the successful negotiation of a new, tougher MFA that expanded coverage to fibers such as ramie,
linen, and silk blends and would prevent "destructive import surges." The override
motion was subsequently defeated, but textile and apparel workers had accomplished their main goal. Despite Republican support for free trade in principle,
highly mobilized textile workers received more political responsiveness from the
Reagan administration in the 1980s than from Bill Clinton in the 1990s.[77]

As events unfolded, the worst fears of the trade-liberalization critics were
realized. Over the next fifteen years, employment fell far more rapidly than industry analysts expected.[78] Most economic studies of job displacement identify
the 2001 entry of China into the World Trade Organization as the key turning
point.[79] But in the South, the break came earlier: in the leading textiles-and-
apparel states, more factory jobs were lost before 2001 than after. Economists
Shushank Hakbyan and John McLaren use census data for 1990 and 2000 to
identify the effects of NAFTA, finding dramatically lowered wage growth for
blue-collar workers and for affected localities.[80] NAFTA may have been a con-

tributing factor, in that textile and apparel imports from Mexico surged between 1994 and 2000 (before being displaced by Chinese imports), but the demise of the MFA precipitated rapid growth of textiles and apparel imports from many other countries as well, including Pakistan, Bangladesh, Vietnam, Indonesia, and Canada.[81] The expansion of Chinese imports after 2001 added another inflection point to the downward spiral, helping explain why early projections underestimated the speed of change so severely.

To be sure, the South was a full participant in the boom of the late 1990s. But that burst of prosperity had little relevance for most displaced millworkers. Detailed studies by the Bureau of Labor Statistics show that former textile workers typically experienced long bouts of joblessness and found new jobs only at substantially reduced pay and benefits, especially health insurance. These effects are confirmed by Autor and his coauthors, who find that workers who lost jobs to Chinese imports experienced more unemployment, lower labor-force participation, lower wages, and little sectoral or geographic mobility.[82] These losses were not exclusive to the South, of course, but evidence from Trade Adjustment Assistance certifications confirm that states most heavily invested in low-wage manufacturing had the largest shares of their workforces affected by trade, southern states leading the lists.[83] Reports in recent years of a "comeback" for the domestic textiles industry have little relevance for most former textile workers: the new jobs are a small fraction of previous levels and the required skill levels now far higher.[84]

This account should not be understood as a suggestion that switching party allegiance was a rational response to economic distress, or that displaced textile workers were the cutting edge of southern Republicanism. The argument instead is that the political-economic basis for a biracial coalition was undermined by deindustrialization. The campaign to protect textile and apparel jobs was a biracial group with a common economic goal in a setting that could not be stigmatized in racial terms. By the 1990s, nearly 30 percent of nondurable-manufacturing employees in leading textile states, and about 35 percent of operatives, were Black. Layoffs were roughly proportionate to this racial composition, implying that the majority of job losses were suffered by whites.[85] Through their unions as well as through impromptu political groups, the races cooperated on appeals to preserve jobs, just as they had on campaigns for industrial development in earlier decades. The South was never highly unionized, but labor organizations punched above their weight in political contests, especially with working-class voters. Deindustrialization decimated union membership as well as factory jobs (see figure 14.7). Once the structural basis for that coalition was removed, it was only to be expected that the attractiveness of alternative appeals was a function of regional culture, including but not exclusively racial attitudes.

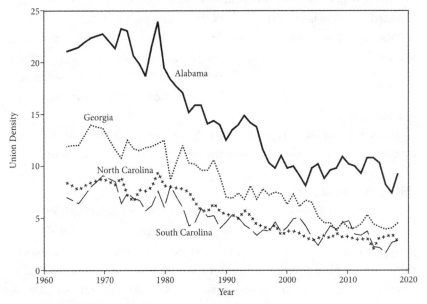

Figure 14.7. Union Density in Textile States, 1964–2018
Source: Barry T. Hirsch, David A. McPherson, and Wayne Vroman, "Estimates of Union Density by State," *Monthly Labor Review* 124 (2001). Updated annually at unionstats.com.

Under the circumstances, it is hardly surprising that Black and Black found that low-income white southerners "displayed little working-class solidarity in their partisan preferences" in 1996, more than half preferring Republicans on the basis of religion, abortion, and gun-owner rights as well as opposition to racial preferences. What deserves emphasis is that this pattern of non-class-based voting by white southerners was a change from the previous generation. Ray Texeira and Alan Abramowitz show that Democratic identification among lower socioeconomic white southerners fell dramatically in the 1990s and even more dramatically afterward: "Class differences in party identification have not disappeared but are considerably smaller than they were thirty or forty years ago."[86] In an update to their 2006 book, even Shafer and Johnston acknowledge a post-2000 Republican shift among low-income southern white voters, "the people who for forty years rejected the new southern Republican party."[87]

Across broad swaths of the region, deindustrialization and economic stagnation have been the dominant facts of life for white southerners in recent decades. The travel writer Paul Theroux spent three years on the road in the South and reported: "If there is one experience of the Deep South that stayed with me it was the sight of shutdown factories and towns with their hearts torn out of them, and few jobs. There are outsourcing stories all over America, but the effects are stark in the Deep South. . . . I found towns in South Carolina, Mississippi, Alabama, and Arkansas that looked like towns in Zimbabwe, just as overlooked and beleaguered."[88]

This essay's modest proposal is that the change in southern white voting behavior was associated with this deterioration in economic conditions.

CONSEQUENCES: RACIAL POLARIZATION

Whatever the combination of economic, ideological, and racial motivations for the southern swing to the Republican Party, the effect was to exacerbate racial polarization in southern political life. Increased racial polarization in presidential voting has been documented by three MIT faculty members in two studies prepared in connection with judicial review of the VRA.[89] The authors compare states covered by the act (primarily southern) with those uncovered or only partially covered using exit polls from presidential elections since 1984. The gap between Black and white voters (as well as between Hispanic and white voters) was always higher in the covered states, a regional contrast that increased over time, with a spurt between 2004 and 2008 presumably associated with the candidacy of Barack Obama. Regional differences in polarization by these measures increased again between 2008 and 2012. Although partisanship in presidential votes is more easily tracked over time, the evidence suggests that similar patterns held in state and district voting. In one sense, we already knew this because the southern Republican voters had been virtually all-white throughout the post–civil rights era, while Democratic voters were biracial.[90]

As Republican majorities have emerged in the southern states, many state legislatures have taken on attributes of one-party regimes, with manifest consequences for racial relationships. Table 14.2 shows that prior to 1994, Black legislators were in the majority party in virtually all southern state legislatures. Their numbers actually increased between 1992 and 2010, but many lost majority status following the 1994 midterm elections. The decisive blow came with the 2010 midterms, after which 95.5 percent of southern Black state legislators had minority status. (Both houses of the Arkansas legislature became majority-Republican in 2014, completing the cycle.) Although Republicans made gains outside of the South during these years as well, more than half of nonsouthern Black state legislators belonged to the majority party throughout the period. In Alabama, Florida, Mississippi, and Georgia, more than half the Democratic state legislators were Black by 2010, constraining the party's ability to appeal to white voters.[91]

Table 14.2. Status of Black State Legislators, Southern States, 1994–2011

Status	*Pre-1994 Midterms*		*Post-1994 Midterms*		*Pre-2010 Midterms*		*Post-2010 Midterms*	
	State House	*State Senate*	*State House*	*State Senate*	*State House*	*State Senate*	*State House*	*State Senate*
Majority Party	158 (99.3%)	43 (100%)	174 (81.7%)	61 (91.0%)	117 (47.8%)	47 (58.8%)	11 (4.5%)	4 (5.6%)
Minority Party	1 (0.7%)	0 (0.0%)	39 (18.3%)	6 (9.0%)	128 (52.2%)	33 (41.2%)	231 (95.5%)	67 (94.4%)
Total	159	43	213	67	245	80	242	71

Source: David A. Bositis, "Resegregation in Southern Politics?," Joint Center for Political and Economic Studies Research Brief (Nov. 2011), table 1.

An immediate consequence was to end what had been a steady advance of Black legislators into leadership positions. In Georgia, the Legislative Black Caucus was highly effective in the 1990s; by 1999–2000, caucus members chaired four committees in the house and five in the senate, including the powerful Rules Committee. The loss of Democratic control in 2004 greatly diminished African American legislators' influence, reducing them to token chairmanships of minor committees. African Americans gained several chairmanships in the Florida Senate between 1988 and 1996, but all of these were lost with the new Republican majority in 1996. In North Carolina, African Americans held powerful committee chairmanships and leadership positions in both houses, progress that largely ended with the Republican majorities of 2012. In South Carolina, "with the loss of control by Democrats [in 2002], African American legislators have little prospect of playing significant roles in the South Carolina legislature, though black clout in the Democratic caucus is enhanced."[92]

Although earlier studies reported that greater Black representation tended to move policy outcomes toward the preferences of Black voters, more refined analysis finds that these effects are vitiated when the parties are highly racialized and the opposite party is in power—as in most southern states in the twenty-first century.[93] Even where the Democrats were extremely conservative, the change in party control has seen a major diminishment of Black representation. In Alabama, three-decade state senator Hank Sanders lost the chairmanship of the Finance and Taxation Education Committee when Republicans gained the majority in 2010. Sanders had used his position to increase the level and equitability of state resources for education and other forms of infrastructure. But with the Republican takeover, he and other Black legislators were almost completely excluded from major decisions. According to Auburn political scientist Gerald Johnson: "There's been a total collapse of Madisonian Democratic government. There's no debate, no compromise, and no minority participation—and by minority, I mean Democratic or African-American."[94]

This is not to suggest that the South has returned or will return to the pre–civil rights era in its political race relations. Black influence in state legislatures may be limited, but overall Black political participation remains high, and representation in municipal and county offices provides a considerable measure of self-determination and racial equity. Republican control of state government has not prompted mass dismissals of Black public-sector employees. Some observers believe that the South has settled into a "New Racial System" in which separate political spheres are largely respected, just as the dualistic system of higher education has essentially been recognized by the courts, with biracial approval.[95]

This regime may have some virtue in maintaining racial peace, but there are at least two major drawbacks. One-party dominance creates both an incentive and an opportunity to limit access to voting in order to maintain partisan advantage. When the parties are racially polarized, "partisan advantage" has inescapable racial implications. In an exhaustive review of the voting rights record since 1965, J. Morgan Kousser shows that proven violations have been overwhelmingly concentrated in the same jurisdictions covered by the triggering formula set down in 1970.[96] These largely southern states have led the way in measures making registration and voting more difficult for low-income voters, particularly since the Supreme Court's ruling in *Shelby County v. Holder* (2013) invalidating the VRA coverage formula. The second drawback is that policies adopted by the new Republican administrations do not appear to reflect the interests or preferences of a majority of state residents.

CONSEQUENCES: SUPPORT FOR EDUCATION AND ECONOMIC GROWTH

If the transition to Republican voting were constrained primarily by organizational inertia and switching costs, then we would not expect to find that attainment of Republican control led to substantive changes in public-policy choices. If southern Democrats were merely those conservatives who had not yet found it convenient to relabel themselves, why should their votes on policy issues change when the relabeling actually occurred? Yet policy continuity in southern states is not what we see. The first major disrupter was the VRA itself. With the ascendance of competitive two-party politics, a cohort of progressive New South governors (mainly Democrats) led campaigns to upgrade state school systems, escaping divisive racial issues to mobilize broad support for a pro-growth agenda that would benefit all residents.

South Carolina is a case in point. As of 1971, the state's chronically underfunded school system had long suffered dropout rates above 50 percent. Because teacher salaries fell 25 percent below the national average, more than half of recent teacher-education graduates left to work in other states. After defeating a segregationist opponent in 1970 with the help of Black voters, Governor John West launched a major effort to reduce dropout rates, particularly among Black students. Increased state spending between 1965 and 1975 was largely driven by surging state revenues rather than by higher taxes (reflecting the booming Sun Belt economy), but the share of the budget allocated to education also sharply increased. At the end of West's term in office, the conservative newspaper *Columbia State* gave the governor credit for "major advances in the economy and race relations," concluding, "We much prefer this New South thinking and goals to the moonlight, magnolias, and political hell-raisin that characterized the old Solid South." Although West was unable to change the state's system of school finance, his example paved the way for Governor Richard Riley's more sweeping Education Improvement Act of 1984.[97]

Similar patterns prevailed over much of the post–civil rights South. Figure 14.8 portrays per-pupil spending on K–12 education for eight southern states from 1948 to 2016 as a fraction of the national average. Despite fears that school integration would weaken support for public schools, Georgia, North Carolina, South Carolina, Virginia, and Tennessee actually accelerated their progress after 1965. Only in Alabama and Mississippi did relative public-school spending decline during the turbulent years 1966–70, after which these states, too, resumed the convergence trend toward the national average. Some of the increase reflected new federal support for public schools in low-income areas, but most of it was the result of new state-policy priorities and economic growth.

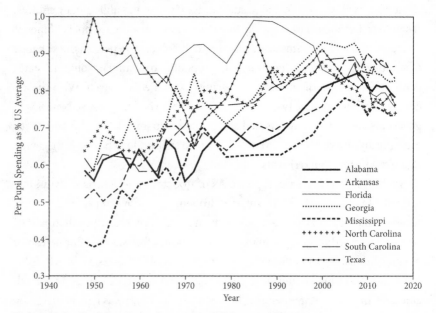

Figure 14.8. Per-Pupil Spending as Percentage of US Average, 1948–2016
Source: National Center for Education Statistics, *Digest of Education Statistics,* various years.

In Alabama, Governor Albert Brewer (who assumed office after the death of Lurleen Wallace) steered a major educational-reform package through the state legislature in 1969, saying, "Our problem is not race [but education]." When funds ballooned in the Special Education Trust Fund, he allocated them to teachers' salaries and capital improvements in the schools. Brewer was defeated by George Wallace in 1970, but an atmosphere of expansionary optimism continued into the

1980s, culminating in the Education Reform Act of 1984.[98] Sarah Reber shows that rising expenditures in Louisiana were instrumental in facilitating school desegregation, as the legislature allocated additional funding to districts where whites would be particularly affected.[99]

Even Mississippi, long the most educationally backward state in the nation, belatedly got into the reform act. The state's compulsory-education law, repealed in 1956 during the desegregation crisis, was reenacted in 1977. Gubernatorial candidate William Winter ran on an education-reform platform in 1979 and got most of his plan through the state legislature in 1982. With biracial support, state funding for kindergarten was introduced, teacher pay increased, and performance-based accreditation instituted. Performance gains from a new assistant-teacher program were said to be "one of the most visible signs of educational progress in the state."[100] Mississippi was the last state to provide funding for kindergarten; every other state in the former Confederacy enacted this reform between 1968 and 1978.[101]

The resurgence of southern public schooling did not survive the counterrevolution of partisan realignment: progress toward national spending levels was halted or reversed in each of these states (as shown in figure 14.8). In some cases, like Mississippi and North Carolina, the reversal predates Republican legislative control. Elsewhere, the reversal largely tracked the advent of Republican governors and state-legislative majorities. Cutbacks were particularly severe in Florida, Georgia, and North Carolina, reversing decades of relative progress. Florida and Texas, having distinctive political histories, were well ahead of other southern states in earlier decades. But these states joined the budget-cutting trend in the 1990s, ending the period in the middle of the regional pack. True, spending levels are in part a function of state per-capita income, which has declined relative to the national average in recent years (see figure 14.9). But even controlling for income, Republican control of the state legislature was associated with a significant fall in relative per-pupil spending in virtually all southern states.

The transition to Republican majorities may have been the proximate cause of these spending cuts, but an important background factor—perhaps jointly contributing to both developments—was the fact that a majority of public-school students were now people of color. This milestone was reached in 2007, prior to the Great Recession, but the trend had been underway for at least two decades. Unlike many urban school districts, this compositional shift was not driven primarily by white flight into private schools but by the influx of Hispanics, whose share of the total students increased from 6 percent in 1978 to more than 20 percent in 2008. Although the broad trends were similar nationwide, the South is the only region of the country to have a majority of both low-income students and students of color in the public schools.[102]

Southern institutions of higher education fared little better. In a turn-of-the-century assessment of the South's progress, historian Thomas G. Dyer calls attention to the extraordinary rise in the size and quality of the region's research universities from the 1960s through the 1990s. The growth had many sources, but "most important was the rolling of unprecedented large sums of tax money into public higher education from the late 1950s into the 1990s, in complete contrast to the pattern earlier in the century."[103] Dyer speculates ruefully that this period of expansive growth and enthusiasm for higher education might turn out to be an anomaly in the region's history, and trends in the twenty-first century suggest that such misgivings may be well founded. To be sure, tight state budgets and cuts to higher education have been experienced throughout the nation. But according to recent surveys, three of the five states with the largest cuts between 2008 and 2016 were southern: Louisiana was most drastic, with a 39-percent decrease, followed by South Carolina and Alabama. Seven of the twenty states with the most severe reductions between 2010 and 2015 were southern: Louisiana, Mississippi, Tennessee, Kentucky, South Carolina, Alabama, and Virginia. Most tellingly, five of the ten states with the greatest declines in university enrollments were in the South: Louisiana, Georgia, Alabama, North Carolina, and West Virginia.[104]

The rise in quality of southern schools and universities was an important feature of regional economic development in the postwar era—both a reflection of and a contributor to growth—persisting through the civil rights decades and even exemplified by the apparently successful response to the stresses of desegregation. A *Wall Street Journal* article on the relative decline of the southern economy in recent decades states: "Many economists say the most effective way for the South to regain its momentum would be to invest more in education, which would over time create a more skilled workforce to attract employers. But Mississippi State University economist Alan Barefield notes that it is difficult to reconcile with southern states' historical desire to keep spending and taxes low."[105] Both the article and Barefield fail to note that the region had somehow overcome this contradiction for nearly half a century.

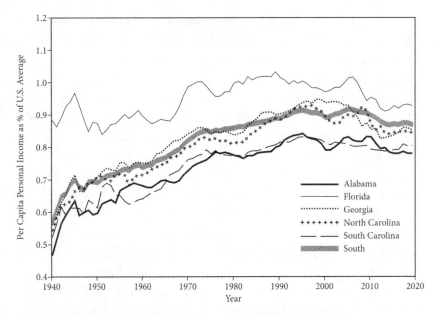

Figure 14.9. Per-Capita Personal Income as Percentage of US Average, 1940–2019
Source: Bureau of Economic Analysis. "South" is the BEA Southeast Region, which includes Kentucky and West Virginia but excludes Texas.

Tax cuts are sold as a stimulus to economic growth, but the track record instead shows a net contribution to the downward spiral. Figure 14.9 shows that the long era of southern convergence toward national per-capita income levels came to an end in the mid-1990s, closely corresponding to the shock of trade-led deindustrialization. Following a brief resurgence between 2000 and 2005—led by Florida and Texas—the trend has been steadily downward in the twenty-first century in every southern state but Virginia. Republican state policies cannot be blamed for the trend reversal of the 1990s, but these policies have done little to improve economic performance since then.

CONSEQUENCES: POLICIES TOWARD LOW-INCOME PEOPLE

After surveying dozens of studies and datasets, political scientist Matt Grossmann argues that the Republican ascendancy in state government has had only modest effects on policy trajectories. States that became "red" were usually conservative already, and policy overreach typically generates countervailing responses from interest groups and the courts. Grossmann concludes, "Republicans have few, if any, widespread real-world policy results to show for their state gains."[106] To this, the only appropriate response is Stephen Potter's famous quip, "Yes, but not in the South." Indeed, Grossmann acknowledges that welfare cuts represent an exception to his thesis, and that the South is an outlier. He writes: "The best case for Republican impact may be distributional," citing Katherine Newman and Rourke O'Brien's evidence that southern states have shifted their tax burdens away from income and property taxes toward sales taxes that fall disproportionately on poorer residents.[107] It is undeniable that the South has long been conservative, but Newman and O'Brien show that regional differences in tax regressivity widened sharply after 1990, coincident with the rise of Republican political control.

One of the earliest and clearest effects of the VRA was an increase in welfare coverage and payments. The change was most marked in Black Belt counties, where plantation elites had long managed relief programs in their own narrow interests. This effect came primarily through the election of Black county officials.[108] Over a somewhat longer period, studies find broader influence at the state level. Haynie reports that greater Black representation in state legislatures have tended to raise spending on health, education, and social welfare.[109]

Although local political control was always important, from the 1960s through the 1980s, welfare policy as such was largely constrained by federal rules. A feature of the conservative drift in national politics was the call to return more discretion on policy and spending allocation to the states. During the first Bush administration (1989–92), states were encouraged to apply for waivers under the Aid to Families with Dependent Children (AFDC) program to experiment with such features as time limits, family caps, and workfare. The real turning point, however, was passage of the Personal Responsibility and Work Opportunity Reconciliation Act in 1996 during the Clinton administration. This law ended the entitlement status of AFDC, replacing it with a time-limited assistance and work-requirement program called Temporary Assistance to Needy Families (TANF). The major policy change was to assign block-allocation grants to the states, which gained far more discretion on detailed conditions of welfare access.[110]

Responses to this newfound freedom varied widely among the states. Because benefit levels were not greatly affected by the change, the main variation was in the stringency of access rules and, by extension, the pace of decline in welfare enrollment. Analysts consistently report that the single most powerful variable associated with adoption of "get tough" policies was the share of African Americans on state welfare rolls.[111] Although social scientists seem averse to any mention of "region" in their interpretations, it is appropriate to point out that this key variable corresponds closely to the states of the former Confederacy. Table 14.3 shows that African American families constituted a majority of the TANF population in all of these states except Florida and Texas, where the share was smaller because of the large Hispanic population. In the other nine southern states, two-thirds of TANF families were Black in 1996, compared to an average of less than one-third in the rest of the country. The table also displays the reduction in the TANF population relative to the poverty population in these states, showing that the cuts were far more drastic in the South than elsewhere.

A more recent state-policy juncture was the decision to support or oppose Medicaid expansion under the 2010 Patient Protection and Affordable Care Act (or Obamacare). These choices were not intended as part of the legislation, but in upholding the act itself in June 2012, the Supreme Court ruled that states could not be compelled to implement expansion of Medicaid coverage for the low-income population not previously covered. The financial incentives to do so remained in place, however, in that the federal government would assume initially all and eventually 90 percent of the additional cost. This subsidy was sufficient to induce most governors to support expansion: all of the Democrats and about half of the Republicans, including many conservatives from otherwise red states. As Governor Rick Scott of Florida, a longtime opponent of Obamacare, put it, "I cannot in good conscience deny Floridians access to healthcare." Expansion in Florida was blocked, however, by the Republican-controlled legislature.[112]

Rejection of Medicaid expansion initially spread through the Midwest and Mountain West as well as the South, but over time the remaining holdouts have become increasingly southern. The exceptions and partial exceptions are as interesting as the core pattern. Kansas, South Dakota, and Wyoming are in various stages of deliberation and negotiation toward probable expansion (in some cases with restrictive provisions). Idaho, Maine, Missouri, Nebraska, Oklahoma, and Utah approved expansion by referendum votes. Wisconsin has rejected Medicaid funds but covers adults below the poverty line under Medicaid. In other words, virtually all of the uncompromisingly rejectionist states are southern.

Table 14.3. TANF-to-Poverty Ratios, 1995-1996 and 2016-2017

	TANF Families/Poverty Population		TANF Families by Race, 1995 (%)	
	1995–1996	2016–2017	Black	Hispanic
Alabama	32	9	72.9	0.1
Arkansas	33	5	58.1	0.5
Florida	55	13	47.2	17.7
Georgia	82	6	72.3	1.1
Louisiana	48	4	81.6	0.8
Mississippi	39	6	86.2	0.2
North Carolina	74	7	63.4	1.8
South Carolina	40	10	72.5	0.7
Tennessee	67	23	55.2	0.6
Texas	47	4	32.1	46.6
Virginia	56	19	65.0	2.0
South	53	9	56	15
Non-South	76	31	31	23
USA	68	23	36.9	20.8

Sources: Center on Budget and Policy Priorities, "State Fact Sheets: Trends in State Caseloads and TANF-to-Poverty Ratios," https://www.cbpp.org/research/family-income-support/state-fact-sheets-trends-in-state-tanf-to-poverty-ratios (updated Nov. 28, 2018); US Department of Health and Human Services, Office of Family Assistance, "FY 1996 Characteristics and Financial Circumstances of TANF Recipients," Sept. 1, 1996, https://www.acf.hhs.gov/ofa/data/characteristics-and-financial-circumstances-tanf-recipients-fiscal-year-1996 (updated Apr. 30, 2019). Race for families is identified as "race of natural or adoptive parent."

The exceptions within the South are equally interesting. In Virginia, Democratic governors recommended expansion after taking office in 2015 but were unable to gain legislative approval until 2018. Kentucky implemented Medicare expansion under Democratic political leadership, but Republican governor Matt Bevin actively campaigned against Obamacare in 2015 and, once in office, imposed a restrictive waiver. The waiver was rescinded by newly elected Democratic governor Andy Beshear in December 2019. Arkansas approved its own version of Medicaid expansion in 2013 under Democratic governor Mike Beebe. Republican governor Asa Hutchinson stated in 2016, "I hope that Washington replaces

Obamacare, but, until then, we would only be punishing Arkansans by turning down federal money."[113]

A remarkable deviation from the pattern is Louisiana, perhaps the exception that proves the rule. The state rejected Medicaid expansion under Republican governors, but conservative Democrat John Bel Edwards campaigned actively on this issue in 2015, pledging to begin implementation on his first day in office. Edwards also portrayed himself as a champion of public schools, frequently mentioning that his wife is herself a public-school teacher. Most notably, he courted the Black vote aggressively, speaking at five churches on the Sunday before the election and appearing with Black and Latino political leaders in New Orleans on Election Day. The result was an above-average turnout and a comfortable 56–44 victory in the runoff election. The new governor was true to his word, issuing an executive order on January 12, 2016, to begin the process of Medicaid expansion. Edwards was reelected in 2019.[114]

The larger point is that the responses of most southern states, willingly leaving federal money on the table for political reasons, are very different from those of the 1960s and 1970s, when these states reluctantly acquiesced in such policies as desegregation of schools and hospitals because of what seemed to be the irresistible power of federal funding. The racially charged character of the topic is difficult to miss: States like Arkansas, Kentucky, and West Virginia have large white-poverty populations but relatively small black shares, so Medicaid expansion is less easily color coded than elsewhere. Virginia is now a "blue" state because Black voters are part of a larger coalition dominated by metropolitan Washington, DC. The example of Louisiana shows that, under the right combination of circumstances, it is still possible to reassemble multiracial coalitions on economic issues, even in states where Blacks comprise a large minority share of the population. Once in place, such popular benefit programs are difficult to reverse. That resistance may in turn help sustain the multiracial coalitions.

CONCLUSION

The promise of voting for Black southerners was long delayed. But since passage of the Voting Rights Act of 1965, voting has been a powerful force for racial progress: beyond improved respect in political discourse, objective gains include greater access to public services and public-sector employment and a fairer share of state expenditures on education and other public goods and services. The increase in Black public officials occurred primarily in districts where Black voters constituted a majority or near-majority. In contrast, gains at the state level came through biracial coalitions, enacting measures that benefited white as well as Black constituents.

Between the VRA and the mid-1990s, the median white southerner voted for liberal-to-moderate Democrats, no doubt conservative by outside standards but well within the spectrum for the national party. Class-based partisan voting emerged during this period, which observers saw as a sign of a diminished role for race and for region. If anything, the southern income-partisan relationship during this era was steeper than elsewhere, suggesting that the persistence of conservative regional culture was largely an upper-income phenomenon.[115]

This apparently stable pattern then changed, beginning with an abrupt right-ward shift in 1994 and more-or-less steadily persistent thereafter, punctuated by decisive Republican gains in the midterm elections of 2010 and 2014. The swing had many causes, but an important contributing factor was change in economic conditions, attributed by voters, with some justification, to removal of barriers to import competition in industries that were central for regional prosperity. Many votes against Democratic legislators in 1994 constituted direct retaliation against President Clinton for his trade policies. The longer-term trend more likely reflected the loss of manufacturing jobs, associated with stagnant or falling real incomes, increased joblessness, and the decline of formerly robust industrial communities.

One way to frame these developments is to argue that racial tolerance and economic generosity are easier in a context of rapid economic growth. The suggestion here, however, is that the promotion of local and regional industries formed a basis for interracial cooperation based not on generosity, but on enlightened mutual self-interest. Removing that structure opened the door to emotional appeals rooted in regional culture or racial and ethnic scapegoating.

Readers will note that the name of Donald J. Trump has so far appeared nowhere in this essay. The political-economic transition chronicled here was firmly established well before Trump's improbable ascendancy to the presidency in 2016. To be sure, the South provided his firmest base of support. But most of his rhetorical tropes—abortion, guns, immigration, distrust of national media—were already familiar to southern Republicans. A phrase often heard among supporters was, "He's one of us." Mississippi Republican strategist Henry Barbour observed,

"It is ironic that the warrior they have found is a billionaire from New York, but he really speaks their language fluidly."[116] Trump's innovation, following the example of George Wallace in 1968, was to take this message national. In doing so, attacks on NAFTA and Chinese imports were important parts of the package, with powerful appeal to working-class voters nationwide.

Despite his popularity, Trump's presence on the ballot did not particularly advance the political standing of southern Republicans. True, the Democratic share of state presidential votes fell by an average of 2.5 percentage points from 2012 to 2016. But most of this shift was reversed by 2020, albeit with much variation among states. In statewide elections for senator and governor during the Trump years, Republican vote-share gains and losses were virtually equal. The largest Democrat swings were in Georgia, South Carolina, Texas, and Virginia.

If anything, Trumpism may have accelerated the rise of a new multiracial coalition: African Americans, Hispanics and other immigrants, and college-educated metropolitan-area residents (especially women) with liberal views on social issues. This alliance has turned Virginia into a blue state, and high turnout among its constituents flipped Arizona and Georgia in 2020 and elected two Democratic Georgians to the Senate in January 2021. Whether the white working class rejoins this coalition any time soon may be questionable. But the track record suggests that an equitable pro-growth program might be good for them as well.

NOTES

For comments on earlier versions, the author thanks Tom Ferguson and Economic History Workshop members at Yale, Columbia, NYU, and the University of Michigan. The outstanding research assistance of Danielle Mitalipov and Binh Thai Nguyen is greatly appreciated.

1. "The Late President Lincoln on Negro Suffrage: A Letter from Him to Gov. Hahn of Louisiana," *New York Times*, June 23, 1865; "Last Public Address," Apr. 11, 1865, Abraham Lincoln Online, http://www.abrahamlincolnonline.org/lincoln/speeches/last.htm (accessed Jan. 9, 2020).

2. Steven Hahn, *A Nation under Our Feet: Black Political Struggles in the Rural South from Slavery to the Great Migration* (Cambridge MA: Harvard University Press, 2003), 211–12, 244–49; Trevon Logan, "Do Black Politicians Matter? Evidence from Reconstruction," *Journal of Economic History* 80 (Mar. 2020): 1–37.

3. See the discussion and statistics in Walter Dean Burnham, *Voting in American Elections: The Shaping of the American Political Universe since 1788* (Palo Alto, CA: Academica, 2010), which also looks at state races. For the 2014 North/South close-up in turnouts, see Walter Dean Burnham and

Thomas Ferguson, "Americans Are Sick to Death of Both Parties," *Alternet*, Dec. 17, 2014: https://
www.alternet.org/2014/12/americans-are-sick-death-both-parties-why-our-politics-worse-shape
-we-thought/.

4. Edward M. Kennedy, quoted in Gary May, *Bending toward Justice: The Voting Rights Act and the Transformation of American Democracy* (New York: Basic Books, 2013), 217. The quotation is from 1981, but Kennedy repeated this assessment throughout his career. He devoted his maiden Senate speech to voting rights and voted for all four renewals of the act.

5. Elizabeth Cascio and Ebonya Washington, "Valuing the Vote: The Redistribution of Voting Rights and State Funds Following the Voting Rights Act of 1965," *Quarterly Journal of Economics* 129 (Feb. 2014): 379–433.

6. Kerry L. Haynie, *African-American Legislators in the American States* (New York: Columbia University Press, 2001), chap. 4. The states covered were Arkansas, Illinois, Maryland, New Jersey, and North Carolina for the legislative years 1969, 1979, and 1989. For evidence of broader effects on southern state budgets, including allocations for hospitals, roads, and libraries, see also Richard M. Vallely, *The Two Reconstructions: The Struggle for Black Enfranchisement* (Chicago: University of Chicago Press, 2004), 199.

7. Joseph A. Aistrup, *The Southern Strategy Revisited* (Lexington: University Press of Kentucky, 1996), emphasizes structural constraints and what Larry Sabato calls "30 years worth of rolling realignment in the South" (p. 60). M. V. Hood, Quentin Kidd, and Irwin L. Morris, *The Rational Southerner: Black Mobilization, Republican Growth, and the Partisan Transformation of the American South* (New York: Oxford University Press, 2012), describe a dynamic process whereby Black mobilization drove whites into the Republican Party, which then took time to become electorally competitive. Angie Maxwell and Todd Shields, *The Long Southern Strategy: How Chasing White Voters in the South Changed American Politics* (New York: Oxford University Press, 2019), attribute realignment to a long-term strategy by Republican leaders to adapt party positions and appeals to deep-seated southern-white attitudes and prejudices.

8. The most prominent critic of these arrangements is Abigail Thernstrom, *Whose Votes Count? Affirmative Action and Minority Voting Rights* (Cambridge, MA: Harvard University Press, 1987). Thernstrom's views were somewhat modified in *Voting Rights—And Wrongs* (Washington, DC: AEI, 2008).

9. Eric Foner, *Freedom's Lawmakers: A Directory of Black Officeholders during Reconstruction* (New York: Oxford University Press, 1993). See also Vallely, *Two Reconstructions*, 23–97.

10. The landmark quantitative study of disfranchisement is J. Morgan Kousser, *The Shaping of Southern Politics: Suffrage Restrictions and the Establishment of the One-Party South* (New Haven, CT: Yale University Press, 1974). Similar patterns, with great emphasis on informal modes of voter suppression (including lynching), are reported in Daniel P. Jones, Werner Troesken, and Randall Walsh, "A Poll Tax by Any Other Name: The Political Economy of Disfranchisement," National Bureau of Economic Research Working Paper 18612 (2012).

11. Robert Margo, *Disfranchisement, School Finance, and the Economics of Segregated Schools in the U.S. South, 1890–1910* (New York: Garland, 1985), table I-1.

12. Jim Gerber, "Public School Expenditures in the Plantation States," *Explorations in Economic History* 28 (1991); Dennis Halicoussis, Kenneth Ng, and Nancy Virts, "Property Ownership and Educational Discrimination in the South," *Journal of Educational Finance* 35 (2009); Pamela Barnhouse Walters, David R. James, and Holly J. McCammon, "Citizenship and Public Schools: Accounting for Racial Inequality in Education in the Pre- and Post-Disfranchisement South," *American Sociological Review* 62 (1997).

13. J. Morgan Kousser, "Progressivism for Middle-Class Whites Only: North Carolina Education, 1880–1910," *Journal of Southern History* 46 (1980): 191.

14. V. O. Key, *Southern Politics in State and Nation* (New York: Knopf, 1949).

15. Margaret Price, *The Negro Voter in the South* (Atlanta: Southern Regional Council, 1957); Price, *The Negro and the Ballot in the South* (Atlanta: Southern Regional Council, 1959).

16. Pat Watters and Reese Cleghorn, *Climbing Jacob's Ladder: The Arrival of Negroes in Southern Politics* (New York: Harcourt, Brace, and World, 1967), 376; David J. Garrow, *Protest at Selma: Martin Luther King, Jr., and the Voting Rights Act of 1965* (New Haven, CT: Yale University Press, 1978), 11, 19. This paragraph also draws upon Steven F. Lawson, *Black Ballots: Voting Rights in the South, 1944–1969* (New York: Columbia University Press, 1976), 23–85.

17. Lawson, *Black Ballots*, 261–87. On the 1962 turning point, see Richard J. Timpone, "Mass Mobilization or Government Intervention? The Growth of Black Registration in the South," *Journal of Politics* 57 (1995).

18. Lawson, *Black Ballots*, 307–30; US Commission on Civil Rights, *Political Participation* (Washington, DC: Government Printing Office, 1968), 11–13.

19. Ari Berman, *Give Us the Ballot: The Modern Struggle for Voting Rights in America* (New York: Farrar, Straus, and Giroux, 2015), 76–78, 82–86, 95–99, 105–13, 118; Bennett quoted in Steven F. Lawson, *In Pursuit of Power: Southern Blacks and Electoral Politics, 1965–1982* (New York: Columbia University Press, 1985), 130–57, 226–53 (quote, 252).

20. Berman, *Give Us the Ballot*, 136–58, 233–44. The unanimity of the 2006 renewal should not be taken to mean that there were no signs of impending change in Republican political strategy. D. King-Meadows argues that members of Congress, even while supporting renewal, "sowed and watered the seeds of judicial skepticism," laying the groundwork for the coming effort to weaken the VRA through the courts. *When the Letter Betrays the Spirit* (Lanham MD: Lexington Books, 2011), 93–112. A comprehensive account of the campaign to dismantle the protections of the act appears in Jim Rutenberg, "Overcome," *New York Times Magazine*, Aug. 2, 2015.

21. US Commission on Civil Rights, *The Voting Rights Act: Ten Years After* (Washington DC: Government Printing Office, 1975), 336. The figures on Black elected officials in covered states are from ibid., 328. The early electoral successes are described in Lawson, *In Pursuit of Power*, 99, 107.

22. US Commission on Civil Rights, *Political Participation*, 19–31. An update, reporting some progress but much persistence, appeared in the 1975 report (*Ten Years After*), 131–72.

23. Lawson, *In Pursuit of Power*, 168–88; Chandler Davidson and Bernard Grofman, eds., *Quiet Revolution in the South: The Impact of the Voting Rights Act, 1965–1990* (Princeton, NJ: Princeton University Press, 1994), 21–37.

24. Davidson and Grofman, *Quiet Revolution*, 335–50. An account of the politics behind the reapportionments of 1992 appears in Berman, *Give Us the Ballot*, 186–92.

25. Quoted by Lawson, *In Pursuit of Power*, 301.

26. Quoted in Thernstrom, *Voting Rights—and Wrongs*, 14.

27. Christian R. Grose, *Congress in Black and White: Race and Representation in Washington and at Home* (New York: Cambridge University Press, 2011), 7–9, 87–109, 110–33.

28. Frederick M. Wirt, *"We Ain't What We Was": Civil Rights in the New South* (Durham NC: Duke University Press, 1997), 69.

29. Davidson and Grofman, *Quiet Revolution*, 278. North Carolina elected a Black attorney general in 1992 and state supreme court justices in 2014 and 2016. Georgia elected African Americans to various state offices in 1998, 2002, and 2006. The election of Raphael Warnock to the US Senate in January 2021 is a significant breakthrough.

30. Davidson and Grofman, *Quiet Revolution*, 215. The South Carolina chapter was written by Orville Vernon Burton, Terence R. Finnegan, Peyton McCrary, and James W. Loewen.

31. William Havard, ed., *The Changing Politics of the South* (Baton Rouge: Louisiana State University Press, 1972), 509. The Mississippi chapter was written by Charles N. Fortenberry and F. Glenn Abney.

32. Nadine Cohodas, *Strom Thurmond and the Politics of Southern Change* (New York: Simon and Schuster, 1993), 412–13, 451; Harold W. Stanley, *Voter Mobilization and the Politics of Race* (New York: Praeger, 1987), 142–43. George Wallace himself dropped racial rhetoric from his third inaugural address in 1975, and in 1979 he told the *New York Times*: "It's good that it's a racial situation being changed. It's good that the civil rights bill has passed. It hasn't been the evil that we thought." Quoted in Waldo W. Braden, "The Speaking of the Governors of the Deep South, 1970–1980," in *A New Diversity in Contemporary Southern Rhetoric*, ed. Calvin M. Logue and Howard Dorgan (Baton Rouge: Louisiana State University Press, 1987), 199.

33. May, *Bending toward Justice*, 181–91.

34. Frederick W. Wirt, *Politics of Southern Inequality: Law and Social Change in a Mississippi County* (Chicago: Aldine, 1970), 166–75; Lawson, *Black Ballots*, 339; Lawrence J. Hanks, *The Struggle for Black Political Empowerment in Three Georgia Counties* (Knoxville: University of Tennessee Press, 1987), 65–66.

35. James W. Button, *Blacks and Social Change: The Impact of the Civil Rights Movement in Southern Communities* (Princeton, NJ: Princeton University Press, 1989), 71. The data on paved streets is presented in table 5.1.

36. Jason R. Gainous, James Button, and Barbara Rienzo, "African Americans and Municipal Employment: A Test of Two Perspectives," *Social Science Journal* 44 (2007): 535–45; James W. Button, Barbara Rienzo, and Sheila L. Croucher, *Blacks and the Quest for Economic Equality: The Political Economy of Employment in Southern Communities in the United States* (University Park: Pennsylvania State University Press, 2009), 75–102; Wirt, *"We Ain't What We Was,"* 72–74.

37. Peter K. Eisinger, "Black Employment in Municipal Jobs: The Impact of Black Political Power," *American Political Science Review* 76 (1982): 385.

38. Michelle D. Byng, "Responding to Black Municipal Interests in the Post–Civil Rights Era," *Sociological Inquiry* 68 (1998): 209–33.

39. John V. C. Nye, Ilia Ranier, and Thomas Stratmann, "Do Black Mayors Improve Black Employment Outcomes?," *Journal of Law, Economics, and Organization* 31 (2014): 1–48.

40. Joel A. Thompson, "The Voting Rights Act in North Carolina: An Evaluation," *Publius* 16 (1986): 144, 149, 151; Abhay P. Aneja and Carlos F. Avenancio-Leon, "The Effect of Political Power on Labor Market Inequality: Evidence from the 1965 Voting Rights Act," Washington Center for Equitable Growth Working Paper 101620 (2020); Andrea Bernini, Giovanni Facchini, and Cecilia Testa, "Race, Representation, and Policy: Black Elected Officials and Public Spending in the US South," University of Nottingham Working Paper (2017); Giovanni Facchini, Brian G. Knight, and Cecilia Testa, "The Franchise, Policing, and Race: Evidence from Arrests Data and the Voting Rights Act," National Bureau of Economic Research Working Paper 27463 (2020).

41. Cascio and Washington, "Valuing the Vote," 379–433.

42. Wirt, *"We Ain't What We Was,"* 67. Similar accounts appear in Hugh L. Perry, "The Socioeconomic Impact of Black Political Empowerment in a Rural Southern Locality," *Rural Sociology* 45 (1980): 207–22; and Laughlin McDonald, *Voting Rights Odyssey: Black Enfranchisement in Georgia* (Cambridge: Cambridge University Press, 2003), 238–45.

43. Bonnie Lefkowitz, *Community Health Centers: A Movement and the People Who Made It Happen* (New Brunswick, NJ: Rutgers University Press, 2007), 137. See also Melissa Fay Greene, *Praying for Sheetrock* (New York: Fawcett Columbine, 1991), 250. Greene presents an account of McIntosh County, Georgia, where Black political representation was delayed until 1978 but was then followed by an extensive influx of federal funding for health and sanitation facilities.

44. J. Mills Thornton, *Dividing Lines* (Tuscaloosa: University of Alabama Press, 2002), 370–79; Hugh L. Perry, "The Evolution and Impact of Biracial Coalitions," in *Racial Politics in American Cities*, ed. Rufus Browning, Rogers Marshall, and David H. Tabb, 3rd ed. (New York: Longman, 2003); Charles E. Connerly, *"The Most Segregated City in America": City Planning and Civil Rights in Birmingham, 1920–1980* (Charlottesville: University of Virginia Press, 2005), 102–28.

45. Stephen Samuel Smith, *Boom for Whom? Education, Desegregation, and Development in Charlotte* (Albany: University of New York Press, 2004), 217–20.

46. Jarrod Apperson, "An Afterward to White Flight: Atlanta's Return to Community & Long Road toward Integration," *East Atlanta Patch*, Feb. 10, 2013.

47. Mark Stern, *Calculating Visions: Johnson. Kennedy, and Civil Rights* (New Brunswick, NJ: Rutgers University Press, 1992), 211.

48. Quoted in Vallely, *Two Reconstructions,* 198.

49. J. David Woodard, *The New Southern Politics,* 2nd ed. (Boulder, CO: Lynne Rienner, 2013), 259; Virginia H. Gray, Russell L. Hanson, and Thad Kousser, *Politics in the American States,* 11th ed. (Singapore: SAGE Publications Asia-Pacific, 2018), table 3.2.

50. Ronald Keith Gaddie and Donna R. Hoffman, "Critical Events in Contemporary Southern Politics," in *The South and Congress in an Era of Change,* ed. John C. Kuzenski, Lawrence M. Moreland, and Robert P. Steed (Westport, CT: Praeger, 2001), 31.

51. Ebonya Washington, "Do Majority-Black Districts Limit Blacks' Representation? The Case of the 1990 Redistricting," *Journal of Law and Economics* 55 (2012): esp. 266; John R. Petrocik and Scot W. Desposato, "The Partisan Consequences of Majority-Minority Redistricting in the South, 1992 and 1994," *Journal of Politics* 60 (1998): 613, 630.

52. Hood, Kidd, and Morris, *Rational Southerner*, 94; Seth C. McKee, *Republican Ascendancy in Southern U.S. House Elections* (Philadelphia: Westview, 2010), 15; Glenn Feldman, ed., *Painting Dixie Red* (Gainesville: University Press of Florida, 2012), 319. The need to build the party from the top down is stressed by Aistrup, *Southern Strategy Revisited*. The concluding quotation is from Kevin Drum, "Why Did the Democrats Lose the South?," *Mother Jones*, Nov. 25, 2015, https://www.motherjones.com/kevin-drum/2015/11/why-did-democrats-lose-white-south/.

53. Jack Bass and Walter DeVries, *The Transformation of Southern Politics* (New York: Basic Books, 1976), 407.

54. Alexander P. Lamis, *The Two-Party South* (New York: Oxford University Press, 1984), 5, 232.

55. Alexander P. Lamis, *The Two-Party South: Expanded Edition* (New York: Oxford University Press, 1988), x.

56. Laurence W. Moreland, "Ideological and Issue Bases of Southern Parties," in *Political Parties in the Southern States*, ed. Tod A. Baker, Charles D. Hadley, Robert P. Steed, and Laurence W. Moreland (Westport, CT: Praeger, 1990), 131. John Van Wingen and David Valentine are even more emphatic: "Absolutely nothing in the data indicates that the Republicans will soon shed their minority standing." Wingen and Valentine, "Partisan Politics: A One-and-a-Half, No-Party System," in *Contemporary Southern Politics*, ed. James F. Lea (Baton Rouge: Louisiana State University Press, 1988), 144.

57. *The Rise of Southern Republicans* (Cambridge, MA: Belknap Press of Harvard University Press, 2002), 3. Two years later, John A. Clark and Charles L. Prysby wrote: "In almost every [southern] state, both parties have a reasonable chance of winning important statewide contests." Clark and Prysby, *Southern Political Party Activists* (Lexington: University Press of Kentucky, 2004), 3.

58. Richard Nadeau and Harold W. Stanley, "Class Polarization and Partisanship among Native Southern Whites, 1952–90," *American Journal of Political Science* 37 (1993): 915.

59. Richard Nadeau, Richard G, Niemi, Harold W. Stanley, and Jean-Francois Dodbout, "Class, Party, and South/Non-South Differences," *American Politics Research* 32 (2004): 61.

60. Byron E. Shafer and Richard Johnston, *The End of Southern Exceptionalism: Class, Race, and Partisan Change in the Postwar South* (Cambridge, MA: Harvard University Press, 2006), 177–85.

61. *A Question of Justice: New South Governors and Education, 1968–1976* (Tuscaloosa: University of Alabama Press, 2002), 173. See also Earl Black, *Southern Governors and Civil Rights* (Cambridge, MA: Harvard University Press, 1976); and Randy Sanders, *Mighty Peculiar Elections: The New South Gubernatorial Elections of 1970 and the Changing Politics of Race* (Gainesville: University Press of Florida, 2002).

62. William R. Shaffer, "Ideological Trends among Southern US Democratic Senators," *American Politics Quarterly* 15 (1987): 299–324; Richard Fleisher, "Explaining the Change in Roll-Call Behavior of Southern Democrats," *Journal of Politics* 55 (1993): 327–41.

63. The literature is too large for a comprehensive listing, but a convenient introduction may be found in the essays by Dan T. Carter and by Byron E. Shafer and Richard Johnston in *Unlocking V. O.*

Key Jr., ed. Angie Maxwell and Todd G. Shields (Fayetteville: University of Arkansas Press, 2011). Leading statements of the two positions are Dan T. Carter, *From George Wallace to Newt Gingrich* (Baton Rouge: Louisiana State University Press, 1996); and Shafer and Johnston, *End of Southern Exceptionalism.* Angie Maxwell and Todd Shields depict an ongoing strategy by Republicans to appeal to white southerners, by adopting themes related to race, feminism, and religion, writing, "The economic masks the racial, so much so that many do not even see it." Maxwell and Shields, *Long Southern Strategy*, 91.

64. Kuziemko and Washington, "Why Did the Democrats Lose the South? Bringing New Data to an Old Debate," *American Economic Review* 108 (2018): 2830–67.

65. James H. Kuklinski, Michael D. Cobb, and Martin Gilens, "Racial Attitudes and the 'New South,'" *Journal of Politics* 59 (1997): 323–49.

66. Nicholas Valentino and David Sears, "Old Times There Are Not Forgotten: Partisan Realignment in the Contemporary South," *American Journal of Political Science* 49 (2005): 672–88.

67. Key, *Southern Politics in State and Nation*, 5.

68. Alexander P. Lamis, ed., *Southern Politics in the 1990s* (Baton Rouge: Louisiana State University Press, 1999), 30–32.

69. Bullock, introduction to *The New Politics of the Old South*, ed. Charles S. Bullock III and Mark J. Rozelle, 5th ed. (Lanham, MD: Rowman & Littlefield, 2014), 14.

70. Black and Black, *Rise of Southern Republicans*, fig. 4.3.

71. Gaddie and Hoffman, "Critical Events in Contemporary Southern Politics," 36.

72. Adam Bonica and Gary W. Cox, "Ideological Extremists in the US Congress: Out of Step but Still in Office," *Quarterly Journal of Political Science* 13 (2018): 207–36. Bonica and Cox do not particularly emphasize redistricting, though it could have contributed to the prospects of a Republican House majority. Alan I. Abramowitz, Brad Alexander, and Matthew Gunning, however, show that the decline in party competition within districts cannot be explained by redistricting. Abramowitz, Alexander, and Gunning, "Incumbency, Redistricting, and the Decline of Competition in US House Elections," *Journal of Politics* 68 (2006): 75–88.

73. Gary C. Jacobsen, "The 1994 House Elections in Perspective," *Political Science Quarterly* 111 (1996): 208. Political scientist Daniel Hopkins documents the increasing alignment between southern presidential and gubernatorial voting, "especially after 1994," in *Increasingly United States: How and Why American Political Behavior Nationalized* (Chicago: University of Chicago Press, 2018), 47–48.

74. "The Geography of Trade and Technology Shocks in the United States," *American Economic Review* 103 (2013): 222–23.

75. Sarah Anderson, "Supporting NAFTA Was the Kiss of Death for Democrats," *Alternet*, June 8, 2015, https://m.usw.org/blog/2015/supporting-nafta-was-the-kiss-of-death-for-democrats-why-dems-should-think-twice-about-voting-for-tpp.

76. US Department of Labor, *Report to Congress: The Past, Present, and Future of Employment in the Textile and Apparel Industries: An Overview* (Washington DC: Government Printing Office, 2004), 35–37.

77. Timothy Minchin, *Empty Mills: The Fight against Imports and the Decline of the U.S. Textile Industry* (Lanham, MD: Littlefield, 2013), 57–85 (esp. 84–85), 91–117.

78. Mark Mittelhauser, "Employment Trends in Textiles and Apparel, 1973–2005," *Monthly Labor Review* (August 2007): 24–34. Mittelhauser predicted in 1997 that the industry would still employ 1.3 million workers in 2005. The true figure was less than 0.5 million. As late as 2004, the Bureau of Labor Statistics projected "fairly modest changes" over the decade 2000–2010. US Department of Labor, *Report to Congress*, 46–51.

79. David Autor, David Dorn, and Gordon Hanson, "The China Syndrome: Local Labor Market Effects of Import Competition in the United States," *American Economic Review* 103 (2013): 2121–68; "The China Shock," *Annual Review of Economics* 8 (2016): 205–40. Congress voted to approve President Clinton's proposal to award Permanent Normal Trade Relations status to China in 2000.

80. Shushanik Hakobyan and John McLaren, "Looking for Local Labor-Market Effects of NAFTA," *Review of Economics and Statistics* 98 (2016): 728–41. The authors report that the nine most vulnerable counties were all in Georgia and the Carolinas. Ibid., table 3.

81. US International Trade Administration, Office of Textiles and Apparel, "Trade Data: U.S. Imports and Exports of Textiles and Apparel," http://otexa.trade.gov/msrpoint.htm.

82. Autor, Dorn, and Hanson, "China Syndrome," 2141–51.

83. Kevin Schaul and Dan Keating, "The States Most Threatened by Trade," *Washington Post*, Aug. 22, 2014. Survey studies show that opposition to free trade is strongest among low-skilled workers. See Kenneth F. Scheve and Matthew J. Slaughter, *Globalization and the Perceptions of American Workers* (Washington, DC: Institute for International Economics, 2001); and Scheve and Slaughter, "What Determines Trade Policy Preferences?," *Journal of International Economics* 54 (2001): 267–92. See also Bruce A. Blonigen, "Revisiting the Evidence on Trade Policy Preferences," *Journal of International Economics* 85 (2011): 129–35.

84. Minchin, *Empty Mills*, 222–33. Examples of textile "comeback" stories include Stephanie Clifford, "U.S. Textile Plants Return, with Floors Largely Empty of People," *New York Times*, Sept. 19, 2013; and Marsha Mercer, "Textile Industry Comes Back to Life, Especially in South," *USA Today*, Feb. 5, 2014.

85. US Equal Employment Opportunity Commission, *Equal Employment Opportunity Report: Job Patterns for Minorities and Women in Private Industry* (Washington, DC: Government Printing Office, 1990).

86. Ray Texeira and Alan Abramowitz, "The Decline of the White Working Class," Brookings Working Paper (Apr. 2008), esp. fig. 2.

87. Black and Black, *Rise of Southern Republicans*, 263–66; Byron E. Shafer and Richard Johnston, "Partisan Change in the Post-Key South," in Maxwell and Shields, *Unlocking V. O. Key Jr.*, 168–70. Shafer and Johnston use averages by decade in their analysis, so the timing of the shift they describe cannot be determined with precision. But their case that southern working-class Republicanism was late in coming is persuasive.

88. Paul Theroux, "The Hypocrisy of 'Helping' the Poor," *New York Times*, Oct. 2, 2015.

89. Stephen Ansolabehere, Nathan Persili, and Charles Stewart III, "Race, Region, and Vote Choice in the 2008 Election," *Harvard Law Review* 123 (2010): 1385–1436; "Regional Differences in Racial Polarization in the 2012 Presidential Election," *Harvard Law Review* 126 (2013): 205–20.

90. See, for example, the chart for US Senate elections in Black and Black, *Rise of Southern Republicans*, 135.

91. David A. Bositis, "Resegregation in Southern Politics?," Joint Center for Political and Economic Studies Research Brief (Nov. 2011), table 3.

92. Charles S. Bullock III and Ronald Keith Gaddie, *The Triumph of Voting Rights in the South* (Norman: University of Oklahoma Press, 2009), 93, 177, 207–8; Charles E. Menifield and Stephen D. Shaffer, *Politics in the New South* (Albany: State University of New York Press, 2005), 55–59, 82–85.

93. Robert R. Preuhs, "The Conditional Effects of Minority Descriptive Representation: Black Legislators and Policy Influence in the American States," *Journal of Politics* 68 (2006): 585–99.

94. Jason Zengerle, "The New Racism—This Is How the Civil Rights Movement Ends," *New Republic*, Aug. 11, 2014.

95. Glen Browder, *The South's New Racial Politics* (Montgomery: NewSouth Books, 2009), 81–95. Browder is a former Alabama legislator, secretary of state, and Democratic congressman.

96. J. Morgan Kousser, "Do the Facts of Voting Rights Support Chief Justice Roberts' Opinion in *Shelby County?*" *Transatlantica* 1 (2015), https://doi.org/10.4000/transatlantica.7462.

97. Gordon E. Harvey, *A Question of Justice: New South Governors and Education, 1968–1976* (Tuscaloosa: University of Alabama Press, 2002), 138–68, 173.

98. Ibid., 41–63; Charles F. Rudder, "Educational Reform in Alabama, 1972–1989," in *School Reform in the Deep South*, ed. David J. Vold and Joseph I. DeVitis (Tuscaloosa: University of Alabama Press, 1991).

99. Sarah Reber, "From Separate and Unequal to Integrated and Equal?," *Review of Economics and Statistics* 93 (2011): 404–15.

100. Robert J. Jenkins and William A. Person, "Educational Reform in Mississippi," in Vold and DeVitis, *School Reform in the Deep South*, 82–107; Charles C. Bolton, *The Hardest Deal of All* (Jackson: University Press of Mississippi, 2005), 217.

101. Elizabeth U. Cascio, "Maternal Labor Supply and the Introduction of Kindergarten into American Public Schools," *Journal of Human Resources* 41 (2009), table 1.

102. Southern Education Foundation, "A New Diverse Majority: Students of Color in the South's Public Schools" (2010), 5, 10–11, 14–15, https://www.southerneducation.org/publications/anewdiversemajority/. See also Southern Education Foundation, "A New Majority: Students of Color in the South's Public Schools," 2007, https://files.eric.ed.gov/fulltext/ED524109.pdf; "A New Majority Update: Low Income Students in the South and Nation," Oct. 2013, https://www.southerneducation.org/publications/newmajorityupdate/; and "A New Majority Research Bulletin: Low Income Students Now a Majority in the Nation's Public Schools," Jan. 2015, https://www.southerneducation.org/publications/newmajorityresearchbulletin/.

103. Thomas G. Dyer, "A New Face on Southern Higher Education," in *The American South in the Twentieth Century*, ed. Craig S. Pascoe, Karen Trahan Leathem, and Andy Ambrose (Athens: University of Georgia Press, 2005), 293.

104. Timothy Pratt, "The New North-South Divide: Public Higher Education," *The Atlantic*, Aug. 25, 2016.

105. Sharon Nunn, "The South's Economy Is Falling Behind," *Wall Street Journal*, June 10, 2019.

106. Grossmann, *Red State Blues: How the Conservative Revolution Stalled in the States* (New York: Cambridge University Press, 2019), 119.

107. Ibid., 125, 132–34; Kathrine Newman and Rourke O'Brien, *Taxing the Poor: Doing Damage to the Truly Disadvantaged* (Berkeley: University of California Press, 2011).

108. Richard F. Bensel and M. Elizabeth Sanders, "The Impact of the Voting Rights Act on Southern Welfare Systems," in *Do Elections Matter?*, ed. Benjamin Ginsberg and Alan Stone (Armonk, NY: M.E. Sharpe, 1986), 56–63; James C. Cobb, "'Somebody Done Nailed Us on the Cross': Federal Farm and Welfare Policy and the Civil Rights Movement in the Delta," *Journal of American History* 77 (1990): 912–36.

109. Haynie, *African-American Legislators*, chap. 4.

110. Michael J. New, "State Sanctions and the Decline in Welfare Caseloads," *Cato Journal* 28 (2008): 515–17.

111. Joe E. Soss, Sanford F. Schram, Thomas Vartanian, and Erin O'Brien, "Setting the Terms of Relief: Explaining State Policy Choices in the Devolution Revolution," *American Journal of Political Science* 45 (2001): 378–95. Other variables with statistically significant influence also seem closely related to region, such as political ideology and two-party competitiveness. Matthew C. Fellowes and Gretchen Rowe confirm the prominence of race but add other influences, such as the policy choices of neighboring states, in "The Politics of the New American Welfare States," *American Journal of Political Science* 48 (2004): 362–73. New, "State Sanctions," shows the effectiveness of restrictive policies in reducing caseloads.

112. Charles Barrilleaux and Carlisle Rainey, "The Politics of Need: Examining Decisions to Oppose the 'Obamacare' Medicaid Expansion," *State Politics and Policy Quarterly* 14 (2014): 437–41. The authors' statistical analysis concludes that governors' decisions on Medicaid expansion have been driven almost entirely by political factors—partisanship, public opinion, and ideology—and that the level of need among the citizenry plays almost no role.

113. David Ramsey, "Gov. Asa Hutchinson Seeks to Debunk Argument That Supporting His Arkansas Works Plan Is Supporting Obamacare," *Arkansas Times*, Feb. 16, 2016.

114. John Nichols, "How a Democrat Can Win in the South," *Nation*, Nov. 23, 2015.

115. Andrew Gelman, in *Red State, Blue State, Rich State, Poor State: Why Americans Vote the Way They Do* (Princeton, NJ: Princeton University Press, 2008), argues that regional cultural differences boil down to differences between the upper-income classes in rich and poor states.

116. Maggie Haberman, "He's 'One of Us': The Undying Bond between the Bible Belt and Trump," *New York Times*, Oct. 14, 2018.

Afterword

ORVILLE VERNON BURTON and PETER EISENSTADT

"Four score and one year ago," wrote Private First Class Willard D. Bristol Jr. in June 1944, "our fathers were freed within a new nation."[1] Private Bristol was an African American soldier stationed at Fort Jackson, near Columbia, South Carolina, a segregated military base serving a segregated army in a segregated state. He was not alone in linking the 1940s to the 1860s. In early 1945, civil rights activist and newly elected New York congressman Adam Clayton Powell Jr., in his book *Marching Blacks,* wrote that what he called "Civil War II" had begun on December 7, 1941. This was a war between "the irresistible force" of the "awakened and united new Negro and the new white man" and "the immovable object" of "intolerant, anti-democratic, fascist prejudice."[2] Bristol's "New Gettysburg Address," published in the *Pittsburgh Courier,* a prominent African American newspaper, agreed: "Now we are engaged in a great struggle for economic and social freedom . . . testing whether that nation or any nation so conceived can deny its citizens inalienable rights." He dedicated his version of Lincoln's address to "the brave men, living and dead, who did struggle and are struggling valiantly to refute the heresy that relegates the Negro to the realms of the apes, have considered it far above our power to add or to detract. The world will little remember what has been said here, by men such as Rankin, Bilbo, and Talmadge [three notorious southern race-baiting politicians] and their cohorts, but it can never forget what our predecessors have done toward the welfare and the building of this nation. It is for us, the living, rather to be dedicated to the unfinished work that those who struggled here so nobly advanced."[3]

Two decades later, in August 1963, several hundred thousand people gathered in front of the Lincoln Memorial, participating in the March on Washington for Jobs and Freedom. Walter Reuther, president of the United Auto Workers, a stalwart supporter of both civil rights and a socially progressive labor movement, told the crowd that "this rally is not the end, it's the beginning. It's the beginning of a great moral crusade to arouse America to the unfinished work of American democracy. . . . We have much work to do."[4] The following February, in celebration of Lincoln's birthday, President Lyndon Johnson spoke of the "unfinished work to which we the living must dedicate ourselves." He said that "the American promise will be unfulfilled, Lincoln's work—our work—will be unfinished so long as there is a child without a school, a school without a teacher, a man without a job, a family without a home," and "so long as there are Americans, of any race or color, who are denied their full human rights," or Americans "of any place or region, who are denied their human dignity."[5] At the time, President Johnson was in the midst of a months-long process to enact a comprehensive civil rights act. After defeating a prolonged attempt by southern senators at a filibuster, the landmark legislation was signed into law that July.

Decades later, a few minutes past noon on January 20, 2021, on a platform on the West Front of the US Capitol, Amanda Gorman, a twenty-two-year-old African American poet from California, read her poem "The Hill We Climb" in honor of the newly inaugurated president, Joseph R. Biden. As everyone watching her was aware, Gorman was speaking on the same portico that a mere two weeks earlier had been swarmed over by insurrectionists attempting to block the certification of Biden's election, an attack on Congress that had been incited by the now-former president, Donald Trump. Her poem did not directly speak to this or to other recent crises, the murder of George Floyd and protests against police violence, or the still rampaging COVID-19 pandemic. Instead, Gorman told Americans that, "while we've braved the belly of the beast," not to give in to despair. Whether or not she was deliberately citing another president, or summoning another inauguration 156 years earlier, she used Lincoln's language: "Somehow we weathered and witnessed a nation that isn't broken but merely unfinished."[6]

The essays in this book explore the meaning of Lincoln's unfinished work. It permits no single or simple definition. For Lincoln, in the last years of his life, the most immediate work was winning the war, extinguishing the rebellion, and restoring the Union. And after the issuance of the Emancipation Proclamation on September 22, 1862, it also meant the creation of an America, and a South, without the institution of slavery. Lincoln was fully aware of the magnitude of this step and how it would mark a sharp severing with the constitutional history

of the nation's first eighty years. In December 1862, he concluded his message
to Congress, most of which was consumed by a discussion of emancipation, by
insisting that "the dogmas of the quiet past are inadequate to the stormy present.
The occasion is piled high with difficulties, and we must rise with the occasion.
As our case is new, so we must think anew, and act anew. We must disenthrall
ourselves, and then we shall save our country."[7]

This sense of radical newness pervades many of his most important statements
in his last years. Many scholars have written of Lincoln's profound sense of operating on a new, uncharted terrain. For Garry Wills, the Gettysburg Address
envisioned a new sort of nation, a unified nation, organized around the idea
of genuine equality.[8] For Orville Vernon Burton, it represented the "hopeful
determination of the human spirit . . . for freedom."[9] In this, it formed a sharp
contrast with the freedom envisioned by the writers of the Constitution, who,
steeped in Enlightenment political theory, created a structure that they thought
balanced the sovereignty of the people with the need for elites to maintain control
of the main institutions of governance, avoiding both the tyranny of the executive and the rule of the mob (as well as recognizing the existence of slavery as a
constitutional reality).[10] They saw the work of democracy as creating a definitive
structure, perhaps at most requiring from time to time some amending and tin-
kering. When Lincoln at Gettysburg spoke of a "new birth of freedom" and the
creation of a "government of the people, by the people, for the people," he was
setting for himself, and for all Americans, a new kind of unfinished work—the
task of democratic inclusion and expansion, one open ended by its very nature,
its boundaries unfixed. The magnitude of this task, and the unbounded ambition
of some of its proposed solutions, has led a number of scholars to speak of the
period as a "second American revolution" or a "second founding."[11]

The unfinished work was never Lincoln's alone to formulate, to enact, or
to try to advance. As much of the best recent scholarship on the president has
demonstrated, Lincoln's unfinished work was the collective creation of a remarkable generation of abolitionists and antislavery activists. It included the women
and men who went behind US Army lines to escape slavery; African American
civilians and soldiers; a Frederick Douglass, a Harriet Tubman, a William Lloyd
Garrison, a Robert Smalls, and a Charles Sumner; and those whose voices remain obscure, forgotten, or unrecorded. And this literature often sees Lincoln
as much of a follower as a leader, someone who gained the courage to listen and

abandon long-held beliefs, carefully walking toward, with the occasional misstep, a new conception of American democracy and the need for effective African American citizenship in a reconstructed United States.[12] In the words of Manisha Sinha, "abolitionists, especially Black abolitionists, had played a crucial role in the coming of emancipation and in challenging Lincoln to abandon colonization and accept Black rights. . . . It had been the pioneering efforts and ideas of Black abolitionists crystallized in the broader interracial abolition movement . . . [that] introduced the idea of interracial democracy under the presidency of Abraham Lincoln."[13] It is this rich polyphony of voices for change that pushed, prodded, and provoked Lincoln to reexamine long-held views, the same reexamination that he now urged the nation as a whole to consider. If we honor Lincoln, we must also pay equal tribute to his contemporaries. It was their dreams that Lincoln, due to his high office, was in a unique position to help realize.

To the end of his life, Lincoln's views on such crucial matters as African American citizenship and suffrage were evolving. In his so-called final speech—though of course it was not intended as such—on April 11, 1865, what comes across is not finality; rather it is his evolving and the unfinished nature of his thinking. He told the audience gathered beneath his White House window that while his deepest beliefs were firm, "so new and unprecedented is the whole case, that no exclusive and inflexible plan can safely be proscribed for details and collaterals."[14] The *New York World* wrote of the speech the following day, "Mr. Lincoln gropes . . . like a traveler in an unknown country without a map."[15] This seems unfair—his specific proposals about Black suffrage in Louisiana were unambiguous—but it was true enough that, in April 1865, all Americans, regardless of their race or political allegiances, were traveling in the same uncharted country, a United States that had ended and abolished slavery. The Age of Lincoln did not end on Good Friday 1865. But Lincoln would no longer be able to advance, amend, or rethink his unfinished work.

What is "unfinished work"? "Unfinished" is a relatively straightforward word, though it has a number of synonyms with slightly different meanings—"incomplete," "imperfect," "unconsummated," and even "half-baked" or "rude" (an unfinished idea or person). "Work," on the other hand, is one of the more complex words in the English language. The *Oxford English Dictionary* has approximately 360 distinct senses of the word, dating back to its Old English roots. Here are a few. Work is "a thing to be done; a task to be carried out." Work is also an "action or activity involving physical or mental effort undertaken as a means of making one's living or earning money"—in other words, work is a job, and no president of the United States has been more identified with the work of hard physical labor than Abraham Lincoln. (Moreover, Lincoln believed fervently that "labor [is] the true standard of value" and that "labor is the great source from which nearly all, if not all, human comforts are drawn.")[16] Work can also be defined as "the part of an activity that requires the most effort"; that is why we call it work, or as Lincoln observed to a prospective lawyer, "the main thing" one needs to do to learn something is just "work, work, work."[17] Work is also an "improvement necessary to reach a more complete or satisfactory state," or to "strive or endeavor strenuously to accomplish something or achieve some end." In his initial political campaign, running for the Illinois General Assembly in 1832, when speaking on internal improvements, Lincoln stated, "it is folly to undertake works of this or any other kind, without first knowing that we are able to finish them—as half finished work generally proves to be labor lost."[18] If this was so when addressing "the People of Sagamo Country" in 1832, it was just as true thirty years later at Gettysburg and at his second inauguration, when addressing the people of the United States as a whole, if not the entire world, and speaking of another kind of internal improvement. The purpose of starting a job is to finish it. No one is going to pay you for half digging a canal, praise you for half building a bridge, or applaud you for half abolishing slavery. Results, not intentions, are what matter. Lincoln retained this practical sense of work his entire life.

On the other hand, some kinds of work do not come with easy or unambiguous endpoints. The word "work" has a number of religious connotations, such as "a good or moral act considered in relation to justification before God" in Christian theology. However one views Lincoln's religious beliefs, he was not a Calvinist.[19] He always believed in the saving power of good works, the sort of work that is a permanent obligation and is never ending. Before God and our ultimate duties, we are all unfinished. There is perhaps something fundamentally religious in this idea of a "higher unfinished work," even in its secular guises. Lincoln's notion of history was as something unfinished, in accord with his deep but nondenominational Christian belief that the "Great Disposer of Events" was working out a plan for human history, sometimes giving it a needed but subtle providential shove when human efforts seemed to falter. The idea of a task that by its nature cannot be finished, a debt that cannot be repaid, is common to many religions. Sometimes, as in the Greek myth of Sisyphus's stone, the task is merely unending and futile, a punishment. In the Jewish and Christian traditions, unfinished work can be both positive and cumulative. The third century CE rabbinic text *Pirke Avot*, the Ethics of the Fathers, in describing the responsibilities of Jews to improve the world through study of Torah and the law, expresses it thusly: "The day is short, the work formidable, the workers lazy, the wages high, the employer impatient. It's not your job to finish the work, but you're not free to walk away from it."[20] This is the sort of work that is an honor to pass on, in the words of the psalm, "from generation to generation."[21] As Lincoln said in Springfield, Illinois, in June 1857, the Declaration of Independence's invocation of "Life, Liberty, and the Pursuit of Happiness" for all men included African Americans, and this should be "the standard maxim for free society . . . revered by all, constantly looked to, constantly labored for, and though never perfectly attained, constantly approximated, and thereby constantly spreading and deepening its influence."[22]

For many, this sort of unfinished work, the unfinished work of democratic expansion, has become a cornerstone of civil religion, an American metaphysic. The more one works to complete it, the more there is to do. It was one of Lincoln's signal achievements to argue that democratic government will involve the latter sort of unfinished work. To be unfinished is to be alive, and to be alive is to be alert to the possibilities and pitfalls of American democracy, to be able to correct and atone for past errors, to be capable of change, and to be sensitive to the possibility of growth. A living constitution, a living America, will always be unfinished. To be finished is to be dead, inert. Eric Foner, in his classic study of Reconstruction, calls it "America's Unfinished Revolution."[23] And surely it was. But how do you finish a revolution? When, at last, is it complete? Do you ever want to announce that all of your goals have been met, that the mission is accomplished, and that everyone is now free to turn their attention to other things? Even if you could finish a revolution like Reconstruction, it will remain unfinished.

Lincoln's Reconstruction was only unfinished in this metaphorical sense. Because of an assassin's bullet, it was not only unfinished, it was essentially unstarted. Those wishing to consider how Lincoln's Reconstruction might have unfolded have evidence from his treatment of captured regions of the Confederacy during the war and his postwar plans, but these are at best hints and intimations of how he would have actually responded to events subsequent to April 15, 1865.

All of this has produced a mountain range of counterfactual speculation, but as LaWanda Cox has noted, most of this has been of fairly recent vintage, since it is premised on a positive appraisal of the aims of Reconstruction, when the "identification of the southern policy of Andrew Johnson with that of Lincoln ... no longer [was] an unquestioned verity of Reconstruction historiography."[24] Some historians, including several in this volume, take a fairly skeptical view of whether Reconstruction would have had a different outcome had Lincoln lived.[25] Like Cox, others disagree, but even those on her side of the argument would probably agree with her that "possible is not probable."[26] But neither can we say what actually happened was the only plausible outcome.

The editors side with those who think a Lincoln-led Reconstruction would have had a very different trajectory than Johnson's. Lincoln did not worry about the hobgoblins of consistency; he grew and expanded his thinking as he learned, especially from African American leaders like Harriet Tubman, Robert Smalls, and Frederick Douglass. As he did with the Emancipation Proclamation, preparing a reluctant nation for the end of slavery, Lincoln at the end of his life was preparing the nation for Black citizenship. He was committed to order and the rule of law and would not have tolerated the white riots of 1866 in New Orleans or Memphis, nor the clandestine and terroristic undermining of the legitimately elected interracial Republican governments that occurred in 1875–78. Especially important would have been his presidential appointments. During his life, he appointed committed abolitionist Salmon Chase to the Supreme Court and supporters of Black civil rights in all levels of government—for example, for Saint Helena's Island, South Carolina, Lincoln appointed tax commissioners who protected African Americans landownership during Reconstruction.[27] Moreover, Lincoln had a firm commitment to the idea that those who fought for the United States deserved citizenship. In response to pressure to revoke the Emancipation Proclamation, he wrote a public letter on August 26, 1863, about African American soldiers and their heroic efforts for the Union: "If they stake their lives for us they must be prompted by the strongest motive—even the promise of freedom. And the promise being made, must be kept."[28] He was determined to make that freedom real. And who is to say that a popular Abraham Lincoln in 1868, arguing that the turbulent times required an experienced hand in charge, would not have broken the third-term taboo more than seventy years before Franklin Roosevelt?[29]

Still, it is worth remembering that even with Andrew Johnson as president, Reconstruction did not somehow just fade away; it was destroyed by persons who believed that interracial democracy was a direct threat to every political and social principle they held dear, and they used all of the influence, energy, guile, and violence at their command to assassinate it. Having just lost the bloodiest war in American history against a largely white though interracial army, southern Democrats had no confidence or assurance that northern whites would, as a matter of racial comity and solidarity, take their side against Black and white Republicans in the battle for control of the South. The members of the Ku Klux Klan did not complacently take for granted that interracial democracy was an impossibility, or that Reconstruction was doomed to failure from the outset. Their greatest fear was that it might succeed.

For many decades, the so-called Dunning school dominated the historiography of Reconstruction, apart from a few lonely voices like W. E. B. Du Bois.[30] The main thesis of the Dunning historians was that, because of the African American incapacity for self-government, Reconstruction was an aberration, its failure was foreordained, and only sentimentalists would argue otherwise. At times, we feel that much recent historical work on Reconstruction, while rejecting the racism of the Dunning school, has simply turned that perspective on its head, still arguing that Reconstruction's success was an impossibility, though this time placing the blame on the tenacity and violence of white racism. If white racism has emerged as an unchanging, constant, invariant, defining characteristic of American history, the successes of Reconstruction (or the civil rights era) become quixotic. But the course of Reconstruction was not predetermined; its demise was not a product of some ironclad law of historical necessity. Recent historians of the Civil War have been much more willing than their predecessors to acknowledge that the war could have taken very different turns. But Reconstruction is generally not granted the same sort of possible contingency. There were strong forces on both sides: African American self-determination, federal resolve, and idealism on one side, and the toxic stew of emasculated masters and embittered white yeomen on the other. Like the Civil War, Reconstruction had its turning points, each a node of alternative histories. The struggle continued in its violent, topsy-turvy fashion for at least twice the number of years the soldiers of the US and Confederate armies had fought and killed one another. Reconstruction did not have to fail. It was a combination of circumstances and the choices people made at that historical time that determined its fate—and the direction of history.

The logical extension of this argument is that Reconstruction was ahead of its time or that it could not have succeeded given the circumstances of the United States in the post–Civil War period. Often lurking in the background of the historiography is the belief that Reconstruction set back race relations so severely it was not even worth trying. This interpretation oversimplifies the racism and reactions of whites and makes other concerns, such as class, labor, the economy, women's rights, and westward expansion, secondary in what is a complex, evolving, and mutable idea and social reality. It also undercuts, if not dismisses, the possibility of African American agency as well as the importance of white antiracism as a social force. It is a paradox that the current interest in exposing "whiteness" and "white privilege" sees itself as unique and can be myopic or dismissive about the long history of white antiracism and the history of interracial collaboration against racism. Without underestimating the immense challenges involved in creating a true interracial democracy, we refuse to accept the conclusion that it is an impossibility. America at its best has always been able to challenge its limitations. Reconstruction was not an exercise in futility and foolhardy optimism. That it and similar episodes in American history have always been met by fierce opposition is evidence of their potential strength and not their inherent weakness.

That said, few now disagree that the destruction of Reconstruction was an unmitigated disaster for African Americans, for the South, and for the United States. It marked the decisive turn toward almost a century of one-party, white-segregationist rule in the states of the old Confederacy. The disputed Hayes-Tilden 1876 presidential election was resolved in Rutherford B. Hayes's favor in 1877, after which military protection for the remaining biracial state legislations was withdrawn (but federal troops were not withdrawn and were still stationed in the former Confederacy).[31] If we recognize that "1877" has become a shorthand for a lengthier process that unfolded both before and after that year, it becomes one of the darkest years in American history—and one of the most significant. In recent years, there has much talk of the year 1619, the year the first ship with captured Africans bound for labor arrived in Jamestown, Virginia, in British North America, or alternatively, 1776 as the year for the real beginning of American history. (We discuss the much-publicized 1619 Project in more detail below.) Let us suggest that 1877 is another candidate for America's key year, certainly for the century and a half that has followed. Much of the recent work on Reconstruction in its totality perhaps constitutes an "1877 Project." The year 1877 was when the "new birth of freedom" had a near-death experience and the second American revolution was defeated by the first American counterrevolution.[32]

Stanley Engerman has written that "the emancipation of the slaves in most parts of the world aroused high expectations but ended with a major sense of disappointment about what had been accomplished."[33] Perhaps nowhere was the initial expectations as high, and the final disappointment as great or the loss of political, economic, and social power as complete, as it was in the United States. With the destruction of Reconstruction, the legacy of slavery was unaddressed, reinforced, and allowed to expand and fester. And, as much recent literature on the end of Reconstruction has pointed out, this was part of a more general rightward swerve in the nation's politics that saw most of the country's political institutions line up with the new industrial capitalists against a resurgent labor movement, the use of the Fourteenth Amendment to defend the rights of corporations rather than defending those of African Americans, anti-Chinese immigration restrictions, and the final push for the full extinction of Indian sovereignty in the West. And yet, if the Reconstruction era sometimes showed America at its worst, it could also show America at its best. The emancipatory fervor unleashed after 1865 was never entirely quashed. These two Americas have done battle against each other ever since.

Reconstruction's demise provided much of the context for the evaluation of Lincoln's reputation and legacy for the century after his death. We do not have the space to comment on all of the Lincolns that have emerged like facets of a kaleidoscope in the century between 1865 and 1965 or how this influenced the understanding of his unfinished work. In the most influential study of Lincoln's posthumous reputation, Merrill Peterson has suggested there were five main ways in which Lincoln was lauded and admired during his first posthumous century, often as the archetypal American: Lincoln as the Savior of the Union; Lincoln as the Great Emancipator; Lincoln as Man of the People; Lincoln as Frontiersman; and Lincoln as Self-Made Man.[34] The president's imprimatur was sought on every side of almost every conceivable political issue, and it was stretched very thin. If an apposite quote from Lincoln could not easily be found, one could be easily invented. No American, with the possible exception of Yogi Berra, has a more extensive apocrypha.[35] Lincoln was a union man, a populist, a liberal, a socialist, and a communist; at the same time, he was an outspoken defender of small business and small government, of free enterprise, and of freedom from Washington's intrusive policies; he was pro-immigrant and xenophobe; and there was even one Lincoln for the NAACP and another for the Ku Klux Klan.[36] Lincoln was never universally admired, of course, and every myth generates its own countermyth. There is also a long history of Lincoln-haters and Lincoln-skeptics, ranging from unreconstructed former Confederates to scholars who have found the prospect of pricking the immense bubble of his reputation irresistible.[37] If there was a dominant depiction during this period, it was Lincoln as the savior of the Union and would-be reconciliator and healer of the nation's wounds. Lincoln as emancipator was always important in evaluations of his legacy, even in the post-Reconstruction Jim Crow nadir of Black civil rights, but for many whites, the abolition of slavery was usually separated from considerations of the contemporary situation of African Americans.[38]

Barry Schwartz has suggested that Lincoln's prestige peaked four score years after his death, in 1945.[39] If this is so, it was because, in the following years, the African American quest for full citizenship clawed its way back to the center of the American political agenda, a place it has yet to relinquish. This would have a profound influence on how Americans viewed Abraham Lincoln. In part, this is because white America began to listen to the complex African American discourse on Lincoln, pro and contra.[40] And, in part, this was so because, as American politics became consumed with the civil rights struggle, comparisons between the 1960s and 1860s became irresistible. The paradoxical result is that if, on the one hand, Lincoln became ever more identified with the cause of civil rights and African American citizenship, on the other, a new generation of historians began asking more searching questions about his civil rights record and attitudes toward Black civic and political equality. Increasingly, Lincoln's attitudes toward race and racism, not just slavery, were a focus of scholarly attention. Moreover, the rise of social history argued for a more complex explanation of social action than history made solely by presidential proclamation. Few contemporary historians would accept without qualification the bald statement of old that "Lincoln freed the slaves" without paying attention to enslaved peoples' efforts on their own behalf. A new generation of historians often viewed the radical abolitionists, Black and white, as the real heroes of the struggle against slavery, those who pushed and prodded Lincoln to a fuller embrace of emancipation and Black citizenship.

In recent discussions of Lincoln, a notorious statement he made on September 18, 1858, during his fourth debate with Stephen Douglas in Charleston, Illinois, has loomed almost as large as the Gettysburg Address. There he said, "I am not, nor ever have been in favor of bringing about in any way the social and political equality of the white and black races." In 1961, Leon Litwack argued that Lincoln's comments in Charleston and elsewhere demonstrate "that he accurately and consistently reflected the thoughts of most [white] Americans." Mark Neely has stated that Litwack's comments mark a "new era" in Lincoln studies, the growing prominence of increasingly searching critiques of his racial attitudes. Lincoln's detractors have argued that he remained a captive of his biases against Blacks until the end of his life, a reluctant and inadvertent emancipator who was at best, in the words of Lerone Bennett, "forced into glory."[41]

The counterargument begins by acknowledging Lincoln's imperfections, that his comments in Charleston, one of the lowest points in his career, were made in the heat of an intense political battle as he was attempting to rebut an opponent who regularly charged that his antislavery convictions were nothing less than a call and cover for racial amalgamation. But Lincoln, before and after the Charleston debate, including just one month later in Alton, a town in one of the most South-like regions of the state, affirmed that the Declaration of Independence's invocation of "life, liberty, and the pursuit of happiness" applied to all men, including African Americans. As Kate Masur has argued, this was for Lincoln a deeper commitment to Black equality beyond the end of slavery.[42]

That deeper commitment is seen also in the Thirteenth Amendment, bringing universal freedom throughout the land, which Lincoln championed and used his incredible political skills to get through Congress. That amendment was not a one-time historical event that became irrelevant once the institution of slavery no longer existed. The Thirteenth Amendment continues to promise to uproot the badges and incidents of slavery, root and branch; to guarantee equality; and, ultimately, to end discrimination and to eliminate racial prejudice.[43]

So, was Abraham Lincoln a hero? Perhaps we should ask if we need Lincoln to be a hero, or the same sort of heroic figure he was to previous generations. Barry Schwartz has suggested that Americans' admiration of Lincoln has declined because we live in a "post-heroic" age, suspicious of and cynical about claims for outsized heroism. (We wish Americans were quite as over past hero-worshipping cults of "greatness" as Schwartz suggested.)[44] But many today seek heroism in the humble, the extraordinary in the ordinary, in the resistance of the weak rather than in the actions of the powerful, and they see heroism as less martial, less masculine, and more shared and collective than just enthroning a single individual in a colonnaded temple of fame high above a reflecting pool. Still, for many, Lincoln remains that sort of singular hero. He remains a man who became president at what remains the most perilous moment in the nation's history, who mastered the necessary but often ugly skills to be an effective politician and commander in chief, and yet as a thinker and writer crafted a new vision of America that reoriented the country toward its better angels and highest aspirations. Torrents of biographical studies, most of them highly laudatory, continue to flood from our publishing houses. In rankings of presidents by historians, Lincoln remains the perennial number one, with a substantial gap between him and the others.[45] As we were writing this afterword, Ayala Emmett, an Israeli-American peace activist in both countries, informed us that, when she was growing up in Israel in the 1950s and studying English, she had to memorize the Gettysburg Address. She "fell in love with the sheer beauty of the sound" and knew that "the Lincoln I met in Israel was speaking of a liberty that was inclusive and meant not just for men but all—women, slaves, the tired, survivors of the Holocaust, and immigrants; all are created equal." For her, "the English [language] would forever be Lincoln. I came to America on the wings of Lincoln's promise of freedom." Cognizant of his flaws, she still thinks Lincoln is one of the greatest and most inspiring of Americans, one of the greatest political leaders the United States or any other country has ever had. She is not alone.[46]

That said, much of the contemporary debate about our sixteenth president is as much about the possibility of racial progress, understanding, and reconciliation, and whether it is even desirable, as about Lincoln himself or his actions. Our attitudes toward Lincoln have always reflected our broader views on what it means to be an American. Black attitudes toward him, from Douglass to Du Bois, Merrill Peterson has noted, have long been a mixture of ambivalence and admiration. In the early decades of the twentieth century, Archibald H. Grimké, lawyer and early leader of the NAACP; socialist radical Hubert Harrison; and Carter G. Woodson, founder of the Association for the Study of Negro Life and History, all offered criticisms of Lincoln for his slow embrace of complete abolitionism and his hesitancy in allowing Black troops into the US military. If these authors' views of Lincoln were less than worshipful, neither did they anathemize him, and they found much to praise in his actions as president. In any event, these critiques must be seen as a cross-current to the more widespread positive African American views of Lincoln, such as *Lincoln and the Negro*, by the prominent Black historian Benjamin Quarles, which acquitted him of the charge of being "anti-Negro."[47]

By the 1960s, Black views of Lincoln generally showed less of both ambivalence and admiration. Here, as in so many other ways, the views of Malcolm X were a touchstone. His comments about Lincoln to an interviewer in 1964 matched what he was saying about him in public: "Negroes have been tricked into thinking that Lincoln was a Negro lover whose primary aim was to free them and he died because he freed them. I think Lincoln did more to deceive Negroes and to make the race problems worse in this country than any man in history." In the same year, whether or not he was directly influenced by Malcolm X, Lerone Bennett Jr., editor at the influential *Ebony* magazine and a popular historian with a Black-nationalist bent, was describing Lincoln as "of course, the godfather of American liberals," the model for so many contemporary "liberals and other white hopes" who he thought talked much but did little to actually advance the cause of Black citizenship. In 1968, Bennett published an article in *Ebony*, "Was Lincoln a White Supremacist," answering in the affirmative. The Black press, for the most part, applauded this debunking. Still, Lincoln continued to have many defenders among Black historians. In 1985, the historian John Hope Franklin criticized Malcolm X, Bennett, and Black anti-Lincoln scholars for an overly narrow view of the president that did not allow for his "flexibility" and "capacity for growth." He argued that it was often Lincoln's image as the Great Emancipator as much as what he actually did or did not do that attracted so much animus, commenting on the "rather remarkable and perverse ways in which the Lincoln legacy has been associated with many of the disorders of our society."[48]

Bennett's assault on Lincoln culminated in 2000 with the publication of the definitive anti-Lincoln tract for our times, the six-hundred-page *Forced into Glory: Abraham Lincoln's White Dream*. Unlike earlier African American and left-wing critics, as John McKee Barr notes, Bennett argues that it "was not simply that Lincoln was coerced into freeing the slaves but that he was an actual *hindrance* to their emancipation." For Bennett, Lincoln was both "in and of himself, and in his objective being an oppressor," arguing that the president was the sort of person who would have supported, or at least done nothing about, apartheid in South Africa or the Nazi Party in Germany. He then indicts the mainstream historical profession as "academic accomplices of the oppression and slavery that Lincoln supported." (But one should note that Bennett concentrated his animus on Lincoln himself and did not extend this to white abolitionists whom he considered to be genuine supporters of racial equality. The dedication page of *Forced into Glory*, honoring "the Real Emancipators," names John Brown, Wendell Phillips, Charles Sumner, and Thaddeus Stevens, among others.)[49]

There have been a number of recent accounts of African American history that, much like Bennett, basically see Lincoln as an opponent or false friend of Black freedom. Historian Ibram X. Kendi, an acknowledged leader of the antiracism movement, does not allow that Lincoln grew and tempered his racism as he met with African American leaders such as Robert Smalls and Frederick Douglass, giving him no credit for his accomplishments—by as early as mid-1862, slavery was prohibited in the territories, the transatlantic slave trade was ended, the United States recognized Haiti and Liberia, and the US Army no longer returned fugitives to the South. Kendi offers a standard misinterpretation of Lincoln's 1862 letter to Horace Greeley (see James Loewen's essay in the present volume) and minimizes the significance of the Emancipation Proclamation.[50]

The widely discussed 1619 Report says much the same, although in even stronger and more hyperbolic language. Its lead editor, Nikole Hannah-Jones, argues in her introductory essay that Lincoln was in many ways America's archetypal racist. She asserts that "the fleeting moment of Reconstruction" did not last because "anti-Black racism runs in the very DNA of this country, as does the belief, so well articulated by Lincoln, that Black people are the obstacle to national unity." This seems to imply that Lincoln's failure, even from the grave, to prevent white racial violence was somehow responsible for Reconstruction's demise, not bothering to distinguish between Lincoln's racial ambivalences and, say, the murderous racism of a Nathan Bedford Forrest or a Ben Tillman. The basis for Hannah-Jones's statement is not clear. If what she says of Lincoln was so, it is difficult to see why, in the months after his election in 1860, Lincoln did not waver in his antislavery convictions and spurned a number of proposed compromises to preserve "national unity."[51]

The only substantial account of Lincoln in the 1619 Project is a lengthy discussion of the notorious White House meeting with Black leaders on August 14, 1862, in which he urged them to consider a colonization scheme. Hannah-Jones concludes, "like many white Americans, he [Lincoln] opposed slavery as a cruel system at odds with American ideals, but he also opposed black equality." This is a too one-dimensional view of Lincoln's thinking before August 1862 and is inadequate for his subsequent thinking, which was influenced by his growing friendship with and learning from Black leaders such as Frederick Douglass, who had been disgusted by the president's proposal at the August 1862 meeting.[52]

As a whole, the 1619 Report, which sees anti-Black racism as basically unchanging throughout American history, has difficulties explaining abolitionism, the Civil War, and the civil rights movement, topics it says little about. Matthew Karp suggests it is overly shaped by its dominant metaphors of slavery and racism as America's "original sin" and being part of its "DNA." The point of original sin, in Augustinian theology, is that it can be alleviated, not that it is permanent. As for DNA, leaving aside the question of whether this greatly overused metaphor is useful for discussing nonbiological entities like the United States of America, it is not a fixed material. Indeed, no one has the same DNA as their parents—that is inherent in sexual reproduction—and to the extent that a country has metaphorical DNA, it is always changing. While Americans, like all people, are surely in part the products of our cultural and political inheritances, we need not succumb to a determinism that argues we have no say in our destinies, that our inheritances are our destiny. Historians of American and African American history need to pay attention to our discontinuities as well as the continuities. The struggle against racism, as well as racism itself, is also a key part of our legacy as Americans.[53]

At the same time, there have been a number of prominent historians—Eric Foner, Orville Vernon Burton, and David Blight among them—taking full cognizance of Lincoln's racial missteps, his hesitancies, his colonization follies, and his occasional backsliding, who argue that Lincoln did exhibit, in John Hope Franklin's words, "flexibility" and "capacity for growth," in leading the United States through its greatest crisis, steering it toward the permanent abolition of slavery. The conflicting interpretations of our sixteenth president is, if nothing else, a continuing invitation to study Lincoln the man and Lincoln the president, including the weight he has borne in subsequent histories of the United States over the past century and a half. On this, perhaps, the contending sides in our latest history wars agree. Lerone Bennett wrote, "Lincoln is a key, perhaps the key, to the American personality, and what we invest in him, and what we hide in him, is who we are." Foner has said of Lincoln that he "provided a lens through which we Americans examine ourselves." Perhaps Franklin said it best: "Even if some tend to misuse the Lincoln legacy, that very act is an affirmation of its importance and of its enduring quality."[54]

The African American religious thinker Howard Thurman, in 1949, urged white Americans to acknowledge and challenge their "white necessity" and for all Americans to wrestle with political, cultural, or religious inheritances that they falsely believed were outside of their capacity to alter. He hoped that America could become a "common ground," where those with unearned and unwarranted advantages would learn to take "their place alongside all the rest of humanity," mingling their "desires with the longing of all the desperate people of all the ages," and create a true democracy of equals. Perhaps Lincoln would have called this the process of "disenthrallment." The extent to which he reached, or to which America as a whole has or can achieve this, will continue to be debated.[55]

One reason to admire Lincoln and his contemporaries is their sense of urgency with the imperative of attending to the "unfinished work." Time is never on the side of those seeking sweeping changes, and real openings for social transformation are rare. Lincoln and his contemporaries were operating in the knowledge of what the late historian of slavery David Brion Davis called, in a different context, "the perishability of revolutionary time," knowing their efforts to remake America might soon be lost and would not soon come again.[56] If the 1860s were one such time, the 1960s were another, when Martin Luther King Jr stood in front of the Lincoln Memorial speaking of the "the fierce urgency of now." People spoke of a "Second Reconstruction." A half century later, as we contemplate what the civil rights movement accomplished and the burden of their unfinished work, we might be standing at the precipice of another such moment, a time to take up the unfinished work of a previous generation. There is renewed talk of the need for a "third" Reconstruction.[57]

There is also, however, talk of a second civil war. In the third decade of the twenty-first century, the question of whether the United States will endure as a democratic republic has become all too pertinent. Like the presidential election of 1876, the election of 2020 has been bitterly and violently contested. (Although unlike in 1876, there was no serious ambiguity as to who actually was its winner.) The January 6, 2021, insurrection to prevent the certification of the electoral vote saw, for the first time ever, the waving of the Confederate battle flag in the halls of the Capitol (by supporters of the one-time "party of Lincoln"). In its aftermath, much as after Reconstruction, many state legislatures are enacting laws that will restrict voting in future elections, targeting their efforts against urban areas of minority populations. And as in 1877, at the core of the conflict are bitter divisions over the status of African Americans and the meaning of citizenship, arguments that also touch on every significant political question: the rights of labor and corporate power, the rights of women, the rights of immigrants, control of the environment, and the place of the United States in the world.

We return to the Lincolnian moment. Preservation of the United States as a democracy and the expansion of citizenship rights for all Americans are not separate choices—they are a single cause, one and indivisible. Even with all our differences, the United States must remain united. Let us hope that no successor to the *Charleston Mercury* ever again runs a banner headline as it did on December 20, 1860: "The Union Is Dissolved!"[58] Just five years later, in November 1865, in the same city, with the world turned upside down, delegates to the Colored State Convention met in the Zion Presbyterian Church on Calhoun Street and proclaimed themselves "Americans by birth." They asserted, "in spite of all the wrongs which we have long and silently endured in this country," they were also "Americans by feeling." They demanded "the rights of citizenship," the right to "acquire homesteads" for their families, the removal of legal and social "barriers in the way of their educational and mechanical improvement," and above all, to be treated with "equity" and "even-handed justice."[59] The members of the Colored State Convention recognized that with the abolition of slavery, many kinds of "unfreedom" still persisted. They still do.

It is always a danger to write about contemporary events in a work of history. It is our fond hope that our successors will pick up this book in a few years or a few decades and smile at our overblown worries about the future of American democracy. At the same time, it is our deep worry that future readers will find our concerns all too prescient. So what is our unfinished work? When Lincoln concluded his second inaugural by saying that he would try to reunite the United States by governing "with malice toward none, with charity for all," wanting to do right as "God gives us to see the right" and to "strive to finish the work we are in" by addressing the underlying roots of the country's bitter political divisions, he was summoning, with both pragmatism and idealism, the unfinished work of America, with all of its tensions, harmonies, dilemmas, and contradictions. It remains our unfinished work.

NOTES

1. PFC Willard D. Bristol Jr, "New Gettysburg Address," *Pittsburgh Courier,* 17 June 1944. For Fort Jackson during World War II, see Andrew H. Myers, *Black, White, and Olive Drab: Racial Integration at Fort Jackson, South Carolina, and the Civil Rights Movement* (Charlottesville: University of Virginia Press, 2006), 1–74.

2. Adam Clayton Powell Jr., *Marching Blacks: An Interpretive History of the Rise of the Black Common Man* (New York: Dial, 1945), 3.

3. Bristol, "New Gettysburg Address." John E. Rankin (1882–1960) was a Mississippi congressman from 1920 to 1952. Theodore G. Bilbo (1887–1947) was a Mississippi governor and, from 1935 to 1947, a US senator. Eugene Talmadge (1884–1946) was a three-term governor of Georgia. All three were notoriously outspoken racists.

4. "Excerpts from Addresses at Lincoln Memorial during Capital Civil Rights March," *New York Times,* Aug. 29, 1963.

5. "Text of President's Lincoln Tribute," *Washington Post,* Feb. 13, 1964.

6. Amanda Gorman, *The Hill We Climb: An Inaugural Poem for the Country* (New York: Viking, 2021).

7. Abraham Lincoln, *Speeches and Writings: 1859–1865,* ed. Don E. Fehrenbacher (New York: Library of America, 1989), 425.

8. Garry Wills, *Lincoln at Gettysburg: The Words That Remade America* (New York: Simon and Schuster, 1992), 145, 146.

9. Orville Vernon Burton, *The Age of Lincoln* (New York: Hill and Wang, 2007), 3.

10. For two different views on slavery and the Constitution, see David Waldstreicher, *Slavery's Constitution: From Revolution to Ratification* (New York: Hill and Wang, 2019); and James Oakes, *The Crooked Path to Abolition: Abraham Lincoln and the Antislavery Constitution* (New York: Norton, 2021). See also William W. Freehling, *Becoming Lincoln* (Charlottesville: University of Virginia Press, 2018).

11. James M. McPherson, *Abraham Lincoln and the Second American Revolution* (New York: Oxford, 1991); Gregory P. Downs, *The Second American Revolution: The Civil War–Era Struggle over Cuba and the Rebirth of the American Republic* (Chapel Hill: University of North Carolina, 2019); Eric Foner, *The Second Founding: How the Civil War and Reconstruction Remade the Constitution* (New York: Norton, 2019).

12. For Lincoln and Black suffrage, see LaWanda Cox, *Lincoln and Black Freedom: A Study in Presidential Leadership* (Urbana: University of Illinois Press, 1981); Eric Foner, *The Fiery Trial: Abraham Lincoln and American Slavery* (New York: Norton, 2010), 134–35, 256–83, 331–35.

13. Manisha Sinha, "Allies for Emancipation? Lincoln and Black Abolitionists," in *Our Lincoln: New Perspectives on Abraham Lincoln and His World,* ed. Eric Foner (New York: Norton, 2008),

196. See also Sinha, *The Slave's Cause: A History of Abolitionism* (New Haven, CT: Yale University, 2016); and Kate Masur, *America's First Civil Rights Movement from the Revolution to Reconstruction* (New York: Norton, 2021). For colonization, see Eric Foner, "Lincoln and Colonization," in Foner, *Our Lincoln*, 135–66.

14. Lincoln, *Writings, 1859–1865*, 701.

15. *New York World*, Apr. 13, 1865, cited in Foner, *Fiery Trial*, 331.

16. Speech in Pittsburgh, Feb. 15, 1861, in *The Collected Works of Abraham Lincoln*, ed. Roy P. Basler et al., 9 vols. (New Brunswick, NJ: Rutgers University, 1953–55), 4:215; Speech in Cincinnati, Sept. 17, 1859, in Lincoln, *Writings, 1859–1865*, 83. For Lincoln on labor and the labor theory of value, see G. S. Boritt, *Lincoln and the Economics of the American Dream* (Memphis: Memphis State University Press, 1978); and Eric Foner, *Free Soil, Free Labor, Free Men: The Ideology of the Republican Party before the Civil War* (1970; repr., New York: Oxford University, 1995), ix–xxxix, 11–40.

17. Abraham Lincoln to John M. Brockman, Sept. 25, 1860, in Lincoln, *Writings, 1859–1865*, 180.

18. "To the People of Sagamo County," Mar. 9, 1832, in Abraham Lincoln, *The Essential Lincoln: Speeches and Correspondence*, ed. Orville Vernon Burton (New York: Hill and Wang, 2009), 2.

19. See Richard Carwardine, "Lincoln's Religion," in Foner, *Our Lincoln*, 223–48.

20. Jacob Neusner, *The Mishnah: A New Translation* (New Haven, CT: Yale University Press, 1988), Abot 2:14–15, p. 678.

21. The phrase "from generation to generation," or in Hebrew "L'dor v'dor," is taken from Psalm 146:10. It is also found in the Amidah, one of the central prayers of Judaism. The editors thought it an apt description of the scope of this book and of the reach of the unfinished work.

22. Speech on the *Dred Scott* decision at Springfield, IL, June 26, 1857, in Abraham Lincoln, *Speeches and Writings, 1832–1858*, ed. Don E. Fehrenbacher (New York: Library of America, 1989), 398.

23. Eric Foner, *Reconstruction: America's Unfinished Revolution, 1863–1877* (New York: Harper and Row, 1988).

24. LaWanda Cox, *Lincoln and Black Freedom: A Study in Presidential Leadership* (1981; repr., Urbana: University of Illinois Press, 1995), 142.

25. See J. William Harris, "Abraham Lincoln's Unfinished Work and the South's Long Self-Reconstruction," and Jerald Podair, "Lincoln and the Two Reconstructions: The Unfinished Work of American Equality," printed in the current volume. Gregory P. Downs, in "The Problem of Enforcement: The Republican Struggle to Protect Voting Rights in Peacetime," also printed in the current volume, makes a somewhat different argument and makes the case for the weakness of enforcement mechanisms available to Republicans.

26. Cox, *Abraham Lincoln and Black Freedom*, 183.

27. Orville Vernon Burton, *Penn Center: A History Preserved* (Athens: University of Georgia, 2014), 19–20, 29, 31; Burton and Armand Derfner, *Justice Deferred: Race and the Supreme Court* (Cambridge, MA: Belknap Press of Harvard University Press, 2021), 40, 42, 72.

28. Lincoln to James C. Conkling, Aug. 26, 1863, in Burton, *Essential Lincoln*, 147–52.

29. On comparison of Andrew Johnson and Lincoln's policies, see Burton and Derfner, *Justice Deferred*, 39–43. See also Burton, *Age of Lincoln*, 272–73, 276; Burton, "The Gettysburg Address Revisited," in *1863: Lincoln's Pivotal Year*, ed. Harold Holzer and Sara Vaughn Gabbard (Carbondale:

Southern Illinois University Press, 2013), 137–55; and Burton, "Lincoln at Two Hundred: Have We Finally Reached Randall's Point of Exhaustion?," in *The Living Lincoln: Essays from the Harvard Lincoln Bicentennial Symposium*, ed. Thomas A. Horrocks, Harold Holzer, and Frank J. Williams (Cardondale: Southern Illinois University Press, 2011), 204–25.

30. See John David Smith and J. Vincent Lowery, eds., *The Dunning School: Historians, Race, and the Meaning of Reconstruction* (Lexington: University Press of Kentucky, 2013). For alternative accounts of the history of Reconstruction, see Alrutheus A. Taylor, *The Negro in South Carolina during Reconstruction* (Washington, DC: Association for the Study of Negro Life and History, 1924); Taylor, *The Negro in the Reconstruction of Virginia* (Washington, DC: Association for the Study of Negro Life and History, 1926); Francis B. Simkins and Robert H. Woody, *South Carolina during Reconstruction* (Chapel Hill: University of North Carolina Press, 1932); and W. E. B. Du Bois, *Black Reconstruction: A History of the Part which Black Folk Played in the Attempt to Reconstruct Democracy in America, 1860–1880* (New York: Harcourt Brace, 1935).

31. C. Vann Woodward, *Reunion and Reaction: The Compromise of 1877 and the End of Reconstruction* (New York: Oxford University, 1951); Gregory P. Downs, "The Mexicanization of American Politics: The United States' Transnational Path from Civil War to Stabilization," *American Historical Review* 115, no. 2 (Apr. 2012): 387–409.

32. The original version of the 1619 Project composed the entirety of the *New York Times Magazine* for August 14, 2019. Some of its right-wing critics proposed in *The 1776 Report*, sponsored by then-president Donald Trump and issued on January 18, 2021, an alternative key year along with a through-the-looking-glass view of American history, one in which John C. Calhoun somehow becomes a forerunner of progressive antiracism because affirmative action "was not unlike those [policies] advanced by Calhoun and his followers." And, of course, Calhoun was "perhaps the leading forerunner of identity politics," with Lincoln becoming a premature opponent of "wokeness," "critical race theory," and all forms of racially conscious politics. President's Advisory 1776 Commission, *The 1776 Report*, Jan. 2021, pp. 15, 29, trumpwhitehouse.archives.gov/wp-content/uploads/2021/01/The-Presidents-Advisory-1776-Commission-Final-Report.pdf.

33. Stanley Engerman, "Comparative Approaches to the End of Slavery," in *After Slavery: Emancipation and Its Discontents*, ed. Howard Temperley (London: Frank Cass, 2000), 281. For the comparative history of emancipation, see Frederick Cooper, Thomas C. Holt, and Rebecca Scott, *Beyond Slavery: Explorations of Race, Labor, and Citizenship in Post-Emancipation Societies* (Chapel Hill: University of North Carolina Press, 2000); Carl N. Degler, *Neither Black nor White: Slavery and Race Relations in Brazil and the United States* (New York: Macmillan, 1971); Stanley Engerman, *Slavery, Emancipation, and Freedom* (Baton Rouge: Louisiana State University Press, 2007); and Jeffrey R. Kerr-Ritchie, *Freedom's Seekers: Essays on Comparative Emancipation* (Baton Rouge: Louisiana State University Press, 2015).

34. Merrill D. Peterson, *Lincoln in American Memory* (New York: Oxford University Press, 1994), 26–35. This framework was utilized by Barry Schwartz in his works on the remembered Lincoln, *Abraham Lincoln and the Forge of National Memory* (Chicago: University of Chicago Press, 2000) and *Abraham Lincoln in the Post-Heroic Era: History and Memory in Late Twentieth-Century America* (Chicago: University of Chicago Press, 2008).

35. See Paul F. Boiler Jr. and John George, *They Never Said It: A Book of Fake Quotes, Misquotes, and Misleading Attributions* (New York: Oxford University Press, 1989), 71–82. Lincoln has by far the longest section in the book.

36. For Lincoln cited in defense of segregation, see Schwartz, *Abraham Lincoln in the Post-Heroic Era*, 108–9. The *Richmond News-Leader*, a stalwart and influential defender of segregation, on February 7, 1959, quoted Lincoln as saying, "I can conceive of no greater calamity than the assimilation of the Negro into our social and political life as our equal." The quote was taken from Thomas Dixon, *The Clansman* (New York: Grosset and Dunlap, 1905), 46.

37. See John McKee Barr, *Loathing Lincoln: An American Tradition from the Civil War to the Present* (Baton Rouge: Louisiana State University Press, 2015). For those seeking a larger serving of anti-Lincoln invective, see the original, and quite longer, version, "The Anti-Lincoln Tradition in American Life" (PhD diss., University of Houston, 2010).

38. David W. Blight's argument in *Race and Reunion: The Civil War in American History* (Cambridge, MA: Harvard University Press, 2001) that the price of sectional reconciliation was rejecting or obscuring the emancipationist meanings of the war has been challenged by Barbara A. Gannon in *The Won Cause: Black and White Comradeship in the Grand Army of the Republic* (Chapel Hill: University of North Carolina Press, 2011). Caroline E. Janney, in *Remembering the Civil War: Reunion and the Limits of Reconciliation* (Chapel Hill: University of North Carolina Press, 2015), argues that for US Army veterans, by the 1890s, the war was much more likely to have been seen as one to end slavery than it had been for them in the 1860s. See also Julie Roy Jeffrey, *Abolitionists Remember: Antislavery Autobiographies and the Unfinished Work of Emancipation* (Chapel Hill: University of North Carolina Press, 2008). Thomas J. Brown, in *Civil War Canon: Sites of Confederate Memory in South Carolina* (Chapel Hill: University of North Carolina Press, 2015), likewise argues that memorialization of the Civil War in South Carolina had less to do with sectional reconciliation than with espousing a stridently anti-northern neo-Confederate ideology. These scholars complicate but do not refute Blight's main argument that, by the turn of the twentieth century, the "lost cause" of Black civil rights was often reinforced by slanted memories of the Civil War.

39. Schwartz, *Lincoln in the Post-Heroic Era*, xii.

40. For African American attitudes toward Lincoln, see Peterson, *Lincoln in American Memory*, 165–76, 348–58; and Kate Masur, introduction to John E. Washington, *They Knew Lincoln* (1942; repr., New York: Oxford University Press, 2018), xi–lxxx. For Black criticism of Lincoln, see Barr, *Loathing Lincoln*, 141–47, 194–99, 248–50, 277–82; and Edna Medford, *Lincoln and Emancipation* (Carbondale: Southern Illinois University Press, 2015). Two papers at the Clemson conference on Lincoln dealt with this topic: Edna Greene Medford, "'The Unsettled Relation between the 'Great Emancipator' and the 'Emancipated'"; and Kate Masur, "They Knew Lincoln: Writing the History of African Americans and Abraham Lincoln during the New Deal Era."

41. Lincoln, *Essential Lincoln*, 50; Leon Litwack, *North of Slavery: The Negro in the Free States, 1790–1860* (Chicago: University of Chicago, 1961), 276; Mark Neely Jr., "The Lincoln Theme since Randall's Call: The Promise and Perils of Professionalism," *Papers of the Abraham Lincoln Association*, vol. 1 (1979), 60. For the early stirrings of this new, more critical phase in Lincoln studies, see Barr,

Loathing Lincoln, 241, 247. Lincoln's statement is used as an introductory epigraph to Lerone Bennett Jr., *Forced into Glory: Abraham Lincoln's White Dream* (Chicago: Johnson, 2000).

42. Kate Masur, *Until Justice Be Done: America's First Civil Rights Movement, from the Revolution to Reconstruction* (New York: Norton, 2021), 262–64.

43. Burton and Derfner, *Justice Deferred*, 44–48, 77–80, 90, 116.

44. Schwartz, *Lincoln in the Post-Heroic Era*.

45. "Presidential Historians Survey 2021," C-Span, June 30, 2021, www.c-span.org/presidential-survey2021/. Ranked on a scale of 1 to 10 in ten categories, Lincoln finished with a total score of 897, with a substantial gap between him and the next-highest-ranked president, George Washington. Lincoln led in six categories: Crisis Leadership, Economic Management, Moral Authority, Administrative Skills, Vision/Setting an Agenda, Pursued Equal Justice for All, and Performance within the Context of His Times.

46. Ayala Emmett, "Falling in Love with Lincoln and Coming to America," printed in the current volume.

47. Peterson, *Lincoln in American Memory*, 248–350, 367; Barr, *Loathing Lincoln*, 142, 143–46, 193; Benjamin Quarles, *Lincoln and the Negro* (New York: Oxford University Press, 1962).

48. Malcolm X, interviewed by Robert Penn Warren, June 2, 1964, Robert Penn Warren Collection, Vanderbilt University Archives, whospeaks.library.vanderbilt.edu/interview/malcolm-x; Lerone Bennett Jr., "Liberals and Other White Hopes," in Bennett, *The Negro Mood and Other Essays* (Chicago: Johnson, 1964), 98; Bennett, "Was Lincoln a White Supremacist," *Ebony* 23 (Feb. 1968); John Hope Franklin, "The Use and Abuse of the Lincoln Legacy," *Papers of the Abraham Lincoln Association*, vol. 7 (1985), 30–42. See also "A Black Muslim Speaks Out," *Chicago Defender*, Apr. 25, 1963; Dave Taylor, "Malcolm X and Lincoln," Dec. 17, 2020, LincolnConspirators.com/2020/12; and Lerone Bennett, "Lincoln and the Liberal Tradition," in Bennett, *The Challenge of Blackness* (Chicago: Johnson Publishing, 1972), 156–75. For the Black press, see "A New Lincoln," *Chicago Defender*, Feb. 12, 1968; and "A New Lincoln," *Pittsburgh Courier*, Feb. 17, 1968.

49. Bennett, *Forced into Glory*, 76, 137; Barr, *Loathing Lincoln*, 278. Other historians rejected both Lincoln and white abolitionism. Vincent Harding, a close friend of Bennett and a fellow radical Black historian, had similar views of Lincoln, writing in 1967 that the president "seemed ready to leave the freed men to the mercies of their former masters," going on to say that unless Americans and their leaders can "far exceed that of Abraham Lincoln in the realm of racial justice and compassion . . . we may expect difficulties far greater than we dare to dream." Harding, "Lincoln's Views on Racial Justice [letter to the editor]," *New York Times*, Aug. 19, 1967. In his major work of African American history, Harding expresses a similar disdain for the white abolitionist tradition and those he felt to be too closely aligned with it, such as Frederick Douglass, for seeking a peaceful resolution of the slavery question. See Harding, *There Is a River: The Black Struggle for Freedom in America* (New York: Harcourt, Brace, Jovanovich, 1981). For Bennett and Harding as historians, see Peter Eisenstadt, "Three Historians and a Theologian: Howard Thurman's Impact on the Writing of African American History," in *Reconstruction at 150: Reassessing the Revolutionary "New Birth of Freedom,"* ed. Orville Vernon Burton and Brent Morris (Charlottesville: University of Virginia Press, forthcoming 2022).

50. Ibram X. Kendi, *Stamped from the Beginning: The Definitive History of Racist Ideas in America* (New York, Bold Type Books, 2016), 214–20; Orville Vernon Burton, review of *Stamped from the Beginning, Journal of Southern History* 84, no. 3 (Aug. 2018): 698–701.

51. Nikole Hannah-Jones, "America Wasn't a Democracy until Black Americans Made It One," *New York Times Magazine,* Aug. 14, 2019. The subsequent book, Nikole Hannah-Jones et al., eds., *The 1619 Project: A New Origin Story* (New York: New York Times Corporation, 2021), was not available when this essay was prepared. Serious discussion of the 1619 Project's strengths and weaknesses has been largely drowned out by the voices of those offended by its placing slavery and racism at the center of American history. We are unequivocally opposed to legislative efforts currently underway to ban its use for classroom teaching, which will extend far beyond the 1619 Project itself.

52. Ibid. For additional information on this meeting and for Lincoln's friendship with Douglass, see Foner, "Lincoln and Colonization," 155–66; and John Stauffer, *Giants: The Parallel Lives of Frederick Douglass and Abraham Lincoln* (New York: Twelve, 2008).

53. Matthew Karp, "History as End: 1619, 1776, and the Politics of the Past," *Harpers,* July 2021.

54. Burton, *Age of Lincoln;* Foner, *Fiery Trial,* xv; Bennett, *Forced into Glory,* ix; Franklin, "Use and Abuse of the Lincoln Legacy."

55. Howard Thurman, *Jesus and the Disinherited* (New York: Abingdon-Cokesbury, 1949), 100, 103.

56. David Brion Davis, *The Problem of Slavery in the Age of Revolution, 1770–1823* (1975; repr., New York: Oxford University Press, 1999), 306.

57. For the Second Reconstruction, see Numan V. Bartley and Hugh Graham Davis, *Southern Politics and the Second Reconstruction* (Baltimore: Johns Hopkins University Press, 1975); and Carl M. Brauer, *John F. Kennedy and the Second Reconstruction* (New York: Columbia University Press, 1977). For the "third" Reconstruction, see William Barber II and Jonathan Wilson-Hartgrove, *The Third Reconstruction: How a Moral Movement Is Overcoming the Politics of Division and Fear* (Boston: Beacon, 2016); Mondaire Jones, "Now Is the Time for a Third Reconstruction—Abolishing Jim Crow Once and for All," *Washington Post,* Apr. 12, 2021; and Randall Woodfin et al., "What the South Needs after COVID-19: A New Reconstruction," *Washington Post,* June 16, 2021.

58. "The Union Is Dissolved!" *Charleston Mercury,* Dec. 20, 1860.

59. "Address of the Colored State Convention to the People of South Carolina," Nov. 24, 1865, in *Reconstruction: Voices from America's First Great Struggle for Racial Equality,* ed. Brooks D. Simpson (New York: Library of America, 2018), 129–33.

Falling in Love with Lincoln and Coming to America

AYALA EMMETT

I was seventeen, in high school in my hometown in Israel in the 1950s, and I fell in love. I grew up in a small agricultural town and went to our local, academically demanding high school, speaking Hebrew and studying English for the college matriculation exam. School, friendships, and romance occupied us in unequal amounts. We worked hard at school and arranged late-evening outings, breathing the scent of citrus blooms and feeling giddy and guilty when we joined the boys in raiding watermelon patches.

We obviously knew that there were all kinds of ways to make our hearts soar and break. Some of the attractions that we felt and whispered and cried and sighed about materialized into adolescent relationships; a few went beyond high school, leading to marriages. For many of us, it was more about passions than materializing them. My enduring love belonged to the secret kind, one that for some reason we kept to ourselves.

In my last year in high school, I fell in love with Abraham Lincoln. It happened when I read his Gettysburg Address. The material for the matriculation exam had a reader with select passages from English and American literature. I liked most of the readings but fell in love with the sheer beauty of the sound of "Fourscore and seven years ago our fathers brought forth on this continent a new nation, conceived in liberty and dedicated to the proposition that all men are created equal."

While I knew the word "liberty," I did not know the word "feminism," one that only came into the Hebrew vernacular long after my high school experience. Yet I knew right away that the Lincoln I met in Israel was speaking of a liberty that was inclusive and meant not just for men but for all—women, slaves, the tired, survivors of the Holocaust, and immigrants; all are created equal. For me, the Hebrew Bible was part of my education, and Lincoln offered an American version of Genesis 1 that assured me that I, and all women and people, were created in God's image.

Like the language of Isaiah, Jeremiah, and the rest of the prophets, Lincoln's Gettysburg Address was singing, with soaring great ideas to be remembered, recognized, and recalled. I was thinking how words could be melodious, and Lincoln's language touched my heart and lifted my spirits by its sheer beauty.

When I read Lincoln's second inaugural address, I wept at the thought that people on the opposite sides of conflict over slavery prayed to the same God; yet only those who opposed slavery could be heard by the One who created us in the Devine's image. I understood Lincoln to say that the prayers to support oppression, to maintain slavery, to take away people's rights, they are unlikely to be granted because they are an offence to God. And that was before Martin Luther King Jr. gave his "I Have a Dream" speech, before his heartbreaking speech to sanitation workers in Memphis.

For me, English would forever be Lincoln. I came to America on the wings of Lincoln's promise of freedom.

Acknowledgments

"Acknowledgment" is too weak a word; a mere honorable mention, a polite round of applause. For the people who made this book and the conference from which it was birthed possible, and in the spirit of Abraham Lincoln, who in 1863 first proclaimed such a national holiday, let us call this a "thanks giving." The giving of thanks was very important to Lincoln. In his Thanksgiving Proclamation of 1864, he thanked God for providential guidance and inspiration and many of his fellow Americans for their "fortitude, courage, and resolution" in their "adherence as a nation to the cause of Freedom and Humanity, to afford us reasonable hopes of an ultimate and happy deliverance from all our dangers and afflictions." Amen. Seven months later, in his final speech delivered a few days before his assassination, he spoke again of giving thanks and how, after a victory, "honors" must be "parceled out." And if Lincoln was speaking of an incomparably vaster achievement in 1865—the destruction of American slavery—his unfinished work still calls to us, and it summoned this book into existence. So there remains our happy task of parceling out the many honors to whom they are due.

Vernon Burton had long dreamed of convening a major scholarly conference on Lincoln's legacy understood in its broadest possible scope, what the president referred to as our "unfinished work." The congressional Abraham Lincoln Bicentennial Foundation (ALBF), committed to honoring Lincoln and to addressing his "unfinished work," generously made this gathering a reality. The conference was held at Clemson University November 28–31, 2018. Several organizations and individuals provided further crucial financial support to make it possible: the Thomas Watson Brown Foundation, the South Carolina Council for the Humanities, the Self Family Foundation, the South Caroliniana Library at the University of South Carolina, Jean Soman (former chair and member of ALBF), and Friends of the Library and Special Collections of the College of Charleston. Further financial assistance was provided by Clemson University, specifically the College of Art, Architecture, and the Humanities (CAAH); the Clemson University Library; the Office of Inclusion and Equity and the Harvey and Lucinda Gantt Multicultural Center; the Watt Family Innovation Center; the CAAH Humanities Hub; the Department of History and Geography; the Department of English; the Department of Sociology, Anthropology, and Criminal Justice; the Department of Political Science; the Pearce Center for Professional Communication; the Rutland Institute for Ethics; the Pan African Studies program; the Department of Philosophy and Religion; the Department of Historical Properties; and Clemson University Press. At Clemson University, a number of persons helped facilitate the conference: Karen Land, Provost Robert H. Jones, Dean Richard Goodstein, Dean Christopher Cox, Lee Gill, Moryah Jackson, Roy Jones, Susan McCall, Jeannette Carter, Angel M. Perkins, and Rob Atkinson. Georganne Burton was utterly indispensable in the planning and execution of every phase of the conference. We could not have completed our tasks without her help.

The campus of Clemson University is not terribly close to the nearest major airport. A number of persons, most of them graduate students in the History Department, organized and volunteered to participate in the substantial logistical effort needed to transport conference participants to and from campus, among them Amanda Arroyo, Harris Bailey Jr., Mikkaela Bailey, Ruthie Calvino, Megan Gaston, Zach Gilbert, Matthew Long, and colleagues David Barkley, William Haller, and Jane DeLuca.

A group of middle and high school students from economically disadvantaged areas of the state attended the conference, interviewed and videotaped presenters, and shared their impressions of the proceedings with the audience. The South Carolina Social Action Team, the Middlebury Bread Loaf NextGen Network, funded by the Ford Foundation's Civic Engagement and Government initiative, made these students and their teachers' attendance possible. Dixie Goswami, Clemson University, emeritus, organized and facilitated their participation in the conference. A workshop on teaching secondary-school students about the difficult issues of the history of race relations was led by James W. Loewen, Vernon Burton, Bobby Donaldson (Civil Rights Institute, University of South Carolina), Paul Harleston (Green School, Baltimore, and Teach for America), Carmen Harris (University South Carolina Upstate), and Amanda Arroyo.

A number of conference participants were unable to contribute essays to the current volume. The presenters who do not have essays in this book are Stephen Berry, Vernon Burton, Catherine Clinton, Armand Derfner, Don Doyle, Paul Finkelman, Alan Grubb, Nicholas Gaffney, Thavolia Glymph, Steve Hahn, Darlene Clark Hine, William Hine, Kwame Holmes, Randall Kennedy, J. Drew Lanham, Matthew Long, Kate Masur, Edna Medford, J. Brent Morris, Bennett Parten, Heather Cox Richardson, Christopher Span, Robyn Spencer, Marjorie Spruill, and the photographer and chronicler of South Carolina's civil rights struggle, Cecil H. Williams. A number of Clemson scholars served as session moderators or introduced speakers—Rod Andrew, Susanna Ashton, Stephanie Barczewksi, Abel Bartley, James Jeffries, Edwin Moise, Maribel Morey, Michael Silverstri, and Lee B. Wilson—as did Dan Littlefield of the University of South Carolina, Georganne Burton, and Carmen Harris. Tullen Burns and his staff at the Watt Innovation Center were the expert videographers for the conference sessions. A special shout-out and debt of gratitude is owed to the extraordinary Eduardo Nieves, who orchestrated documenting the conference and created the website for Lincoln's Unfinished Work. For those who wish to have a fuller sense of the conference proceedings, we urge them to visit the Gallery and Videos section of the website, where every conference session is available for viewing: https://www.clemson.edu/caah/sites/lincoln-conference/gallery/index.html.

William D. Hiott, senior executive director and chief curator of the Department of Historic Properties, gave a thoughtful tour of Calhoun's mansion, Fort Hill. Professor Richard Saunders led a bar crawl for participants. Georganne Burton generously hosted a reception each evening in the Burton townhouse. Henry Ronald "Snake" Lowrey did a special "Ninety Six" country-style barbecue at the Southern Living Center in the South Carolina Botanical Garden. Excellent restauranteurs at Calhoun Corners, the Blue Heron, and the 1826 Bistro—located in a hall where, a few years after its founding, John C. Calhoun denounced the abolitionists—kept us fed. (If the conference disturbed the shades of Calhoun, we achieved our purpose.)

At LSU Press, let us especially thank series editor Michael Parrish, who had early solicited a volume from the conference for his outstanding series Conflicting Worlds: New Dimensions of the American Civil War, and the incomparable Editor in Chief Rand Dotson, Catherine L. Kadair, and Sunny Rosen. The meticulous work of freelance copyeditor Kevin Brock and the suggestions of the anonymous outsider reader were greatly appreciated. The argus-eyed indexing skills of Human Enterprises' Beatrice Burton, who attended and participated in the conference, improved the book. To all mentioned, our heartiest giving of thanks.

One person who participated in the conference as a presenter, a facilitator in the conference's workshop, and as an essayist in the present book was Dr. James Loewen. Sadly, he will never see the book you are reading; Jim died in August 2021. He was one of Vernon's closest friends, having met in 1980 while working for the NAACP with civil rights lawyer Armand Derfner in a South Carolina voting-rights case. Jim Loewen was a scholar of many and varied talents. He achieved considerable renown as an indefatigable gadfly, both generous and cantankerous, attacking the falsification of American history in our textbooks and at our historical sites. One of the things Jim hated the most was the Confederacy and its latter-day apologists, and as we write these words, a month after his passing, the news of the day is that in Richmond, Virginia, the equestrian statue of Robert E. Lee, which has loomed as a massive symbol of white supremacy since 1890, has finally been hoisted from its plinth. Jim mentioned the statue in his essay printed in this volume, and nothing would have pleased him more than to see the statue brought down. Jim's tireless advocacy helped bring about this great day. His article in this volume is titled "Our Textbooks and Monuments Have Flattened Lincoln, Just When We Need Him the Most." No one could ever flatten Jim Loewen. And we lost him just when we need him the most.

Vernon Burton dedicates this book to his grandchildren, two of whom—James Tucker Morris Burton, his youngest, and Charlotte Burton Harleston, already a teenage social-justice warrior—attended the conference at Clemson University. James, an infant, came with his mother, while Charlotte actively participated and interviewed historians. Peter Eisenstadt dedicates this book to his brother, Eric; and to Fay, Ariel, and Lia. We both dedicate the book to all who have advanced or will advance the "unfinished work"—in the words of Psalm 146:10, "L'dor v'dor"—from generation to generation.

Contributors

Orville Vernon Burton is the Judge Matthew J. Perry Distinguished Chair of History at Clemson University and Emeritus University Teacher/Scholar at the University of Illinois. He has published more than two hundred articles and authored or edited more than twenty books, including the award-winning *The Age of Lincoln* (2007). His most recent book, with Armand Derfner, is *Justice Deferred: Race and the Supreme Court* (2021).

Richard Carwardine is the Rhodes Professor of American History Emeritus at the University of Oxford. His books include *Evangelicals and Politics in Antebellum America* (1993); *Lincoln: A Life of Purpose and Power* (2006), winner of the Lincoln Prize; *The Global Lincoln* (2011), coedited with Jay Sexton; and *Lincoln's Sense of Humor* (2017), winner of the Abraham Lincoln Institute Annual Book Award. His current project is a book on the politics of religious nationalism in the Civil War era.

Joshua Casmir Catalano is an assistant professor in the Department of History and Geography at Clemson University and the coordinator of the public history program. Prior to his arrival at Clemson, he was a graduate research assistant at the Roy Rosenzweig Center for History and New Media. His research focuses on the role of symbolism and language in the process of settler colonialism.

Gregory P. Downs is professor of history at the University of California–Davis and the author of three books on the US Civil War era, most recently *The Second American Revolution: The Civil War Era–Struggle over Cuba and the Rebirth of the American Republic* (2019). With Kate Masur, he coedits the *Journal of the*

Contributors

Civil War Era, cowrote the National Park Service's first-ever theme study on Reconstruction, and lobbied for the creation of the first-ever national park site devoted to Reconstruction, proclaimed by President Barack Obama at Beaufort, South Carolina, in January 2017. With Scott Nesbit, he created Mapping Occupation (www.mappingoccupation.org), a digital history of Reconstruction. With Masur, Scott Hancock, and Hilary Green, he directs the We Want More History public-history effort.

Peter Eisenstadt, affiliate professor of history at Clemson University, is the author or editor of many books on urban history and African American history, including *Against the Hounds of Hell: A Life of Howard Thurman* (2021); the award-winning *Rochdale Village: Robert Moses, 6,000 Families, and New York City's Great Experiment in Integrated Housing* (2010); and *The Encyclopedia of New York State* (2005).

Ayala Emmett is professor emeritus of anthropology at the University of Rochester and the author of *Our Sisters' Promised Land: Women, Politics, and Israel-Palestinian Co-Existence* (1996). She has published numerous journal articles and book chapters on politics, gender, and religion; has received the Humanistic Anthropology Fiction Award; and is the founder of the digital publication *The Jewish Pluralist.*

Eric Foner is DeWitt Clinton Professor Emeritus of History at Columbia University and the author of numerous books on the Civil War–Reconstruction era, most recently *The Second Founding: How the Civil War and Reconstruction Remade the Constitution* (2019).

J. William Harris is professor emeritus at the University of New Hampshire. His books include *The Making of the American South: A Short History, 1500–1877* (2006) and *Deep Souths: Delta, Piedmont, and Sea Island Society in the Age of Segregation* (2001), which was a finalist for the Pulitzer Prize in 2002.

Stephen Kantrowitz is the Plaenert-Bascom and Vilas Distinguished Achievement Professor of History at the University of Wisconsin–Madison. He is the author of *Ben Tillman and the Reconstruction of White Supremacy* (2000), *More Than Freedom: Fighting for Black Citizenship in a White Republic, 1829–1889* (2012), and

Settlers, Citizens, and Civilization: The Ho-Chunk Confrontation with Colonialism, 1825–1881 (forthcoming).

James W. Loewen was emeritus professor of sociology at the University of Vermont and the author of many books and essays on the falsification of historical memory, including the best-selling and award-winning *Lies My Teacher Told Me: Everything Your American History Textbook Got Wrong* (1996; revised edition, 2008): *Lies across America: What Our Historic Sites Get Wrong* (1999); *Sundown Towns: A Hidden Dimension of American Racism* (2005): and most recently, *Up a Creek, with a Paddle: Tales of Canoeing and Life* (2020).

Lawrence T. McDonnell is assistant professor of history at Iowa State University and author of *Performing Disunion: The Coming of the Civil War in Charleston, South Carolina* (2018). His research focuses on the American transition to capitalism in the Civil War era.

Adrienne Petty codirects, with Mark Schultz, the oral-history project Breaking New Ground: A History of African American Farm Owners, part of the Southern Oral History Program Collection at the University of North Carolina at Chapel Hill. Petty is associate professor of history at the College of William & Mary and the author of *Standing Their Ground: Small Farmers in North Carolina Since the Civil War* (2013).

Briana L. Pocratsky is a lecturer in the Department of Sociology, Anthropology, and Criminal Justice at Clemson University. She is a public sociologist whose research focuses on popular culture, identity, and everyday life.

Jerald Podair is the Robert S. French Professor of American Studies at Lawrence University. His books include *The Strike That Changed New York: Blacks, Whites, and the Ocean Hill-Brownsville Crisis* (2002); *Bayard Rustin: American Dreamer* (2009); and *The Routledge History of the Twentieth-Century United States* (2018, coedited with Darren Dochuk).

Mark Schultz codirects, with Adrienne Petty, the oral-history project Breaking New Ground: A History of African American Farm Owners, part of the Southern

Oral History Program Collection at the University of North Carolina at Chapel Hill. Schultz is professor of history at Lewis University and the author of *The Rural Face of White Supremacy: Beyond Jim Crow* (2005).

Randall J. Stephens is professor of American and British studies at the University of Oslo. He is the author of *The Fire Spreads: Holiness and Pentecostalism in the American South* (2008); *The Anointed: Evangelical Truth in a Secular Age*, coauthored with physicist Karl Giberson (2011); and editor of *Recent Themes in American Religious History* (2009). His latest book is *The Devil's Music: How Christians Inspired, Condemned, and Embraced Rock 'n' Roll* (2018). Stephens is also an Organization of American Historians Distinguished Lecturer.

Rhondda Robinson Thomas is the Calhoun Lemon Professor of Literature at Clemson University, where she researches and teaches early African American literature. She is the author of *Claiming Exodus: A Cultural History of Afro-Atlantic Identity, 1770–1903* (2013); the award-winning *Call My Name, Clemson: Documenting the Black Experience in an American University Community* (2020); and "Locating Slave Narratives" in the *Oxford Handbook of the African American Slave Narrative* (2014.) Additionally, she is the faculty director for the Call My Name Project, which documents African American history at Clemson.

Gavin Wright is the William Robertson Coe Professor of American Economic History Emeritus at Stanford University. His publications include *Sharing the Prize: The Economics of the Civil Rights Revolution in the American South* (2013) and "Slavery and Anglo-American Capitalism Revisited" (*Economic History Review*, 2020).

Index